The Children of Pride

Books by Robert Manson Myers

HANDEL'S MESSIAH: A TOUCHSTONE OF TASTE (1948)

FROM BEOWULF TO VIRGINIA WOOLF (1952)

HANDEL, DRYDEN, AND MILTON (1956)

RESTORATION COMEDY (1961)

THE CHILDREN OF PRIDE (1972)

A GEORGIAN AT PRINCETON (1976)

The Children of Pride

A NEW, ABRIDGED EDITION

Selected letters of the family of
the Rev. Dr. Charles Colcock Jones
from the years 1860–1868,
with the addition of several
previously unpublished letters

ROBERT MANSON MYERS

Yale University Press

NEW HAVEN AND LONDON

Set in Garamond No. 3 type by Brevis Press.
Printed in the United States of America by
Vail-Ballou Press, Inc., Binghamton, New York.

Library of Congress Cataloging in Publication Data
Main entry under title:

The Children of pride.

1. Jones, Charles Colcock, 1804–1863. 2. Jones
family. 3. United States—History—Civil War, 1861–
1865—Personal narratives, Confederate. 4. Georgia—
Biography. 5. Georgia—History—Civil War, 1861–1865—
Sources. 6. Reconstruction—Georgia—Sources.
I. Jones, Charles Colcock, 1804–1863. II. Myers, Robert
Manson, 1921– .
E559.9.C46 1984   975.8′03   83–10377
ISBN 0-300-04053-9

10 9 8 7 6 5

TO
SHIRLEY STRUM KENNY

He beholdeth all high things: he is a
king over all the children of pride.
Job 41:34

Contents

Illustrations

to Jefferson Davis, . . . by Frank E. Moran. Baltimore, Maryland: Printed for the Family of the Author, n.d.

Sketch of the hospital at Andersonville. From *Life and Death in Rebel Prisons,* by Robert H. Kellogg. Hartford, Connecticut: L. Stebbins, 1865.

A Confederate Army ambulance wagon. From *Atlanta Illustrated. Containing Glances at Its Population, Business, Manufactures, Industries, Institutions,* . . . by E. Y. Clarke. Third edition. Atlanta: Jas. P. Harrison & Co., 1881.

"Rebels moving south from Atlanta." From *Harper's Weekly,* October 15th, 1864.

View of Atlanta, 1864. From *Harper's Weekly,* November 26th, 1864.

Preface

IN abridging *The Children of Pride* I have inevitably created a new book—swifter and more sharply focused, with its own shape and its own meanings. Here, as before, I have been guided by a single purpose: to select from the voluminous family papers of the Rev. Dr. Charles Colcock Jones (1804–1863), of Liberty County, Georgia, letters which, when brought together in chronological order without editorial links, would form a coherent, independent narrative related entirely in the words of the characters themselves. What has emerged is a true story told in letters—something akin to an epistolary novel: an account of family life in coastal Georgia before, during, and after the Civil War. It is a story of intelligent, perceptive, well-to-do plantation people remote from the public eye—people who lived out their lives with little feeling that they were making history or changing destiny, and who went to their graves with no suspicion that their letters, written in the heat of the moment and posted without delay, would ultimately see print. It is a quiet story of births and marriages and deaths, of daily joys and sorrows, of the response of a proud people to one of the great crises of American history. For eight years (from 1860 to 1868) we follow their fortunes and misfortunes in multifarious detail—from prewar plenty through wartime privation to postwar ruin. As the story mounts to its terrible climax we see three generations caught in the grip of a national tragedy.

The Jones family correspondence comprises some seven thousand letters in repositories in Georgia and Louisiana. Some five hundred of these letters appear in the present volume; six letters are printed here for the first time (on pp. 80–81, 91–94, 144–45, 490–91). The source of each letter is indicated at the end of its title by the appropriate superscript: *g* (University of Georgia, Athens) or *t* (Tulane University, New Orleans). For permission to publish the letters I am obliged to the authorities of the Tulane University Library and the Library of the University of Georgia, as well as to the Seago family of New Orleans and the Waller family of Augusta, Georgia.

To facilitate reference I have regularized all datelines, supplying at the head of each letter the name of addressor and addressee, together with place and date of writing; within letters I have retained all dates in their original form. A few undated and misdated letters I have correctly dated on the basis of internal evidence; datelines so altered I have terminated with an asterisk. Obvious discrepancies in dates I have silently corrected wherever possible.

Readers will note that a few letters begin on one date and continue on another without indication of change of date, thus causing apparent (but not actual) discrepancies between date and text. All omissions within the letters are marked by ellipsis dots; three dots at the end of a paragraph may indicate the omission of the remainder of that paragraph or of one or more subsequent paragraphs; in the few instances where postscripts are deleted I have disregarded the omission. An extended dash (———) following the title *Mr.* indicates a name omitted for reasons of prudence.

The Joneses and their friends wrote extraordinarily careful English, but for ease of reading it has seemed wise to reduce a varying text to a consistent standard. To this end I have normalized all spelling, capitalization, punctuation, and paragraphing. I have retained the italics of the original letters; in addition I have silently italicized titles of books, names of ships, and foreign phrases in accordance with modern usage. I have expanded abbreviations at will. A few clear inadvertencies I have set right without notice. On rare occasions, to prevent misreading, I have silently introduced a pronoun or a conjunction or an article or a form of the verb *to be.* A journal kept jointly by Mrs. Mary Jones and her daughter, Mrs. Mary S. Mallard, and surviving only in a later draft in the handwriting of Mrs. Mary Jones, I have sectioned according to author on the basis of internal evidence.

Seeking to make *The Children of Pride* a happy blend of accuracy and readability, I have resisted all temptation to intrude upon the text with explanatory notes. As Dr. Johnson observed two centuries ago, "Notes are often necessary, but they are necessary evils. . . . The mind is refrigerated by interruption; the thoughts are diverted from the principal object; the reader is weary, he suspects not why; and at last throws away the book which he has too diligently studied." In editing the letters I have preferred to keep the reader in the nineteenth century rather than force him to shuttle between the nineteenth and twentieth. I have let the story speak for itself.

At every stage in the production of this book Ellen Graham of the Yale University Press has proved indispensable. I record with pleasure my appreciation of her energy, her enthusiasm, and her thoroughgoing editorial support. I also wish to thank the people who assisted us so generously in obtaining the illustrations for this edition: Mrs. Mary Seago Brooke, Mr. Harcourt Waller, Mr. Malcolm Bell, Jr., and Mrs. W. H. Cohan.

R. M. M.

Washington, D.C.
September 10th, 1983

The Children of Pride

The Principal Characters

At Maybank, Montevideo, and Arcadia

Rev. Dr. Charles Colcock Jones, *a retired Presbyterian clergyman*
Mary (Jones) Jones, *his wife*

In Savannah

Charles Colcock Jones, Jr., *a lawyer, elder son of Dr. and Mrs. C. C. Jones*
Ruth Berrien (Whitehead) Jones, *his wife*
Julia Berrien Jones, *their daughter*

In Augusta

Joseph Jones, *a doctor, younger son of Dr. and Mrs. C. C. Jones*
Caroline Smelt (Davis) Jones, *his wife*

In Walthourville

Rev. Robert Quarterman Mallard, *a Presbyterian clergyman*
Mary Sharpe (Jones) Mallard, *his wife, daughter of Dr. and Mrs. C. C. Jones*
Mary Jones Mallard ⎫
Charles Colcock Mallard ⎭ *their children*

At Social Bluff (Point Maxwell)

Rev. David Lyman Buttolph, *a Presbyterian clergyman*
Laura Elizabeth (Maxwell) Buttolph, *his wife, daughter of Mrs. Susan M. Cumming*
Susan Mary (Jones) (Maxwell) Cumming, *twice-widowed sister of the Rev. Dr. C. C. Jones*

At Springfield

Colonel William Maxwell, *a planter, widowed brother-in-law of the Rev. Dr. C. C. Jones*

3

At Woodville and South Hampton

Julia Rebecca (Maxwell) King, *widow of Roswell King, Jr.*

James Audley Maxwell King, *eldest son of Mr. and Mrs. Roswell King, Jr.*

Kate (Lewis) King, *his wife*

Mary Elizabeth (King) Wells, *a widow, elder daughter of Mr. and Mrs. Roswell King, Jr.*

George Frederick King
William Henry King
Roswell King III
Isabel Couper King } *younger children of Mr. and Mrs. Roswell King, Jr.*
Julian Clarence King
Bayard Hand King
John Butler King

In Rome

Rev. John Jones, *a Presbyterian clergyman, brother of Mrs. Mary Jones*

Jane Adaline (Dunwody) Jones, *his wife*

James Dunwody Jones
John Carolin Jones } *their sons*
Joseph Henry Jones

In Marietta

Eliza Greene (Low) (Walker) (Robarts) Robarts, *thrice-widowed half-aunt of the Rev. Dr. C. C. Jones*

Mary Eliza Robarts
Louisa Jane Robarts } *her daughters*

Joseph William Robarts, *her son, a widower*

Mary Sophia Robarts
Elizabeth Walton Robarts
Ellen Douglas Robarts } *children of Joseph William Robarts*
Joseph Jones Robarts

Friends in Various Places

Rev. Dr. George Howe, *professor at Columbia Theological Seminary in Columbia, South Carolina*

Rev. Dr. I. S. K. Axson, *pastor of Independent Presbyterian Church in Savannah*

Thomas Cooper Nisbet, Esq., *an iron manufacturer in Macon*

Hon. John Elliott Ward, *a lawyer in Savannah*

Katherine Clay (Kitty) Stiles, *a lady of leisure in Savannah*

Prologue

SOUTH OF SAVANNAH the Georgia landscape stretches broadly to the sea. Long, low islands, crowned with cedar, myrtle, and palmetto, fringe the coast and beat back the thundering surf; wide, waving salt marshes, everywhere broken by sluggish streams, spread to the encircling sandy bluffs; here and there bold estuaries reach their giant fingers past the shore to the boundless green beyond. The growth is rank and wild: dense forests of long-leaf pine are intersected by dark, languid cypress swamps, where the gray moss floats from every branch and twig like the beard of some hoary patriarch, and the yellow jessamine wreathes itself in clusters amongst the tangled vines, and the butterflies flit eternally in the mysterious half-light. Overhead the sun shines as it seems to shine only in a southern sky; and everywhere the soft sea breeze mingles with the fragrance of jessamine and magnolia and pine.

To the motorist speeding south along the coastal highway linking Savannah and Jacksonville this semitropical landscape offers little that is striking or dramatic. His route passes through a monotonous expanse of swampland and primeval undergrowth; on built-up causeways and modern bridges he traverses a maze of ponds and creeks and branches and drainage canals, with now and then a glimpse of a farmer's shack, or perhaps in a clearing a majestic avenue of live oaks calling up the grace of a day that is dead. From Chatham County he crosses the Great Ogeechee River into Bryan; from Bryan County he soon passes into historic Liberty; then suddenly, some thirty miles out of Savannah, he finds himself irresistibly drawn to a commanding structure on the left. A white frame church, reminiscent of a New England meetinghouse and now venerable with age, stands facing south in a grove of pines and moss-draped oaks a short distance to the east of the highway at the fork of two roads. Shuttered, small-paned windows line each clapboarded side in a double row; two small circular openings adorn the pedimented front gable; rising from the roof is a slender square tower surmounted by an open belfry and a tall hexagonal spire. Inside the church the same chaste mood is sustained. Stiff pews with old-fashioned hinged doors stand on a wide-planked floor in three sections, separated by aisles. Eight sturdy wooden columns support a circular gallery designed expressly for the use of Negro slaves. A high pulpit, superbly paneled and approached on either side by a flight of steps, occupies the north end and places the clergyman in equal touch with his hearers above and below.

Altogether it is a strict, solemn place—beautiful in its restraint and touching in its evocations of a noble past.

A bronze tablet to the left of the entrance identifies this imposing landmark as Midway Congregational Church, erected in 1792, but organized some forty years before by descendants of an English colony which had migrated to Massachusetts in 1630, to Connecticut in 1635, to South Carolina in 1695, and to Georgia in 1752. The church has been called "the cradle of Revolutionary spirit in Georgia": two of its sons, Lyman Hall and Button Gwinnett, were signers of the Declaration of Independence; two others, Daniel Stewart and James Screven, became brigadier generals in the Revolutionary army. In recognition of the marked patriotism of the Midway community during the Revolutionary War the county of which the parish later became a part was honored by the name of Liberty. Six counties in Georgia today bear the names of Midway sons: Lyman Hall, Button Gwinnett, Daniel Stewart, James Screven, John Baker, and Augustus Octavius Bacon. Four sons of Midway became early governors of Georgia: Lyman Hall, Button Gwinnett, Richard Howley, and Nathan Brownson. Among distinguished Midway pastors were Abiel Holmes, father of Oliver Wendell Holmes, and Jedidiah Morse, father of Samuel F. B. Morse. The scientist Louis LeConte, world-famed for his botanical gardens, was a communicant of Midway Church; his two sons, John and Joseph LeConte, also distinguished scientists, were instrumental in founding the University of California, and John LeConte served for a time as its president. Descendants of the Midway community have found their way even to the White House: Theodore Roosevelt was a great-grandson of General Daniel Stewart, of Revolutionary fame; and Ellen Louise Axson, the first wife of Woodrow Wilson, was a granddaughter of the Rev. Dr. I. S. K. Axson, for seventeen years pastor of Midway Church. It would be impossible to name or even to number here the countless clergymen, doctors, lawyers, professors, teachers, scientists, judges, legislators, and soldiers who have left this tiny church to assume positions of influence and distinction throughout the nation and the world. For a rural community which at no time boasted more than a few hundred souls, and which was dispersed only a little more than a century after it was settled, such a record is indeed astonishing if not unique.

When the first colonists removed from South Carolina in 1752, they emigrated in a body under their pastor and officers and established themselves in a district some thirty miles south of Savannah and some ten miles west of the sea islands at the headwaters of the Medway and Newport Rivers, two short tidewater streams draining what was afterwards known as St. John's Parish and what ultimately became Liberty County. These hardy settlers were sober, pious, God-fearing Calvinists of English, Scottish, and French Huguenot extraction; they found the low swamplands readily adapted to the culture of rice, and the rich, alluvial soil of the higher lands ideally suited to the culture of cotton and corn. Their first concern was to provide for the services of religion. For a time they met in private houses, but early in 1754 they built a temporary log meetinghouse three-quarters of a mile east of the spot where the present structure stands. The first church was called Midway, its situation being midway between Savannah and Darien, or midway between the Savannah and Altamaha Rivers. Here the first sermon was preached on June 7th, 1754, and here the colonists convened on August 28th, 1754, to frame articles for the civil and religious government of their community. On this historic occasion the people formally instituted the Midway Church and Society, a governing body consisting of two coordinate branches: the Church, comprising all male communicants, was to administer spiritual affairs; the Society, comprising all male residents whether communicants or not, was to administer temporal affairs. Annual meetings of the Midway Church and Society were to be held on second Wednesdays in March, when a pastor, a clerk, and three or more selectmen were to be chosen. Though nominally Congregational, the church was from its incorporation essentially Presbyterian; it was so understood and so universally styled, and every pastor in its history was Presbyterian with but two exceptions.

Plans for a permanent structure were drawn up at the organizational meeting in August 1754. The first rude meetinghouse was accordingly replaced by a frame building, thirty-six by forty-four feet, with pitched roof hipped at one end, facing the Sunbury road on the site of the present structure; here services were first held on January 2nd, 1757. This building was not destined to survive long. After twenty-one years, on November 27th, 1778, it was burned by the British; the community was overrun, and the congregation was for a time scattered. A third structure, a "coarse meetinghouse" designed to be temporary, was erected near the site of the second church in 1784. Finally, on August 23rd, 1791, the Midway Church and Society agreed on specifications for a fourth church:

Voted, that the selectmen contract with some person or persons to build a meetinghouse. Voted, said house be built sixty feet by forty; also agreed it shall be twenty feet in the stories. Voted, that the form of the roof be as our old meetinghouse was; that is to say, a pitched roof hipped at one end, and a steeple at the other; and also to stand in the same manner as the former house did. Voted, that the number of lights in said house be left to the selectmen to determine. Agreed also the above house be built of the best wood. [James Stacy, *The Published Records of Midway Church* (Newnan, Georgia, 1894), p. 51]

This handsome meetinghouse, weatherboarded in cypress and fashioned with hand-wrought nails, was completed in 1792. Originally there were three doors, one opening north, one opening west, and one opening south. A high pulpit stood on the east side with a great sounding board overhead; a gallery extended across the south end with two flights of steps providing access directly from the outside. In 1849 the pulpit was removed to the north end, its present position; and the gallery was extended to the three sides opposite. At the same time two of the three doors were closed, thus confining access to the south—a measure intended, it is said, to encourage members of the congregation to mingle as they passed out. Adjacent to the church at convenient distances were thirty or more little houses, something like booths or pavilions, to which the various families retired for rest and refreshment during the intermission between morning and afternoon services.

The district settled by the South Carolina colonists in 1752 abounded in swamps and stagnant pools; it was an insalubrious region, and the culture of rice, with its system of canals and ditches and dams and backwaters, multiplied the hazards of disease. In an age of primitive hygiene malaria was a menace against which only the Negro was proof, and the mortality rate among the early settlers was appalling. To escape the exposures of the sickly months the planters soon sought healthier spots on higher ground, where it became their custom to live through half the year in summer retreats. To these retreats, clustered in villages among the pine forests, they withdrew with their servants late in the spring; almost without exception they visited their plantations at least twice a week during the summer months; in late autumn, after the first killing frost, they returned in safety to their winter homes. As the community grew, the retreats prospered. In the early days a number of planters resorted to Sunbury and Colonel's Island, where the pleasures of social life and the sport of angling and the cool sea breeze brought relief from the scorching suns. But the coast was distant and hence inaccessible to many plantations, and in time it became necessary to establish retreats contiguous to the outlying districts. As early as 1795 a rich planter, Andrew Walthour, settled some fifteen miles southwest of Midway Church in an area known as the Sand Hills, afterwards called Walthourville in his honor. By 1814 several families were summering eleven miles northwest of Midway Church at Gravel Hill, later renamed Flemington after its first settler, William Fleming. Meanwhile the people in the neighborhood of Riceboro had penetrated the piney woods below Bulltown Swamp and had joined Samuel Jones, the first settler, in establishing a village called Jonesville some eight miles south of Midway Church. And in 1843, with the decline and eventual abandonment of Sunbury as a result of its increasing unhealthiness, a group of planters nearer the coast withdrew to form the village of Dorchester some six miles east of Midway Church on the Sunbury road. With the passing of years a number of these families came to find their semiannual migration from plantation to retreat, from retreat to plantation, both expensive and inconvenient; and inevitably some of them chose to reside permanently at their summer homes.

Throughout the antebellum South the Midway people were justly known for their remarkable way of life. No planting community could boast deeper religious convictions, higher intellectual cultivation, gentler social refinement, or greater material wealth. The church was the very cornerstone of their being; their piety was orthodox, practical, unpretending, and exalted. Education was second only to religion: in each of the four retreats—Walthourville, Flemington, Jonesville, and Dorchester—an academy was

8

promptly established, and schools also flourished from time to time at Sunbury, Newport, Riceboro, Hinesville, and Taylor's Creek. Often parents engaged private tutors to live in their households and instruct their children; and promising sons were sent to the state university in Athens if not to Princeton or Yale or Harvard. In a society thus fixed on the things of the mind and the spirit the people were virtuous and accomplished. If few were extravagantly rich, all were comfortably disposed; equality of rank and fortune generally prevailed, and social life was leisurely, gracious, and polite. Describing this world in an *Address Delivered at Midway Meetinghouse in Liberty County, Georgia, on the Second Wednesday in March 1889,* Charles Colcock Jones, Jr., distinguished Georgia historian and himself a son of Midway, recalled the society he had known so well as a youth:

When the centennial was celebrated in 1852 everything relating to this congregation and county was in a prosperous and satisfactory condition. While there were few who could lay claim to large estates, the planters of this community were in comfortable circumstances. They were industrious, observant of their obligations, humane in the treatment of their servants, given to hospitality, fond of manly exercise, and solicitous for the moral and intellectual education of their children. The traditions of the fathers gave birth to patriotic impulses and encouraged a high standard of honor, integrity, and manhood. The military spirit survived in the person of the Liberty Independent Troop; and on stated occasions contests involving rare excellence in horsemanship and in the use of the saber and pistol attracted the gaze of the public and won the approving smiles of noble women. Leisure hours were spent in hunting and fishing, and in social intercourse. Of litigation there was little. Misunderstandings, when they occurred, were usually accommodated by honorable arbitration. Personal responsibility, freely admitted, engendered mutual respect and a most commendable degree of manliness. The rules of morality and of the church were respected, acknowledged, and upheld. The community was well-ordered and prosperous, and the homes of the inhabitants were peaceful and happy. Of all the political divisions of this commonwealth none was more substantial, observant of law, or better instructed than the county of Liberty. Enviable was her position in the sisterhood of counties. In bringing about this satisfactory condition of affairs the influence of Midway Church and its congregation was very potent. [pp. 14–15]

Till the coming of the Civil War the fortunes of the Midway people continued to rise. Their economy was founded on Negro slavery, and they were reputed to be among the largest slaveholders in the South. Some four thousand Negroes lived and toiled in Liberty County alone. The concern of the Midway community for the spiritual state of these Negroes was sincere and active; the efforts of masters to instruct their servants in religious matters became nationally and even internationally known. That veteran traveler, Frederick Law Olmsted, journeying on horseback through the seaboard slave states in the 1850s, observed the religious instruction of the Negroes in Liberty County firsthand; in his two-volume work, *The Cotton Kingdom,* published in New York and London in 1861, he gave a picture of the conditions surrounding Negro slavery in the South that had great influence on British as well as American opinion during the critical years to follow:

In the county of Liberty, in Georgia, a Presbyterian minister has been for many years employed exclusively in laboring for the moral enlightenment of the slaves, being engaged and paid for this especial duty by their owners. From this circumstance, almost unparalleled as it is, it may be inferred that the planters of that county are as a body remarkably intelligent, liberal, and thoughtful for the moral welfare of the childlike wards Providence has placed under their care and tutorship. According to my private information, there is no body of slaveowners more, if any as much so, in the United States. I heard them referred to with admiration of their reputation in this particular even as far away as Virginia and Kentucky. I believe that in no other district has there been displayed as general and long-continued an interest in the spiritual well-being of the Negroes. It must be supposed that nowhere else are their circumstances more happy and favorable to Christian nurture. [II, 215]

In promoting the spiritual welfare of the Negro population in Liberty County and throughout the South no man was more active or zealous than the Rev. Dr. Charles Colcock Jones, "Apostle to the Blacks," a lifelong member of Midway Church, who now lies buried in the historic graveyard directly across the way. This extraordinary man, father of the Georgia historian quoted above, was a rich planter, a gentleman of liberal education, and a Presbyterian clergyman of radiant Christian character, aptly described by his son-in-law as "one of the noblest men God ever made." He was born in Liberty County at his father's plantation, Liberty Hall, on December 20th, 1804. His paternal grandfather, Major John Jones (1749–1779), a native of Charleston, South Carolina, had migrated shortly before the Revolutionary War to coastal Georgia, where he had purchased a plantation in St. John's Parish and commenced the cultivation of rice. A few years later, at the siege of Savannah, he had met a patriot's death in a bloody and futile assault upon the British lines on the morning of October 9th, 1779. Jones Street in Savannah was named in his honor. He left a widow, Mary (Sharpe) Jones, who in 1783 married Major Philip Low, a cousin of General Nathanael Greene, and had one daughter, Eliza Greene (born September 29th, 1785); he also left two sons: John (born November 25th, 1772), who became the father of Charles Colcock Jones; and Joseph (born November 26th, 1779), who became the father of his wife, Mary Jones.

The elder son, Captain John Jones, a successful planter in Liberty County, was said to be an admirable type of the English country gentleman; he was fond of everything English, and he imported everything possible from England—his horses and hounds and his guns and pistols as well as his pictures and books. He represented Liberty County in the state legislature in 1796, 1797, and 1798. In 1793 he married Elizabeth Stewart, sister of General Daniel Stewart, by whom he had one daughter, Elizabeth (born September 11th, 1794); soon after the death of his first wife in 1801 he married Susannah Hyrne Girardeau, daughter of John Girardeau, of French Huguenot descent, by whom he had two living children, Susan Mary (born October 22nd, 1803) and Charles Colcock (born December 20th, 1804). In his early thirties this generous, attractive, popular man was thrown from his horse while chasing a deer; he died from the effects on March 28th, 1805, leaving his two infants to the care of his widow, a woman of singular piety and great strength of character, and to the guardianship of his younger brother, Captain Joseph Jones, a gentleman of large wealth, known throughout Liberty County as "the guardian of widows and orphans." His grandson, Charles Colcock Jones, Jr., later characterized Captain Joseph Jones as "a man of imperious will, of great personal courage, quick in quarrel, impatient of restraint, intolerant of opposition, and of mark in the community." He married three times and fathered twenty-six children, the youngest born in his sixty-fourth year. He died on October 18th, 1846, from injuries sustained when he was thrown from his buggy three days before.

Fatherless at three months, the boy was also motherless at five and a half years. Susannah (Girardeau) Jones died on July 1st, 1810; on her deathbed she committed her two young children, Susan and Charles, to the custody of her deceased husband's half-sister, Eliza Greene Low, then Mrs. Robarts, widow of James Robarts. In November 1810 Captain Joseph Jones carried the two children to Mrs. Robarts at her home in Greene County, eight miles from the village of Greensboro. Some weeks later, following the marriage of Mrs. Robarts to her deceased husband's cousin, David Robarts, she removed to Greensboro, where Susan and Charles attended school until late in 1811, when Captain Joseph Jones brought the children back to Liberty County to live with their half-sister, Elizabeth, recently married to Colonel William Maxwell. In December 1813 Mrs. Robarts, following the death of her third husband, returned to Liberty County with her three small children, Mary Eliza, Joseph, and Louisa Jane. Thereafter for several years the Jones children, Susan and Charles, divided their time between their half-sister, Mrs. Maxwell, and their half-aunt, Mrs. Robarts; they summered with Mrs. Robarts and her children at Sunbury; they wintered with Colonel and Mrs. Maxwell, a childless couple, at Yellow Bluff on Colonel's Island; and at frequent intervals they visited their uncle and guardian, Captain Joseph Jones, at his plantation home, the Retreat. These kind relatives—Aunt Eliza Robarts, Sister Betsy Maxwell, and Uncle Joseph Jones—were the three mainstays of Charles's orphaned childhood; to him they ever stood *in loco parentis,* and to them he ever looked with respect, obedience, and cherished affection.

Upon their return to Liberty County Susan and Charles were placed at the Sunbury Academy, then one of the finest schools in Georgia, where they mastered the rudiments of an English education under the tutelage of the Rev. Dr. William McWhir. Early in 1819 Charles was sent to Savannah, where at the age of fourteen he became a clerk in the countinghouse of William Neff, a prosperous commission merchant. Here for four years he prepared himself for a mercantile career; and such were his energy, integrity, and practical gifts that his services were soon in demand and his prospects for business were bright. Noting his extraordinary powers, the Hon. John Elliott, United States senator from Georgia and a warm friend of the family, urged Captain Joseph Jones to send his ward to West Point Military Academy, and volunteered his influence in securing him a place. But the versatile young man was ordained to nobler work: a near-fatal illness had proved the instrument of his spiritual awakening. When nearly eighteen, on the fourth Sunday of November 1822, he became a member of Midway Church along with some forty others, including his sister, Susan, and his cousin, Mary Eliza Robarts. The Rev. Murdoch Murphy, then pastor at Midway, urged him to study for the ministry; he at once became active in the Sunday school and church, and after profound and prayerful deliberation he felt the call to preach. In May 1825, having already passed his twentieth birthday, he entered Phillips Academy, Andover, Massachusetts, where for the first time he took up a Latin grammar. Two years later he proceeded to Andover Theological Seminary, where he remained till October 1829. Without graduating from Andover he went on to Princeton, and there he received his diploma from Princeton Theological Seminary on September 27th, 1830, having been licensed to preach the gospel the preceding spring. Returning to Liberty County, he was married at Retreat plantation on December 21st, 1830, by the Rev. Dr. William McWhir, to his first cousin, Mary Jones, an intelligent and pious young lady of twenty-two years (born September 24th, 1808), daughter of Captain Joseph Jones, his uncle and guardian.

Thus opened the public career of the Rev. Dr. Charles Colcock Jones. In May 1831 he was called to the First Presbyterian Church of Savannah, where he labored earnestly and successfully for eighteen months. But the cry of the Negroes of his native county was too urgent for him to resist; to their needy spiritual state he had been drawn while a student at Princeton, and he now felt constrained to devote himself to their evangelization as well as to their moral and social uplift. With some regret he resigned from the Savannah church in November 1832: his first pastoral charge was destined to be his last. Returning once more to Liberty County, he gave himself body, mind, and soul to the great work of his life.

Nothing contributed more to Dr. Jones's success in the spiritual elevation of the Negro race than his *Catechism of Scripture Doctrine and Practice,* first published in Savannah in 1837. This volume, designed chiefly for "the oral instruction of colored persons," was used extensively in families and schools throughout the antebellum South; it was translated into Armenian and Turko-Armenian by the Rev. John Bailey Adger, missionary at Smyrna, in 1842; it was also translated into Chinese by the Rev. John Winn Quarterman, missionary at Ningpo, in 1853. A second volume, *The Religious Instruction of the Negroes in the United States,* published in Savannah in 1842, considerably augmented the usefulness of the first.

Through his publications as well as through his labors among the blacks Dr. Jones won nationwide recognition. In November 1836 he was elected professor of ecclesiastical history and church polity at the Presbyterian Theological Seminary in Columbia, South Carolina. Early in 1837 he removed with his family to Columbia, where he remained until December 1838, returning at that time to resume work among the Negroes of Liberty County. For nine consecutive years—from January 1839 to the close of 1847—he continued his chosen work, devoting the prime of his manhood to the cause nearest his heart. In November 1847 he was again elected professor of ecclesiastical history and church polity at the Columbia seminary; again he accepted the call, and early in 1848 he returned to Columbia to remain for two more years. Then came the challenge of his life. In the spring of 1850, at a time of peculiar national tension over the slavery issue, he was elected corresponding secretary of the Board of Domestic Missions of the Presbyterian Church, a position bringing him conspicuously before the whole church both North and South, and necessitating his removal to Philadelphia. It was a distinction altogether fitting and deserved. As *The Southern Presbyterian* noted on July 25th, "There is probably no other minister in our connection whose thorough knowledge of the state of things at the South, whose personal experience in missionary life, whose sound judgment and conciliatory manner are calculated at once so effectually to check the rabid zeal of Northern fanatics and secure the confidence and hearty cooperation of the South in sustaining missions among our own people, as is our highly esteemed and long-tried brother, Dr. Jones."

To Philadelphia Dr. and Mrs. Jones removed in October 1850. Their two sons, Charles Colcock and Joseph, were taken from the South Carolina College in Columbia and entered as undergraduates at Nassau Hall, Princeton; their only daughter, Mary Sharpe, was placed at a seminary for young ladies in Philadelphia conducted by the Misses Gill. In his new and most responsible position Dr. Jones manifested all his executive talents: his untiring energy and zeal, his common sense, his systematic business habits, his manly independence, his unfailing tact, and his thorough comprehension of the field. And his efforts were crowned with success: he infused new life into the operations of the Board of Domestic Missions, and he awakened the national church to the religious plight of the Negro. But he was not to continue long in the North: his constitution, never vigorous and now debilitated by the shock of his missionary labors, declined appreciably under the incessant demands of his office. As a boy at play he had accidentally fallen against a stick and pierced his lungs; an abscess had developed, and for a time he had been desperately ill. From this injury he had never fully recovered; his lungs had always been delicate, and in consequence he had suffered increasingly from a mystifying "inaction" or "paralysis affection"—a phenomenon considerably aggravated by cold and often accompanied by an overwhelming sense of weariness in his vocal cords. To his already enfeebled condition the burdens of his Philadelphia post measurably contributed, and after three years of unremitting labor he collapsed. There was no alternative: he was compelled to resign his secretaryship and seek restoration in the quiet of his Georgia home. In October 1853, leaving his two sons in the North, he returned with his wife and daughter to Liberty County to live out his days as a semi-invalid, teaching and preaching as his strength permitted, but growing progressively weaker with the months and years. His disease was known as the "wasting palsy"; it gradually but fearfully consumed his frame, leaving his mind untouched to the end. As his daughter wrote to a friend in 1860, "His inaction increases, so that it is with difficulty that he gets about at times. . . . He seldom preaches now, and is always compelled to sit while doing so. There is one great comfort: the nervous inaction has never affected his lungs or his head."

It was in many respects an agreeable and gracious world to which Dr. Jones returned in the autumn of 1853. He was a man of large property, chiefly in land and slaves. In the Federal Census of 1850 he was recorded as the owner of 107 slaves; by 1860 the number had increased to 129. In addition he and his wife were joint owners of three plantations. The largest of these, Arcadia, was also the farthest from the coast; it stretched from Midway Church to McIntosh Station and comprised 1996½ acres. Evidently Arcadia was never a favorite residence; although the Joneses visited the "long-deserted mansion" from time to time and actually wintered there in 1855, they occupied it as a settled home only in 1862, when its distance from the coast seemed to render it safe from Yankee raids. Dr. and Mrs. Jones deeded Arcadia to their three children, to be held by them jointly, early in 1857.

Far dearer to the Joneses was their fixed winter residence, Montevideo, a rice and sea-island cotton plantation comprising 941 acres, situated on the south bank of the North Newport River about a mile and a half below Riceboro. The first house at Montevideo was built in 1833; some twenty years later it was substantially altered and enlarged, and in November 1856 the Joneses first occupied the remodeled structure. It was, as Mrs. Jones wrote at the time, "a double two-story house, new, nicely painted and finished throughout"; there were fifteen rooms, with four large corner rooms on each of the two main stories. The dining and drawing rooms, each twenty-one feet square, communicated by means of a large folding door; from the drawing room projected a wing for a library eighteen feet square; from the dining room projected a corresponding wing "fitted up with closet and locked and open cupboards and all the appointments of a pantry and eating room." On the same floor there were two chambers seventeen feet square, separated by an "entry" or hall; on the floor above there were four more chambers and a laundry. As Mrs. Jones went on to say, in an undated note preserved at Tulane University:

The house is beautifully located, on one side fronting a lawn of twenty or thirty acres covered with live oak, magnolias, cedars, pines, and many other forest trees, arranged in groves or stretching out in lines and avenues or dotting the lawn here and there. On the other front passes the North Newport River, where all the produce of the place may be shipped to Savannah and water communication obtained to any point. In the gardens will be found both sweet and sour oranges and the myrtle orange, pomegranates, figs, the bearing olive, and grapes. . . . Attached to the house lot are a brick kitchen, brick dairy, smokehouse, washing and weaving rooms, two servants' houses, a commodious new stable and a carriage house and wagon shed, various poultry houses and yards attached, a well of excellent water, and a never-failing spring. On the plantation settlement are a two-story cotton house, gin and ginhouse, barn, cornhouse, ricehouse, winnowing house, millhouses, and fifteen frame houses, a brick shed and yard of excellent clay, and a chapel twenty by thirty feet.

Through the lawn or park in front of the house a straight avenue led approximately a mile from the chapel to the plantation gates. Midway Church was six and a half miles away; McIntosh Station was ten, Flemington fourteen, Walthourville thirteen, and Dorchester four. To the Jones family Montevideo ever remained "a happy, happy home." At the height of the war the widowed mother found consolation in returning to its welcoming embrace: "This precious home," she wrote on December 21st, 1863, "had always peculiar charms for me. Your beloved father often asked if I was conscious of always singing as I came in sight of the house."

From Montevideo the Joneses removed each year, late in May or early in June, to the healthier climate of their summer retreat, Maybank, a sea-island cotton plantation comprising 700 acres, situated fifteen miles to the east of Montevideo and overlooking the mouth of the Medway River at the northwest end of Colonel's Island. This picturesque island, actually an elevated tract of land surrounded by low salt marshes and hence free from malaria-bearing mosquitoes, lay between St. Catherines Island and the mainland, to which it was connected by means of a causeway. It was originally known as Bermuda Island, having been settled prior to the Revolutionary War by emigrants from the Bermudas; it was renamed Colonel's Island about 1778 because, it is said, as many as six colonels had established their summer retreats on a tract not more than three miles wide. To the Joneses and their friends it was known simply as "the Island." The soil there was exceedingly fertile, and the oyster beds were extraordinarily fine. Maybank had been bequeathed to Dr. and Mrs. Jones, together with some thirty Negro slaves, early in 1834 by Major Andrew Maybank ("Uncle Maybank"), a brother of Mary Maybank, the first wife of Mrs. Jones's father, Captain Joseph Jones. The original house, known as the Hut, had been the Joneses' residence for seven summers; in 1840 a new house had been built on an adjacent site and the Hut had been demolished; the Joneses had first occupied the new house in the summer of 1841. "We must ever hold Uncle Maybank in grateful remembrance," wrote Dr. Jones in his journal on June 2nd, 1860, "for bestowing upon us this quiet and healthful retreat, where we reared and educated our children until prepared for college, and where we have experienced unnumbered mercies from above." It was a house with many happy associations; for years the Jones children looked back nostalgically upon its simple domestic pleasures. Charles Colcock Jones, Jr., wrote thus on October 10th, 1857:

Some of the pleasantest recollections of youthful days are connected with the first fall fires on the Island, shedding their cheerful rays around the parlor while the rude northeast wind came dashing its watery gusts against the windows. Well do I remember the first gathering of the little basket- and net-makers around the genial hearth and the delights there experienced. Oh, the happy days of youth—they come not again!

On one occasion Mrs. Jones described Maybank as an unpretentious place, offering "such comforts as a plain country residence can furnish"; but her son Charles Colcock, writing to his only daughter, Mary Ruth, on May 11th, 1888, recalled that the plantation houses were "ample and very comfortably furnished" both at Maybank and at Montevideo:

These were generous homes, and the hospitality there extended was profuse and refined. Daddy Jack was the majordomo. Patience and Lucy were the chambermaids. Phoebe and Clarissa were the seamstresses. Marcia was the cook. Gilbert was the carriage driver. Flora and Silvy were the handmaidens. Jupiter and Caesar were the gardeners, and sundry younger servants were commissioned to sweep, scrub, brush flies, and run on errands. Niger was the fisherman, and there was a lad to bring the triweekly mail. There was no lack of service, and everything about the establishment was conducted upon the most liberal scale. . . .

That my sister, my brother, and myself might be well instructed, Father engaged the services of private tutors who resided in the family. At Maybank and also at Montevideo schoolhouses were built by Father. At the former the children of our neighbor, Mr. Roswell King, united with us, and at the latter were also convened the children of Mr. John Barnard. The teacher was generally the graduate of some approved college. The general direction of our studies was indicated by Father, and he not infrequently gave his personal attention to the manner and scope of our studies. The school hours were from eight in the morning until two o'clock P.M. in summer, and from nine until three in winter. Saturday was a holiday, and was devoted to hunting and fishing. Every Monday morning we read compositions and declaimed. Very rarely the tutor was absent, and then my dear father took upon himself the burden of our instruction. . . . The 4th of July, the 22nd of February, and three days at Christmas constituted our only vacations during the year.

The country abounded in deer, wild turkeys, ducks, squirrels, rabbits, raccoons, quail, woodcock, doves, ricebirds, fishes, alligators, and crabs, and we enjoyed every opportunity for hunting and fishing. We had our sailboat also; and that we might be encouraged in the art of riding and in swordsmanship, a little cavalry company was formed which paraded weekly at home and at the residences of our neighbors. . . . Fourth of July celebrations were held under the great live oak on the lawn at Maybank, the speeches of the youngsters being preliminary to a generous spread to which the neighbors were invited. On the 22nd of February we always repaired to the parade ground of the Liberty Independent Troop to listen to the oration and to witness the prize contest with saber and pistol. . . . I look back upon this boyhood period with unalloyed pleasure and gratitude. No son could have had kinder or more indulgent parents, or fuller opportunities for indulging in those pastimes which a plantation life afforded.

It was at Maybank, "the house that has been so dear to us," where "the climate is so healthy, and the advantages of the salt water so great," that the Joneses were settled in October 1860, when the story of this book begins. The elder son, Charles Colcock, "the Judge," born in Savannah on October 28th, 1831, and now nearing his twenty-ninth birthday, was practicing law in Savannah, having graduated from Nassau Hall, Princeton, in 1852 and from Dane Law School, Harvard, in 1855, and having married Ruth Berrien Whitehead on November 9th, 1858. The second son, Joseph, "the Doctor," born in Walthourville on September 6th, 1833, and now in his twenty-eighth year, was practicing medicine in Augusta, having graduated from Nassau Hall, Princeton, in 1853 and from the Medical College of the University of Pennsylvania in 1856, and having married Caroline Smelt Davis on October 26th, 1859. The youngest child, Mary Sharpe, born at Lodebar, the plantation of Colonel and Mrs. William Maxwell near Dorchester, on June 12th, 1835, and now in her twenty-sixth year, was residing in Walthourville, having become the wife of the Rev. Robert Quarterman Mallard, a Presbyterian clergyman, on April 22nd, 1857. It was generally agreed by family and friends that Charles Colcock and Joseph were exceptional young men destined to brilliant public careers. As their uncle, the Rev. John Jones, wrote in 1856, "I am acquainted with no young men who have had equal advantages and who have made so diligent improvement of them. They bring to their professions minds not only well stored but (what is better) well disciplined. With patience of investigation and persevering purpose they are bound to excel." And Mary Sharpe was felt to be equally promising in the private sphere to which young ladies were then confined; a family friend remembered her as "a sprightly, intelligent, well-informed young woman . . . bright, quick, merry, joyous." Typical was the response of Laura Elizabeth Maxwell, first cousin and lifelong friend of the Jones children, who wrote pleasantly in 1855: "I am proud of my cousins, and have every reason to be. To my mind none are *more polished;* and I must hide my diminished head, having never had the advantages of a *polished Philadelphia* school."

Few friends were as well qualified to assess the merits of the Jones children as Laura Elizabeth Maxwell, daughter and only living child of Dr. Jones's beloved sister, Susan, now Mrs. Cumming. As a girl Susan Mary Jones had attended the Sunbury Academy for several years with her brother, Charles; in 1818 she had proceeded with her cousin, Mary Eliza Robarts, to Charleston to attend a select boarding school for young ladies. Returning to Liberty County in 1819, she had resided with her half-sister, Elizabeth, wife of Colonel William Maxwell, until her marriage in September 1823 to James

Audley Maxwell, grandson of Colonel James Maxwell, one of the first settlers of the Midway community. Three children blessed this union: Laura Elizabeth (born July 20th, 1824), who survived all three of her Jones cousins and lived past the turn of the century; Charles Edward (born May 18th, 1826), who when about to graduate from the Medical College of the University of Pennsylvania was stricken with dysentery and died tragically in Morristown, New Jersey, on April 3rd, 1852; and Georgia (born March 7th, 1828), who died in infancy. On December 1st, 1828, Mrs. Maxwell had been left a widow with three small children; ten years later (on November 21st, 1838) she had married Joseph Cumming, a Savannah widower with four children: William Henry, Mary Cuthbert, Montgomery, and Wallace. She had been widowed a second time on December 5th, 1846. Although she owned two plantations in Liberty County—Lambert and White Oak—she had preferred to live much of the time between her first and second marriages in the household of her brother, where her two surviving children, Laura and Charles, had come to feel toward the Jones children more as brother and sister than as cousins. After the death of her second husband in 1846 she had again lived at intervals in her brother's family; in October 1850 she and her daughter, Laura, had accompanied the Joneses to Philadelphia, where her son, Charles, was then studying medicine; and in October 1860, still mourning the untimely death of her son eight years before, she was living at Point Maxwell, a beautiful retreat occupying the northeast portion of Colonel's Island, sharing the household of her daughter, Laura, who had become the wife of the Rev. David Lyman Buttolph, pastor of Midway Church, on June 10th, 1856.

Between Mrs. Cumming and Dr. Jones there existed from the first "an affection not often witnessed and never transcended." So wrote Charles Colcock Jones, Jr., years later in an obituary of his aunt. And the Jones letters provide ample evidence of this deep and abiding devotion which through the years brought the two families to feel virtually as one. "I have never known any difference between your interest and my own," wrote Dr. Jones to his sister in 1855; "and *yours* have always been to me as mine own children." "Your dear children," wrote Mrs. Cumming in 1864: "dear to me as my own, they are constantly on my heart." Living for many years in the same household, Laura and Mary Sharpe were brought up as sisters, and they ever regarded each other as such, despite a difference in age of nearly eleven years. "She is *my* little sister," Laura once said; and her affection was fully reciprocated. "When I am with Aunt Susan and yourself," wrote Mary Sharpe to her cousin in 1856, "I feel as though I were in another home." Mary Sharpe was to name one of her children for Mrs. Cumming's deceased infant, Georgia Maxwell; Mary Sharpe's children were to call Laura "Aunt Laura" and Mrs. Cumming "Grandma Susan"; and eventually Mary Sharpe was to say to her cousin: "I feel to your children as though they were my sister's children."

Also summering on Colonel's Island was the family of Roswell King, Jr., a "kind friend and good neighbor," whose two plantations, Yellow Bluff and Woodville, occupied the east and southeast portions of the island overlooking the waters of St. Catherines Sound. The Kings divided their year between Woodville, their pleasant summer retreat high on Half Moon Bluff, and South Hampton, their handsome winter residence a few miles east of Montevideo. Roswell King sprang from long-established New England stock. His father, also Roswell King, had come to Georgia from Windsor, Connecticut, in the 1780s and settled at Darien, then an important mercantile center, where he had commenced a thriving business in lumber, rice, and sea-island cotton. In 1825 Roswell King, Jr. (born 1796), had married Julia Rebecca Maxwell (born 1808), a sister of James Audley Maxwell, the first husband of Susan Mary Jones. Mrs. King was therefore sister-in-law to Mrs. Cumming and aunt to her daughter, Laura Maxwell; and by easy extension she became "Aunt Julia" to the three Jones children, who looked on Laura as a sister. The Joneses and the Kings were the closest of neighbors and the dearest of friends. In crises they were quick to come to each other's aid; in joy as well as in sorrow they were often united; and at Maybank and Montevideo their children attended the same school. As Mrs. Jones observed in 1858, "the many, many years of kind intercourse and unbroken friendship we have enjoyed make them all especially near and dear."

By all these relatives and friends Dr. Jones was cordially esteemed; by those in his intimate family circle he was greatly beloved. Members of the Jones family felt bound together by ties of extraordinary affection—partly, perhaps, because first cousins had married; and the center of that affection was Dr. Jones: beloved as nephew, cousin, brother, father, husband. "The anguish of my heart is great, for I have indeed lost a son," wrote Mrs. Eliza G. Robarts at the time of her nephew's death. "This day the tears of a mother and sisters are shed for one who has ever been to them a son and brother," wrote Miss Mary Eliza Robarts. "To *me* he ever stood more in the relation of a parent than a brother," wrote Henry Hart Jones; "from early childhood he was my counselor and guide, and I can truly add that no mortal man ever wielded such influence over me for good." "I loved him more than any man on earth," wrote the Rev. John Jones; "he came very near to my own father." "The memory of my father is the richest legacy I have on earth," wrote Charles Colcock Jones, Jr.; "and I can never be sufficiently grateful for all his goodness and example, for all his precept and principle." "For thirty-two years," wrote Mrs. Mary Jones, "it pleased the Lord to honor me with his companionship—with his guidance, his support, his spiritual instruction, his wise counsels, his intellectual light and knowledge, his daily example, his prayers and his precepts, and all that tender and affectionate intercourse which as a wife I felt was the cherished boon of my life. Oh, that I had been found worthy of such a blessing!"

Mrs. Jones was indeed found worthy, and by no one more feelingly than her husband, who was ever articulate in sounding the praises of his "model wife." On October 19th, 1859, writing to his son Charles, he enlarged on a favorite theme:

Her industry, her economy, her prudence, her foresight, her resolution, her intelligence are uncommon. She has done her husband good all the days of his life, and has never stood in the way of his advancement, but has taken the liveliest interest in his office and duties, and made sacrifices for it, and kept up her mental improvement, and been at home in all circles in which she has moved and in all the company we have so numerously entertained. And how she manages her household, and how she discharges her duties therein, and above all what a mother in all respects she has been to her children, they best know. And so she continues to be and will ever be. And so you can well understand how my esteem and admiration and affection for her continues and grows.

It was a mutual happiness which husband and wife bestowed: their relationship was one of selfless interdependence. "My anxiety knows no abatement when I am separated from you." So wrote the wife to her husband. And the husband responded in kind. On June 21st, 1851, sojourning briefly at Maybank, he wrote to his wife, then far away in Philadelphia, of the peace of their summer home:

I am upstairs in my old quiet pleasant study. Not a sound about the house. Perfect quiet within. But the whole world without is filled with the melody and notes of a hundred birds. Their voices are not silent a second of time. They seem to have entered in and taken possession more perfectly than when we were here. The calmness, the quiet is delightful. The lot looks so grown, so fresh and green. The house all open, so clean and pleasant from top to bottom. Everything just as you left it, and all reminding me of my love, my sweet Mary. If I look out on the flowers and smell their fragrance, she planted and trained them with her own hands; if I look at the trees and the garden with its fruits, its oranges and figs and pomegranates, its pears and peaches and plums and apples, they were all set out under her eye and pruned and fostered by her care; if I walk in the piazza, in imagination she is at my side, and we are leaning in the cool breeze upon the shaded banister, sharing our thoughts and our love together. In the parlor, in the passage, in our chamber, her image is before me. There is not a part of the dwelling—no, not a single part of it—which does not furnish some scene of affection, some moments of love between us. Oh, if you were here, you would know how my heart beats towards you, my own, my dearest Mary!

I

MR. CHARLES C. JONES, JR., *to* REV. *and* MRS. C. C. JONES[8]
                                          Savannah, *Tuesday,* October 9th, 1860
My dear Father and Mother,

By today's papers you will see that I have been elected mayor of the city of Savannah. This appointment was on my part *wholly unsolicited,* the nomination having been made during my absence from the city. It was also a nomination and ratification by the citizens of Savannah irrespective of party. Under these circumstances I did not feel at liberty to decline, and must admit that the compliment of the election comes home with peculiar effect, conferred as it is by the city of my birth, of my choice—a city, too, whose soil covers the honored dust of Great-Grandfather.

The theory of the citizens' movement in this campaign was *in municipal elections to ignore national politics,* and consult only such questions as concern the interests of our city. Party, factions, and intrigues were ignored, and men of all parties united in the support. The policy pursued by the Breckinridge and Lane party, as represented by the executive committee of this city, was suicidal. Every overture was made to induce them to unite in the general plan of a citizens' ticket irrespective of party, and thus avoid any bias by this election for or against the Presidential candidates. They foolishly refused, and defeat ensued. This is not, however, a test vote of the popularity of Breckinridge and Lane in this city, as many of our citizens had not registered, and the citizens' ticket received the votes of at least three hundred Breckinridge and Lane Democrats.

I trust to see you both soon, my dear parents, and will explain then more fully the theory of this election. I sincerely hope, in view of the important duties thus devolved upon me, that I may receive strength and guidance from above.

Tonight I leave for Augusta. Ruth will return in a week or two. I go to bring her from Bath to Augusta, and will, D.V., come back here myself on Thursday. All friends well. With warmest love, my dear father and mother, to you both, and sensibly alive to the feeling that the chief delight which I experience in this confidence of my fellow citizens arises from the fact that you, my dear parents, and Ruth will be gratified by the result and the course which I have pursued, I am, as ever,

                              Your affectionate son,
                              Charles C. Jones, Jr.

Maybank, *Monday,* October 15th, 1860

My dear Son,

Your election was unexpected to us, as we had no intimation of your being in nomination until it appeared in the newspaper a day or two before the election took place. It is a high honor, coming unsolicited, and the expression of the confidence of a majority of your fellow citizens; and we esteem it such, and are gratified that your conduct and character have been such as to attract to you their suffrages, which place you in the highest office in their gift. And we sincerely hope that they may not be disappointed in their expectations of you, but that you will conscientiously seek to discharge your very responsible and in many respects difficult duties with all sobriety, industry, impartiality, justice, and integrity, and with kindness and decision and intelligence. I look upon the office as one of very high responsibility, and trust you are of the same impression. Otherwise you may fail in filling it as you ought.

You will, as you remark in your letter, need aid from *above*; and I hope, my dear son, that *you will seek* that aid. Since "the powers that be are ordained of God," and in His providence you have been called to preside as the chief executive officer over a large city, you should acknowledge the Lord's hand in it and seek from Him wisdom to direct and power to stand. "In all thy ways acknowledge Him, and He shall direct thy paths." Elevation to station and influence involves a responsibility which awakens solicitude in the bosom of every right-minded man; and instead of inflation and self-sufficiency he is prompted to humility and watchfulness. And knowing the fickleness of popular favor, and how trivial events cast down those who seem to stand firmest, he will trust but little to it, and take his satisfaction in doing his duty and making himself useful to his friends and country. And such lose not their reward. *Hoc nempe ab homine exigitur, ut prosit hominibus: si fieri potest, multis; si minus, paucis; si minus, proximis; si minus, sibi. Nam, cum se utilem ceteris efficit, commune agit negotium.* So writes Seneca, and his views are just. And may you make yourself useful to others, and so be reckoned a common good, or a benefactor.

Our first desire and prayer for our sons and our daughter has been that you all might be the true children of God, and our second, that your lives might be spent in usefulness to your fellow men. And our advice (and I trust example) has been, never *to seek office,* but let *office seek you.* If it is tendered, and you hope you are qualified to fill it, and it is proper to accept, do so. Honors to be well worn and well borne need to be well merited. You are perhaps the youngest mayor Savannah has ever had; therefore you must so act that no man may despise thy youth.

You are just twice as young as Socrates was when he consented to take public office in Athens. He was fifty-six. You have that to aid you which that great and excellent heathen never had: the knowledge of the living and true God and of His Holy Word. You will let me as your father insist, my son, that you do conscientiously read God's Word carefully *twice* a day. Do not speak or think of the want of time when God gives you all your time and can stop it when He pleases; and you can make no better use of it than by conversing with Him through His Holy Word and by prayer. This will strengthen and enlighten you for all the cares and businesses of life. Try it faithfully, and you will find it so. As you advance and become more and more involved in the affairs of this life, the more anxious your parents feel for your everlasting interests, and pray you *not to neglect them.*

Mother sends much love, and congratulations upon your honors, and her best wishes and prayers for your success under them. Am happy to say she has been better of late. Our kind friend and good neighbor Mrs. King has had a severe fall, and is confined to her bed and suffers much from pain; but the doctor thinks she is not dangerously injured, though her confinement may be protracted. We were glad to hear from Ruthie and Julia and from your brother and Carrie. Love to Ruthie for us when you write, and kisses for Julia. We long to see you all. Weather very cold for the season. God bless and keep you, my dear son!

Your ever affectionate father,
C. C. Jones.

Mrs. Mary Jones *to* Mrs. Mary S. Mallard[t]

Maybank, *Monday,* October 15th, 1860

My dear Daughter,

It has just occurred to me as we were retiring that I might send you a line by Gilbert, who goes to the depot with Joe's box tomorrow. Your beautiful little sacque and gown have been safely deposited with the other articles.

On last Friday week your Aunt Julia was standing in her pantry door when one of the horses she has been in the habit of petting was brought up, and she took hold of the halter whilst the servant drew water for him. She turned around to speak to someone. He threw up his head and jumped off, jerking her out of the door and dashing her upon the ground at least ten feet from the door. She fell upon her left side and was taken up insensible, and has been in bed unable to move ever since, except as she is assisted from one side to the other. I was sent for immediately, and reached her before Dr. Harris, who made (as soon as she could bear it) a thorough examination and said there was neither fracture nor dislocation. But her sufferings continue so great that he now requests a consultation with Dr. Bulloch. I have been as much with her as possible. They are truly a distressed family. . . .

When may we expect to see Mrs. Stevens and yourself? We have almost winter. You have seen the honor conferred upon your brother; pray for him that he may be found faithful. Father unites with me in best love to Robert and yourself. Kisses for our dear grandchildren.

Ever your affectionate mother,
Mary Jones.

Walthourville, *Tuesday*, October 16th, 1860

My dear Mother,

I was just going to get my pen today when the mailbag came, and in it your welcome letter. I am truly sorry to hear of Aunt Julia's injury, and feel very much troubled about her; but I hope our kind Heavenly Father will spare her life. I feel for Cousin Mary and Isabel. And I know the burden of nursing falls upon you, dear Mother; I hope you will not make yourself sick. I wish I were with you to help in some way.

I saw Mrs. Stevens this evening, and if nothing prevents, we hope to be with you on next Tuesday evening. Mr. Mallard expects his father's carriage on Monday next, and we will leave early Tuesday morning, dine in Dorchester, and I will probably take a seat with Mrs. Stevens in her carriage from that place. Mrs. Stevens anticipates a great deal of pleasure in going down, and I have no doubt the change will do her good. She will remain until Friday. . . .

I received a very pleasant letter from Brother Charlie today in reply to one I wrote him offering my congratulations. He expects Ruth next Monday. Julia can say a good many little words.

Last week I had a long, interesting letter from Carrie, in which she sends a great deal of love to Father and yourself and begs me to tell Father that she has written a letter on large paper; and I can testify that every part of it was well filled. Brother Joe sent us quite a flaming placard advertising the Planters' Convention. We intend sending it to the station tomorrow and having it posted there. Perhaps some of the planters may be induced to attend.

What cold weather we have had for several days past! This early cold always carries me back to Maybank. *Well* do I remember the first fires that were kindled in the fall, and how we used to gather around the hearth—Father reading aloud, Mother knitting or sewing, Brother Charlie sitting upon the floor with a bunch of wire grass and ball of flax thread making mats with *Taddy* at his side (or else sinewing arrows), Brother Joe with his paint box and some megatherium skeleton model before him, and I think I used to make mittens or sew my hexagon quilt. Sometimes a hoarded stock of chinquapins would engage the attention of all the children, each one counting his store. I think Father's reading was often interrupted on such evenings by questions as to the *probable* time when frost would come; and if Daddy Jack made his appearance in the room, his opinion was sure to be asked. We all have hearths of our own now, but I do not think any of them will ever burn as brightly or possess the same attractions of that one at Maybank. There was always something peculiar about the first autumn fire. . . .

Our little ones are quite well. Charlie develops daily, and is very good. Mamie often says something about her "danma" and "danpa." Mr. Mallard unites with me in warmest love to dear Father and yourself, dear Mother.

Your affectionate daughter,
Mary S. Mallard.

HON. CHARLES C. JONES, JR., *to* REV. C. C. JONES[g]

Savannah, *Thursday,* October 18th, 1860

My dear Father,

I am in receipt of your kind and valued letter of the 15th inst., and sincerely thank you for the same.

No one can form any idea of the multifarious and important duties which devolve upon the mayor of this city until called upon practically to discharge them. The accumulated ordinances of a century and a quarter have to be carefully understood, and administered with firmness and discrimination. Interests varied in their character must be duly considered and protected. Much lies in the discretion and sound judgment of the mayor, and in many things a nice sense of right, of justice and propriety, is his only guide. The summary jurisdiction of the police court, held every morning at ten o'clock, also involves in its proper exercise no little firmness, intelligence, and discrimination. You are aware that over this court the mayor presides every morning at ten o'clock. In fine, he is expected to have a care for every interest and for the every protection of the city at all hours of the day and night. I am feelingly alive to the responsibilities which are thus devolved upon me; and it will be my constant endeavor, with an humble and ever-repeated prayer for assistance from above, to bring to the discharge of the incumbent duties a firm resolution, a clear judgment, and an enlightened perception of right and justice.

Our city, since these recent frosts, improves in health. The broken-bone fever decreases. The summer absentees are returning, and business has received an upward impulse. I must, however, make a special exception in our profession. Legal matters are quite stagnant. The doubt which attends any attempt to conjecture what another month may bring forth in the political and social status of our country exerts in all probability its depressing influence. The election of Lincoln seems now almost a fixed fact, in view of the recent advices received from Pennsylvania, Ohio, and Indiana. The Republicans claim New York by a clear majority of forty thousand. Should Lincoln be elected, the action of a single state, such as South Carolina or Alabama, may precipitate us into all the terrors of intestine war. I sincerely trust that a kind Providence, that has so long and so specially watched over the increasing glories of our common country, may so influence the minds of fanatical men and dispose of coming events as to avert so direful a calamity.

Ruth and little Julia are expected on Monday night next. I shall be truly happy when they return. "It is not good for man to be alone." Especially is this true in the case of a married man.

We have but little of interest with us. I was pained to learn the severe indisposition of Aunt Julia, and sincerely hope for her speedy relief. With warmest love to you, my dear father, and to my dear mother, I am, as ever,

Your affectionate son,

Charles C. Jones, Jr.

25

Maybank, *Tuesday,* October 23rd, 1860

My very dear Son,

We are this afternoon in expectation of the arrival of your dear sister and the little ones with Mrs. Dr. Stevens and some of her family to make us a visit; and whilst waiting to receive them I will send you a few lines, as I shall not have the opportunity of writing again this week.

I trust your own fireside has ere this been gladdened by the presence of your dear wife and sweet little daughter. How I long to see you all! Julia's likeness stands open upon the mantelpiece, and we look upon it daily. Precious child, may she long be spared to you, and prove an angel of mercy to direct your heart to the Giver of such a gift!

My feelings of interest and congratulations upon the distinguished position which you have been called to occupy by the voice of your fellow citizens have been already conveyed to you through your good father in his letter of wise and affectionate counsel and advice, which I trust and believe you will reverence and obey. It surely is no common honor for one at your age to be called to preside and direct the interests of fifteen or twenty thousand people! I trust you will realize the high responsibilities which rest upon you. God grant you, my child, *fidelity* in your lot, and uprightness in all your ways! My daily—my *special*—prayer for you is that you may have the teachings and guidance of the Holy Spirit in all that you are called to say or do. I feel that just at this time above all other periods in our national history special grace, wisdom, and decision are needed by all our rulers.

(*Just here* the ladies arrived.)

Yesterday your uncle and Mr. Buttolph spent with us, and we had a pleasant day. Mrs. Stevens has never visited the Island before. She admires both scenery and atmosphere, and yesterday we had a fine display of fish upon the table: sheepshead, young drum, whiting, and yellowtail.

Our good friend and neighbor Mrs. King is more comfortable, but in a very suffering condition, and likely to be so for a great while. If you see Willie, tell him his mother is becoming more accustomed to her confinement, and the family are well, excepting their servant Jaque.

The coming Sabbath, my dear child, will be your birthday, and Father and Mother now send you our blessing and best wishes upon it. God bless and save you with His everlasting salvation! . . . Enclosed is an order for the railroad dividend, and I wish you to take sixty-five dollars and buy a *desk* or *bookcase* for your nice new study as a *birthday gift from your mother, or any other article* that would be useful and acceptable. The remainder you can send by any private opportunity.

When shall we see you? Our best love to our dear daughter and little darling Julia, in which Sister unites.

Ever your affectionate mother,
Mary Jones.

October 25th.

HON. CHARLES C. JONES, JR., *to* MRS. MARY JONES^r
Savannah, *Saturday,* October 27th, 1860

My very dear Mother,

I was yesterday favored with your precious letter of the 25th inst., and must thank you for all the kind congratulations and valuable advice which it contains. You never forget my birthday, and each recurrence brings me a message of love and interest, full of the tenderest maternal solicitude and of the purest Christian counsels. How much, my dear mother, do I owe to you and to dear Father! . . . Time does but consecrate you and all your virtues in my heart of hearts. Amid the varied scenes and phases of life, amid the perplexities and cares which present not infrequently questions in morals hard to be answered by some, I have always some precept of former years, taught by you, which solves the doubt and indicates the path of duty and of honor; while your examples are ever before me—by far the best lesson, the most perfect illustration of the principle. Twenty-nine years of my life have passed away. Solemn thought! And how little have I accomplished! . . .

The duties of the mayoralty are heavy upon me—more particularly so when the present political status of the country is considered, and the further facts which grow out of it—that scoundrels are seen, and suspicious persons found, tampering with our Negroes and attempting to induce them to leave the state. I have now under arrest a crew of Negro sailors—free men of color—who are charged with this offense. The case comes up before me on Monday next. I find also that great laxity has obtained in reference to the conduct of the Negro population. The consequence is that they have forgotten their places—are guilty of gambling, smoking in the streets, drinking, and disorderly conduct generally. To the remedy of this I intend to devote, and am devoting, my every energy. I mean also to bring to justice those offenders of foreign birth, the rum-sellers, who at the corners of our streets in their shops are demoralizing our servants and ruining them in every point of view. Any mayor who is sensibly alive to the duties which are devolved upon him, and who endeavors conscientiously to discharge them, has, I can assure you, his hands full.

I have again to thank you, my dear mother, for your handsome and valued present. It is just what I most coveted. The remainder of the dividend (say, one hundred dollars) is now in my hands, and I will embrace the earliest opportunity for sending it to you. . . .

You and Father we will expect and hope to see at least during the meeting of Presbytery if not before. From Mr. Porter we learn that this body convenes here on Thursday the 8th prox. Do, my dear parents, come if you can find it in your power to do so. Ruth has nicely arranged and fitted up her new house. Your room is all ready and waiting for you, and we wish you to see your little granddaughter. You will not be ashamed of her. All well, and unite in warmest love. As ever,

Your affectionate son,
Charles C. Jones, Jr.

REV. C. C. JONES *to* HON. CHARLES C. JONES, JR.[g]
Maybank, *Saturday,* October 27th, 1860

My dear Son,

Your last favors are at hand, and we congratulate you on the return of your dear wife and sweet little daughter. We long to see you all, and will try and pay you a visit after a while.

Enclosed is a draft on Mr. Anderson for two hundred dollars, the amount of my note, which please take up and end the long run. And I hope we may be favored so as to need no more help of the kind. Mr. Anderson has that amount in his hands on my account, which we reserved for contingencies; but as the crop will be going to market, we now use it.

Mother wrote you last mail. Sister and the little ones are on a visit to us. Robert left this morning with Mrs. Dr. Stevens, who has been spending a few days with us. Mrs. King is doing well.

I do not apprehend any serious disturbance in the event of Lincoln's election and a withdrawal of one or more Southern states, which will eventuate in the withdrawal of all. On what ground can the free states found a military crusade upon the South? Who are the violators of the Constitution? Will the conservatives in the free states make no opposition? If the attempt is made to subjugate the South, what prospect will there be of success? And what *benefit* will accrue to all the substantial interests of the free states? The business world will think very little benefit. Under all the circumstances attending a withdrawal there would be no *casus belli.* Is not the right of self-government on the part of the people the cornerstone of the republic? Have not fifteen states a right to govern themselves and withdraw from a compact or constitution disregarded by the other states to their injury and (it may be) their ruin? But may God avert such a separation, for the consequences may in future be disastrous to both sections. Union if possible —but with it we must have *life, liberty, and equality.*

I pray for your just and prosperous administration of the trusts reposed in you by your fellow citizens. Kiss Ruth and little Daughter for us all. All send much love. Don't hold any courts *Sunday!*

Your ever affectionate father,
C. C. Jones.

REV. C. C. JONES *to* HON. CHARLES C. JONES, JR.[g]
Maybank, *Monday,* November 5th, 1860

My dear Son,

I send by your Cousin Lyman a manuscript volume (the fourth of my *History*) which you will express to Mr. ——, Columbus, Georgia, according to the address, and much oblige me. I wrote Mr. —— that it would be expressed on Thursday of this week, D.V. Some 170 or 180 pages are to follow, and the first volume will be closed, and I shall be grateful. So soon as Mr. —— finishes the copy, will put it to press, D.V.

Also your mother's spectacles: *broken*. Please have the same magnifying power, pebble glasses if to be had, and return them as soon as possible—by mail if you have no direct opportunity out. We have but one available pair of specs between us.

Also my faithful watch: broken in winding up. Please have it well repaired for me.

Sorry to give you so much trouble, as you are so busy.

Moving up this week. Mother worn out gardening and packing. Late, and she has retired. Sends much love to Ruthie and yourself with me, and many kisses for the dear little granddaughter. Must refer you to Cousin Lyman for all the news our way.

Your ever affectionate father,
C. C. Jones.

MRS. MARY JONES *to* HON. CHARLES C. JONES, JR.[g]

Maybank, *Tuesday,* November 6th, 1860*

Thanks many, my dear son, for your affectionate and valued letter. *Gilbert* begs me to say he can get you eight turkeys at a dollar apiece if you are willing to give it and will send word by *Thursday*. They are very scarce. With much love,

Your affectionate mother,
M.J.

HON. CHARLES C. JONES, JR., *to* REV. *and* MRS. C. C. JONES[g]

Savannah, *Wednesday,* November 7th, 1860

My dear Father and Mother,

We are happy today to hear from you so directly. Mr. Buttolph came in while we were at dinner and gave us the latest news from you. The watch and spectacles are already in the hands of the jeweler, and will be repaired so soon as practicable. You shall have them by the earliest opportunity thereafter. The volume is now in charge of the express company, and will be duly forwarded to Mr. ——. In consideration of the fact of my being His Honor the Mayor, the agent refused to receive any pay for the transportation of the same.

The telegrams announce the fact of Lincoln's election by a popular vote! South Carolina has today virtually seceded. Judge Magrath of the U.S. Circuit Court for the District of South Carolina, Hon. William F. Colcock, collector of the port of Charleston, and other government officers have resigned, and we learn that the Palmetto flag will be hoisted on the morrow. A meeting of the citizens here is called for tomorrow evening. We are on the verge of Heaven only knows what.

I write in haste for the mail. You have my congratulations, Father, upon the near completion of your first volume. May you have increasing mind and strength to conclude your most valuable labors! Ruth will, my dear mother, be very happy to get the turkeys at some convenient and early day. Our little Julia is recovering from her attack of broken-bone fever, but my dear Ruth is quite unwell, and has been suffering much for nearly a week. They unite with me, my dear parents, in warmest love to you both. As ever,

Your affectionate son,
Charles C. Jones, Jr.

HON. CHARLES C. JONES, JR., *to* MRS. MARY JONES[g]
Savannah, *Tuesday,* November 13th, 1860

My dear Mother,

We are happy through Sister to hear from you today. She expects, I believe, to be with you on Thursday of this week, unless we can persuade her to remain with us until Robert, who left us this morning, returns from Columbus. My dear Ruth continues quite unwell, and little Julia is not as bright as she might be.

I have my hands completely filled day and night. The duties devolved upon me at this important crisis are many and onerous. Our country needs the prayers of the good and the counsels of the wise. I trust that we may soon see a Southern confederacy. If we are true to ourselves, it may be formed upon a substantial and viable basis.

I have only time to say, my dear mother, that we all unite in warmest love to self and dear Father. As ever,

Your affectionate son,
Charles C. Jones, Jr.

MRS. MARY JONES *to* HON. CHARLES C. JONES, JR.[g]
Montevideo, *Thursday,* November 15th, 1860

My dear Son,

We were happy to receive your affectionate favor by today's mail, and to know that you were well and again at the post of duty. No festive greetings were ever mingled with more elevated feelings of friendship, honor, patriotism, and courage than those recently enjoyed by the citizens of Charleston and Savannah. We are much obliged to you for the *Mercury,* and felt honored that our son bore so high a place. Your opening speech at the Pulaski gave evidently a tone to the meeting.

Be assured, my dear child, of your parents' warmest sympathy at this time, and of our united and special prayer that you may be divinely guided and ever act with wisdom and fidelity in your sacred and responsible station. It is a new era in our country's history, and I trust the wise and patriotic leaders of the people will soon devise some united course of action throughout the Southern states. I cannot see a shadow of reason for civil war in the event of a Southern confederacy; but even that, *if it must come,* would be preferable to submission to Black Republicanism, involving as it would all that is horrible, degrading, and ruinous. "Forbearance has ceased to be a virtue"; and I believe we could meet with no evils out of the Union that would compare to those we will finally suffer if we continue in it; for we can no longer doubt that the settled policy of the North is to crush the South.

But I am wandering quite beyond my object in writing, which is specially to ask if dear Ruth cannot come out with our little granddaughter and spend some time with us until they both recruit. The weather is now delightful, and we would do all in our power to make home pleasant to them. Our little Mary has been a great comfort and source of amusement, and we shall feel lost without her.

Today we sent Gilbert to Sunbury for the turkeys, and tomorrow Sam will take them to Stepney with directions to feed them well, that they may be ready for your use when ordered. They are young birds and not as large as they will be. Poultry is scarce, and we got them as a favor.

Father has just returned from the chapel, and unites with me in best love to Ruth and yourself, and many kisses for our granddaughter.

Ever your affectionate mother,
Mary Jones.

REV. C. C. JONES *to* HON. CHARLES C. JONES, JR.[8]

Montevideo, *Thursday,* November 15th, 1860

Your position is a very responsible one. Go calmly and quietly about your duties, and discharge them with integrity and fidelity, and avoid excitements and too frequent speaking on public occasions. I was much gratified with your speech at the dinner to the Charlestonians in Savannah.

The times are remarkable; the questions before the people momentous. The final issues are with Him who rules among the nations. A nation to be born in a day, without a struggle, would be a wonder on earth. If the Southern states resolve on a separate confederacy, they must be prepared for any emergency, even that of war with the free states; as their arrogance and confidence in their power may urge them to attempt our subjugation—although I do not fear it if the Southern states are united. We have a heavy Northern element, and a Southern element Northernized, to contend with in our own borders, and may perhaps lead to some embarrassment; but the majority the other way is so decided that it cannot—at least it is so to be hoped—effect much. Certainly we do need "the prayers of the pious and the wisdom of the wise." Portions of Governor Brown's special message are excellent. Having no access to the leading spirits of the day, I cannot discern the drift of affairs beyond the light of the newspapers, which we read with interest. We have no knowledge of the course which Maryland, Virginia, North Carolina, Tennessee, Kentucky, and Missouri will pursue.

The Lord keep and bless you and yours, my dear son, and give you a place in that Kingdom which cannot be moved, is the prayer of
Your affectionate father,
C. C. Jones.

REV. C. C. JONES *to* HON. CHARLES C. JONES, JR.[8]
Montevideo, *Monday,* November 19th, 1860
My dear Son,

I shall send, D.V., our shoe measures tomorrow to Messrs. Butler & Frierson to fit and forward by Friday's freight train. Will you do me the favor of calling and selecting the quality and price for me? The first I wish substantial, the second not extravagant. Have notified them that you would do so.

Your sister reached us in safety, and improved by her pleasant visit to you. The little ones pretty well, and very engaging. We want Ruthie and little Julia to come and see us. The change will do them good, and we will do all in our power to make it agreeable in our quiet home.

Preached yesterday at Midway, and do not feel the worse for it today.

Tomorrow the county holds a meeting on Federal affairs. Captain Winn tells me our esteemed friend Judge Law is expected out. We shall be glad to see him; his influence will be good. Shall attend, Providence permitting; and Mother says she will go with me *to represent her father,* being the oldest child of his family now living. You know her patriotism. She has taken possession of your pistol with the shooting apparatus underneath, and Gilbert is ordered to clean and put it in perfect order. And she says she has *caps* for it. I trust the measures of the state will be calmly considered and resolutely taken, and the convention of the people duly called.

Mother and Sister unite with me in love to Ruthie and yourself, and kisses for Julia. I am longing to see the child. The letter of your brother to Mr. Cobb, president of the Cotton Planters' Convention, was a *private* one and never intended for any other eyes than Mr. Cobb's. He should not have published it; and some things your brother ought not to have put in it.
Your affectionate father,
C. C. Jones.

REV. C. C. JONES *to* MRS. RUTH B. JONES[8]
Montevideo, *Thursday,* November 22nd, 1860
My dear Daughter,

We were pained to learn through Robert on Tuesday that our dear son, your good husband, was sick with perhaps the broken-bone fever. He said if he should be seriously sick that you would not delay but write and let us know; and as we have heard nothing by mail today, we trust through God's mercy he is doing well if not entirely recovered. Write us, if you please, by return of mail (Saturday's) and let us know the truth. His Honor the Mayor has necessarily a great deal of care and of business, and is obliged to be at least occasionally out at night; and therefore it becomes him to be as careful of himself as he possibly can, and defend himself from the night air when he goes out. And I know you will try like a good wife to relieve him as much as possible from domestic cares, and make his hours at home hours of enjoyment and repose. And so you will do him good and be a helpmeet to him. A cheerful and an affectionate wife is the joy of her husband and the life and light of his home, and I am sure you are such a one. Don't you think a change from town to country would be good for yourself and Julia when you can make it? It will give us great pleasure to have you with us, and we much regret that our son cannot promise to be one of your party.

Robert and Daughter with their little ones left us this morning, and the house has been very silent since. Little Charlie really seemed to verge towards broken-bone, but perhaps it was his teeth. Daughter said she had a most pleasant visit to you, and Joe and Carrie wrote us that they enjoyed your visit to them very much in Augusta.

Mother has been busy all day both without and within the house, and is now measuring off clothing for the plantation to be given out this evening so soon as I return from the chapel; and am expecting the bell to call me over every minute to the lecture. There appears to be some interest in religion among our people, and our hope and prayer is that it may be the work of the Holy Spirit, and result in the saving conversion of some of them. The cases of several are very encouraging.

Our county had its public meeting on Tuesday on Federal affairs, and you will see the proceedings in the papers. Judge Law delivered an excellent address. The substance of the Savannah resolutions was embodied in our resolutions.

Mother unites in much love to our dear son and yourself; and kiss our dear little granddaughter for us many times. Howdy for all the servants. Their families are all well out here.

Your affectionate father,
C. C. Jones.

Bell just ringing. Half-past 7 P.M.
Quarter to nine. Just come back. Full and pleasant meeting.

Hon. Charles C. Jones, Jr. *to* Rev. *and* Mrs. C. C. Jones[t]
Savannah, Wednesday, November 28th, 1860

My dear Father and Mother,

We are all pretty well this evening, and unite in warmest love. The day has been pretty generally observed in the city.

Charlie West has just returned from Princeton. His mother has ordered him home, ostensibly on account of the present political condition of the country. I must say I think she acts without judgment.

33

Nothing new. The monetary pressure still continues. Governor Brown promises to veto the Alleviation Act, but the legislature will probably pass it by a constitutional majority over his head. As ever, my dear parents,

Your affectionate son,
Charles C. Jones, Jr.

It is rumored that Secretary Cobb and Chief Justice Taney have resigned.

MRS. MARY JONES *to* MRS. MARY S. MALLARD[t]

Montevideo, Friday, November 30th, 1860

My dear Daughter,

We had a very pleasant visit from your brother and Ruth. Little Julia improved, but Charles was still very unwell when he left. I feel anxious about his state of health.

A letter from Carrie by the last mail. She is bright and well. Joe will deliver his address in the early part of the fair, which commences on Monday the 3rd December. I would be delighted to hear him. Do you know of anyone going up?

Your aunt and cousins came out on Friday to dinner and left us yesterday. Laura was in bed several days with pain in her face. Jimmie is the most wonderfully improved child mentally and physically I ever saw. He says everything, and knows the short questions in the catechism, and a great many little verses. . . .

Today I rode to Arcadia. Have not been there for a long time. Found all well. I am very tired tonight. In consequence of your father's not feeling able to ride so far this Sabbath, we will not be with you. Remember you are all to come home at Christmas. Charles and Ruth will be with us, *God willing*. We have missed you so much—particularly little Mary. Father has retired, but unites with me in best love to Robert and yourself, and many kisses for our grandchildren.

Ever your affectionate mother,
Mary Jones.

MRS. MARY JONES *to* HON. CHARLES C. JONES, JR.[g]

Montevideo, Tuesday, December 4th, 1860

My dear Son,

The jars arrived safely yesterday and are very nice, and I am greatly indebted to dear Ruth for selecting them. They could not be better.

One little favor more: I want *two yards* of *very narrow blue* satin ribbon to make a *cockade* for the center of the arrowroot cake designed for the fair. I intend to surround it with a wreath of magnolia and live oak, with sprigs of rice and pods of cotton interspersed, and on the top in some form or other the fifteen Southern states with the cockade in the center. You see I am going to send up a "sentiment" from at least one of the Liberty County ladies—an echo from old St. John's Parish. Will Ruthie send me the ribbon the next time you write in your letter?

A letter from your brother today informs us in consequence of the delay of the European goods that the fair will open a week later than was advertised. It would give us great pleasure to hear his address, but I fear it will not be until Christmas week.

We are very happy to hear of dear little Julia's improvement. Continue the medicine as long as necessary, and be careful of her diet. And do, my dear child, avoid exposure to the night air and overfatigue. Everyone tells me the effects of broken-bone fever are very lasting. . . .

If Charlie West is still with you, please say we would be very happy to see him. The removal of a father's influence is a sad loss to a youth about his age. I regret that his course at Princeton was not completed.

Father has long since retired. Excuse this hurried note. Our best love to Daughter and yourself, and kisses for our little Julia. God bless you, my son!

Your affectionate mother,
Mary Jones.

REV. C. C. JONES *to* MRS. MARY S. MALLARD[c]
Savannah, *Thursday,* December 13th, 1860

My dear Daughter,

Mother went up with Brother Joe Monday evening to Macon with her trunk of contributions. Your brother was in waiting. Very thin, but said he was "very hearty," and that Carrie and he had not had "a finger ache" the whole summer. He read me his address, which is to be delivered today, D.V.; and I consider it an excellent one, and hope it may be appreciated and published by the Cotton Planters' Convention and circulated through the state. It will take him an hour and a half to deliver it. You will see in the *Morning News* of this morning a letter written by a lady giving an account of her visit to the fair. You will read it with interest and be glad to know that the fair will be "a decided success." A little energy is a great matter, and what others do we may do. Am so glad Mother went; it will be such a treat and recreation. And Mr. and Mrs. Nisbet will do all in their power to make her stay agreeable. I wish we *all* could have gone. I should have paraded my three little grandchildren and run for the prize at the baby show—if there is such an exhibition at the fair. I could not accompany Mother, fearing the effects of the fatigue, and especially the encumbrance and bother I would have been to the party.

There was a grand secession meeting and nomination here last night. *Vide* the papers. Your brother (His Honor the Mayor) and I went early, and on the opening of the hall he placed Major McIntosh and myself (two old gentlemen) on the front seat. Uncrowded and pleasant location. Hall densely packed; three or four times as many outside. Your brother presided with ease and dignity, and delivered an admirable opening address of eight or ten minutes, rapturously applauded. The speaking followed the nomination from the balconies, the hall emptying itself into the sea of people in the streets. We stayed behind to avoid the crowd, thinking we could stand in the balconies with the speakers—Judge Jackson, Mr. Bartow, and others. But they were so crowded we retired and, taking seats, passed the evening most pleasantly with numerous old friends and acquaintances until, having sent Major McIntosh home, we took our carriage and returned a little before ten. Not a late hour, but we left the meeting when it was at its height.

While the committee was out, Father O'Neill, being called for (he was sitting on the platform), made an entertaining speech, in which he declared himself "a *ra*publican and a *sa*cessionist and *sa*tizen of Georgia; and in case there should be war, he would be the first to *lade* them into battle, he would!" Popery and republicanism make a funny figure together. It was a funny speech altogether, and some good points very well put. I laughed heartily in the progress of it.

When your brother went out on the balcony to put the resolutions and nomination to the multitude in the streets, amidst the universal hurrah of ayes, off went the cannon, and into the sky flew the rockets, illuminating the scene. Then the pause: "Contrary minds, no!" A dead silence—when one man cried out: "There's *narra no,* Mayor Jones!" The meeting was remarkably peaceful and orderly and elevated, with an entire absence of folly and rowdyism. . . .

Politics and stringent times and an earnest looking forward to shortly-coming secrets is the order of the day here and everywhere. . . . The aspect of Charleston is impressive. Their theaters and places of public amusement are closed, and seriousness pervades the city. This is the report.

Ruthie and your brother unite in much love to yourself and Robert and to the little ones. Charles is still very unwell from the effects of the broken-bone fever, and has no rest from one day to another. If he does not get better, he will be obliged to take it. Your Uncle John and family are expected down today or tomorrow; and I hope to see Mother back, God willing, tomorrow night. She said she would return home on Saturday. The carriage is ordered to meet us. Much love to Robert. Tell Little Daughter Grandfather sends love and a kiss for her. And kiss Charlie for me. Howdy for all the servants. All well here. The Lord keep and bless you and all yours, my dear child!

Your affectionate father,
C. C. Jones.

HON. CHARLES C. JONES, JR., *to* REV. *and* MRS. C. C. JONES[t]
Savannah, *Monday,* December 17th, 1860
My dear Father and Mother,

We trust that you reached home safely, and that you have recovered from any fatigue which you may have experienced upon the way.

Our citizens are anxiously awaiting the action of the South Carolina convention, but as yet we have no news. I sincerely trust that there will be no hesitancy or faltering on their part. It is suggested, in consequence of the existence of smallpox in Columbia, that the convention will adjourn to reassemble at once in Charleston.

No movement as yet of a submissive character in this city, although there are intimations to that effect; and there is no doubt of the fact that there are those in our midst who do not sympathize with us upon the question of state action and secession.

A letter from Aunt Mary Robarts states that all in Marietta are well. Ruth and little Julia unite in warmest love. I am, my dear parents, as ever,

Your affectionate son,
Charles C. Jones, Jr.

MRS. MARY JONES *to* HON. CHARLES C. JONES, JR.[8]
Montevideo, *Thursday,* December 20th, 1860

My dear Son,

We felt disappointed that your letter today gave us no information when we might look for dear Ruth and yourself and our little Julia. I hope she continues to improve, and that you will be with us next week. Your sister and the children are with us, and we have been enjoying the visit of your uncle and Aunt Jane and their noble little boys. They leave us tomorrow.

Our hearts were filled with joy and gratitude at the good tidings received from Augusta on last Tuesday. We have now two granddaughters and two grandsons!

Will you, my dear son, be good enough to draw the dividend and *transmit to your brother* for me (if the present amount of the dividend is the same as the last) sixty-five dollars. I would like the remainder in gold, if you could conveniently obtain it; and you can bring it out when you come.

They are all talking loudly around me, so that I scarcely know what I am writing. This is your father's birthday, and tomorrow will be the thirtieth anniversary of our wedding day! All unite with me in best love to Ruth and yourself, and kisses for our little Julia.

Ever, my dear son, your affectionate mother,
Mary Jones.

REV. C. C. JONES *to* HON. CHARLES C. JONES, JR.[8]
Montevideo, *Monday,* December 24th, 1860

My dear Son,

Niger leaves, D.V., tomorrow on a trip to Savannah to see his daughter Adeline, and Mother embraces the opportunity of sending by him to Ruthie and yourself a piece of fresh beef for your Christmas dinner. We are sorry it is no fatter; our dry fields could afford no better. It may, however, taste like *home*. We regret you could not come out and make part of our circle tomorrow. Small: your sister and Robert and Uncle William, God willing. Your Uncle John and family left us Friday, and the county for McIntosh Saturday of last week.

We dined at Henry's on Friday, the thirtieth anniversary of our wedding day (nearly a generation), and in the same house we were married. It was easy to recall the past and paint in memory the cheerful scenes of the wedding day and evening. I saw the figures, the countenances, the dress, the smiles, and heard the conversation, and saw myself and your mother too, and the wedding party (but four in number), and our venerable friend performing the ceremony, the supper and all things else—a bright and pleasing vision. Since then what changes! I could more than fill my sheet with them. But let me record the mercies of the Lord in one particular, not to mention ten thousand others: He has spared us to rear and educate our dear children, and to see them settled in families, adding *three more* to our children and permitting us to see our *children's children,* and each of you occupying most honored and influential stations in society, and five out of the six members of the Church of Christ! Surely these are special mercies, calling for the greatest gratitude; and we felt that our cup would have been full had our dear *first-born* been added to them. For this mercy we daily and earnestly pray.

Mother received your letter. We all unite in much love to Ruthie and yourself, and kisses for little Julia.

Your affectionate father,
C. C. Jones.

. . . We were much rejoiced to hear of your brother's blessing, and wrote him and Carrie our congratulations immediately. Please have the enclosed letter mailed to him: to go up by the night train of the 25th.

MRS. MARY JONES *to* HON. CHARLES C. JONES, JR.[8]

Montevideo, *Thursday,* January 3rd, 1861

My dear Son,

Your affectionate favor was this day received, and from our heart of hearts we respond to your kind wishes—"A Happy New Year!"—although every moment seems fraught with the sad foreboding that it may be only one of trial and suffering. But "God is our refuge and strength, a very present help in trouble. Therefore will not we fear." Read Psalm 46. I trust the Lord of Hosts will be with us!

An indescribable sadness weighs down my soul as I think of our once glorious but now dissolving Union! Our children's children—what will constitute their national pride and glory? *We* have no alternative; and necessity demands that we now protect ourselves from entire destruction at the hands of those who have rent and torn and obliterated every national bond of union, of confidence and affection. When your brother and yourself were very little fellows, we took you into old Independence Hall; and at the foot of Washington's statue I pledged you both to support and defend the Union. *That Union* has passed away, and you are free from your mother's vow.

Your father thinks the occupation of Fort Pulaski will produce more effect than anything that has occurred. How can the South delay united and decided action? . . . The results may be awful unless we are united.

Did your father tell you old Montevideo gave forth her response on the night of the 26th in honor of Carolina and in sympathy with Savannah? Strange to say, as we walked out to view the illumination from the lawn, we discovered that there were thirteen windows on the front of the house, each of which had one brilliant light resembling a star; and without design one of them had been placed far in the ascendant—emblematic, as we hailed it, of the noble and gallant state which must ever be regarded as the polar star of our Southern confederacy.

And now, my dear son, we will look within the home circle. I trust you have regained your accustomed strength, and dear little Julia still improving. Your sister and Robert and the little ones have been with us for two weeks, and left us today. So did your uncle, who spent the day and night with us.

Enclosed I send your brother's letter, with the hope that you may yet help him to obtain the appointment. Would it be possible for you individually, or through Colonel Lawton or anyone else, to see *Governor Brown* whilst he is in Savannah, and if possible to secure the appointment for him? Poor boy, my heart sympathizes very deeply with his disappointments and perplexities. I know you will do all you can to aid him. I believe him worthy of and qualified for the trust, or I would not ask it even for my child.

Your dear father is very unwell from a severe cold. I want to write Ruth a few lines, and my paper is at an end. . . . With love from Father and myself to you both, and kisses for our little darling,

Your affectionate mother,
M. Jones.

HON. CHARLES C. JONES, JR., *to* MRS. MARY JONES[8]
Savannah, *Monday,* January 7th, 1861
My very dear Mother,

Your kind letter of the 3rd inst., with enclosures as stated, has been duly received, and I sincerely sympathize with you in all your reflections upon the past and present memories of our country.

We are now in a state of very reliable preparation at the fort, and when a few more heavy guns are received, the fortification will be invincible by almost any force that may be sent against it. Everything within its walls is conducted upon strict military principles, and it is truly wonderful what changes the discipline of even a few days has accomplished. My engagements here are of so imperative a character that I am precluded from spending as much time there as I could wish. . . .

I sincerely sympathize with Brother in his disappointment, and had I known the fact earlier would certainly have conversed with Governor Brown on the subject. As it is, I will write the governor and see if something cannot be done for him. While here I saw the governor every day, and upon the most confidential terms. He grew in the esteem of everyone, and received every attention from our citizens. He is a truly honest, strictly upright, pious man, temperate in all things, and is not afraid of responsibilities.

Little Julia is the very picture of health, Ruth quite well, and both unite in warmest love to self and dear Father. I am, my dear mother, as ever,

Your affectionate son,
Charles C. Jones, Jr.

How can I get the hundred dollars to you?

MRS. MARY JONES *to* MRS. RUTH B. JONES[8]

Montevideo, *Tuesday,* January 22nd, 1861

My dear Daughter,

Your kind favor was received by Saturday's mail. . . . We rejoice to know that our dear little granddaughter has entirely recovered. How many teeth has she out? Do tell us all about her when you write.

Mr. Jones has just written Mr. I. W. Morrell that we wished him to furnish a crib for our little grandson in Augusta; and will you, dear Daughter, be so kind as to call at your earliest convenience and select it for me? I wish one *like Julia's;* but perhaps it had best be of *black walnut* to suit Joe and Carrie's bedstead, which is of that material. Mr. Morrell is to forward it as soon as you have selected it.

Our hearts are rejoiced to learn the fact of a daily prayer meeting in Savannah in view of the state of the country and our convention now in session, and to see that on last Sabbath religious services were held in the fort. May God overshadow us all with the guidance and protection of His own Holy Spirit! You and I—a wife and mother—need surely to keep near our Father's throne when we know not what perils are awaiting one who is dear to us as our own life, and who is yet unreconciled to our gracious and Divine Redeemer. I think of him daily—I may say hourly. Oh, that I could be assured that he was the child of God! This one great interest possesses my mind above all others. In all that concerns the honor or welfare of his country in this righteous conflict I know he will be brave and true.

Dear Daughter, do write us often. You know not how anxious we feel when we do not hear from Charles. It is late, and I must close. Father unites with me in much love to you both, and kisses for our dear little Julia.

Ever your affectionate mother,
Mary Jones.

Tell Adeline on next Saturday night her sister Judy expects to be married to Sam, and her brother Niger to Tenah, Daughter's nurse, at Montevideo. Howdies for all your servants. *Patience* has a daughter.

REV. C. C. JONES *to* HON. CHARLES C. JONES, JR.[8]

Montevideo, *Thursday,* January 24th, 1861

My dear Son,

Sam, Abram's brother, expects, D.V., to be married on Saturday evening *the*

26th, and begs me to enclose Abram three dollars (enclosed) to buy him a coat for the occasion. And as the time is very limited, and the case an urgent one, he requests Abram to get his master to write the direction on the coat and to send it out by Adams' Express to Riceboro by railroad and stage *on Saturday morning without fail.* Direct it to me. Sam says the coat that fits Abram will fit him. Please help this cause if you can.

Have just dismissed fourteen (9 P.M.) who have been for religious instruction. A long time since we have had such an awakening on the plantation. May it prove to be a genuine work of the Spirit!

Was not the Missouri Compromise occasioned by the opposition of the anti-slavery North against the reception of Missouri as a slave state? And was not Henry Clay the author of it? I am, at Mother's instigation, engaged in writing an answer to Dr. Hodge's Black Republican article in the last number of *The Princeton Review.* Am sorry to see the doctor so much astray. Hope to finish it in a few days, D.V.

We are all pretty well, and are at the end of a four day's northeaster. More rain fallen than for months.

No special news today. Trust things may remain in forts, etc., *in statu quo* until the convention of the seceding states in February. And then, if on a united application our demands are not responded to, we may go to work. By that time a peaceful solution may be obtained, which is desirable for all parties concerned. Our cooperation members of the convention are acting as well as could be expected in the premises. Wish the convention had more elbow room and we fuller reports.

Mother sends to say she wants room for a *postscriptum.* Love to Ruthie, and a kiss for my little granddaughter. She ought to be walking.

Your affectionate father,

C. C. Jones.

In the judgment of your mother, my dear son, your father's reply will be a twelve-inch columbiad fully charged—and discharged not in offensive but defensive warfare: in the cause of truth and justice!

MRS. MARY S. MALLARD *to* MRS. MARY JONES[t]

Walthourville, *Friday,* January 25th, 1861

My dear Mother,

What a week of rain we have had! From present appearances I fear the sun will not shine upon the brides tomorrow. Tenah seems quite merry on the occasion. I have been busy getting her dress ready. Her heart was set upon a swiss muslin, so I have given her one. She has been a good, faithful servant to me and always a kind nurse to my children, so I felt she was entitled to a nice dress. Lucy, you know, is labor-saving and self-sparing in her notions, so she preferred to buy bread and cake rather than "bother with the making." She is quite long-faced, as she has had toothache nearly all week. For my own sake I would have been glad if Tenah had been otherwise-minded. I tell her it is a

41

most inconvenient arrangement, and she has taken us by such a surprise that Niger and herself will have to do the best they can until we can provide a place for them to occupy. Little Daughter thinks getting married means having a plenty of cake, for when I was fixing Tenah's cake, she asked: "Mama, can't I get married too? The cake is so nice I want some!"

Mr. Mallard has been waiting all week for fair weather to go and see his father. This afternoon he concluded he would go anyhow, so he went off in the rain. The last time we heard, he was suffering very much and was threatened with another rising.

How do you feel now, dear Mother, that *we* are in a foreign land? Did you illuminate when you heard of Georgia's secession? Savannah does not seem to have made as great a demonstration as when Carolina seceded. What is to be done with those Georgians who unfurled the Stars and Stripes when the news reached them? I think it is a pity the whole county—land and all—could not be transferred immediately to New England. I received a letter from Kitty this week; she is quite stirred up, and rejoices at our freedom. . . .

I was quite amused yesterday morning by some of little Mary's capers. She was playing with a little china doll, and after showing me how she had fixed its dress, she said: "Now, do give me a little basket to shut it up in, so that when the king's daughter comes, she will say: 'Bring me that basket.' And when she opens it, the little baby will cry, and then the king's daughter will say: 'Call somebody to *norse* the baby.'" She told her father today to give her love to Grandma and Grandpa and Grandma's pussy. She often comes to me and says it is time for me to "tell Daddy Dilbud to fix the carriage dood so that we can go to Danma's home."

I am sorry you will have all the trouble of the wedding. It seems Sam had determined to take Elvira if he could not get Judy, and Elvira said if Sam did not marry Judy she would accept him. So Lucy tells me. Accept kisses from the little ones for Father and yourself and the warmest affection of

Your attached child,
Mary S. Mallard.

HON. CHARLES C. JONES, JR., *to* REV. C. C. JONES[8]

Savannah, Monday, January 28th, 1861

My dear Father,

In reply to your query, "Was not the Missouri Compromise occasioned by the opposition of the anti-slavery North against the reception of Missouri as a slave state? And was not Henry Clay the author of it?" I would say yes. Mr. Clay has always had the credit of being the author and the most powerful advocate of that compromise of 1820. During the pendency of the compromise measures of 1850 he alluded to the fact of his position in 1820 and called upon the good and true men of the North to rally to his support then as they had done in 1820. A fatal mistake in both instances. Had we manfully resisted the first aggression, we might have stifled the serpent in its den, and not now have been suffering from the poisonous brood which with hissing tongue and noxious breath are crawling everywhere and polluting the otherwise wholesome air of this once pure and happy country. It is a sad sight to see our national flag lowered, our union of states dissolved, and our unparalleled peace and prosperity interrupted for cause so foul as this. I have long since believed that in this country have arisen two races which, although claiming a common parentage, have been so entirely separated by climate, by morals, by religion, and by estimates so totally opposite of all that constitutes honor, truth, and manliness, that they cannot longer coexist under the same government. Oil and water will not commingle. We are the land of rulers; fanaticism has no home here. The sooner we separate the better.

I really regret the action of our convention in its appointments of delegates to Montgomery. Hill, Kenan, Wright, and Stephens should not have been sent. The convention should have selected representatives not of themselves. Personal ambition and love of preferment, although not so designated by the metaphysicians, should be classed, at least among public men, both as innate and inalienable ideas.

I sincerely trust that you will have health and strength to complete all the most valuable labors in which you are now engaged. Do, Father, let me have a copy of your reply to Dr. Hodge so soon as it is finished. Ruth and Julia, who are both quite well, unite in warmest love to dear Mother and self. Ruth selected the crib for Brother, and it went forward this morning. As ever,

Your affectionate son,
Charles C. Jones, Jr.

II

REV. W. M. CUNNINGHAM *to* REV. C. C. JONES^t
LaGrange, *Monday,* February 18th, 1861

Many, many thanks to my dear Brother C. C. Jones for his manly and masterly review of Dr. Hodge on "The State of the Country." By this timely and able service you have made the whole South and—what is more—the cause of truth and righteousness your debtors. The cause you defend is the cause of God and of the country, and indirectly of all mankind; and the man you met was a foeman that demanded your steel.

Though a more vulnerable article than that of Dr. Hodge I never read, yet a more *plausible* and *pernicious* one, I verily believe, was never published. Under an air of candor and kindness he disguises a most *bitter* and *blinding* prejudice, of which not even the writer himself was conscious. Behind the cooing of the dove, the poison of the asp is bitter toward the South. In him Black Republicanism has become an angel of light, without one sin *as a party* to confess or one concession of *right* to make; and the Southerners resenting and resisting its rule are perjured covenant-breakers, as reckless of their interests as they are recreant of their duty. And yet we have only to lift the veil that covers this angelic embodiment of candor and kindness and truth and righteousness to see that in thus canonizing and sanctifying the Republican party Dr. Hodge has himself become assimilated to and imbued with the spirit of that foul and fiendish party, whose advocate he has become. The angel, in representing the devil, has, unbeknowing to himself, become a devil.

This seems to be one of the most uniform and deplorable of the consequences of the abolition heresy. It is, as you well say, an *ever-contracting iron band* around the soul that squeezes out and kills all the charity of piety and the humanity of our nature from the heart. How else can we account for it that the naturally mild and prudent and Christian Dr. Hodge should conceive of and compare all the tried patriots of the South who favor secession to Benedict Arnold! And class all the Christian ministers and members in the South—and amongst them his own brethren in the church—who sustain secession, with those who approved and sustained the executions of the Inquisition! How can he maintain Christian fellowship with such traitors and *unnatural monsters?* And what communion can we have with men who so feel and think and speak of us? As much as I deplore it, nothing, I verily believe, will be left for us at the South to do but to separate from the church as well as the state at the North.

In your review you show off finely some of Dr. Hodge's inconsistencies. I would have been gratified if you had remarked upon this in addition. In holding up secession as involving all the crimes of *perjury* and *covenant-breaking* and *treason* and *rebellion*, he yet speaks most *complacently* and *encouragingly* of withdrawing Canada from its allegiance and uniting it by revolution to the Northern confederacy! No sin here! If the North propose to aid in this *awful enormity*, Dr. Hodge thinks it would be a noble achievement, and he would open his arms to receive this perjured and covenant-breaking Canada!

But I did not intend to write a letter, but only to express to you my *gratification and thanks* for your very able and timely review. Without being awed by reverence and conquered by kindness and flattery, *as has been Brown of The Central Presbyterian,* you yet show all that respect and kindness due from one Christian minister to another. And without being quite so bitter and so pungent in your terms as our good Brother Porter, you yet give full expression to your manly indignation and at times *make the truth awfully cutting* and *scathing.* Dr. Hodge will feel it to his innermost soul—as he ought. I only wish it could be read by all the thousands that have read Dr. Hodge's article. Could we not contrive some way to get it into *The New York Observer,* even if it should mean *a supplement to be paid for?* I for one would bear my full proportion of the expense. In haste and in love, I remain,

As ever,
W. M. Cunningham.

Rev. Joseph R. Wilson *to* Rev. C. C. Jones[t]

Augusta, *Tuesday,* February 19th, 1861

. . . Having just finished the perusal of your masterly review of Dr. Hodge's late political article, I cannot resist the impulse which compels me to write you my humble word of thanks therefor. You have followed him through all his doublings, have met his arguments at every point, have placed him at your mercy. I am deeply thankful that *you* of all men have undertaken and accomplished this task—you whose whole life has been devoted to the study of the "slavery" subject; you whose reputation is national for wisdom, piety, and learning; you whose official sojourn in the North has made you intimate with the Northern peculiarities of mind.

May I beg of you to have this piece published in pamphlet form and distributed among the ministry of our church at the North? It will do much good. It may indeed have the effect of stopping the prematurely exultant boasting of such abolitionized brethren (of whom there are many at the North) who are, I doubt not, already beginning to hail Dr. Hodge as a leader of their hosts, and his article as an entering wedge to the disruption of our church. Pardon my freedom.

Your brother in Christ,
Joseph R. Wilson.

HON. CHARLES C. JONES, JR., *to* REV. C. C. JONES[c]
                              Savannah, *Wednesday,* February 20th, 1861
My dear Father,

I have just finished the perusal of your able and most valuable reply to the article of Dr. Hodge, for the receipt of which I am today indebted to you. You have done the cause of truth and justice great service, and your reply is unanswerable: Dr. Hodge must wince helplessly under it. I trust that he may be brought to realize the error of his ways.

I write this evening to the editor of *The Southern Presbyterian* for several copies of your article. Would it not be well, Father, to have it published in permanent pamphlet form? I wish that you would consent to have this done. All should be in possession of the article, and it ought not to be allowed to remain in its present ephemeral form. Cooper can attend handsomely to the republication, and I will, with your permission, see with pleasure to the correction of the proof sheets.

Did dear Mother and yourself receive copies of my little work upon *The Monumental Remains of Georgia?* I posted to your address the first copies issued, and hope that the perusal may afford you some pleasure.

We are expecting Brother, Sister Carrie, and their little son tonight. Nothing new with us. With our united love to dear Mother and yourself, I am, as ever,
                              Your affectionate son,
                              Charles C. Jones, Jr.

HON. CHARLES C. JONES, JR., *to* REV. and MRS. C. C. JONES[c]
                              Savannah, *Friday,* February 22nd, 1861
My dear Mother and Father,

D.V., Ruth and little Julia hope to be with you on Thursday next. Will write you again. With our united love,
                              Your ever affectionate son,
                              Charles C. Jones, Jr.

REV. C. C. JONES *to* HON. CHARLES C. JONES, JR.[8]
                              Montevideo, *Tuesday,* February 26th, 1861
My dear Son,

We are happy to learn by yours of last evening that we should have the pleasure of seeing Ruthie and little Julia on Thursday, and will send the carriage for her to the depot (No. 3) on Thursday. The cars, you know, come out in the afternoon, and she will not reach Montevideo until 8 P.M. The pleasure would be increased could you become her escort. Tomorrow, D.V., we send for your sister and little ones, and on Friday Robert hopes to be down, and your Uncle William comes tomorrow. So we have the prospect of having all our children (except yourself) and grandchildren together in the

46

course of the week, which will be a joyful event to us, and one calling for sincerest gratitude. . . .

Your mother and I read your *Monumental Remains* immediately as we received them with great pleasure and instruction. It is written in a graceful and scholarly manner, and is a credit to you and a valuable contribution to the history of the Indian races that once inhabited our country. Your theory of the migration of the Mound Builders from Mexico north up our rivers is new to me and appears reasonable and has facts in its favor. Verily the traces are dim; and the absence of a written language in any character shuts out access to the real history and character of these strange men.

We are passing through historic times, and I have thought some man amongst us should be laying up material for a history of these times—the dissolution of the greatest republic that ever existed, and the formation of two if not more. The work might be appropriately divided into three parts: first, the causes leading to the disruption; second, the disruption and formation of a new confederacy; and third, the settlement of the same: resources and prospects. The material should be laid up of the passing events *ab initio:* many striking facts, speeches, meetings, acts of the people, of governors, legislatures, conventions, Congress (United States and Confederate States), the religious element pervading the whole, and all such like matters. There is much in the newspapers of the day well worth laying by as it comes out, which would save much laborious turning over of leaves afterwards. Patience and perseverance might give us a worthy history of these times.

May it please God so to dispose the hearts of those who have it in their power to plunge us in war to refrain from it! We may be punished for our sins, but my hope is that the confessions and prayers of the true Israel may come up in remembrance before God and that He may grant us peace. I still think we shall have no war—although the prospects are darker.

We all unite in much love to dear Ruthie and in kisses for Julia. We long to hear her prattle. Your brother is devoting himself to exercise and health, which he much needs. The Lord bless and keep you and yours, my dear son! We highly appreciate the inscription of your little work.

Your affectionate father,
C. C. Jones.

9 *P.M.* A letter from your sister says little Charlie is sick and she cannot come tomorrow. Am sorry for the cause and the fact.

REV. C. C. JONES *to* MRS. MARY S. MALLARD[t]

Montevideo, *Saturday,* March 2nd, 1861

My dear Child,

We were truly sorry to hear of little Charlie's sickness, and that you could not come down. It was a great disappointment to us all. Your brother and family came out on Thursday. He returns this morning; Ruthie and little

Julia remain. She is a sweet child, and Little Daughter will be delighted to see her. It would have been so pleasant to have had you all together; but we must be thankful for the mercy we enjoy, and hope the pleasure another time.

Little Stanhope will be baptized, if possible, on Sabbath. Ruthie expects to go back next week—perhaps Thursday; and Miss Davis and Joe and Carrie may go down to the Island. I hope our dear little grandson is better; and not having heard from you, conclude he is better. All are well, D.G., and unite in much love to yourself and Robert, and kisses for the children. Shall ride with Charles this morning as far as Arcadia.

Your ever affectionate father,
C. C. Jones.

You can write us by Niger, who anticipates seeing his family this evening.

C.C.J.

Hon. Charles C. Jones, Jr., *to* Mrs. Mary Jones[8]

Savannah, *Saturday*, March 2nd, 1861

My dear Mother,

I forgot to hand you the enclosed chestnuts. They were gathered from a tree which grows very near the tomb of Washington. I thought you might wish to plant and endeavor to rear them. They may grow in our climate if the heat of summer does not prove too severe. The memory of Washington is still as dear, and every association connected with his home and grave as sacred, as ever it was; and I know by no one is that memory more patriotically cherished, or those relics more sincerely valued, than by yourself. The dissolution of this Union cannot silence those consecrated voices of the past; nor can it rob us of the relationship which we bear to, or of the veneration which we shall ever cherish for, the virtues and the great deeds of the Father of our Country. He was of us.

Hoping that under the soft influences of the sweet airs and gentle dews of spring these little seeds may soon burst and expand into a living green, and that among the many beautiful trees which now adorn and render our beloved home so attractive (all of them the offspring of your superintending taste and culture) you may number in a few short years the bright foliage and symmetrical forms of five Mount Vernon chestnuts, I am, with warmest love,

Your ever affectionate son,
Charles C. Jones, Jr.

Rev. C. C. Jones *to* Hon. Charles C. Jones, Jr.[8]

Montevideo, *Monday*, March 4th, 1861

My dear Son,

Will you see our friend Major Porter and know if the bank is discounting and if we could be accommodated in some eight hundred dollars if we should need it? I think fully as much as that I will need for a special purpose.

48

Your brother had his fine little son baptized in old Midway yesterday. The little fellow followed the example of all our grandchildren and never uttered a sound, but displayed unusual good humor. May the outward sign of covenant blessings be followed by the inward blessings themselves, and parents and children all be bound in the sure bundle of life!

Ruth begs you to have the rooms fixed for your Aunt Susan and Cousin Lyman, who will accompany *her down on Thursday*. And so I will defer my visit. Dr. Axson and Brother Buttolph are exchanging pulpits.

I hear little Julia's voice—"Pudna! Pudna!"—prattling in her room, dressing. Ruth sends much love, and intended to write you, but have written for her and myself too. She and Julia quite well. Julia is getting very fond of her grandmother, and is trying to call her *grandma*. I showed her the sheep and told her to say *sheep,* and she made the effort and said *pheep.* All unite in love to you.

Your ever affectionate father,
C. C. Jones.

HON. CHARLES C. JONES, JR., *to* REV. C. C. JONES[t]

Savannah, *Tuesday,* March 5th, 1861

My dear Father,

In reply to your last favor I would say that Major Porter promises the required discount of eight hundred dollars. Whenever you make the note, be pleased to see that it is drawn payable to my order, and at the Bank of the State of Georgia. Enclosed you have receipts for amounts paid, as per statement rendered in my last.

Say to Ruth that the rooms will be all ready on Thursday as desired. I am very sorry to hear you say that you will not come in yourself.

Lincoln's inaugural is before us, and a queer production it is. What does it mean? It means this, and it means that; and then it may mean neither. That sly fox Seward, I expect, has had the shaping of it.

Our large guns are not here as yet. They are, however, daily expected. With warmest love to self, dear Father, dear Mother, Ruth, Julia, Brother, Sister Carrie, and Stanhope, and with respects for Miss Davis, I am, as ever,

Your affectionate son,
Charles C. Jones, Jr.

MRS. MARY JONES *to* HON. CHARLES C. JONES, JR.[8]

Montevideo, *Thursday,* March 14th, 1861

My dear Son,

The visit of dear Ruth and little Julia was very delightful to us—only far too short. Your sister, too, enjoyed it—especially bringing all our dear little grandchildren under the old roof. I wish it was so in God's providence that we could oftener surround the family altar, the domestic hearth, and the social board together. I dread the alienation which long separations produce even with the nearest and dearest. Your little Julia is a most interesting child: intellectually bright with a loving little heart.

Have you observed the notice of your *Indian Remains* to be found on the last side of *The Southern Presbyterian?* . . .

Father asks for a little space, so I will close, with the united love of Carrie and Joe and your father and myself to Ruth and yourself, with kisses for our little darling.

Ever your affectionate mother,
Mary Jones.

REV. C. C. JONES *to* HON. CHARLES C. JONES, JR.[8]
Montevideo, *Thursday*, March 14th, 1861

My dear Son,

Your favor advising Major Porter's kind answer has been received, and as your brother hopes to be in Savannah next week, will send the note down by him, and you can get the money and hand to him. . . .

Papers today indicate brightening skies at Washington—if the news be *true*. The sooner *our* convention adjourns the better after ratifying the permanent Constitution of the Confederate States. Some two hundred and fifty or three hundred men (and many raw recruits) kept together for any time are apt to breed mischief or nonsense.

Your affectionate father,
C. C. Jones.

HON. CHARLES C. JONES, JR., *to* REV. *and* MRS. C. C. JONES[8]
Savannah, *Wednesday*, April 17th, 1861

My very dear Father and Mother,

You will, I am sure, excuse me for not oftener writing you when I tell you that in addition to the discharge of the duties devolved upon me in an official, professional, military, and civil way I last week agreed at the request of my company to deliver an address before the Chatham Artillery on the 1st of May next. With such short notice and so little time to devote to its preparation, you may well believe that very few leisure moments are at my command.

Recent telegrams inform us of the probable passage of an ordinance of secession by the Virginia legislature. The North Carolinians are realizing the importance of decided action. A noble reply to Lincoln's demand for troops has been returned by Governor Magoffin of Kentucky. Thus act succeeds act in this wonderful drama. Lincoln has made requisitions upon the Northern states for one hundred and fifty thousand more troops. Every indication points to a prolonged and sanguinary struggle.

We are endeavoring to prepare for the conflict. Colonel Lawton has, as you have observed, been appointed a brigadier general of the Confederate States, and is charged specially with the defense of our city, harbor, and coast. Tybee Island is now occupied by more than two hundred troops. Batteries are soon to be erected there. Near two hundred men from the interior of the state arrived last night, and will take post also upon Tybee. Fort Pulaski is garrisoned by four hundred men, and Fort Jackson by one hundred and twenty. The volunteer corps of the city are at present held as a reserve—subject, however, to orders at any moment. When the plot thickens and the day of battle comes, they will be where stout hearts and brave hands are most needed.

The ladies of Savannah are not idle. They are daily engaged singly and in concert in the preparation of cartridges both for muskets and cannon. Thousands have been already made by them, and the labor is just begun. Others are cutting out and sewing flannel shirts. Others still are making bandages and preparing lint. Their interest and patriotic efforts in this our cause are worthy of all admiration.

We have now three full batteries of field pieces in the city—one in the possession of our company, another in the keeping of the Savannah Artillery, and a third at the barracks. Upon Tybee Island they have two six-pounders and two twelve-pound howitzers. Heavy guns are needed there, and I doubt not but that General Lawton is directing his immediate attention to the preparation of batteries both at the northern and southern extremities of the island. The work of mounting columbiads at Fort Pulaski progresses slowly. Eighteen-pounders have arrived for Fort Jackson, are lying now upon the parade and upon the parapets of that fortification, and will be mounted so soon as carriages can be prepared. The workshops of the Central Railroad are busily occupied with their construction. Our company has been constantly engaged in putting our battery in thorough order, and in the manufacture of fuses (a very delicate and responsible duty) for the forts and for ourselves.

It is today officially announced that our mails are cut off, and that there will be henceforth no further communication through their agency with the Confederate States.

Can you imagine a more suicidal, outrageous, and exasperating policy than that inaugurated by the fanatical administration at Washington? The Black Republicans may rave among the cold hills of their native states, and grow mad with entertainment of infidelity, heresies, and false conceptions of a "higher law"; but Heaven forbid that they ever attempt to set foot upon this land of sunshine, of high-souled honor, and of liberty. It puzzles the imagination to conceive the stupidity, the fanaticism, and the unmitigated rascality which impel them to the course which they are now pursuing. I much mistake the policy of this Confederacy and the purposes of our worthy President (at once soldier and statesman) if in the event of our pure rivers and harbors being blockaded by Northern fleets, a great Southern army is not put in motion, attracting to itself the good and true men of every section, whose object it shall be to redeem the tomb of Washington from the dominion of this fanatical rule, and to plant the standard of this Confederacy even upon the dome of the capitol at Washington. This is a favorite scheme with President Davis, and he has brave men such as Major McCulloch and General Pillow to sustain him in carrying the idea into practical effect.

Nothing from Fort Pickens today. Mr. Ward is daily expected. Colonel Jackson has gone upon professional business to Atlanta, and on Saturday of this week expects to deliver an oration at Marietta commemorative of the virtues and of the character of the late Charles J. McDonald. It will be a finished production.

We are much obliged, my dear parents, for your kind remembrance of us. We enjoyed the strawberries for dinner today. They were the first we had tasted, and were regarded as a great treat.

Robert, who left us yesterday, took with him a package which arrived from Mr. —— for you, Father. I presume it has to do with your work, and will, I hope, reach you safely.

These troubles are seriously interrupting our professional labors, and diminishing our receipts. We will all have soon nothing but war to engage our attention. Ruth and little Julia are both quite well. Ruth is energetically devoting herself every day to the work of cartridge-making. Julia is a sweet child—affectionate, good, and very intelligent. She already takes great delight in her little linen books, and will explain the pictures. We hope, my dear father and mother, that we may soon have the pleasure of welcoming you here. We all unite in warmest love to you both, Brother, Sister Carrie, and little Stanhope. As ever,

Your affectionate son,
Charles C. Jones, Jr.

REV. C. C. JONES *to* HON. CHARLES C. JONES, JR.[8]
Montevideo, *Saturday,* April 20th, 1861

My dear Son,

We are aware of your numerous engagements, and never think anything of your not writing as frequently as usual, for we know that you will always write us whenever you can. Your two last came last night with the papers.

A kind Providence seems to watch over our Confederacy. Whoever read or heard of so important and desperate a battle as that of Fort Sumter without the loss of a man on the side of the victors or on the side of the vanquished? And how remarkable that the only men killed were killed saluting their own flag as it was lowered in defeat! May this battle be an earnest of all others that shall be forced upon us in its merciful and glorious success. All honor to Carolina! I hope our state may emulate her bravery and patriotism—and *her self-sacrificing generosity,* in that she has borne out of her own treasury the entire expense of her army and fortifications and all matériel of war, and has not and will not call upon our government for one cent of it. Georgia is well able to do the like for her own seaport and her own territory, and there must be some movement of our chief men to secure so honorable an act. It will relieve our new government, and enable it to appropriate its funds in other directions for our honor and our defense.

We are favored again, in providence, by the belligerent acts and declarations of Mr. Lincoln, which have precipitated the border states upon a decision in our favor precisely at the moment most favorable to us. I never believed we should have war until after Lincoln's inaugural address—and not altogether then, thinking that there were some preventing considerations of interest and self-preservation, and some residuum of humanity and respect for the opinions of the civilized world in the Black Republican party. But in this I have been mistaken. Christianity with its enlightening and softening influences upon the human soul—at least so far as the great subject dividing our country is concerned—finds no lodgment in the soul of that party, destitute of justice and mercy, without the fear of God, supremely selfish and arrogant, unscrupulous in its acts and measures, intensely malignant and vituperative, and persecuting the innocent even unto blood and utter destruction. That party is essentially *infidel!* And these are our enemies, born and reared in our own political family, for whom we are to pray, and from whom we are to defend ourselves!

The conduct of the government of the old United States towards the Confederate States is an outrage upon Christianity and the civilization of the age, and upon the great and just principles of popular sovereignty which we have contended for and embraced for near an hundred years, and brands it with a deserved and indelible infamy. We have nothing left us but to work out our independence, relying, as our good President instructs us, upon "a just and superintending Providence." The ordering out of such large bodies of men is an easy matter; but to *officer,* to *equip,* to *maintain,* and (*more than all*) to *maneuver and bring these forces into safe action with the enemy*—these are the burdens and the arts and realities of war. And we wait Lincoln's success. He is not training and educating the people up to the point of war gradually and familiarizing them with it, but he plunges them up to their necks in it at once. But enough. What is it all for? Are the people of the free states going to attempt *the subjugation* of our Confederacy under the fanatical and brutal lead of Black Republicans? I agree with you fully in your view of the character and conduct of this party. It would be a sublime spectacle to see the conservative portion of the free states uniting with our Confederacy in overthrowing the present government in Washington and installing a better one in its place—not for us, but for themselves. But I fear that portion of the free states have not the decision and daring and patriotism for the effort. *Douglas* leads off for coercion! A miserable politican and patriot he.

No man can even conjecture where this strife is to end. Yet it is under the control of God. He can "still the tumult of the people," and we can but cast this care upon Him and humbly await His interposition. It may be long delayed; it may be immediate. We must maintain our equanimity, go to our daily duties and by His help faithfully discharge them as in times past, and stand ready for emergencies when they arise, and keep in good heart all around us. The Lord keep you, my dear son, and strengthen you to serve Him and to fear His great and holy name, and to discharge your various and responsible duties to your family and country with cheerfulness and self-possession, with purity and integrity, and with intelligence, decision, and kindness. Seek to do all things well, and everything in its proper time.

Am glad you have consented to deliver the address to your company the 1st of May. You may do good by it, and should like to come and hear you.

The package from Mr. —— was his finish of the copy of the first volume of my church history. Arrived safe. . . .

The news from Baltimore and Washington is out here in the form of rumor. The events of the morning are old by the evening. The scenes succeed almost as rapidly as those of a play. Marvelous if Lincoln, who gave us twenty days to disperse, is in less than ten dispersed himself! As our mails North are stopped, send us what news of interest you can spare. Special prayer should be offered for the *life* of our President; I hope he will not expose his person.

Your affectionate father,
C. C. Jones.

REV. DAVID H. PORTER *to* REV. C. C. JONES[t]

Savannah, *Saturday,* April 27th, 1861

Reverend and dear Sir,

Since the last meeting of our presbytery actual hostilities have commenced between the North and South; or rather, the conflict was raging while our presbytery was in session, though we knew it not at the time. Under these circumstances a question has suggested itself to my mind which troubles me no little, and for the solution of which I turn to you, my revered father in the ministry, and one who I know is always ready to give counsel to his younger brethren, though God may not permit him through bodily infirmity to meet with them in presbyterial assembly.

The question is this: ought not our presbytery to have a called meeting to *reconsider* our action in appointing commissioners to the next assembly? We are in a state of war—an unholy, unjust, *brutal* war forced upon us by the North. It has been made painfully evident that many of our brethren of the assembly sympathize with the political principles of our enemies in this contest. And how can we meet with them in General Assembly with a proper self-respect? Is it possible that our delegates could sit with them in counsel or communion when at the very time, perhaps, our brothers and friends were falling in battle? And yet I tremble at the possibility of giving a wrong touch to the Ark. I am anxious that our presbytery should do right in the premises, but I am not able to decide what *is* right.

My own judgment suggests the course I have indicated, but I am afraid to rely upon that judgment alone in a question of so much moment. What do you think? . . .

My dear doctor, I *do* feel very much exercised on this subject, and beg that my anxiety and great desire to be and do *right* may stand as my excuse for troubling you. With Mrs. Porter's and my kindest regards to Mrs. Jones, I am

Very truly yours in Christ,
David H. Porter.

Rev. C. C. Jones *to* Rev. David H. Porter[t]

Montevideo, *Tuesday,* April 30th, 1861

Reverend and dear Brother,

Your kind favor of 27th reached me last evening. Brother Mitchel of Darien, one of our commissioners, wrote me last week on the subject of your note, and I answered him that were I a commissioner to our coming assembly under existing circumstances I should not go. The inauguration of war upon the South by the Black Republican government, backed by the entire North, is a sufficient reason.

The church must be divided. There is no help for it, Dr. Hodge in his late article in the last number of *The Princeton Review* to the contrary notwithstanding. Have not read but a few pages of it—enough to make the impression that it is ecclesiastically what the first article on "The State of the County" was politically. We are two people distinctly and politically now—what we have been in fact for the last ten or fifteen years. To continue the union of the church after we are divided nationally is contrary to the usage of the Church of Christ in all ages. Ecclesiastical connections conform to civil and political. Our political separation is in part upon a subject which will ever remain a tender and vexed question, and be able at any assembly to break up our harmony; and our being citizens of separate confederacies will but tend to bring up the question. The sympathy of the ministers and elders of the Old School in the North and West with the monstrous doctrine of coercion, and their silence in the crisis, will not breed confidence and that charity which fosters union. Our people will not go for a continued union: confidence is measurably destroyed. Union and good feeling will be better promoted by living under our own vine and fig tree and shaking hands across the hedge and sending delegates over to each other to express love and good will.

The boards are all without our territory save one. Foreigners cannot act for us as we can for ourselves. We cannot afford to pay duties for our books to circulate. The present assembly is too large now. The country is large enough to support *two* or more efficient assemblies. An assembly of our own would promise to be continuously harmonious. The powerful influence of Old School Presbyterianism would be promoted in the South by division; we could act more directly upon our people and call out more talent in the conduct of the great work of the church on earth. We can use the assembly's organization in the free states if we desire—for a time, at least. Nor is there

55

division of the assembly but in the sense (if I may so express it) of jurisdictions of government. We remain doctrinally, spiritually, and in organization one: the Old School Presbyterian Church under *two* assemblies —one in the old union of states, the other in the Confederate States. I have no qualms about such a separation. Dr. Hodge is haunted with the notion of *centralization*. He considers division sin, crime, treason—like secession in the state!

But enough. I had written a page or two on the subject for *The Southern Presbyterian,* but when Sumter was bombarded I considered it useless and threw the paper in the fire. Sumter or no Sumter, I believe in division.

The conduct of the old United States government and of the North is a disgrace to the civilization and Christianity of the age, and an outrage on the great principles of political and civil liberty upon which our former government was laid and upon which it has stood for eighty years. We can do no more than humbly commit our cause to God and meet the issue forced upon us unjustly, iniquitously.

Yours very truly in our Lord,
C. C. Jones.

HON. CHARLES C. JONES, JR., *to* REV. C. C. JONES[8]

Savannah, *Saturday,* May 4th, 1861

My dear Father,

I am under many obligations to you for your recent kind favor, and am happy to know that all at home are well.

My address is pronounced by my friends and the company to have been a perfect success, although you must excuse me for repeating the compliment. The peculiar circumstances attending its delivery—the state of the country, the presence of several old and respected ex-captains on the stage, and the inspiration growing out of the monuments and the memories of the past, the absorbing questions of the present, and the prospects of the future—all conspired to invest the occasion and the theme with unusual attractions. For the first half hour or more I labored in speaking, and for this reason: my throat had become filled with the dust of the morning parade, and as usual my voice had grown husky from the issuing of orders. It improved, however, as I proceeded. The delivery of the oration occupied about two hours. The stage was filled with army and commissioned officers of our city companies, with ex-members of one company, with clergymen and many prominent citizens. The theater was crowded almost from pit to dome, and heard me one and all with marked attention. The address will be published by the corps, and it will give me great pleasure to send to dear Mother and yourself the first copy issued from the press.

We had on that day ninety-three members in full uniform, and paraded with a battery of six six-pounder guns and two twelve-pounder howitzers and a full brass band. This parade in point of numbers is unprecedented in the history of our company. In the morning a Confederate flag was presented to the corps by the wives and daughters of our noncommissioned officers, Lieutenant Hartridge making the presentation address and Captain Claghorn responding on behalf of the company. Our exercises in the theater were commenced with a prayer offered to Almighty God by the chaplain of the corps, Private William S. Bogart. The entire proceedings of the day will be published in substantial form, and will constitute, I trust, a pleasant and interesting chapter in the history of our esteemed and time-honored company.

I heartily wish, my dear father, that you could all have been with us upon that occasion. Twenty-five years hence, when the hundredth anniversary will be celebrated, probably but few from out those well-filled detachments will be there to recount the memories of this day. An inexorable past is forever unfolding within its silent embrace the men and the manners of the present, and but few are the memories which escape a shipwreck in the deluge of time.

But a moment since I returned from the Pulaski House, whither I had been summoned in haste. It appears that some of our citizens observed upon the books of the hotel the names of two officers, Miller and Hook by name, connected with the U.S. army. This fact was rapidly circulated, and an excited number of citizens soon assembled there. Immediately upon my arrival at the Pulaski House I requested the proprietor, Mr. Wiltberger, to arrange an interview with them for me in his private parlor. They immediately responded to the call. I found them to be two young lieutenants, recent graduates of West Point, far gone in consumption, who had been upon leave of absence for several months, and had been endeavoring to recruit their enfeebled constitutions in Florida. They were returning home to die, and with them some ladies also sorely burdened with that terrible disease. They were both gentlemanly men. I was touched with some remarks which they made—such, for example, as this: "Why, sir, so far from taking any part in the existing troubles, we have long since ceased to take any interest in anything other than the restoration of health. And now that this appears impossible, we are more nearly concerned about the affairs of a future world than with any excitements of the present. We will neither of us ever see service again," etc. I was fully satisfied with their statements, corroborated as they were by certificates, etc., and by the more emphatic attestation of their consumptive indications, that they were subjects for commiseration rather than for suspicion and hatred. I made a brief statement to the crowd of the result of my interview, and am happy to state that they confessed themselves satisfied therewith, and retired without any noise or acts of violence. The poor fellows will resume their journey, if physically able to do so, on the morrow.

If there is any one thing which I detest more than another, it is any exhibition of mob law. There is always a remedy for almost any evil, and it is a grave reflection upon the good order of any community whenever its citizens disregard the obligations resting upon them first to resort to the exercise of authority provided by the ordinances of the city and the laws of the land and exhaust the remedies therein provided before resorting to lawless and violent manifestations of feeling and act.

It is a proud and enviable peculiarity of our Southern cities that while riots and lawless mobs are perpetrating all kinds of excesses at the North, reminding of the darkest hours of the French Revolution, we have up to this time been law-abiding citizens, preserving the peace, the good order, and the dignity of the community in which we live. Should any disturbances of this character occur, however, many allowances are to be made. Our feelings, our rights, our cherished privileges have all been grossly invaded by a blinded, a malignant, and a fanatical enemy. Daily are we receiving new indications and proofs of their iniquitous policy, and it would not be strange if retaliation should with not a few become the law of the hour.

We have some private intimations today—how reliable we are as yet unable to judge—that several of the companies composing the Volunteer Regiment of this city will soon be ordered to Virginia. We will soon be informed.

I should think that it would be a wise plan for Brother and his family to remain with you this summer. Aside from the pleasure which they would enjoy in being with you, my dear parents, much expense would be spared. He will find that all business matters are most seriously interrupted—that the minds of men are busied with other subjects. And besides, he will enjoy an excellent opportunity for prosecuting his botanical and ornithological studies. Apart from this, the calm quiet rest of the summer will prove most grateful and salutary after several years of unremitting labor and toil. If I were he, I would think twice before I returned to Augusta, at least for the present. A month will demonstrate the probabilities of the future. And, my dear parents, should the war cloud descend along our coast, I may have to commit to your kind keeping Ruth and little Julia.

We are all well, and unite in warmest love. Julia is a perfect gem. As ever,

Your affectionate son,

Charles C. Jones, Jr.

P.S. I almost forgot to say that we will send the tea, etc., by express on Monday, D.V.

Dr. Fraser charged me eighty-five dollars for his attentions to Clarissa. Do you not think the bill heavy? I certainly find it so these "hard times."

MRS. MARY JONES *to* HON. CHARLES C. JONES, JR.[8]

Montevideo, *Tuesday,* May 7th, 1861

My dear Son,

After a day of nursing and constant attendance upon the sick I close with a few lines congratulatory upon the success of your late oration. We have heard with no small degree of pleasure—and ought I to say pride?—of the approbation and praise bestowed upon it. I thought a great deal of you on the 1st, and if I had "wings to soar" would certainly have been present to witness the well-earned honor bestowed upon my son. Your dear father and brother, too, deeply regretted that the sickness on the plantation detained them at home.

We have had some cases of critical illness; and whilst I write, your brother is compounding doses for at least a dozen now suffering from violent colds, many of them with pneumonia symptoms. Patience's daughter Miley is very ill, and one poor little infant I scarcely think will live out the night. I never knew as much sickness in all my life. It is a great comfort to have Joe's skill and unwearied attention. No one could do more than he is now doing, and we can but hope that God's blessing will own the means. It all appears the result of an epidemic, and we hear prevails elsewhere. The servants thus far have not had anything of the kind at Arcadia.

Please say to dear Ruth that we are very much obliged to her and yourself for the delightful tea and Chinese fruit, both of which we have already enjoyed. And I shall do my best with the yucca seed.

Margaret has proven herself a great comfort to me, and says if Ruth can spare her she will remain one week longer and not return before week after the next. Please let me know if this will answer.

Your brother thinks it is to his interest to return to Augusta and commence the practice of medicine, and says I must tell you he hopes to see you very shortly. Had it consisted with his interests, we should most happily have kept Carrie and Stanhope and himself with us all summer. And if in God's providence you should commit your loved ones to our care, I hope they will ever receive a father and a mother's welcome. If we had only a good physician within reach at Maybank, and dear Ruth and yourself would consent to such an arrangement, it would be my highest pleasure to have her come home and let me wait upon her in her approaching hour of trial. Please assure her how welcome she would be; and I place the matter before her.

On last Saturday Laura and Mr. Buttolph became the parents of another fine little *boy*. All doing well. We saw your name proposed for the colonelcy; Father says he wants to write you about it. I must close, with the united love of Father, Brother, Sister Carrie, and Mother to Ruth and yourself. Kisses for our little darling. God bless you, my child, and keep you in His fear!

Ever your affectionate mother,
Mary Jones.

REV. C. C. JONES *to* HON. CHARLES C. JONES, JR.[8]

Montevideo, *Thursday,* May 9th, 1861

My dear Son,

Mother wrote you to express our great gratification at your success in your oration. Nothing affords us more sincere pleasure than the fact that our children are filling up their days usefully and honorably on the earth. We endeavored to bring you up to that end, and when we connect with it piety towards God in all, then we can go no higher. Your good friend Rev. D. H. Porter wrote me in the kindest and most complimentary form of the oration. Send us a copy when it comes from the press.

Your brother returns with his family to Augusta next week, God willing. We shall miss them a great deal. He has been for the past week constantly occupied with the sick on this place, and I deem it a special providence in our behalf that he was with us. Since writing the foregoing, today (Saturday the 11th) the sick list has greatly diminished, and all remaining are convalescing. And what contributes to health is the seasonable warm weather. Thermometer 80° in the coolest part of Lyons & Trask's store, Riceboro, this morning.

I do not know how many visits Dr. Fraser paid to Clarissa, but eighty-five dollars strikes me as a large bill. His office cannot be above seven miles from Arcadia. *She was, however, very dangerously ill, and for a considerable time required close attention.* The specific charges, if given on the bill, will best show the justice of it.

Now that your oration is over and everybody is pleased, be grateful for your success and go on as before as though nothing had happened, and stand in your lot to meet the next call, and do the best you can, whatever it may be, for God and your fellow men. The command of the Volunteer Regiment is highly honorable and tempting to one ambitious of military honors, and withal a most useful and *deeply responsible position.* And a man should well understand what he is about who seeks it. It must require a great deal of knowledge of military science (tactics, as they call them) and practice of them—the composition, organization, drill, disposition, movement, and support of large bodies in service. War is both a science and an art, and a man wants an education for such a position. The lives and fortunes of thousands—sometimes the fate of the country—turns upon a single pivot, and that not a very large one. And yet nearly every man thinks he can be a captain, a colonel, and even a general! You have about as much business in the city and in the artillery company as you can well attend to. If you become colonel in these war times, you will have to qualify yourself thoroughly and make a serious business of it. Nothing but an absolute call of duty ought to incline you to accept such an appointment.

I agree with you perfectly in relation to mob law. It is the beginning of the overthrow of justice, mercy, truth, and order. So reads history. Self-preservation should aim every man against it, to go to no higher motive. The law-abiding mass of the American people lies south of Mason and Dixon's line.

Your brother will leave next week for Augusta. He is very anxious to make an effort to get into practice; and although times are deranged, yet sickness comes at all seasons. Besides, Carrie is not acclimated; her family are at a distance, and we know how circumscribed are our associations and privileges on the Island. And your brother at home with his library and laboratory would no doubt do more in a professional way than with us. We appreciate his kind offer to stay with us in these times; yet for that reason alone we could not wish him to do so, especially as we cannot calculate certainly how things are going to turn out. And besides, he has joined our troop, and will come down in case of necessity whenever required to do so.

Our united love to Ruthie and yourself, and kisses for Julia.

Your affectionate father,

C. C. Jones.

Can you let me know what prospect is there of bacon being *higher* or *lower?* And what are clean good sides worth? And what can *good* West Indies molasses be had for by the *tierce?* Ask Aaron Champion among others.

HON. CHARLES C. JONES, JR., *to* REV. C. C. JONES[g]

Savannah, *Tuesday,* May 14th, 1861

My dear Father,

Mr. Robert Hutchison, your old friend and companion in youth, died last night. For some time he has been suffering from debility, and has been looking and feeling badly. The proximate cause of his death I understand to have been a stoppage of the intestinal canal. His funeral took place in a private way this afternoon at five o'clock, and his remains will leave tonight for Virginia.

You have doubtless noticed that the port of Charleston has been blockaded by the *Niagara.* We are daily expecting the arrival of a blockading fleet for this harbor. The clouds thicken, and we know not when the sun of peace will again dawn upon this distracted country. But let them gather as darkly as they may: with a holy cause and manly breasts we can and will fight as bravely and as cheerfully under a shadow as under the brightest skies. We are preparing for the struggle here. Our companies hold themselves in readiness to march upon shortest notice. We have placed ourselves under the command of General Lawton for the defense of this city and the coast of our state.

In reference to the colonelcy, I have determined not to accept the invitation to become a candidate. The responsibilities and the duties involved require more attention and careful consideration than I am able under present circumstances to give to them. The engagements incident to the discharge of the mayoralty and my obligations to my company sufficiently engage my time and attention, and do not allow much opportunity for the consideration of other matters. The office of colonel of this regiment should command and receive at this time the attention of an experienced, efficient man. I trust we may be able to secure the services of such an one.

Bacon is now held at a very high figure. Expectations are entertained that a supply may be soon obtained. I will obtain and send you a statement of the prices of this article and of West Indies molasses.

We are all well, and unite in warmest love to self, dear Mother, Sister Carrie, Brother, and little Stanhope. . . . As ever,

Your affectionate son,
Charles C. Jones, Jr.

P.S. The note matures soon in bank, and I send renewal. Have you the discount, or shall I pay it?

MRS. MARY JONES *to* HON. CHARLES C. JONES, JR.[8]

Montevideo, *Monday*, May 20th, 1861

My dear Son,

Tom has just come in from the mail, and I take the earliest opportunity of expressing my great pleasure and gratification at receiving thus early a copy of your oration, which I shall prize most highly, and hope to read early tomorrow, not having leisure tonight, as we are all busy helping to get things in readiness for your brother's departure early in the morning.

We feel very sad at their departure. Joe has been unwearied in his medical attentions to your father and myself, and I know not what we would have done without his skill and attention to the servants. For the past three weeks the plantation has been almost a hospital. We have never known as many cases of sickness, but have great reason to be grateful that their lives have all been spared thus far.

Did you remember that I had your *army glass*—the gift of your old friend Mr. Helm—in possession? *Patience* has taken great pride in brightening it up today, and I send it down to you by the present opportunity. Please let George take the cans, etc., to King & Waring. I must now close, with our united love to dear Ruth and yourself, and kisses many for our little granddaughter.

Ever your affectionate mother,
Mary Jones.

HON. CHARLES C. JONES, JR., *to* REV. *and* MRS. C. C. JONES[8]

Savannah, *Tuesday*, May 21st, 1861

My dear Father and Mother,

We were a few hours since gladdened by the arrival of Brother and his family. I am sorry to see that Sister Carrie is troubled with a very bad cough. As usual they tell us that they can only pay us a flying visit. I must confess I doubt the expediency of Brother's returning to Augusta this summer when he might remain with you upon the Island. My fear is that he will find such a derangement existing in every department, in consequence of the presence of this war, that it will be a very difficult matter to sustain the depressing influences of small fees and poor pay. But of this he must be the best judge.

At his hands, dear Mother, I was favored with your very kind letter, for which you will accept many thanks. Hope that you will not be disappointed upon a perusal of the address. I regret that I did not have the pleasure and honor of delivering it in the presence of yourself and dear Father; for I am well aware that there were many circumstances attendant upon its delivery which conduced no little to the interest and the effect of the occasion. My friend Deitz promises me a bound copy, which I will take great pleasure in sending to you so soon as it is finished.

The news has just reached us from the harbor that the *Harriet Lane* is lying outside blockading the port. A Spanish brig was this morning chased by her, but succeeded in forcing the blockade. The *Harriet Lane* fired at her, but without effect, and the brig is now lying secure from all harm under the guns of the fort. The *Harriet Lane* declined to come within range of the guns of the fort; indeed, she did not dare even an entrance within the sound. The above I give you as the report of a pilot just arrived from below.

Upon Tybee Island we have as yet no battery of heavy guns. Some four hundred troops are stationed there as sharpshooters. The erection of a battery of probably eighteen- and thirty-two-pounder guns is in contemplation. The reason why no very heavy guns will be mounted there is in order that if the battery be taken, there shall be no guns which would be of sufficient size to be turned and used with effect upon the fort.

At Thunderbolt an earthwork has been thrown up mounting one columbiad and three eighteen-pounder guns. The former is in position, and commands the approach for more than two miles. The latter, I believe, are not as yet mounted.

Fort Pulaski is believed to be in a capital state for defense. Some eleven columbiads, I am informed (I have been so much occupied that I really have had no time of late to visit the fort), are in position—most of them *en barbette,* a few in the casemates. These are terrible engines of war, and can be used with fearful effect upon any attacking force. One gun in position in a fixed battery is worth more than a dozen upon a floating battery. The garrison of the fort numbers about six hundred men. The troops have been suffering much from measles, but are now getting better.

The Volunteer Regiment of Savannah are expecting orders for the field early next week. There will then be probably a movement of troops along the coast, with a view to the occupation of exposed points liable to attack. Nothing definite has as yet, however, been determined upon. My own impression is that the troops of this city should not be ordered away from their homes except under a pressing necessity. The avocations of citizen-soldiers who have wives and children dependent upon their daily exertions should not be interrupted until the very latest moment. Distress and want follow at best close upon the heels of war, and it is the part of prudence to postpone their coming as long as possible. The companies here might be drilled every afternoon in regimental and battalion movements to their great advantage without withdrawing them from home and placing them in camp.

This may be a long and exhausting war, and the longer we can retain our citizen-soldiery at home—in the bosoms of their own families, engaged in their support and comfort, and thus relieving them from the sad necessity of becoming pensioners upon public charity—the better.

Mr. Hutchison died very quietly and in full possession of his mind. He expressed himself prepared for the last great change, and made every arrangement in reference to his property and worldly affairs. He dismissed all his friends during the night, and died early in the morning with only his servants around him. Major Porter, Mr. Duncan, Colonel Lawton are, I believe, named as his executors.

In consequence of these disjointed times our business engagements are very nearly suspended. We all, my dear parents, unite in warmest love. As ever,

Your affectionate son,
Charles C. Jones, Jr.

HON. CHARLES C. JONES, JR., *to* MRS. MARY JONES[8]

Savannah, *Saturday,* May 25th, 1861

My dear Mother,

Enclosed please find an ambrotype likeness of General Beauregard, the hero of the battle of Fort Sumter. I thought you might like to have it.

The ladies have concluded their fair for the benefit of the soldiers and of their needy families with considerable success. The profit realized is not yet definitely ascertained, but I presume it will not be less than several thousand dollars. They should now see that this sum is judiciously expended and not wasted in trifles.

Our regiment is under marching orders, and will probably be upon the move early next week, taking post at points most eligible for the defense of the coast. Charlie Whitehead has been elected to the position of major of one of the Georgia regiments in Virginia, and is now stationed at Portsmouth. The present indications are that we shall soon hear of severe and bloody hostilities in that state. The Lincolnites are occupying Alexandria, upon Virginia soil. . . .

We are all well, and unite in warmest love to self, dear Mother, and to dear Father. Although in much haste, I am, as ever,

Your affectionate son,
Charles C. Jones, Jr.

MRS. MARY JONES *to* HON. CHARLES C. JONES, JR.[8]

Montevideo, *Tuesday,* May 28th, 1861

My very dear Son,

I read your oration with intense interest, and your father and myself regret more than ever that in providence we were not permitted to hear you deliver it. Your father says he was greatly pleased with it, and will write you particularly about it. Accept many thanks for your favor by the last mail enclosing the picture of our gallant hero General Beauregard. All honor to his name!

Our esteemed friend Dr. Howe spent a day with us last week. He was in Charleston on Saturday at the time of the surrender, saw the white flag raised, and heard Major Wigfall give the account of his interview with Major Anderson. He confirmed what the papers stated, that in the center of the fort was placed an immense gun prepared and pointed for shelling the city and destroying defenseless women and children. There were several remarkable providences connected with the engagement and defeat. The barbette gun designed to play upon the iron battery recoiled at the first fire and was rendered useless, and the outer metallic doors to the magazines became so warped that they could not be opened. Dr. Howe says the burning of the officers' quarters was singular, as there was not a particle of wood about them—even marble mantels, and handsomely fitted out. If the truth was known, I would not be surprised to hear that they were fired by Anderson himself. His whole course has been marked by duplicity and falsehood. Our good friends are feeling very deeply for their brave boy Willie. He was stationed on Stono River during the fight, and is now in Virginia in Colonel Kershaw's regiment, which I see by the papers will probably be one of the first to meet the enemy. Here it is that the sword pierces into our own bosoms!

Last Sabbath was our Communion season at old Midway, and a peculiarly precious and solemn time it was. And I doubt not every heart present bore a bleeding country to the Prince of Peace. . . . The afternoon service was a prayer meeting especially in view of our present condition, and the church engaged to devote—or rather it was suggested that every evening at sunset we remember our country, our rulers, and those who have gone forth to battle, that God would shield them and crown our arms with victory.

We shall no doubt be soon surrounded by all the horrors of war; and it becomes every heart to be fixed, trusting in God, and every arm to be nerved for the righteous conflict. In my poor way I want to testify my interest in those who are called to defend our homes and firesides, our lives and liberties. I have had all the sage and balm from the garden dried, and if you think it would be acceptable I will send it for the sick. And following out the suggestions of the governor, I would like to prepare clothing for *four* soldiers. I have enough for two suits, and would be much obliged if it does not give you too much trouble to call at Mr. Lathrop's and request him to send me enough for two suits of such material as is used by the army soldiers—thread and buttons, etc., etc.—and materials for four shirts of such as is used in service.

Your father requests you to call at King & Waring's and ask them to send our articles if not already sent, and write us when they do send them.

Please ask dear Ruth to send me *by mail six skeins* of linen thread—or by any other way that I can get them soon—*for embroidering flannel.*

Enclosed is a certificate of church membership for Adeline; your father says she must present it to Dr. Axson.

It is late, my dear son, and I must close. Packing all day; begin to move tomorrow, *D.V.* I long to see you and dear Ruth and our darling little granddaughter. What can I do for Ruth? Did you get your army glass? No word from Joe since he left. . . . Father unites with me in best love to you both and kisses for Julia.

Ever your affectionate mother,
Mary Jones.

HON. CHARLES C. JONES, JR., *to* REV. *and* MRS. C. C. JONES[8]

Savannah, *Wednesday,* May 29th, 1861

My dear Father and Mother,

I trust that a kind Providence is dealing mercifully with you, and that all the sick servants are well again. We have not heard from you for some time, and feel very anxious to do so.

Still in the dark as to the true status of affairs in Virginia. Daily anticipating accounts of an engagement between our troops and the Lincolnites. One would think that a collision must inevitably at a very early period ensue. The Fabian policy of our administration may be all for the best, as the Black Republican administration is fast exhausting its resources, and must sooner or later crumble and become the prey of mobs and intestine feuds. You have noticed the heroic death of Jackson in Alexandria—a modern Tell whose name will not be forgotten.

We are adopting measures to provide for the destitute families of our volunteers. A battery is in process of erection on Tybee Island. Our regiment is daily expecting orders from General Lawton. All well, and unite in warmest love to you both, my dear parents. As ever,

Your affectionate son,
Charles C. Jones, Jr.

REV. C. C. JONES *to* HON. CHARLES C. JONES, JR.[8]

Montevideo, *Thursday Evening,* May 30th, 1861

My dear Son,

Tom has just returned from the office with your letter, and we are thankful to learn that you and Ruthie and our sweet little granddaughter are all well. We are as much so as usual. I think your dear mother has greatly improved under your brother's treatment, and is much better than she was before he came down.

We received a letter from Carrie last night in which she expresses regret that their visit was cut short to you by the sickness of little Stanhope and the invalid condition of the servants. And all three of them have been fairly in bed since they reached Augusta. Stanhope has been unwell too, but is better. We regretted to part with them, but your brother thought he ought to return and see what he might do in the way of practice, unpromising as the times are; and I could not reasonably object. Something may turn up in his favor. And then Carrie is near her own family, which is a great matter in troublous times. I do not know what we should have done without your brother in our late epidemic of colds. He is an excellent physician, and of many resources; and to him I am indebted for great help in my case; and he is the only doctor who seems fully to comprehend it. It is a little remarkable—he left two cases convalescing, and not another has occurred, and our people, D.G., are enjoying their usual health.

I have received a copy of your oration and thank you for it, but had already read Mother's copy. And I must congratulate you on it as an admirable one—well conceived and well written, with some eloquent passages, and adapted to the occasion. And I can well appreciate the praises bestowed upon it well delivered before the audience that honored you with their attendance. I understand some of your best passages were impromptu and do not appear in the text. Please send a copy to Mr. W. F. Colcock; also to *Miss Sarah Jones, Charleston,* and to your Aunt *Sarah Howe, Columbia, South Carolina.*

Robert dined with us today. His family all well. Reported that Captain Lamar's Mounted Rifles were expected in Sunbury this week, to be stationed there till the Liberty Troop is mustered into service. This is all I know about it. Certain it is the Liberty Troop *cannot leave the county* for prudential reasons. The citizens meet at Hinesville on Tuesday next on *public affairs,* Governor Brown's address, etc. Want to attend if possible. Had spasm of throat after preaching on Sabbath.

The Fabian policy is the best for us. Meanwhile our every effort should be put forth thoroughly to arm and equip and ammunition every state in the Confederacy, and put everything in the best state of defense. War or no war, this is the true policy; for if we are to be independent, we must be independent, and ever keep up such a state of preparation for war that the Federal states shall never have us at an advantage. Am glad to know that Lincoln's finances are running low. Did not suppose it, since the cry has been "men and money in abundance—no lack and no stint." I cannot divest myself of the impression that there will be some effectual interposition of a kind Providence in our favor and for our repose. It may be only what I desire; but surely we are right, and whatever be our sins that call for judgment—and *they are many*—yet so far as the North is concerned, we have not sinned against it, and therefore may pray for a blessing.

It is another providence in our favor that Ellsworth, heading those miscreant Zouaves, from whom so much was expected by the Black Republican President and his party, should have been shot dead the first man! Jackson will long be remembered and honored.

What Lincoln and Scott mean to do, time only will show. We can only wait on our arms, trusting in God.

We have now a *third* confederacy—a single one, however. This honor is reserved for *Kentucky!* She has ascended to the pinnacle of state sovereignty and declared herself independent of both the other governments, and warns them both from her soil on penalties most severe to the trespasser.

But enough. Hope Mr. Anderson sold my cotton to go out in that ship that left you last week. Please ask King & Waring if they have sent out our little order of articles. Note all right. We are hoping to be at Maybank Saturday for the summer. Moving this week. . . . Mother says I am writing you a very long letter. She unites in much love to Ruthie and kisses for Julia. May every blessing of God, my dear son, ever rest on you and yours!

Your affectionate father,
C. C. Jones.

HON. CHARLES C. JONES, JR., *to* REV. C. C. JONES[g]

Savannah, *Saturday*, June 1st, 1861

My dear Father,

I am today favored with your kind letter of yesterday, and am truly happy to hear from you and dear Mother. Am deeply pained to know that you have recently suffered from another attack of spasm of the throat.

The knowledge of your favorable opinion of my recent address is most pleasing to me. I did extemporize during its delivery, and could not find time or memory to locate positively the spoken words—the offspring of the moment—which were there given to the passing air. You well know how these sparks are struck from the heated iron.

Ruth and little Julia went to Howard's plantation on Wednesday last on a visit of a few days. I am glad they are gone, and for this reason: the very day after they left, a little Negro of Dr. Harriss' was taken violently ill with scarlet fever and diphtheria, a throat affection which has proven very generally fatal. Neither Ruth nor our little Julia has had either of these diseases, and they are both contagious. While I write, they are momentarily expecting the demise of the poor little Negress. It is impossible for her to live through the night. Were Ruth and Julia here, my anxiety for them would be very great. In these tenement houses the diseases of your next-door neighbor are almost certain to become those of your own yard. Do you know whether any of our servants here have ever had the scarlet fever? In Ruth's present situation I am informed that the disease is greatly to be dreaded.

Our regiment, with the exception of one company which is at present held as a reserve corps, has left the city. Lamar's company of Mounted Rifles has, I understand, been ordered to take post for the present at Sunbury. It has not been as yet, however, mustered into service.

Without wishing in any manner to quarrel with the orders of General Lawton, it strikes me his dispositions are to a great extent ill-judged. The theory of his operations is not correct. He has withdrawn from this city between six and seven hundred men at a time when most of all they should be here. Points exist all along the coast where an enemy might readily land. That enemy has command of the sea, and can without let or hindrance transport troops at pleasure, and by means of transports land unmolested at almost any given point. It is unnatural to suppose that Fort Pulaski, strongly built and well fortified, will be attacked when a landing equally effective can be had at other points not far distant, by means of which the fort may be taken in the rear, Savannah attacked from the land, and Pulaski, thus isolated, forced to surrender. The fact is, the Lincolnites, in full force at the Tortugas with a full navy, might any day make a demonstration upon our coast, either by land or by sea. And what at the moment have we to offer as a means of successful resistance to an invading force of four or five thousand men fully appointed and precipitated upon us unexpectedly? As it is now, the regiment is completely scattered—some at Pulaski, other companies at Thunderbolt, others on Skidaway Island, and little or no reserve in the city.

Another mistake of the generals, it appears to me, is this: the companies of our regiment are, *quoad hoc,* pretty well drilled, but there is but little familiarity with battalion and regimental movements. The men rely upon company capabilities and not upon regimental. What we need is a camp of instruction. The regiment should have now while we have the opportunity been ordered into service, and a camp of discipline organized. We would then have learned how to act in concert, and a reserve force of certainly not less than twelve hundred men (than whom no better volunteer troops can anywhere be found) be fully prepared to act promptly and efficiently and in concert wherever and whenever opportunity occurred. As it is, scattered at various points, such general discipline, concert of action, and mutual confidence have all to be subsequently acquired; and it may be that the first lesson will have to be acquired in the face of an invading foe and under the fire of advancing columns. A capital place for brave action, but a poor opportunity for perfection in regimental drill.

An isolated company here and there, with no reserve corps to support it, can do little more than watch the movements of the enemy and report his advance. What we need is a regular system of fortifications at the most accessible points along our coast, with heavy batteries well manned and reserve corps to support in the event of hostile demonstrations.

The withdrawal of a thousand men from our city just at this time gives me no little uneasiness. I am trying to get everything in trim for any emergency.

Tybee Island is now occupied by nearly one thousand regulars, as I am informed, and the battery there progresses rapidly.

We have a telegraphic rumor that fighting has commenced in Virginia. It needs confirmation. . . .

I forgot to thank dear Mother for the army glass, which came in such admirable condition. It may serve me a good turn before long.

Do let me know, my dear father, whenever I can serve you in any way. When I called at Captain Anderson's counting room to inquire whether the cotton had been sold, I found it shut: all hands gone to the wars. Will endeavor to ascertain, however, on Monday. Our streets have lost many familiar faces by the withdrawal of our regiment. With warmest love, I am, as ever, my dear father and mother,

Your ever affectionate son,
Charles C. Jones, Jr.

A letter from Uncle John, just received, states that Dunwody has gone to Virginia with a company from Rome—as a private, I believe.

REV. C. C. JONES *to* HON. CHARLES C. JONES, JR.[8]

Maybank, *Friday,* June 7th, 1861

My dear Son,

We were happy to hear from you last evening that the case had terminated at Dr. Harriss' without spreading. Poor little sufferer! You have had scarlet fever, but I think neither of your servants. Ruthie must be careful; but should she take it, in God's providence, remember that thousands have it, old and young, and are spared, and therefore do not despond. And thousands never take it.

When I think of the *realities* of life, my dear son—sickness and its solemn issues—I long, long for your conversion, that you may be the priest and spiritual stay of your own dear family, and have yourself a God and Saviour to go to and trust in and fear not; for even death is vanquished by our Lord. Let neither business nor pleasure nor cares of any kind cause you to neglect so great salvation. All else is perishing.

We find the change to Maybank very pleasant. Your sister and the children and Miss Kitty Stiles are now with us; and wish all our children and grandchildren were with us. I greatly desired to go down and see you and Ruthie and Julia before moving, but was so unwell that I feared to venture; and you must take the will for the deed. All on the Island well and doing well. And all in the house unite in much love to Ruthie and yourself and kisses for Julia. Embrace an opportunity by Mr. McDonald to send you this hasty line today; may go down tomorrow.

Your ever affectionate father,
C. C. Jones.

P.S. Will you please ask Dr. Axson if he has a copy of Lardner's *Credibility of the Gospel History* in his library? If not, Mr. Porter. If not, is there a copy in their knowledge in the city? It is in eight or ten volumes. My copy was burnt up, and expected to replace it sometime this summer, when I should need to refer to it; but the state of the country forbids it until our ports are open to England. We must import our books direct, and pay no more toll and high tariff.

C.C.J.

Meeting at Hinesville: committee of safety appointed. The assessment of the governor for support of the government and a contingent fund for support of families of such as may go to the war out of the county to be *raised by general tax on the county*. Best way. Nothing done further. Was not able to go to the meeting; report through Rev. D. L. Buttolph.

C.C.J.

MRS. MARY JONES *to* HON. CHARLES C. JONES, JR.[8]

Maybank, *Friday*, June 7th, 1861

Please say to dear Ruth that I will send the flannels next week. My heart is with her especially at this time, and wish my presence could be also. Nothing but your dear father's extreme feebleness prevents my leaving him. Do advise us constantly of the state of her health. I wish she could be with us in her approaching trial, that we might render her every attention in our power. I hope she will be prudent for the next two or three weeks, living plainly and taking an occasional dose of cooling medicine, looking well to the state of her digestion. Some persons derive great benefit from drinking flaxseed tea daily, taken cold; and to make it palatable she could add lemon juice. (This part of the letter is for her eye.)

We long to see you all. Had you not best send us Julia at least? Did you give my order to Lathrop for the soldiers' garments? With warmest love,

Ever, my dearest son, your affectionate mother,

M.J.

HON. CHARLES C. JONES, JR., *to* REV. *and* MRS. C. C. JONES[8]

Savannah, *Monday*, June 10th, 1861

My dear Father and Mother,

Ruth has returned after her short visit to Amanda looking pretty well. She suffered one day from an acute attack, but was soon relieved.

I presume you have observed the appointment of Judge Jackson as a brigadier general in the Confederate service. It is a position he has long and most ardently desired, and I doubt not when the hour of combat comes he will do the states no little service.

That hour must soon arrive. Sincerely do I trust and believe that the God of Battles will in that day send the victory where it of right belongs. I cannot bring my mind to entertain even the impression that a God of justice and of truth will permit a blinded, fanatical people, who already have set at naught all rules of equality, of right, and of honor; who flagrantly violate the inalienable right of private liberty by an arrogant suspension of the privilege of habeas corpus, a writ of right than which none can be dearer to the citizen—and that in the face of judicial process issued by the Chief Justice Taney, renowned for his profound legal attainments, respected for his many virtues and high position, and venerable for his many useful labors and constitutional learning; who set at defiance the right of private property by seizing Negroes, the personal chattels of others, without offer of remuneration or consent of the owner; who permit their mercenaries to trifle at will with private virtue; who trample under foot sacred compacts and solemn engagements; who substitute military despotism in the place of constitutional liberty; and who without the fear of either God or man in their eyes recklessly pursue a policy subversive of all that is just and pure and high-minded—to triumph in this unholy war. We have our sins and our shortcomings, and they are many; but without the arrogance of the self-righteous Pharisee we may honestly thank God that we are not as they are. Should they be defeated in this fearful contest, how fearful the retribution! Who can appreciate the terrors of this lifted wave of fanaticism when, broken and dismayed, it recoils in confusion and madness upon itself? Agrarianism in ancient Rome will appear as naught in the contrast.

You will observe that I have issued a proclamation requesting the citizens of Savannah to abstain from their ordinary engagements on Thursday next, the day set apart by the President as a day of fasting and prayer, and with one consent to unite in the due observation of the day. You may also notice an anonymous communication in our city papers signed "Citizen," in which I recommend that the suggestion in reference to the taking up of a collection in all places of public worship on that day for the benefit of our army and of our government should meet with a generous, practical, and patriotic adoption. If this plan be pursued generally on that day throughout these Confederate States, the amount received will be large, and the fund thus realized will prove most acceptable to the present finances of the government. The idea is a good one, and should be everywhere carried into effect. I intend myself conscientiously to observe the day. We should all do so.

We are kept very much in the dark with reference to the true movements of our army in Virginia, and it is proper that this should be so. President Davis' presence inspires great enthusiasm and confidence. He appears to be in every respect the man raised for the emergency. At once soldier and statesman, he everywhere acknowledges our dependence upon and our hope in the guiding influence and the protection of a superintending Providence. I regret to know that his health is feeble. In the event of his death, where would we look for a successor?

The Central Railroad Company have declared a semi-annual dividend payable on and after the 15th inst. of five percent. Very acceptable to all stockholders at the present. I send by this post a copy of Judge Jackson's recent eulogy upon the life and character of the Hon. Charles J. McDonald. We are all well, and unite, my dearest parents, in warmest love to you both. As ever,

Your affectionate son,
Charles C. Jones, Jr.

What was done at Hinesville last Tuesday?

72

REV. C. C. JONES *to* HON. CHARLES C. JONES, JR.[8]

Maybank, *Monday,* June 17th, 1861

My dear Son,

I embrace a moment to write to acknowledge your last favors. Hope your dear wife and child are with you now, and your home is more cheerful and happy. We are all, through divine mercy, in good health. Your sister and Miss Kitty Stiles have been paying us a most pleasant visit; leave us the last of this week. The little children interest us a great deal, and we long to see Julia.

Your responsibilities are very great, and energy and decision and wisdom and justice must characterize your administration. You have been enabled to succeed so far, and I trust the Lord will be with and bring you successfully to the end. It is positively difficult for a man to believe—to realize—the condition of our country. The sun has never shone *on the like before!*

Chief Justice Taney's exposition of the Habeas Corpus Act and Lincoln's usurpation is exceedingly fine. It is as clear as a bell: his style eminently legal. It forms a graceful close to his term of office, if he should go out. Yet the fanatical Northern people will pay no manner of respect to it.

Gilbert has come for the letter, and I must abruptly close. Mother sends much love to Ruthie and yourself, and many kisses for Julia.

Your ever affectionate father,
C.C. Jones.

P.S. Your mother inquires if you ever received her letter enclosing Adeline's certificate of membership and dismission to the Independent Church, Savannah. She fears you never did, as you have never mentioned it.

MRS. MARY JONES *to* HON. CHARLES C. JONES, JR.[8]

Maybank, *Tuesday,* June 18th, 1861

My dear Son,

Robin has just arrived bringing the box of books, for which your father is very much obliged; and I embrace the opportunity of sending by him a few little articles of flannel for dear Ruth. There are some other little articles which I hoped to have completed and sent at the same time, but the demands upon time have been so varied and constant I have not been enabled to complete them. The flannel she may want soon. That God will grant her deliverance from protracted sufferings, and make her the joyful mother of a perfect babe, and spare her life and restore her speedily to usefulness in her family, the church, and community is my daily prayer. As soon as possible I hope she will come out and spend some time with us. We long to see our dear little granddaughter, and wish she was here now with her little cousins, who would love and amuse her very much.

We moved down on Saturday two weeks. Miss Kitty Stiles and Daughter came down early the following week, and we have had a delightful visit. Today they are at the Point. . . . In addition to other matters your sister and myself have molded and made up about a hundred and twenty-five or a hundred and fifty bullets and cartridges for Joe's carbine, in case he is called into service with the Liberty Independent Troop, of which corps you know he is now a member. . . . By the last mail we received letters from Carrie and himself. Both she and Stanhope are suffering still from coughs. I feel uneasy about them.

Your father has not recovered from the exhaustion consequent upon preaching at Midway. He is very feeble, and suffers from his throat and pains in his chest. I hope after a while that rest and our sweet Island atmosphere, with God's blessing, will restore him to his usual strength and comfort.

Your father has ridden to see your uncle and consult with him about a singular affair. Last evening we sent Gilbert to Montevideo; he returned early this morning, making the following statement: *Jackson* was sent by Cato very early yesterday morning (Monday) to go throughout the pasture and report if all things were right. As he was going through a piece of brushwood back of Dogwood Swamp he came suddenly upon two white men lying down, two others coming up immediately. They asked him to whom he belonged, where his owner was, who took care of the place—all of which he answered in great alarm. They then told him to pass on his way, but to tell no *white person* that he had seen them. He says he kept on as quietly as he could, but as soon as he was out of their sight he ran home and informed Cato; and they sent immediately for Mr. McDonald, who got one or two men from the Boro and some of our Negroes and made search for them without discovering anyone. Jackson describes them as being dressed in caps and clothes alike and looked somewhat like soldiers. He was so frightened he did not see if they had guns. It certainly is a strange matter, and in these war times must be looked into. We are dealing with an enemy whose aim is our destruction by all or any means. Your father has just come in and reproves me for telling the strange story. I know you will receive it for what it is worth. Some suggest they may be deserters.

I got Mr. McDonald to make trial of the carbine. He stood in the front piazza and sent a ball into the *old cedar tree* (the target tree) upon the lawn *six inches deep*. I had the ball bored out and measured the depth of the hole.

We observed the day of fasting and prayer with our whole household both at Montevideo and Maybank, and presume they did the same at Arcadia. We were very much pleased with your proclamation and the piece signed "Citizen," but do not know if any contributions were taken up in the county.

I do not think you could have received my letter written before leaving Montevideo. It contained a certificate for Adeline of church membership to connect herself with Dr. Axson's. Please let me know if you did do so.

It is time for Robin to start, and I must close this hurried scrawl. Friends are all well on the Island. Your father joins me in best love to Ruth and yourself and kisses for our dear little granddaughter.

Ever, my dear son, your affectionate mother,
Mary Jones.

Our Confederate flag now floats in the Atlantic breeze upon the bay in Sunbury, and "the deserted village" presents a novel sight: white tents upon the plain, all the military arrangements of camp life, officers in command, soldiers on duty, horses ready for service. Two eight-pounders have been taken from the old fort in perfect preservation. They ring like bell metal, and are said to be French pieces. Captain Lamar intends to have them mounted.

I shall feel so anxious about dear Ruth that I hope you will write us as often as you can.

HON. CHARLES C. JONES, JR., *to* REV. *and* MRS. C. C. JONES[g]

Savannah, *Tuesday*, June 18th, 1861

My dear Father and Mother,

I am sorry to tell you that our dear little Julia is suffering from scarlet fever. She was very restless all last night with fever, which continues hot and high today. Her little head appears to be unaffected, as she talks and remains quite sensible. Ruth is greatly distressed, and filled with fearful apprehensions. I try to make her look on the bright side of the future. Her heart is so completely bound up in the life, the health, and the happiness of this our dear little daughter that any distress or indisposition affects her very sensibly. I never have seen such devotion as she has and bears for Julia; it has been a marvel to me for many days. The tender love which a mother cherishes for her child—at once so pure, so disinterested, so self-sacrificing —is perhaps the holiest emotion of which this fallen human nature is capable. Dr. Harriss hopes that the attack may not prove very severe. Most of the cases—and there have been many in the city this season—have proved manageable, yielding to treatment. We ardently hope for the best.

I have sent George for Mrs. Hall, that she may be with us and relieve Ruth as much as possible—or rather, as much as she will suffer herself to be relieved. I believe none of our servants have had this fever. Nothing new in the city. With warmest love to you both, my dear parents, in which we all unite, I am, as ever,

Your affectionate son,
Charles C. Jones, Jr.

Did you receive the box of books forwarded yesterday by Stepney?

III

Mrs. Mary S. Mallard *to* Mrs. Mary Jones[t]

Maybank, *Saturday,* June 22nd, 1861

My dear Mother,

We were rejoiced last evening to hear of your safe arrival and dear little Julia's improvement. I hope she is quite out of danger now, and that she will soon be well. Captain Winn was kind enough to send Brother Charlie's note down last night. The servant came just as we were going to bed. I was very much startled, fearing little Julia was worse; but we were greatly cheered to know she was better. . . .

Yesterday and today have been the warmest I have felt this season. The heat has been intense. The thermometer stood at 95° today, and we heard it was as high as 99° yesterday in Sunbury. I neglected to look here.

Uncle Henry spent last night with us. He had dined with Captain Lamar, and I believe carried a lamb and some vegetables to the soldiers. He says Captain Lamar told him the people of Liberty had been so kind to him that he would love them all the days of his life.

Little Mary has just come in, and says: "Do tell my dear danma that I send my love to her and want her to send me the candy now, and I send my howdy to her." She has made frequent inquiries about you and *chère amie.*

I have been busily engaged in finishing the cartridges, and was very glad my occupation called me in the basement, for it was so much cooler than any other portion of the house. I have finished all—a hundred and twenty-five in number.

Today was so warm that Rex spent a good part of his time in the horse trough.

Father has felt the heat very much, and was very much debilitated by it this morning. I will try and take good care of him, and will stay as long as you wish to be absent.

I feel very anxious about Ruthie, and hope she will be spared the scarlet fever. Do give her much love and my best wishes. I hope she will be spared great and protracted suffering. I know it must be a great comfort to Brother Charlie to have you there. Give much love to him also, and kiss little Julia for me.

Mom Patience has just brought me two dollars and Miley's measure for a pair of shoes. She would like heels; and if any money is left, please bring some hickory stripe. If you are able to go out, will you get for me, dear

Mother, some pretty chintz for a bedspread? I would like a light ground and something that can wash. Don't trouble yourself with this unless you feel able to go out, for I know you will have fatigue enough without walking in the sun. We deal at Nevitt's, so please get Mamie's stockings and the calico there.

Pulaski is waiting to go, so I must close, with kisses from your little grandchildren, and love from us all.

Your affectionate daughter,
Mary S. Mallard.

REV. C. C. JONES *to* MRS. MARY JONES[t]

Maybank, *Saturday,* June 22nd, 1861

My dear Wife,

I had written a page to you, and Daughter sent up her letter to me with this space, and on reading find she has said all I had written and more too. So will add no more. But much love to you and to Ruthie and Charles, and kisses for the dear little patient. Do get something to make me a couple of *thin waistcoats.*

Your ever dear husband,
C. C. Jones.

HON. CHARLES C. JONES, JR., *to* REV. C. C. JONES[g]

Savannah, *Sunday,* June 23rd, 1861

My dear Father,

Dear Mother suffered from fever last night, but is better this morning, and hopes so soon as the medicine has accomplished its desired effect that she will be entirely relieved.

We trust that our dear little Julia is better, although what the final result will be is known only to Him in whose hands are the issues of life and of death. We hope for the best, and the attending physician thinks that the severity of the attack is well-nigh overpassed.

With our warmest and united love, I am, as ever,

Your affectionate son,
Charles C. Jones, Jr.

HON. CHARLES C. JONES, JR., *to* REV. C. C. JONES[g]

Savannah, *Monday,* June 24th, 1861

My dear Father,

Mother is quite relieved from her attack of fever, and we trust she will have no return of it. Julia, we hope, is somewhat better this morning. The fever appears to be abating somewhat, leaving the little sufferer very prostrate, however.

77

In consequence of the amount of electricity along the line of the telegraph between Charleston and Augusta last evening, we received no telegrams, the operators not being able to communicate. We are hourly in anticipation of startling accounts from Virginia. All the indications point to a general and very sanguinary battle. May the God of Battles send us the victory in that day!

All unite in warmest love. As ever,

Your affectionate son,
Charles C. Jones, Jr.

HON. CHARLES C. JONES, JR., *to* REV. C. C. JONES[g]

Savannah, *Tuesday,* June 25th, 1861

My dear Father,

Ruth was this morning at nine o'clock delivered of a fine little daughter. Her previous sufferings were not protracted, but after the birth of the child she was brought to death's door in consequence of the failure of the womb to contract, and the enormous effusion of blood. This has been stopped, but she lies very weak. Dr. Harriss thinks that the danger is overpassed, but she will have to remain perfectly quiet for hours to come.

Julia, we hope, is better. The febrile action is diminished somewhat, but she continues quite restless. I do not know what we would have done in the absence of dear Mother. She is better this morning, and I sincerely trust that her exertions may not induce a return of her fever.

We all unite in warmest love. As ever,

Your affectionate son,
Charles C. Jones, Jr.

REV. C. C. JONES *to* MRS. MARY JONES[t]

Maybank, *Wednesday,* June 26th, 1861

My dear Wife,

My apprehensions were realized: I feared the long and hot ride, first in the carriage and then in the cars, would prove too much for you. But I am truly happy to learn by Charles's notes of the 23rd, 24th, and 25th that you had had no return of fever. May it please God to restore you speedily!

And so you were just in time to aid in the care of the little patient, and to welcome your third granddaughter! How opportune! Our prayers have been heard. We shall be anxious to know that Ruthie is well over it, for Charles writes she was extremely ill immediately after. I wish Joe was nearer to his brother, though he is distant but a few hours after all. He is a most excellent and prompt physician. Do present Ruthie my hearty congratulations, and many kisses of welcome to my little nameless granddaughter. And say to Mrs. Hall that she must take the same good care of it she did of Julia. Remember: if you have any more fever, I shall come down and nurse you.

The weather has been intensely hot: Saturday 95° and Sunday 99° in the entry—figures I never saw reached at Maybank before. Three showers for three successive evenings; last evening a fine one. Think it was general. Greatly needed.

All well on the Island. Our little ones afflicted with the heat. Daughter is great company and a great comfort to me in your absence. We try to get along as well as we can. I keep the little fry busy within and without doors to let things look cared for when you come back.

We are invited to witness the marriage ceremony of Miss Matilda Jane Harden to Mr. T. Sumner Stevens in Walthourville Presbyterian Church tomorrow evening. And this is the greatest news we have on hand to send you.

Our letters come to Dorchester every evening this week, where we send Tom for them, by an arrangement made with Robert, who is there for the week. His father is no better. . . . Daughter sends a great deal of love to you and to Brother Charlie and Sister Ruthie, with her congratulations on the birth of their little daughter. Shall write to Charles. Kiss Julia for Grandpa. Do write me and let me know how you are, and all in the house. Time for Tom to go. I remain, my dear wife,

Your ever affectionate husband,
C. C. Jones.

REV. C. C. JONES *to* HON. *and* MRS. CHARLES C. JONES, JR.ᵗ
Maybank, *Wednesday,* June 26th, 1861
My dear Son and Daughter,

I congratulate you both and unite with you in thanksgiving to our Heavenly Father for His great mercy in making you a second time the living parents of a living and a perfect child. Receive it as His gift; and may your lives be spared to train it up for His honor and glory, which will bring the greatest happiness both to parents and child. Your responsibilities are increasing: two precious immortal beings are now committed to your trust. And God only can by His grace enable you to fulfill that trust. May both be spared! What pleasant and happy companions will the two little sisters make for each other! Am so happy Mother is with you; but was distressed to hear she had been sick.

Your uncle William was exceedingly pleased to hear the good news of the little stranger this morning. Daughter sends her hearty congratulations. Write us daily, and keep us advised how you all are. The recovery from scarlet fever, you know, is generally quite slow, and Julia will require much care. Kiss the two little ones for me, and their mother also, with my love. I am, my dear son and daughter,

Your affectionate father,
C. C. Jones.

Do take *good care* of Mother.

79

HON. CHARLES C. JONES, JR., *to* REV. C. C. JONES[g]

Savannah, *Wednesday,* June 26th, 1861

My dear Father,

By God's blessing we hope that Ruth and Julia are both better this morning. The little infant is doing very well. Dear Mother has endured much fatigue, but is resting this morning, and we trust will after a refreshing sleep feel restored. We are more than grateful to her for her great kindness. Her tender attentions to dear little Julia have been unceasing and most valuable.

The presence of these delightful showers will, we hope, produce a beneficial change in the health of the city. We all unite in warmest love. As ever,

Your affectionate son,
Charles C. Jones, Jr.

HON. CHARLES C. JONES, JR., *to* REV. C. C. JONES[g]

Savannah, *Thursday,* June 27th, 1861

My dear Father,

Little Julia had a more comfortable night than she has had for some time. Her fever has somewhat increased this morning, but we hope that a good God will preserve her precious life. No decided change has as yet occurred. Ruth seems tolerably well—perhaps as well as we might reasonably expect under the trying circumstances. Dear Mother enjoyed an excellent night's rest, and feels quite well this morning. All unite in warmest love. As ever,

Your affectionate son,
Charles C. Jones, Jr.

Ruth calls her little infant (who appears to be getting along very well) *Mary* after her grandmother.

DR. JOSEPH JONES *to* REV. C. C. JONES[t]

Savannah, *Saturday Morning,* June 29th, 1861
Four o'clock

My dear Father,

You will see from the date of this that I am with Brother in Savannah. Day before yesterday I received his letter informing me of the extreme illness of little Julia and Sister Ruthie, and came immediately down by the day train, hoping that I might be able to render him some assistance, and relieve Mother from some care and anxiety.

I am very sorry to inform you that I entertain little or no hope of the recovery of dear little Julia. For twelve days she has had no sleep, tossing from side to side, throwing herself with violence against the sides of her little crib; high fever; small running pulse; great difficulty of swallowing;

throat greatly swollen. She is now apparently sinking under the protracted nervous derangement and fever.

Ruth is critically ill. She came near perishing from hemorrhage at the birth of her little one, and now has quite a fever. She has never had scarlet fever, and I trust that through a merciful Providence she may escape it now. If she takes it in her present situation the result must be uncertain in the extreme.

Brother is very unwell himself with inflammation of the throat and tonsils and fever.

Truly the hand of God is upon us, and we must look to Him for help and comfort. I will do all in my power to assist them in their sickness.

I am happy to inform you that dear Mother is very well. I relieved her last night, and am now relieving her this night in setting up.

I sincerely hope that you will not think of coming down, my dear father, as it would be at the great risk of your health. I know that you could not possibly stand the fatigue and anxiety. Besides this, all the rooms in the house are now occupied, and we have as many sick as it is possible for us to attend to. Will write you every mail of the true state of affairs.

Eleven o'clock A.M. Julia the same if not worse. Ruthie better. Brother better. In haste,

Your affectionate son,
Joseph Jones.

MRS. MARY JONES *to* REV. C. C. JONES^t

Savannah, *Saturday,* June 29th, 1861

My dear Husband,

I have not had time to write. Joe says on your own account you should not come down. I am extremely anxious about *Charles,* and think him very sick. If you think best to come—although every room is occupied here—you could stay with Dr. Axson nearby. Should you come be sure and bring Tom, and tell Patience to give him his new clothes and the new shirt I gave Jack, and see that his clothes are clean, and bring your new shirts. I would like two chemises, one petticoat, white sacque, and blue muslin, and the *brillanté* skirt.

I must close. Love and kisses to my dear daughter and the children.

Your affectionate wife,
Mary Jones.

MRS. MARY JONES *to* REV. C. C. JONES^t

Savannah, *Monday,* July 1st, 1861

My dear Husband,

I trust our letter of Saturday may not induce you to come in; I feel that it would be attended with great injury to yourself and could do the sick no good. Charles is much better today; Ruth more comfortable, though still in a very critical condition. Little Julia lies extremely ill: little or no change. If she was not a child of vigorous constitution, I should utterly despair of her recovery. Joe is much worn by nursing and anxiety. The responsibility is now mainly cast upon him, although the *cases* belong to Dr. Harriss, with Drs. Arnold and Sullivan in consultation. Yesterday prayer was offered in both of our churches for this afflicted family. May the Lord in mercy hear and answer!

Do not feel uneasy about me. I must close, with best love for yourself and Daughter, and kisses for the dear children, and howdy for the servants. I should be glad to have a *dozen* chickens (not more) and a few eggs and a little fresh butter sent in. The chickens could be sent in the bird cage. In haste,

Your ever affectionate wife,
Mary Jones.

REV. C. C. JONES *to* MRS. MARY JONES[g]

Maybank, *Monday,* July 1st, 1861

My dear Wife,

Your letter of this morning is just at hand by Gilbert (11 P.M.), and am distressed at the afflictions which lie upon our dear children. We received no letter on Saturday; none ever came. I will send in the morning the chickens in the bird cage and some fresh butter and all the eggs we can collect by the passenger train, with a note to the conductor or express agent to have the things sent immediately up to the house on arrival. Do not fail to write by *tomorrow's mail out in the afternoon,* and we will get the letter from the Boro here at 10 P.M. And whatever you want can be sent down any day.

Am truly glad and thankful to know that our dear son Joe is with you. I have great confidence in his skill and care. And may it please our Heavenly Father to direct the consultations of the physicians aright, and bless the means to the recovery of our dear son and daughter and little granddaughter, and so in mercy hear the prayers of many on their behalf, and on behalf also of you, who have the great care and responsibility of nursing. What may a day bring forth? The Lord is dealing with us, and it is all right, and we can do no more than submit to His hand and wait His will.

Daughter and I want to know what is the matter with Charles, as we did not get your letter. Write us particularly about all tomorrow. Nothing prevents my attempting to go down tomorrow but my *weakness,* which seems to increase, and the fear that I would but add another invalid and increased care to all you now have. I hope through divine mercy there may be no occasion for me to make the attempt.

Daughter unites in a great deal of sympathy and love to dear Ruthie and to our dear son and little Julia. Kiss them all for us. And love to our dear son Joe. Hope he left Carrie and our little Stanhope better if not entirely recovered. Kiss the little stranger for us. And much love to you, my dear

82

wife. I feel in such a time as this my affliction, that prevents me from being with you and helping in time of trouble. May you have strength for the day from on high!

We are getting everything fixed and ready tonight, that Gilbert may be off very early in the morning. It is going on to one o'clock.

Your ever affectionate husband,
C. C. Jones.

Will send all the chickens the bird cage can hold. Fear we shall not be able to get an egg tonight: none on the place. Will get and send some.

Tuesday Morning. Thought the shortest way would be to send Gilbert down and return this evening. Write by him.

Mrs. Mary Jones *to* Rev. C. C. Jones[t]

Savannah, Tuesday, July 2nd, 1861

My dear Husband,

Our little sufferer died this morning about nine o'clock. The physicians decide that there must be an early interment—this evening about seven o'clock. From the nature of the disease and poor Ruth's situation this is necessary. She lies extremely ill—often wandering but mostly unconscious of surrounding objects, but rational when roused, and able to nurse her little babe. Joe thinks her in a very critical situation. She has as yet no symptoms of scarlet fever, but decided ones of puerperal fever. The infant, too, has ulcerated sore throat and a little rash, which we hope may not move into scarlet fever. Charles has been very sick with sore throat and fever—threatened almost with suffocation; can now scarcely speak or swallow. Truly the hand of our God is upon us. Oh, that we may feel and act aright under the rod! We can only have prayer offered ere our dead is removed; Ruth is too ill for any service.

I am thankful you did not come in. And such is the state of the family here I know not when I will be able to leave them. Pray for us: God alone can sustain us. Joe is not well. All unite with me in tenderest love, and kisses for the children.

Ever your affectionate wife,
Mary Jones.

Mr. Henry H. Jones *to* Rev. C. C. Jones[t]

Savannah, Tuesday, July 2nd, 1861

My dear Brother,

At the request of Sister Mary and my nephew Joseph I write to inform you of the distressed condition of the family of your eldest son Charles Colcock. After a painful illness of the most violent character, the daughter of the latter (little Julia) breathed her last at eight o'clock A.M. of today. The disease was scarlet fever of the most virulent type. Ruth, the mother, is also critically ill with puerperal fever, attended with occasional delirium. At this time she is rather more comfortable, but with no decided change for the better. Your son Charles is up and much better, but greatly distressed in mind. Sister Mary and Joe, though much fatigued, are pretty well, though both have a little sore throat. The babe is quite unwell with sore throat, though no decided symptoms of scarlet fever have developed themselves. Of course poor Ruth is kept in ignorance of her painful bereavement, and kept in a separate chamber to avoid if possible any danger from contagion. Joe's presence is an unspeakable comfort to them all. I have been assisting him in making the necessary arrangements for the funeral and burial. Mr. Porter will perform the services in a private manner sometime this afternoon, and the little remains will be deposited for the present in the Neely family vault.

I regret that intelligence just received through Dr. Stevens of the extreme illness of one of my Negroes, and the indisposition of my dear wife and youngest child, render my return home today indispensable. May a merciful God spare the wife and surviving child of your dear son, and sanctify to the parents the terrible bereavement they have sustained! With much love,

Your affectionate brother,
Henry H. Jones.

REV. C. C. JONES *to* HON. CHARLES C. JONES, JR.[8]

Maybank, *Tuesday,* July 2nd, 1861

My dear Son,

Gilbert has just come, and I cannot express to you my sympathy and grief at the loss of dear little Julia and the extreme illness of your affectionate and devoted wife, my dear Ruth.

Sweet child! A child of the covenant, and removed, we trust and believe, to be with God. She is not dead, but sleepeth. We must think of her as with the spirits of the redeemed in heaven. Your heart is torn; you feel what you never felt before. It is a great affliction; I wish I knew how to bear it for you. That sweet child was given you by the Lord, and *He has removed her.* Acknowledge His right, and humbly pray to Him for submission to His will, and that He may bless the stroke to your own eternal welfare. *He* alone can bind up the brokenhearted.

I feel the greatest anxiety for Ruthie, and am so glad your dear mother and brother are with you in this hour of your sorest trial. I am on the point of coming to you, and what to do I know not. Mother says it will be best for me not to do so. Nothing makes me hesitate but my physical weakness and inability to render any aid, and the probability of my adding another care to all. Am not as well as common on account of a recent throat attack, and having it now in an inflamed state. If I do wrong in not undertaking the journey for the reasons given, I hope I may be pardoned. It is my desire to spend and be spent for my dear children, and it adds to my affliction that the ability to do all I desire is no longer mine. Assure yourself, my dear son, of the deepest sympathy and affection of your own father. I am distressed for dear Ruthie. God in mercy to you and to the little one and to us all bring her through this extreme illness! Our hope is alone in Him. You have the best medical attendance and the best nursing, but the issue is with God. You have many prayers ascending for you. Your sister is now writing you, and will express her feelings and Robert's. . . .

When you can, kiss my daughter for me, and express to her my true love and sympathy in this dark hour, and my hope that her soul may find peace under all in her gracious Saviour. Kiss the baby for me. God be with and bless you, my dear afflicted son, is the prayer of

Your afflicted and affectionate father,
C. C. Jones.

REV. C. C. JONES *to* MRS. MARY JONES[g]

Maybank, Tuesday, July 2nd, 1861

My dearest Wife,

The sad intelligence in your note and Henry's has filled us with deep grief. Alas, the dear little sufferer! It is now all over, and nothing remains of her short pilgrimage but sweet memories of her smiling face and gentle voice and winning ways, and her trying passage through the valley of death to the bright world beyond. How comforting to believe that the Saviour has gathered this little lamb into His fold above!

My dear son! I feel for him in this dark day that has come so unexpectedly upon him, and can but hope and pray that it may be the hand of God leading him to Himself. That hand is upon us all, and with you I pray that we may be made to feel and act aright under it. I am so anxious about dear Ruthie! The Lord spare her life, if it be His holy will!

I do not know what to do. Have just written my dear afflicted son and stated the reason why I have not come down. Still my mind is not satisfied. Daughter thinks I ought not to go. You say you are thankful I did not come.

Daughter says she will come down any time you may need her. She is writing her brother.

We send four dozen eggs in the blue basket and your underclothing in the little black portmanteau by Mrs. King's Cain, who goes in to Savannah tomorrow morning. You did not mention anything about your clothes in your note, or they would have been sent by Gilbert. The articles sent are three chemises, one petticoat, one gown and cape, one pair drawers, two calico dresses, two pair stockings, four handkerchiefs, two aprons, and two collars, and one flannel sacque.

Audley comes out tomorrow, and if you can write by him we will be very glad. If not by him, please write by the mail. *Perhaps you had better write by the mail anyhow* and let us know *particularly* how Ruthie and the baby are.

My dear son Joe, am so happy you are with your brother in his deep sorrows. I know how you feel for him, and trust God may bless your skill and spare his own life and the life of his dear wife. Hope you left Carrie and Stanhope better if not well. Do take care of your sore throat and Mother's. So soon as it may please God to relieve the sick, they should change the air. If you can come out and see us for a day or so, it would be a great happiness to see you. Nothing but my weakness and recent throat attack keeps me from coming down to your brother.

It is going on to one o'clock July 3rd, and I must close and get all ready for Gilbert to go over to Mrs. King's very early. Daughter sends with me love to you and Brother. Do not fail to write, and don't forget to say how you yourself are. The Lord watch over and bless and keep you up in mind and body!

Your ever affectionate husband,
C. C. Jones.

MRS. MARY JONES *to* REV. C. C. JONES[t]

Savannah, *Wednesday,* July 3rd, 1861

My dear Husband,

Cain has just arrived with your very acceptable cargo. Thanks to you and Daughter and all the dear friends.

Last evening at five o'clock Mr. Porter came. The doors were closed in the dining room, and prayer offered. We took our precious little body—Joe and Mr. Porter with it in one carriage, Mrs. Harriss, Mrs. Neely, and myself and Susan her nurse in another—and took her to the cemetery, and there laid the remains in Mr. Neely's vault.

But my time for writing is short. Dear Ruth still lies *very ill*. No change for the better; all the symptoms very distressing. The doctors forbid the infant to receive any more nourishment from her; so we must feed the poor little one, which has been more quiet today. Ruth says ask you to pray for her every moment that you are awake.

Charles is exceedingly feeble and cast down. I am very anxious about him. Pray for us. Do not come down: it would only increase our trouble. With best love to Daughter and all friends,

Your affectionate wife,
Mary Jones.

MRS. SUSAN M. CUMMING *to* REV. C. C. JONES[t]

Point Maxwell, *Thursday,* July 4th, 1861

My dear Brother,

I have decided to go to Savannah. Mr. Buttolph will go with me to the station. I send Dick to get any note or anything you may wish to send, so as to save the distance and arrive at the station in time. He will meet us at the causeway. I shall tell Charles your great desire was to come, but that we had done all we could to dissuade you from it. With much love to you and Mary,

Your affectionate sister,
S. M. Cumming.

REV. C. C. JONES *to* MRS. SUSAN M. CUMMING[g]

Maybank, *Thursday,* July 4th, 1861

My dear Sister,

Am glad you are going down on account of the afflicted ones. Please see that we hear by mail daily. Audley has a boy that comes out today by whom you can write. He will call at Charles's. I do not think I can stand the fatigue. And you see what Mary says. And Joe writes the same. Do tell my dear son how much we sympathize with him, and that my heart is with him and his all the time. Give my love to dear Ruthie. Tell her I will pray for her all the time. . . . May God hear our prayers and spare her life!

I write seeing dimly through tears. Kiss the stranger for me. Thank my dear wife for her letter. The Saturday letter came to hand this morning. Daughter is not awake. Love to Brother Buttolph.

Your ever affectionate brother,
C. C. Jones.

REV. R. Q. MALLARD *to* MRS. MARY S. MALLARD[t]

Dorchester, *Thursday,* July 4th, 1861

My darling Wife,

My dear father left us this morning at a quarter past one o'clock, I confidently believe for a better world. He fell into a gentle sleep and yielded up his spirit to his dear Redeemer without a groan or even sigh. . . .

I go to Savannah today to return this afternoon. I am advised against going to see your brother's family. If I could be of any assistance, I would cheerfully encounter the risk; but on account of our little ones I ought not merely for a visit of sympathy to incur the risk. I will communicate with them, however.

Let us know by the bearer of this note when you wish to come to Dorchester, and the carriage will be sent for you.

Your husband,
Robert Q. Mallard.

P.S. The funeral at Midway tomorrow at eleven o'clock A.M.

HON. CHARLES C. JONES, JR., *to* REV. C. C. JONES[g]

Savannah, *Thursday,* July 4th, 1861

My dear Father,

I know not how to express my heartfelt thanks for your kindest and tenderest sympathies for me in this dark day when the light of life, of hope, and of joy seems wholly withdrawn, and a home of sunshine, of happiness, and of peace converted into the abode of chaos and of black ruin. I pray earnestly to God that I may recognize Him and His will in all this affliction—and that without murmuring or rebellion. Our dear little Julia is in heaven, and in all human probability my dearest wife will not long be separated from her. She never has been made acquainted with the fact of her decease. Her first intimation will be when they are united in the bonds of eternal love around the throne of God.

Just as the precious little sufferer was breathing her last, just as the last breath was escaping from her tranquil little frame, without a single groan, without a single tremor or contortion of her angelic face, I was sitting at her side; and from the eye next to me, as her spirit winged its flight to that holy and happy home where the wicked cease from trembling and the weary are at rest, started one little teardrop, pure as crystal—the only one she had shed during all her lingering and severe illness. It was her farewell to earth, and to her sorrow-stricken parent. It may have been purely accidental, but there was and is in this little circumstance a world of tenderest import which melts my soul to deepest sadness.

My dear Ruth does not improve. Brother tells me that there is little or no hope, and that she must, humanly speaking, soon die. My soul dies within me at thought of the utter wreck of cherished hopes, of present happiness, of future plans, of everything that makes life desirable. . . .

Dear Mother and Brother have been most tender and unremitting in their kindnesses. I shall never have heart enough to thank them for all their goodness. The Doctor is head and shoulders ahead of his medical brethren here; and it will be a never-failing source of consolation to me to know that my dear Ruth and Julia had the benefit of his superior skill and fraternal attentions.

Today is the anniversary of our original independence, but these weeping skies seem to be bemoaning the distracted condition of our poor country.

Saw Robert Mallard for a moment just now. Poor fellow, he also is passing through deep waters.

I am glad, my dear father, that you have not undertaken the fatigue of a visit to us just at this time. Most glad as I would be to see you now, I know all the sympathies of your generous, Christian, fatherly heart; and most sensibly do I feel them and thank you for them. I pray you, however, do not venture upon the trip. Brother, Mother, all agree in this. We all hope to see you soon. Trusting that God will grant you every needful strength and favor, I am, with warmest love to self, Sister, and little cousins,

Your affectionate and afflicted son,
Charles C. Jones, Jr.

Mother and Brother are quite well. We are truly happy to have Aunt Susan with us. She has always been little less than a mother to me.

REV. R. Q. MALLARD *to* MRS. MARY S. MALLARD[t]

Dorchester, *Thursday,* July 4th, 1861

My dear Mary,

I have just returned from the city, having successfully accomplished the business which carried me. I went with Aunt Susan to Charlie's and saw Mother and both your brothers. Charlie I found reclining in his library, still suffering from sore throat, but able to accompany me down to the front door. Mother did not seem to be well. Brother Joe looked pale, but better than I expected. The little baby is better, but our poor sister I fear will not recover. Brother Joe told me it was a hopeless case. I now almost regret that I did not go in to see her. I did not expect to be asked, and feared that seeing me might injure her.

I told our afflicted brother that I felt for him from my heart, but well knew that he needed a Power higher than man to comfort him. He seems to give Ruthie up. Oh, it is so sad an affliction that I am loath to admit its probability! "Ah, Lord God, thou hast made the heaven and the earth; is there anything too hard for thee?" Poor Charlie, he has no religion to comfort him. It is a severe discipline he is receiving. God grant that it may prove salutary!

I hope to see you tomorrow and talk over our plans. Assure dear Father of my love and heartfelt sympathy with him in his painful and trying position. I am truly glad that he did not go down to Savannah. I have but one living father and one mother now. God bless you all!

My darling, your own
Robert.

REV. C. C. JONES *to* MRS. MARY JONES[g]

Maybank, *Thursday,* July 4th, 1861

My dear Wife,

We have just received a note from Robert and a letter from my dear afflicted son, and my heart is sore-broken with his sorrows and the dreadful trial which seems ready to fall upon him. I trust his soul is turned in the right direction—even unto God our Saviour; and from Him I hope he will find salvation and consolation. I am unable to reply to his letter now. Dear, dear Ruthie! All day long Daughter and I have been hoping, hoping for good news of a change for the better tonight. But alas, it is not so. We have been weeping over what has come to hand, and cannot think it will be so. With God all things are possible, and we could but pray again together just now that if it were possible this cup might pass from us. What an affliction! The Lord enable us to understand it, and sanctify us under it!

Am so happy you are all with the chief mourner. He seems filled with comfort that Mother, Brother, and Aunt are with him. Would that I were with him also. Nothing but the positive opinion of all to the contrary has kept me here. If I have done wrong, may I be pardoned for it!

If dear Ruthie can receive it, express to her my fond attachment and sympathy. Kiss her for me. Tell her I have tried to fulfill her request, and we have been praying constantly for her; and I hope that she is resting upon her Saviour, and that all is peace with her. What a trial that I cannot see her! The Lord Jesus receive her spirit! Yet I cannot but hope.

My dear wife, when you do come out let me suggest that you all come out to Walthourville to Daughter's to save a long night's ride from the depot to Maybank. You will reach Walthourville early in the evening. *Should* Daughter not be at home, her key is over at Mr. Samuel Mallard's; and by sending for it everything is open to you, and Lucy and the servants are there. And then at your leisure you can come down afterwards. Daughter begs you to do so. Please write me—someone—*every mail*.

I send Tom up early in the morning with this letter to Riceboro for the mail. The clock strikes twelve. My tenderest love to my dear Ruthie and Charles, to my dear son, and to Sister. And kiss the little one for me. The Lord be with you all!

Your ever affectionate husband,
C. C. Jones.

July 5th. Daughter goes to Mr. Mallard's funeral today. Am feeling so badly, do not think I have heart or strength to go. All well.

HON. CHARLES C. JONES, JR., *to* REV. C. C. JONES[8]

Savannah, *Friday,* July 5th, 1861

My very dear Father,

Brother tells me that he regards the case of my dear wife as more favorable today. We trust from the bottom of our hearts that God in His infinite mercy will interpose in her behalf. We are endeavoring to do for her all that human skill, care, and attention can suggest or accomplish; and we must leave the result with Him in whose hands are the issues of life and of death. I can but hope that in His great goodness He will spare her precious life.

Her bedding is now being changed, and when everything is again clean and cool, I trust that she will feel better. My heart goes out in thankfulness every hour to my dear mother and brother, and now also to Aunt Susan, for all their unwearied kindness and tender care.

All unite in warmest love. The little infant, who is named Mary after Mother, is pretty well. Hoping, my dear father, that renewed health and strength may be vouchsafed to you from on high, and with united love to Sister and little Nephew and Niece, I am, as ever,

Your affectionate son,
Charles C. Jones, Jr.

REV. C. C. JONES *to* HON. CHARLES C. JONES, JR.[8]

Maybank, *Saturday,* July 6th, 1861

My dear Son,

Yesterday was a day of distress, and as the hours drew near for the coming of the mail, it became more intense. I retired at nine, and lay awake listening for the footsteps of the letter boy. He came; and in a few moments your sister and Robert, who had come home with her from the funeral, I heard running upstairs. The door opened, and your sister with a beaming countenance said: "Father! Good news! Good news, Father, from Sister Ruthie! Brother Joe says her symptoms are more favorable today. Here is Brother Charlie's letter." The letter was read over twice. Oh, what a burden passed off! What a mercy to us! I cannot say it was unexpected, for all day Daughter and I were entertaining *hope* that the Lord, who can quicken even the dead, would hear the many prayers offered and interpose and raise your dear wife up again. We could do no more than rejoice with trembling, and we knelt down and returned thanks to our Heavenly Father for His great mercy to us. . . .

Kiss dear Ruthie for me. Tell her we pray for her constantly, that I hope she is able to cast her all into the Saviour's hands, and that He will raise her up to love Him more and serve Him better all the days of her life. But I must beg her to do one thing: to remember she professes to be God's child. God is her Father; He knows what is best for her; and she must pray and say: "Father, Thy will be done."

Our united love to dear Mother and Brother and Aunt. All friends anxiously send or come every day to know what we hear from you. Robert must soon leave, and I must close. The servants all send howdy, and are much rejoiced to hear that Miss Ruthie is better. Kiss for us your little one. She is now in the place of her sister.

Your ever affectionate father,
C. C. Jones.

HON. CHARLES C. JONES, JR., *to* REV. C. C. JONES[g]

Savannah, Saturday, July 6th, 1861

My dear Father,

Dear Ruth is no better this morning. She spent a distressing night, and enjoyed little or no rest. She is at present a little more comfortable, and is quite rational. During her illness her mind has for a good portion of the time wandered. Her strong constitution contests the progress of the poison in her veins inch by inch; a feebler would have yielded long ago. We are doing everything that we can to prolong her precious life, and can only look to God for His blessing. We fear the worst.

The little infant is rather better this morning, and eats heartily. All well, and unite in warmest love to you, my dear father, and to Sister and Nephew and Niece. As ever,

Your affectionate son,
Charles C. Jones, Jr.

DR. JOSEPH JONES *to* REV. C. C. JONES[t]

Savannah, Saturday, July 6th, 1861

My dear Father,

I hope that you will excuse my not writing you oftener. Since my arrival here I have sat up almost every night, and have administered most of the medicines; my time has therefore been so much occupied that I have had but little time to write.

I am sorry to inform you that poor Ruthie is very low, and I see no hopes whatever of her improvement. She has suffered from a severe attack of puerperal fever, complicated with *phlegmasia dolens* (inflammation of the coats of the veins induced by the absorption of the disorganized matters from the uterus). I have regarded her disease, from the time that the symptoms were well marked, as due to the poisoning of the blood by the absorption of the disintegrating and we might almost say putrefying matters within the cavity of the uterus. The first accident determined, I think, her fate; and the disease has been aggravated by the peculiar state of the atmosphere of Savannah, and especially by the presence of the scarlet fever poison in her own residence. Strange as it may appear, profuse hemorrhages, instead of preventing puerperal fever, tend greatly to induce it, and when induced to aggravate.

Last night and this morning she was wandering. Her mind was dwelling upon many incongruous subjects in turn, without any special purpose or reason. Now (12 M.) her reason is more clear. I believe that she is resigned; for although she has not been informed of her near end, still she has always expressed the belief that she was very ill and would not in all probability recover. Day before yesterday I prayed with her at her own request, and her mind at this time appeared calm and resigned.

We have carefully avoided informing her of the death of little Julia, in whom her heart was centered. If she is to be taken, it would be far better to spare her the painful news; and she will make the happy discovery in a far better place.

I am very glad that you have not, my dear father, attempted to come down. You might have suffered most seriously, and we all beg you not to come, as the atmosphere of the city is very unhealthy, and there is an especial tendency to sore throats. Mother has had an attack, but is now almost entirely relieved. Besides this, Ruthie may linger a day or two in this only partially conscious state.

Before my return to Augusta I will come out and pay you a short visit. I am very anxious to make some prescriptions for your throat and lungs. Have heard from Carrie; all well. The hour for the starting of the mail has arrived, and I must close. With best love to you, my dear father, and to Sister, I remain

Your affectionate son,
Joseph Jones.

DR. JOSEPH JONES *to* MRS. CAROLINE S. JONES[t]

Savannah, *Sunday*, July 7th, 1861

My dear Wife,
Our poor sister Ruth died this (Sunday) morning at eight o'clock. The

hand of God has indeed been very heavy upon us. My poor brother is indeed afflicted. His wife and child are taken, and his home left desolate. He has been a devoted husband and father, and his afflictions are correspondingly great. We must all pray that they may be sanctified to his eternal salvation.

Ruthie made a happy and triumphant end. Yesterday and the day before at her request I prayed with her several times. She sent for Messrs. Axson and Porter, who gave her great comfort. She expressed her entire resignation to the will of God. Yesterday Brother told her of the death of little Julia; she replied that she had been certain that she was dead for more than a day, and expressed her joy at the thought of meeting her so soon in heaven. Last night she sent messages to all her relatives and friends. To you, my dearest Carrie, she begged me to say: "Tell dear Carrie that I loved her and hoped to have passed a long time in life with her, and enjoyed her friendship for many years." All the servants were assembled at her request, and appropriate messages delivered to each one. The poor creatures appeared to be deeply affected, and the scene was one of great solemnity.

She had a long and solemn conversation with her husband, and left with him at this interview her dying requests. My dear brother has this morning written down these requests and shown them to me. The first is that he "should seek the Saviour, and that right early." Her little child she gives to dear Mother to bring up for her. The poor little thing is indeed an object of compassion. The mother's milk has greatly deranged its health, and I hardly think that it will live long. Mother will take it out as soon as possible to the county and place it in the charge of a good nurse. She says that it will be a great comfort to Father and herself. Would it not be too sad if this the last member of my poor brother's family should be taken?

The funeral services will be held tomorrow morning at 9½ o'clock, D.V. Mother, Brother, the little baby, and Aunt Susan and myself will go out to Liberty in the evening train. Mother and Brother and Aunt Susan will go on to Walthourville, as we have not and will not be able to get word for the carriage to meet us at the No. 3 station. I will get off at the No. 3 station (the same, you remember, from which we went last winter) and obtain a conveyance from thence to Arcadia, and there obtain a conveyance to the Island, which I hope to reach tomorrow (Monday) evening. The horses and carriage will be sent up early the next morning to Walthourville for them. I will remain Tuesday on the Island with dear Father, who is very feeble, and anxious to see me.

If Providence permits and I am not detained by the illness of the baby or of Father or of Mother, who has suffered severely in Savannah and is now sick, I will return to Savannah on Wednesday and leave that night at 11½ P.M. for Augusta, and hope to be with you, my own most precious wife, Thursday morning. Would be glad to have Titus at the station then. If I should not come then, do not be alarmed, my dearest, for there are many things to detain me over which I can have no control. I hope, however, that a merciful Providence will stay His hand from our afflicted family.

My own most precious darling Carrie, I long to be with you. My heart has been with you, my faithful devoted sweet wife, every moment since I left you, and I cannot tell you how anxious I have been about you and my own most precious little Samuel. I turn to you in every trouble. You do not know how much all my relatives love you. Mother says that you are a noble-hearted woman, full of affection and sweetness. God bless you, my own, and my dearest son!

Your affectionate husband,
Joseph Jones.

REV. C. C. JONES *to* MRS. MARY JONES[t]

Maybank, *Monday,* July 8th, 1861

My dear Wife,

Our dear son arrived at ten this evening, and our fears were all realized! Oh, how I feel for my dear son! How I longed to see that dear child once more! And she died so calmly, so peacefully. What a consolation! I cannot write now.

As you requested, Gilbert leaves very early in the morning with the carriage; but I do not think it advisable for you to attempt coming down tomorrow (the same day) on account of the *heat* and *the ride,* which for the *horses* would be some fifty miles. Your travel would be *slow,* and *very late* in the evening. A day's rest would perhaps benefit you all, and the dear little sufferer in particular. And the next day you could make an early start and get here by eleven or twelve o'clock. I have just sent Joe over with a note to Brother Buttolph to send up the buggy for Sister in the morning. And I think she will have to stay over the day also.

Tom goes up in the morning to Cato to send Peggy down, and she will be here in the afternoon. Daughter stays to see her brother when he comes down, but her little ones will be sent to Dorchester. Our love to my dear son and to Sister. Kiss the baby for us. It is going on to twelve o'clock. I long to see you, my dear wife, and learn all concerning our sad affliction. Love to Robert from us all. His wife and little ones are quite well.

Your ever affectionate husband,
C. C. Jones.

IV

MRS. MARY S. MALLARD *to* MRS. MARY JONES[t]

Walthourville, *Thursday*, July 11th, 1861

My very dear Mother,

We arrived safely today at half-past twelve. Found Mr. Mallard and all quite well. We had a clouded sky and pleasant breeze, so the heat was not at all oppressive. Mamie was so glad to get home and to see the servants that she laughed until she almost cried. She ran over the house trundling her little wheelbarrow and looking at all her toys, riding in turn her babies, marbles, etc. Charlie, seeing his sister's delight, thought there really was something amusing going on, so he "sculled himself" after his sister, laughing merrily and calling out "See da! See da!" to everything she said or did. When he went into the drawing room, he remembered the little girl with the chickens and commenced *shooing* and calling them. . . .

I wish I could have stayed with you this morning, for I feel I scarcely saw you; but my children were both so well I was afraid to have them remain too long in Dorchester, as they would have to make another change in coming here. I have thought of the dear little baby all day, and wish I could take care of it for you. I hope if it is consistent with our Heavenly Father's will its little life may be spared. I wish Brother Charlie could remain out several weeks. What will become of him when he goes back to his lonely home? I do feel so much for him, and think of him all the time. Uncle Henry thinks of going down tomorrow, as he wishes to see him before he returns to Savannah.

I have cut the coat pattern, so don't return this that I send, but please send the coat back by Uncle Henry. I thought you would rather see it on Father before cutting out his coat. If you would send it to me and mark where the buttonholes are to be made, I will make it.

Little Mary says she is so glad for the candy, and says she is "must obiced to Danma" for it. Mr. Mallard and our little ones unite with me in warmest love to Father, Brother Charlie, and yourself, and kisses for the dear little baby. Love to all at Maxwell and Woodville.

Your affectionate daughter,
Mary S. Mallard.

I will fix the mantle and send it as soon as possible. I think your things will come out on Saturday or Monday. If you could send me a skirt to measure by (by Uncle Henry) I could help you make them.

MRS. MARY JONES *to* MRS. MARY S. MALLARD[t]

My dear Daughter,

James arrived in good time this morning, and I am very much obliged to you for the things; also for the mantle and collar. I have sent you what I conceive to be the best of the dress patterns; the other one is much worn in holes, but it will answer my purpose, and looks like delaine. Tell my dear little granddaughter Grandma sends a little quilt for her bed. I wanted to have quilted it this summer, but there is no prospect now. I had nothing new to bind it, but send a curtain (not old, but stained with mildew); it will answer very well, and perhaps you could make Lucy quilt it, if not run the two together. The sacque for Charlie I meant to scallop, but I really feel too weak and badly to do anything. My whole system feels prostrated. I am suffering very much from dyspepsia and pain in my side, and am as one struggling to awake from a terrible dream. . . .

Our dear son left us on Monday and returned to his desolate dwelling. He said it was his duty to do so, although he knew not what would become of him. I think he realizes the solemn circumstances into which the Lord has placed him, and whilst with us was engaged in religious reading and frequent conversations with your dear father, who tried to direct his mind to the great work of repentance and faith. I know dear Robert and yourself will remember him constantly. Will not our Redeemer hear and answer us *even now?*

Our dear little babe improves. I think the emaciation has ceased. The nourishment agrees well with her, and she takes a plenty. The discharge still continues from the ear, but in other affections she is better. Sometimes very fretful. We have moved into the rooms below your father (in the smallest), so I am much more comfortably situated, and if I were better, would get pretty good rest at night; but my throat and cough keep me awake.

I have wanted to accept your offer to help me with your father's flannel coat. Have made two attempts to cut it out, but failed. I am too weak at present. I was on the bed all day yesterday. . . .

Your Uncle John writes: "My church have unanimously given me leave of absence for three months to visit our soldiers—particularly the 8th Regiment, to which they belong—to labor as a minister among them. I expect to leave on the 17th inst. for Richmond and Winchester. There is risk in taking my family with me, but I believe it would make Jane ill to leave her. They will return if they should be in danger." I shall feel very anxious about him.

Do return Kitty my best thanks for the things, and enclosed is her change due. . . . Pay Kitty, and buy a hat for Charlie with the rest. Father unites with me in best love to Robert and yourself and many kisses for our dear grandchildren.

Ever your affectionate mother,
Mary Jones.

Howdies for the servants.

REV. C. C. JONES *to* HON. CHARLES C. JONES, JR.[8]

Maybank, *Saturday*, July 20th, 1861

My dear Son,

Am happy to inform you that your dear little baby continues to improve. Her complexion is natural, and is assuming the ruddiness of healthy infancy. She has no new eruption; the old has disappeared excepting under one arm, and that is fast healing up. Nurses heartily. Everything right: sleeps soundly, and gives no more trouble at night than is common. Her only affection is that of the ears. The running of the first has much diminished; the second commenced yesterday, but is not excessive; and we hope with Mother's good care and your brother's prescriptions both will soon be well. She enjoys her warm bath every morning, takes quietly the pouring of the water on her little person, which is gaining flesh, and when Mother syringed her ears she held her head still and seemed to feel the comfort of it. We think she is a bright little thing: notices a good deal, and combines a likeness of both her sainted mother and sister, though the shape of the head favors yours. And if, by God's blessing, she continues to improve in time to come as since you left, you will scarcely know her when you see her again. She evidently had scarlet fever; her tongue, her mouth, her surface, and the affection of the ears all prove it; and now the cuticle rubs off in the bath. Your mother thinks so, and I believe it was your brother's impression also. How wonderful that she should have come through so many trials—only three weeks old last Tuesday!

Mother has been very unwell with something of a return of the attack she had in Savannah, but has kept up, and is better today, and—what is specially promising—has had a fair appetite for two days, takes the doctor's prescriptions, slacks off some of her work, and rides out every afternoon. The weather too has been pleasant, with good showers.

You are daily in our thoughts, and are with us in our conversations and in our closets and in family worship. We do feel, my dear son, more for you than we can express; and if "the oppressive silence which reigns around you and the spirit of deep desolation which broods over everything in your once happy home" and your own uncommon sorrows could be removed by your parents, it would so be done. But we are afflicted in your afflictions; and what can we do but to weep with you and for ourselves, and go with you to our Heavenly Father, from whom the afflictions have come, and pray that He who has wounded will heal us, and He that has broken will bind us up. "Is any among you afflicted? Let him pray." God is our only sure and satisfying refuge in times of trouble. . . .

Mother unites in much love to you. We beg you to be careful of your health. Make George sleep near you. Tell all the servants howdy for us. Susan begs that we should "tell her master howdy for her, that she is well, and the baby is well, and sends howdy for the servants."

From your ever affectionate father and mother,

C. C. Jones
M. Jones.

97

HON. CHARLES C. JONES, JR., *to* REV. C. C. JONES[g]

Savannah, *Wednesday,* July 24th, 1861

My dear Father,

Amid the heavy engagements which are upon me I have not had an opportunity until this moment for replying to your kind and valued letter of the 20th inst. I thank God that you are all better at Maybank, and that dear little Mary Ruth improves. There is scarcely an hour of the day that my heart does not melt in sincerest gratitude to you both, my dear parents, and rejoice that our precious little motherless infant in the absence of her who gave her birth has been entrusted to the guardian care of those whose hearts will melt in tenderest sympathy for the darling little orphan. Should her life be spared, she will be a standing monument of God's great goodness and mercy.

Our city is filled with mingled exultation and sorrow at the news of the recent triumph of our arms at Manassas—a victory without parallel in the history of this western world, an engagement continental in its magnitude, a success whose influence must be felt and acknowledged not only within the limits of our own Confederacy and of the United States but also throughout the civilized world. Surely the God of Battles is with us.

The price of that victory, however, was great. Colonel Bartow and some of our best young men have fallen, and our city is filled with mourning. A meeting of the citizens last night sent five persons (whose names you will see in the daily journals) to Richmond to attend to our dead and wounded. Colonel Bartow's body will be brought home. The bar had a meeting yesterday afternoon; the resolutions are mine. If the accounts we have of his death are true, he died the death of a hero. None ever for one moment doubted his bravery, and he has left to our army and to his country a signal illustration of true Southern valor.

What a world of heroism in that act of our worthy President—leaving Richmond and in person leading the center column on that fearful battle-field! I presume Dunwody Jones was in the fight. I see in the reports no mention of his being either killed or wounded, but we will not have full details for several days. I have telegraphed the mayor of Richmond for particulars so soon as they can be obtained. He was absent at Manassas when my telegram reached that city.

Mr. Colcock writes me that a miniature of my dear wife can be painted by an artist of Charleston, and I am about sending my locket to him for that purpose. A letter from Brother, this morning received, states that all are well. You will see, my dear parents, that I have written in great haste in my office, and must close for the mail. You have ever the warmest love of

Your affectionate son,

Charles C. Jones, Jr.

Howdy for Susan and all the servants. Old Mama at Dr. Harriss' says give her best love to Susan, and say to her that all the sisters send love and bid her hold on to her faith.

MRS. MARY JONES *to* HON. CHARLES C. JONES, JR.[8]

Maybank, *Thursday,* July 25th, 1861

My dear Son,

Mr. McDonald has just brought your last favor, and as he returns immediately, I have only time to send you a few lines to assure you of our tenderest love and constant remembrance and of the continued improvement of our dear little babe. If the discharge from her ears would cease, I should have every hope of her perfect restoration. Already she looks up into my face and smiles, and is very bright for her *days*—one month old today! What an age of sorrow that one month has brought to our hearts! . . .

Our hearts are filled with gratitude to God for our victory over our enemies, and at the same time we weep at the costly sacrifice. I feel especially for Mrs. Bartow, and shall look most anxiously for further accounts. . . . Enclosed we send you twenty dollars. Please forward it as you know best to some official in Richmond for the use of our suffering and wounded soldiers. I wish it was an hundredfold. I thought it best to send it direct to Richmond.

Your father asks you to order *from Richmond* to the office here one of the Richmond *city newspapers,* and he leaves the selection to yourself—either triweekly or otherwise. . . . He unites with me in best love to you, and kisses from your little daughter. Susan and the servants beg to be remembered. In haste, my dear son,

Your ever affectionate mother,
Mary Jones.

HON. CHARLES C. JONES, JR., *to* REV. *and* MRS. C. C. JONES[8]

Savannah, *Saturday,* July 27th, 1861

My dear Father and Mother,

I have only a moment in which to thank you for your recent kind letters, and to rejoice in the glad tidings of the good health of dear little Mary Ruth.

You cannot imagine the pressure that has been upon me during the past week. We have been in the midst of the greatest excitement consequent upon this glorious victory at Manassas, and last night we received the body of General Bartow. It now lies in the exchange long room under a guard of honor; will be buried tomorrow afternoon.

Judge Fleming's sons both safe. Saw one of them (William O.) this morning; the other (Johnnie) was slightly wounded at Manassas.

It seems to me that I am living in a graveyard. I never have passed through such a period in my life before. The impression will never fade from my memory. Nothing from Dunwody. As ever, my dear father and mother,

Your affectionate son,
Charles C. Jones, Jr.

Kiss my dear little daughter for me.

I will see to it that the generous contribution to the sick and wounded soldiers is forwarded by earliest opportunity.

HON. CHARLES C. JONES, JR., *to* REV. *and* MRS. C. C. JONES[g]

Savannah, *Monday,* July 29th, 1861

My very dear Father and Mother,

By the express of today I have the pleasure of sending you herewith box containing:

1. Copies of obituary of my sainted wife. How I wish in its preparation that my pen could have been permitted to shadow forth those feelings of truest love, devotion, and honor for her precious memory which possess me ever! But these emotions belong not to the public but to the sacred recesses of my own heart, where they will ever be most sincerely cherished.

2. Daguerreotype of Ruth, a copy of the one contained in the medallion which I wear—her gift to me during our engagement. It was the best impression that could be obtained by the artist here after repeated trials. This, Father, is for you. I deeply regret that it does not do my dear wife justice. The original I have forwarded to Mr. Colcock, who will place it in the hands of an artist who he assures me will execute for me an accurate and beautiful miniature on ivory. This I am to expect in three weeks. I sincerely trust that he may succeed in his undertaking, for now that the bright original is gone, nevermore to gladden the eye of affection by her coming, never again with her loves to gladden this sorrow-stricken heart, these shadows become sacred beyond expression.

3. A mourning pin for you, my dear mother, containing the commingled hair of Ruth and of our sweet little Julia. You will, I know, accept and preserve it in cherished remembrance of them. Oh, how precious to me every object which speaks of them! For three weeks yesterday has my dear wife been lying in her last long home, and our little Julia a little longer. During that period what I have suffered is known only to my desolate heart. Everything around me appears invested with the habiliments of the grave. And yet amid all these scenes of shadows and of silence there are consecrated associations, happy memories, hallowing by their precious influences every object and every hour. . . .

4. A hair comb for you, Mother. You remember that yours was broken while I was with you on the Island.

5. A mourning pin for Aunt Susan, which I will trouble you to send to her. It also contains the hair of Ruth and Julia.

6. This letter.

Yesterday I attended in an official capacity the funeral of our gallant and lamented fellow townsman, Colonel Bartow. His body lay in state (as they call it in this country, although the application of that term would be inappropriate if we adopt the true European acceptation of the custom) in our city hall (the exchange long room having been draped in mourning and suitably prepared for its reception) ever since Friday night last, until Sabbath afternoon, attended day and night by a guard of honor detailed from Company B of the Oglethorpe Light Infantry, a portion of his former command who did not go to Virginia. The outer box had to be removed, and the metallic case reenclosed in a coffin lined with lead. This was done on Friday night after its arrival, and every unpleasant feature connected with his remains was dissipated. The coffin was covered with the Confederate flag and with numerous tokens of respect, such as chaplets of laurel appropriately entwined, the offerings of the ladies of Charleston and of Savannah. The funeral services were performed by Bishop Elliott from Christ Church, whither the body was transferred from the exchange about four o'clock on Sabbath afternoon. While it lay in the exchange long room hundreds of our citizens paid their farewell respects.

The funeral cortege embraced all the military companies and all the officers of the army, navy, and militia of this city and its vicinity under the command of Colonel Mercer, who was recalled for a day from Fort Pulaski specially for that purpose. It also included, directly and indirectly, the larger portion of the whole population, white and colored, of Savannah. The mayor and city council attended in a body. During the moving of the procession all the bells were tolled, flags displayed at half-staff, a detachment from the Chatham Artillery firing minute guns, and each one rendering every tribute of respect for the memory of the brave departed. The sidewalks and windows of the houses along the line of march were filled with silent spectators. The commons beyond the jail were thronged with Negroes. No noise or confusion: everyone seemed to realize the solemnity of the occasion. Colonel Bartow's name will live in the history of these Confederate States, and his noble daring on the field of Manassas be remembered by all, and especially by those whose state he illustrated in such a signal way by his undaunted courage and chivalrous valor. I have had a most interesting account of the battle from Lieutenants Berrien and Mason, aides to Colonel Bartow, who both passed unharmed through the dangers of that fearful struggle.

Our company will probably during the course of the present week be mustered into service for twelve months. As the first lieutenant of that company I expect to join them so soon as my term of service as the mayor of this city expires, which, D.V., will occur about the 15th October next. Until that time General Lawton will grant me a furlough. I feel it to be my duty, upon a careful comparison of obligations, if I have life and ability, to execute to the end the trust devolved upon me by my fellow citizens of Savannah. I therefore, much as I desire to go with my company, will not resign the mayoralty. But when my term expires, I feel it to be equally my pleasure and my duty, however great the sacrifice, to aid by my own arm in defending these our homes and our national honor. And I trust, and fain would believe, my dear parents, that if the day of battle does come, and I am permitted to share in its dangers and its carnage, you shall not blush at mention of the name of him who owes under the good providence of God his life to you, and all about him that is just and honorable and manly and of good report to your kind teaching and parental example. With my whole heart, from the very inception of the agitation of that question, did I endorse and earnestly advocate our secession movement; and now when it is evident that our national independence can be secured only at the point of the bayonet and at the cannon's mouth, I shall not shrink from testifying even with my blood, if that should in the good providence of Him who doeth according to His pleasure among the armies of heaven and among the inhabitants of earth become necessary, my fixed devotion to the sacred cause of truth, of honor, of religion, of property, and of national independence. A freeman's heart can beat in no nobler behalf, and no more sacred obligations can rest upon any people than those now devolved upon us to protect our homes, our loves, our lives, our property, our religion, and our liberties, from the inhuman and infidel hordes who threaten us with invasion, dishonor, and subjugation.

I have sometimes thought, my dear parents, that my precious Ruth and our darling Julia were taken in the tender mercy of a good God from the evil to come. At least it is most pleasant for me to view their deaths in this light, for even this naked thought robs these dark bereavements of somewhat of their terrors. I now know that it is all well with them. . . .

My dear little Mary Ruth is rejoicing in that tender care and affection which you alone, my dear parents, can give.

It does seem to me at times that the finger of Providence points me to the path of duty, and bids me stand in my lot upon the tented field with the brave defenders of our country's honor and our country's rights.

My impression is that our company, identified as it has been with the history of our city and state for the past seventy-five years, will be reserved for home and coast defense, and will not be ordered to Virginia. Without doubt, if we may believe the signs of the times, there will be a diversion along our coast during the coming autumn or winter. The two regiments stationed there have been ordered to Manassas, and have already gone. We must therefore from our own firesides furnish the men and materials for our own defense.

Dr. Axson on yesterday morning gave us a remarkably fine thanksgiving sermon, preached in compliance with the recommendation of our Confederate Congress and municipal proclamation. Did your eye rest upon my proclamation? His son was uninjured in the recent battle at Manassas. What a glorious victory! Surely the Lord of Hosts is with us, and it is both proper and pleasant to see the people of these Confederate States, both rulers and the governed, civil and military, referring all our successes to Him, and upon every occasion acknowledging His superintending providence, and imploring His aid and guidance in all our engagements and purposes.

An interesting fact connected with the formation of our Confederate Constitution is that it was born of prayer, and acknowledges in the most emphatic manner the existence and superintending powers of the Living

God. The old Federal Constitution was a godless instrument. May it not be the fact that God is now punishing this nation, as He does individuals, for this practical atheism and national neglect in not by organic law, legislation, and in a public manner acknowledging His supremacy? All good governments are ordained of God. Government is a divine institution. It is therefore a fatal error—one which He will not overlook—in the organic act to ignore His existence.

I have sent pins with the hair of my dear Ruth and Julia to Philo, Vallie, Amanda, Mrs. Randolph Whitehead, Sister, Mrs. Harriss, and Sallie Berrien. They will all prize them sincerely.

I trust, my dear father and mother, that I have not wearied you with this long letter. It is so seldom that amid the burdens which are resting upon me I have an opportunity to write you fully. I have embraced this leisure hour for doing so. Kiss little Mary Ruth for me. May God in His great goodness soon restore her to perfect health! With warmest love, my dear parents, I am always

Your affectionate son,
Charles C. Jones, Jr.

Howdies for Susan and for all the servants. Tell Susan the old mama next door says she must hold fast to her profession, and sends her much love.

MRS. MARY JONES *to* HON. CHARLES C. JONES, JR.[8]

Maybank, *Friday,* August 2nd, 1861

On Wednesday night Tom returned bringing the box containing the precious memorials of our beloved ones and mementos of your own affection, for which we shall ever feel grateful to you.

I cannot express the emotions that fill my heart as I gaze upon the pin. It was my last office to arrange those flaxen locks upon the angelic brow of my precious little granddaughter, and to comb and part the beautiful brown hair of my ever dear daughter upon her calm, pure forehead, where rested the expression of that heavenly peace and joy into which her redeemed spirit had entered. Dear precious Ruth! I received her when you married as my own child, and she was ever such to me in all that was respectful, affectionate, and kind. I knew it not if a shadow ever rested between us, and now day and night the unbidden tears are resting upon my worn face for my loved and departed ones. But most of all for you, my beloved son. They have entered into all the happiness and glory which the Divine Saviour has prepared for His own redeemed ones! But you are left to mourn the withdrawal of all that rendered your life most happy on earth—the sweet affection of one of the most devoted wives, and all the winning loveliness of one of the sweetest children—your bright and happy heart and home suddenly clothed in mourning and silence. . . .

The proclamation we saw in a *Daily News* taken at Woodville; our paper did not contain it. It gave us great satisfaction. Your father was delighted with it, and I begged him to cut it out for me, as I wanted to save it. We could hardly wish for you the perplexities of the mayoralty another year. I feel for the past you could have served your fellow citizens in no more important sphere. The courage and *honor* of *my sons* is the *last thing on earth that I could doubt. Assure me* but that they are *Christians,* and I freely yield them up to any service which my Heavenly Father appoints; and none more noble than the defense of truth, honor, religion, and all that we hold dear as a nation.

Father returns grateful thanks for the likeness, and I for the comb, which is very handsome. Some of the copies of the obituary I want to send to some friends.

Did it occur to you to send dear Carrie, *your brother's wife,* some little memento of your dear wife? I think it would be greatly prized by them. Carrie has written me twice since I came home; she seems greatly affected by your deep affliction in the death of Ruth and Julia. She is an affectionate woman and an excellent and devoted wife to Joseph.

Is there anything, my dear son, that I can do for you? Have you got your drawers? It would not give me the least trouble to make them for you if you would select the cloth and send me a pair to cut by. I think they would be stronger than the bought ones. If you go into camp, would it not be best to have some made of flannel? Do send me any work you may have to do, and it shall be immediately attended to. Or if I can render you any assistance in any of your arrangements, I trust you will let me know.

Do you remember to use the *quinine daily,* and to apply the iodine to your throat every now and then? Your father has derived great benefit from the chlorate of potassium as a gargle, and thinks the wine you so kindly sent him has done him good. You and he should both remember and follow Joe's directions.

I am happy, my dear son, to inform you that your dear little babe improves daily. I did not think when we brought her out that she could live many days, but now we have every hope that God will bless and spare her precious life to us. She is very good, especially at night, and begins to notice wonderfully. Your father fancies that she knows my voice. And I must tell you what I know will gratify you—that everyone thinks she will be the image of her dear mother. Susan is very attentive and obedient and fond of her little mistress. She begs to be remembered to you and to Adeline and George and Grace and the old mama at Dr. Harriss'.

My kind remembrances to *Mrs. Harriss.* She was a kind and sympathizing friend, and I shall always remember her affectionately. I trust Mrs. Howard has recovered, and that Mrs. Neely and her family escaped the fever. We have an ill Negro (*Cinda*), which may take your father to Montevideo tomorrow. He has just retired, leaving his best love for you. All the servants desire to be remembered. Your darling little daughter sends her kisses and smiles. That the love of Christ may be shed abroad in your heart ever prays

Your affectionate mother,
Mary Jones.

Have you heard anything of my nephew Dunwody? I feel very anxious about him.

HON. CHARLES C. JONES, JR., *to* REV. *and* MRS. C. C. JONES[g]

Savannah, *Tuesday,* August 6th, 1861

My dear Father and Mother,

I am in receipt of your kind favors of the 2nd and 5th inst., and am truly happy to know that all at home are well, and that precious little Mary Ruth improves daily and bids fair to reflect the features of my sainted Ruth. I sincerely trust that she may, and that her life may long be spared for much usefulness, piety, and happiness. . . .

I hope within two weeks to have a miniature painting on ivory of my dear Ruth. My locket for that purpose and also an ambrotype of her are in the hands of Mr. Bounetheau of Charleston, an artist of considerable reputation. Mr. Colcock has been very kind in assisting me in this matter, and I do hope most sincerely that I may be able to secure a truthful picture.

In reference to the mayoralty, I have been pressed to serve for another year, but have declined. I feel that the service of the past year has been sufficient to warrant my declining a second term, especially when I am inclined to believe that a graver duty calls me into the field with my company.

I thank you sincerely, my dear mother, for your kind offer, and if I need anything I will most assuredly let you know.

Dr. Bulloch, who returned today from Virginia, tells me that he saw Dunwody Jones and that he was safe, well, and without a wound. He also saw Uncle John, who was also quite well.

I write in much haste, my dear parents, but with much love to you both, and many kisses for my dear little Mary Ruth. As ever,

Your devoted son,

Charles C. Jones, Jr.

REV. C. C. JONES *to* MISS MARY JONES MALLARD[t]

Maybank, *Friday,* August 9th, 1861

My dear little Granddaughter,

Don't you know that you have a sweet little cousin, Mary Ruth, at Maybank—Uncle Charlie's and Aunt Ruthie's little baby? And she has got no mother to take care of her. Your dear Aunt Ruthie and Cousin Julia are no longer in this world. They have gone to heaven, where all good people go, and where you will go when you die if you are a good child and love and serve our Saviour Jesus Christ. Do you want to know who takes care of Mary Ruth? Grandmother takes care of her. She sleeps in the little crib every night by Grandmother, and sleeps so good she does not wake at night more than two or three times, and then don't cry, or cries very little, and goes to sleep again. She has gotten 'most well and is gaining every day. Do you want to know who she looks like? She looks like her mother, Aunt Ruthie, and looks like Cousin Julia too. When you come to see Grandma and Grandpa you shall sit down and hold her. Won't that be pleasant? Grandma says you and your brother Charlie must call her Sister, and we must all love her very much and take care of her, for she has no mother. But Grandma will be her mother.

Kiss your mama and papa for Grandma and Grandpa, and your little brother too. Grandpa sends you a roll of peach leather and a piece of candy—all he has in the house. Give Brother some. We heard from Uncle Charlie and Uncle Joe and Aunt Carrie and little Stanhope, and all are well. Uncle William came to see us yesterday, and is well. Jimmie and Willie Buttolph are growing finely. Grandpa and Grandma want to see you and little Brother and Mama and Papa very much, but you know we can't come and leave the little baby. Niger is waiting, and Grandpa can't write any more now. The Lord bless you, my dear child! Give our love to Aunt Lou, and tell all the servants howdy for us.

Your ever affectionate grandfather,
C. C. Jones.

Oh, here is Aunt Susan and Uncle Buttolph and Jimmie just come! And your Aunt Laura sends you a bonnet, and Aunt Susan made it. And send much love.

Miss Mary Jones Mallard *to* Rev. C. C. Jones[t]
Walthourville, *Monday,* August 12th, 1861

My dear Grandpapa,

Mama read your letter to me, and I asked her again and again if you wrote it all for me, and thought you were so good to write a letter to a little girl like me. I will love Cousin Mary Ruth and will call her a sweet little baby; and I want to know if I must take her in my lap when I call her Sister, for you said I must *take* her for my sister. We all want to see her very much.

Uncle Charlie sent me a beautiful necklace last week, and says I must remember my little Cousin Julia in heaven when I wear it. I wanted to wear it now, but Mama has locked it up and will keep it until I grow larger.

I often ask Mama when she is going to take Bubber Charlie and myself to the Island to Maybank to see you and Grandma and Cousin Mary Ruth. Last week Grandma sent us some nice red potatoes, and they were so nice that I begged Mama to let Elvira cook some for breakfast, dinner, and supper; and whenever Mama opened the pantry, Bubber would beg "Ta-a-a" until he got one, and then he would carry it himself to the kitchen. Oh, Grandpa, you don't know how well he can walk! And he says a great many words.

Do tell Aunt Susan I am much obliged to Cousin Laura and herself for the nice bonnet. Mama says it is a little large for me, but she is glad of that, as it will last the longer. . . . Do give my love to Grandma Susan, Aunt Laura, and Cousins Jimmie and Willie. You must kiss Grandma and Cousin Mary Ruth. Mama and Papa send their best love.

Your affectionate little granddaughter,
Mary Jones Mallard.

Mrs. Mary S. Mallard *to* Rev. C. C. Jones[t]
Walthourville, *Monday,* August 12th, 1861

The letter I have written you, dear Father, is pretty nearly all in Mamie's own language. We are all quite well, and have much good health for which to be grateful.

Johnnie Fleming has returned wounded in the shoulder, but able to be at church yesterday. Mr. John Baker has also returned. His brother was not well enough to travel, but will come as soon as he can without injury. His wound was very severe, but no bones broken—shot between the elbow and shoulder in the left arm. Mr. Baker saw Uncle John, who was very busy visiting the wounded. Dunwody's wound made him limp a little. Cousin Marion Glen has gone on, and is now in Richmond with her brothers.

The gentlemen that have returned are full of the horrible scenes of the battlefield. Mr. Baker says for miles around the air was awful—so many men either unburied or partially covered, and such numbers of dead horses upon the field. General Beauregard made the prisoners bury the dead, and they would frequently put the bodies in gullies and throw a little earth over them. They represent the New Orleans Zouaves as quite equal to the New York in wickedness. These young men confirm the statement that a Mississippi regiment fired into the Oglethorpes, mistaking them for the enemy; and their fire was quite destructive. They say that the Federals did fight under a Confederate flag. Is not this the most outrageous piece of cowardice you ever heard of?

Our ladies have entered into the soldiers' work with a great deal of zeal. We had a meeting last week. Mrs. E. S. L. Jones was appointed first directress, Mrs. Walthour second, and myself secretary and treasurer; and an executive committee of twelve appointed whose duty it will be to cut out and distribute work. Seventy dollars have been expended, and I have in hand about ninety more. This is doing well, I think. We meet in the upper room of the academy, and a busy scene it is—ladies all at work, some cutting out, some working on machines, others with their needles, etc.

I received a most interesting letter from Kitty on Saturday. She is quite well. Her brother has just gone to Virginia with his company, the Cobb Guards. Mr. Mallard unites with me in warmest love to Mother and yourself and kisses for the baby.

Your affectionate child,
Mary S. Mallard.

Hon. Charles C. Jones, Jr., *to* Rev. C. C. Jones[g]
Savannah, *Thursday,* August 15th, 1861

. . . By this post you will receive, as desired for Uncle William, a copy of the map of the seat of war. Also the New York *Daily Tribune* of the 7th inst. It is a perfect wonder to read now and then issues from that Northern press. I enclose this number that you may judge of the spirit of our quondam brothers as manifested in an article which you will find on the fourth page, marked. Was ever anything more infidel, outrageous, and inhuman? These devils incarnate not only slander the living but endeavor with their polluted tongues to blacken the memory of the dead—and with impious appeals invoke the intervention of a just God.

The "In Memoriam," kindly prepared by Rev. Mr. Porter of this city, I have had printed, and enclose a few copies of the same to you, my dear parents. How earnestly do I desire to show every mark of the profoundest and tenderest respect to the memory of my beloved Ruth! I know she would have done the same for me. I have purchased two lots in Laurel Grove Cemetery, and anxiously desire to have her removed from the vault in which she now lies with dear little Julia (Mrs. Neely's vault), and both of them interred in accordance with her request in those consecrated limits. But in consequence of the distracted condition of the country—the absence of laborers and materials—it is at present impossible to compass the fencing of the lots and the erection of a suitable monument. And here, my dear parents, I desire to record it as my *last wish* that in the event of my dying before I am able in person to see to this, that the bodies of my dear Ruth and little Julia be removed as soon as convenient from the vault in which they now temporarily rest and be interred in these lots which I have recently purchased for this purpose. I desire further that these lots be suitably enclosed with a stone and iron fence, and that a monument be erected over my dear wife and child. In case of death (if my body can be identified in the event of my falling in battle) I desire to be laid by the side of my dear wife. It was her dying request, and most sacredly do I desire its fulfillment.

Our city, through the kind providence of God, continues in the enjoyment of much health. I sincerely trust that this great blessing will be continued.

I have just been tendered the captaincy of the Savannah Artillery, and its acceptance is very warmly pressed upon me. My attachment to the Chatham Artillery is, however, so great that I do not feel inclined to separate from my first love—especially when, upon learning the fact at the fort where the Chatham Artillery is now posted, a delegation was sent by that company to urge me by every consideration not to dissolve my connection with the old Chatham. As yet I have given no positive answer. The command tendered is a remarkably fine one, and under ordinary circumstances I would have no hesitancy in accepting the honor.

I am rejoiced to know that dear little Mary Ruth improves daily; and my heart goes forth ever in thankfulness to the Giver of All Good for this His special mercy, and to you, my dear parents, for all your many and great kindnesses. Kiss her for me. And think of me ever as

Your devoted son,
Charles C. Jones, Jr.

V

Rev. C. C. Jones *to* Mr. ———^r

Maybank, *Monday,* August 26th, 1861

Sir,

You entered my family on a friendly arrangement for copying my church history, on your own proposal, the 28th of July 1860, and left it on the 20th of the September following, and became first particularly known to me a short time previous when a guest of my neighbors, Rev. D. L. Buttolph and Mr. J. A. M. King. You were introduced as an educated man, the son of a venerable and highly esteemed minister of South Carolina, whose full name you bear; as a married man, having but recently married your second wife, who was then absent at the North for her health; as a prominent member of the Presbyterian church in Columbus, Georgia, the superintendent of the Sunday school, the president of the Young Men's Christian Association, and the principal of a female high school in that city, and recommended on your school circular by names of the first respectability. You had also taught a school within the bounds of our own congregation in Liberty County, and had associated with the active members of the church resident in the village, and taken part in their religious meetings, and I believe aided them in their efforts to give religious instruction to the Negroes. You came to my acquaintance under these favorable circumstances, and were received for what you were considered and professed yourself to be—a gentleman, a married man, and a Christian. You had my confidence as unreservedly as any stranger possibly could have, and enjoyed the kind hospitality of my family from the day you entered to the day you left it. You rendered yourself agreeable, and conducted yourself with every mark of respect and propriety; were always present morning and evening at family worship, and sometimes took part in that worship, and also in our weekly neighborhood prayer meeting. You were the guest of a gentleman, a professing Christian and minister of the gospel, and witnessed from week to week his efforts to instruct religiously the servants of his family and household.

You were under my roof but a short time before you debauched a young Negro girl—a seamstress, and one of our chambermaids. And you continued your base connections with this Negro woman week after week until you took your final leave! Of the hundreds of men of all classes and conditions and professions—men of the church and men of the world, married and unmarried—who have been guests in my house for days, weeks, months, and some for years, you, ——, are the only man who has ever dared to offer to me personally and to my family and to my neighbors so vile and so infamous an insult. You are the only man who has ever dared to debauch my family servants—it being the only instance that has occurred—and to defile my dwelling with your adulterous and obscene pollutions. Had you been detected, I should have driven you instantly out of the house and off the premises, with all the accompanying disgrace which you merited; and I regret that the law affords me no redress under so serious an indignity and injury.

The proof of your criminality is of so clear a character as to remove all doubt. *There is the free, unconstrained confession of the Negro woman herself in full detail; there is the correspondence between the time of your connection with her and the birth of the child—a mulatto, now some time born; and there is a resemblance to you beyond mistake.* In this last proof I do not rely upon my own convictions. I have submitted the child to the inspection of three gentlemen in the county who know you well personally and are familiarly acquainted with your countenance and physiognomy, and they without hesitation declare its resemblance to you to be as striking as possible. And all who have seen it are of the same opinion. The evidence is amply sufficient to warrant the submission of the case to the session of the Columbus church for action.

And now, sir, what are your former Christian friends to think of you? You have sinned under the most forbidding and aggravating circumstances, and it is difficult to conceive of a more degrading and hypocritical course of wickedness and folly, or one which argues a greater destitution of principle or more callousness of conscience! I never have been more deceived in a man in all my life. How have you wounded the Saviour, and brought disgrace upon religion, and given occasion for the ungodly to triumph! What an injury have you done to the soul of the poor Negro! What disgrace and ruin of character have you brought on yourself! I pity you, and try to pray for your redemption. You well know what your duty is both toward God and man, and I hope you may find grace to perform it.

I voluntarily offered you my name on your school circular. I request you to take it off. You have betrayed my confidence and injured me grievously, and I cannot look upon you as I once did nor hold any further intercourse with you.

C. C. Jones.

HON. CHARLES C. JONES, JR., *to* REV. *and* MRS. C. C. JONES[g]
Savannah, *Saturday,* September 7th, 1861
My very dear Father and Mother,

After my short but delightful visit to you and to our sweet little Mary Ruth (for whose continued good health and daily improvement I render constant thanks to God and gratitude to you, my dear parents) I left Savannah on Saturday afternoon and spent Sabbath with Brother and Sister

Catrie in Augusta. Found them both well, and their interesting little son Stanhope the very picture of health. They are all happy, and are getting along very well. The Doctor as yet has not secured much practice except among the poorer class, where professional services are to be regarded rather as a matter of love and charity. He will not, however, lose his reward.

Arrived in Atlanta on Monday. Governor Brown absent in attendance upon a sick brother. On Tuesday went to Marietta and dined with Aunt Eliza and family. All well. Aunt Eliza is far better than she has been for years; the improvement in her health and strength was marked. Aunt Mary just as fat and good-natured as ever. Cousin Louisa thin, but well. The girls all with them, and Joe employed as a clerk in Mr. Denmead's flour mill. They all desired much love.

Returned to Atlanta that afternoon, and the next day had an interview with Governor Brown. He has given me an order for fifty horses for the use of our company, with a view to placing it upon a war footing as a flying artillery company, and promises an increase at no distant day. He is expected here this evening, and will undertake a tour of inspection along the coast on Monday in company with Commodore Tattnall and General Lawton.

Philo and Amanda were both at Atlanta. The latter, when I left, was suffering much from one of her severe attacks, accompanied with fever. Saw Fred King at his tannery. Please say to Aunt Julia that I spent a pleasant hour with him, and delivered her letter. He is prospering in business. On my arrival at Atlanta, saw our friend Mr. Rogers. He called several times to see me. He is as genial as ever. Philo, Amanda, and myself rode out to his farm, met him there by invitation, enjoyed his fine grapes, and visited his wine cellar. His success in the culture of the vine has been marked. Atlanta is a most thriving place, and already claims a population of sixteen thousand inhabitants, a growth unexampled in the history of our Georgia towns. It bids fair to become the largest city in Georgia.

On my return I stopped for a day at Bath. This little retreat is deserted of the male inhabitants. Most of them are in Virginia. Tarried with Mrs. Randolph Whitehead, with whom Vallie is spending the summer. My visit to Bath was at once pleasant and mournful in its character. Lights and shadows were strangely commingled. And yet as I dwelt upon the pictures which memory evoked from a consecrated past, I found that the shadows rested only upon my own desolate heart, while a pure, a holy, a heavenly light illuminated every recollection of the precious lives and loves of my dearest Ruth and our sweet little Julia. How did the recollections of our earliest loves—of those days when the heart throbs almost to bursting with its first, its ardent affections; of the places, the roads, the drives, the walks, the seats, all consecrated by our engagement vows hourly renewed; of that room and hour which gave her to my heart a blushing bride, who never once for even a short moment after ever forgot her vows in married life, or withheld the ready precious offerings of her daily kindnesses and truest loves—come crowding thick and fast, each moment filling my eyes with gushing tears and my heart with sorrow unutterable! . . .

Leaving Bath on Friday afternoon, I spent that evening with Brother and Sister Carrie, leaving Augusta at midnight and reaching my lonely home this morning. Found all the servants well. All friends desired kindest remembrances to you both, my dear parents. And our kinsman, Mr. Charles Jones Colcock of Charleston, an accomplished and Christian gentleman, whom I met in Atlanta (we traveled from that city towards Augusta together, and passed almost the whole of Wednesday night in the most pleasant conversation), asked me to remember him very especially to you.

I thought while I had the opportunity (it is so seldom that I am able to leave the city) I would improve it by seeing as many friends as I could. They all appeared glad to see me.

I sincerely trust, my dear father and mother, that you are both feeling better, and that little Mary Ruth still continues in the enjoyment of her remarkable health. With warmest love to you both, my dear parents, and kisses for Daughter, I am, as ever,

Your affectionate son,
Charles C. Jones, Jr.

REV. C. C. JONES *to* HON. CHARLES C. JONES, JR.[8]
Maybank, *Wednesday,* September 11th, 1861
My dear Son,

We were happy to receive your interesting letter last evening, and entered into your feelings on revisiting scenes of your friendship and love towards one now no longer here to cheer and bless you with sweet returns. . . .

Your dear little daughter, Mother says I must tell you, grows daily, and is developing in mind and body. She has her ups and downs, but sleeps well, and has an excellent appetite, and enjoys her waking hours. She is now on a course of treatment directed by your brother, who sent the medicines prepared by himself by express. Her ear is not yet well, but better. . . .

Am glad you succeeded so well with Governor Brown. You ought to have presented to you by the state a battery of *rifled cannon* from the Rome, Georgia, foundry. They have been sending them on to Virginia. Cannons decide battles. Did you observe that the Hatteras forts were taken by the guns of the ships at long ranges *throwing shell two miles?* Have we any guns to return such salutes *in Fort Pulaski?* If not, General Lawton must look out for the loss of that as well as of the small batteries he is putting out on the coast islands. I have little faith in them. If the enemy are in any force and know what they are about, they may land in two or more divisions in a calm day or clear night at different points on any one of the islands; and what can one or two hundred men do with a thousand or two—and the breastwork open in the rear? We need a camp or camps of six or eight thousand men on the line of the coast that may be gotten together at short notice upon an invasion to attack the enemy instantly; and at different available points on the main, forts that may be holden against any force—at least for a time, to allow succorers to come in, if no more. However, I am only giving my impressions. Our general in command may be doing all he can, but there is much dissatisfaction with him among the people, I understand.

Your Aunt Abby begs to be remembered to you. Mother sends much love. "My love to my dear father." (I held the pen in your dear baby's hand, and she writes you her first little letter. You will be able to read it.) The Lord bless and keep you, my dear son!

Your very affectionate father,
C. C. Jones.

HON. CHARLES C. JONES, JR., *to* REV. C. C. JONES[g]

Savannah, *Saturday,* September 14th, 1861

My dear Father,

I am favored with yours of the 11th inst., and am happy to know that all at home are well. Sister left me yesterday morning, after giving me the pleasure of a short sojourn of a few days. I wish that I could have prevailed upon her to have tarried longer, but the claims of a happy home would not admit an additional absence from their duties and their pleasures.

I agree with you fully in your views of the character and efficiency of the batteries erected for the protection of our coast. They may answer the purpose of preventing the ingress of marauding parties in gunboats and vessels of light draught, but they are wholly unable to cope either with a fleet or even with a single ship of the line armed with rifled cannon or with a battery of heavy guns such as those now used on board the U.S. sloops and steamers of war. Should any one of them be taken, and the guns fall into the hands of the enemy, we will be most effectually blockaded by our own batteries. I have just had an interview with Adjutant General Wayne, and he assures me that troops are to be concentrated at once at convenient distances for the defense of the coast, and a system of signals established from the mouth of the Savannah to the mouth of the St. Marys. We need at least ten thousand men in addition to the numbers now in service for the protection of the state. The batteries already erected are to be to a certain extent remodeled, and the garrisons strengthened.

Governor Brown returned last evening from his tour of inspection. The nomination of Judge Nisbet does not carry with it much enthusiasm in this city. On the contrary, I think Governor Brown's chances for reelection have been materially confirmed. In consequence of the smallness of the convention, Mr. Ward refused to allow his name to go before that body for a nomination. I presume from all I can learn that Joseph E.

Brown will be our next governor; and if for a third term, why not for life?

I heartily wish that we had some efficient, competent military leader to take in hand and vigorously prosecute this whole matter of our seacoast defenses. Carolina is far ahead of us.

We have not as yet received our horses for the Chatham Artillery. Governor Brown telegraphed to Secretary Walker to know if the Confederacy would pay for one hundred horses with a view to placing the Chatham Artillery upon a war footing as a light battery. The reply was that the expenses would be defrayed by the War Department. Instead of acting at once upon this, he orders the quartermaster here to send on an estimate of the probable expense of the purchase. Nothing has been had in reply, and we are yet without horses, or any reasonable expectation of having them until a further reply is had from Richmond. The delay is very prejudicial and unfortunate at this time, when every moment should be devoted to the efficient drill of men and horses. The drill of a light battery is the most difficult in the service, and we should have been in camp some time since.

The recent intelligence from Kentucky is very unfavorable. Unfortunate people, they will soon experience all the horrors of war without the sympathy of those whom they had not the manliness to acknowledge as friends.

Nothing new in our city. We are enjoying the blessings of health in a remarkable degree. On Tuesday or Wednesday next I hope to send out the crib, etc., for dear little Mary Ruth. Will direct the parcels to No. 3, and will have to trouble you to have a cart sent for them from that point. Mother will find some of Mr. Ward's nice oolong tea, which I send because you, my dear parents, will enjoy it much more than I will. With warmest love, my dear father and mother, to you both, and many kisses for dear little Daughter, who has her father's tenderest thanks for her first remembrance, I am, as ever,

Your affectionate son,
Charles C. Jones, Jr.

Mrs. Mary Jones *to* Hon. Charles C. Jones, Jr.[8]
Maybank, *Saturday,* September 14th, 1861

My very dear Son,

Your two last favors since your return have been received. We were happy to know that you had the pleasure of seeing so many friends and measurably accomplishing the principal object of your visit. Well does my heart sympathize with you in the melancholy but yet attractive sadness of your visit to Bath, the scene of your early and devoted loves. The recollection of our beloved Ruth and sweet little Julia is ever present with me. What must it be to you in the home once so happy but now so desolate—in your affectionate and generous heart, whose greatest earthly happiness was centered in your wife and child! . . .

Your father wrote you this week, but as Gilbert goes up this afternoon and is now waiting, I send you these hurried lines. Our precious little baby grows every day more and more interesting and intelligent. I am carrying out your brother's directions faithfully, and hope in time that she will be entirely relieved of the affection of her ear. She has had a cold, and today I gave her my old remedy (castor oil), and she appears much better—I may say relieved.

I am glad to know that your sister has been paying you a visit.

Sister Abby and her sick little boy have been with us the past week; he is much better, and I hope the change will do him permanent good. . . .

Our friends are all well. I am feeling much better, and think your dear father is no worse. When shall we see you? And what can I do for you? Father unites with me in best love, and Little Sister sends her sweet kisses to her dear papa. God bless and save you, ever prays

Your affectionate mother,
Mary Jones.

HON. CHARLES C. JONES, JR., *to* MRS. MARY JONES[g]

Savannah, *Wednesday,* September 18th, 1861

My very dear Mother,

I am in receipt of your last kind favor, and sincerely thank you for it, and for your tender sympathy and Christian counsels. I never will be able, the longest day I live, to be sufficiently grateful to you and to dear Father for all your great goodness to me and to my precious little daughter. Regret to know that she still suffers from her ear, and trust that the treatment which she is now undergoing will soon relieve her entirely.

The monotony of our city was on yesterday morning relieved by the arrival of the steamship *Bermuda,* direct from Liverpool, with a cargo consisting among other things of eighteen rifled cannon, some seven thousand Enfield rifles, any quantity of percussion caps, fixed ammunition, blankets, shoes, etc. Her coming is most opportune. She saw nothing whatever of Lincoln's famous blockade. This cargo was brought over in chief, I am informed, for account of the Confederate States. The *Bermuda* came in under English colors, and is an ironclad steamship of some fifteen hundred tons burden. Our Confederacy could not do better than to purchase her and convert her into a sloop of war. She would very easily bear a battery of, say, six or eight guns, and some of the rifled cannon which she brought over might very advantageously be used for that purpose. She is the first of a line of passenger and freight steamships intended for direct communication between Charleston, South Carolina, and Liverpool. We have intelligence that Captain Bulloch and Mr. Edward C. Anderson will soon leave England, each in command of fully appointed steam vessels of war. Were they here, they might very readily levy contribution upon these small fry hovering about our coast.

A letter from Sister, today received, tells me that all are well.

Did you receive the articles sent by Tuesday's train, a list of which I enclosed to Father? I hope they reached you without accident.

Our city, through a kind Providence, still continues in the enjoyment of an unusual degree of health. The dealings with our entire Southern coast during the present season have been remarkable. Myself, Grace, and George have been for some days suffering from colds; mine I contracted at a fire some nights since. With warmest love to you both, my dear parents, kisses for dear little Daughter, and remembrances for Susan and the servants, I am, as ever,

Your affectionate son,
Charles C. Jones, Jr.

MRS. MARY JONES *to* HON. CHARLES C. JONES, JR.[8]

Maybank, *Wednesday*, September 18th, 1861

My very dear Son,

Your last favor was received yesterday. Today your father went to Montevideo and returned, and we were just arranging for Gilbert to go to the depot early in the morning when Robin drove up with the precious memorials of our beloved child in heaven. They opened all the fountains of grief! I shall almost feel as if she is around me. Your father says he realizes more than ever now that he shall see them no more in the flesh. . . .

I hope you will find you have a loving little heart left you in your sweet little daughter. She grows daily more and more interesting, and has the warmest place in her grandparents' hearts. I long for the time to come when you will be with us to enjoy her sweet smiles. She cannot take the place of those who are gone, but she will have her own place in your heart.

When would you like me to come down and assist you in putting away such articles as you would like to preserve for our little one as mementos of her dear mother? Any time you think best will suit me, and I want you to say exactly what you would desire.

I had prepared a bag of dried shrimp, a few sheepshead corned, and red potatoes to send by Gilbert up to the depot, and now forward them by Robin to go by express, hoping you will enjoy them. Father asks you to request Lathrop & Company to send him one piece of Cobb cloth and one piece brown homespun at about nine cents, care of Lyons & Trask, Riceboro. Ask George to take care of the basket with buckets, etc., left in Savannah belonging to Sister Susan with a few articles of my own. You need not send them out. Father is very tired. He unites with me in tenderest love to you, with kisses from your little daughter. Friends all well.

Ever your affectionate mother,
Mary Jones.

HON. CHARLES C. JONES, JR., *to* MRS. MARY JONES[c]

Savannah, *Thursday*, September 19th, 1861

My dear Mother,

I send you herewith a map giving a partial view of the seat of war, which

116

I have just received from one of the officers now on service near Manassas. It may afford you some interest, although it is not as minute as we could wish it.

Mr. Ward left last night for Europe—under the most trying circumstances. He has just heard of a severe accident to his little son Jimmie. Mrs. Ward is in great distress, and he has braved all the dangers of imprisonment, etc., etc., to join them. I feel most deeply for him. He is completely overcome. I sincerely trust that there is some humanity left at the North, and that they will not molest him in passing through the enemy's country. He will bring his family immediately home.

Nothing new in the city. We are better of our colds. Warmest love to you both, my dear parents, and many kisses for dear little Mary Ruth. I am, as ever,

Your affectionate son,
Charles C. Jones, Jr.

HON. CHARLES C. JONES, JR., *to* MRS. MARY JONES^t
Savannah, *Sunday,* September 22nd, 1861*

My very dear Mother,

John has just come in for a ticket to go out in the morning, and I embrace the opportunity offered for acknowledging the receipt of your last kind letter and of thanking you for it.

Am happy to know that the articles sent have all been received. They are precious memorials, and it is almost like sundering my heartstrings to part with them; and yet under the circumstances I do it the more cheerfully because they go into the keeping of those who are dearest to me, and are for the use and benefit of that precious little daughter who will never know the tender loves of the mother who made and the sister who gave them. I pray you, Mother, save me one of the dresses—any one which you may deem best—that I may keep it ever near me, although I need no remembrancer of that character to keep the memory of the dear departed in living, cherished recollection. . . .

In reference to the disposition of the wardrobe of my dearest Ruth, any day, my dear mother, that you may name as convenient I will be most happy to see you, and will submit the whole matter to your determination.

I saw Messrs. H. Lathrop & Company, and they have executed the commission.

Mr. Ward has left for Europe with a view to bringing his family home. His determination to do so was suddenly formed, and was based upon a letter received last Tuesday in which he received tidings of a severe injury sustained by his little son Jimmie in falling from a swing. Mrs. Ward was in a very distressing condition of mind, and urged him by every consideration to come to her. In obedience to his duties to his family he has braved the dangers of imprisonment, etc., etc., and has entered upon the attempt to reach them.

He had made ample provision for the support of his family in Europe—if necessary for several years. It was a terrible trial to him to leave the country just at this important juncture, when she so much needs the services of every true and loyal son. His own conscience, however, will approve the act, let those who are ignorant of the facts of the case say and think what they may. He has the sincere sympathy of all his friends here. He said he would go—or make the attempt—if it blasted every hope of subsequent profit and preferment, and if he was imprisoned for years. To remain was to refuse to listen to the voice of the most sacred affection. I never saw a strong man more sorely moved than he was upon the receipt of the letter.

We are all better again, through a kind Providence. With warmest love to you, my dear mother, and to dear Father, and with many kisses for my darling little daughter, I am, as ever,

Your affectionate son,
Charles C. Jones, Jr.

HON. CHARLES C. JONES, JR., *to* MRS. MARY JONES^t

Savannah, Monday, September 23rd, 1861

My very dear Mother,

On yesterday evening I wrote in reply to your recent kind letter and stated that I would be most happy to see you any day you might find it convenient to come to the city. I write this evening to say so still, but to suggest that for the present you had better defer your visit, and for the simple reason that the weather is at present very trying, and our city not quite so healthy as it has been. I fear that you might suffer from the exercise of travel and the change of atmosphere. Soon we may hope for more pleasant days, and then I shall eagerly anticipate a visit from yourself and dear Father. . . . With a heart full of love for you all, I am, as ever,

Your affectionate son,
Charles C. Jones, Jr.

HON. JOHN JOHNSON *and* MR. A. G. REDD *to* REV. C. C. JONES^t

Columbus, Tuesday, September 24th, 1861

Reverend and dear Sir,

On the 30th ult. —— of this place showed to the subscribers (members of the session of the Presbyterian church of Columbus) a letter from you dated August 26th, 1861, addressed to said ——, containing a charge against him of a very serious character—namely, adultery—and that, too, under very aggravating circumstances. If the charge be true as stated, we could not be astonished at any degree of indignation and contempt that might be felt and manifested by the injured party.

Your letter bears date 26th ult., but is postmarked 28th. It was shown by Mr. —— to us on the 30th, so that there was no delay after he received it before he made it known to others. He (Mr. ——) most positively, solemnly, and unequivocally denies the charge altogether. He submitted the letter to us as members of the church session (the pastor being absent) for such action in the matter as might be deemed necessary. After some consultation we decided to write to you on the subject, but a severe attack of bilious fever has prevented our writing earlier.

We find stated in your letter, among other things: "The evidence is amply sufficient to warrant the submission of the case to the Columbus church for action." Now, dear sir, the evidence is what the session wants if it takes any action in the matter. And in such cases reliable legal evidence is what is usually most difficult to obtain. You appear to be fully satisfied of the fact. There may be circumstances connected with such cases that may produce conviction in the minds of those well acquainted with them, but it may not be practicable to produce evidence according to established forms and usages sufficient to convince others, or such evidence as would warrant a conviction by an investigating tribunal.

In looking at the evidence so far as appears by your letter, it is: first, the birth of a mulatto child at a time corresponding to the time Mr. —— was in your family; second, the declarations of the mother of the child; and third, the resemblance of the child to the accused. The first part of the evidence—time—is satisfactory as far as it goes. The second—the mother's declaration—is what usually has to be mainly relied upon in similar cases when the mother is a free white woman; but courts and juries have not always convicted the accused when the mother's declaration upon oath has been positive. The third—to wit, resemblance—is of very doubtful character at best. You can doubtless readily call to mind the very striking resemblance that is often found to exist between persons where there can be no kindred, and then again the absence of resemblance between brothers and sisters, parents and children, where the fidelity of the parents would not be questioned by anyone acquainted with them. Suppose the session should take action in the case upon the state of facts as presented by your letter and should pronounce —— guilty. What would be said of the action by an appellate court?

But let us turn aside a moment and look at the facts of the case and the parties. In a majority of cases that have fallen under our observation tried before the courts of the country for bastardy, the mother, being the complainant and a free white person, has pleaded *promise of marriage*. In this case such plea could not be urged, for in addition to the fact of Mr. ——'s being a married man, the law of the country does not tolerate such marriages. Look at the parties. The woman is a servant—a slave. We have no doubt but that she has been carefully trained and instructed in morals and religion; that she has been taught to observe the strictest rules of chastity. But all this is true of Mr. ——, and in addition thereto he has a character to sustain for himself and his family; and his success in the vocation in which he is engaged must depend in no small degree upon the purity of character he may sustain. He is also much older than the woman—perhaps nearly twice her age; and so far as is known to the subscribers, he has always sustained a fair character.

It is the opinion of some of our ablest legal men who have had much experience in the investigation of cases of bastardy that the propensity in woman is to conceal the true father. The cases that differ from this, they say, are the exceptions, and usually arise from a spirit of revenge for what the woman considers a breach of promise, false pretenses, etc. So strongly impressed have some of our lawyers and judges been with these facts that some effort has been made in the general assembly of the state to have the law so altered as to make the mother incompetent for a witness unless the complaint be made at the time or very soon after the illicit intercourse.

Now, dear sir, the fact is apparent that your woman, the mother of the child, has departed from the rules of chastity. She can plead no breach of promise of marriage. She gave no alarm of any coercive measures having been used. Her own declaration is the only positive evidence. The only corroborative evidence is the coincidence in time and resemblance of the child—that is, so far as the facts appear from your letter. On the other side there is the unequivocal denial of the accused, his former character and position in society, and the interest he must have in maintaining a good moral character. Certainly these are entitled to consideration.

We do not write to you for the purpose of screening Mr. —— from the full measure of any penalty which he may have incurred; but he is a member of the church of which we are officers, and while we grant that it is our duty to look closely to all offenders, yet it is no less our duty to protect and defend innocent members of the church. We make this communication to you in all frankness and candor, with a desire that you reply to us as early as convenient, and if any additional evidence or developments have come to light, that you will inform us. We have given no publicity to this charge, and shall not until time shall have been given to hear from you. The character of Mr. —— is in great jeopardy, and with his character goes his prospects for success even in his secular vocation.

With due consideration and esteem, we are, dear sir,
Truly yours, etc.,
John Johnson
A. G. Redd.

REV. C. C. JONES *to* HON. CHARLES C. JONES, JR.[8]
Maybank, *Friday,* September 27th, 1861
My dear Son,

Your last favors by mail and by John have been received, and Mother says she will not visit you until she hears particularly from you, as she is ready at any time. . . .

I cannot but feel that God is dealing very closely with you, my dear son, and am exceedingly anxious that you make your peace with Him, and do it now. Do not postpone so important a matter. He has broken up your precious family by a direct personal affliction; and now your home is to be broken up by a general judgment of a cruel war upon the country, and you are to be thrown into new scenes, and it may be new sorrows. For who knows the issue of war? Do not come out of that home but under the protection and leadership of the Great Captain of our Salvation. And come what will, you will be safe, and saved in Him.

Your dear little daughter is doing as well as possible, and everyone says is growing finely. Mother unites in much love to you. I remain, through God's mercy,

Your ever affectionate father,
C. C. Jones.

HON. CHARLES C. JONES, JR., *to* REV. C. C. JONES[g]
Savannah, *Tuesday*, October 1st, 1861
My dear Father,

I was two days since favored with your very kind letter of the 27th inst., and have most seriously considered its injunctions, and reflected upon the most important counsels which it contains. . . .

I was last evening with Mr. Porter, who has suffered much from several hemorrhages. He is quite weak, and we know not yet what the result will be. He was unable to preach last Sabbath, and is now closely confined to his bed. The doctor hopes that the bleeding comes from the throat and not from the lungs. He is a good man, and I sincerely trust that he may be soon restored to health and usefulness. . . .

The fortifications of our coast are progressing more rapidly than they have been at any time heretofore. The question of field fortifications around this city is being considered.

You will see that I have declined a reelection as mayor of this city, and also the appointment as representative from this county in the state legislature. The reasons I will give you in full, for I hope to be with you in a short time. My present term of office expires on the 21st inst.

With every love for yourself, my dear father, dear Mother, and my precious little daughter, I am, as ever,

Your affectionate son,
Charles C. Jones, Jr.

REV. C. C. JONES *to* HON. CHARLES C. JONES, JR.[g]
Maybank, *Thursday*, October 3rd, 1861
My dear Son,

Your deeply interesting letter of the 1st we received last evening, and your dear mother and father returned thanks to God for what it contained of your views and feelings and purposes in relation to your eternal interests. . . .

We have had a serious affliction this week in the death by typhoid fever of Dinah, Andrew's daughter. She died on Sunday evening at nine o'clock in the washroom, where we removed her for more ready attention. The first case of such a fever we have ever had in our household, and the first I ever saw in my life. Her death has cast a gloom over the place; and it was unexpected to us all, the fever making rapid progress the last two days. She was the life of the place, and a consistent member of the Baptist Church. . . .

Just as your mother and I returned from laying our poor servant in her grave, as the shadows of the evening were deepening into night and we were very sad, your dear sister, Robert, and the children drove up. Their visit seemed a special mercy under the circumstances. They left us on Wednesday.

Your dear little daughter is growing finely, everyone says, and certainly more and more interesting day by day. She is perfectly well all to the ear, which is much better under your brother's treatment. She rode round and round the lot yesterday in the buggy, and when she was brought in, her grandmother put the coconut dipper to her little mouth and she drank heartily like an old person. . . .

In an interesting letter received from your Uncle John last evening from Manassas, he expresses a most anxious desire to get Dunwody transferred from Virginia to our Georgia coast army, fearing the cold of winter upon his constitution, which has been shaken twice with pneumonia. He asks if he could not be elected in some company a lieutenant and so be transferred, and begs us to do what we can for him. I do not see how such an election could be brought about, nor how the removal can be accomplished. I wish you would make some inquiries on the subject and let me know. Your Uncle John returns this month about the 14th. He asks you in the letter to help him.

Am happy to learn our coast defenses are advancing. There are complaints on that score everywhere. It is past time for it—if the enemy are coming either to Brunswick or Savannah. The defenses of Savannah should not be delayed a single moment, and the city be protected by land as well as by water. I learn Captain Anderson had two or three guns sent him naked as they left the foundry, with not a pound of ammunition, but files ready for spiking!

Mother goes to Montevideo tomorrow and returns immediately. She has a bad cough. She sends much love. Mary Ruth is sleeping sweetly: quarter past 10 P.M. We have had meeting for the people this evening. The Lord bless you, my dear son!

Your affectionate father,
C. C. Jones.

HON. CHARLES C. JONES, JR., *to* REV. C. C. JONES[8]
Savannah, *Monday*, October 7th, 1861
My dear Father,

I am much indebted to you for your very kind letter of the 3rd inst., which would have received an earlier reply but for the numerous engagements which are ever pressing upon me.

In addition to the duties of the mayoralty, since the absence of Mr. Ward the entire burden of the office has devolved upon me; and now under the pressure of the Confiscation Act business engagements are greatly multiplied. I presume several hundred thousand dollars' worth of alien enemy property will be sequestrated in this city. The Confederate receiver, Dr. William C. Daniell, is pressing the matter. So intimate have been our business relations with the North that the complications growing out of copartnership transactions and joint interests in property owned here are endless. Hardships occur in not a few instances. But the old sore must be soundly probed before the purifying process will begin. The more absolute the separation the better. I have seen an estimate that the alien enemy property at the South will amount in value to some three hundred million dollars. This in our treasury, we will the better be able to prosecute the war and sustain the expenditures incident thereto, although all these sequestrations must eventually be accounted for by treaty stipulations—unless, forsooth, we are eventually overturned, which is simply a matter of impossibility. Even the Lincolnites admit this now, and justify the war upon the plea that it is with them a domestic necessity—that unless public attention be kept away from home, they will suffer from internal dissensions, civil war, and every manner of turmoil, eventuating in absolute destruction.

Kentucky is paying the penalty of her indecision, and reaping the legitimate fruits of her pretended neutrality. The scenes of "the dark and bloody ground" are come again. I regretted to see that two of Governor Helm's sons had been arrested by the Lincolnites and sent for confinement to Lafayette Prison.

Have you noticed the brief account of the recent and successful engagement of General Henry R. Jackson? There is no question of his bravery; I fear for his prudence.

You may observe in the morning papers a proclamation in reference to the immediate defenses of Savannah. The work will commence on Thursday of this week, and the expectation is that it will be completed in ten days. It is expected that three or four hundred hands will report themselves on that day for duty. The principal approaches to the city will be protected by strong earthworks, and these will be connected by a redoubt. The circumvallation will be almost complete. These defenses are constructed in anticipation of a land attack. Captain Gilmer is here, and General Lawton is getting the benefit of his views.

Our military operations have progressed very rapidly during the past two weeks, and troops are being concentrated daily along the coast. Our company is at present stationed at the Isle of Hope, about nine miles from the city. We are busily engaged in getting our horses, men, and drivers in proper training—by no means a light task. My duties here expire about the 22nd of this month, and I expect then to join my company.

There are sundry aspirants for the mayoralty. No nominations by the people have yet been made.

Had the pleasure of a night from Brother on Friday last. Was surprised to find that he was on his way to join the Liberty Troop and serve as a private in the ranks. What do you think of this step? We talked the matter over, and I advised him to ask your judgment of the propriety of the course, all things considered.

I was pained, my dear father, to hear of the death of Dinah. She was a faithful servant, and her loss to her little family and to the circle on the plantation must be severely felt. Her disease was very singular.

In reference to Dunwody, I fear that there will be but little prospect for his obtaining a commission in any of the coast companies. In the formation of companies the officers are those first chosen, and they are men who have the influence necessary to secure the enlistment of the men who are to compose them. It is no easy matter, then, to put aside those who have borne the heat and burden of the day, and who have devoted their time and labor and money in recruiting, for one who has not in any manner contributed "in getting the organization up." You will find that the same is true of regiments. The colonel empowered to raise the regiment confers his field and staff appointments—as many as are at his command—to those whose influence can secure the companies necessary to perfect the organization. I know not of a single commission on our coast which could be secured by Dunwody. He can act as a private almost anywhere. We can give him a place in our company, but offices we have none. I have just endeavored, but without success, to secure a lieutenancy for Edgeworth Eve, who returned a week since from the Army of the Potomac, where he had been acting as a lieutenant in one of the companies of the 4th North Carolina Regiment.

I am truly happy to hear such good news of my precious little daughter. May God in His great mercy bless her every day! I am trying in weakness, my dear father, to lead a new life, and will remember all your kind counsels and those of my dear mother. I hope to see you both very soon. Mr. Porter is recovering. Our city is not as healthy as it was. It would not be prudent for Mother to come, much as I desire her to do so. Give her my warmest love. Kiss dear little Mary Ruth for me. And believe me ever

Your affectionate son,
Charles C. Jones, Jr.

Did you receive a copy of my annual report?

REV. C. C. JONES *to* HON. CHARLES C. JONES, JR.[8]

Maybank, *Wednesday,* October 9th, 1861

My dear Son,

We received your two favors of the 7th and 8th this afternoon, and were happy to learn your continued good health. Do be careful of these October *suns* and *dews,* and make use of the preventive recommended by your brother whenever it is needful for you to do so. He thinks it might be a preventive of yellow fever if used in cities liable to that terrible affliction. But it would require a world of quinine, and not now to be had.

Your annual report as mayor of Savannah your brother sat down and read for us so soon as it came to hand, and it gave us great satisfaction. And as far as country folks are capable of judging, we thought it in composition clear, in sentiment admirable, and in suggestions judicious. I wish (had your space permitted) you had recommended the plan we spoke of touching the sewerage of the city. Your brother tells me it is the *plan of Paris*. High example, certainly. I never knew it before. Perhaps you have done so in council. Savannah never can be a healthy city until these intolerable and accumulating nuisances are entirely obliterated. What people would think of tolerating an acre excavated from six to eight feet deep and made a pool of such matter in the heart of their city for public convenience, and the receptacle of tens of thousands of rats, and millions of cockroaches, centipedes, and all manner of vermin! The difference is very little, having the offense to life and comfort put into smaller receptacles and distributed throughout the city. Your reign has been a prosperous one, for which we should be grateful, although from war influences your expenses have exceeded your income.

The Confiscation Act works finely. There will be money enough to pay for all the Negroes stolen and emancipated. Dr. Daniell, my old friend and physician, is an excellent man for carrying out the act; and I agree with you it ought to be carried out *in extremis* and break up the connection totally. The Federals have outwitted themselves for once in the speculation.

May it please God to deliver us from their iniquitous warfare, and enable us on the seacoast to repel their piratical invasions! If we are favored in giving them one or two decided repulses, it would go far to open their eyes; for they would see that our weakest points (in their estimation) are sufficient for their most powerful demonstrations. And on this account particularly I have felt the greatest anxiety that our coast defenses should be as nearly perfect and invulnerable as possible. And it is aggravating to think that golden months have been lost in almost absolute idleness, and that at the last hour things are hurried to preparation. If we are saved in case of an invasion from the sea, it will be a kind Providence over us blessing us when we have not put forth our efforts and done our duty. I apprehend, by all accounts, that the sea and coast defenses of Savannah need overhauling. A poor battery on Tybee with two poorly mounted guns and a force of fifteen hundred raw men! And guns of *limited range* in Fort Pulaski! But I will say no more on this subject; it is an unpleasant one to the people generally.

Your brother felt that he could not reconcile it to his conscience to remain quietly in professional pursuits when his country was imperiled; that the reflection in the future would be disagreeable when all would be over and he never to have borne any part in so good a cause; that he could not call upon up-countrymen to defend his own home and property and he remain behind; that he regards it a duty, and that every true patriot should be willing to make sacrifices; that he is not a military man, nor does he seek position or fame, but opportunity to testify devotion to his country and to aid in achieving her independence; and things being so, there is no better corps for him to serve in—for convenience, for acquaintance, for character—than the Liberty Independent Troop; that the mustering-in will be but for six months to begin with; and he will be, you may say, at home. This is the view he takes, and I do not feel at liberty to interpose any objection when he has made provision for his family for six months or more. And if camp life agrees with him, the relaxation from years of close study and the daily exercise cannot fail to restore his constitution to better health and strength. The truth is, your brother is not liable to military duty at all. You know the weakness of the left arm once broken; he could not carry a musket for any time conveniently, and a horse company is the only arm of service he could well serve in. He has been practicing his fine horse to the use of the pistol and the saber, and he stands fire and the rattle of the scabbard very well. Jerry, mounted by Titus, took part in the practice, but he made a sorry figure under the circumstances as a war horse. . . .

Dunwody would be glad to get a place as a private in our coast army if such a thing can be compassed. He says "he will give all the Confederacy over him and fifty dollars beside to any man who will take his place, and he will serve the Confederacy in the South, and begs his Cousin Charles to help him if he can." His direction is J. Dunwody Jones, care of Captain Magruder, Rome Light Guards, 8th Regiment Georgia Volunteers, Manassas, Virginia. Could he be allowed to get a substitute in Virginia and then come and join here? Do help him if you can.

Waring ought to be closely watched. His property is in Washington; he would be as a surgeon in the very place for a spy.

Your sweet little daughter is growing daily. Took a ride in the little carriage today and was quite delighted. Opens her mouth for you to kiss her, and observes everything. Mother and Brother send much love. May your way be clearer and clearer, my dear son, in the new life in Christ Jesus you are endeavoring to lead! Cast your all into His hands. Am glad to hear Mr. Porter is better.

Your ever affectionate father,
C. C. Jones.

Hon. Charles C. Jones, Jr., *to* Rev. *and* Mrs. C. C. Jones[8]
Savannah, *Thursday,* October 10th, 1861
My dear Father and Mother,

The pleasant change in temperature which this morning brings will, I trust, restore the health of our city. It certainly is delightful, and the warm breath for the first time this fall was cloudy on the early air.

Today I purchased a service horse—a fine animal, bay, six years old, of good action, and I think in every respect reliable. The officers in the flying artillery are required to furnish their own horses, trappings, etc., etc.—quite an item at the present rates. Our battery is still stationed at the Isle of Hope: camps located under those beautiful live oak trees which adorn the old Bulloch lot. With the spot I am familiar, although I have not as yet visited the encampment. The preparation of a mounted battery for efficient service, involving as it does the drill of men and horses, is exceeding onerous. The drill itself is the most difficult and complicated in the service. After frost we will probably be nearer the city. The men having been for more than two months since at Fort Pulaski, it was not deemed prudent to transfer them to open camp on the outskirts of Savannah.

My term of office expires, D.V., on the 21st inst., and I expect so soon thereafter as practicable to join my company. It is quite a sacrifice for me to do so, but I think that I am in the line of duty; and that, ascertained, should be complied with.

I am at quite a loss to know what disposition to make of my furniture. There is no sale for it. To have it boxed and stored is rather an expensive operation; and to store it in a public wareroom without covering would be ruinous. Mr. Morrell says he has no room for it. Today Mr. G. B. Lamar spoke with me about renting the furniture for a year. He did not say definitely whether he would do so or not, and will probably determine on the morrow. It seems to me that if the furniture can be left in the house in the hands of a careful person (as I take Mr. Lamar to be), and thereby the expense and the injury of removal be avoided, that this would be the best disposition that could be made of it. What do you say, my dear mother? It is an utter impossibility for me to retain the house, as I could not afford to pay the rent, all income being at an end.

All friends well. With much love to you both, my dear parents, and to Brother, and many kisses for my dear little daughter, I am, as ever,

Your affectionate son,
Charles C. Jones, Jr.

HON. CHARLES C. JONES, JR., *to* REV. C. C. JONES[g]
Savannah, *Friday,* October 11th, 1861

My dear Father,

I am this afternoon favored with your kind letter of the 9th inst., and rejoice to hear that all at home are well.

Very easily and heartily do I appreciate the feelings which induce Brother to enter the service in the manner he does. The more readily do I sympathize with him in them because my own heart responds to the promptings. How would it do in after years (if in the good providence of God life be spared to attain that age) for the father, when the question is asked by his child just learning the history of his country and studying that chapter, interesting in the extreme, which will be devoted to a record of this eventful period, "Did you fight for our country then?" to answer, "No, my son (or my daughter), I did not." And when the other question, the logical sequence of the first, comes, "Why not, Father?" how awkward and unsatisfactory alike to the parent and the child to respond, "I was too much engaged with private business to do so." A clear record whether in peace or war is the most precious legacy that a parent can leave for a child.

Above all other considerations, however, whether of interest, of inclination, of convenience, or of prudence, rises the desire to stand in one's lot and serve in that capacity in which his services are most needed. I could very easily have avoided active enlistment by consenting to another term of office. Only yesterday (and I say this only at home) a renomination was virtually unanimously tendered to me by the nominating committee appointed at the recent citizens' meeting. They could not agree upon any one of the candidates named, and asked whether I would not allow my name to be used, with a direct assurance that if an affirmative answer were given, no opposition would be made by any of the candidates whose claims were urged before the committee. While sensible of the good feelings of my fellow citizens, and thankful that I commanded their respect and confidence, I could not in all good conscience, and with the apprehension of duty now resting upon my mind, consent to retain the office for another year.

The truth is, I am weary of the office and its continued routine of duties, which this year have been unusually exacting and important. My heart is heavy, and my mind is weary. I am at times—and especially during the silent watches of the night—so nervous that I spring almost out of the bed when dozing. This is not natural to me. The slightest thing which startles for the moment sets my heart to beating at such a rapid rate that I almost grow faint. This also is not what it should be.

Besides, I regard it as a matter vital to our interests here that the Chatham Artillery should be placed upon a proper footing as a mounted battery. You have, my dear father, no idea of the labor and continued care and study and drill and discipline which are required not only to organize but also to keep in a state of efficiency such a company. The conduct of a regiment of infantry is far easier. The members of the company will not hear to my leaving them, and have waited upon me with committees to protest against my doing so.

Above all, as a matter of personal duty and of private example, I think I ought to render service in the field. Were I to consult my own private inclinations as based upon principles of comfort, considerations of interest, and prospects of gain, I would not go. The service will be arduous, involving sacrifices great in their character; but I am of opinion that my duty requires it, and I will go.

Judging from the morning papers, we are to have several aspirants for the mayoralty. The election occurs on Monday next. I trust a competent and honest man may be secured. It is all-important.

I am happy to know that you were pleased with the annual report. My highest earthly ambition is to secure the approbation in whatever I do of dear Mother and yourself. Your opinions I value more than those of all else.

In my letter of yesterday I mentioned that Mr. G. B. Lamar contemplated renting my house with the furniture and servants. I do not see what better I can do. Today he looked at everything, but will not give a decided answer until next Tuesday or Wednesday. The whole matter is as yet quite open. The furniture, etc., will probably be in as good hands as they could be under similar circumstances. To have everything covered and placed in a store- or wareroom would involve an expense of at least one hundred and fifty dollars. I have not the money to pay for this. And to place everything in store in an open condition would be simply ruinous. What the cockroaches and rats and dust and mold would leave would scarcely be worth retaining.

Adeline tells me that she would be glad to remain with Abram, who is hired at the depot, until January next, and says that she will see that Grace does not fall into any bad habits. In these seasons of financial depression every source of reasonable income should be husbanded.

It makes me very sad to part with the possession—even for the time being—of the furniture so nearly and dearly associated with all the precious memories of my beloved Ruth and sweet little Julia, and to bid farewell to those rooms which are consecrated with all the recollections of their inestimable loves. But though times and places may change, the sweetest influences which belong to their memories will abide with me forever, and at all seasons. In their steads no substitutions can ever be had; a home in the heart—such a home as they had in my heart—can never be occupied by others.

I learn today that Mr. Ward arrived safely in Canada. Before this he has sailed from Quebec. I hope for him a speedy return. Our office will be temporarily closed until he does reach home again.

All friends here are well.

Do, Father, say to dear Mother that I sincerely regret that this (to a certain degree, at least) unhealthy condition of our city has rendered it imprudent for her to come in and select, as she kindly purposed, such articles from the wardrobe of my dear Ruth as should be preserved for my sweet little daughter in precious remembrance of her kind mother, whose loves she never in person can appreciate. When I leave I shall have her wardrobe sent to Philo's house. Would it not be well for me to select and send out some articles? I might bring them with me when I come; for I must see you, my dear parents and my little daughter, before I leave for camp. My duties here expire on the 22nd inst., D.V. I wish also to hand to Mother, to be kept for Mary Ruth, a little box containing some seventy dollars in gold and silver which belonged to her dear little sister Julia. It was her savings bank, and the sweet little thing had learned to take great delight in depositing in it ten-cent pieces, quarters, etc. It will be a matter of great interest to her. I will let you know what day I can come out.

With warmest love to you both, my dear parents, and to the Doctor, and with many kisses for my little daughter, I am, as ever,

Your affectionate son,

Charles C. Jones, Jr.

I will see what can be done for Dunwody.

MRS. MARY JONES *to* HON. CHARLES C. JONES, JR.[8]

My dear Son,

An opportunity occurring to No. 3, I send you a hasty line to say that through divine favor we are all well in our *white* household. One or two cases of autumnal fever with the servants, which we trust will soon yield to your brother's skill, under God's blessing.

Your precious little daughter is very bright and sweet. Every day develops some new charm to her grandpapa and grandmama. Susan takes her walking into the yard, and she is much interested in feeding the chickens. . . .

I have nearly completed a warm camp blanket for your brother, and would like to make the same for you, as I have another large thick blanket, *if you would like to have it.* It is lined throughout with dark striped Cobb cloth, which makes a very warm covering and relieves the unpleasant contact of the wool from the blanket and does not materially increase the size. You have never sent me your *drawers* to make. I am now perfectly at leisure to do them or any other work you may wish done. Only send the materials and a pair to cut by and they shall be made immediately. Write me if you wish any coarse shirts or pants made for George. I have materials for such in the house.

Many thanks for the delightful tea and gumdrops. Your uncle dined with us yesterday, and I gave him a cup; he said it was superb. We will have to touch such luxuries daintily if the blockade lasts. One thing is certain: we will endure privations joyfully rather than yield an inch to the vile miscreants that are now seeking our destruction.

I am rejoiced to know that active efforts are making for the defense of *Savannah* and our coast. Public feeling has been greatly exasperated by the apparent apathy and neglect of our general in command.

Your brother goes into service on Monday next. Your father has expressed our views of the matter.

Whenever, my dear child, you feel that I can help you in any way, do let me know. Your mother's heart is ever filled with sympathy for you in your deep sorrow. When you think it prudent, I will come down and assist you in any arrangements. Your bedding and carpets I can have put up in such a way as will never be troubled by moths, and you could send them home for safekeeping. Did it ever occur to you to retain the rooms in the third story of your house, where you could store your furniture, and rent out the rest of the building? *The office* itself would be valuable. And in these hard times they ought to reduce your rent at least one hundred dollars. They have done so in other places. I make this suggestion as it may relieve you of the trouble of moving your furniture for the present and save you some expense.

Your father and brother unite with me in much love to you. Many kisses from your little daughter. God bless and save you!

Ever, my dear son, your affectionate mother,
Mary Jones.

HON. CHARLES C. JONES, JR., *to* MRS. MARY JONES[g]

Savannah, *Monday,* October 14th, 1861

My very dear Mother,

I am in receipt of your kind letter of the 11th inst., and am very happy to know that all at home are well, with the exception of one or two cases of fever among the servants, which I trust have before this yielded to treatment.

The delightful sprig of verbena which you were so kind as to enclose in your letter, the perfume of which still lingers about me as I write, is most acceptable to me. I never see or smell this flower without having all the happy associations connected with Maybank revived in all the fullness and freshness of their earliest existence. There is the breath of a pious, generous, quiet, intelligent, beloved home about the perfume of that little flower which is exceedingly precious to me. You know, in eastern lands they talk in flowers; and I can assure you the language of this is soft, sweet, and most attractive.

I am happy to know that my dear little daughter still continues to enjoy health, and that she is daily attracting to herself the renewed loves of her kindest grandparents. I sincerely trust that it may please God to spare her precious life, and that He will at an early age change her heart and cause her to live ever a life of piety and of usefulness. . . .

I much regret, Mother, that the past tendency to ill health in the city has postponed your anticipated visit, which I have so anxiously hoped for. In the event of my leaving the city before you are able to select from the wardrobe of my dear Ruth such articles as you think should be preserved for little Mary Ruth, and such also as you yourself might like to keep, I will have them all packed up and leave them with Mrs. Harriss next door, who will, I know, take every care of them until such time as you may find it prudent and convenient to make the disposition. Philo I have asked to distribute among her sisters the other articles. She was Ruth's favorite sister, and she will faithfully execute this melancholy and sacred trust. It is hard indeed to part with a single memorial of her whom I loved so tenderly; and yet, sad as the parting is, I cannot think of any other more appropriate disposition than the one contemplated.

In my former letters I told you what my anticipated plans were in reference to my furniture, and I hope under the circumstances that they will meet with your approbation. I know not what else can be done; and just now, with all the expenses which are upon me, I do not feel at liberty to decline an arrangement of this character and incur the additional expense of not less than one hundred and fifty dollars for the packing and removal of furniture to a wareroom. I presume by Wednesday of this week I shall hear from Mr. Lamar, who is now in Macon, in reference to the matter. Meanwhile I hope to hear from you.

I would be very much obliged to you, my dear mother, if you would have the blanket made for me. It will be very acceptable, and just at this time it is a matter almost of absolute impossibility to obtain a blanket of any sort or description. My drawers I have had made here (four in number) of white flannel. The coarse shirts and pants for George would be very acceptable.

I expect, D.V., to leave the city for our camp, which for the present is located at the Isle of Hope, some nine miles from the city, about the middle of next week. Before doing so, however, I expect to come out and see you and Father and my dear little daughter.

The probability is that we will be in the vicinity of Savannah for some time to come, unless ordered off upon special duty upon the coast in expectation of an attack from the enemy at some conjectured point. We are promised by the general a prominent position in the first engagement. I hope and trust that the Lord of Hosts will be with us. . . .

There is, Mother, some of that excellent tea left, and you shall have it all. If this blockade continues, we will be almost entirely deprived of these luxuries which in times of peace and plenty came to be regarded as absolute necessaries. For myself, I can very readily dispense with them.

I hope the health of our city is improving. The temperature is very delightful. Give much love to Father. Kiss my precious little daughter for me. And believe me ever, my dear mother,

Your affectionate son,
Charles C. Jones, Jr.

MRS. MARY JONES *to* HON. CHARLES C. JONES, JR.[8]
Maybank, *Tuesday,* October 15th, 1861
My dear Son,

Your affectionate favor, received this afternoon, gives us the delightful assurance that we may hope to see you before long. I cannot bear to think of your going into service without seeing us and your precious little daughter.

Your father and myself fully approve of your renting your house and furniture to Mr. Lamar. He is in every respect a reliable gentleman, and it would be a relief not to make any changes either in your furniture or servants, if he will take Adeline and Grace and allow Abram to be with his family as heretofore. . . . When would Mr. Lamar wish to take possession? I would be glad to come down at any time you thought it prudent, and will probably be compelled to do so as early as is safe.

I write in haste, as Mr. McDonald is waiting to go. This morning your brother was mustered into the Confederate service. We rode down to see him. Henry and himself are in the same tent, but they are very much crowded. I will have the blanket and George's clothes made immediately. What more can I do for you? Unless it is customary I do not think you ought to rent your carpets. Father unites with me in best love to you. Sweetest kisses from your little daughter.

Ever, my beloved child, your affectionate mother,
Mary Jones.

Hon. Charles C. Jones, Jr., *to* Rev. C. C. Jones[g]

Savannah, *Wednesday,* October 16th, 1861

My dear Father,

I am in receipt of your kind note at the hands of Titus, and am happy to know that all at home are well.

If you will be so good as to send the buggy for me to No. 3 on Saturday morning next, I will try and be with you and dear Mother and my precious little daughter on that day. I would have been out before, but it has been a matter of utter impossibility for me to escape from the numerous engagements which have been pressing upon me.

As you observe from the daily journals of this city, there has been no election of my successor by the people. In that event it is provided by an act of the legislature that after the board-elect has been fully organized, that they shall at once proceed to select a mayor from the two candidates who shall have received the largest popular vote. I presume from present appearances that Mr. Thomas Purse will be the mayor for the ensuing year, as the board-elect seem to be in his favor. He is a good man in the main, but quite too pliable in his composition and, as I respectfully conceive, unfit for emergencies like the present. Dr. Arnold, his competitor, would possibly on the whole have been more reliable, but even he is not the man for the times.

I am happy to think that in retiring from the office, the duties of which for the past year I have endeavored faithfully and honestly and fearlessly to discharge without favor or affection, that I carry with me the esteem, the confidence, and the approbation of the good men of this community, and withal have preserved my own sense of self-respect and rectitude of purpose. That lost, everything else is of no avail. The annual report is now in the hands of the printer, and will soon appear in pamphlet form. So soon as completed, you shall have copies. . . .

Successes have crowned our arms in every quarter recently. We are loudly called upon to return earnest thanks to the Giver of All Good for His continued interposition in our behalf. The health of our city is improving; the pleasant change in temperature has exerted a most beneficial influence. . . . All friends are well. Mr. Porter improves, but not very rapidly. . . . With much love, my dear father, to self, dear Mother, and many kisses for my dear little daughter, I am, as ever,

Your affectionate son,
Charles C. Jones, Jr.

Rev. C. C. Jones *to* Hon. John Johnson *and* Mr. A. G. Redd[t]

Maybank, *Wednesday,* October 16th, 1861

My dear Sirs,

Your letter in relation to Mr. —— reached me on the 30th ult., and as you requested, I embrace my earliest convenience to reply to it. You make several points on my letter to him, and I presume with the desire of eliciting some notice of them from me.

Your first point is that "there may be circumstances in a case sufficient to produce conviction in the minds of those well acquainted with them, but it may not be practicable to produce evidence according to established forms and usages sufficient to convince an investigating tribunal." This at times is most unfortunately so—unfortunately so for the innocent, as they must ever lie under suspicion; and unfortunately so for the guilty, as they escape punishment.

Your second point is that "such appears to be the nature of Mr. ——'s case." The first proof submitted in my letter of his guilt was "the free, unconstrained confession of the Negro mother herself." The plea urged by you against it, drawn from the illicit intercourse of whites under promise of marriage, is irrelevant, since no contracts of marriage obtain between whites and blacks. Nor is it essential to the truthfulness of the mother's declaration that she was not forced and gave no alarm. The consent of the woman was all that was required, and her declaration is that she so consented, and that she had repeated criminal conversation with the said ——, and that the mulatto child is his. And she makes the declaration without revenge and without compulsion. Her evidence you allow to be positive evidence. The second proof submitted was "the correspondence of the time of his criminal connection with the Negro and the birth of the child." This you allow to be satisfactory as far as it goes. The third proof submitted was "a resemblance beyond mistake." Your answer to this is that "resemblances may be traced between individuals utter strangers to each other," and that "they are wanting between brothers and sisters, parents and children." These are rare exceptions when you compare man with man, and the members of the same families with each other. And the exceptions prove the rule. The resemblance of progeny to parent is *a law of nature,* and runs through the whole animal kingdom, and can neither be gainsaid nor resisted. The resemblance of the mulatto child to Mr. —— is uncommonly and unmistakably distinct and perfect.

The third point you make is "the character and, by consequence, the credibility of the parties." The party of the first part is the woman—a Negro and a servant, whom you doubt not has been well instructed and morally and religiously brought up. But servants are not always liars, and are particularly slow to father their children upon white men without the best of reasons, and because of their humble and exposed condition are more open to the seductions of their superiors (not in character but in station in society). The careful training of our servant has proved no defense. She says "Mr. —— told her not to make him known if anything should happen." The party of the second part is Mr. ——, who you say has also been well and religiously trained, is respectably connected, has a character to sustain, a family to support, his success in business is dependent upon his good reputation, has always sustained a fair character, and is much older than the woman. Age is too frequently an overmatch for inexperienced youth, and Mr. ———'s age is an immaterial circumstance, for he is in good health and in the prime of life. The circumstances of Mr. ——— to which you allude as well calculated to bind him to a life of integrity and virtue are forbidding enough against a life of contrary character, and were all fully drawn out in my letter to him. But in themselves they do not prove him innocent of the charge preferred against him by the Negro girl, although backed by his denial. They afford ground of presumption that he would not perpetrate so vile a crime, but nothing more. Previous good character and standing may mitigate the sentence of condemnation or aggravate it, just as those who try a case are led by the testimony to view it, but can never be admitted of the nature of proof against charges of wrongdoing. Otherwise some of the greatest offenders would escape justice. Our civil and ecclesiastical courts furnish examples of transgressors in high places, and we cannot be forgetful of like examples recorded in the Holy Scriptures for our warning.

You say finally: "So far as is known to us, Mr. ——— always sustained a fair character." And your remark obliges me to note the point. So far as was known *to me*, Mr. ——— when he came to my house had sustained a fair character. But to my amazement, after he left my house I learned that he had been charged by a Negro girl in the village where he taught school in our county with having had criminal connection with her and with being the father of the child with which she was then pregnant; that he had denied the charge before the trustees of the academy and demanded that the Negro should be punished, which punishment was inflicted previously to the birth of the child; and the trustees acquitted him, there being no evidence but that of the Negro girl against him. Nor did the matter come abroad in our community, so kindly did the people act towards him; at least, it circulated but to a limited extent. The Negro girl, however, persisted under punishment that he was the father of the child. The child was afterwards born, and born a mulatto, and she persists in the charge to this day. And while some in the village believe him innocent, others believe him guilty. Now, here are two Negro women living twenty miles apart, without any knowledge of or correspondence with each other, preferring the same charge against the same man and holding to it. Had I known the first charge when Mr. ——— came into our neighborhood, I never would have permitted him to become the inmate of my family without having first assured myself that he was truly an innocent man. And after it came to my knowledge, and before the birth of the mulatto on my own place and the confession of its mother, I had a charitable hope that it might not be true. Nor did I recall this charge to Mr. ———'s remembrance in my letter, for the reason that I did not wish to aggravate his case and go beyond the crime committed in my own household.

When remarking in that letter that "the evidence was amply sufficient to warrant the submission of the case to the Columbus church," I left Mr. ——— to act as he chose in the matter; and he has done what he could not well have left undone: he has submitted the case himself.

I have nothing further to add in reply to your letter. You cannot be more surprised nor grieved than I have been, nor more desirous of seeing Mr. —— cleared—not on technical grounds for want of legal evidence to convict, but upon absolute grounds of innocency, there being no evidence of any kind to convict him. But in my judgment this is impossible. If my servant were a white woman, with the evidence before you, she would carry a prosecution for bastardy against him in any common court of justice. My own belief is settled, which I pronounce with sorrow: that with all the circumstances and evidences before me, he is a guilty man. Nor am I alone in that belief.

I thank you for your Christian letter, and for your kind appreciation of my feelings in so unhappy an affair, and do highly honor the charity and integrity you manifest—charity to protect as far as possible the character of the innocent, and integrity in searching into the matter in order that you may carry out the discipline of the church to the fullest extent necessary without respect of persons, and so preserve the purity and character of Christ's Church, which He has bought with His own Blood, and over which He has set you as rulers. That you may have grace to direct and enable you so to do is the sincere prayer of

Very truly yours,
C. C. Jones.

VI

LT. CHARLES C. JONES, JR., *to* REV. *and* MRS. C. C. JONES[8]

Camp Claghorn, *Saturday,* October 26th, 1861

My dear Father and Mother,

You will see by the date of this letter that I have joined our battery, and am now fairly entered upon the duties of camp life—a change quite marked from the routine of civil and professional duties which have for many years received my undivided attention. I left the city on yesterday morning, and found our entire command in good health and fine spirits.

Our time is fully occupied with the numerous duties which devolve upon us in preparing our battery for active service. What those duties are, no one can know who is not charged with their constant and faithful discharge. There is, I can assure you, a deal of hard labor in the efficient drill of men and horses, and in the careful conduct of all the details which appertain to a mounted battery. The men, however, who compose our company are unusually efficient. They are gentlemen all, and bring to the discharge of the duties incumbent upon them a degree of intelligence, industry, and cheerfulness quite remarkable. I trust that our shores may never know the pollution of the enemy's presence; but if he does come, I sincerely hope that our battery may be detailed to resist his first attempted landing, and to dispute every inch of ground in his contemplated march of desolation. I am beginning to appreciate the practical entertainment of the *Dulce et decorum est pro patria mori.*

Our camp is advantageously located nine miles from Savannah on the Isle of Hope, upon a bluff overshadowed with some of the noble live oaks which impart such dignity to the forests of our coast region. We occupy the site of the old Bulloch house, a few years since passing from the possession of the former owners and becoming by purchase the property of our present worthy and efficient captain. You would be pleased with the appearance of our encampment. Our pure white tents contrast beautifully with the dark, overhanging foliage of these attractive trees, and our burnished battery gleams brightly in the morning sun. Our garrison flag is floating freely in the quick air, and within a stone's throw of the guard tent a bold river moves onward between its low-lying shores toward the far-off sound. Our reveille is answered by no less than three encampments at distances of several miles above and below us along the coast, while the transmissive wave and the evening air carry to them unimpaired our nightly tattoo.

As I write, the campfires are all dead save that which burns brightly still in front of the guard tent, where "the watchers keep their vigils sharp"; and the stillness is unbroken save by the lazy flap of the tent curtains, the soft ripple of the tide as it gently chafes with the shore, and the occasional note of some waking songbird among the overshadowing branches. All else is hushed. Not a sound from the stables. No challenge from the sentinels. They are keeping their posts, however; for every now and then I can detect the clank of the scabbard against the slings as they come to the about. Even the quiet breathing of the captain, whom I can touch with my hand as he lies sleeping behind me on his camp cot, I cannot hear. And I am holding silent converse with you, my dear parents; and my heart is going forth in warmest love towards you and my sweet little daughter. May a kind Providence prove ever near you to bless and keep you from every harm!

George is with me, and attends well to his duties and to my horse Yorick, who I think will make a very fine parade horse. Did you receive my packages, etc., per Savannah, Albany & Gulf Railroad? With much love to you both, my dear father and mother, and many kisses for dear little Mary Ruth, I am, as ever,

Your affectionate son,
Charles C. Jones, Jr.

Direct to me as usual at Savannah.

MRS. MARY JONES *to* LT. CHARLES C. JONES, JR.[8]

Maybank, Saturday, October 26th, 1861

My very dear Son,

This is your third night in camp, and my thoughts and heart have dwelt with you, within those thin cloth coverings wet with the dews and rains and swept by the cold northeasters that have been blowing uninterruptedly since you left us. Your couch perhaps has been the damp earth, and sad fears for your health amid such exposures are rising up before me. Oh, this cruel, cruel war! I am every moment forced to feel and realize it has been so from the commencement, in sympathy with my suffering relatives and country-men; but now it is brought to my own bosom when yielding up our beloved sons.

I feel that you have both acted noble parts in going into active service upon the tented field. You, my son, might have yielded to the solicitations of your fellow citizens in continuing the occupancy of the mayoralty, in the discharge of high and honorable duties, and also in the prosecution of your professional engagements, surrounded by the comforts of home. But it has been your choice to lay these aside and share every hardship and privation with your gallant company, which from its being the most effective arm of service is also the most exposed in the day of battle. I know not one of your men personally, but I pray for them all, from your captain down. I know that the Lord's arm is mighty to protect and save in the day of battle and to make you valiant and victorious. Your brother, too, had every reason to continue his profession, and was exonerated from military duty by the injury in his arm and many considerations.

But it strikes ten o'clock, and I must close. God watch over and bless you this night, and with the light of the coming day grant you the sweet influences and teachings of the Divine Spirit, that you may "Remember the Sabbath Day to keep it holy"!

Monday Morning, October 28th. Yesterday was very dark, damp, and cloudy. Your father worshiped in Sunbury; I remained with my precious charge at home. Your brother from fatigue and exposure was unwell Saturday, but quite recovered and at church.

This is a clear, cool, and I may say brilliant October day—just such an one as thirty years ago was made most memorable in your mother's life when our kind friend Miss Lavender laid a beautiful boy in her arms, and she first felt that new and quenchless fountain of love opened up by her firstborn which will cease only with her existence. Did time permit, I might sketch a pleasant review of these long years, in which the mercy and goodness of God have followed you all your days. . . .

Mr. McDonald expects to leave in a short time. I have closed hurriedly for want of time. Your sweet babe is very bright and well. Colonel Charles Spalding is keeping our coast guarded: seventeen men from the troop at Can't-Help-It, *couriers* at Riceboro, a guard at Harris Neck, etc., etc. It is very inspiriting to know that we have an active officer in command. Father unites with me in best love and good wishes on your birthday. He remembered you especially this morning. Kisses from your little daughter.

Ever, my dear son, your affectionate mother,

Mary Jones.

REV. C. C. JONES *to* MRS. MARY S. MALLARD[t]

Maybank, *Saturday,* October 26th, 1861

My dear Daughter,

The past two weeks have been of unusual interest to your mother and father. On the 5th came your dear "Bubber Dodo" to be mustered into service in the Liberty Independent Troop. His summons was one week too early, but none too soon; for the week he spent at home breaking his fine charger to the use of the sword and to the fire of guns and pistols. Carrie has fitted him out handsomely, comfortably, and amply for six months or even more; and he has provided against dews and rains with waterproof coat, and in uniform on his horse accoutered makes a fine-looking trooper. The change of life will be a great advantage to his health, provided it pleases God to avert sickness in camp from him, to which so many fall victims.

On the 14th he joined the troop in Sunbury and went into camp and took quarters in your Uncle Henry's tent, with Prime from Arcadia for his body servant. The old man is vastly pleased, and very attentive, active, and handy, but in a few days lost a nice new blanket and one of his new working shirts your mother gave him. Stolen, of course—although he was very emphatically warned on that common vice of camps. He felt himself perfectly competent to take care of his own blanket, but in this he was mistaken.

On the 15th Mother and I rode down to Sunbury to see the form of mustering the soldiers into service, but we arrived just too late. We understand the form to have been: Forming the line on horse, armed and equipped, the Confederate officer sent for the purpose read the articles of war and the oath, and dispensed with the form of swearing the officers, and then the men in squads; and calling out their names, said every man who answered to his name would be considered *sworn*. And so the thing was done. The other and regular way would have been better, because more direct, personal, and solemn.

Your brother has been on the go, attending the sick here and there, ever since he has been in camp, and on the 21st was appointed surgeon of the post by Captain Winn, which appointment we hope General Lawton will confirm. It is in Joe's line, adds to his comfort and pay, and relieves him from guard duty. The two upper rooms in Mr. Screven's house he has fitted up for his hospital, and I believe occupies one for his quarters, where he keeps also his surgical instruments and medicines, etc. He expects to make some requisitions on the different retreats for hospital bedding and stores. He will have his department all ready and in good order. Mother gave him a cot and mattress and a large blanket lined with Cobb cloth and a camp stool and some candles, etc., so he is pretty well fitted out. He and your Uncle Henry save their flour and send it to Mother, and she has it turned into nice loaf bread and biscuits for them.

Your dear brother Charlie came on the evening of the 19th. He looks thin—through much labor, care, and sorrow. It is wonderful how he has thus far borne his griefs—and all alone. The lonely nights in the desolated home! I feel deeply for him. We hear no complaints, no murmur. We went to church at Dorchester next day, and his brother came and spent the night with him. We sang together some of our old hymns in the evening, and we wished you and yours had been with us. In the afternoon, after our return from church, I had a long and encouraging conversation with him. I can but indulge the pleasing hope that there is a good work begun in him. . . . He is going into camp; but what are all the temptations and trials that can be gathered together against our poor, weak, depraved souls if God be with us? . . . He was much gratified at the growth and improvement of his dear little baby. The little thing seemed to have an instinctive turning to him. Mother made him a double blanket also for camp and a nice gray flannel shirt after Carrie's pattern of Joe's, and trimmed it with some pieces which dear Ruthie gave her, left over from the sacque she used to wear. He recognized it immediately. He had the mayor's office tendered him twice—the last time by the committee of citizens, who could not agree upon a candidate, with the assurance that if he offered, there would be no opposition. Mr. G. B.

Lamar takes his house and all his furniture (except the silver) and Adeline and Grace. A great relief, and an excellent arrangement. George becomes his body servant in camp. He was to have gone into camp with his company on the 24th (Thursday) at the Isle of Hope, but soon to be encamped near the city. As in the Doctor's case, so in his—I think the change, provided his throat can stand it, will be very beneficial to his health. He needs change and activity.

Our only sons—and both in the army! They have made great personal sacrifices, and upon a principle of duty. Both could without any reflection upon their patriotism have been usefully employed—and for the public—in important stations; but they preferred to share in the privations, labors, and dangers necessary to their country's independence. There is true nobility in their action. They are conscientious in it. I commend them for it. And we can commend them to God for His care and blessing, and hope He will take care of and bless them.

My physical strength is exhausted; otherwise I should endeavor to find some active employment in my country's service. The Revolutionary struggle was not more important than the one in which we are now engaged. The Lord thus far has evidently been on our side. Let us rejoice with trembling, and pray that His goodness may lead us as a nation to greater and more universal repentance. His countenance will not be turned towards us in full favor until the judgment is removed by Him.

Maybank, Springfield, and Woodville assembled at Maxwell on Thursday in honor of Jimmie Buttolph's third birthday. A squad of troopers on a scout dined with us and fired a salute in Jimmie's honor when they left. The day was closed by united prayer for ourselves and all ours.

Tell Little Daughter Grandma put Little Sister yesterday in a big cotton basket, and she lay like little Moses, but did not cry. And Gilbert and Susan held the pole and swung the basket, and Grandpa weighed her, and she weighed *eighteen pounds*. And she was four months old yesterday.

Tried to get some fish to send to you today, but the northeaster continues to blow, and Niger has had poor luck. Mother unites in much love to Robert and yourself, and in many kisses for our dear little granddaughter and son.

Your ever affectionate father,
C. C. Jones.

Grandmother sends some apples *from Tennessee* for Little Daughter. Her Uncle Charlie brought them out. Her ducks are all well and much grown.

Howdy for the servants. Tell Kate I am glad to hear good news of her. She must watch and pray to the Saviour to give her strength to hold on and to hold out to the end.

MRS. MARY S. MALLARD *to* REV. C. C. JONES[r]
Walthourville, Sunday, October 27th, 1861
My dear Father,

Niger arrived about eleven o'clock Saturday night, bringing your valued letter and the fruit from Mother.

Your letter carried me home and told me just what I wanted to know about all the dear ones there, and particularly about my dear brothers. I read with many tears of joy what you wrote in regard to Brother Charlie's conversation with you, and I could scarcely sleep all night for thinking of him and praying that our Heavenly Father would perfect any good work begun in his heart. I wish he could see his way clear to make a public profession before he fairly enters upon his life in camp. . . . I am sure if Mother and yourself feel that both your sons are soldiers of the Cross, you can cheerfully bid them go forth to fight the battles of our country; and I know they will never be wanting in courage. I regret exceedingly that I did not see Brother Charlie when he was in the county, as I fear it will be long before he has an opportunity to come out again. I hoped he would have taken us in his route. As soon as I can, I will see Brother Joe. Mamie is greatly delighted to hear that he is one of "our Confederate soldiers." She seems to think "our Confederate soldiers" ought to be loved and admired by everyone.

The children are both well, though little Mary is very thin. She charged me to give her love to "Danma" and "Danpa" and to kiss her Little Sister and "beg Danpa please not to leave her when she moved to Montevideo, for she wanted to make her coo and laugh." . . .

I am glad to think you will move so soon. We will come and see you as soon as we can. I shall not be able to go much from home for some weeks to come on Tenah's account. Her mother is so easily frightened by sickness that I would not feel satisfied to leave her. She has always been a kind, good nurse to the children.

Do give much love to all at Woodville and Maxwell and to Uncle William. Mr. Mallard and our little ones unite with me in warmest love to dear Mother and yourself, dear Father. Howdy for the servants.

Your affectionate daughter,
Mary S. Mallard.

REV. C. C. JONES *to* LT. CHARLES C. JONES, JR.[8]

Maybank, *Wednesday,* October 30th, 1861

My dear Son,

Your two favors of the 24th and 26th reached us this evening, Robin bringing the first with the articles from the depot excepting the champaign basket of sundries which you mention. Have written to Mr. Quarterman to inquire for it at the depot. A trunk, a box, and dear little Julia's chairs were all that came. . . .

Your ambrotype (as we take it to be) is exceedingly fine. It is a handsome picture and fine likeness, and Mother and I greatly prize it. And our hope is that you may be spared in a kind providence, and your brother also, and all your comrades in arms, the perils of battle; and that your likeness may only remind us of your soldier's life and of what you were, by

142

God's help, prepared to do for your country had you been called upon. Not a ray of light relieves our contest with our malignant enemies. We have nothing before us but self-sacrifice and devotion to a cause which exceeds in character that of our first revolution—and an unshaken trust in the righteousness and goodness of God.

Mother wrote you on your birthday, the 28th. On that day thirty years ago I carried your mother from Mr. King's, where we then lived, in Miss Lavender's practicing gig quietly to the entrance into her yard just after breakfast; and at about half-past 2 P.M. we beheld the face of our firstborn —and firstborn son: an uncommonly large and healthy infant. And when I first looked upon him I was as conscious of the flowing of a new affection through my soul towards him as my son as I would have been of a warm stream flowing over the most sensitive part of my person. And that stream has been flowing towards him ever since, and will continue to do so while my heart continues to beat. . . .

Your dear sister, Robert, and the little ones are quite well; and so is your brother now—but had well-nigh made himself sick last week from too much exertion in his calling. I wish his excellent corps was *better officered.* . . .

By Colonel Spalding's order seventeen men are stationed at *Can't-Help-It,* relieved every four days, and four couriers at the Boro relieved in the same time. And so the active colonel has all the coast in his command under watch.

Your dear little daughter was weighed by her grandmother on the day she was four months old (the 25th) in a big cotton basket, at the bottom of which she lay perfectly quiet and carefully watching all our operations. Gilbert and Susan swung the basket on a short stick, and she weighed *eighteen pounds*—pronounced by all the neighbors and friends an excellent weight for one of her age. She slept the entire night last night and never woke once. Mother sends much love. Be careful and run no risks in breaking your horse.

Your ever affectionate father,
C. C. Jones.

MRS. MARY JONES *to* LT. CHARLES C. JONES, JR.[8]

Maybank, *Wednesday,* October 30th, 1861

My dear Son,

I will look over the sacred contents of the trunk and set a seal upon it for our dear little Mary Ruth. If my life is spared, she shall be taught to love and honor her father and her mother. Did you remember to take the wax doll, etc., from the bureau drawer in the third story? It may be ruined if left there. Mrs. Harriss would doubtless take care of it and send it out, to be preserved for Baby when she is old enough to value it. Do write us as often as you can. Many kisses from your little daughter.

Your affectionate mother,
Mary Jones.

Lt. Charles C. Jones, Jr., *to* Rev. *and* Mrs. C. C. Jones^t
Camp Claghorn, *Monday,* November 4th, 1861

My dear Father and Mother,

I am today favored with your very kind letter of the 30th ult., and am happy to know that all at home are well, and that my dear little daughter weighs so roundly. Eighteen pounds is a capital weight. I sincerely trust that she may continue in the enjoyment of that good health with which a kind Providence has recently so signally blessed her.

We are in daily expectation of active service, and know not at what moment our battery may be put in motion. Our position is a peculiarly central one, and we can within the hour by a forced march advance to the relief of at least three encampments, any one or all of which may be at any moment attacked. This week may and probably will, if we may credit the reports now current, develop important movements upon our Southern coast.

We have in our encampment every moment during the day fully occupied. Reveille at 6 A.M. Stable call at 6:25 A.M. Drill in the manual of the piece from 7 to 8 A.M. Breakfast at 8 A.M. Guard-mounting at 9 A.M. At 9:30 A.M. the battery leaves the park and takes up the line of march for the drill ground, distant from the encampment some three miles, where we spend from three to four hours in active drill, and thence return to camp in time to park the pieces and stable the horses by 2 P.M., when dinner is served. At 3 P.M. fatigue duty, such as making cartridges, fuses, filling shell, etc., etc. At 4 P.M. practice at the target, with solid shot and shell: target located seven hundred yards from our parade on a small island across the river. At 5 P.M. retreat. At 6 P.M. supper. From that hour until 9 P.M. in quarters. At 9 P.M. tattoo. At 9:30 P.M. taps. And so the day passes. On Sabbath all exercises are suspended except reveille in the morning at 6, inspection at 9, and retreat at 5 P.M., with tattoo as usual. We have preaching every Sabbath, and the men attend very generally.

Our camp is beautifully located; and quiet, sobriety, good order, and attention to duty and discipline prevail. Our battery has made remarkable progress in the drill of both men and horses. Yorick bears his training quite well, and is already pretty well used to the drill, to the sword, drum, and the cannon. He is, however, so full of life and spirit that his rider can never remain for a moment off his guard. He threw one of our drivers the other day who was riding him near the drum. In time he will, I think, make a very fine parade horse.

With much love to you both, my dear parents, and many kisses for little Mary Ruth, I am, as ever,

Your affectionate son,
Charles C. Jones, Jr.

George tells me that the champaign basket was not sent. The wax doll, etc., I locked up carefully in my bookcase recess below.

Excuse this paper—perhaps a little too patriotic in its pretensions. It is the fancy of our orderly, a red hot little South Carolina secessionist who has just named a son for me: Charles Jones Askew.

LT. CHARLES C. JONES, JR., *to* REV. *and* MRS. C. C. JONES[g]

Camp Claghorn, *Tuesday,* November 5th, 1861

My dear Father and Mother,

Environed as we are by the exacting engagements of camp duty and daily drill, and removed from the companionship of those we love and from the pleasant influences and the comforts of home, you cannot think how much enhanced is the joy of receiving letters of kind remembrance from those to whom we are bound by the ties of sincerest affection. I fear my letters may prove at times uninteresting, devoid as they often must be of that variety which is the spice equally of life and of epistolary correspondence; but I can at least tell you that my heart is ever turning to you, my dear father and mother, and to my precious little daughter.

The duties of organizing this battery and of drilling our men and horses have devolved entirely upon Captain Claghorn and myself. Besides the engagements thus incumbent, we have been busily employed in manufacturing fuses, filling shell and cartridges, etc., etc. We know not how soon the hour of battle may come, and we desire to be as fully prepared as practicable for the contest.

The boasted armada of Lincoln is now upon our coast, and we know not at what hour, or where, the attempted invasion may begin. Forty-three sail are today reported off Port Royal in sight of Tybee Island. The attack may be made upon our own coast or upon that of South Carolina or upon both. We have an inhuman enemy to meet, and in great force in all probability. The struggle may be desperate, but our trust is unshaken in the justice and the manhood of our cause, and our reliance firm in the outstretched arm of Him who is mighty to save, and who has already in such signal manner, and on so many occasions, covered the heads of our brave soldiers in the day of battle. There can be but little doubt but this fleet is quite perfect in all its appointments—except in men: they are at heart, I believe, in the main cowards, for "conscience doth make cowards of us all." Either that, or they are inhuman fanatics, to be classed with mad dogs and shot accordingly. Doubtless every effort will be made to produce a powerful and startling effect upon our coast, but of the result we may rest satisfied. The victory beyond a question must, with the blessing of a kind Providence surely with us, eventuate in our favor. The enemy can never penetrate into the interior.

The Lincoln government is forced to make this demonstration, and in so doing the full power and energy of their navy will be expended. Failing in their present project, their capital besieged, the navigation of the Potomac stopped, defeated at every point, and shut up at home to the workings of their own leaven of unrighteousness, infidelity, rascality, violated faith, broken credit, lawlessness, and corruption, the entire North must sink even lower in the esteem of the world, and remain of all nations the most miserable—and with no one to pity, because with a blind fanaticism and a blackhearted malice, with their own hands they have removed the pillars of the temples of religion, justice, honor, integrity, and common humanity. They have surely worked out their own destruction, and must perish in the ruins which their own hands have made.

I learn from a gentleman that he has received intelligence from a private and reliable source that our independence is in all probability before this acknowledged by England, France, and Spain.

Commodore Tattnall with a portion of his mosquito fleet had a bloodless brush with the enemy off Port Royal last night. We are almost in hearing of the guns. Our battery is located within supporting distance of three batteries on our coast, either one of which we can reach in an hour by a forced march. Their morning and evening drums are answered by ours. Our orders are to support in the event of an attack.

I was here interrupted by tattoo, and have just learned from a member of our company fresh from the city that the fleet which had concentrated to the number of forty-three off Port Royal has gone to sea again, steering south. Brunswick may be the threatened point. Should such be the case, we will in all probability soon be on the move. No arm of the service is more efficient than a light battery in holding an advancing column in check.

Our practice here with six-pounder guns charged with solid shot, and with twelve-pounder howitzers with shell, has been excellent. Our shells explode beautifully, and we are confident that with half a chance we will be able to render effective service and send destruction into the ranks of our enemies. In our morning drill we fired in battery blank cartridges to practice the men in rapid firing and to accustom our horses to the sound of the cannon. The horses are becoming somewhat accustomed to the discharge. Yorick cannot quite like the sight and sound as yet, but he is manageable. I wish that you could witness our drill. It is imposing, and our proficiency will soon be quite creditable.

I have been for several days suffering from an attack of sore throat, but am glad to say that my throat is better. It was probably induced by the change from close and warm apartments to the airy covering of the canvas. Our men are all well. You have, my dear father and mother, my warmest love. Kiss my sweet little daughter for me. And believe me ever

Your affectionate son,
Charles C. Jones, Jr.

Captain Claghorn, Father, begs that I would convey to you his sincere and respectful regards.

Lt. Charles C. Jones, Jr., *to* Rev. C. C. Jones[t]
Camp Claghorn, *Friday,* November 8th, 1861

My dear Father,

. . . Today has been a gloomy one with us. Each hour fresh advices arrive of our disaster at Port Royal. The enemy's fleet is represented to be in full possession of everything—forts, islands, and harbor. The batteries seemed to produce no impression upon their men-of-war and ships of the line. From our post every gun was heard yesterday. We had expected—and had confidently anticipated—a successful resistance on the part of our batteries. But so it is: we are repulsed, and this will prolong the war and necessitate much heavy land fighting. I presume the enemy will be occupied several days in landing and entrenching. We learn this afternoon that in Savannah preparations are being made immediately to impede the channel of the Savannah River. A crushing responsibility rests upon the heads of those highest in military authority for the present helpless posture of affairs. We confidently anticipated orders to leave our present position for the support of the batteries at Port Royal, but none arrived. I presume, however, it will not be long before we will be on the move.

These reverses must produce their effect upon the public mind, and that effect should be to gird our loins one and all for the contest, with an earnest prayer that the God of Battles would at an early day grant us a triumphant deliverance from the presence of these violators of public and private peace and happiness, despisers of law, justice, integrity, and truth, and scoffers at the great law of the Living God.

The drill and discipline of our men and horses are excellent, and I trust that whenever the opportunity occurs, you will hear a good account from us. We are in hourly expectation of orders for change of post. I write in great haste, but with warmest love to you, my dear father, to dear Mother, and many kisses for my precious little daughter. As ever,

Your affectionate son,
Charles C. Jones, Jr.

LT. CHARLES C. JONES, JR., *to* REV. *and* MRS. C. C. JONES[8]
Camp Claghorn, *Saturday,* November 9th, 1861
My dear Father and Mother,

Three years ago this very night I led my beloved Ruth, a young, beautiful, and loving bride, to the altar. In your presence those sacred vows were taken, the memory of which will live ever with me. As I look back upon that evening and think of the many joys which that union brought, as I remember the loves which were there cemented and the happy days which succeeded, as I cherish the living recollection of the truest loves of my dear Ruth and dwell upon all the hallowed remembrances of her life and affection, and then turn to these recent days of saddest affliction, of present loneliness and sorrow, my eyes fill with tears, and my heart grows weighty with grief. And yet there is sunlight—bright, holy sunlight—in the midst of this gloom. The sorrows are mine only, but the joy is also mine—to know that she, my dearly beloved wife, and our precious little daughter are both far beyond the reach of all evil, fear, change, and harm; that upon their ear will break no rude alarms of war; that for them an eternal home full of peace and joy and holiness has been securely prepared; and that into it they have already entered. It is thus in the midst of this great sorrow, and amid the depressing influences by which we are surrounded, that my heart, while bowed to the dust, blesses God for the precious deaths which they died, and almost rejoices that they have been taken from the present and the evils which seem soon about to overtake us.

We have nothing new today from the scene of our recent reverse, and have as yet no orders for the removal of our battery. General Lee has, I understand, directed that all the guns be removed from the seacoast islands, with a view to planting them at important points on the main. He is represented as severely condemning the policy adopted by our general. You remember the opinion you expressed in reference to those mantraps. Savannah, I fear, is in rather a precarious condition. We are without the munitions of war requisite for a proper resistance in the event of an attack, and the preliminary labor which should have been accomplished has not been commenced. This will necessitate a desperate resistance on the part of the defenders, fighting as we will have to do under disadvantages.

But the enemy must expect every resistance before success. That success may be temporary, but it will never prove abiding. For one I will most cheerfully give my life in defense of our common and beloved home, and in support of the honor, nationality, and principles for which we are contending. I say this not boastfully, but in all earnestness and calmly. And should it be my lot to fall in this struggle, I will die in the legitimate discharge of the most solemn duty which ever devolves upon a free citizen—the obligation resting upon him to make every sacrifice in support of national honor and in the protection of that soil from which he sprang from the infamous pollution of a lawless and inhuman enemy. . . .

General Lee, now in South Carolina, is expected very soon in Savannah. That city is in great commotion—many moving away, and more attempting to send forward articles of value. A storm of indignation is reported against General Lawton. Vessels have been sunk in the Savannah River near Fort Pulaski and in Wall's Cut with a view to impeding the passage of the enemy. Mayor Purse is represented as being quite inefficient. He could not be found last night when his presence was greatly needed. The firing of the fleet upon the Port Royal battery is represented as being perfectly awful. Thirteen-, eleven-, and ten-inch guns were used by them, and they completely enfiladed the fort, almost all the guns having been dismounted so soon as position had been taken by them. No impression was made by the batteries. All the talk you see in the papers about Colonel Stiles's having two horses shot under him is simple nonsense. But more of this anon. Randolph Spalding is represented to have been so drunk that he could not take command of his regiment when ordered to the relief of the Port Royal batteries. As yet we have no orders other than notice to hold ourselves in readiness to march at a moment's warning.

The accompanying rough sketch will give you a general idea of the position of the Port Royal batteries, and show how completely the position taken by the fleet enfiladed the fort. It appears that in constructing the fort they never once contemplated the contingency of the enemy's passing Fort Walker and making the attack from the side and rear. They had anticipated that they would be able to prevent all ingress. The fact was that the navy passed in with perfect ease, and by an enfilading fire soon silenced almost every gun in the fort.

I cannot think Savannah in immediate danger. My impression is that they will securely entrench themselves at Port Royal before advancing.

Do, my dear parents, let me know whenever I can be of assistance to you at any time. You have my warmest love. Kiss my dear little daughter for me. And believe me ever

Your affectionate son,
Charles C. Jones, Jr.

LT. CHARLES C. JONES, JR., *to* REV. C. C. JONES[t]

Camp Claghorn, *Monday,* November 11th, 1861

My dear Father,

Enclosed please find notice for renewal of note in Bank State of Georgia. On the other page I have sent renewal note, which you will please sign and return.

All well, and nothing new today. We are in the midst of trying times, and must look to Him from whom all our help cometh for our deliverance, and use every exertion to repel this iniquitous invasion. You may, I think, expect a good report from our battery when the occasion occurs. With warmest love to self and dear Mother, and many kisses for my dear little daughter, I am, as ever,

Your affectionate son,
Charles C. Jones, Jr.

REV. C. C. JONES *to* LT. CHARLES C. JONES, JR.[g]

Maybank, *Monday,* November 11th, 1861

My dear Son,

Serious events since I last wrote you a week ago! We are to reap the bitter consequences of an imbecile administration of the coast defenses of our state. And to cap the climax, *Pulaski* untenable under a serious attack like that on Hilton Head battery, and the city itself totally at the mercy of the enemy! The best thing now to be done is *to obstruct the channel as in the last war and compel the enemy to come by land,* and we may have a chance. I see nothing before us but a protracted hand-to-hand conflict, and God our hope. The Lord shield your person and life, my dear son! Live close to Him, and lean upon Him.

We are thinking of removing a part of our people up the country—at least for the present. Could you not write your friend Dr. Howard, or any other

149

you have in or about Burke, how many he could take care of or *employ or hire,* so that they might be profitable, and in a safer position; and we can send them up from Arcadia, leaving a part on the plantation.

Unless we can collect twenty or thirty thousand on this side the Savannah and keep the city, our seaboard will be overrun. In Carolina they will need as many more. Georgia can raise speedily thirty thousand men if we can *arm* them. We can pray for *a special interposition of Providence;* without it we shall suffer.

Your dear little daughter, unconscious of the sorrows of life, is in excellent health and full of life. Mother sends much love. We pray for you constantly. Your brother with the troop, now quartered at Riceboro. We leave for Montevideo tomorrow, God willing; your Aunt Susan and family and Uncle William move to Arcadia.

Your ever affectionate father,
C. C. Jones.

Present my very friendly salutations to your excellent captain, and am pleased to be remembered by him.

If the city is to be taken, the banks ought to send their specie away.

LT. CHARLES C. JONES, JR., *to* REV. C. C. JONES[t]
Camp Claghorn, Wednesday, November 13th, 1861

My dear Father,

I am today favored with your kind letter of the 11th inst., and am happy to know that all at home are well. I have this moment written to Dr. Howard and to Neely inquiring how many of our Negroes they can accommodate, and upon what terms. I will probably in a few days hear from them.

We have no advices of any movements on the part of the enemy. General Lee is now in Savannah. So is General Walker.

We learn this afternoon that a vessel has arrived and is safely moored at the wharf at Savannah. Her cargo consists of many thousand Enfield rifles, several rifled cannon, sabers, ammunition, shot and shell, blankets, etc., etc. This cargo comes on account either of the State of Georgia or of the Confederate States. This arrival is most opportune, and looks like a direct interposition of Providence in our behalf. Again and again are we called upon to lift up our hearts in earnest gratitude to the Giver of All Good for His continued and most marked interposition in our behalf. These munitions of war will enable us to prepare a determined—and without doubt a successful —resistance in the event of any attempt on the part of the Lincolnites to penetrate in the interior. I doubt very much if any immediate effort is made to advance, unless the attempt be made upon the city of Savannah or Charleston.

Our battery is in excellent order, and our men are ready to expend their every energy in defense of our homes and of all that we hold dear.

Do, Father, let me know if I can serve you in any way. I am pretty well. My throat has been giving me some trouble, but I hope that it will soon be better. With warmest love to self and dear Mother, and many kisses for my dear little daughter, I am, as ever,

Your affectionate son,
Charles C. Jones, Jr.

The name of the vessel, an ironclad propeller, is the *Fingal*. Edward C. Anderson comes in her. She was cleared for "the Island of Madeira and the west coast of Africa."

REV. C. C. JONES *to* LT. CHARLES C. JONES, JR.[8]

Montevideo, *Thursday*, November 14th, 1861

My dear Son,

Your three welcome letters of the 8th, 9th, and 11th came all together last evening, and were read with great interest by your mother, your brother, and myself. I agree with you that the unexpected success of the enemy in carrying the forts on Port Royal Sound will vastly elate the Northern and Western people and serve to protract the war, and *may* give us much hard and hand-to-hand fighting on land.

I say *may*, for the enterprise of their armada carries two faces. The first, to "repossess and hold" (to use President Lincoln's language in his inaugural) all the forts once belonging to the old United States on the coast of the Confederate States, and such other valuable points on the same which might be conquered; and well fortify and garrison the same for the purpose of commanding our available outlets to the sea, and so rendering the blockade perfect and perpetual; and from which forts and points naval and land forces might be sent to make attacks upon the mainland at their pleasure, and keep the seacoast in a state of uneasiness all the time; while their light draft and heavily armed gunboats would, running between and inland, destroy our coasting trade to the last fishing smack. The second face is to do all this, with the addition of "pouring in" (as the enemy terms it) "an overwhelming land force" of horse, foot, and cannon, and carry our great export cities by storm, inflict summary vengeance upon them, desolate the whole seaboard, liberate the great and oppressed "Union party" of the South, and finally "crush out the rebellion"—and perhaps, if it cannot be done otherwise, "proclaim liberty to the captives" and blot out the remembrance of the people from the earth!

All this sounds mighty, and no doubt our enemies would be glad of one or the other, and many of both projects. But the first is perhaps their more probable purpose for the present. The idea of sending large land forces to operate as armies of subjugation and of conquest on the coast of the Southern states, to be fed and clothed by supplies drawn from distances of from three hundred to a thousand miles—and that by sea—and added also their whole matériel of war; and these armies to quit their supply ships and depots and march into a country unfavorable to the movements of large masses of men, difficult to traverse, in the face of a determined resistance of men fighting for

151

their liberties, their property, their homes and firesides—I think it, to say the least, an experiment which none but infatuated men would try with the hope of any permanent success. The capture of the forts, the capture of some of our principal seaports, the occupation of districts on the mainland, would have no power in bringing about our subjugation. Savannah, the seaboard of Georgia, Charleston, the seaboard of South Carolina—nay, all the coasts of the Old Thirteen, and vast portions of their territory—were all under British power in the Revolution; and we are as well able, by the blessing of God, to meet similar calamities, if need be, as our fathers were. We have nothing to do but, relying upon the righteousness of our cause and upon the aid of God, who has thus far left us not without witness of His favor, gather our forces and meet the enemy in every one of his schemes and do our best to convince him of the fruitlessness of his undertakings.

It is certainly matter of devout thankfulness that we have had time allowed us to collect some force and to make some preparations after so miserable an administration and so much absolute exposure to danger and loss. I never hear the name of our commanding general mentioned but with disapprobation, and all rejoice that General Lee has come—we hope in time to save us, under God. A resignation of General Lawton, if not graceful at the present time, would certainly be altogether agreeable to the great body of our people civil and military. I was happy to learn through Judge Fleming, who came from Savannah yesterday, secondhand through Captain Winn, that Savannah was now deemed safe, and that Pulaski could withstand the combined navy of the Federal states—and hope *it is all true.*

You must embrace the opportunity when it offers of making not only the military but the personal acquaintance of General Lee. You know his reputation in the army: he has checkmated Rosecrans in Western Virginia. And he is Miss Kitty Stiles's great friend. Should he make a progress through these regions I should be happy to know and to receive him at our house.

We moved up from Maybank this week. Reached home last evening, and your brother spent the night with us. He is quite well, but full of practice and very popular with all his patients and with his company. He has been attending our old neighbor Mr. John B. Barnard, who is suffering from a severe attack of chill and fever, but is better, but quite feeble. The weather is so warm, sickness may ensue. No frost of consequence yet.

Robert preached for the troop on last Sunday, and your sister came down with him. All well. By invitation of Captain Winn, who called on me this morning, I hope to conduct the religious exercises of the camp tomorrow, D.V., our day of national fast and prayer by order of our good President. Shall have to give them something extempore.

On the 9th your dear mother, who never forgets you, recalled the day as the anniversary of your marriage with one who proved in every respect a blessing to you and a comfort to us. We cherish her precious memory, and think over and over, with gratitude to God, her last sufferings and triumphant death. My dear son, you have the constant sympathy and prayers of your parents in your great sorrows. . . . We read with emotion your remarks on that hallowed wedding day.

Your little one is becoming more and more interesting. Her mind expanding as well as her body; is getting some more use of her voice, and shows some new tricks; takes an interest in all around her; and has been out all the morning amusing herself with the chickens and the ducks and the pigeons and the pig; has a strong will, but pleasant disposition; and all the people say: "She is a little beauty."

Thank you for the sketch of the position of the Hilton Head battery, Fort Henry, and that of the enemy's fleet in the late engagement. The wonder is that the fort held out against such fearful odds and under such disadvantages of construction and guns so long—near six hours. Had the battery been well constructed and well mounted, the fleet might have spent the whole day and done no great harm. The battery guns were of too short range to do much execution. How much was done we shall never know.

Enclosed is the note for the bank signed, and am obliged to you for sending it. The discount—the bank having funds of mine on deposit—can pay itself.

Will you be kept on the Isle of Hope all the winter as an advanced post, or be quartered in Savannah? Have the batteries on Tybee and Green Island been withdrawn by General Lee? Who commands at Fort Pulaski? And what is his value as an officer in that post so important? We feel much anxiety for our commercial emporium.

Mother sends much love. Is very tired, and as I close is lying on the couch in my study enjoying a deep and quiet slumber. And Susan is downstairs making her usual efforts and noises to direct Little Sister. I hear her little voice.

Your ever affectionate father,
C. C. Jones.

Lt. Charles C. Jones, Jr., *to* Rev. C. C. Jones[8]

Camp Claghorn, *Saturday,* November 16th, 1861

My dear Father,

I am this evening in receipt of your very kind and interesting letter of the 14th inst., and am very happy to know that all at home are well, and that peace and quiet still are exerting their sweet influences there.

A moment since, one of our men returned from Savannah bringing with him an extra, by which it appears that the New York *Herald* claims and reports Savannah and Charleston as both in the actual possession of the Lincolnites. This is news to us, and may possibly be accounted for upon the supposition that the wish is father to the thought.

It is indeed a fortunate circumstance for us that the enemy did not immediately advance with the ferryboats and armed steamers of light draft through Wall's Cut up the Savannah River. Had this been done, the city would have been found almost entirely at the mercy of our hated foes. As it is, time has been afforded for arming Fort Jackson and for concentrating troops. While on parade yesterday we heard the garrison practicing with their guns recently mounted upon the ramparts of Fort Jackson.

My own impression, from present indications, is that the Lincolnites purpose a regular siege with a view to the reduction of Fort Pulaski. Nothing prevents their at once occupying Daufuskie Island; and as you are aware, our forces have been withdrawn from Tybee. Nothing would be easier than for them thus to obtain command of the back river, by means of which predatory bands might work their devastations upon the plantations of the Savannah River. To prevent this, batteries should at once be executed below the city capable of beating back their gunboats, etc. Fort Jackson commands the entrance from Wall's Creek, and when put in proper condition will constitute a most valuable fortification, indispensable for the protection of the city.

Fort Pulaski is one of the strongest fortresses on the line of our coast. It is said to be much more powerful than either Sumter or Moultrie or the Mobile and New Orleans forts. Several guns of heavy caliber have recently been added to its armament. In the event of an attack it ought to prove invincible by almost any force which might be sent against it. The enemy will find a vast difference between open sand batteries and regularly constructed casemates. The object of the Lincolnites will probably be to reduce that fortress by getting into the rear; and we should see to it at once that measures are adopted in advance to prevent this.

I have no doubt but that the enemy will advance very cautiously, and be quite circumspect in any attempt to penetrate into the interior. Unless wholly blinded and given over to believe a lie, one would think that at last the fact must find an acknowledgment even from those fanatics that they are now upon a soil where no Union element can lift its friendly arm of protection and of support, but where every bush and swamp has become a fortress bristling with "masked batteries" (which they so much dread), and every man, woman, and child the cannoneers ready and anxious to apply the portfires.

We cannot cope with them upon the sea, for the simple reason that we have not the means for so doing; but when they leave their boasted armada and attempt to penetrate our shores, then, by the blessing of a just and righteous God, they will find that a people armed in the holy cause of liberty, in such a country as this which we possess, are invincible by any force which they may send against us. They may possess themselves of our seacoast; they may desolate our exposed plantations, and to a certain extent compass their cherished plans of theft and lawlessness; but they can no more consummate their avowed designs of subjugation and of annihilation than can the occasional shadows which flit across the sky extinguish forever the bright beams of the risen sun. The lesson which you educe from the history of our own Revolutionary period is conclusive, and of itself, independently of every other consideration, should afford assurances of success of the most satisfactory character.

We have now some eight hundred men on Skidaway Island, within two miles and a half, as the crow flies, from our camp. That post, commanding as it does one of the approaches to Savannah, is to be strengthened; and a battery is in process of construction which when completed will mount some ten or more guns. The bridge which connects this island with the main, a structure passing over a river more than the quarter of a mile wide, is now held by us. Our battery is posted within supporting distance of the commands at Skidaway, at Thunderbolt, and at Green Island. The battery on Green Island will be held, and is the strongest earthwork on the coast. It is garrisoned by the Savannah Volunteer Guards, one hundred and ninety strong, under command of Captain Screven. Although an open battery, in the angles there are casemates, which it is expected will effectually protect the garrison from shell. In the event that any of these commands are compelled to retire, our battery will be essentially requisite to cover the retreat and to oppose a landing of the enemy.

Fort Pulaski is garrisoned at present by six companies—say five hundred men—under command of Major Olmstead of Savannah, a graduate of the Marietta Military Institute and a young officer who is highly esteemed.

Our battery is in good order. We have now some eighty men. Would be glad to recruit up to one hundred and fifty. Are adding daily to our numbers. Our company has lost more than twenty-five members, who are all now in service bearing commissions in other companies. To such an extent has this obtained that it has become a trite remark that the Chatham Artillery has had to officer most of the other companies.

Enclosed, Father, I send a letter this afternoon received from Dr. Howard. Do you think it necessary to remove the Negroes at present?

The renewal note is at hand, and I will endeavor at an early day next week to go to Savannah and have the matter arranged.

We have preaching every Sabbath, and our men attend very generally. The captain and myself always do so. Grace at every meal, and good order, sobriety, and attention to all duties characterize our command. The captain desires his respectful and kind remembrances. He is a brave, high-toned man, fully imbued with our high and holy cause, and will not be found wanting in the day of trial. He enjoys the reputation of being the best-informed and most accomplished artillerist in the state.

Do, my dear father, accept for yourself and my dear mother my warmest love. Kiss my precious little daughter for me. And believe me ever

Your affectionate son,
Charles C. Jones, Jr.

The orderly reports news from the city to the effect that nineteen of the Lincoln armada started from the North, went down in the recent gale at sea, and have not been heard of.

Will be very happy when occasion occurs to form the acquaintance of General Lee. His appointment is a cause for public rejoicing.

As yet we have no orders; for the present we continue in the occupancy of this post.

Hon. John Johnson *to* Rev. C. C. Jones[t]
Columbus, *Monday,* November 18th, 1861
Reverend and dear Sir,

Some time ago the writer of this and A. G. Redd addressed you relative to certain charges made against ——, a member of the Presbyterian church of this place, to which you replied. At that time the pastor of the church was absent. After his return early in October the matter with the correspondence was submitted to him. The pastor, Redd, and myself had several conversations with each other and with ——, he (——) most positively affirming his innocence all the while.

Desiring to do the accused no harm needlessly, the matter has not been laid before the session, nor has it been made known to anyone beyond the above-named persons. —— from the first declared his willingness to swear to his innocence. He has now done so, and a copy of his statement of denial of the charges upon oath is herewith enclosed.

I, being session clerk, have been requested by the pastor to send you this, with a respectful request that you reply as early as convenient, and that from your extensive experience and observation in church judicature you will please suggest what course should be adopted here by session. Will you become prosecutor, or can the case be so made out that the session of this church can take action upon it?

With due consideration and esteem, I am
Yours, etc.
John Johnson.
[Enclosure]

Charges have been made against me by Rev. C. C. Jones embracing adultery and therewith unchristian conduct. I do hereby solemnly deny the truth of such charges and do pronounce them to be utterly false and unfounded.
[signed] ——.
Sworn to and subscribed before me this 9th day of November 1861.
John Johnson, *Ordinary,*
Muscogee County, Georgia.

VII

Rev. C. C. Jones *to* Lt. Charles C. Jones, Jr.[8]

Montevideo, *Monday,* November 18th, 1861

My dear Son,

I write to say that your brother *or* myself will, God willing, be in Savannah on Wednesday afternoon at the Pulaski House, where we would be glad to meet you if you could ride in and see us, if only for an hour or two. The visit is one purely of business, and we return next day. Your brother thinks the fatigue will be too much for me, and thinks it will be better for him to make the trip, and you may expect to see him more than myself.

Your aunt and family are with us for a few days while fixing up Arcadia. They unite in love to you. . . . Your dear little daughter is quite well, growing daily, and is a pet for everybody. The Lord bless you, my dear son, ever prays

Your affectionate father,
C. C. Jones.

Lt. Charles C. Jones, Jr., *to* Rev. C. C. Jones[8]

Camp Claghorn, *Saturday,* November 23rd, 1861

My dear Father,

Your kind note of the 18th inst. has been duly received. On Wednesday evening after retreat I left camp for Savannah, expecting the pleasure of seeing you and Brother, thinking that you would both come by the Savannah, Albany & Gulf Railroad. About four miles from the city I was accosted in the darkness of the night by someone on horseback who inquired the way to Captain Claghorn's camp. To my surprise and pleasure I at once recognized the voice of the Doctor, who told me that you had not come. We returned to camp, and he spent the night with us. He will tell you of our camp, etc., etc. I have been quite concerned to know how he endured the fatigue of his return journey, following so closely as it did upon his long ride from Riceboro to Savannah.

I regret, my dear father, that we did not enjoy the pleasure of your company also, and was very sorry to hear from Brother that your recent pulpit exercises had given you considerable uneasiness. From this I sincerely trust you have entirely recovered.

The miniature of my dearest Ruth was received from the artist a day or two since, and is as yet in an unfinished condition. Mr. Bounetheau has sent it to me for suggestions. The painting is exquisite, and the picture beautiful; but it lacks the expression of my precious wife, especially about the mouth. Dear little Mary Ruth will never remember the person of her good mother, and I most earnestly desire to secure for her the best likeness that the art of this Confederacy can afford. I deeply regret that in the present instance the artist has failed to embody a correct shadow of the precious original.

We are all anxiety to know how the battle at Pensacola progresses. It commenced yesterday.

I am tonight the only commissioned officer at this post, and in command. Everything is quiet, and all sound asleep except the guard. Our battery progresses finely, and our men are in an excellent state of drill. . . .

With warmest love to you both, and with many kisses for my dear little daughter, I am, as ever,

Your affectionate son,
Charles C. Jones, Jr.

REV. C. C. JONES *to* LT. CHARLES C. JONES, JR.[8]
Montevideo, *Monday,* November 25th, 1861

My dear Son,

Yesterday was the thirty-ninth anniversary of my membership with the church, having united with Midway the fourth Sabbath in November 1822. . . . The congregation of whites and blacks was large, and the day seemed one of interest. Audley had his fine little daughter baptized. We would have wished your dear little Mary Ruth baptized, but thought as you could not be present (neither could her aunts) it ought to be postponed. The dear little thing is quite well and growing, and develops every day. She looks very much like her mother, and reminds us of her daily.

Your brother reached the Boro safely, though he was a little perplexed finding his way out to the Ogeechee road; and when he dismounted, Mr. Barnard's buggy was in waiting to take him out to see him. He took a late tea with us and went on to Mr. Barnard's. He is sent for from all parts of the county, and although kept so much on the go, improves under it. We were happy to hear through him so good accounts of your health and comfort, and of your camp and corps. Your brother's visit to you was very much enjoyed by him.

Look out—if the enemy's gunboats come your way—for Skidaway bridge and the forces on that island. One or two shots will settle the bridge in the river, and neither your battery nor Cumming's horse and foot could stand their broadsides—you having no batteries of any kind on shore, not even such batteries as were put up on the islands and are now to be seen on the Ogeechee road in the outskirts of Savannah!

The supineness and inefficiency of the military commander in Savannah, and *the perfect indifference of the citizens* to the dangers of an attack on the city, amaze every observing man. The attack on Savannah *by water,* the enemy holding Daufuskie and raising the obstructions in the channel in Wall's Cut (is it called?), is the point to be guarded with the greatest care. And it seems nothing is done! Nor is there the first gun mounted on the bluff at either end of the city on the river—positions twenty feet or more above the water which would command the approaches by the river and keep off an attacking force. And nothing is done! The enemy has given full warning, and yet we suffer the city to lie all exposed in this way! It is amazing that no one is awake in the city for its preservation. The cry is: "No danger. No danger. We have forces sufficient to repel any attack." The forces should be a third more, ranging on to twenty thousand men. I confess that I cannot contain my indignation at a condition of things which can be remedied. Our great commercial emporium lies at the mercy of the shot and shell of an enemy.

Send me Mr. Neely's letter so soon as you receive it. . . . Mother sends you much love. And kisses from your sweet baby.

Your ever affectionate father,
C. C. Jones.

Lt. Charles C. Jones, Jr., *to* Rev. C. C. Jones[f]
Camp Claghorn, *Monday,* November 25th, 1861
My dear Father,

Enclosed please find a letter which was this day received from Neely in reply to my inquiries in reference to the removal of the Negroes. Should the necessity arise, I think our Negroes might be accommodated with him and with Dr. Howard. I sincerely trust, however, in the good providence of God, that we may be spared the desolating presence of our enemies.

Nothing new with us. A fire large and bright on Tybee Island (to judge by the eye) last night. All well. With warmest love to dear Mother and yourself, my dear father, and with many kisses for my sweet little daughter, I am, as ever,

Your affectionate son,
Charles C. Jones, Jr.

Lt. Charles C. Jones, Jr., *to* Rev. C. C. Jones[g]
Camp Claghorn, *Wednesday,* November 27th, 1861
My dear Father,

I was yesterday afternoon favored with your kind letter of the 25th inst., and am happy to know that all at home are well.

It would have afforded me the greatest pleasure to have been with you on the past Sabbath, an anniversary filled with such holy memories, and to have had my dear little daughter Mary Ruth baptized. But I found it entirely out of my power to gratify this wish. Captain Claghorn was compelled to absent himself on account of sickness in his family, and the command of this post consequently devolved upon me. Under the circumstances I could not leave. I hope, however, that it may soon be in my power to be with you and my dear little daughter. I am anxious that she should be baptized, and trust that this may be done at the ensuing Communion Sabbath, when I will make every effort to be there. Philo and Vallie are very desirous to be present also.

The plot thickens on our coast. This afternoon twelve vessels are reported off Tybee. The enemy has landed on that island, and it is said a force is upon Wassaw some twelve miles in a direct line east of us. What General Lawton is doing I cannot divine. The Lincolnites with probably not more than seven hundred men landed on Tybee Island last Sabbath afternoon in the face of day, and without the slightest opposition, and have remained there ever since without molestation. The Federal flag flies in sight of Fort Pulaski—and not more than two miles distant. Six thousand men are within less than a half hour of Savannah, ready and desirous of the liberty of attacking these vandals, and yet nothing is done. Five hundred men in the darkness of the night might have driven them in utter consternation into the sea; and there are ten times the number who would have held it a high privilege to have resolved themselves into Spartan bands for the accomplishment of this purpose. But no: General Lawton goes down in a steamboat, takes a look, returns home to a good dinner, and there the matter ends. The enemy meanwhile fortifies and reinforces, and flaunts his flag under our noses—and all forsooth because our general does not think it prudent to attack.

Laocoön tampered idly with the venomous serpent until its powerful folds encircled both him and his sons, confining them in helpless bondage. Nero fiddled while Rome burned. And while these Lincoln troops are thus quietly possessing themselves of our coast, to all appearances there exists a strange indifference or want of action on the part of those who are charged with the conduct of our military affairs. Would that the days of Sumter and Marion were come again! Idle troops are all about us; transportation sufficient can be had at any moment; and yet not the slightest effort is made to repel the invasion! I sincerely sympathize with you in all you have said in your letter in reference to the conduct of our military affairs. . . .

The idea of the Lincolnites appears to be to establish themselves upon those islands which command the mouths of our rivers, and thus to interrupt all commerce. I do not think that they will venture—at least for the present—away from the range of their guns.

Captain Claghorn desires his respectful remembrances. Am happy to know that the Doctor did not suffer from his long ride. Do give warmest love to my dear mother. Kiss my dear little daughter for me. And believe me ever, my dear father,

Your affectionate son,
Charles C. Jones, Jr.

Since writing the above I have learned that the enemy's forces on Tybee

Island are to be attacked tonight, the attack to be conducted by Commodore Tattnall. All success if it be true! It should have been done on last Sabbath night.

REV. C. C. JONES *to* REV. R. Q. MALLARD[t]

Montevideo, *Saturday,* November 30th, 1861

Dear Robert,

If the Doctor can secure a furlough for a few days, we hope to leave in the cars at No. 3 on Monday for Augusta and the General Assembly. We hope to learn if the furlough will be granted this evening. If not, I feel scarcely able to venture alone.

I write now to request you to be at court at Hinesville on Monday the 2nd. A meeting of the citizens of the county then and there present who are not in military service may be called for the purpose of preferring a request to General Lawton that in case of a necessity for the withdrawment of the forces now in the county to any other point on our coast, that he would leave such a military force behind as will be sufficient to keep our colored population under supervision and control, and so prevent anything like an effort on the part of many or few of them to abandon the plantations and escape to the enemy. And also a force sufficient to give assurance and confidence of protection to our many families who are left without their protectors, fathers and sons having gone off to the war; and in case the Negro population is ordered back into the interior, sufficient to insure their going without giving any trouble. These are important considerations; and although they may be known to General Lawton and to General Lee, yet an expression from the citizens directly will not fail to produce some good result. The county can make this request with a good grace, since two-thirds of her voting population are in the ranks.

Take part in the meeting; and I authorize you to sign my name to the action of the meeting, which will no doubt embody the views here expressed. Should I fail in going to Augusta, will try and be at the meeting. Will you let Messrs. J. B. Mallard, W. Q. Baker, J. McCollough, R. Cay, and others know of the contemplated meeting? We must not request that the Liberty Independent Troop be retained in the county, or any other troop or company, but merely request a military force, and let the commanding general appoint what troop or company *he pleases.*

Mother says Daughter must let her know by Niger upon what day she must send for her next week—Tuesday or Wednesday. . . .

Mother unites in love to Daughter and yourself, and many kisses for our dear grandchildren.

Your affectionate father,
C. C. Jones.

LT. CHARLES C. JONES, JR., *to* REV. C. C. JONES[8]

Camp Claghorn, Saturday, November 30th, 1861

My dear Father,

By the enclosed letter, received today, you will observe that I am tendered the command of the Oglethorpe Light Infantry from Savannah, now in service for the war, and forming a component part of the Army of the Potomac under Generals Johnston and Beauregard. Although but a few months in service, this company has already lost two captains, Bartow and Couper, and has suffered severely. You remember their conduct upon the plains of Manassas. The application comes upon me unexpectedly. It is highly flattering, and should be considered.

The inclination of my own mind is to decline. My company will not listen for a moment to my leaving them; and I cannot reconcile it with my own ideas of duty for the sake of name and perhaps some military reputation to desert the soil of my native state in this the hour of her immediate peril. But the question is still open, and the letter unanswered; and I write at this early moment to beg that you and my dear mother would give me your views and wishes in the matter.

Can you make it convenient to let Gilbert meet Val Whitehead and myself at the depot on *Thursday* next, the 5th inst., say at No. 3 (McIntosh Station)? She is most anxious to see dear little Daughter, and I hope to be able to spend the night of that day with you, my dear parents, and with her. Such is the nature of my obligations here that I find it almost impossible to leave the camp even for an hour; but I must if practicable see you on the day named, D.V.

We have now mustered into service and belonging to our battery one hundred and twenty-five men—a splendid command. I very much doubt whether a finer can be found within the limits of the Confederate States. With warmest love to you both, my dearest parents, and many kisses for my precious little daughter, I am, as ever,

Your affectionate son,
Charles C. Jones, Jr.

MRS. MARY JONES *to* LT. CHARLES C. JONES, JR.[8]

Montevideo, Tuesday, December 3rd, 1861

My dear Son,

Several weeks have passed since I have had leisure to write you a line. Our semi-annual migration brings many additional cares, whose weight I find increases with my own increasing years—to say nothing of the infirmities which must necessarily cluster around advancing age. I can only say that you are constantly in my thoughts and in my poor prayers.

I know that you are now every moment exposed to the attack of our perfidious and merciless enemy; but your sword will be drawn in a righteous cause, and I fervently implore my God and Redeemer to protect and save you in the day of battle, and to encourage your heart and the hearts of your commander and of all your noble company, and to strengthen your arms for the conflict, that in your full measure you may be enabled to repel the infidel invaders who are now at our own doors with their work of ruin and destruction. Their intentions are now openly declared, and nothing but Omnipotent Power will keep them from making this not only a civil but a servile war.

Savannah is still said to be in a defenseless condition! Not a gun on the water approaches! Of course I know nothing about the matter, saving that the *mistakes* of our commanding general have now to be rectified in hot haste at the last moment, and that his name is never mentioned with either respect or confidence as a military leader. Why in such a state of public sentiment and public peril is he not at once superseded and someone of judgment, ability, and tried valor placed in his stead? When General Jackson arrives, will he rank General Lawton?

Your father and brother left yesterday for Augusta—both commissioners to our first General Assembly of the Presbyterian Church in the Confederate States. The meeting will be one of vital interest to our church, and I am glad they are both members. They may not remain longer than Saturday, as Joe's furlough will then be out.

I sent you by them, care of Messrs. Claghorn & Cunningham, a light little mattress for your camp bed, and a pillow. And the mattress I had made long enough to double at the end, thus forming a pillow. I am sorry to send it made of such coarse materials, but I had nothing better in the house, and hope it will add to your comfort.

I was very happy to learn through your brother how pleasantly you were associated. I hope, my dear son, you find time to read your Bible and commune with your God and Saviour. . . .

Your dear little daughter improves daily. She is the light of our dwelling. Has cut one little tooth without trouble, saving a little restlessness for two nights. Is very bright and playful, delighting herself in the cats and dogs and poultry. Tomorrow, D.V., I expect to send for your sister and the children, to be with me in your father's absence. Little Mary calls the baby "Little Sister," and so do Charlie and Jimmie. They are all in ecstasies with her when they come, and she enjoys seeing them. She sends here kisses for her dear papa. Susan and all the servants send many howdies to you and to George. I write in haste for the mail. God bless and save you, my dear son!

Ever your affectionate mother,
Mary Jones.

Mrs. Mary Jones *to* Lt. Charles C. Jones, Jr.[8]

Montevideo, *Tuesday,* December 3rd, 1861

My dear Son,

Your letter of the 30th November was not received until today. I wrote you this morning before its reception; and failing to reach the mail in time, my letter was handed to Mr. S. S. Barnard, who promised to see that you received it in Savannah.

I am rejoiced to think you will be with us, *D.V.*, on Thursday, accompanied by our friend Val. The carriage will await your arrival at No. 3, and I shall expect you to dinner. It will ever afford me great satisfaction to have the relatives of our beloved daughter visit us and take an interest in our precious little babe, and I hope they will recognize as we do her striking resemblance to her sainted mother. At times it is so marked I wish that I could pick her up and place her with her sweet expression before the artist now painting her likeness.

Your unanimous election by the officers and men of the Oglethorpe Light Infantry, now (it may almost be said) upon the battlefield in Virginia, is indeed a compliment to be valued. As their captain you would doubtless fill a post of distinction much more in the line of military promotion than the one you now occupy. But that, I conceive, would be the only advantage. Your usefulness I do not think would be increased, for I believe you are now occupying one of the most important positions in the most effective arm of service on our coast. It seems to me you are now especially defending your native soil, your own home and servants, your infant daughter, your father, your mother, the graves of your loved ones, the temples where we long have worshiped God. The strong ties which bind you to your present company I know you fully appreciate. I hope that I would not throw even a shadow between you and any post of duty which you may be called in God's providence to occupy, but I must say a change like the present one would grieve me. May the Lord direct you, my dear child, by the unerring influences of His Divine Spirit in this and every other point of duty!

I must close now, as I wish to write your father tonight.

Ever your affectionate mother,
Mary Jones.

MRS. MARY JONES *to* REV. C. C. JONES[t]

Montevideo, *Tuesday*, December 3rd, 1861

My dear Husband,

I trust our dear son and yourself had a comfortable journey to Augusta, although I could not but fear that you must have encountered the thunderstorm that seemed to be raging last evening in the northwest. Soon after Gilbert's arrival the rain fell in torrents with us, and all today it has been very cold and cloudy. . . .

Tomorrow I expect to send, D.V., for Daughter and the children; and by a letter received by the mail our dear Charles and Miss Val Whitehead will be with us on Thursday. He did not know of your absence; says he can stay but one night. Enclosed he sent the letter of a committee from the Oglethorpe Light Infantry, now in camp near Centreville, Virginia, stating his unanimous election by officers and men to their captaincy, and urging his acceptance. He wrote for our views. In your absence I could only say what I thought and felt, and told him I did not think it his duty to leave his present post, where he was defending his native soil, his home and servants, his infant daughter, his father and mother, the graves of his loved ones, and the temples where we long have worshiped God—all now invaded by the merciless enemy at our doors.

I hope you have found our dear Carrie and precious little grandson well; and if she thinks it safe, I hope she will accompany you home. I am sure it would greatly increase our pleasure to have her with us.

The weather has become quite cold, and reminds me that our servants are yet unprovided with Negro clothing. Do see about the cloth. And if to be had, bring a pair of light leather shoes (No. 6) for Sue, Flora, and Peggy, and Kate (No. 7), a pair for Jack (a little smaller than for Tom), and a thin pair for Elsie (you can judge of her size by Fanny). *Patience* wears the *largest* woman's size. I would be glad to get for the house servants at least.

I am glad you got off on Monday morning, for that evening Captain Winn received orders not to give a furlough beyond thirty-six hours. . . . I must now close, as it is late. Hoping that the divine blessing will rest upon our first assembly convened in the Confederate States. Best love to Carrie and Joe. Kisses for the dear boy. Respects to Dr. and Mrs. Davis and Julia.

Ever your affectionate wife,
Mary Jones.

MRS. MARY JONES *to* REV. C. C. JONES[t]
Montevideo, *Wednesday,* December 4th, 1861
My dear Mr. Jones,

I wrote you last night, and now at Robert's desire to say if our son Joe must return on Saturday that you must remain longer, and he will come up on Monday next and accompany you and take care of you on your return home. He appears very anxious to attend our first assembly, and will gladly come and help you back. He begs that you will write without fail so as to inform him by Saturday. Direct to Riceboro: he and Daughter and the children are with me, and all well. Tomorrow, D.V., we send for Charles.

It is very late, and I must close, as I have a little headache. Our united love to Carrie and Joe, and kisses for the dear baby. It is extremely cold tonight; hope you will not suffer from its effects. I trust the divine blessing will rest upon all the acts of our first General Assembly.

Ever your affectionate wife,
Mary Jones.

REV. C. C. JONES *to* MRS. MARY JONES[t]
Augusta, *Thursday,* December 5th, 1861
My dear Wife,

Through a kind Providence we reached this city on Tuesday at 5 P.M., having been detained twelve hours by the throwing of the cars off the track sixty miles from Savannah, which Joe will explain to you. No one was injured save a scratch or two upon the baggage master. I refer you to him to describe to you also the case of the sick soldiers who came along with us. We took Carrie upon an agreeable surprise, and found her and little Stanhope in the best of health and spirits. The little fellow is much grown, and is a very fine and interesting and sensible child.

The assembly is more numerously attended than I anticipated. Called to order Wednesday the 4th by Dr. McFarland of Virginia. Dr. B. M. Palmer of New Orleans preached the opening sermon, according to request of the convention last summer, and was elected our moderator. We were in session today some four hours. Business is advancing. Am chairman of the Committee on Domestic Missions. Report on next Tuesday. Gives me opportunity to open the great subject of the religious instruction of the Negroes before the assembly. Do not see how I can return before I fulfill this duty, which is an important one.

And as I am up here, it seemed a good opportunity for me to look at the places in Burke that might be occupied in case of necessity, and learn how a portion of our people might be disposed of favorably. Our kind friend Mr. Gideon Dowse says he thinks he can aid us, and will take me to see several advantageous locations, and says he will do all in his power to help us. I think it may be well to embrace his kind offer, which may keep me a few days longer; for there is no telling what our enemies may venture upon. . . .

Will you please tell Cato to start the gin on Monday and handle the cotton for the bag with three or four of the best motors (no more). If Niger wants any buckskin for the bands, you will find it in my black square trunk in the study, and have a strip cut off for him. The dark calico for Susan and the homespun for Martha cannot be bought for less than twenty-five cents per yard. Shall I give that? Please write me by Monday's mail, and your letter will reach here on Tuesday.

Give much love to my dear daughter and Robert, and kiss Little Daughter and Charlie and Little Sister for Grandfather. Howdy for the servants. I write tonight, as tomorrow we may not have the time. I shall be thankful to return home. The days of activity in public assemblies are passing away to me; and after a man becomes too feeble for much locomotion and labor, he had better stand out of the way and let others encounter the labor. Love to Sister and all at Arcadia. . . . I remain, my dear wife,

Your ever affectionate husband,
C. C. Jones.

Rev. C. C. Jones *to* Lt. Charles C. Jones, Jr.[8]

Augusta, *Friday,* December 6th, 1861

My dear Son,

Judge Law informed me of your election to the command of the

Oglethorpe Light Infantry on Monday in the cars as we came down to Savannah.

My impression is that Providence has indicated your duty. Your own state is threatened with invasion, and we know not at what moment it will be upon us. You are in a responsible command in the oldest and most respectable artillery company in the state, and perhaps inferior to none in the Confederacy. Your company is already in position for the enemy, and its efficiency in action depends much upon your continuance, and you may serve your country as ably here as in Virginia.

Besides, the climate of Virginia would not be as well suited to your constitution. You are well aware of the difficulties which you experience with your throat even in our own mild and open climate—the best climate perhaps in the world for a winter campaign. And if you should be seriously ill, you will be at home with your own relatives and friends.

If you wish to be in action, there is as great a prospect of having a chance here as in Virginia. It is not military promotion that you would seek in going, for you have had that offered to you abundantly at home. And under all the circumstances I think that your allegiance is due to your own state as a battleground. We cannot afford to lose officers at the present time.

These are my impressions of the call made upon you, and I trust that you may be divinely directed in your decision. The object in life is not to glorify ourselves but to be useful to our fellow men in the fear and love of God; and I think that you are in as useful a position where you are as you would be at Manassas.

Carrie and Joseph unite with me in best love. You see your brother has been my scribe.

Your affectionate father,
C. C. Jones.

Lt. Charles C. Jones, Jr., *to* Rev. C. C. Jones[g]

Camp Claghorn, *Saturday,* December 7th, 1861

My dear Father,

I am this evening favored with your kind letter of the 6th inst., and fully coincide with you in the views therein expressed as to the propriety of my accepting the command of the Oglethorpe Light Infantry, now in Virginia, which has been unanimously tendered to me. Immediately upon the receipt of a communication from that corps expressive of their wishes I wrote you upon the subject, and am happy to find that my own sense of duty agrees with that expressed by you. My own company, hearing of the application, immediately, without my knowledge, held a meeting and passed a series of most complimentary resolutions entreating me not to sever the relationship which exists between us. Those resolutions, as well as all the correspondence in the premises, I will be happy to lay before you at some early day, when I can fully explain the reasons which induce me to remain in the position which I now occupy.

Last Thursday night I had the pleasure of spending at Montevideo with dear Mother and my precious little daughter. Sister and Robert and the little ones and Val Whitehead were there also. I was much disappointed in not seeing you also, and was not aware that you had gone to Augusta until I reached Station No. 3, Savannah, Albany & Gulf Railroad.

I trust, my dear father, that you may find it convenient to visit our camp on your way home. It is only nine miles from Savannah, and a delightful shell road connects it with that place. We will be most happy to welcome you here, and to show you everything connected with our battery. I think you might spend a day with comfort and pleasure. If you did not return from Augusta on Saturday with Brother, Robert intends coming up to Augusta and accompanying you home. . . . Do let me know when you will be in Savannah, and whether you cannot visit our camp. Our parade ground is some five miles from the city, and directly on the shell road leading to camp. We are there almost every morning from half-past 10 A.M. to 1 P.M.

With warmest love to you, my dear father, and kindest remembrances for the Doctor, Sister Carrie, and the little one, I am, as ever,

Your affectionate son,
Charles C. Jones, Jr.

LT. CHARLES C. JONES, JR., *to* MRS. MARY JONES[8]
Camp Claghorn, *Saturday,* December 7th, 1861

My dear Mother,

I arrived in camp last night about ten o'clock after my short but very pleasant visit to you. For the valuable basket the officers' mess is under many obligations, and Captain Claghorn begs that I will present his especial acknowledgments for your very kind remembrance of him. He begs that you will favor him with the receipt for preparing the Russian sauce.

In consequence of the loss of our mailbag, neither of your kind letters have been received, and the letter of the committee of the Oglethorpe Light Infantry tendering me the captaincy of that corps has been lost.

Received a letter from Father this afternoon in which he fully coincides in the views expressed by you, and acted upon by me, with regard to an acceptance of that command. My letter of acknowledgment and declination has already been written and sent forward.

I trust that Father on his way home may be able to visit our camp. We will be most happy to see him, and I think that he will find somewhat to interest him. Our men are all pretty well. Do remember me affectionately to Sister, Val, Robert. Kiss my precious little daughter and Sister's little ones for me. And believe me ever, with warmest love, my dear mother,

Your ever affectionate son,
Charles C. Jones, Jr.

REV. C. C. JONES *to* MRS. MARY JONES[t]

Augusta, *Monday,* December 9th, 1861

My dear Wife,

Our dear son left us on Friday afternoon, and it depressed me a great deal to part with him; and I could fully realize the social and other sacrifices he has made for the service of his country. Poor Carrie came back from the depot, where she parted with him, with weeping eyes, and has been about her family duties with her usual cheerfulness since, but feels his absence greatly. Mrs. Cuthbert is staying with her, which is a great relief to her loneliness. Stanhope is a fine, good-natured, lively little fellow, and has got quite acquainted with me. Sits in my lap, but never long, for he is in perpetual motion.

Our assembly has some ninety-three commissioners, and has come into existence full grown, and goes on in its business like an ancient body. We have an excellent representation for talent, especially in the legal line, having several judges of distinction. Dr. Palmer delivered an excellent opening sermon and was elected moderator, which office he discharges with ability and dignity. The debates on various questions have been interesting, and harmony has prevailed throughout. Dr. Thornwell is the author of the assembly's "Address to All the Churches of Christ," which you will read with interest, for it is a paper upon which he has bestowed much labor. I am chairman of the standing Committee on Domestic Missions, and tomorrow we report to the assembly, and propose to have a meeting in the evening to bring forward the colored field for missionary and pastoral labor. And the committee have laid the duty of an address on that subject upon the chairman before the assembly, and, God willing, I shall endeavor to speak. Instead of boards, as under the old General Assembly, our assembly will organize *committees;* and this morning was spent mainly in discussing the mode of organization: to be resumed tomorrow. I took part in the debate today for the first time, having nothing to call me up before.

Have seen many brethren—old acquaintances—who appear as glad to see me as I am to see them. . . . *Mrs.* and *Miss* Eve called to see me on Friday afternoon, and then again on *Sunday* evening, as I was not in at their first call. There is something special in this. . . . Yesterday all the pulpits in town were filled by our ministers. Dr. Palmer preached in the Presbyterian church to an overflowing congregation, but not as ably as I have heard him. . . . I have not been out to preaching at night, as the walk is too much for me; and we are tonight missing a meeting on foreign missions which no doubt will be most interesting. An Indian (full-blooded) from the Choctaws speaks, and I believe he is a minister or exhorter. All the Indian missions are under our care now.

The weather has been mild for two days. The first few days were cold; and suffering from cold at night, Carrie advised me to sleep between blankets, which I did; and have continued to do so, to my great comfort; and consider it a discovery of no mean value to an invalid. It has been an entire relief from all chilly sensations.

Will try and fill your order for shoes if possible, but they are very dear: $2.50 for the commonest kind, and money quite scarce. The express charged $2.50 for the coop of poultry, and $1.00 for your *little* box of sundries for Carrie. War prices!

Hope to see Robert tomorrow. Carrie unites in much love to you and Daughter, and kisses for my dear little grandchildren. I told Mrs. Cuthbert and Carrie about little Mary Ruth's saying her prayers, which interested them very much. Love to my dear son. His family all well, and send much love. Have written Charles about his election to the captaincy of the Oglethorpe Light Infantry. Howdy for all the servants. The Lord bless and keep you, my dear wife!

Your ever affectionate husband,
C. C. Jones.

REV. R. Q. MALLARD *to* MRS. MARY S. MALLARD[t]
Augusta, Wednesday, December 11th, 1861

My darling Wife,

Through the favor of a kind Providence I arrived in this city in due time and found all our friends well.

As you might have anticipated, I was very cordially welcomed by Sister Carrie; and I believe Father was very much pleased not only to see me but to have my assistance. I arrived too late to assist him in his writing, his report having already been prepared, Mrs. Cuthbert aiding him with her pen. But I have had the pleasure of lending him a helping hand in our walks to the church. Dr. Davis frequently sends his carriage for him, but this is not always convenient at the hour needed. But I do not think the walk at a deliberate speed and with my arm to aid him seems to injure him.

He was looking rather badly last evening—the effect of a long and in some respects exciting morning session; but last night's exercises seem to have refreshed him greatly. He was by a vote of the assembly requested to address the body on one suggestion of the report of the Committee on Domestic Missions touching the religious instruction of the Negroes. His address (one hour long) was simple in language, interesting in the facts related, and powerful in its feeling appeals. It was listened to throughout with profound attention; and the remarks of Dr. McNeill Turner and Dr. Lyon expressive of their gratification and the profit received were no doubt an echo of the feelings of the whole assembly. God grant that the good communicated to my soul and stimulus imparted to my ministry may prove permanent! You may be sure that it is highly gratifying to me to observe the marked and respectful attention with which the assembly listens to him on all occasions.

The assembly is a noble one. All the presbyteries of the South excepting those of Missouri, Kentucky, and Maryland are fully represented. The number of delegates present is ninety-one. In the delegation from the eldership, which is a large one, there is quite an array of judicial talent and learning. There are some distinguished ministers in attendance as visitors. Drs. Howe and Axson are here.

I am enjoying myself very much, and only wish that my beloved Mary was here to participate in the pleasure and profit of an attendance upon the General Assembly. If it had not been for the trouble which our children would have occasioned Mother, I would have insisted more upon your coming up with me. Many inquiries after you have been made by friends. I have had the great pleasure of meeting with Brothers McAllister, Porter, Harris, and Boggs—all fellow seminarians.

Today we are to dine on The Hill at Dr. Davis'. Father has just declined a pressing invitation from Mrs. William Eve to dine with her today. She is *very polite* to *him,* I hear.

Father unites with me in much love to yourself and Mother, and in many kisses for the darling little ones, in which Sister Carrie would join if she were present. Providence permitting, I will give you due notice of my future arrangements. I will probably stay until the close (I mean if the Yankees do not forbid it), and will accompany Father to Burke County if he goes. Would give much for a warm kiss from your sweet lips this morning. God bless you!

Your husband,
R. Q. Mallard.

Rev. C. C. Jones *to* Mrs. Mary Jones^r

Augusta, *Wednesday,* December 11th, 1861

My dear Wife,

Robert arrived safely on Tuesday morning to breakfast, bringing the pleasing intelligence that you were all well. The attendance upon the assembly for four or five hours at a sitting, and committee business in addition, and walking generally to the church, has been fatiguing.

By the invitation of the assembly I delivered an address on the religious instruction of the Negroes before that body and such citizens as attended last evening in the Presbyterian church; and although there were but two or three hours to prepare it in, it was well received. And the assembly this morning requested me by resolution to prepare and publish it as delivered before them, and appointed me as chairman to prepare a pastoral address to the churches on the same subject, to be presented at the next assembly. The first I assented to; but on account of health and uncertainty of being at the next assembly, the second was respectfully declined.

The business of the assembly has been conducted with harmony, but slowly, and there will be no adjournment before next week; and I do not feel that I can remain away from home so long at the present time, and under the peculiar circumstances of our country. So Robert and I purpose to leave here, God willing, on Friday, remain over Sabbath in Burke County, and take the cars on Monday for Savannah. Charles begs that I will pay him a visit at his camp, and if we can, will do so for a day and then turn our faces homeward.

Should we come out on a mail day, will take the stage to the Boro, and if not, will go on to Walthourville and get Robert's buggy and come down. So you need not send for me to the station, as I can appoint no day.

We dined with Dr. and Mrs. Davis today. Carrie went with us. Mrs. Smith sends her affectionate regards to you particularly and to Daughter. Mr. and Mrs. and Miss Davis also. A pleasant visit. . . . *Mrs. Eve* invited me to dine with her today and meet Mrs. Colonel Cumming, but the engagement at Dr. Davis' prevented. Have returned no calls and paid no visits and accepted no invitations but this one. . . . The weather has been remarkably mild and good, but is changing colder this evening.

We have no news in the papers different from what you have read in the Savannah papers. There is some appearance of returning reason in our enemies. How far it will reach to a peaceful conclusion of difficulties remains to be seen.

A pretty full report of the proceedings of the assembly you will find in *The Southern Presbyterian.* Please keep the numbers for me.

Mrs. Cuthbert, Carrie, and Robert are sitting around me—Mrs. Cuthbert hemming pocket handkerchiefs, Carrie knitting, and Robert giving an account of the meeting of the assembly this evening, from which he has just come in (10 P.M.). And each of them severally and particularly send a great deal of love to you and to Daughter and to the Doctor, and kisses for the dear little ones, in which I join. . . . I am anxious to be with you. Dreamed of you last night. I esteemed the address before the assembly last evening as one of the special occasions granted me of doing good, and hope God will own and bless it. Howdy for the servants. I remain, my dear wife,

Your ever affectionate husband,
C. C. Jones.

Mrs. Caroline S. Jones *to* Mrs. Mary Jones^t

Augusta, *Tuesday,* December 17th, 1861*

My dearest Mother,

If I did not know that you were "the dearest, kindest, and most lenient" of mothers, I should begin my letter with some fear that you would decline reading it when it reaches you and entirely disown me as a correspondent. I have before me a long, delightful letter you wrote me soon after Joe went away, which stirred my heart so at the time of its reception that I did not think a week would go by without my answering it. Yet these many weeks have passed, and I am just now writing! But, dear Mother, I have been in such a vicissitude of *busy-ness* that seemed hardly to leave me time to write, and sadness that quite took away from me the power of writing, that I really think I may plead some excuse.

I hope Joe gave you all my messages of love and thanks for the delightful box you sent me. There was not a thing in it that was not delightful. I do assure you I never received anything more acceptable to *me,* or that met with such unqualified satisfaction from all who shared my good things. . . .

I hope that this evening Father is comfortably seated at home recounting all the events of his absence. . . . I know well how glad he is to be at home. We all enjoyed his visit to a degree I fear he did not himself. But I hope at all events he will not feel any disadvantage from it. All his friends seemed to have taken so much pleasure in his presence at our first assembly that he ought to feel repaid for all the trouble and fatigue. My only regret was that you and Mary were not with us. I am sure you would have enjoyed it; and as to me, I should have been so delighted I would have gone in the strength of it for many a day. It was very grievous to me to see them going away without me. I had fixed all my hopes on going down under Mr. Mallard's care, but I suppose I must bear it as one more of the many trials of this sad winter.

Last night the assembly was dismissed. Mother had been spending the day with me, and at night Father came down for her, and we all went to the church to be present at the evening services. After reading the minutes of the day there were devotional services which were very interesting. Poor old Dr. McFarland, who had heard that day of the serious illness of two sons belonging to the army, offered a very affecting prayer for the country and prayed most earnestly for peace. After the dismission it was very interesting to witness the leave-takings.

Yesterday was the baby's birthday. I tried to persuade myself that he was brighter and better and *older* than he had ever been before, but I am obliged to confess he did not distinguish himself in any way whatever. He persisted in crawling and making himself just as dirty as he possibly could, was as gay as a lark, ate a great deal, and was very sweet, but no more so than usual. I am trying to teach him to say his prayers, but he is such a perfect little fidget I find it hard to hold his attention. I took a kiss from him to send his dear grandmother, meaning to have written yesterday, but was prevented, so send it now.

Dear Mother, I wish that instead of writing you this poor little letter I were talking with you face to face. I am sure I could make myself much more interesting. At least I may say so, with this forlorn prospect of never having an opportunity of proving the difference to you! Do give a great deal of love to Father. Tell him his departure was so sudden at the last that to this moment I do not know whether he made his visit to Mrs. Eve or whether I am to do it for him along with the others. Take a great deal of love for yourself, and many kisses from Baby and me. God bless you, dear Mother.

Most affectionately your daughter,
Carrie.

Lt. Charles C. Jones, Jr., *to* Mrs. Mary Jones[g]
Camp Claghorn, *Wednesday,* December 18th, 1861
My very dear Mother,

I have heard for many days neither from yourself nor Father. I trust, however, that all at home are well.

From the report of the proceedings of the General Assembly I observe that many matters of the utmost importance are claiming and have already received the attention of that body. Dr. Palmer's opening sermon, as reported in *The Southern Presbyterian,* I read last Sabbath with great interest. I observe that Father is one of a committee to prepare a report declaring to the world the causes which induced the present separation of the Presbyterian Church of the Confederate States from that of the United States. The report—or circular, as it might properly be termed—will, I doubt not, be a very able paper, and we will anxiously await its coming. Its effect upon all candid minds must be imposing, and in the history of the church it will be regarded as a declaration of independence.

I still hope that we will have the pleasure of a visit from Father at this camp on his way home. Several days since, I addressed a letter to him at Augusta begging this favor. The ride from Savannah will not be fatiguing to him; and he will, I trust, find the visit agreeable in more respects than one.

How is my precious little daughter? Many kisses for her.

A strange inactivity seems to exist on the part of the enemy. One is at a loss to conjecture the plans of our threatened invaders—if indeed any they have. It does seem to me that God has given them over to blindness and madness. Like Ephraim, they are joined to their idols of fanaticism, of infidelity, of lawlessness; and the God of Nations has let them alone to work out their own destruction. The expenditures on the part of the Federalists are said now daily to reach the enormous sum of two million dollars, and yet they are accomplishing literally nothing—defeated in every engagement. The prospects of the United States—political, social, moral, and religious —are of all most miserable.

I rejoice to see that the public voice of England, as reported in the morning's papers, is lifted against the recent outrage offered to their national flag in the matter of the capture of Messrs. Mason and Slidell. If the government sympathizes with the popular feeling, the Yankee government will soon find ample cause for defeat or dire humiliation in the eyes of the world.

We are all pretty well. A heavy rain is greatly needed. With warmest love, I am, as ever, my dear mother,

Your affectionate son,
Charles C. Jones, Jr.

REV. C. C. JONES *to* LT. CHARLES C. JONES, JR.[8]
Montevideo, *Friday,* December 20th, 1861

My dear Son,

I was happy to receive your letter in Augusta and to learn your decision in respect to the Oglethorpe Light Infantry election. I think you reasoned correctly in declining it.

Our meeting of our new General Assembly, independent of the old, was full, every presbytery in the Confederate States being represented (and also from the Indian Territory) except Missouri, from which state in its present agitated condition we looked for none. . . . The occasion was one of deep interest to all the commissioners. It marked an era in our ecclesiastical history, and we were laying foundations which, by God's blessing, we hoped would endure for ages, and prove a blessing to our country and to the world. The address to the churches, of which you speak in your letter to your mother, was drawn up by Dr. Thornwell, and approved by the committee of which he was chairman, and adopted by the assembly; and I think you will be pleased with it, as it is an excellent paper. . . . By request of the assembly I delivered an address before that body, the Tuesday evening after it commenced its sessions, on the religious instruction of the Negroes—one of the rare opportunities granted me of doing good. And although there were but two or three hours to arrange it in my mind, I never spoke with more comfort to myself nor with more acceptance to others. And the assembly requested me afterwards to reduce it to writing and publish it, which I will endeavor to do if I can recall it properly.

The whole meeting was a refreshment. Saw many brethren not seen for years, renewed old friendships, and formed new acquaintances; and indeed I never was received and treated by my brethren with more respect and consideration. But daily walks to the assembly and long sittings began to weary the weak tabernacle; and as Robert, who kindly came up in good part to see me safe home (your brother having returned the week he came up), was obliged to be in Liberty at the division of his father's estate on Tuesday the 17th; and wishing to spend a day in Burke with Mr. Gideon Dowse to look at a place there and make inquiries in view of a removal of our people if it should be necessary, we left Carrie's on Friday (4 P.M.), spent Saturday with Mr. Dowse and his excellent lady and daughters. Sabbath Robert preached in Waynesboro, and in the evening I preached to Mr. Dowse's people. Monday we dined at Mrs. Harlow's, one of the most pleasant old ladies we have met with in a long time. Took the cars at 5½ P.M.; reached Savannah 11½. Night at the Pulaski, and home by 2 P.M. next day, finding all, through God's great mercy, well and doing well.

And no part of my purpose in leaving home was unaccomplished but a visit to my dear son in camp on the Isle of Hope, which I had set my heart upon, and was compelled to forgo on account of my fatigued state, and defer for a little time. And I will now say that your Uncle William, who was with us last night, says he will go with me to pay you a visit; and our purpose, God willing, is to do so after Christmas, taking the buggy and driving from home directly to your camp, which will be the most expeditious and agreeable mode of reaching you—of which you shall have due notice. We shall both be greatly gratified with the sight and evolutions of your fine battery.

Saw Dr. Howard and his lady in Waynesboro. He said he could make arrangements for twenty or thirty among his neighbors for their bread and clothing if necessity was laid upon us to remove. Saw nothing favorable at

Mr. Dowse's for such a matter. Saw at Waynesboro also Major Charles Whitehead, since gone back to Virginia, and Mr. Randolph Whitehead, and Captain Morris with his wounded hand.

The up country is alive—at least on the lines of travel—with soldiers, many returning home to recruit their wasted constitutions. Disease slays tenfold more than the sword in war, and is invariably attendant upon war. The day we left Liberty for Augusta one poor young man died on the cars between No. 3 and Savannah, and his corpse went up with us on the Central Railroad.

Received calls while in Augusta, and among the rest Mrs. and Miss Eve. They called Friday, and then Sunday afternoon, not seeing me on Friday! And was invited the week following to dine at Mrs. Eve's—one I never saw nor knew before! And putting one thing with another, I could not divine the intent of these attentions.

Your brother has a fine, noble little boy. Nearly walking. Resembles his mother's family. Carrie bears her separation as well as she can, and is much favored in having Mrs. Cuthbert living with her. . . .

What times! The enemy permitted unmolested to occupy and fortify Tybee—in one and a quarter mile of Fort Pulaski—with the avowed design of reducing that fort with heavy ordnance and fleet, and then Savannah afterwards! We shall have another Fort Sumter affair—but not in our favor! Can nothing arouse Savannah and the commander in chief from fatal apathy? The defenses on Green and Skidaway Islands and Thunderbolt will avail nothing when Pulaski falls. And not a gun mounted in the city! It is amazing and distressing to me. We must let England and France and all the world go, and depend upon ourselves, trusting in God.

Do not let camp life nor business nor pleasure nor company nor anything rob you, my dear son, of time daily to read God's Word and meditate thereon and pray to Him in secret. I hope you are coming into clearer and happier views and hopes. Mother wishes to add a line.

Your ever affectionate father,
C. C. Jones.

MRS. MARY JONES *to* LT. CHARLES C. JONES, JR.[8]

Montevideo, *Friday,* December 20th, 1861

I design, my very dear son, to write you at least once a week, but such are my numerous engagements I often fail to do so. I am glad the Russian sauce pleased the captain, and I will send him the recipe as you desired in my next letter.

Will it be possible for you to be with us on Christmas? It would be so delightful to us to have you at home; and I hope your sister and brother will be with us.

Your precious little daughter improves daily. She has now two teeth, and is a perfect specimen of health and cheerfulness. We think she grows more and more like our dear Ruth.

Your father says he will write you particularly about the miniature. I feel that his criticisms may benefit the artist, as he can not only point out defects but their remedy.

We see from the papers that our valued friends the Misses Jones are amongst the sufferers in Charleston, and presume the old family mansion was destroyed by the fire. I have really felt my spirits weighed down in sympathy with the distress in Charleston from that awful conflagration. The defenseless state of our own city and the insulting occupancy of Tybee gives us fears that Georgia ere long will be worse off than Carolina. . . .

This is your dear father's birthday; and if spared to behold the light of tomorrow, it will be the thirty-first anniversary of our marriage. . . . Your father has retired, and I hear the voice of our little darling calling for her nurse. She sends sweet kisses for her papa. *Susan's* lover has not returned; *Old Andrew has not* a very good opinion of him. Father unites with me in best love to you. . . . God bless you, my child!

Ever your affectionate mother,
Mary Jones.

Lt. Charles C. Jones, Jr., *to* Rev. C. C. Jones[g]
Camp Claghorn, *Saturday,* December 21st, 1861

My dear Father,

It is with much regret that I learned from George, who went to Savannah a day since on business, that you had already passed through the city on your way home, and that we would not enjoy the anticipated pleasure of seeing you and Robert at this camp. I had earnestly hoped that you would have found time and convenience to spend at least a day with us, and we were prepared to show you some excellent drill and shell practice. An hour's drive would have conducted you over a capital shell road to this beautiful encampment. I presume, however, that the fatigues attendant upon your recent protracted engagements in Augusta and your anxiety to return home after a considerable absence prevented. I have had no letter from home for more than two weeks, but trust that all are well.

The recent advices from England are most important in their character, and in the event of a refusal on the part of the Federal government to acquiesce in the reported demands of the British government, we may expect comparative quiet here. With the heavy guns of English men-of-war thundering about their ears, they will have but little time and strength and opportunity for stealing Negroes and colonizing sea islands.

The conduct of the Lincolnites in the forcible arrest of Mason and Slidell to my mind involves a gross violation of the laws of neutrality, and a positive insult of the most flagrant character to the British flag. By the law of nations the deck of the *Trent* was as emphatically a portion of British soil, and as exclusively entitled to the protection of the British flag, as any part of the territory of that nation. The *Trent* had violated no blockade. She was an accredited mail steamer plying between neutral ports; and upon the broad highway of nations Messrs. Mason and Slidell, as ordinary passengers, were entitled to the full protection of that flag by the law of common carriers. If they were accredited envoys, they were doubly protected, not only by that law but also by the law of nations. If, on the other hand, they are to be regarded as political refugees and upon British soil, the United States had no right whatever to violate that territory and arrest them by the application of the rule of the *major vis*. In either event the act was lawless in the extreme, and the insult most violent. My only fear is that the United States will, with characteristic Yankee timidity, recede from the position at present taken, and make any apology demanded by England. In that case the unmitigated contempt of the world will be their portion. If a compliance with the demand be refused, then our war is practically at an end. The English and French navies will sweep their blockading squadrons from the coast, our ports will be again open, our staple commodities will go forward, and practical peace and plenty again lie down at every door. To my mind the future of the Lincoln government is of all most gloomy: a God- and man-forsaken people left to work out alone their own destruction.

The health of our camp is excellent, and our men in fine drill. With warmest love to you both, my dear parents, and to my dear little daughter, I am, as ever,

Your affectionate son,
Charles C. Jones, Jr.

Lt. Charles C. Jones, Jr., *to* Rev. C. C. Jones[8]

Camp Claghorn, *Wednesday*, December 25th, 1861

My dear Father,

Christmas Day! Many happy returns to you and my dear mother and precious little daughter! And long before the coming of another anniversary may these storm clouds which now hover about us have been succeeded by the pure light of love, of peace, and of righteousness! This is my hope, but whether it will be realized within the time specified, and by whom, is known only to Him who disposes all things in infinite wisdom and according to His own great pleasure. Of the ultimate success of our cause I have no doubt; but I am persuaded that the struggle will be not without privation and (it may be) great personal danger and perhaps death to many into whose immediate keeping is committed the defense of all we hold dear in life and sacred in death.

The enemy with a force of five vessels is now within a few miles of us, threatening the Skidaway battery, an earthwork mounting seven guns. Night before last our company bivouacked on Skidaway Island in supporting distance of the battery, without shelter and to a great extent without food, having moved from our camp at very short notice. A slight skirmish took place that afternoon between a portion of Commodore Tattnall's fleet lying

178

under the guns of the battery and the enemy's vessels, in which several shots were fired but neither man nor vessel injured on either side. Yesterday we returned to our camp. Today heavy firing heard to the seaward, and this afternoon the vessels of the enemy again in the neighborhood of the Skidaway battery. An attack is expected upon the Skidaway battery tomorrow, and we are in expectation of orders to move in the morning. There may be nothing in the present demonstration of the enemy; but everything appears to indicate a contemplated effort to possess themselves of Skidaway Island, which will enable them effectually to cut off our inland navigation, and would also afford additional facilities in the event of any direct operations upon Savannah.

Our bivouac night before last was the first real taste of soldier's life. Our caps were all frosted in the morning, and the canteens of the men sleeping around the fires had ice in them. It was quite cold, but clear, bracing; and no evil effects have been experienced by either men or horses.

George goes home in the morning to see his mother and family, and I send these hurried lines by him. . . . I much regret to see that the Lincolnites are reported prepared to surrender Mason and Slidell in obedience to the demands of the British government, although I must say I fully expected the result. . . . It is late, and I must bid you all good night. My warmest love to self, dear Father, and to my dear mother, with tenderest kisses for my precious little daughter. May a good God continue ever to bless you all at home! As ever,

Your affectionate son,
Charles C. Jones, Jr.

Rev. C. C. Jones *to* Lt. Charles C. Jones, Jr.[8]
Montevideo, *Wednesday,* December 25th, 1861
My dear Son,

With the shadow of God's judgment and displeasure still resting over our beloved country, and no ray of absolute light breaking from any quarter, I do not know that we can greet each other with a "Merry Christmas." But the Apostle bids us to "Rejoice in God always," and this is the privilege of His people. Hoping we are such, we can rejoice that He reigns, that His ways are just and true, that His judgments are right, that we can commit ourselves and all that concerns us into His merciful care, and so rest upon Him to keep and to sustain and bless us. . . .

Our waking eyes have been saluted with the light of as brilliant a sun and as beautiful a day as ever this world saw. Your dear little one put her hands together and said her prayers as the sun arose; and soon after, the servants came with their "Merry Christmas," and our venerable old man wishing us and all ours "peace all the days of our life, without difficulty or trial in the way; the Blessed Jesus was the Lord and Master, in whom was all power and grace, and He was and would be to us the only Giver of all peace." Next followed your sister's two sweet children, rejoicing in their stockings stored with all manner of things pleasing to their eyes and their ears and their tastes. She and Robert are with us. We remembered you at family worship —as we do always in all our prayers—and your brother and all his.

He took tea with us last evening. Is full of occupation in his profession. Said he did not expect that Mr. J. B. Barnard would live out the night. And Cato informed me this morning *that he had died last night*—so reported by a boy from that neighborhood. Do not know that is so from any other source. Your brother has been in almost daily attendance upon him, and without hope from the beginning.

Mr. B. S. Screven gives his man Andrew a character in the following words: "Andrew as far as I know him is honest and of a submissive spirit. He is not what I wish—a Christian." The appearance and conversation of the boy are good. Susan says she wishes to marry him, but only with your and our approbation. Please write on receipt of this and signify your will. I promised Andrew an answer next week—so soon as I heard from you.

We had no mail yesterday, and between nine and eleven this morning we heard cannonading—in direction of Savannah, we thought. It did not continue long, and hope our coast defenses have suffered nothing from the enemy. I cannot say that I am in daily expectation of an attack upon Savannah or the approaches to it, but shall not be surprised to hear of an attack any day. It is to be hoped that all arrangements are perfect for getting our troops off the islands where they are stationed if there shall come a necessity for their withdrawment. The Johns Island retreat in South Carolina should settle the propriety of looking into this matter.

The Liberty Independent Troop have a meeting today of all the families and friends of the troopers, and a contribution dinner, as no one can go home on Christmas to his family. Shall not go on account of a cold, and think none from our house will.

Mr. Barnard is really dead, and his funeral takes place tomorrow at 12 M. The measles have appeared in the troop, and a considerable number have never had them. Your brother is well, but has too much sickness to attend to. Hope it may not last. The *firing* today, I learn, was *south*. Mother, Sister, and Robert and Brother send much love. Little ones quite well. Respects to Captain Claghorn.

Your affectionate father,
C. C. Jones.

REV. C. C. JONES *to* HON. JOHN JOHNSON[t]

Montevideo, *Wednesday*, December 25th, 1861

My dear Sir,

I beg you to excuse my apparent neglect of your note of November 18th in relation to the case of——. It reached me a few days before I left for Augusta to attend the session of our General Assembly, from which I returned home last week, and embrace the first leisure to reply.

Mr. —— denied from the beginning; his denial under oath makes no change in my own convictions. Acquaintance with persons charged with crimes, and with prosecutions for crime before both ecclesiastical and civil courts, has taught me to rely for the truth more upon the evidence than upon the asseverations of the accused.

It would be highly improper in me at the request of your honored pastor to suggest what course should be adopted by your session, as this would carry me beyond my sphere, being neither prosecutor nor member of your session. And also unnecessary, since in reply to your letter written upon the said ——'s report of his case to you, I have laid pretty fully all the evidence relating to it before you; and upon which, with the first six chapters of our book of discipline in your hands, you are well able of yourselves, independent of all assistance, to decide what course should be pursued without the intervention of any prosecutor at all. I am

Respectfully and very truly yours in our Lord,
C. C. Jones.

VIII

MRS. MARY JONES *to* LT. CHARLES C. JONES, JR.[8]

Montevideo, *Thursday,* January 9th, 1862

My very dear Son,

The clock reminds me that it is hastening on to midnight, and yet if I seize not the waning moments of this day, tomorrow may not with its many cares and interruptions afford me one hour for writing you. . . .

Your dear father enjoyed his visit to you exceedingly, and Robert and himself have been unsparing in their admiration of the Chatham Artillery, and the truly military appearance of Camp Claghorn, and (though last, not least) the hospitable entertainment extended to them by your honored commander. I quite envied them the visit. God bless you, my very dear child, your captain, your officers, and your brave men! If called to meet our enemies, may the Lord shield you all in the day of battle, and nerve every heart with courage and every hand with strength for the conflict! . . .

We have had a delightful visit from your Uncle John, Aunt Jane, and the two little boys. The interesting incidents of the past eventful summer which he has treasured up, and the events of historic moment, would fill a volume. He went upon the battlefield of Manassas the day after the great victory of July 21st, and has lived since then mostly with our Army of the Potomac, acting directly as chaplain to the 8th Georgia Regiment. He has been instrumental in doing great good to our suffering and dying soldiers. Your sister and the children left us on Monday afternoon. Your Uncle John brought an exploded shell from the battlefield, and when showing it little Mary burst into tears and said: "Those Yankees want to kill my Uncle Charlie!"

Your precious little daughter grows more and more interesting every day. When, my dear son, could you spend a Sabbath with us? We desire not to delay her baptism. I want to know that she has been publicly dedicated to her mother's and I trust her father's and her grandparents' God and Saviour. Do write me your wishes; I desire to do nothing contrary to them.

Susan would like to know if you consent to her marrying the man Andrew. I expect it is just as well. I have told her she takes the risk of separation.

Your brother has been quite unwell. We expect Carrie and dear little Stanhope on Saturday. Father has long retired, leaving best love for *you.* With many kisses from your little daughter,

Ever your affectionate mother,
Mary Jones.

The servants all send howdies.

Lt. Charles C. Jones, Jr., *to* Mrs. Mary Jones[g]

Camp Claghorn, *Saturday,* January 11th, 1862

My very dear Mother,

I am this moment favored with your kind letter of the 9th inst., and sincerely thank you for it. I am truly happy to know that all at home are well. The very earliest Sabbath that I can be excused from this post shall be named to you as the baptismal day of my precious little daughter. I am exceedingly anxious that this sacred rite should be performed. . . .

I have been tendered by General Jackson the judge advocacy of his division, which comprises the brigades of Generals Walker, Capers, and Harrison, with the rank of major, and as chief of artillery. This places me in immediate command of all the artillery in the state service, amounting at present to three batteries numbering in all nineteen pieces. General Jackson regards it—as it is, in fact—the most important position on his staff. The truth is, the position is much superior to that of a colonelcy, and is second in consequence to that of a brigadier general. The duties and responsibilities consequent upon an acceptance will be most responsible. The truth is, the science of artillery and the knowledge of that drill are but little understood as a general rule in our state, and it is no easy matter to find one to fill the position. The only inducement which would influence me in accepting the appointment would be the desire of accomplishing as much good as I could in behalf of my state and country in the present emergency. The labor in preparing these batteries for the field will be great, but must be undertaken by someone.

As yet I have the matter under consideration. Enclosed I send for the perusal of yourself and dear Father the letter of General Jackson, which I must beg that you will preserve and return to me with your views as to the propriety of an acceptance. My mind inclines favorably at present. My greatest regret will be at parting with my own company, to which my attachments are very strong. Do let me hear from you by return mail if practicable.

We have nothing new with us in camp. With warmest love to you both, my dear parents, and many kisses for my precious little daughter, I am, as ever,

Your affectionate son,
Charles C. Jones, Jr.

I have no objections to Susan's marriage if you think it proper.

Rev. C. C. Jones *to* Lt. Charles C. Jones, Jr.[g]

Montevideo, *Monday,* January 13th, 1862

My dear Son,

Yours of the 11th enclosing General Jackson's of the 9th was received by your mother this afternoon, and as she is weary and unwell I undertake to answer for her.

The appointment is tendered you in a frank and kind spirit, is superior to the one you now hold in position, importance, and emolument, and brings you more into service and in the view and knowledge of your own state and fellow statesmen; will certainly give you far more labor and no more exposure in event of your being called into action. To put in good order and efficiency the artillery of the state will be rendering no mean service in such a time as this. We think favorably of the appointment, and your brother, who has read the letters, thinks you ought to accept decidedly. We can well conceive the pain it will give you to separate yourself from the officers and privates of the old Chatham Artillery, from whom you have received so many proofs of their confidence, and to whom you are so much attached. I shall feel it myself, and for your good captain in particular. Mother adds that there will be a great increase of care and of responsibility and also of usefulness, and is an important position. And as we really do not comprehend all involved in it, we feel rather like acquiescing in your decision, believing you will do what you think is right. General Jackson is very candid in his letter; he wants a *working man,* and will expect you to work. Mother says the state has greater claims on you than a single company. Let us know your decision, and if you change, where your quarters will be. We think hotels are miserable places for headquarters for single or married men either. And we are always hoping that your public engagements may not draw off your mind from your higher and immortal interests.

We shall be glad to see you whenever you can come out.

Your dear little daughter has an eruption around her mouth and on her hand which is the effect of her biting my silver pencil and getting on it a little of the iodine ointment which had been rubbed on the back of her ear and on a little sore on her head. At least, that is the supposition. But it is nothing serious, we hope. She sat near me on the sofa this afternoon, playing with the cloth baby her dear mother made for little Julia, of which she is very fond, and for some time was laughing out most heartily with her nurse. She is now in her crib, gone to bed for the night.

Carrie and little Stanhope reached us safely on Saturday. Both in fine health, and it will be a comfort to your brother to have them near him. . . . Mother and Carrie unite in love to you. Our respects to Captain Claghorn. Excuse the blots: they came in some unseen manner. As ever,

Your affectionate father,
C. C. Jones.

Lt. Charles C. Jones, Jr., *to* Rev. C. C. Jones[8]
Camp Claghorn, *Monday,* January 20th, 1862

My dear Father,

I beg at greater length to acknowledge the receipt of your very kind letter of the 13th inst.

Upon reflection I have concluded to decline the appointment tendered by General Jackson. The truth is, I think he acted rather unadvisedly in the matter, and without consulting the organic act of the legislature providing for the raising of the state forces now in the field. By that act it is provided that whenever *four or more* artillery companies should be received and mustered into the service of the state, *a colonel* of artillery should be commissioned by the governor, to be elected by the commissioned officers of the artillery companies, and to be attached to the staff of the commanding general. General Jackson has only *three companies* of artillery in his division. The law makes no provision for a *major of artillery*. The general proposed to fill this hiatus by commissioning me as judge advocate with the rank of major, and assigning me to the specific command of these and of all future batteries which might be mustered into the state service and attached to his command, as *chief of artillery*. I question his right to do this. He certainly finds no warrant for it in the organic act. And besides, Governor Brown has already appointed Colonel Boggs, recently of the Confederate service, and chief of ordnance at Pensacola, as chief of engineers and of artillery for the State of Georgia. You see at once, then, where a conflict of jurisdiction may arise, and the question of rank might lead to difficulty.

Moreover, these batteries attached to the state forces never will be concentrated at any one point so as to be under the immediate direction of a general officer. They are attached to the respective brigades, and in case of an action will in all probability—and in fact, of necessity—be posted with those brigades under the command of their respective officers. The truth is, light batteries always act, and are so regarded, as distinct commands. Seldom in the history of warfare have they been associated together. So that the idea of an intelligent separate command of these batteries upon the field cannot be entertained. There is no field in the vicinity of Savannah where they could be drilled in battalion movements.

The truth is, I very much doubt if Judge Jackson, when he wrote me that letter (which has been already submitted to you) tendering me the appointment, had any very definite idea of what he wished me to do, or of the extent and practical operation of the duties which he desired me to assume. And of this I think I convinced him in a conversation which I had with him. The whole matter, then, resolved itself into a mere appointment upon his staff as judge advocate with the rank and pay of major.

If ease and personal interests were consulted, I would accept the appointment. The emoluments are considerably greater and the labors much less than those devolved upon me in my present position. But I sacrifice personal considerations in my honest endeavor to sustain the efficiency of the Chatham Artillery, a company to which I am attached in no ordinary degree, and in the firm conviction that I will be able in my present subordinate position to render more essential service to the great cause which enlists our every sympathy.

Speaking freely, Hartridge is in very bad health; Davidson is almost crippled with rheumatism; and Captain Claghorn tells me if I should leave the battery he knows not where or how the loss could be supplied. The men urge me not to leave them, and Captain Claghorn has been much depressed at the idea of my doing so. I speak freely because I am writing to you, Father.

All things considered, I believe I am right in remaining where I am. Had the office tendered proved upon examination to be what General Jackson conceived and represented it to be, I would have accepted. But as I said to you before, it resolved itself simply into an appointment upon his staff as judge advocate with the rank of major, with little to do except to conduct causes before a division court-martial. Now, I desire, in as emphatic a manner as possible, to testify my personal devotion to the interests of our young Confederacy, and in common with tens of thousands of our brave soldiers to endure the inconveniences and the privations of actual service. Besides, this desire to hold office merely for the rank and the emoluments, and without discharging any material duties or rendering any essential services, has been and still continues to be a great bane. My idea is that it is a mistake to change a position in which you already are performing valuable services, and where you enjoy the esteem and respect of your associates, unless by that change you can advance the interests of a common cause and enlarge your sphere of usefulness.

We are anxiously awaiting the movements of this Burnside expedition. As yet it has not made its appearance upon our coast. Should a land attack be made upon Savannah, it will probably be attempted in this vicinity. We have now upon the coast of Georgia in both Confederate and state service about sixteen thousand men.

My impression is that along the limits of our Confederacy we will have heavy work during the next three months. The Lincolnites now have ready for the advance an army of four hundred and eighty thousand, exclusive of sick, etc., etc., and of the naval force. With this vast army they propose to overwhelm us by hurling heavy columns upon us simultaneously from different quarters, with the hope (in the language of Seward) to "crush out the rebellion" at once. Vain expectation! But certain it is that we must in meeting the invasions suffer much, and many a brave man surrender his life in the defense of all we hold pure in honor, true in principle, honest in religion, dear in life, and sacred in death. But I earnestly pray, and confidently hope, that the same good and great God who has hitherto so signally interposed in our behalf will continue to bless our exertions and crown our struggle with success. There can be no retreat. The ultimatum with every true lover of his country who is able to bare his breast in support of the principles for which we are contending must be *victory or death*. . . .

Our pickets on Skidaway were fired upon by a barge of Lincolnites who approached the island through a creek in Romney Marsh on Saturday night last about eleven o'clock. The shots were distinctly heard at our camp; also the long roll at Stiles's camp, and also at the camp of the Louisiana battalion. None of the pickets were wounded, nor are we aware that any of the enemy were killed. One of our company who visited the spot picked out of a tree one of the balls fired by the rascals.

Will you my dear father, at some leisure moment let me know whether you think the miniature painting of my precious wife can be altered by the artist so as to make it at all a likeness? Where do the defects lie? To me it conveys scarce an idea of my dearest Ruth. Her sacred image is with me ever, and the memory of all her loves is with me morning, noon, and night. Never will love like that kindle again in this breast. It will live alone—pure, separate, ever bright—although other affections may possess the heart. I am especially anxious on account of my dear little daughter to obtain a good likeness of her.

It is late, and I must say good night. Do give warmest love to dear Mother, and many kisses to my precious little daughter. And believe me ever, my dear father,

Your affectionate son,
Charles C. Jones, Jr.

Kindest remembrances to the Doctor, Sister Carrie, and little Stanhope.

REV. C. C. JONES *to* LT. CHARLES C. JONES, JR.[8]

Montevideo, *Friday*, January 24th, 1862

My dear Son,

Yours of the 20th reached us yesterday. We were aware of the peculiarity of the appointment tendered you by your friend General H. R. Jackson, but presumed that he had secured all the necessary and regular steps thereto, so that you would in accepting be free from every objection and embarrassment. You have done what I was sure you would do—search into the matter and give it proper consideration and then decide; and all your reasons for declining the appointment meet our approbation. There being no law for it settles the question. And what was desirable in the appointment being thereby taken away, and its becoming dwarfed into a mere office of rank and emolument, puts it beneath the consideration of a man who wishes to serve his country in action on the field and in the camp from disinterested and patriotic motives. Changes to meet the approbation of the wise and the good, and especially the approbation of a man's enlightened conscience in the public service at a time like this in our country's need, should be made on the *ascending* scale of *usefulness* in the common cause. In this you are right, and I never wish you to act differently. Your loss to your company I believe would have been a serious one, and much felt by Captain Claghorn.

The *reported armament* of the Burnside expedition, which has been gotten up with much secrecy, is more formidable than that of Sherman's, and if managed with skill and spirit will give us work to do on whatever point on the coast it descends. I cannot comprehend the movement of the selection of the North Carolina coast about Hatteras for that purpose unless that be only *a part* of the program. A flotilla of thirty to fifty vessels carrying hundred-pound rifled cannon and columbiads and other guns proportionally heavy would render an attack on our small sand batteries and short ranges a pretty serious affair. Am happy to learn that there are sixteen thousand men on our coast. Is it true that the lower end of Savannah at the gasworks is now being fortified? And that there is a battery at the lower end of Hutchinson's Island commanding the back river? Ogeechee River should be looked after; a night expedition might destroy the railroad bridge there. The battery on that river is feeble.

There has been a *lull* in Federal war operations for several weeks, preparing, they say, for the grand move of four hundred and eighty thousand men of which you speak on all our borders simultaneously, land and water. Their finances are in a critical condition, as it appears to *outsiders*. But it is not their impression: they are lacking for neither men nor means; and although, through God's mercy towards us, thus far much foiled, they seem as determined as ever to "crush out rebellion" (their favorite phrase); and not one ray of light appears on the horizon indicative of returning peace.

The hope of aid from England or France in our struggle is the faintest possible. The policy of England, indicated months ago, is to "tide over," as they expressed it, the cotton deficit of the present year, 1862, and to put a strain upon her cotton manufacturing interest, and if possible demonstrate their ability to *do without American cottons,* and consequently her independence of us in all time to come. That is, *if it be possible.* The direst necessity alone will force her to interfere in American affairs.

We have nothing to do but humble ourselves under the afflicting hand of God, and committing our cause to Him, go forward making every arrangement for a protracted and deadly struggle, and doing our best, God helping us, in conquering a peace with as vile and tyrannical enemies as any nation has ever been called to resist. The Lord be with you and bless and keep you, my dear son, from all evil, and unto His Heavenly Kingdom!

Your dear little one has been very unwell with the affection I wrote you about. Is still suffering from it; has lost much flesh; but is in good spirits, and we think better. Your brother is prescribing for her, and sees her almost every day. Mother is somewhat better. All the rest well. And all unite in much love. Will write about the likeness of dear Ruth another time at more leisure. Respects to Captain Claghorn.

Your affectionate father,
C. C. Jones.

MRS. MARY JONES *to* LT. CHARLES C. JONES, JR.[8]

Montevideo, *Sunday,* January 26th, 1862

I have but a moment to say to you, my very dear son, that through the goodness of God we are all well, and your dear little daughter almost entirely relieved of her cold and the eruption on her face and head. She grows sweeter and sweeter every day.

Please arrange to meet a box or basket at the depot on Thursday evening. I want to send you a few home remembrancers. With our united love, and kisses from your babe,

Ever your affectionate mother,
Mary Jones.

LT. CHARLES C. JONES, JR., *to* MRS. MARY JONES[8]

Camp Claghorn, *Wednesday,* January 29th, 1862

My dear Mother,

I am this afternoon favored with your kind letter of the 26th inst., and cannot tell you how happy I am to know that all at home are well, and that my dear little daughter is almost entirely relieved from her cold and the eruption on her face and head. I never will be able even to express to you how thankful and more than grateful I am and ever will be to you for this your great kindness in assuming the tender care of my dear little daughter now that she will never know the sympathy and love of my precious Ruth, and while stern necessity prevents me from even seeing her. . . . I long to see you both, my dear parents, and my dear little daughter; but the dangers which environ us preclude the possibility of my leaving this post at this time.

Over twenty Lincoln vessels, war and transports (principally the former), are lying in Wassaw Sound, only a few miles below our batteries. For two days they have been drilling in column, deploying in line of battle, etc., etc., and practicing with their guns. Today they have been testing the currents with floats; and as the tide suits about eight o'clock in the morning, we are expecting an attack upon the Skidaway batteries at that hour. What the result will be is known only to the Sovereign Disposer of all events. From our camp we could distinctly see the shelling from the gunboats behind Wilmington Island.

The convoy of the provision steamboats from Savannah to Fort Pulaski by Commodore Tattnall and his little fleet in the face of the enemy's gunboats on either hand was a most gallant act, and the wonder is that the feat was accomplished. Both from Wall's Cut and from Freeborn's Creek they poured shot and shell upon him from guns of vastly superior metal. One of his vessels, the *Samson,* was struck four times, three shots passing through her and one shell exploding in her storeroom, and, as if by a miracle, no one injured or killed. Commodore Tattnall replied, but with what success is not known. Certain it is that in the face of this opposition he safely convoyed the steamers to Fort Pulaski; and that fortress has now a store of seven months' provisions. Commodore Tattnall's name will live in the grateful remembrance of us all. A truer, nobler, braver man does not breathe. I love him almost as a father, and I believe it is my good fortune to enjoy his positive friendship and esteem, a possession of which I am proud. He stands in strange contrast with some others, high in military preferment, whose names it becomes me not to mention.

General Lee is in Savannah, and every effort is being made to place the city in a state of defense. I learn that the citizens are calm and resolved to meet any emergency which may arise. The enemy are not in possession of Savannah yet by a great deal, and I confidently trust that a kind Providence will continue to vouchsafe His favor to us all.

Our battery is performing laborious picket duty, and now occupies three points. Tonight I bivouac with a section of the battery under my command at the western terminus of the Skidaway bridge for the protection of that structure from a night attack, which is apprehended. The object of the enemy appears to be to get in our rear and to isolate Fort Pulaski and our forces on Skidaway and Green Islands. If this bridge is destroyed, nearly two thousand troops will be cut off. We expect with the rising sun to hear the enemy's guns at the Skidaway batteries. I must mount Yorick and join my command at the bridge.

Many thanks, my dear mother, for your kind remembrance, which I will try and get from the depot. Did you ever receive from Vallie a box containing some articles for Daughter? She asked me some time since if you had received it. With warmest love to you both, my dear parents, and many kisses for my dear little daughter, I am, as ever,

Your affectionate son,
Charles C. Jones, Jr.

Captain Claghorn begs his remembrances to you and Father.

Rev. C. C. Jones *to* Lt. Charles C. Jones, Jr.[8]

Montevideo, *Wednesday,* January 29th, 1862

My dear Son,

We were favored with letters last evening from Captain Claghorn and yourself, and were happy to hear from both of you that you were both well and at the post of duty. May God enable you to do your duty; and if called into danger may He preserve you safe in person and in life, and spare you for usefulness to your country and to your families and to His own Heavenly Kingdom! Our kind regards to the captain.

Events are taking the course of which the enemy gave us timely warning very shortly after the Port Royal affair, and about the time that he was beginning to realize the extreme difficulty of operating on Charleston. Savannah is far more accessible from having more approaches by water directly and fewer fortifications, and his attention was turned in that direction. The obstructions in Wall's Cut and Freeborn's Passage have been quietly removed, and our authorities were not aware of it! Pulaski may be considered cut off, and its reduction begun. Next follows the Burnside expedition, and a trial upon our batteries on Green Island and Skidaway, which if carried reduces the seaboard down to St. Simons and Jekyll. And then attempts may be expected there. Our hope is that it may please God to enable us to repel their attacks upon our batteries. If so, we shall do well; if not, we fall back upon the main and repel their advance into the interior and upon the city—which, however, if they approach near enough, may be shelled and damaged. We cannot prevent these naval expeditions: we have no navy. And the taking of our seaboard cities, which cannot be long held, and our coast islands, although subjecting us to great inconveniences and (many of us, perhaps) to pecuniary losses and ruin, will not "crush out rebellion," to use the favorite expression, nor "wipe out the South." The enemy can make no progress inland. Separation from their fleet is starvation and death. And our brave men, fighting for everything dear to men in home and country and in honor and religion, will beat them back inch by inch.

We appear to be at this time, throughout our whole Confederacy and in our foreign relations, at one of the most important periods of our revolution; and I pray that the Lord may pardon our sins and espouse our just cause, as we hope He has heretofore done, and be a wall of fire round about us and a glory in the midst of us. I am obliged to believe that He will hear our prayers ascending from every part of our land and maintain our right. We cannot expect to escape reverses; but they should humble our pride, remove our self-confidence, but increase our courage and resolution in the Lord to meet our cruel and unjust enemies in every battle to the end. . . .

Am happy to inform you that your dear little daughter, we hope, is nearly herself again. She is remarkably intelligent, and Mother says "the most *earnest eyes* she ever saw," and very much like dear Ruth. How often does her image and remembrance come up in my mind! Have not had time lately to give the miniature a careful study; will do so early. Your sister and Little Daughter with us. She, Carrie, and Mother unite in much love; and all continually pray for you. All relations, friends, and servants generally well.

Your ever affectionate father,
C. C. Jones.

MRS. MARY JONES *to* LT. CHARLES C. JONES, JR.[8]

Montevideo, *Thursday,* January 30th, 1862

I hope, my very dear son, the basket will reach you in safety and prove acceptable at this time. The weather is so very warm you will have to use the sausages and white puddings at once. The turkey is a present from your sister, and I thought it best to have it roasted.

I need not say how anxiously we are feeling, and hope we will hear as frequently as you can possibly write. God bless and protect you and your whole company and our united army and country! I cannot trust myself to write on this subject. At times I feel that my heart would almost break when I think of what may be the suffering of my own sons and my relatives and countrymen, and the wrongs inflicted by the diabolical enemy upon our country. But God reigns, and I commit all into His just and wise and holy keeping!

Our dear little babe has quite recovered. Your sister left us this morning. Your father, brother, and Carrie unite with me in best love to you. Sweetest kisses from your little daughter. I have received the captain's polite acknowledgment of the recipe, and send you three bottles of the Russian sauce, which I fear is not so good, being prepared of *domestic vinegar* and *mustard*. I must close, or we shall lose the cars.

Ever, my dear son, your affectionate mother,
Mary Jones.

LT. CHARLES C. JONES, JR., *to* MRS. MARY JONES[8]

Camp Claghorn, *Friday*, January 31st, 1862

My very dear Mother,

I am this afternoon in receipt of your note of yesterday and also of your very kind remembrance in the most acceptable basket of sundries, all of them delicious and tempting. You have not only my own but also the hearty thanks of the officers' mess. Such favors are, I can assure you, highly prized, and I promise you the many good things you have sent will be enjoyed with honest appetites. . . . The wax tapers and candles have elicited much praise. One of them is now burning upon the table, and we are admiring its fine light and the slowness with which the material is consumed. Do thank Sister for the turkey. It arrived just in time for dinner, and was greatly enjoyed by us and some officers who dined with us.

The enemy has retired from the immediate vicinity of Savannah, but no less than seventeen vessels remain in Wassaw Sound, only a few miles below our batteries. For what they are waiting, or what their purposes are, we are unable to ascertain with any certainty. This morning, as the tide was favorable, we confidently anticipated an attack. It may have been postponed on account of the dense fog which overshadowed everything until about eight o'clock. Now we have the promise of a regular northeaster, which may further postpone active operations on their part. Every indication points to an attack upon the Skidaway batteries, which have recently been considerably strengthened. . . .

General Lawton visited our camp today. We are in a state of very creditable preparation, although our battery is at present divided. To us are entrusted Montmollin's Point, the Isle of Hope settlement, and the defense of Skidaway bridge. Tonight I will be on picket duty at the latter point. It is so dark that we will have to keep a very sharp lookout. And the skies promise rain—just the time for an attack. The burning of this bridge will isolate no less than eighteen hundred of our troops at present on Skidaway Island.

We have today a rumor of a desperate battle at Bowling Green, Kentucky, in which we are victorious. I trust and pray that a kind Providence will watch over us and deliver us from the threatened devastations from an inhuman enemy.

With warmest love to you, my dear mother, to Father, to Sister Carrie, the Doctor, and little Stanhope, and many kisses for my precious little daughter, I am, as ever,

Your affectionate son,
Charles C. Jones, Jr.

With the termination of this day six months of our term of service expire. Where we will be at the end of the next six months God only knows. I sincerely hope that before that period elapses we may see the arts of peace restored, our independence established, our honor vindicated, the temples of learning, of justice, and of religion again fully opened, and God acknowledged and fervently worshiped throughout all our borders.

Lt. Charles C. Jones, Jr., *to* Rev. C. C. Jones[8]

Camp Claghorn, *Saturday,* February 1st, 1862

My dear Father,

Last night I enjoyed the pleasure of replying to Mother's note and of thanking her for her very kind remembrance, which duly reached us and is sincerely appreciated. Today I write to acknowledge the receipt of your valued favor of the 29th ult. and to express to you my obligations for it and my unqualified acquiescence in all the views therein presented.

The casualties which attended the Sherman expedition to the careless observer might have been referred to the chance effects of an idle wind; but now that forty vessels of the Burnside fleet have been swallowed up and stranded amid the angry billows which guard our coast—vessels freighted with elaborate munitions of war and filled with those who breathed devastation and destruction to our homes and lives—can even the Lincolnites fail of perceiving that there is a God who rides upon the whirlwind and directs the storm? Truly each day—each hour—we are called upon in this, as in everything else, to lift up our hearts and voices in gratitude to the Giver of All Good for His renewed interpositions in our behalf.

We have been in daily expectation of an attack upon our Skidaway batteries. A courier just arrived reports an addition this morning of five vessels. The tide has been favorable, and we are at a loss to conjecture the designs of the enemy, or to explain the reason of this apparent delay. My own impression is that a combined movement is intended against Savannah, both by land and water.

We are now experiencing the realities of the bivouac; nearly fifty members of our company are upon picket duty. Picture a bed of clean pine straw with a couple of blankets and the overarching branches of a generous live oak, and you have my sleeping apartments for the past night—by no means to be despised, even if a regular Scotch mist was settling over everything. . . .

Give warmest love to dear Mother. Kiss my precious little daughter for me. And believe me ever, my dear father,

Your affectionate son,
Charles C. Jones, Jr.

193

Lt. Charles C. Jones, Jr., *to* Rev. *and* Mrs. C. C. Jones[g]
Camp Claghorn, *Monday,* February 3rd, 1862

My dear Father and Mother,

I send by express for my precious little daughter a silver cup and spoon which she will accept as a token of the tender love and abiding affection of her absent father.

Heavy firing today on the Carolina shore. As yet we know not the cause. My own impression is that a combined attack is meditated against Savannah. Whether the enemy will have the courage and the ability to consummate their designs time alone will show.

We have a rumor that France and England have entered into an agreement to recognize the Southern Confederacy and raise the blockade. It is quite improbable, and it would be better for us to look less for foreign aid and rely more firmly upon ourselves, by the blessing of Heaven, for the ultimate and favorable solution of our present difficulties.

No change in the disposition of the enemy's forces near Wassaw batteries —or rather I should say Skidaway batteries. As ever, my dear parents,
Your affectionate son,
Charles C. Jones, Jr.

Lt. Charles C. Jones, Jr., *to* Rev. *and* Mrs. C. C. Jones[g]
Camp Claghorn, *Wednesday,* February 5th, 1862

I have only a moment, my dear father and mother, to convey my warmest love to you both and to my precious little daughter. We are all well, and there is no change in the military status of affairs. The Lincolnites appear to be waiting for reinforcements. Their ships are lying idly below our batteries on Skidaway Island, and no new demonstrations are made in our vicinity. This delay is very tedious. The defenses of Savannah have been very materially strengthened during the past few days. Previously the city was, comparatively, at the mercy of the enemy. As ever, my dear parents,
Your affectionate son,
Charles C. Jones, Jr.

Mrs. Mary Jones *to* Lt. Charles C. Jones, Jr.[g]
Montevideo, *Saturday,* February 8th, 1862

My very dear Son,

I have risen a half hour earlier than usual that I might have time not only for my usual family duties but to send you a line of love by today's mail. I am writing in the western wing. The sun in all his glory is just above the trees, and his brilliant rays, darting through the deep green foliage of the old cedar in the yard, fall with fanciful effect all around me. I have just read the 25th and 27th Psalms. They appear this morning possessed of peculiar beauty. I commend them to you at this time. . . . Tomorrow two weeks will be our

Communion at Midway. I wish it could be possible for you to be with us and have our dear baby baptized on that day.

It is more than probable that Daughter and myself may come to Savannah on Monday next. I have some dental work which is really necessary to be done by Dr. Parsons. We will stop at the Pavilion, and should I come, will put a line in the mail on Monday for you, hoping you may be able to see us, if only for a moment, on Tuesday.

The beautiful cup and spoon for our little darling was duly received, and she returns her dear papa sweetest kisses for it. She seems to understand that they are her own; stretches out her little hand for the cup, and holds the spoon, upon which already may be traced the print of her little teeth. She is one of the most interesting infants I have ever seen, and the joy of our home.

I wrote Vallie acknowledging the receipt of the box. As she did not write, it was not received as soon as it might have been from the depot.

Your Uncle John is now with us. His account of the battle of Manassas is deeply interesting. He has brought your father a fine map of the battlefield, and myself some valuable relics.

What can I do for you, my dear child? I would be glad oftener to send in articles to you. Would you like to have more of the "Confederate green lights"? I have made quite a supply.

Your father has improved within a few days, but has suffered from a severe cold. Your brother also is better. He has too much to do: *a nurse and surgeon's duty* and a private's reward.

Yesterday we heard of the death of *Willie Howe* at Centreville. He was in Colonel Kershaw's regiment; had been made orderly sergeant; was in the battle of July 21st. A noble, gallant youth. My heart is filled with grief and sympathy for our dear friends Dr. and Mrs. Howe. May God sustain them! Such are the *priceless treasures* this vile enemy demands and receives from our hearts and homes. Father, Carrie, your uncle unite with me in best love to you. Sweetest kisses from your daughter.

Ever your own affectionate mother,
Mary Jones.

REV. C. C. JONES *to* LT. CHARLES C. JONES, JR.[8]

Montevideo, *Monday,* February 10th, 1862

My dear Son,

The execution of Mr. Bounetheau's miniature is very fine, but the likeness is not satisfactory. He has copied the larger of the two daguerreotypes, neither of which is satisfactory. The best you have is the one Ruthie gave you before your marriage. I would prefer a copy from that to any other. Mother thinks the one Mr. Bounetheau copied excellent.

It is difficult to point out the variations of the copy from the original on paper. Yet let me say, according to my eye the change of the dress to a low-neck, and a cross to the necklace, is no improvement, while the chest between the arms is too narrow. The entire face and head is more oval than in the original—the top of the head running up more to a point, and the falling of the hair on each side of the forehead and face made to correspond, while there is a considerable flattening of the hair over the left side of the forehead. The face is not as full, looking more *from* you than *to* you or *at* you. The distance between the eyes is less, and the eyes not as deep and earnest in the copy as in the original. The eyebrows rather sharply defined. The nose not as perpendicular, the mouth not as expanded as in the original, and the rounding of the chin too full.

Whether these observations would benefit Mr. Bounetheau I do not know. I am sure if he could hit the *likeness* he would make the *execution* most excellent, and do sincerely hope he may succeed. Your mother showed the daguerreotype to Mary Ruth and told her it was the likeness of her dear mother, and the little thing held it with her hands; and when Mother told her to kiss it, she kissed it two or three times.

Mother has just left for Walthourville, where your sister joins her; and they go on their way to Savannah this afternoon, and put up at the Pavilion to be near Dr. Parsons. She hopes to get a sight of you, if but for a moment, while in town, and if Dr. Parsons finishes her work, will return about Wednesday. . . .

Am hopeful that General Lee may put the city and its surroundings in such a state of complete defense that our enemy may be discouraged from making an attack beyond the Green Island and Skidaway batteries, which it is presumed he has made up his mind to attack anyhow. If these batteries are commanded by *brave* and *cool men,* they will find it hard to take them. The defense of the Port Royal battery, manned and worked as it was, ought rather to encourage than discourage us, your brother thinks.

Is it not monstrous that these brutal creatures should come near a thousand miles in gratuitous wrath and cupidity to make war upon us in our very homes and firesides? May the Lord decide for us in the day they come upon us! If Georgia does not do her duty, we shall hang our heads in overwhelming shame and sorrow. Surely if she has fought so gallantly on every field in sister states, will she not fight with equal gallantry in defense of her own sacred soil? I believe, by God's blessing, she will.

We are all pretty well this trying weather. Hope your health is good, and that you are as careful of yourself as can be, and live in watchfulness and prayer before God. Respects to Captain Claghorn. Love from all, and kisses from your little one.

Your ever affectionate father,
C. C. Jones.

Lt. Charles C. Jones, Jr., *to* Rev. *and* Mrs. C. C. Jones[8]
Camp Claghorn, *Monday,* February 10th, 1862
My dear Father and Mother,

I sincerely trust that these dark and gloomy days, with their somber shadows and weeping skies, may not be symbolic of the coming fortunes of our young Confederacy for the next few months. I cannot divest myself of the impression, formed as it is with the aid of the best lights at command, that our struggle for national independence and national repose must for some time to come be characterized by unprecedented effort and bloody details. While the Northern armies have been gathering strength, improving in discipline, and recovering from the effect of the reverses to which they were subjected at an early stage of the war, I cannot perceive a corresponding increase of strength on our part, or such an accumulation of the materials of war as will enable us successfully to combat with these barbarian hordes now thronging our borders, except through the continued intervention in our behalf of a gracious superintending Providence and the most desperate exertions of our brave soldiery.

Not only are we sensible of the want of a proper supply of the munitions of war, but we will also soon be forced to recognize in the failure of many whose terms of service are on the eve of expiring to reenlist a prime mistake committed at the outset of our difficulties. That mistake is simply this: in enlisting soldiers for six and twelve months, when they should have been mustered in for the war. The latter could, at the inception of our present contest, have been accomplished without much doubt or difficulty. Men anticipated a short war. They were attracted by the novelties of a soldier's life. They were eager to serve their country and (many of them) to win distinction upon the tented field. They were practically ignorant of the dangers and the inconveniences, the hardships and the privations in store for them. Under such circumstances—the early and strongest tide of patriotism throbbing in their veins—they stood ready to assume any obligations, and to enter with alacrity upon the discharge of all engagements which might have been represented as vital to the best interests of the homes they loved and of the government so recently and so heroically inaugurated. But the opportune moment was permitted to pass unimproved; and the consequence is that we only here and there find a regiment in for the war, while almost entire brigades will soon be disbanded, their terms of enlistment having expired. Wet tents, thin blankets, scanty rations, heavy marches, sleepless nights beneath the canopy of a dripping sky, and long hours of sickness and of pain are the severest tests to which devotion to country can be subjected; and many a soldier with this experience fresh in his remembrance so soon as his term of service expires will return to his home satisfied with past duties, and avoid a repetition of like labors and similar scenes unless forced from his retreat by the searching draft or the near approach of the enemy.

The Lincolnites are evidently watching with great care the result of the expiration of the term of service of many of our troops in April next. I trust that they will freely reenlist, that others will come to the rescue, and that our cause may not suffer repulse or temporary reverse for lack of strong arms and stout hearts upon the field of battle. I have before me a letter from a friend, an officer in the Army of the Potomac, in which, alluding to this question of reenlistment, he uses the following language: "I cannot conjecture how we are to meet the advancing columns of McClellan in the coming spring. Of this grand Army of the Potomac, supposed to number about seventy thousand men, but *twenty regiments,* with a maximum average of five hundred men each, are mustered in for the war. The rest are twelve-months volunteers, whose terms of service will expire in April; and not one of the many whom I have heard express their intentions have any idea of reenlisting. The Georgians all say they will go to the coast of Georgia, the Carolinians to the coast of Carolina, etc. The candidates for home defense are above par. The raging fever to go to Virginia, so prevalent in Savannah and throughout Georgia last summer, has expired at last, and with its dying gasp proclaims the Army of the Potomac, the Army of the Northwest, and the Army of the Peninsula armies composed of fools. Unless the provisional Congress moves vigorously in the matter, Jeff Davis will find himself minus a force sufficient to oppose the advance of McClellan. Great indignation prevails among the higher officers of the army on account of the carelessness of Congress in not providing some remedy for the emergency."

You see, my dear parents, that this picture illustrates rather the dark shadows of West than the bright colorings of Guido.

The Lincoln government foresaw the difficulty and provided against it. It is represented that there are now over six hundred thousand Lincoln troops in service who are in for the war. The only changes, therefore, which can interfere with or diminish this large force are those which result from disease, death, mutiny, etc., etc. Our Congress should at once give to this matter the gravest consideration and devise such remedies as the emergencies of the occasion demand. There is but little philosophy in organizing a grand army, training, arming, and posting the same, with the fact inevitable that at the expiration of a few short months entire brigades will retire to civil life and leave vacancies to be filled with raw recruits, if filled at all.

It sometimes seems to me that our President and those high in authority have misconceived the true theory of the war. We have from its very inception acted solely and exclusively upon the defensive. This has in the main grown out of the peculiar character of our position. But occasions for "carrying the war into Africa" have occurred, which if vigorously improved would have produced good effects and inspired our enemies with a wholesome dread.

One thing is certain: we cannot contend with the enemy on the seas, for the very simple reason that we have no navy. And it has often seemed to me little less than ridiculous, this idea of endeavoring to fortify every avenue by light sand batteries, which must be silenced so soon as the heavy metal of the Lincoln gunboats is brought to bear. The day belongs to the past when open earthworks and palmetto forts can successfully contend with the heavy batteries of modern fleets. And the difficulty is that the rascals will scarcely ever venture beyond the range of their guns. If we could only get them beyond this cover the victory would be ours.

The inaction of the Federals has been most fortunate for us. General Jackson has now large working parties engaged in throwing up a series of earthworks and fortifications which will extend from Causton's Bluff to the Springfield plantation. They will be completed in a few days, and will be very formidable. General Jackson is most sanguine of his ability to defend the city against almost any land force which may be brought. He promises that the history of the defense shall be as famous as that of the success at New Orleans under the veritable "Old Hickory." The river defenses have also progressed very rapidly, and between thirty and forty guns are in position at various points above Fort Pulaski. Live oak is being thrown into Freeborn's Cut and Wilmington River to prevent the passage of gunboats in that direction.

From present indications I have serious doubts whether the enemy really contemplates an attack upon the city. Certainly the requisite force is not present. . . .

I sincerely trust, my dear parents, that you are both well and in the enjoyment of many blessings, and that my dear little daughter has quite recovered. I cannot tell you how anxious I am to see you and her, but it is out of my power to leave this camp at this time. When does Brother's term of enlistment expire? With warmest love to selves, many kisses for my precious daughter, kind remembrances to Sister Carrie, the Doctor, and little Stanhope, and howdy for the servants, I am, my dear father and mother, as ever,

Your affectionate son,
Charles C. Jones, Jr.

Lt. Charles C. Jones, Jr., *to* Rev. *and* Mrs. C. C. Jones[8]
Camp Claghorn, *Thursday,* February 13th, 1862
My dear Father and Mother,

I only write to acknowledge the receipt of your recent favors and to reiterate the thanks for them which I had the great pleasure of expressing in person to you, my dear mother, two days since in Savannah.

No change of any moment in the military status of affairs in our vicinity. The enemy, having landed a considerable force on Wassaw Island, are busily engaged in drilling upon the beach in sight of our batteries. They are reported to be dredging out Wall's Cut and removing the obstacles placed there. An attack upon Savannah is apprehended—and that at no distant day. This is an inference from their apparent movements. I am glad to see that the city council have named tomorrow as a day of humiliation, fasting, and prayer. May a good God hearken in mercy and send us deliverance!

With warmest love to you both, my dear father and mother, many kisses for my precious little daughter, and kindest remembrances for the Doctor, Sister Carrie, and Stanhope, I am, as ever,

Your affectionate son,
Charles C. Jones, Jr.

LT. CHARLES C. JONES, JR., *to* REV. *and* MRS. C. C. JONES[8]

Camp Claghorn, *Monday,* February 17th, 1862

My dear Father and Mother,

The news of our recent deliverance in Tennessee fills every patriotic heart with joy and with sincere thankfulness to the God of Battles for sending us the victory. I sincerely trust that the result of our success may be as decided as it is represented to be, although it is very difficult to place absolute reliance upon early telegraphic reports. This victory shows the silver linings of those clouds which seemed to overshadow us so darkly.

There is but little change in the military status of affairs here. Every exertion is being made to render certain the defenses of Savannah. The great neglect was in not effectually preventing, either by batteries or by obstructions of a permanent character, the ingress of the enemy by means of his gunboats through Wall's Cut into the Savannah River. Fort Pulaski is now virtually isolated, and the guns of that strong fortress, which under other circumstances would have proved of such incalculable advantage in defending our city and its approaches from the sea, are entirely valueless. The neglect is an outrageous one, and grievously must condemnation fall upon the guilty one. General Lee, I understand, expresses his belief that the fortifications in the Savannah River located between Venus Point and the city will be able to repulse any force the enemy will be able to bring. Torpedoes and fire rafts will be called into requisition. Several of each are already prepared. General Lawton has taken the field. His headquarters are now upon Skidaway Island. The rivers leading from Wassaw Sound into the Savannah River are being obstructed with live oak trees. We learn that St. Simons and Jekyll Islands have by order of General Lee been abandoned, and the troops withdrawn with the heavy guns to the mainland.

We are all pretty well. Some of our men have colds and sore throats—the effect of exposure upon picket these wet, bleak nights. With warmest love to you both, my dear parents, and many kisses for my precious little daughter, I am, as ever,

Your affectionate son,
Charles C. Jones, Jr.

REV. C. C. JONES *to* LT. CHARLES C. JONES, JR.[8]

Montevideo, *Tuesday,* February 18th, 1862

My dear Son,

. . . Professor Brumby's son is just on from Manassas—in not good health—and is staying with us. Your classmate in Columbia. He says that the decided turn in the Army of the Potomac when he left was *for reenlistment for the war,* and the great majority will be found true to the country on that point. This is what I anticipated; and your friend, I hope, who wrote so discouragingly will be happily disappointed. Governor Brown's proclamation in answer to the President's requisition for twelve more regiments from

Georgia is a patriotic and excellent one. Our government is thus active, and will forestall the deficiencies of those that will not reenlist. We are engaged in a long and desperate war, and our only hope is in the Lord and in the wise, energetic, and determined use of every means in our power to obtain our independence.

As a country we must disabuse ourselves of any reliance upon *foreign nations*. We ought not to expect them to fight our battles for us. If they choose to go to war with the old United States for their own interests, well and good for us. But after tendering them our friendship and offering them favorable commercial treaties our business with them is at an end. They have treated us not as they did Greece and the South American republics and Belgium and Italy, and we have no reason so far to expect any special favors from them. And I believe if our people are true to themselves we can be free; of course I mean with God's blessing upon our cause, which I believe to be just.

We must disabuse ourselves also of two other notions. The first: that the Federals cannot cope with the Confederates in open and fair battle. Whatever blessing has attended our arms heretofore, we should thank God and take courage, but not presume upon the want of resolution in our foes. To stand firm in battle is much the result of custom; their armies are for the war, and men will fight desperately for interest, for glory, and for their own cause, whatever it be. And the second is that the enemy will exhaust his resources. He will find some way to raise them. There are many ways left. He balks not at the most enormous expenditures. The Federals are displaying the energy of a despotic government laboring to maintain its life. They say "they are fighting for the life of their government." Then we must gird up our loins for the war—develop all our agricultural and manufacturing resources, produce the materials of war, and live as independent of the world as we can. The credit of the government and its existence is with our people. The whole old United States is one workshop of war. The war gives the masses their daily bread and rolls up fortunes for thousands. It is to them now the great pursuit for support and fame, and their furor runs in this channel.

The Fabian policy is and must be ours still. There has been no time in the war that we could safely have departed from it.

The ravaging of our coasts we must submit to for a time, but it goes but a small way to a *conquest—a subjugation* of over eight hundred thousand square miles of territory. The expeditions will not accomplish what the enemy anticipates from them. We should withdraw every cannon and soldier from our seaboard islands. They are barren possessions. The enemy commands the entrances already. We cannot afford loss after loss of the men and munitions of war. Small as they may be, the effect is not good.

Excuse my long letter on the all-absorbing subject. Hard fighting in Tennessee! Your dear little daughter is better; three teeth out, one coming. Mother not very well. The Doctor and family well. So is your Uncle John and family, and all others around us. People generally well. Weather very rainy. Take the best care you can of yourself. All send love to you. Do, my dear son, live near to your God and Savior.

Your ever affectionate father,
C. C. Jones.

Respects to Captain Claghorn. Mail closing.

Lt. Charles C. Jones, Jr., *to* Rev. C. C. Jones[8]

Camp Claghorn, *Friday,* February 21st, 1862

My dear Father,

I thank you for your very kind favor of the 18th inst., which was yesterday received, and I am happy to know that my dear little daughter is so much better. I cannot tell you how anxious I am to see you all at home; but the threatening attitude assumed by our detested enemy, and the necessity existing for the presence at his post of every soldier at this hour of danger, forbid my absenting myself from the battery at this time.

And here I take great pleasure in saying to you that the Chatham Artillery is in a very flourishing condition. We already number some hundred and thirty-five men, and the prospect is that before many days our muster roll will show one hundred and sixty. Every day the application of some good and true man is submitted for membership. You are aware of the peculiar character of our company. No one can be admitted who is not vouched for by at least two members of the company, and then the application is submitted to the corps. If the applicant receives four-fifths of the votes cast, he is admitted; if not, he is rejected. This rule relieves us of the presence of all who are objectionable; and the consequence is, we have a company of companions and of gentlemen—men of true courage and men (many of them) with large private interests at stake. I have often thought that if the Chatham Artillery does not render a good account of itself, by the blessing of God, in the day of battle, then one's faith in character, blood, and social position may well be shaken.

I had the pleasure of seeing at our camp a day or two since Lieutenant Cass of the 1st Georgia Regulars, who has just returned from Manassas. He assures me that the Army of the Potomac will largely reenlist when the terms of service expire—he thinks to the extent of seven-eighths. Our soldiers feel the responsibility resting upon them, and the wants of our Confederacy in this the day of perhaps her greatest peril. Mr. Brumby's views and Lieutenant Cass's are coincident on this subject. You may remember Cass; he studied law in our office. He is a reliable man, and courageous. I have a great attachment for him, and obtained for him a lieutenancy in the service.

The time has emphatically arrived when nearly every man capable of bearing arms within the broad limits of our Confederacy should be in the field. We are pressed on every hand, and by overwhelming forces. Our deliverance is from above, and I feel more and more deeply every day the duty which rests upon every one of us to humble himself before God, to

202

repent of our transgressions, individual and national, and invoke His interposition in our behalf. I believe that the rod will be lifted just so soon as its chastening influences have brought forth the legitimate fruits of penitence, sorrow, and reformation.

Our people must also disabuse themselves of any erroneous impressions as to the inability of our enemy to cope with us upon a fair field. The history of the world shows that the southern race as a general rule triumphs; but it also teaches us that the Puritan stock will fight, and that a feud between kindred races is always the most desperate. We have erred in this particular, and have speculated too much in regard to foreign intervention. I sincerely trust that our recent disasters will inure to our benefit, and that every arm may be nerved for the desperate struggle. We must depend upon ourselves, under God, and upon ourselves alone.

General Lee expresses the opinion that we will be able to resist any attack by water; and I am quite confident that a terrible fate awaits any force attempting an attack by land.

I presume you are aware that St. Simons and Jekyll Islands have been abandoned, and our troops withdrawn upon the main. The guns lately in position there have been brought to Savannah and are being mounted on the river. The delay on the part of the enemy in not advancing at once upon the city when the demonstration was first made was most opportune, and I may say providential.

Yesterday afternoon the enemy struck their tents on Wassaw Island and embarked their troops. This looks like an attack. It may be that they purpose taking possession of the islands recently abandoned by us in the vicinity of Brunswick. . . .

Do give warmest love to dear Mother, to my dear little daughter. And believe me ever

Your affectionate son,
Charles C. Jones, Jr.

Kind remembrances to the Doctor, Sister Carrie, and little Stanhope. My respects to Mr. Brumby.

I have directed Messrs. Claghorn & Cunningham to send to you a cask of porter which is said to be very fine. I trust that you and Mother will be benefited by it. The cask will reach No. 3 on Monday next.

Captain Claghorn desires his special remembrance.

IX

Montevideo, *Friday,* February 21st, 1862

My very dear Son,

My thoughts have often reverted to the evening we spent together in Savannah. We are living in such solemn and alarming times that we must realize that those who part today may never meet again on earth. God grant you His special care and protection, fidelity in your lot, a holy faith and trust in Him at all times, which will support you in the hour of conflict, deliver you from every fear, and arm you with wisdom and deathless courage!

The hour has arrived when men and women too in the Southern Confederacy must seek to know and to do their duty with fearless hearts and hands. Our recent disasters are appalling. The thought of Nashville, the heart of the country and I may say granary of our Confederacy, falling into the hands of those robbers and murderers casts a terrible gloom over us all. That point in their possession, it really appeared that they might touch every other in North Alabama and Georgia. I trust this day's mail will bring us some encouraging news!

Tomorrow, with the divine blessing, our worthy President will be inaugurated and our government established. Through a suggestion of your father's we are to have religious services and special prayer throughout our county, that God's favor might rest upon the events of the day, upon all placed in authority over us, and upon the whole constitution and government of our beloved country, civil, military, and religious. Your father wrote Mr. Axson upon the subject, and I see there is to be an observance of the day in Savannah. Without the regenerating, sanctifying influences of the religion of our Divine Lord and Saviour we cannot be established in justice, truth, and righteousness.

On last Sabbath your Uncle John preached one of the best-adapted sermons on the present state of things and our duties growing out of them that I ever heard. The place of meeting was the Riceboro hotel, and his audience the Liberty Independent Troop. I wish every camp in the country could hear it. I asked if he could not go and preach it at Camp Claghorn. Would it be practicable?

Next Sabbath will be our Communion. If you could have been present, we wanted to have our precious little Ruth baptized. We are fearing that she will take the measles, as two cases have appeared on the place, and her *nurse* has never had it. Your brother thinks they would not affect the baby seriously, but I would be glad to keep them off. She is now cutting her fourth tooth, and while I am writing is sitting by herself on the carpet. When I reached home from Savannah, Susan met me with her at the gate, when she reached out her little arms with delight and clung to me.

Your letter containing the autograph of our noble old commodore has been received, and I am truly obliged to you, my dear son. I shall prize and preserve it. My relics of war, warriors, and battlefields are increasing. In a letter of much interest recently received from Dunwody he sends me a portion of the nostril of General Bartow's horse. It looks almost like a flake of isinglass.

The day after we saw you Daughter and myself had the pleasure of seeing Commodore Tattnall. He was slowly promenading in the square before the Pulaski House with his son, recently released from the North. We walked up and passed him for a good view, and our hearts went up with the fervent: "God bless and preserve you, noble and bravest of men and patriots! If I had the power, you should command the proudest fleet that ever floated on the ocean." As it is, let us rejoice that our infant navy can claim such a paternity.

Your Uncle John and family are with us. He has a pair of artillery epaulettes from Manassas for you. All unite in best love to you, with kisses from your own babe.

Your affectionate mother,
Mary Jones.

Lt. Charles C. Jones, Jr., *to* Rev. *and* Mrs. C. C. Jones[g]
Camp Claghorn, *Monday,* February 24th, 1862
My dear Father and Mother,

I write to hope that all at home are well, and to send my warmest love. We have nothing of interest with us.

The recent reverses in the West, most severe as they are, will, I trust, bring our people to a nearer trust in God and to a more faithful and energetic use of those means which are placed in our hands for the preservation of our national honor and for the defense of our soil. Every man capable of bearing arms should be in the field; and the country should be thoroughly alive to the sense of the imminent dangers which surround us.

Our battery is receiving almost daily accretions; and we trust, with the blessing of God, to do the state some service when the day of battle comes. Our expectation is, if we can obtain additional horses, to make our battery *an eight-gun battery,* recruiting up to one hundred and seventy-five men.

Give many kisses to my precious little daughter. And believe me ever, my dear parents, with warmest love,

Your affectionate son,
Charles C. Jones, Jr.

LT. CHARLES C. JONES, JR., *to* MRS. MARY JONES[g]
Camp Claghorn, *Thursday,* February 27th, 1862
My very dear Mother,

Many thanks for your very kind and interesting letter, which reached me a day since. I am happy to know that all at home are well. In addition to other duties I have been all the week busily engaged in the capacity of judge advocate in a series of cases at an adjoining encampment.

We can from this camp hear the morning and evening guns from one of the Lincoln batteries recently erected in the Savannah River.

Our recent reverses are exerting a salutary effect, and I trust they will continue to do so. Last evening we admitted thirteen new members, and are expecting many more petitions. Tomorrow is a day of fasting, humiliation, and prayer. This evening at retreat our captain published an order suspending on that day all customary drills and requesting each member of the corps to observe the occasion with becoming solemnity and earnestness. To humble ourselves before God and to repent of our sins, national and individual, and to invoke His interposition in our behalf is now our first duty. And I believe He will hear our cry.

I sincerely wish that I could be at home on Sabbath, but the enjoyment of that privilege does not lie in my power.

There is but little change in our military status. Our defenses are being strengthened daily. General Mercer is now in command of Skidaway Island and of the adjacent forces. Do give much love to Father. Kiss my precious little daughter for me. And believe me ever, my dear mother,
Your ever affectionate son,
Charles C. Jones, Jr.

LT. CHARLES C. JONES, JR., *to* REV. *and* MRS. C. C. JONES[g]
Camp Claghorn, *Monday,* March 3rd, 1862
My dear Father and Mother,

I embrace a moment at this early hour in the morning, while our transportation agent waits with team harnessed and ready for his trip to the city, to send you and my precious little daughter much love. We are all pretty well in camp. The approaching draft has moved the sluggish, and our ranks have materially increased.

The Federal fleet has, with the exception of some four vessels, disappeared from Wassaw Sound. It is rumored that a night attack will soon be made, under the leadership of General Walker of the state forces, upon the batteries recently erected by the Federals in Savannah River. How true this may be time must show. The effect of their capture would be to relieve Fort Pulaski immediately, and indirectly to infuse new spirit and confidence in our troops. The attempt should be made. As ever,
Your affectionate son,
Charles C. Jones, Jr.

Montevideo, *Monday,* March 3rd, 1862

My dear Son,

I embrace a moment to let you know that your last notes have been received, and we are happy and grateful to know that you are in good health and spirits, and that your company is so prosperous. I have no doubt that if you are called to the field that both officers and men will do their duty to God and their country. For I consider you as fighting for the cause which our Heavenly Father approves, and that He will give you all courage and strength in that day. My prayer daily for you and for the company is threefold: first, that officers and men may become the true soldiers of the Cross; second, that you may never see more of war than you now see; and third, if it be ordained otherwise, that the Lord would preserve you in your persons and your lives and bless you with victory.

Our late disasters are arousing our country, and making all a *unit,* and inspiring us with a right spirit. We have been resting on our laurels, and upon the impression of our ability to overcome always. For this good effect we should bless God.

It was indeed fitting that our permanent government should be inaugurated with fasting, humiliation, and prayer; and no doubt the day was devoutly observed throughout the Confederacy. No God was ever acknowledged in the Constitution of the old United States. We have acknowledged "the Almighty God" in our Constitution—the God of the Bible, the only living and true God—as our God; and we take Him as the God of our nation and worship Him, and put our nation under His care as such. This is a blessed fact, and a soul-inspiring fact; and I believe He will own and bless us. And moreover, under the old Constitution of the United States we never had a *Christian President*—never a man who in the Presidential chair openly professed the orthodox faith of the gospel and connected with that profession an open communion with the Lord at His table, and a decidedly Christian walk and conversation. General Washington was a communing member of the Episcopal Church; and while it is hoped and believed that he was a true Christian, yet the evidence is not so clear and satisfactory as we could wish. Our first President is accredited a *Christian man.* We should bless God for this mercy, and pray for him as a brother in Christ as well as our chief magistrate. His proclamation is Christian throughout in language and spirit; and the close of his inaugural address, in prayer to God as the Head of a great nation in such a time as the present, melts into tenderness under a consciousness of weakness and imperfection, and yet rises into the sublimity of faith—the sublimity of an unshaken faith. Oh, for pious rulers and officers! What a healthful influence would flow down from them over our people! Captain Claghorn's order for the day of fasting was an honor to him and acceptable to his companions in arms; and if he will honor the Lord, the Lord will honor him.

Your dear little one is quite bright, full of spirits, intelligent, affectionate; but is thinner than she was, and troubled with an eruption on her head. It seems hard for her to get over her lingering affection. Yet we hope it is gradually wearing away. She and Stanhope are great friends. It is interesting to see them kiss each other. They ring the bell for family prayers every morning between them, and sometimes stay to prayers; but their patience is not always long enough.

Was with Robert on fast day (Friday); your Uncle John with Mr. Buttolph. All relations and friends generally well. Drop your Uncle William a line sometimes.

Your Uncle John takes this letter down to Savannah with him today, where he expects to stay till Thursday. Puts up at the Pulaski, and hopes if possible to ride out and see you—perhaps on Wednesday.

Mother has just come into the study with Little Sister to show me her head, with iodine put on the little eruptions. She is motioning with her hands like a bird, and with her earnest eyes watching my pen, and in great good spirits, and pulling away at her grandmother's buttons. Do not omit your Bible nor your secret devotions daily; camp life is trying to principle and faith. We pray for you constantly.

Your ever affectionate father,
C. C. Jones.

LT. CHARLES C. JONES, JR., *to* REV. C. C. JONES[8]

Camp Claghorn, *Friday,* March 7th, 1862

My dear Father,

I am under many obligations to you for your very kind and valued favor of the 3rd inst., which reached me only last night. Our mail facilities are not as perfect as they might be, and letters are consequently not unfrequently behind their proper seasons.

We have had the pleasure of a visit from Uncle John, which I appreciated and enjoyed, regretting at the same time that he was prevented from extending it. He appeared pleased with our camp and its details. The fact is that it is remarkable for its beauty, cleanliness, and good order. The addition of the tents recently pitched for the recruits has increased the proportions of the encampment almost to those of a regiment.

I have just come in from assisting in dressing the wound of young Samuel S. Law, a son of your esteemed friend Judge Law—a private in our company, and a very exemplary and exceedingly pleasant man. I say *man:* he is about eighteen years old. He was handling his pistol (one of Colt's navy revolvers) with a heavy glove (the day being very cold) when the hammer escaped from his fingers and the cap exploded. The ball passed through the calf of his left leg, barely touching the bone. The wound, although not at present dangerous, is painful, and the accident a sad one.

Today is a day set apart by our governor as a season for humiliation, fasting, and prayer to Almighty God. It is observed as such in our camp. There is a total suspension of all drills and customary fatigue duties. We cannot regard such occasions too frequently or too solemnly. The nation must be brought to feel their sins and their dependence upon God, not only for their blessings but for their actual salvation from the many and huge dangers which surround us.

I believe that one end of this present punishment is being realized: you may observe signs of penitence and of reform. The last is a most important one. I refer to the exclusion of all intoxicating liquors from our camps, and the prohibition of the manufacture of alcoholic drinks. Could we but rid our armies of the presence of this prime evil, there is no estimating the amount of sickness, immorality, neglect of duty, and false courage which would be removed. Never trust any soldier who drinks habitually. His apparent daring under dangers is, in nine cases out of ten, artificial, and vanishes with the fumes which gave it birth. I have seen illustrations of this. The reform has been begun in earnest in Savannah. The military authorities, acting under the orders of General Jackson, are closing the drinking shops. Were the mayor of the city a man of the right stamp, he would have taken the initiative in this matter long ago. There is a plain way for accomplishing reform.

Our reverses seem to be producing the desired effect. If properly improved, they, instead of being as they seem an injury, will really inure to our great benefit.

I thank you, Father, for the picture of my dear little daughter. I am greatly concerned about that affection of the ear; I fear it may prove permanent in its character. I long to see you all, and hope to be able to do so the latter part of this month. Do give warmest love to my dear mother and little Mary Ruth. Remember me sincerely to the Doctor, Sister Carrie, and little Stanhope. And believe me ever, my dear father,

Your affectionate son,
Charles C. Jones, Jr.

Lt. Charles C. Jones, Jr., *to* Rev. *and* Mrs. C. C. Jones[8]
Camp Claghorn, *Friday,* March 14th, 1862
My dear Father and Mother,

In consequence of the absence of Captain Claghorn I have been so much occupied with the details of the battery that I have not enjoyed an opportunity until this moment of expressing my sincere hope that all at home are well, and of sending my warmest love to you both and to my precious little daughter. In all my often remembrances of home there is a constant and heartfelt regret that I am prevented from enjoying the pleasure which I so much crave of at least an occasional visit. I trust so soon as the captain returns I will be able to come out.

There are so many recruits in our company, and the necessity for drill is so urgent, that we are constantly occupied. The efficiency of the battery is rendered the more requisite now that the guns of the Skidaway batteries are retired, as well as those of Green Island. The troops are still upon those islands. The guns thus retired will be remounted, some at the Thunderbolt and others at the Beaulieu batteries on the main. The withdrawal of those batteries, it seems probable, will necessitate a removal from our present camp, as the gunboats of the enemy can now with but little difficulty find access to this point. A field battery can least of all protect itself at an advanced post. Our line of defenses has been very materially changed. There is now a total abandonment of all the islands. It is astonishing what a vast amount of labor and materials has been wasted in our military operations. And these continued evacuations are exerting a most depressing influence upon the troops. We need some decisive action—let the results be what they may—for a moral effect.

We have a bright ray of sunshine from the *Virginia*. Gallant vessel—and gallant men! They have given us memories which will live in proudest remembrance in the history of our present struggle.

I sat down for a long letter, but am prevented by the coming of General Mercer, who calls upon business and will remain for some hours. The troops from Skidaway and Green Islands will probably be retired to this island and the adjoining main. With warmest love, my dear parents, to you, and many kisses for my dear little daughter, I am, as ever,

Your affectionate son,
Charles C. Jones, Jr.

REV. C. C. JONES *to* LT. CHARLES C. JONES, JR.[8]

Montevideo, *Friday,* March 14th, 1862

My dear Son,

The week has almost gone, and you have had no letter. Not that your mother and I have not purposed to write, but there has been a succession of family and social events that have remitted the matter from one day to another.

Last Saturday we had an arrival of friends from McIntosh about 6 P.M.— Mrs. and Miss Dunwody and Mrs. Dean Dunwody and five children, ten servants, two carriages and one baggage wagon, and four horses and two mules—en route for the up country, having broken up their plantation on the Altamaha, leaving a small part of the Negroes behind for future disposal, the bulk moving up by steamboat to Doctortown and through Liberty to No. 3 station, part going to Southwest Georgia and part to vicinity of Columbus. The river bottom of the Altamaha has been pretty much abandoned: Negroes moved up the river, and the greater part of the market crop also, the enemy having free access to every part of the river if he chooses to come up. Darien is pretty well deserted.

Satan seems to have taken advantage of the times at Midway last Sunday by sending up a report that the enemy had taken possession of Darien the night before, which threw many people into a nervous state and set nearly everybody talking; and the good seed fell by the wayside, and the fowls of the air devoured them up, and am afraid not much good was done by two very excellent sermons. The war impinges dreadfully upon the Sabbath and upon all the means of grace. War is the most universal of all the divine judgments in its injurious influences upon man and upon his every interest, temporal and eternal. Nothing escapes it. There was, however, no panic on Wednesday, the day of the annual meeting of the Midway Church and Society; for we met, transacted our business quietly, voted the same officers, the same pastor, and the same salaries, and chose pews and went home as if there was no war at all, which was doing just what our duty required.

Our friends the Dunwodys have left us, and your Uncle John went with one party of them to Savannah to assist them in getting through the town with their people and baggage. We expect him home today.

Colonel Spalding has ordered a detachment of twenty-five men from the Liberty Independent Troop to be stationed at Fort Barrington to arrest the ascent of the enemy up the river and so to protect the railroad bridge. The men with their rifles could not do much with a gunboat in rapid motion. Guns of some caliber are required at favorable points below the bridge to do much good. The Ogeechee is equally exposed, and the destruction of either one bridge would seriously incommode us. We hear of Colonel Stiles's killing some Yankees on an oyster bank and of the shelling of Brunswick in revenge by the enemy; of a skirmish towards St. Marys in which we came off very well, taking three prisoners; of the ascent of the St. Johns by the Yankees and of the abandonment of East Florida, etc., etc.

There seems to be a general movement of our armies everywhere, a concentration of forces at given points and a falling back and change of front in others, all foreshadowing warm work and some new line of policy. We are happily waking up from our lethargy and putting off foreign expectations. My own opinion is that we should resort to a system—to a chain of impregnable fortifications: New Orleans, Mobile, Savannah, Charleston, some point in North Carolina, Norfolk, Richmond, and so round through Virginia, North Carolina, and Tennessee to Memphis, and all inland cities that lie in any exposed condition. They would call for heavy forces from the enemy to reduce them, impede their progress, give us more men for active field service, and strengthen our people. Of course we should require more foundries, more powder mills, etc.; but the outlay would be our gain and add to the happy issue of our war.

Mr. Quarterman has consulted me about the amount of cotton to be planted at Arcadia the present season, and showed me your letter. I told him I should not plant above an acre to the hand, if that, and recommended him to inform you of my opinion. We have the present crop on hand, which will be sufficient if sold this or the coming year to pay expenses for two years. If not, why add to it? And if not, our only dependence is upon a provision crop which we may sell for the support of our armies. If peace comes and finds us with a provision crop, we can sell it for something. And then peace will bring some little credit if we need it. But we are to look matters in the face as they are: there is not the faintest prospect in the world now apparent for a peace. Every farmer and planter should see this and feel that he is called upon in duty to his country to raise all the provisions he possibly can for the support of our armies, especially in the cotton states, since Kentucky and Tennessee are not available sources of supply to us now; and when they shall be no one knows.

I say there is not the faintest prospect of peace, for nothing but a demonstration of the utter impossibility of the North's subduing the South will bring about negotiations for peace. If we beat back their six hundred thousand men and they exhaust all their present revenue and plans of revenue, such is the resolution which they aver, and their desire to save themselves from bankruptcy and disgrace, that they will manage to raise another six hundred thousand men and money in some shape to support them. A great necessity, they feel (of their own wretched creation), is laid upon them to go forward; and they say openly they have the power and the money, and they will crush out the South! And we see how they are rousing all their energies for that purpose. We have nothing to do but to meet it; and I believe that if our people are true to themselves and to their principles, by God's help, they cannot conquer us.

Am glad to see more vigor infusing itself into our government—martial law where necessary, suspension of military officers, liquor reforms, etc. Our reverses are doing us good. May it please our God—the Almighty God whom we have acknowledged and taken in our Constitution to be the God of our nation (and it is a source of great comfort to my mind that we have done so, for under the old United States Constitution we acknowledged no God at all, the Constitution being atheistical)—I say, may it please God to hear our prayers, and accept our fasting and humiliation, and cause us to break off our sins by righteousness, and to show us His favor and redeem us from the hand of our enemies! We are not to faint in the day of reverses, but to grasp the sword more firmly and pray more humbly and fervently and fight more manfully.

Mother is very unwell with her cough at nights and her old complaint; and having so many cases, she has not rest enough.

About our arrangements for the summer we will write you another time, D.V. Have sent twenty-five bales cotton and stored it at Arcadia. Mother thinks it would be safer there than on the river here.

Your dear little daughter is looking like herself again, and is full of life; and her little mind is daily expanding, and she begins now to use her voice, and is becoming very decided in her preferences for individuals, and chooses her grandmother above all. She rings the bell for family worship every morning, and as soon as I come down in the parlor and tell her to ring the bell, she looks and leans towards the mantelpiece and carefully takes it by the handle for the purpose. Her nurse thinks she makes special effort to say "Jack" and "Elsie." But she eschews food, and it is only grains of dry rice that she will pick up in her little fingers and eat.

Carrie and Stanhope are with your sister on a visit; the Doctor is well. Your Aunt Jane and mother unite in much love to you. Thank you kindly for the *porter*;

it is an excellent article, with a fine body to it, and agrees with me well; and the Doctor says I must use it daily. You are remembered always in our prayers in our closets and in the family. Our best respects to Captain Claghorn. The Yankees say within thirty days Savannah and Charleston will be laid in ashes by their ironclad steamers that they are waiting for. Hope General Lawton will stop the river before our batteries and bring them to, and that we may be able to disappoint their plans. Has any general been appointed in General Lee's place? Or has he not resigned?

From your ever affectionate father,

C. C. Jones.

Have the Skidaway and Green Island batteries been *abandoned?*

P.S. I mentioned to Mr. Quarterman that perhaps he might be able to sell a few head of stock cattle at Arcadia. He said they were very poor; he had two he was fattening for sale. We have some stock cattle to sell at Maybank (twelve or fourteen head), but there have been no purchasers out for some time. *All stock cattle are poor now.*

LT. CHARLES C. JONES, JR., *to* REV. C. C. JONES[g]

Camp Claghorn, *Tuesday,* March 18th, 1862

My dear Father,

I am this moment favored with your very kind and valued letter of the 14th inst., for which you have my sincere thanks.

I deeply regret to know that dear Mother has been of late so unwell, and that she still suffers from a return of her old affection. May a good Providence soon restore her to her accustomed health, and keep my dear little daughter in that good health which I am happy to learn she is now enjoying. I long to see you all, and trust so soon as Captain Claghorn returns (which will be certainly within a week from this period, D.V.) that I will be able to obtain from headquarters a furlough of a day or two.

Skidaway and Green Islands have both been entirely evacuated. The guns, provisions, munitions, quartermaster and commissary stores have all been retired, and no advance as yet on the part of the enemy. For some two weeks past only four or five Lincoln vessels have been lying in Wassaw Sound. We have a report today that this number has been increased by the appearance of three more. The evacuation of these islands after the large amount of labor expended in fortifying them, and in the construction of causeways and bridges to facilitate the withdrawal of the troops there stationed in case of actual necessity—when, too, we have no inner line of defenses, except those erected within sight of the city of Savannah, behind which to retire the forces thus removed—seems to me very questionable in a military point of view. The men themselves are sadly disheartened at the necessity which compels them, without firing a single gun, to evacuate forts which they with their own hands had constructed, behind whose ramparts they confidently antici-pated a successful combat with the enemy at no distant day.

It does seem to me that all our operations on this coast have been mere military experiments, conceived in ignorance and brought forth none the more wisely—mere jackleg performances. Look at a few of them. Tybee Island evacuated when it should have been heavily fortified and defended by a force of certainly not less than three to five thousand men. Mistake No. 2: attempting to fortify every inlet on the coast with miserable little sand batteries on isolated points, with here and there a thirty-two-pounder and a few rounds of solid shot. Of course labor and time were only idly expended, and the project fell stillborn. Mistake No. 3: fortifications on the inner islands, which, for want of proper forecast and engineering skill in their location, and in the occupation of neighboring points, were soon pronounced untenable. Mistake No. 4: gross and most inexcusable neglect of the water approaches to Savannah and other points on the coast.

And so they may be multiplied at pleasure. The useless expenditure of means, labor, and time on our coast is fearful to contemplate, and the want of proper knowledge and requisite skill on the part of those in authority is most surprising. The reply is: "Our general has done all he could." That is not a proper answer. If he could do no more, then he should have abdicated and permitted someone else to see if he could not have done something more.

I have more confidence in General Mercer than in any of our officers, as at present advised. He is now with his forces on the Isle of Hope. His brigade numbers in all (the forces at Beaulieu, Genesis Point, etc., etc., included) about thirty-five hundred men.

In consequence of this abandonment of our outer line of defenses, this post is thrown quite in advance; and we will have lively work if the enemy moves from this direction. Skidaway Island will still be picketed with mounted men at the most assailable points, such as at the batteries at Waring's Point, Pritchard's plantation, the Indians' Fort, Adams' Point, Modena Point, etc., to give notice of any movements which may be made by the enemy. This brigade is occupied in strengthening the Thunderbolt battery and the battery at Beaulieu, which latter fort commands the approach by Vernon River and will mount ten guns, some of them of heavy caliber.

The defenses of the Savannah River I have never had an opportunity of examining, but I learn that they are numerous and formidable. Great labor has recently been expended in their construction, and we have obtained almost all the guns we need. The condition of our river defenses previous to the arrival of General Lee was horrible. It was said that we could procure no cannon. The forces were scattered about in various camps, doing little else than drilling and loafing. So soon, however, as General Lee assumed command, seconded by the activity of General Jackson of the state forces, everything indicated a most material change for the better. The earthworks thrown up around the city are quite formidable, and siege guns are mounted at intervals. The forests in front have been felled, and determined men behind them can offer a most effectual resistance.

With all due deference to the opinion of General Jackson, I think he errs in risking everything upon these works. I understand his wish is to throw everything open and invite the enemy in, offering no material check to his advance until within reach of these defenses. This is risking too much upon a single cast. We should meet our enemy where his foot first presses the soil, contest every inch, and look to these fortifications as a last resort. You know the enthusiasm of General Jackson. He will lead his forces as gallantly as probably any living man into action, and will fight to the last extremity; but I think he does not calculate sufficiently the chances of reverse. It is a rule as false in war as in logic to presume upon the weakness of our adversary. Of this we have already been guilty on more than one occasion. Recent events fully demonstrate that no such calculations can with safety longer be made. We have to contend against a power numerically vastly stronger than we are, with armies and fleets perfect in all their appointments, men who have and who will fight, and fight desperately, for they are engaged in a desperate enterprise—one in which they either rule or are ruined. We should therefore embrace every chance on our own soil which presents itself for opposing their progress, and not risk the defense of the only place and section we are actually defending upon the issue of a single battle under the very eaves of the houses of our metropolis.

I am inclined to believe that General Jackson had much influence with Generals Pemberton and Lawton in procuring the abandonment of Skidaway Island. I know that he desired it. Better far have held the forts there and taken the chances of the battle. Two causeways would have conducted the forces to the main in the event of defeat. Even a defeat in the face of superior numbers and after a gallant contest is often worth much in giving a moral tone to a contest. General Mercer regrets the step, but of course could do nothing else than obey orders. Evacuation is the order of the day. The sight or sound of that word is now as bad as a dose of hippo.

It appears that all this show of fleets on our coast has hitherto been intended as a demonstration, to keep our forces here while decisive blows were contemplated and actually struck in the West. Every day seems but to tighten the cords around us. The valley of the Mississippi is virtually almost lost, and our entire seacoast and Gulf coast with but few reservations are completely in the power of the enemy. We have nothing to offer on the seas by way of resistance, and the construction of these ironclad steamers has materially changed the value of coast fortifications. Forts are now scarcely of value, and cannot effectually check an advance.

But we are not conquered yet, nor will we be. And most cordially do I say "Amen" to your remark: "We are not to faint in the day of reverses, but to grasp the sword more firmly and pray more humbly and fervently and fight more manfully." McClellan has planned his campaign with great ability, and has already redeemed his pledge that he would compel General Johnston of the Army of the Potomac to evacuate his lines—and that without firing a single gun. But, as the old adage says, that is a long road which has no turning. We have been fighting in the shade very long, but the dawning of new life and light must come. We needed as individuals and as a nation chastisement to bring us to a sense of our sins and of our many and great shortcomings. We are, I trust, being purified as by fire; and my firm belief is that so soon as we are fairly brought to true humility before God and repentance of sin, He will crown our resistance of these lawless, ruthless invaders with quick and absolute success.

Did you observe what the wretches did at New Bern, North Carolina? I want no black flag raised upon a staff, but I wish to see it carried in the breast of every good and true man armed in behalf of our country and of the homes we love. And every Lincolnite found in enmity upon our shores should be put to the sword as an outlaw, outside of the pale of civilization and of humanity.

The concentration of our forces will enable us when the opportunity presents itself to offer more effectual resistance. In concentrating, however, we give up much—very much—that is most valuable. At present an area of ten miles square in extent will embrace about all the soil of Georgia actually defended. This is a most depressing reflection.

I see by the papers that General Lee has been appointed commander in chief of the military of the Confederate States under the provisions of a recent act of Congress. His loss will be severely felt by us. He is succeeded in the command by General Pemberton, an old army officer and a Pennsylvanian by birth. Most of his reputation is, I think, before him.

I fully concur with you, my dear father, as to the character of the crop to be planted the present year. We should all plant largely of provisions. Every bushel of corn and blade of grass will be greatly needed for the support of our armies.

I am happy to know that you enjoy the porter, and trust that it will prove of benefit to you.

We have a report in camp that thirteen thousand stand of Enfield rifles have arrived in Florida for the State of Georgia.

This evening I assisted in laying out an earthwork on this side of Skidaway bridge, designed for the protection of a section of our battery and three hundred infantry to be posted there in case the enemy occupy Skidaway Island and attempt to use that structure in crossing to the main. A courier just arrived from Skidaway reports all the vessels (nine in number) gone. Rumor says our batteries there are to be blown up tonight by our men.

I trust, my dear father and mother, to see you very soon. Meanwhile I am, with warmest love and with many kisses for my precious little daughter, as ever,

Your affectionate son,
Charles C. Jones, Jr.

216

LT. CHARLES C. JONES, JR., *to* REV. *and* MRS. C. C. JONES[8]

Camp Claghorn, *Wednesday,* March 19th, 1862

My dear Father and Mother,

I write to remind you and my dear little daughter of my warmest love and constant remembrance.

We have nothing of interest in our camp or its vicinity. As yet the Lincolnites have made no demonstrations. A report reached us this afternoon that a few troops had been landed from the fleet upon Green Island, but it has been contradicted. The intention of the enemy as expressed by Commodore Du Pont, and illustrated by their acts, seems to be simply to possess our coast and to threaten without attempting an invasion. Another object doubtless is to keep our troops here and prevent heavy reinforcements in the West.

A delightful thunderstorm this afternoon has quite refreshed us, and the falling rain induces quiet thought and a calm of mind and body quite opposed to the turbulent passions and events of the hour. Captain Claghorn has not yet returned. I sincerely hope to see you very soon. As ever,

Your affectionate son,

Charles C. Jones, Jr.

REV. C. C. JONES *to* LT. CHARLES C. JONES, JR.[8]

Montevideo, *Monday,* March 24th, 1862

My dear Son,

We are in receipt of your two last interesting letters of the 18th and 19th. Mother says you will have to excuse her not writing, as she is not well, and has the constant care of a large family. It has been a long time since we have been alone for a day.

Your dear little daughter is thinner than she was, and has an eruption on her person which Mother thinks may be measles; and your brother has just ordered that she be kept closely housed this very cold, blustering day. She is quite bright, and will not quit her grandmother's arms if she can help it.

Two days ago Peggy took her to nurse, and finding her mumbling something in her mouth, took out a piece of *veritable tobacco* (chewing twist) nearly the size of a quarter of a dollar and somewhat thicker—a piece she got hold of about Susan's person someway, as she uses tobacco (smokes certainly, if she does not chew). It had been in the little thing's mouth long enough to be well moistened; and had she swallowed it, she would have died in a short time and the cause never had been known! It was a special providence, for which we desire to be thankful. Mother has hung the piece of tobacco up by a string in the closet, that Susan may see it morning and evening and at other times when she is washing and dressing the baby. As might be supposed, Susan has not the most remote idea how the baby came by the tobacco.

Last week she was sitting in her grandmother's lap at morning prayers playing with a rose, and several times she plucked off the leaves of the flower, and looking archly into her grandmother's face put them to her lips as if she intended to eat them, and then took down her hand and shook her head. Little Daughter and Charlie and Stanhope and your uncle's boys John and Joseph are very fond of her, and she is delighted with their attentions. Her ear is better. She is somewhat fretful today.

Your sister and family are with us (today at Arcadia), and your brother's family and your Uncle John and family; and if you were with us our little circle would be complete of our children and grandchildren. We bless the Lord for those He spares to us on earth, and we bless Him for those He has taken to Himself in heaven. Dear Ruthie and Julia! How often, how often are they in my mind!

Miss Mary Dunwody and Mr. Howard, who married Carrie Shackelford, are with us, en route to Darien to remove the last of their Negroes from old Sidon up the country.

We have measles both at Montevideo and at Arcadia. Progress very slowly. But no whooping cough as yet. Cold for planting operations. Abundant rains. Planting in hope that we may be permitted to cultivate and harvest.

If the enemy makes no invasion this season and the war continues, arrangements must be made this summer—whoever lives to see it—for a removal back from the coast; for the invasion will come next winter. By present appearances the campaign is to lie westward for the spring and summer, and must prove a heavy one and put our resources to the test. We are changing front from Virginia to Missouri. We are obliged to concentrate and fortify and meet the heavy advancing columns of the enemy. Our people have been ahead of our government. I should like to see more energy and expansion in our government. We have needed and do now need it greatly, although our reverses have had a quickening and salutary effect. We cannot rectify past mistakes except in part. We have to do with the present. If our people are true to themselves, by God's blessing, the issue will eventually be favorable. I tremble for the increasing wickedness of our country. War is the hotbed of iniquity of every kind. The Lord interpose and help us!

Mr. Yancey settles the European intervention! No friend in any government on that civilized continent! This is no news to the historian, nor to the reflecting observer. The republic of America never had any friends in Europe, unless in the Swiss cantons. The forms of government are all opposed to ours. Their wars have been against the power of the people. Opposition to *the form* of our government we have to begin with, then add the dread and abhorrence of revolutions and changes to be found in all despotic and aristocratic governments. And no princes hate revolutions more than those who have risen through revolution into power; to aid revolutionists gives such matters respectability and influence with their own people. All the friendship we shall get is that of interest. Upon this, in the single articles of cotton and tobacco, our government and people have relied most blindly. A kind Providence has so adjusted the provisions for man's necessity that any one product, no matter how largely soever cultivated and used, may be struck out, and after a little temporary inconvenience the world eats, drinks, sleeps, and clothes itself and goes about its business as aforetime. There was a time when the world had neither cotton nor tobacco, and such a time could be again. We are fighting first for our liberty and independence, not for our interests. They certainly are involved, but they are secondary. Give us the first; the second follows surely.

Dr. Axson preached two admirable sermons for us yesterday, adapted to the times.

Mother says I must tell you she is getting on well with her *gunboat fund.* Has killed her stall-fed beef today and says she will corn some up for you, and you must come out and enjoy it. Hope the captain will come soon, so as to give you a chance.

Our men who were sent down to work on the fortifications under General Lawton's requisition have been gone near three weeks. Four have been sent back—one to Arcadia and three to this place.

All unite in much love to you. Our regards to Captain Claghorn. The Lord bless and keep you, my dear son!

Your ever affectionate father,
C. C. Jones.

LT. CHARLES C. JONES, JR., *to* REV. *and* MRS. C. C. JONES[g]

Camp Claghorn, *Monday,* March 24th, 1862

My dear Father and Mother,

The recent demonstrations of the enemy on the South Carolina coast, trivial in fact, have by our commanding generals here been magnified into movements of no inconsiderable importance; and the consequence is that we have been for the past week under orders "to march at a moment's notice." The ensuing days, however, on each occasion brought disappointment, and we subsided into the customary status of a fixed encampment. Wright's Legion (eight hundred strong), a band of brave, hardy fellows, yesterday afternoon took up the line of march for Savannah en route for South Carolina. This morning before day they are again in camp. The island resounded with their shouts of joy when moving towards the anticipated field of battle, and the tap of the drum gave impulse to their active tread. This morning in silence they returned to their former camping ground, disappointed and full of regret that the pretended proved not to be a real demonstration on the part of the enemy, and that the day of battle was again indefinitely postponed.

Our limber and caisson chests have all been packed for several days, and we have anxiously hoped that we would soon enjoy the opportunity of rendering essential service to our section and country in the immediate presence of the hated foe; but the prospect for so doing seems at present quite as remote as ever. There is no telling, however, what a day may bring forth, and our duty is to be always in readiness. For one I profess as much disinclination to danger and fighting, abstractly considered, as generally exists; but it is to me a source of deep regret to find day after day of our present term of enlistment expiring, and this fine battery, than which there is said by Generals Lee and Pemberton to be none superior and but one equal (and that one of the companies of the justly celebrated battalion of artillery from New Orleans) in the Confederate service, never allowed the opportunity of testifying its devotion to our immortal cause, and of proving its efficiency and the bravery of each member upon the field of battle.

I am quite sure that it would do your patriotic hearts good to see our proficiency in drill, the order of the company, and to feel the pulse of true courage which throbs in every breast. Our parade ground is visited almost every day by persons from Savannah. So soon as the news reached us of the landing of the Lincolnites at Bluffton, I immediately wrote (Captain Claghorn being still absent) to General Lawton, expressing our preparedness and urging him to send this battery wherever danger seemed most imminent. A flattering reply is before me in which he says that "he highly appreciates the chivalric and patriotic spirit which induced the tender of the services of this battery, and that whenever the emergency arises it will give him great pleasure to afford us the earliest opportunity to exhibit our discipline and efficiency in front of the enemy." From General Mercer, who is in immediate command of this brigade, I have a like assurance.

Nothing but a sense of duty and the honest desire to discharge it and to serve one's country faithfully in this the hour of her greatest need can give satisfaction in camp life, where none of the excitements of an active campaign and of danger actually present exist. You remember Napoleon's rapid movements and remarkable success in the face of overwhelming forces in the vicinity, I think, of Lake Garda. I have often wondered at the inactivity and slothfulness of many of our officers in command, and have as often wished that some of his spirit, his wonderful enthusiasm, his quickness of perception and activity in execution, could possess them. Price is almost the only one who has any creative genius about him.

Two days since, I rode over to Skidaway Island to our abandoned batteries. They are already to some extent yielding to the disintegrating influences of the winds and rains. Five Lincoln vessels lay in full view. A large sailboat filled with men was amusing itself on the bright waters. The sea gulls and pelicans in large numbers were disporting themselves on easy wing. The first blush of spring was upon the shore, and the waves were gently rising and falling in soothing murmurs beneath the mild sunlight and the evening air. All was perfect stillness—everything emblematic of perfect peace. The antithesis was striking to a degree, and it was difficult to realize the fact that where nature reposed in such sweet, quiet, generous security, peace dwelt not.

For the present I can see in the future no ray of peaceful sunshine. Clouds and darkness are about us. That we shall, if we but prove true to our God and to ourselves, be eventually successful I entertain not the shadow of a doubt;

but this consummation will, as matters now stand, be reached only after months and probably years of severe struggle, heroic endurance, and patient patriotism. Foreign intervention is entirely out of the question. I wish our people had thought it so long ago; we would have gone more earnestly about our work. I am glad it is out of the question, and that no foreign power shall attempt to intervene for the supposed settlement of our present difficulties. No compromise can by any possibility be made. We must make ours a self-sustaining government, developing at home resources of every description and remanding ourselves to the days of Roman virtue and Spartan simplicity. Mr. Yancey, I see in a recent speech, suggests that our ministers, now knocking for admission into the cold reception rooms of European palaces, be recalled. I think his idea more than half correct. The time is, I trust, not far distant when the world will feel our power, and in turn itself honored by our friendship and benefited by our commercial alliances.

You see our gallant commodore has left us to assume the command of the *Virginia*. All success to him! We part with him with less regret because he goes to enlarge his sphere of usefulness. We need his example and his services everywhere. . . . I sincerely trust, my dear father and mother, that you both and my precious little daughter are in the enjoyment of many blessings. With warmest love, I am ever

Your affectionate son,
Charles C. Jones, Jr.

LT. CHARLES C. JONES, JR., *to* REV. *and* MRS. C. C. JONES[g]
Savannah, *Wednesday,* March 26th, 1862
My dear Father and Mother,

The enemy on yesterday afternoon landed a small force on Skidaway Island, burned our batteries under cover of their steamers, and retired, leaving the United States flag flying from a house recently used by us as a hospital previous to the evacuation of the Island. We had only a few pickets at the battery. Three shell were fired at them from the gunboats, but they did no damage. So soon as the enemy retired, which they did after firing the batteries, the pickets returned and secured the flag. It is now in General Mercer's quarters. I do not think the Lincolnites had any intention in making this trifling demonstration other than the destruction of our abandoned works. All is quiet today, and the vessels are lying at their accustomed anchorage. We could see the smoke of the guns from our camp. If they land in force, General Mercer will, I think, give them a fight upon Skidaway. This I deem quite improbable, as I do not believe that they have in their vessels now lying in Wassaw Sound one thousand men.

I am expecting Captain Claghorn every day. Do kiss my dear little daughter for me. And believe me ever, my dear father and mother, with warmest love,

Your ever affectionate son,
Charles C. Jones, Jr.

I am in the city for an hour or two to attend to our quartermaster and commissary supplies for the next month.

MRS. MARY JONES *to* LT. CHARLES C. JONES, JR.[g]
Montevideo, *Thursday,* March 27th, 1862

My very dear Son,

With my large household it seems impossible to find time for writing you, although my thoughts are ever with you, and we are eagerly looking forward to your promised visit.

Our precious little Ruth has had an eruption all over her person which I have hoped would prove to be measles. Joe does not think it is so. We kept her confined all this week to our chamber. This morning the little bird is released from her cage, and she is delighted to be again in the parlor and playing with the children. They are all devoted to her, showing her every mark of the tenderest love. She has lost flesh, but is bright and cheerful, and every day expands her little mind. I wish she could see you every day, and assure you she is the joy and comfort of her grandparents.

The cases of measles on the place multiply daily; some eight or nine in the house at this time. Several of the men who worked on the entrenchments have returned sick, but a few days' rest I hope will restore them. The measles have also broken out at Arcadia.

Your brother's term of service with the troop ends the 1st of April. Carrie and himself speak of going to Augusta next week, but I want him to rest awhile at home.

I have been making some collections for the gunboat, and will soon forward them to Mr. G. B. Lamar. Mrs. John Barnard and Mr. N. L. Barnard have presented your brother with a silver pitcher and two goblets on a silver waiter—an elegant expression of their kind feelings—each marked "Dr. Joseph Jones." Your father enjoys the porter daily, and takes it not only with relish but benefit. Father, sisters, brother, and Uncle John all unite with me in best love to you, with unnumbered kisses from your own little daughter, and the unfailing love and prayers of

Your affectionate mother,
Mary Jones.

In haste.

LT. CHARLES C. JONES, JR., *to* REV. *and* MRS. C. C. JONES[g]
Camp Claghorn, *Monday,* April 7th, 1862

My dear Father and Mother,

I embrace a moment and an opportunity to the mail this morning to assure you and my dear little daughter of my constant love, and to express my earnest hope that a kind Providence is mercifully restoring to health and strength again the sick at home. How is Tyrone? And are all the measles patients recovering?

I regretted very much that I was compelled to leave you on Saturday, and nothing but a sense of imperative duty compelled me to do so. Arrived at camp Saturday evening. Found everything quiet. Some of our men sick. Almost all of the troops retired from the Isle of Hope. We now hold the most advanced post. Nothing definite in reference to the movements of the enemy on our coast. Indications point to an early attack upon Fort Pulaski.

The morning papers have just been received, and we are thanking God for our grand victory near Corinth, the Solferino of the war. I trust the accounts as reported are correct. I do not feel entirely confident as yet. We have been so often overwhelmed by numbers that I fear the effect of the advancing reserve columns of Buell. Should this Army of the West be annihilated, the North will feel it most sensibly, and the effect will be great at home and abroad. If the report of numbers be correct, this is the heaviest battle ever fought upon the western continent. Albert Sidney Johnston will have amply established his claim to that regard which ranks him as our best general in the field. I pray God to consummate the victory which He has so auspiciously inaugurated.

I send fifty dollars for Gilbert. In the hurry of leaving the depot I forgot to hand it to him. Did Brother receive from him one hundred and twenty-five dollars? Mr. Quarterman handed me that sum at the station, and I charged Gilbert with its delivery to Brother, with the request that he would divide it between Sister and himself, sending me receipt for same that I may keep the account of the place correct.

I thank you sincerely, my dear parents, for the volumes. I will read them at the earliest moment, and with care. Pray say to Uncle John that Mr. Lamar promises to meet him and family at the depot on Tuesday afternoon next. I handed the gunboat fund to Mr. Lamar in person on Saturday afternoon. Do kiss my dear little daughter for me. And believe me, my dear father and mother, with warmest love to you both, and with kindest remembrances to all at home,

Your affectionate son,
Charles C. Jones, Jr.

Lt. Charles C. Jones, Jr., *to* Rev. *and* Mrs. C. C. Jones[g]

Camp Claghorn, *Tuesday,* April 8th, 1862

I sincerely wish, my dear father and mother, that we were near enough in person to indulge in mutual congratulations upon the recent glorious success of our arms in the West. Truly we have cause for the proudest exultation and for profoundest thanks to that great God who has in mercy sent us such a signal victory. New Orleans is, for the present at least, safe from any approach of the enemy down the Mississippi valley. Island No. 10 will not now be outflanked. Memphis will remain in undisturbed security. And if the flying legions of the Lincolnites are closely pressed, Nashville may be repossessed and Tennessee delivered from the polluting presence of the insulting invaders, who have of late boasted of the prowess of their arms beneath her beautiful groves, upon her attractive hills, and within the shadow even of her splendid capitol.

We cannot overestimate the importance of this victory, and I trust from the bottom of my heart that the defeat may prove total and awful. The scenes attendant upon the retreat of the British army from Concord and Lexington in the days of the Revolution should be reenacted to the last degree; and every tree, every stone, should be clothed with a voice of thunder. Every man, woman, and child should rise in arms along the line of the retreating foe, and enforce by terrible illustration the lesson to the frightened outlaws how fearful the vengeance of a people armed in the holy cause of liberty, contending upon their own soil for the inalienable rights of life, freedom, religion, and the pursuit of happiness.

Our advices are as yet incomplete, but Beauregard and Polk lead the pursuit. I trust that the reserve columns of Buell may not stay the tide of victory. I do not think they can, with the horrors of defeat in a hostile country resting upon the one army, while the other is jubilant with that enthusiasm which draws its inspiration from such marked, recent, and illustrious success in a struggle whose issues involve all that is sacred in honor, pure in principle, true in religion, and valuable in life. Our troops must have fought with a bravery and a desperation worthy that holy behalf to the support of which they pledged their lives and sacred honors. Think of *eighteen field batteries captured!* This naked fact will give us an idea of the magnitude of the victory, and of the peril and the daring involved in its purchase. They were all probably six-gun batteries of the most approved style, and complete in all their appointments. This would give us, then, 108 field pieces, 3200 men, and at least 2250 horses, as the artillery corps in the "grand army" engaged in the battle, and scattered like the leaves of autumn before the whirlwind of our advancing regiments. The accession of arms, ammunition, camp equipage, and of the general munitions of war thus secured to us by this victory must be enormous and most valuable. The moral effect of this success cannot be overestimated, if we may credit all the accounts we already have. I would most willingly, my dear parents, have given my left arm—yes, both of them, were it necessary—to have been a personal participant in the glories of that day.

But alas, in our garlands of victory the bright and joyous leaves of the laurel are tempered into sadness by the commingled boughs of the mournful cypress. One of our bravest leaders and most accomplished generals, Albert Sidney Johnston, has fallen! And the exultant paeans of victory which rose upon the morning air from ten thousand lips throughout the length and breadth of our Confederacy as the first news of triumph were heralded with lightning speed, melted into strains of genuine sorrow before eveningtide at thought of the great price at which that victory was purchased. And yet I know of no death more grateful to the gallant chieftain—if his peace be made with his God—than to fall, sword in hand, at the head of his victorious legions, sealing by his lifeblood his devotion to country and to the holy cause of her redemption, and consecrating his name for all time upon the living pages of a glorious history as one of the protomartyrs in perhaps the noblest struggle which ever nerved the arms, inspired the energies, and gave impulse to the truest patriotism of man. His labors are ended, and the green grass will soon be growing, the soft airs of spring sighing, and the thoughtless songbirds warbling their accustomed notes of love and joy above the newly made grave of the fallen hero. Although the gleam of his blade shall nevermore amid the smoke and shock of battle point the way to victory, although his brave comrades will not again catch the inspiration of his presence on the field of peril, he will still live in the grateful remembrance of his countrymen; and the valor displayed in his death will prove alike a bright incentive to heroic action and a rich legacy to the record of the triumphs of this momentous struggle for freedom.

The day dawns. God in mercy grant that the rays of the rising sun may shine higher and brighter to the perfect end! . . . Our military status here is unchanged. The enemy, from all that we can gather, seems to be contemplating an attack upon Fort Pulaski at no distant day. The fort, we trust, is prepared to make a formidable and successful resistance. With warmest love to all, I am ever, my dear father and mother,

Your affectionate son,
Charles C. Jones, Jr.

MRS. MARY JONES *to* LT. CHARLES C. JONES, JR⁸

Montevideo, Thursday, April 10th, 1862*

My very dear Son,

Your affectionate and interesting letter was received today, and most heartily do we reciprocate the feelings it contains of gratitude to our Divine Master for our recent victory, and of profound grief at the death of our noble and gallant General A. S. Johnston. Our losses from time to time have been very great in our brave leaders, but we must trust in God and never give up our righteous cause.

I and my dear little Ruth are all alone this evening. Your father left after dinner for Walthourville to attend the meeting of Presbytery convened this evening. Joe, Carrie, and Stanhope are taking tea at South Hampton and will be back ere long. Everything around me exhibits a scene of perfect tranquillity. The trees with their deep dark shadows are reposing upon the lawn, which is irradiated with the soft pure light of a half-grown moon; whilst the melodious notes of the whippoorwill, unfailing harbinger of spring returned and winter gone, is echoing from the grove near the house and reechoing from the distant wood. In strange contrast to all that is beautiful and peaceful in this dear home of ours is the "rude sound of war's alarms" as it breaks even now upon my ear from the cannon's slow and measured thunderstrokes. Oh, the agony that comes over me at times! Where is my child? We will await tomorrow's mail with great anxiety. The Lord bless and spare you, my dear child, and preserve your whole company, and if the hour of conflict has arrived, arm you with courage and wisdom and give us the victory over our merciless foe! I trust that Pulaski will stand out against an attack.

The Liberty Troop have not yet reorganized, so we are without their military protection. They will do so in ten days.

Your Uncle John left the county today.

I am thankful to say that our sick are all more comfortable tonight, and Tyrone and Adam and July and Joe slowly improving. . . .

Our dear Little Sister is delighted with her dog. We call him Captain as a remembrancer of his kind donor. She tries to snap her little fingers at him, and he walks and plays with her, and every time she goes up to bed lies down near her crib. I imagine that he still has a "mother want" about him, and try to supply it by frequent feeding; but he has lost flesh. I must find out what is best for him.

Friday Morning. Our sick all better this morning: eight or nine cases up. The firing was heard again this morning, but the wind is so high and blowing from the west that we cannot now hear if it continues. God grant us strength to resist our enemies, and in His own good time entire deliverance from them!

The cargo of the Halifax vessel is fast discharging. I hope we may secure some of the quinine. Some persons suspect that it is a Yankee speculation; if so, I wish it could be proven, for it would nevermore leave our waters.

Your brother unites with me in best love to you, and says as he passes through he will try and see you. Sweetest kisses from your precious daughter, and the love and prayers of

Your affectionate mother,
Mary Jones.

Lt. Charles C. Jones, Jr., *to* Rev. *and* Mrs. C. C. Jones[g]

Camp Claghorn, *Friday,* April 11th, 1862

My dear Father and Mother,

The all-absorbing matter of interest in our immediate neighborhood at present is the bombardment of Fort Pulaski by the Lincoln forces. The fire against the fort is directed mainly from some seven or eight gun- or mortar boats lying to the north and east of the fort, and from the mortar batteries which the enemy has been for some time erecting on Tybee Island. That fire has been continuous ever since a quarter before eight o'clock on yesterday morning. From our camp we can distinctly see the explosion of the shells and the smoke of the discharges. At the commencement of the bombardment Fort Pulaski was provided with about one hundred and thirty rounds of ammunition to the gun. The barbette guns are, I believe, not casemated, although they are to a very great degree protected by traverses. In the casemates are a few eight-inch columbiads, three or four forty-two-pounder guns. The rest are thirty-two-pounder guns. On the barbette are mounted some ten or more heavy eight- and ten-inch columbiads. I understand that a few guns have been placed in position in the demilune which protects the rear of the fort. Several mortars are posted near the south wharf.

With a view to a more accurate observation Captain Claghorn and myself rode over to the abandoned batteries on Skidaway Island yesterday afternoon, and remained there until sunset. The fort is in a direct line from this point not more than (I should judge) six or seven miles, and is clearly discernible with the naked eye. You look across a wide extent of marsh and water without an obstruction of any character. The flag of the fort was flying freely, and every discharge could be noted, whether from barbette or casemate. The fort fired with deliberation—probably not more than twenty-five shots per hour on an average. There was no indication whatever of any injury sustained. In fact, the simple statement that our brave soldiers were working their barbette guns freely will show that no damage had been done. The distance at which the Lincoln batteries are operating forbids the possibility of breaching the fort. The most that can be done—so far, at least, as we were able to judge—will be to sweep the barbettes of the fort by the fragments of exploding shells and perhaps eventually disable the guns themselves. The batteries on Tybee Island and the gun- or mortar boats fired with great rapidity, and with guns of very heavy caliber. The most of the shells burst high.

While we were at the battery a large steamer which had come in to the south of the fort, and had been engaging the fort for some time, hauled off and crept out to sea very slowly. Our impression was that she was crippled —and that badly. She certainly declined further contest, and moved—or rather crawled—away. We thought with our glass that we could see places where her bulwarks had been considerably shattered, and at one time she appeared to be on fire; but the lights and shadows were so changeful that it was difficult to arrive at any certain knowledge as to her exact condition. Certain it is, however, that she had her fill of the fight, and hauled off with considerable difficulty.

Those rascally gun- or mortar boats lie so low in the water that it will be a difficult thing to strike them at long range. Some very heavy mortars are in position on Tybee Island, and the enemy is using them freely. I have not been over to Skidaway today, but from our camp we can see and hear that the engagement still continues, the enemy firing rapidly, the fort with its accustomed deliberation. At present rate it will be a long time, I think, before any material impression will be made upon the fort. No breach can be effected. Men may be killed at the barbette guns, but all else will be protected. Doubtless as the bombardment continues the enemy will approach nearer, and then the casemate guns will be employed. Olmstead, I think, will do his duty like a man, and offer every resistance. The most painful reflection connected with this affair is that the fort is wholly isolated, and at present we have no means of furnishing reinforcements of men or ammunition. There is no lack of provisions; and powder is there which, if economized, will suffice for many days.

The news has just reached us that the *Virginia* made some captures today in Hampton harbor. Our advices from the West are still unsatisfactory. God help us! We are beleaguered on every hand. But we must only trust in Him, pray more, and fight the harder.

I have written in great haste. I trust all at home are better. With warmest love to you both, my dear parents, many kisses for my dear little daughter, and kindest remembrances for all, I am, as ever,

Your affectionate son,
Charles C. Jones, Jr.

LT. CHARLES C. JONES, JR., *to* MRS. MARY JONES[g]
Camp Claghorn, *Monday,* April 14th, 1862
My dear Mother,

Let me thank you sincerely for your recent kind letter, perfumed alike with the happy memories of home and the attractive fragrance of flowers I love so much—the first tidings I have had since my recent visit to you.

Since I last wrote, a heavy blow has been struck on our coast in the reduction of Fort Pulaski. I must confess the surrender of that fortification after a bombardment of scarce a day and a half, and with only four wounded, has surprised me beyond measure. It is reported that the effect of the Parrott shot upon the face of the fort looking towards King's landing on Tybee Island was wonderful. Heretofore it has been a military rule, deduced from actual and oft-repeated experiment, that breaching masonry walls of six feet in thickness with solid shot could not be accomplished beyond eleven hundred yards. Remarkable modifications, however, have already occurred during the course of this present war. In the present instance the entire battery of the southern face of the fort was silenced and seven casemates knocked into one by the Parrott guns posted near King's house on Tybee Island, a distance of a mile or more. The projectiles used were pointed with steel and were fired with wonderful accuracy. Knowing perfectly the plan of Pulaski, the enemy concentrated their heaviest fire upon the south magazine and succeeded in breaching even the inner walls of that apparently invulnerable retreat. The world has never known before such perfection in heavy ordnance and in artillery generally as that now possessed by the Lincoln government. Some of the recent improvements in rifled cannon are extraordinary; and each day, with the vast appliances of matériel, skill, and labor at their command, serves but to reveal some new and more terrible engine of war. Our artillery will not compare with theirs, and the consequence is that we are too often compelled to retire beyond the range of their cannon.

It is always a difficult matter to sit in judgment upon the actions of others when we are not fully acquainted with all the attendant circumstances; but it does seem to me, no matter how damaged the condition of the fort, that I never would have surrendered it with magazines well supplied with ammunition and not a member of the garrison killed. Too many similar defenses have been made by us during the existing war—so much so that it has become almost (I should suppose) a matter of pastime for Lincoln gunboats to engage and reduce Confederate batteries. We need more heroic action and sterner resistance to restore a moral tone which has been to some extent, at least, lost. Never did man or officer have a better opportunity of giving a name to history and honor to his country than did Olmstead, and I marvel that he did not improve the chance in a more marked manner. Of course it is but a matter of speculation, but it does seem to me that had I been in his place—in command of the best fort garrisoned by Confederate troops, with the eyes of an agonized country upon me, in sight of the home of my birth, and in immediate protection of all God and nature have rendered most dear upon earth—I should have nailed the color halyards hard and fast, fought every gun until it was thoroughly dismounted beyond redemption, clung to the fortification so long as a single casemate offered its protection, and when further resistance was entirely hopeless, have withdrawn the garrison, or what remained of it, and blown the whole concern to atoms. I never would have been charged with the surrender of a fort in the mouth of the Savannah River. I am afraid Olmstead lacked nerve. But I will not judge of his actions until we know the particulars. He may have done the best in his opinion. Had he perished in the ruins of Pulaski he would have lived a hero for all time. As it is, his reputation is at best questionable.

The enemy may soon move upon Savannah. Every exertion is being made, I understand, to impede the progress of the Lincoln vessels by placing physical obstructions in the channel of the river. No time is to be lost. Physical obstructions and submarine batteries only can offer the requisite resistance. If the heavy masonry walls of Pulaski were of no avail against the concentrated fire of those Parrott guns posted at a distance of more than a mile, what shall we expect from our sand batteries along the river? The great mistake was in the evacuation of Tybee Island, which should have been properly fortified and held at every hazard.

The garrison surrendered at Pulaski numbers, I believe, some 383 men all told. Of this number one company was American (part *Yankee*)—the Oglethorpe Light Infantry, Company B; two companies Irish; one company German; and the fifth company, the Wise Guards, from Western Virginia of late, but composed, I believe, of Georgians. The garrison should have consisted entirely of *Georgians*.

Our location is unchanged. How long we will remain here I know not. I write in haste, but with warmest love to you, my dearest mother, to dear Father, and with many kisses for my precious little daughter. Kindest remembrances to Brother, Sister Carrie, and little Stanhope. I trust the servants are better. Will the Doctor remain at home until we know the issue of our impending dangers?

As ever,

Your affectionate son,
Charles C. Jones, Jr.

MRS. MARY JONES *to* LT. CHARLES C. JONES, JR.[8]

Montevideo, *Wednesday,* April 16th, 1862

My dear Son,

Yesterday I received your most welcome and affectionate letter. We watch with anxious hearts the coming of every mail. Today's was without any tidings—not even a Savannah paper.

The fall of Pulaski after so short a bombardment, and the surrender of the garrison without even an attempt at escape and blowing up of the fort, which certainly could have been done, appears both astounding and humiliating! The state of our long-neglected defenses and the results, now to be fatally realized, of ignorance, imbecility, and neglect make us realize when too late for remedy the ruin and misery brought upon us by the general in command, who has had since this time last year to occupy and fortify the positions taken by our enemies within the past four or five months and now used for our destruction. I see no hope for Savannah but in the special mercy and goodness of God; and my only comfort springs from the hope that He will deliver us in the day of battle from our inhuman foes. If so, it will be all of sovereign mercy bestowed through our compassionate Saviour, for our sins and our presumptuous neglect of duty deserve only His just punishment. How dark the clouds are hanging all over our beloved country! The Righteous Judge alone knows the end from the beginning!

Today another deep sorrow has fallen upon our household in the death of *poor Joe,* another of our young and most active and athletic men. He was one of the three who returned first from the fortifications; and although he looked badly, he went about until a week or ten days since. Your brother has felt very uneasy about him from the first, but did not anticipate his death when he left yesterday. His case has been very peculiar; I never knew any like it. . . . Yesterday afternoon I walked over to see him, and found him sitting up on the side of his bed, and had a conversation with him about the state of his soul. He said "it would have been better for him if he had thought more about it before now." I reminded him that for three years he had been a constant and an attentive attendant upon our Sabbath night school, where I had often spoken to him of our Saviour, and asked him where he was now looking for salvation. He said: "Only to the Lord Jesus Christ." I know your dear father has often and most faithfully warned him. Poor fellow, I wish we could entertain a well-grounded hope of him! All is now over. He has passed to the great Judgment Bar, where we too must sooner or later appear when our summons comes. In these repeated and heavy afflictions your dear father and I desire to say from our hearts: "Thy will be done." He died this morning about ten o'clock.

Our old servant Niger continues very ill; unless relieved shortly I see very little hope for him. Tyrone is still very sick; Adam a little better. Some eight or ten other cases, most of them measles. All the men who worked on the fortifications excepting Pulaski seem to have taken some poison from water, food, or atmosphere into their systems which defies the ordinary remedies. The effect of this increased anxiety and sorrow upon your father is very evident. The Lord give us grace and strength that we may be patient and submissive under His chastening rod!

Your brother and Carrie left us yesterday. He was to accompany his family as far as Millen and return today or tomorrow.

Thursday. Our sick are more comfortable this morning. God bless and preserve you, my dear child, and your whole company and all our brave soldiers now about to meet our foes! Although they are a mighty host, yet our God has power to destroy them and to give us the victory if we are true to Him and to ourselves. With best respects to Captain Claghorn,

Ever your affectionate mother,
Mary Jones.

Sweetest kisses from your little daughter, love from Father, and howdies from the servants.

Lt. Charles C. Jones, Jr., *to* Mrs. Mary Jones[g]
Camp Claghorn, *Saturday,* April 19th, 1862
My dear Mother,

I have only a moment in which to acknowledge the receipt of your kind and valued letter of the 16th inst., this afternoon received, and to thank you most sincerely for it. It is with much sorrow that I learn the death of Joe. The finger of God has indeed been heavily laid upon us at Montevideo; and while we bow in submission, we can but hope and pray that the chastening rod may now be lifted, and that all may in good time be restored to wonted health.

The enemy on yesterday afternoon came in three gunboats opposite the abandoned Skidaway batteries and fired some seven shot and shell at our pickets and upon the island without accomplishing anything save a useless expenditure of ammunition. The gunboats thereupon retired to their former position at the mouth of Romney Marsh, no troops having been landed on Skidaway Island. It is the impression of many that the enemy will make his approaches by the way of Whitemarsh Island. It is of the last importance that he should not be allowed to obtain a foothold there, as in that event batteries could be planted which would soon render our batteries at Thunderbolt and Causton's Bluff and along the Savannah River almost untenable. That island is now held in force by us, and General Smith is energetically engaged in strengthening the river defenses.

The fall of Island No. 10 is severe. We are anxiously anticipating the arrival of recent intelligence from Fort Macon, the forts near the mouth of the Mississippi, the Peninsula, and from Corinth. I understand that Beauregard is unable to advance on account of the want of ammunition. I hope such is not the fact. Ammunition went forward to him and to General Van Dorn from Savannah today.

Only fourteen ounces of quinine were brought by the vessel, and these were sold at fifteen dollars per ounce at public outcry. So soon as I can purchase any, you shall have it. A scarce article. Do give much love to Father. Kiss my dear little daughter for me. And believe me ever, my dearest mother, with warmest affection,

Your son,
Charles C. Jones, Jr.

LT. CHARLES C. JONES, JR., *to* MRS. MARY JONES[g]

Camp Claghorn, *Monday,* April 21st, 1862

My dear Mother,

We have nothing of special interest in our vicinity today. The enemy appears to be operating quietly down the river, but the exact character and extent of their labors are not, I believe, definitely ascertained. Most of the ships have returned northward, either with a view to returning with reinforcements at some early day, or for the purpose of swelling the immense force which now threatens our army on the Peninsula.

The approaching conflict there will doubtless be terrific. The shock of that battle will be felt in the remotest bounds of our Confederacy, and its results will exert a most material effect upon the duration of this war. If driven from our positions there and discomfited, God alone knows when the war will end; while on the other hand, if He in mercy crowns the valor of our arms with success, the annihilation of that boasted Grand Army of the Potomac under the leadership of McClellan will, at least for the present, in that direction work a practical cessation of hostilities, and may conduce in no small degree to an early and final restoration of peace.

One after another our fortifications and strong places have fallen before the superior forces and untiring industry of our unrelenting enemy. So far our foe is without a permanent check to his general advance, except upon the memorable hills of Shiloh. But I think if we can hold our own until August, we will see more light and somewhat of joy and immediate hope. The present exertions of the Lincoln government are wonderful, and their resources marvelous. All we have to do—now that the mind of the people has at length been happily turned from a morbid consideration of the chances of foreign intervention, and an underestimate of the power of our adversary and the degree of his hate—is to exhaust our every energy, bend every nerve, and develop every Spartan virtue in the resolute defense of all that is holy in religion, dear in honor, valuable in property, true in principle, and sacred in death, at the same time earnestly and constantly invoking divine guidance and the blessings of a just God upon our efforts. Our men must make up their minds to suffer freely, and if need be, to die freely. They must dare all things, and endure all which may become a noble race whose priceless all is placed in imminent peril by an inhuman, powerful, and relentless foe bent upon subjugation and annihilation. So long as many of our generals are afraid of consequences, ignorant of their duties, negligent of imposed obligations—so long as they shrink from attempting deeds even above heroic (for the odds are against us)—we will continue to give back.

I have no fears of our ultimate success; but as matters now stand, and at the rate at which we have been for some time retrograding, the amount of blood, loss, and deprivation to be incurred before that consummation devoutly to be wished for is reached will be enormous. But it is no time to calculate the chances of either pecuniary or vital loss. We are to be saved *as by fire;* and our duty is to go manfully, fearlessly, and persistently about the work of our country's salvation, humbling ourselves for past and present transgressions, as individuals and as a nation, before a just God who will not look upon sin with the least degree of allowance, praying His intervention in our behalf, and using every means to help ourselves while we invoke His aid. If our troops will quit themselves like men and stand bravely to their guns, the enemy will have heavy work in compassing the capture of Savannah. If, on the contrary, the defense be abandoned when only half made, we may expect nothing else than the fall of our beloved city. For one I trust never to see that day.

The existing difficulties about the continuance of the late state forces in service, and the disagreements which recently arose between those in authority, are peculiarly unfortunate just at this time, and would seem to indicate that the Devil is yet at his work, and that true patriotism and the cultivation of the nobler virtues are not uppermost in the minds of at least many of those who are immediately charged with the defense of our sacred rights and liberties. What we greatly need now is artillery of heavy caliber and long range. We are in great want of guns which will enable us to compete successfully with those of our adversary.

But I fear, my dear mother, that I weary you. I trust that all the sick at home continue to improve, and they may all soon be restored to perfect health. Give much love to dear Father. Many kisses for my precious little daughter. And believe me ever

Your affectionate son,

Charles C. Jones, Jr.

Kindest remembrances for the Doctor if he has returned. Howdy for the servants. Did Gilbert ever receive fifty dollars I sent him? And did he hand to Brother one hundred and twenty-five dollars I sent from the depot to him? Do ask the Doctor, if he did receive it, to send me receipt, that I may keep the Arcadia accounts correct.

REV. C. C. JONES *to* LT. CHARLES C. JONES, JR.[8]

Montevideo, *Monday,* April 21st, 1862

My dear Son,

Your last interesting favors are at hand, and we feel thankful that you are in good health, and your comrades in arms also.

The preservation of the city depends, under God's blessing, upon the wise and energetic and determined action and bravery of our officers and men. No regular approaches should be allowed on the part of the enemy, and nothing left undone to break up and retard their advances. This is fundamental. The loss of Pulaski does not necessarily involve the loss of the city; by no means. It yields the river approach to the enemy, but I see no reason for discouragement in finally repulsing him. Now is the time for General Pemberton and our chief officers to show themselves to be men; and I trust they will, and that God may give us the victory.

The sending our men to work on the Savannah River batteries has been a sad thing to us. Poor Joe died on the 16th with dysentery (river cholera) contracted there, making two of our best men. What is peculiarly affecting in Joe's case is, he died without hope, so far as we have any evidence to the contrary. Tyrone has been extremely ill; is still in bed and something better. Little Adam is just walking about. July has been very sick, and is barely convalescing. Sam was very sick for a short time. And the only one who seems to have escaped the dreadful poison of the place is Pulaski, the youngest of the seven. The plantation, with these extreme cases and the measles with the people, has been going on three weeks *a hospital;* and had not your brother been with us, I do not know what we should have done. Arcadia is suffering also from measles; the men who went to Savannah have suffered much also. Old Niger is suffering from his old chronic complaint and other disorders, and there is little hope of his recovery. But his mind is clear and calm, and his hope in Christ strong and comforting.

You must needs know how much we have been confined at home, and how much care we have had. So has the Lord ordered it, and we are bearing our portion of the judgment of war, for our sicknesses came from the war directly. And we would rather fall in this way into the hands of God than to fall into the hands of man.

Your brother took his family to Augusta on the 15th, stayed a day, and returned kindly for our help on the 18th; and between Montevideo and Arcadia he has had his hands full. I hope it may please God to rebuke our diseases so that he may return to Augusta in a few days. It is a great interruption to him. He has not settled down on any plan for the future, and cannot until he returns to Augusta. The Liberty Independent Troop has split into two companies, neither sufficient in numbers to be mustered in: Lowndes Walthour captain of one and William Thomson of the other. Winn thrown out by both sides.

Mr. Gué, I understand, comes out to No. 3 tomorrow (Tuesday) to purchase cotton for Mr. Molyneaux, who stores it on speculation in Thomas-

234

ville. Offers twenty-one cents. Am inclined to sell him under these conditions a part of what I have ginned out (one-half the crop here *not* ginned out) at that price—to pay my running accounts and keep a little for contingent expenses. I think it would be well for you to sell a part of the Arcadia crop for the same purposes. Will ask Mr. Gué if he will take a part. If your brother and sister desire it, will sell a part. Your Aunt Susan wishes to sell a part of her crop. The cotton is *not sold to go out of the country.* This I would not do. But if men buy and store on speculation and wait the opening of the ports, and we can afford to sell at their offer, I think we may do so.

Your dear little daughter is quite well, and learning *slowly* to eat. And her little dog, which we call *Captain,* is an unfailing source of amusement to her. Mother and Brother unite in much love to you. We pray for you day by day. Our respects to Captain Claghorn.

Your ever affectionate father,
C. C. Jones.

LT. CHARLES C. JONES, JR., *to* REV. C. C. JONES[g]

Camp Claghorn, *Tuesday,* April 22nd, 1862

My dear Father,

Your very kind letter of the 21st inst. was this afternoon received. It finds us under orders to move our encampment in the morning. Whither we know not as yet—probably to some point within a few miles of this beautiful spot, where we have enjoyed an unusual degree of health and quiet for the past seven months. We are loath to leave it, but we are completely deserted by the rest of the brigade, General Mercer in the bargain. It is the first time in my reading or observation that I have ever known or heard of a light battery being kept upon picket week after week at the most advanced post, and for a part of the time, at least, neither cavalry nor infantry to support it in the event of an attack, which might with the utmost ease have been made by the enemy any night. These civilian generals do things in a queer way, and revolutionize all established principles of warfare. While I write, we are the only troops upon this whole island, with the exception of two pickets sent over only an hour since, and at our earnest solicitation. The Isle of Hope will be abandoned by us in the morning—if the enemy does not during the night impel us to a more rapid move. . . . From the very nature of the arm of the service, field batteries with their park of guns and stable of horses are least able to move at a moment's warning, and from the character of camp and weapons least of all capable of self-protection. I think the conduct of General Mercer very reprehensible, but I am forbidden by the articles of war to say so, and I do so knowing that what I say will not be repeated. Our removal will cost trouble and great labor in the preparations of a new camping ground, building stables, etc., etc. This everlasting evacuation, coupled as it is with no apparent disposition on the part of our commanding officers to seek out and check the advance of the enemy, who certainly on our coast have everything their own way, is not only blameworthy in the extreme but also heartily disgusting.

In reference to the cotton, I would sell without hesitancy upon the terms suggested. Do ask Brother to see Mr. Gué if practicable, and to make such arrangements for the disposition of the whole or such part of the Arcadia crop as you may think proper.

I sincerely sympathize with you, my dear father, in all our afflictions at Montevideo, and trust and pray that in the good providence of God the hand of disease may be arrested and all the sick restored to health. The penalty which is exacted by war under the most favorable circumstances is severe. . . . If you do not hear from me for a few days, you will know that we are busily engaged with our change of location and the duties incident thereupon. I have written in great haste, but with much love to self, dear Mother, and many kisses for my precious little daughter. Kindest remembrances for the Doctor. I am ever, my dear father,

Your affectionate son,
Charles C. Jones, Jr.

Captain Claghorn desires his special and respectful remembrances. George well. Howdy for the servants.

X

REV. C. C. JONES *to* LT. CHARLES C. JONES, JR.[8]

Arcadia, *Monday,* April 28th, 1862

My very dear Son,

The news came up from the Island on Friday that two of the enemy's gunboats were in Woodville River at Drum (Timmons') Point below Mrs. King's place; that a part of the troop under Captain W. L. Walthour had gone down to give them a brush should they attempt to land troops or come up the river; and that citizens were going down to aid. Your brother was at Arcadia visiting the sick when he heard it, and posted back to Montevideo, got ready his blanket and camp clothing and waterproofs by the time Mother prepared a hurried lunch; and while he was eating she put up some rations for him; and taking his grandfather John Jones's double-barreled gun with ammunition, he bid us good-bye, and putting spurs to Lewis, hurried away for the fight.

When he arrived at the Island the vessels had passed up and were lying at the Crosstides, and in the midst of divided counsels were not fired on by the small force on the bluffs. He then went with Messrs. Munro McIver and William C. Stevens and George Handley to Carr's Neck, all resolving to fire on anything that should pass, and remained there all night—the rest of the men going, I believe, to Mr. Busby's landing, where the Nova Scotia vessel lay waiting for a cargo. In the morning the gunboats were seen under weigh steaming swiftly, smoothly, and noiselessly up, without a particle of smoke, and out of range. They pushed on for Busby's landing. The Nova Scotia vessel was sunk by the small company there in the channel, and her works above water set on fire. The tide detained the gunboats some hours.

Your brother came on to Montevideo, giving his fine horse a ride that tested his bottom fairly, and reached us about half-past 5 or 6 P.M. He left the gunboats coming up on the flood, and recommended Mother and myself to take the carriage and Little Sister and at once go to Arcadia and be out of the way in case the enemy should either land or shell the plantation.

Mother had that very day sent to Arcadia three or four loads of household furniture, which she had purposed to do, but sickness and interruptions had prevented till then. And Gilbert and the boys were away! There was energetic movement in the house to get things ready on a short notice. The enemy approaching—a complete surprise! You know your mother's energy. Patience, Flora, Elsie, Tom, Sue and Sam, your brother and myself (after a fashion) were all in motion, Susan and Peggy looking after the baby and her outfit in particular, Cook Kate pushing on tea, the horses and carriage getting (and mule-wagon for baggage), Cato called (and Porter) for instructions, Lymus dispatched as a lookout on the lower dam, to run immediately and give notice if he saw or heard the gunboats or any boats at all coming up the river. All astir, but no confusion; and much was accomplished in a very short time. A few principal things out of the house and out of the study, and all the rest left! We had been burnt out once; might be again. We quietly submitted to the will of God. A hasty cup of tea—nothing more.

Just as we were getting into the carriage, Gilbert arrived from Arcadia. The faithful fellow would not let Sam take the box; said "he was fresh and wanted nothing to eat and preferred driving his mistress himself; it was pitch dark, and he knew his horses better than anyone else." It was cloudy and very dark; we took a candle in the carriage, which was a great help in driving, and a comfort. The mule-wagon behind us. Your brother stayed to take care of the people. We had started but a little way when Lymus reported a boat in the river. We had all the lights extinguished, and the people hastened to the brickyard shed, and your brother then went back and reconnoitered. Says it was a boat, but where it went he could not determine; thinks it was a barge sent up on a search and for soundings and then dropped down quietly. (I should have mentioned that he had not reached home fifteen minutes to hurry us off before my neighbor Mr. Calder, managing for Estate J. B. Barnard, sent a boy express to let me know the gunboats were coming up by White's Island not far below the ferry.)

When we reached Arcadia the family had retired; but after some knocking we were let in and welcomed, and after supper and worship went tired to bed.

Your dear brother was up on the watch all night. Gilbert went back to him, and with all the servants packing all night, about daylight the oxcarts were packed with furniture and household matters of every kind and sent off for Arcadia. Meanwhile the carts from Arcadia and Lambert were dispatched. And Sabbath (as it was) we had a stream of carts and wagons running all day between the two places; and by sundown your brother had nearly everything moved out of the house, and nearly all the women and children and some of the sick men moved over also. He says he never saw servants more attentive and active or take a greater interest in the removal and effort to keep clear of the enemy.

When the Negroes ran (on the alarm of the boat) to the brick shed, someone called for the old patriarch Tony to go along.

Said he: "Where is Massa?"

"Gone."

"Where is Mistress?"

"Gone."

"Well, I am too old to run. I will stay and throw myself into the hands of the Lord."

Your mother and Aunt Susan and Cousins Lyman and Laura went to church, but I was too inactive to go and remained at home with the children. But on the report of the boys with the oxcarts that the enemy were coming up in open barges, that your brother had a detachment of men at Montevideo (and *Robert* among them), and others had gone over to Mr. Barnard's, and they were preparing to attack them, I felt I must go, and ordered the buggy. And your aunt got me a little relish, having taken but one sermon with Mother. And putting your little revolver on the seat by me, refusing to let Mother go with me as she desired to do, I drove off, meeting carriages on the road returning from church. At the Boro I learned that the barges proved to be the yawl of the Nova Scotia vessel coming up to the Boro with the seamen. But the gunboats were lying at the ferry—had not gone up to Busby's landing—and had fired a shell at two of Captain Hughes's men near Mr. J. B. Barnard's settlement, but did no one any damage. Part of Captain Hughes's company had come over to aid from their encampment at South Newport.

Riding up to Montevideo house, the scene was lovely: horses hitched about, others grazing with their saddles on, and little groups of soldiers and men here and there, and the stoop full of them. They all gave me a hearty welcome. Robert there, sure enough; had left his church and come down with others on the alarm, armed.

"But where is Joe?"

"Oh, the Doctor! We have all prescribed him to go and lie down and rest, for he has been up the whole of two nights, and has been riding to and fro all day watching for the enemy on the river."

Not long after, he appeared at the upstairs window in his shirt sleeves, looking like a man just out of a nap. He came down in wet stockings: his boots drying. Had ridden, in reconnoitering along the swamp, into a spring bog which came up to his knees on horseback almost and to the crupper of his saddle. The horse by great exertions got out.

Mr. Edgar Way now arrived and reported that the gunboats had left the ferry and were steaming down to the Colonel's Island, where a part of the troop had gone to fire upon them on their way down. About the time they would reach the Island we heard their cannon. And the firing was continuous, but not very rapid, for half an hour or three-quarters, upon which we concluded our men had fired upon them and they had shelled the woods and Woodville and Maxwell settlements.

Nearly all now started for the Island. Two returned to sick families at Walthourville, leaving Mr. Thomas W. Fleming, Rev. D. L. Buttolph (who had come on after church), Robert, Joe, and myself. The enemy being gone, there was no need of any further guard at this point; and about sundown the three ministers and the planter and the doctor retired in single file—the planter in the lead—to our homes, which we reached near 9 P.M. Robert and Joe came home with Brother Buttolph to Arcadia. Supper; family worship, at which we sang "Come, My Redeemer, Come"; then bed.

Such a Sabbath I never spent before—and wish to spend none other like it. We prayed that the enemy might be sent back the way he came; and so it has been done. May all his future visits, if any, prove of like innocent character to our people and their interests!

We have had a hospital at Montevideo for full four weeks. Wally died on the 4th, Joe on the 16th, Old Niger on the 24th, and—last—Cinda on the 25th. (These are the dates, I believe.) Several have been extremely ill. The last case (little James Monroe, George's brother) now better. Three of the Savannah men yet not at work: convalescing. Four deaths and an entire evacuation of house and home for fear of the enemy in four weeks! These are some of the sad changes of life—and all from this unnatural and cruel war. What remains we know not, but ask the presence and blessing of God, and that we may not be hardened under His hand.

All the women have been sent back from Arcadia this morning except those with little children and the little children. We are now hauling and storing the corn from Montevideo in a part of Arcadia cornhouse, and may remove the cotton also. Arcadia is less exposed, we think, than Montevideo. I regret our inability last fall to remove all our people back from the seaboard. We should have been saved much anxiety, and we know not yet what loss. We are planting a crop *in hope* only that we may harvest it. The enemy has for the present everything his own way where he operates with his navy. If he succeeds in the remaining seaboard cities as he has at New Orleans, we may be annoyed in Liberty. But I hope and pray that Savannah may be able to repulse him. General Lovell has done well *not to surrender New Orleans;* he can now attack and retake it as opportunity offers.

I do not know what we should have done without your brother. He has done everything for us he could, and I feel that he has been the means of saving the lives of several of the servants in our recent illnesses. All, thanks to divine mercy, are better. The cotton sold by Mr. Gué for Arcadia and Montevideo is weighing today at No. 3, and Mr. Gué will send you the sale in a few days, I suppose. Jog his memory about it. Your dear little one is quite bright: learning to eat. All in the house unite in much love to you. Write soon.

From your ever affectionate father,
C. C. Jones.

P.S. *Tuesday, April 29th, 1862.* Our citizens and soldiers have had a skirmish at Half Moon (Sellegree's) with the retiring gunboats on Sunday afternoon—the firing we heard at Montevideo. Will write you all the particulars when I learn them. When the men left at the firing, we told them they would be too late. Am glad we fired on the boats. They fired their guns, but the balls and shells went over our men, and we had nobody hurt. They should have been fired upon at the Screven place when they came up. Meet them, fight them at all points, repel them, harass them—keep the war moving. They have a great work to subdue and keep military possession of eight hundred thousand square miles of territory! Conquest! The word can't be found in the dictionary of a people resolute in a good cause, with the Righteous Lord to lean upon.

We are just breakfasting, and there is enough for Captain Claghorn and his military family. Wish you were all here. I think when peace comes we must have the Chatham Artillery—officers, at least—at Montevideo on a picnic. Brother Buttolph goes to the depot this morning to see to the weighing of the cotton. All send much love—old and young. Little Sister is in the best of humors. Received your letter yesterday.

Your affectionate father,
C. C. Jones.

Lt. Charles C. Jones, Jr., *to* Rev. C. C. Jones[g]

Camp Claghorn, Wednesday, April 30th, 1862

My very dear Father,

I cannot sufficiently thank you for your minute, graphic, and deeply interesting letter of the 28th inst., this afternoon received. It grieves me deeply to know that *home*—a place so peculiarly consecrated to peace, quiet, religion, hospitality, and true happiness, the abode of my honored and beloved parents and of my precious little daughter—should have been ruthlessly disturbed in its security and calm repose by the near approach of those lawless bands of robbers and freebooters who are now infesting our coasts, annoying and murdering our people, pillaging our country, and endeavoring to deprive us of everything which we hold priceless in individual, social, or national existence. I presume the immediate object in the contemplation of the enemy in coming up the river was the destruction of the vessel at Busby's landing. Of the fact of that vessel having passed up the river I imagine the blockading fleet had due notice, as they seem to be apprised of almost everything which transpires along our coast. I do not think the gunboats will return.

The burning of the vessel and the alacrity with which all armed upon the first note of alarm are most praiseworthy. Do offer my congratulations to the Doctor for his energy and most valuable services. I am sorry that he did not enjoy the opportunity of discharging at least both barrels well loaded with buckshot from Grandfather's genuine "Mortimer" (placed in his hands by Mother) full in the face, at easy range of the nefarious rascals. I would have given a great deal to have had a section of our battery at Half Moon and treated the Lincolnites to a dose of shell and canister. A light battery is very effective under such circumstances.

It is a most unfortunate circumstance when the holy quiet of the Sabbath is disturbed by the rude alarms of war; but the obligations of national defense and of the protection of our homes and lives and property from the attacks of an invading foe are as sacred on that as on any other day. When our mothers place the arms in our hands, when our fathers by actual presence counsel, aid, and encourage, and when the ministers of the Living God leave their desks, the sermon half delivered, to hasten to the field of danger, the nation, pressed on every hand though it be, must eventually prove invincible by any force our enemy may send against us. The days of 1776 are come again. The record of the virtues, the courage, the self-denial, and the generous interest of our women in the great cause of our national honor and national defense is as bright, as striking, as it was in the days of Martha Custis, Mrs. Otis, and Mrs. Motte. It remains for our men to prove themselves worthy their mothers, wives, daughters—worthy the cause they espouse.

I could but contrast in my mind the appearance of the river disturbed by the Lincoln gunboats—the trees marred by the iron missiles, and the still air rent by the noise of cannon and of firearms and filled with the strange smell of battle—with that presented of late as, in taking your accustomed morning ride, you halted Jerry as was your wont on the edge of Half Moon Bluff, and uncovering your head beneath the grateful shade of the oak, you enjoyed the calm influences of the scene—nothing to interrupt the perfect harmony of nature, nothing to frighten the songbird from its favorite retreat, nothing to obscure the outlines of the low-lying shores, nothing to hush the voice of the refreshing morning air as it gave life to the forest and a gentle ripple to the waters, nothing to divert the thoughts from those peaceful and happy contemplations which lead the mind and heart through nature up to nature's God. . . . Half Moon Bluff has now become somewhat historical. I hope that the enemy suffered loss and harm in the skirmish, in order that they may be deterred from adventuring a second time.

The hand of affliction has indeed been heavily laid upon us at Montevideo. Am truly happy to know that all the sick are now convalescent, and hope that they may all be soon restored to accustomed health and strength.

The fall of Fort Macon does not surprise, as the work has been isolated for some time, and its surrender was simply a question of time. The age of ordinary fortifications has passed. . . . Alexander telegraphs a battle imminent at Corinth. God grant us a signal victory! Our arms need success to restore confidence and lift the depressing influences caused by our recent disasters.

You see General Lawton has expressed his resolution not to surrender the city of Savannah, and the board of aldermen determine to aid in carrying into effect this determination.

Nothing new in our immediate vicinity. I have written amid a perfect cloud of sand flies, and with both my boots filled with fleas. We lost tonight one of our finest battery horses. Blind staggers: I have never seen a poor animal suffer as it has done for many days. Do give warmest love to dear Mother, many kisses to my precious little daughter, kindest remembrances to the Doctor and all good relatives at Arcadia. And believe me ever, my dear father,

Your affectionate son,
Charles C. Jones, Jr.

LT. CHARLES C. JONES, JR., *to* REV. *and* MRS. C. C. JONES[8]

Savannah, *Friday,* May 9th, 1862

My dear Father and Mother,

I am still here as judge advocate of this general court-martial. Some very important cases are before us, and the probability is that our sessions will be protracted. For the past few days I have been continuously occupied during not only the hours of light but until two o'clock in the morning; and as I now indite this hurried letter it is the 10th and not the 9th as above dated.

These imperative and uninterrupted engagements must plead my excuse for having delayed Gilbert so long. Each day I have thought that I would have a leisure moment to go to the house and select the volumes I desired packed for removal; but until this morning I did not enjoy the opportunity for doing so, and then only for a very short time. I have sent only a few volumes and the rest of my Indian remains, which I must trouble you, my dear parents, to have placed for me in a safe place. I thank you for the services of Gilbert.

The most outrageous circumstance occurred about midday today in our river. A Federal transport showing a flag of truce at the fore was permitted to ascend the Savannah until she reached within less than a mile of Fort Jackson, and within pistol shot of one of our batteries. She was then not halted by the sentinels but by a captain of one of the steamers lying in the stream opposite Fort Jackson, who steamed down the river to meet her, and succeeded in bringing her to just before she reached the obstructions in the river. The enemy's vessel (unarmed) when halted was so near the city that the stripes in the Federal flag could be distinctly seen with a glass from any part of the city. Generals Lawton and Smith both posted down in the *Ida* to see what was wanted. The object of the flag of truce I do not know; neither am I acquainted with the results, if any, arrived at. The Lincolnites from below were yesterday taking observations from a balloon; I presume wishing to verify these observations they today adopted the ruse of a flag of truce.

I have always been informed that when an enemy is allowed with a flag of truce within the lines, he should be blindfolded so as to be incapable of possessing himself of any information. But in the present case, in the face of a cloudless sunlit sky, this Lincoln transport is permitted to pass our pickets, come within our lines and opposite to one of the river batteries, occupying for two hours a position from which the very men of the city of Savannah could be observed and every fortification along the river accurately viewed and located, and its exact strength and the metal of its guns definitely ascertained. This act does out-Herod Herod, and shows how grossly culpable is the negligence of the officers in charge, and how monstrous the ignorance of our sentinels on the river. That vessel, despite the white flag, should have been brought to just within range of the heaviest guns of our lowest battery. If a shot across the bows would not have accomplished it, the next through her hull would have done it. But uninterrupted in her course by the

243

batteries, those on board the vessel came on and on, and in all probability, unless Captain King of the *St. Johns* had seen fit to stop her, would have steamed clear up to the city. Monstrous to a degree!

We learn this afternoon that the great battle of Corinth commenced today about 12 M., Beauregard making the attack. It is also said that Stonewall Jackson has had another fight, and that the result of the engagement was favorable to us. We have nothing else of interest. With warmest love to you both, my dearest parents, and many kisses for my precious little daughter, I am, as ever,

Your affectionate son,
Charles C. Jones, Jr.

REV. C. C. JONES *to* LT. CHARLES C. JONES, JR.[8]

Arcadia, *Saturday,* May 10th, 1862

My dear Son,

Gilbert has arrived, and we are happy to learn your good estate through his report and your acceptable letter.

Truly we are fallen upon men of ignorance and imbecility! The coming of that transport up Savannah River is a disgrace to the general in command, and sufficient ground for a court-martial, and may result in the overthrow of the city! I must repeat what I have so often said, in view of the lethargy and weakness of the officers in command and the amazing apathy of the citizens, that if Savannah is delivered out of the hands of our enemies, we shall owe it to the immediate and merciful intervention of a kind Providence. And that the city may be so delivered we should daily pray.

The fall of New Orleans is a terrible blow, and the people should demand to know where the responsibility lies. Lost unquestionably through criminal delay and neglect. And so of the fall of our coast fortifications. We are upon the eve of great events; and I agree with you, my dear son, that all who have an interest at a throne of grace should be continually in prayer to our Heavenly Father for a happy deliverance.

We have to add another to our severe afflictions in our household. Poor *Bella,* Agrippa's wife, died the evening of the 7th on this place unexpectedly from an affection of the heart, from which she has been suffering for some time past. Her attack of measles seemed to have pretty much passed away. Your brother said she was liable to sudden death from it. In conversation with her two or three hours before her death she said: "Massa, if the Lord would come for me this night—this *very* night—I would be freely willing to go, for there is nothing to keep me here longer. I can leave all in His hands." *The Lord came,* and my hope is it is well with her. She was a member of Midway Church. Daphne continues very ill, and we fear the result. Rest of the sick on both places better.

Mother has kept up astonishingly. Sends much love. Your dear little one has been steadily improving since we got her to eat, which she now does in a moderate way three times a day. Is full of life and intelligence. Your aunt and Cousins Laura and Lyman send much love. Their little ones well. Very sickly among the Negroes in the county. Whites generally healthy. . . . Have engaged Mr. Calder, managing for Estate J. B. Barnard, to take care of our business at Montevideo, at least for a season. A great relief.

Gilbert is waiting for the letter to go to the depot and bring your things home at once, and they will be carefully put away. Send for him whenever you need him to help you further. Your change to the city is something, if the business is onerous. Praying for you always, I remain, my dear son,

Your ever affectionate father,
C. C. Jones.

LT. CHARLES C. JONES, JR., *to* REV. C. C. JONES⁸

Savannah, *Monday,* May 12th, 1862

My dear Father,

I am under many obligations to you for your kind favor of the 10th inst.

The telegraphic communications of today cast additional gloom over our prospects: Norfolk evacuated, the navy yard burnt, our vessels, dry dock, and all destroyed, the *Virginia* blown up, the city in the occupancy of the enemy, Commodore Tattnall resigned, and our army in Virginia falling back generally. Add to this that General Beauregard is said to be suffering severely in the Army of the Mississippi for want of provisions; the report that Atlanta is suffering from the supposed Lincoln incendiaries; and the further rumor that both Charleston and Savannah are to be evacuated at no distant day—and we have a chapter of evil tidings which it is almost impossible to consider with composure.

There is no disguising the fact that our country's fortunes are in a most desperate plight, and thus far I see nothing ahead but gathering gloom. Each event but proves more conclusively than the former the power of our enemy, his indomitable energy, consummate skill, and successful effort. General Joseph Johnston, from whom we were led to expect so much, has done little else than *evacuate,* until the very mention of the word sickens one *usque ad nauseam.* There may be a great deal of strategy in all of these movements, but to the eye of the uninitiated there appears but little of real action and determined resistance. This doctrine of evacuation on every occasion robs us of our means of supply, annihilates our ordnance, discourages our troops and people generally, and if persisted in must eventually contract our limits to an alarming extent. Encouraged by an almost uninterrupted succession of decided successes, we cannot wonder that the Northern mind is bent upon a prosecution of the war, and impressed with the idea that the suppression of the rebellion is at hand. Of a mercurial temperament, success works its stimulating influences in a no less marked manner than does defeat exert its depressing effects.

The passage of this conscript law—a law good in itself—just at this time exerts a most disorganizing and deleterious effect upon our armies. The elections thus far evidence the fact that almost all of the good officers have been thrown overboard in the reorganization of companies, battalions, and regiments, and that in their steads men of inferior qualifications—in very many instances mere noses of wax, to be molded and controlled at will by the men whom they should govern—have been entrusted with the command. All the worst phases of low, petty electioneering have been brought to light, and military discipline and becoming subordination are in frequent instances quite neglected. I am sorry to say that in our company there is a strong disposition to depose those officers who have endeavored faithfully to discharge their duties, and to supply their places with men who have not a proper conception of their responsibilities or of the obligations of truth, honor, and of a sacred oath. The election in the Chatham Artillery occurs on Friday or Saturday next. What the result will be I have not inquired. Of one thing you may rest assured: I will compromise neither name nor honor to compass a reelection.

Enclosed I send for your perusal a letter from my friend Cass. Its perusal may interest you. I deeply regret to learn the death of Daphne—*Bella, I mean*—but am truly happy to know that you have hope in her death. . . . The court-martial is still in session. With warmest love to you, my dear father and dear mother, and tenderest kisses for my precious little daughter, I am ever

Your affectionate son,
Charles C. Jones, Jr.

REV. *and* MRS. C. C. JONES *to* LT. CHARLES C. JONES, JR.[8]
Montevideo, *Thursday,* May 22nd, 1862

My dear Son,

We were happy to hear of your safe arrival after your short visit, which was so refreshing to us all, and that the election in your company is satisfactory, and consequently there will be no necessity for a transfer of service either to Virginia or to Tennessee. . . . We heard from Little Sister on Monday. Daughter says she is as well and as happy as possible. It was a wise arrangement of Mother's to take her up to Walthourville and wean her at once, for Peggy is just coming out from an attack of the real simon-pure measles.

We removed home on Monday after a delightful visit at Arcadia of three weeks. I believe this is the best way for relatives to visit—go and spend two or three weeks together, old and young, bond and free, and brighten and tighten up all the cords of affection. Real *family* friends are the friends after all.

Montevideo looks beautifully—all day long vocal with the sweet voices of nature bursting from every tree and cover, the little squirrels playing about, the lawn lighted aslant by the evening sun spread with green and covered with sheep and calves and poultry, and Mother's garden looking as if a rainbow had been broken and showered down and its beautiful and varied fragments had caught on all the plants and shrubbery. It is a beautiful world after all, and as Bishop Heber expresses it in his missionary hymn, "Man is only vile."

The plantation is still a hospital. Near twenty cases of sickness, all connected with measles. Better today. And we trust God will give us our wonted health in a short time. . . . We are trying to get up to the Sand Hills this week, but cannot tell if we shall accomplish it: so much sickness. Mother does not wish Dr. Parsons to send out the work, for in that case she cannot return nor have it altered if it does not suit. She will try and come down so soon as we move to Walthourville. The Lord be with and bless you, my dear son, is the daily prayer of

Your affectionate parents,
C. C. and M. Jones.

LT. CHARLES C. JONES, JR., *to* REV. *and* MRS. C. C. JONES[t]

Savannah, *Thursday,* May 22nd, 1862

My dear Father and Mother,

I scarcely know whether to direct this note to Montevideo or to Walthourville. All, however, that I desire to do is to assure you, my beloved parents, of my constant love and remembrance.

We have nothing of interest today by telegraph, and the enemy appears to be quiet in the river. Indications seem to point to Charleston as a place of early attack. In that event I presume we will be ordered to South Carolina.

I have just this morning received a check from Mr. Anderson for $1131.41. The session of our court today was so protracted that I did not have an opportunity for paying the bills, but I will endeavor to do so tomorrow, and will then forward account, receipts, etc.

Tomorrow morning we enter upon the consideration of a case involving life and death. The responsibility of a judge advocate under such circumstances is by no means trivial. Do kiss my little daughter for me when you see her. And believe me ever, my dear parents, with warmest love,

Your affectionate son,
Charles C. Jones, Jr.

REV. C. C. JONES *to* LT. CHARLES C. JONES, JR.[8]

Walthourville, *Wednesday,* May 28th, 1862

My dear Son,

Enclosed is the note for the bank, signed as requested. I would be glad if you would get a certificate of deposit of the amount you have had placed to my credit in the state bank from the cashier, subject to my check, and send it to me.

Am obliged to you for the memorandum of accounts paid and Mr. Anderson's account current. All right, I think. The memorandum of the investments you have made of Dr. Martin's payment to you of $6778 I will carefully file away with the memorandum of the evidences of your property previously sent me. Your investments, in my opinion, are as good as could be made. If our revolution fails, everything of value in property fails.

Daughter wrote you for me yesterday. We sent for Dr. Stevens this morning to see Little Sister, and he thinks Mother is doing all that is necessary to be done, and that she is getting along very well. She has not slept well for two nights, and has had the fever which accompanies measles; but this morning she plays and laughs, the fever has abated, and the crisis seems to be passing away. It appears to be a genuine attack of measles.

Your sister is not very well today, but is up as usual. Rest pretty well. Much suffering on some plantations, Dr. Stevens tells me, from measles, whooping cough, and dysentery (like cholera), and a tendency to this latter disease more or less in different places. Stepney was ill with convulsions Saturday night last; is better and up. We hope our sickness is abating. Some lingering cases.

Came up for the summer here on Monday the 26th. . . . Hope to get to work now. Tom is unpacking a few cases of books in the nice study Daughter has given me, and Little Daughter is superintending his operations.

James is just in with the morning's *News*. Great and good news from that great and good General Stonewall Jackson. The rout has fallen on the right head this time: Banks. May it be the prelude of what the Lord will do for us at Corinth and at Richmond! If not, collect armies and try it again. Reverses do not indicate in struggles like ours God's final decree concerning our cause; they are often the means He institutes to insure us success. All unite, my dear son, in much love to you. Our respects to Captain Claghorn.

From your ever affectionate father,
C. C. Jones.

If you are passing by the *Morning News,* please order my triweekly sent to *Walthourville.*

LT. CHARLES C. JONES, JR., *to* REV. C. C. JONES[8]
Savannah, *Wednesday,* May 28th, 1862

My dear Father,

I am just favored with your very kind letter of today, and cannot tell you how thankful I am to hear that my dear little daughter is so much better. Since this morning, when I received Sister's letter, I have had nothing but fearful apprehension and ceaseless anxiety; but your welcome assurances of the fact that Mary Ruth is so much better, that she "plays and laughs," and that "she is getting along very well," fills my heart with joy, and gives me the perfect antithesis in feeling to the depression from which I have been suffering. Well do I know how tenderly she will be nursed, and my heart goes out in thankfulness to you both, my dear parents, for your great kindness. . . . Am glad to know that the sickness at Montevideo is abating, and trust that all disease may soon be rebuked.

The enclosed renewal note has been received, and will, D.V., be attended to tomorrow morning. I will endeavor to have it extended until January next so as to avoid the necessity of a renewal every ninety days. The amount which I will deposit to your credit, subject to check, in the Bank State of Georgia at the same time will be $744.53. Besides this amount I will have in hand three hundred dollars to be sent out in current funds by first suitable opportunity, in accordance with your wishes. I will also in the morning attend to the transfer of direction of *Morning News.*

Had a sight of the enemy this morning. Two steamers and one schooner came up the river so near the city that with an ordinary spyglass the stripes (which Butler says we will be made to feel, even if we do not respect the stars) of the United States flag could be distinctly seen. They were careful enough, however, to keep out of range of our batteries. I took a good look at the rascals from the window of the room in which our court-martial is convened, just over Claghorn & Cunningham's store. Reconnoitering, I presume, although the precise character of their mission has not yet transpired.

We have now at the end of the Bay a battery of four guns—two eight-inch columbiads and two long thirty-two-pounder guns; and just to the south of the gasworks, on the brow of the hill, occupying a part of the site of old Fort Wayne, two more guns—eight-inch columbiads. These all have a direct range down the river. These batteries are to be reinforced by some four or six more eight-inch howitzers, I believe, and will form a very valuable addition to the immediate defenses of the city. Thus from the city to Mackay's Point, where St. Augustine Creek enters the Savannah, every available point will present its armament ready to oppose the approach of the enemy by water. On St. Augustine Creek there are two more batteries—one at Causton's Bluff of (I believe) five guns, and a ten- or twelve-gun battery at Thunderbolt. Add to these the battery at Beaulieu and the one at Genesis Point, and you have all our seacoast defenses. I hope in the hour of peril that we will not be found wanting.

General Mercer has been transferred to and put in command of Charleston. General Ripley has been ordered elsewhere. Too much drinking is said to be a besetting sin of both himself and of General Evans.

We will soon be returning the compliment of the enemy by reconnoitering with our own balloon. A member of our company made it, and will make the ascensions. Everything is ready.

To give you an idea of my labors here upon this court-martial, I may state that I today forwarded to General Pemberton two hundred and forty-seven pages foolscap closely written, all in my own handwriting, containing the records of fourteen cases tried and disposed of by this general court-martial. There are some thirty others upon the docket, and new ones coming in every day, so that I cannot tell when we may look forward to a termination of our labors. It is peculiarly unfortunate that I am compelled to be absent from the company just at this time, as Captain Claghorn has been forced on account of ill health to seek and obtain a furlough of thirty days, thus leaving the company in charge of newly elected officers.

I cannot tell you, Father, how happy I am at thought that my sweet little daughter is so much better. Do kiss her for me. Give warmest love to dear Mother, Sister, Robert, and little Niece and Nephew. And believe me ever

Your affectionate son,

Charles C. Jones, Jr.

. . . I am indebted for your letter tonight to the kindness of Mr. Mills, the assistant postmaster, who very kindly kept the office open to me until nearly eight o'clock, and obtained the letter from the bag which would not otherwise have been distributed before half-past nine o'clock tomorrow morning.

MRS. MARY JONES *to* LT. CHARLES C. JONES, JR.[8]

Walthourville, Friday, May 30th, 1862

My dear Son,

I am happy and thankful to say that through the loving-kindness of our Heavenly Father our precious little babe is doing as well as she could in the progress of a painful and distressing disease. It has been a genuine case of measles, and aggravated by the scarlet fever influences remaining in her system. At no stage have I felt that there was anything alarming about her; but we have had Dr. Stevens to call twice and see her—first by your sister and once after we came up—to assure ourselves that all was doing that was right and proper in the case. His only suggestion to what we were already using was *young pine-top tea,* which I have found both agreeable and efficacious. And I would commend it especially to our soldiers in all cases of colds, measles, etc. Our dear one is very bright this morning: is up and dressed, playing with her doll; and when her grandpapa came from his study (where he sleeps during her sickness) to bid her good morning, with one little hand she struck him with her baby, and pinched him with the other, and then laughed at the saucy performance! Your brother thought a genuine attack of measles would tend to eradicate the old disease from her system, and I trust it will prove so, in God's mercy. . . .

I have a subject of interest on my mind which I wish to mention without delay, although very much hurried now. You know the Halifax brig (after which the enemy invaded our river) was sunk at Mr. Busby's landing. *Captain Thomson* is removing her ropes, etc., etc., and I am told pronounces her a staunch, well-built vessel. Only her upper works were burnt, and she floats at every high tide. Why could we not use her for our coast defense— give her a coat of iron, a lining of cotton bales, a boarding prow, a strong engine, a few big guns; man her with brave hearts; and let her go forth from our quiet little stream (where it seems to me this might be done as well as elsewhere) to make her mark upon our insolent foes? Do, my son, if you think anything can be done to use this vessel for the purpose, speak of the matter to the proper authorities. I am convinced she could be made useful in a short time. Your Uncle Henry expects to go to Milledgeville next week on a visit to the governor, and promises that he will name the subject to him. It would do no harm to have the brig examined. Man, woman, and child in our Confederacy must be up and doing for our beloved country.

With sweetest kisses from your baby, and our united love,

Ever, my beloved child, your affectionate mother,
Mary Jones.

MRS. MARY JONES *to* LT. CHARLES C. JONES, JR.[8]

Walthourville. *Sunday*, June 1st, 1862

My very dear Son,

Major Winn has just kindly sent over to say that he expected to see you in the morning, and would take any communication about your precious little one; and I employ a few of the closing moments of this calm and holy day to gladden your heart with the assurance of her continued improvement. She was so well and bright this afternoon that I left her to your sister's care and heard Robert's sermon, an excellent one from Psalm 104:34—"My meditation of Him shall be sweet." The measles eruption is passing off, but the dear little one suffers from small boils over her head and face, which disfigure her completely. But I can but hope, as your brother anticipated, it will eventuate in her permanent benefit. She is cheerful, and her appetite keeps up. She lives in my arms, but amuses herself with the children, who caress her in the tenderest manner. You may rest assured I shall write you of the least change.

Father, Sister, Brother all unite in tenderest love to you, with many kisses from your precious child, now sweetly sleeping in her crib after having enjoyed a warm bath. God bless you, my dear son! May your meditation of Him be sweet!

Ever your affectionate mother,
Mary Jones.

REV. C. C. JONES *to* LT. CHARLES C. JONES, JR.[8]

Walthourville, *Monday*, June 2nd, 1862

My dear Son,

Major Winn very politely sent over and gave us the opportunity of writing a line by him which you were to receive in the courtroom at ten this morning. Your dear little daughter had a warm fever during the night, and of course her rest much disturbed; but Mother does not think that she has any fever now, and that we must expect these fluctuations in the disease when it is passing off. The eruption is subsiding. She will not let her grandmother pass her, and almost lives in her arms, and scolds anybody who offers to take her. She holds her porcelain baby carefully which her Aunt

251

Vallie sent, and is much pleased with it. She pulled off my spectacles just now, and gave them up rather reluctantly. She tries to keep up her spirits, and answer caresses with smiles. It is wonderful how she has stood the attack: is no cry-baby with it at all. The eruption over her face and head has been abundant and large, like cat-boils. Mother has taken off her cap and part of her flannel on account of the heat. We hope she will begin to improve. She has fallen away in flesh and strength, but not so much as you would have supposed. We will keep you advised of her state.

We lost another infant on Friday: effect of measles. Patience's last—little Marcia. The first she and Porter have ever lost. Some lingering cases yet.

The papers are just in. We have cause of gratitude to God for the manifest indications of His returning favor. Great has been His blessing upon His servant General Stonewall Jackson. That pious man and able commander has executed one of the most brilliant passages at arms during the war. Every person who has an interest at a throne of grace should be constantly there for our brave Army of the Potomac now in the heat of *the great battle,* perhaps, of the revolution—at least, so far. The Lord be merciful to us and grant us this victory! *Banky* is here; came last week. Says he left the army in excellent condition and in fine spirits, ready for the enemy. Then there is the army of Corinth; by a short notice in the papers of Generals Price and Van Dorn being ordered to get between the enemy and the river, a battle must be in progress there. My faith is unshaken. Sinners as we are, yet humbly trusting in a just cause and in a just and merciful God, we may confidently hope that He will give us a happy issue.

Mother is much worn by loss of sleep and confinement, but is up, and went to church once yesterday. Daughter stayed with Baby. She is now writing your brother. We feel very uneasy about *little Stanhope.* He was ill with an affection of the bowels last week, and Joe had called in Dr. Ford.

All your boxes came safely and are carefully put away. Mother thanks you for the tea, and says it must be fine to be put up in such nice canisters, and says when Baby gets better she is coming down to see you—and *Dr. Parsons!* The note and your deposit, etc., is all exactly right. All unite in much love to you. And a kiss from your daughter.

Your ever affectionate father,
C. C. Jones.

2 *P.M.* Your dear little daughter is in her crib, enjoying a sweet sleep.

LT. CHARLES C. JONES, JR., *to* REV. C. C. JONES[g]

Savannah, *Tuesday,* June 3rd, 1862

My very dear Father,

It is with great pleasure and thankfulness that I acknowledge the receipt of your very kind letter of yesterday, giving me such a detailed account and so many happy remembrances of my dear little daughter. During the dark hours of this stormy day I have often thought of her and of you all, and have hoped that the change of temperature would not affect her unfavorably. I am this afternoon literally tired out. During the entire day I have been confined to the courtroom with an intermission of scarce half an hour for dinner, having conducted two cases involving life and death, and completed the entire record in them both.

From a private source—how reliable I am unable to say—we have an intimation of the evacuation of Corinth by our forces, who are reported to have fallen back some forty miles. With such generals as Beauregard, Bragg, Price, Van Dorn, and others in command, there must be good cause for the movement; but I confess the intelligence has excited in me no little surprise. Not a word from Richmond, or from that gallant Christian warrior Stonewall Jackson. We are told that the enemy last night made several demonstrations on the South Carolina islands in the vicinity of Charleston. More activity is manifested by the Lincolnites in our immediate vicinity just now than has been exhibited for some time past. I would not be surprised if we are called upon almost any day to meet our foes in a desperate struggle. May we have strength from above in the hour of contest!

I sincerely trust that my dear little daughter may soon be restored to perfect health, and that my dear mother will not suffer from all her kindest care and constant watchings over Mary Ruth. I regret to know that Brother's little boy is so unwell. Will try and write him tonight, and sincerely hope that all may yet be well. When you see Patience, do tell her that I sympathize with her in her recent affliction. With warmest love to all, and many kisses for my precious little daughter, I am ever, my dear father,

Your affectionate son,
Charles C. Jones, Jr.

REV. C. C. JONES *to* LT. CHARLES C. JONES, JR.[8]
Walthourville, *Wednesday,* June 4th, 1862
My dear Son,

We are happy to hear from you this morning. When will your court be over? It seems to be without end, because transgressions will never cease. You should take a ride on Yorick every day for exercise.

Your dear baby had a pretty good night's rest, and we hope the excitement in her system is passing away. Mother rubbed her all over this morning with *fat bacon* and then gave her a *warm bath;* and she has just waked up after a nap of an hour and a half in which she slept sweetly. She is now (12 M.) taking her butter and hominy, and looks as sober as a judge with her bib on, but cannot repress her smiles when her grandmother speaks to her. The eruption is abundant on her head and face, and it seems she will peel off as in scarlet fever. Little Daughter and Charlie are very fond of her, and she kisses them, and is greatly pleased with their attentions. I now hear her little voice talking to her grandmother: "Da, da, da."

Rode with Robert to the depot to hear the news. The great battle at Richmond yet to come off! Beauregard fallen back! Hope Alexander's statement that it leaves the enemy in possession of the Charleston & Memphis Railroad from Memphis to Chattanooga, and gives him Memphis and Fort Pillow, cannot be true. If true, then the Mississippi is gone from the Ohio to the Gulf, and troops may be forwarded to any point inland whether waters be high or low! General Lee's address not published. Glad of the stand he takes. The truth is, the war has just opened in earnest. All heretofore has been preliminary. We now realize all our enemy designs, and learn his inmost feelings towards us. Butler's proclamation gives us the strength of fifty thousand men. It is victory and honor and independence or defeat and abject humiliation and servitude. I hope General Mercer will be adequate to the position he now holds, and that Charleston will never be surrendered, and that Lawton will fulfill his declaration to hold Savannah to the last extremity. What is to be gained by surrender or evacuation? Let New Orleans speak. If it pleases God to enable us to repulse the enemy in these two cities and in Richmond, it will be a mercy that will produce a mighty effect on the country. If all *fall,* then fall back and renew the contest. Subjugation and submission on the part of the South will still be afar off.

We have been blest with a copious and timely rain: much needed. Another little one has been taken from us—Patience's *grandchild,* Beck's little infant boy. Was well on Saturday when I saw it; taken with fever Sunday evening, and died the same night. Do not know what could have been the cause. This makes the *eighth:* four adults and four infants. May we be made to know why these afflictions are sent, and be sanctified under them! We have prayed that we may fall into the hands of God and not of man, and He may thus be answering our prayer. Mother and Daughter and Robert all unite in much love to you. Hope you will write your brother. No letter from him today.

Your ever affectionate father,
C. C. Jones.

REV. C. C. JONES *to* LT. CHARLES C. JONES, JR.[8]
Walthourville, *Friday,* June 6th, 1862
My dear Son,

Your very interesting favor of yesterday is in by the morning's mail, and I write today because if we defer until tomorrow you will not hear from your dear child until Monday. We still think she is improving, but the eruption on her little head is great and continuous; one pimple does not go before another comes, and they are little boils. And her patience and quiet under all are remarkable. For the first time in two weeks Mother has allowed her to go downstairs; and when her straw bonnet was put on and she understood she was to go out, her countenance exhibited the sincerest delight; neither did she want to come up again. We are looking every day to see the eruption pass off. You must come and see her when you can.

I agree with you fully that our country should not be left to the ravages of the enemy. If government meditates invasion, let a force be kept in the Southwest sufficient to keep the enemy in check, and not allow him to possess and fortify the entire valley of the Mississippi. We private citizens can only conjecture and speculate; we are called upon to exercise patience and to pray for our country. Am sorry for our choice troops to be withdrawn from the coast. Is government going to weaken our defense and play the same game of evacuation or shameful surrender of Charleston and Savannah as of other places? We are weak enough—and our commanders appear to be imbecile enough—as we are.

The condition of things down the Savannah River is simply ridiculous: the enemy's boats *within* our obstructions, and chasing our boy-commanders in open day. They must have a contempt for such management. The next thing we hear will be that they have removed every obstruction, and not a soul in the city or on the river knew when they did it! It is difficult to restrain one's feelings at so much neglect when so many interests are at stake. If I had to go to the wars, I should like to go with such fine troops, but not under an untried commander, and one (as far as known) who has made anything but a favorable impression on the public. But I must not speak evil of dignitaries.

All unite in much love to you, with kisses from the baby, who is downstairs. As ever,

Your affectionate father,
C. C. Jones.

Lt. Charles C. Jones, Jr., *to* Rev. C. C. Jones[g]

Savannah, *Saturday,* June 7th, 1862

My dear Father,

I am under many obligations to you for your last kind favor, which reached me this morning. It rejoices me to know that my precious little daughter is so much better, and I hope that it will please God soon to restore her to perfect health.

We have an intimation this evening—but as yet lacking confirmation—that the enemy has shelled and captured Chattanooga. If this be true, Cherokee Georgia will soon be threatened if the avowed objects of the Lincolnites are further consummated. I believe that the statement that General Beauregard is on his way to Richmond with ten thousand men is incorrect. General Mercer has returned to Savannah, and is in command here, General Lawton having left for Richmond last night. General Smith is in immediate command at Charleston. General Pemberton still remains in command of the Department of South Carolina and Georgia.

I have it from good authority that General Pemberton has telegraphed to the department that in consequence of the withdrawal of such a large portion of the forces from this department, he will be unable to defend both Savannah and Charleston, and submitting which of the two cities shall be evacuated. I trust this is not true. We have already become a laughingstock from our continued and in many instances unwarranted abandonment of important points. It seems to me that all that is necessary to cause an evacuation of a chosen position on our part is the simple fact that it may be hazardous to hold it, or that in the event of its being vigorously attacked by the enemy it may be problematical whether or not a defense under an imagined condition of adverse circumstances could be successfully maintained. Thus it is that we have time and again lost ground without reason. Thus it is that by our own culpable timidity the enemy is induced to attempt enterprises and achieve plans which would not but for our own lack of determination have been seriously undertaken. Thus is the moral tone of our army weakened, the expectations of our countrymen disappointed; and thus the great cause of national honor and national reputation suffers to an unpardonable extent. The time long since has come for desperate enterprises and desperate defenses. It came with the very inception of our present difficulties, when without an army, without a navy, without the appliances of modern warfare we took up arms against a people more than twice as numerous as our own, and with every resource on sea and land to aid them in the unequal contest. Our leaders have in very many instances failed to regard our struggle in its true light, and as a natural and necessary consequence we have lost ground.

We have a report that Stonewall Jackson has met and routed the enemy again at Strasburg under command of General Shields of Mexican notoriety.

George goes out on Monday morning, and to his carriage I commit this letter and the enclosed three hundred dollars, which you desired me to retain and send out by earliest opportunity. Of the balance of the amount received from Mr. Anderson I have already rendered you an account.

I trust, my dear father, that you are feeling better, and that we may all be mercifully spared to hail the return of that day when peace shall again spread her white wings over a land smiling in happiness, in plenty, rejoicing in the assurances of honor vindicated, of national existence and national repose firmly established, confident in the hope of a great and of a good future when we shall indeed be that happy people whose God is the Lord. With warmest love to all, I am ever

Your affectionate son,
Charles C. Jones, Jr.

REV. C. C. JONES *to* LT. CHARLES C. JONES, JR.[8]

Walthourville, *Sunday*, June 8th, 1862

My dear Son,

As I promised to let you know how your dear little daughter was from

256

time to time, I write today (Sabbath) to say that she was taken with an affection of the bowels yesterday which continued until eleven o'clock last night, when it was checked until five o'clock this morning. It returned, and Dr. Stevens has come and made a prescription which we hope may arrest the affection altogether. The eruption is drying up on her head and person, and renders such an attack unpleasant, and it requires strict attention. She has shrunk in her person a good deal, but her spirits keep up remarkably well, and so far has suffered no pain.

It would afford us great pleasure for you to come out and see her, if it could be done consistently with your engagements. . . . You might come out in the cars in the morning to the Walthourville station, where we will have a buggy in waiting for you, or in any other mode you might choose.

Mother would be glad to have a syringe for *injections for infants*—the common kind, without any pump or India rubber to it. Also a *quart of brandy* for medical purposes. The dear little baby is quietly asleep as I close this note (1 P.M.), but looks languid. All unite in much love to you.

Your affectionate father,
C. C. Jones.

Lt. CHARLES C. JONES, JR., *to* REV. *and* MRS. C. C. JONES[g]

Savannah, *Monday,* June 9th, 1862

My very dear Father and Mother,

I embrace a moment before retiring to say that I reached the city safely after my most refreshing visit to you, my precious little daughter, and all at home.

The health of my dear little Mary Ruth is ever in my mind, and causes deepest anxiety; but I pray God most earnestly that it may please Him soon to restore her to her accustomed health. I never will be able, my dear parents, to thank you for one tithe of all your great kindness and tender love in this constant care of my motherless infant; but God will reward you, though even your affectionate son cannot.

I trust that Mamie and Charlie will soon be entirely well again.

By the telegraph of today we have the intelligence of another victory by Stonewall Jackson—over Frémont—and an anticipated victory at no distant day over Shields.

It is rumored upon the authority of a gentleman this evening arrived from Florida, whence he came having recently successfully run the blockade with a small steamer, that France has recognized the independence of the Southern Confederacy. He asserts positively that the fact was believed in Havana, and that the news reached that city by steamer *Trent,* arrived in that port the day before he left—namely, the 23rd ult. What degree of credence is to be attached to his statement one cannot judge; it may be, like all of its predecessors on this subject, merely a sensational rumor.

I learn tonight that our battery has been ordered to Causton's Bluff, which will place us within four or five miles of the city. The situation, however, must prove anything else but healthy, exposed as it is directly to the miasmatic influences of the Savannah River and swamp. However, those who are bound must obey. Nothing heard from our detachment in South Carolina.

With warmest love to you both, my dearest parents, many kisses for my precious little daughter, with every prayer and hope for her speedy recovery, and sincere remembrances to Robert, Sister, Mamie, and Charlie, I am ever
Your affectionate son,
Charles C. Jones, Jr.

LT. CHARLES C. JONES, JR., *to* REV. C. C. JONES[8]
Camp Stonewall Jackson, *Friday,* June 13th, 1862

My dear Father and Mother,

The mails of the past two days have not brought me a letter, and I have passed many anxious moments on account of my dear little daughter. Believing, however, that you would have written me had she not have been improving in health, I have trusted that no news was good news. I pray daily for her, and I hope that it will please God to restore her—and that right early—to her accustomed health.

Our camp is located at Causton's Bluff, just opposite Whitemarsh Island. We are now occupying the ground just vacated by the 47th Georgia Regiment, which, as you have observed by the daily journals, suffered rather severely in the recent engagement on James Island. You cannot imagine how filthy we found everything. The effluvium was horrid, and we have done little else until this morning except police the premises. I am quite confident that much of the ill health of our troops, especially typhoid and fevers of a slow and lingering type, are due to a polluted atmosphere generated by the decaying vegetable and animal matter scattered by the men themselves in the immediate vicinity of their tents, and suffered there to remain and fester in putrid corruption under the influences of a scorching sun. Officers in command cannot be too careful in this particular.

Our section is still in South Carolina, and it is said is attracting much commendation and attention. It was expected that by our rifled gun an action would have been opened today. Read's battery and two regiments infantry have already returned; and I understand that the pledge has been given to Governor Brown that Savannah shall be defended at every hazard, and that at least nine thousand troops shall be kept in its vicinity. Here I can only retail the items of news at second hand. This afternoon I had the battery practiced at shell and solid shot firing, and with very creditable success.

Do kiss my dearest little baby for me. Accept every assurance, my dear parents, of my constant and warmest love for you and for all at home. And believe me ever
Your affectionate son,
Charles C. Jones, Jr.

The mosquitoes are fairly putting out the lamp, and I am covered from ankle to knee with fleas.

258

REV. C. C. JONES *to* LT. CHARLES C. JONES, JR.[8]

Walthourville, *Saturday,* June 14th, 1862

My dear Son,

Your two last favors have been received. You have given your new camp a good name. It is a name to inspire the breast of the patriot and nerve the arm of the soldier. Our fine troops have gone to reinforce General Stonewall Jackson; no doubt they will do their duty. By appearances General Pemberton means to hold both *Charleston* and Savannah. He ought so to do—and can do it if he will just go on as he has begun and keep the enemy from *entrenching* on James Island. His first attack badly managed: no reconnaissance, and no support to our brave 47th.

Went to Montevideo yesterday—the reason why you received no letter. A melancholy day. Found *Beck* (Patience's)—that intelligent, fine young woman—*a corpse!* Died about daylight after some ten days' sickness from dysentery consequent upon measles. Dr. Way in daily attendance for a week; says she had pneumonia also, and did his best. A great loss. I never saw her. The message I received was that Mr. Calder had called in Dr. Way and she was mending, which was not true. This, together with the baby's illness, kept me here, and I never knew a word until I went down. This is the seventh case from measles and its consequents, and the *ninth this spring!* It is most affecting and distressing. And the plantation is not over the visitation yet. Little Miley (Beck's sister) is very sick with the same affection, and there is a disposition to it on the place.

Mother has gone down today, from which you may well infer that your dear little daughter is better. The doctor seems to have discharged the case. The affection is checked; her appetite is improving; and she had a fair night's rest last night. But she scolds a good deal more than she has ever done, and it is a sign of a returning sense of her own rights and of a determination to assert them. She will have very little to say to me today. . . .

Little Daughter has had measles, and is out of bed today for the first time. Lucy, Tenah, Kate, and Elvira—all Daughter's servants but James in the yard—down together with measles. Tenah came out yesterday. Rest still down. We sent down for our cook Kate, and with Flora, Elsie, and Tom are doing very well. . . . Am writing for the mail, and must close. *Lime* is a good disinfecting agent about camps, etc. All unite in much love.

Your ever affectionate father,
C. C. Jones.

LT. CHARLES C. JONES, JR., *to* REV. *and* MRS. C. C. JONES[8]

Savannah, *Monday,* June 16th, 1862

My very dear Father and Mother,

I am under great obligations for Father's kind letter of the 14th inst., which relieved me of no little anxiety on account of my precious little daughter. It rejoices me to know that she is so much better, and I thank God for her recovery thus far, and pray that He will restore her fully to her

259

accustomed health. Not a day passes, my dear parents, but brings to my mind and heart a realizing appreciation of the special thanks which I owe to you for your never-tiring care and tender love for my little daughter under the most trying circumstances.

I am shocked and distressed to learn the sad intelligence of the death of Beck, one of the finest and best young women on the place. The hand of God has indeed been most heavily laid upon us, and I am sorry to hear that the progress of disease has not yet been stayed.

Today has been a period of no little anxiety with me. A section of our battery was engaged in the fight on James Island, which has resulted so favorably to our arms. I trust that they have rendered valuable service and suffered no loss. The section numbered thirty-three men, nineteen horses, one Blakely rifled gun, and one twelve-pound howitzer. Everything in the finest order, and the numbers composing the two detachments reliable every way. We will have a good account from them. The day has been unusually propitious for field operations—cool, bracing, and no dust. We should have further particulars tonight. I enclose an extra.

I ought by rights, under ordinary circumstances, to have been in command of that section, and only the peculiar nature of the case prevented. At the time the order was received for the section to move—and that without a moment's delay—Captain Claghorn was absent sick. I was relieved from duty and was in attendance upon general court-martial in Savannah. Lieutenant Wheaton was thus left in command. The order reached camp at night. I knew nothing of it until the section had nearly reached the city en route for Charleston, when I found—as was right and proper under the circumstances—that Lieutenant Askew had been detailed as the officer in charge of the detachments. Although it is all right, I have experienced no little regret that I did not have the opportunity of going in command of the section. It may be, however, that our entire battery may soon have a chance of meeting the enemy, who, although driven back today, if they contemplate a serious demonstration against Charleston will doubtless reinforce themselves and advance again to the attack.

I am happy to know that our defenses on James Island are far more formidable than I had been led to believe. Across the entire island we have entrenchments of strength mounting many siege guns (forty-two-, thirty-two-, twenty-four-, and eighteen-pounders); while at either extremity of our earthworks are protecting forts, located on the streams which respectively wash either side of James Island, mounting considerable batteries containing heavy ten-inch guns and rifle pieces. These forts, it is confidently expected, will be able to resist any advance of the enemy's gunboats. The possession of James Island thus retained by our forces, Charleston may be considered as virtually safe, as I scarcely think an attack will be attempted by way of the harbor—certainly not until the anticipated steel-clad gunboats of the enemy appear upon our coast.

McClellan has, I learn, withdrawn his forces from this side of the Chickahominy. Every day and every account prove more and more forcibly the fact that the recent engagement near Richmond was an important Confederate victory.

Its value is enhancing every moment, and I would not be surprised to learn any day—if Stonewall Jackson is sufficiently reinforced, as doubtless he already is—that the boasted modern Napoleon has been compelled to raise the siege of Richmond and consult the immediate safety of the Lincoln capital.

It is difficult to conjecture the cause of Lord Lyons' leaving Washington just at this time. The English fleet is said to be rendezvousing in the vicinity of Fortress Monroe, and the French fleet in New York harbor. A few weeks at farthest will furnish an explanation.

I fear from all that I can learn that General Beauregard's army is suffering a great deal from sickness. In its present position it appears to be accomplishing little or nothing; and Halleck will hardly pursue, risking the fortunes of a general engagement, when the Mississippi valley is already won.

General Stonewall Jackson is probably awaiting reinforcements. He will not long remain idle. The brigade which General Lawton took with him is one of a thousand, and by God's blessing we may anticipate from their brave deeds results of the most fortunate character.

It appears to me that the Lincoln government is now feeling more than at any previous time the pressure of this war. Although possessed of wonderful resources, it is already a bankrupt government; and a light wind from the wrong quarter may soon send the whole political fabric tumbling about the heads of the misguided race who inaugurated the wretched policy which gave rise to this unholy and most unjust war. The day of retribution, though deferred, must come; and when it does arrive it will be terrible in the extreme. I can imagine no nation with more forbidding prospects in the future than those which look the Lincolnites full in the face. And the most unsatisfactory reflection—if they reflect at all—is that they have themselves made their own destruction sure.

But I fear, my dearest parents, that I tire you, so I will bid you good night, begging that you will kiss my precious little daughter for me. Assure Sister, Robert, and little Niece and Nephew of my kind remembrances. And believe me ever, with warmest love,

Your ever affectionate son,
Charles C. Jones, Jr.

Our court-martial resumed its session in Savannah this morning.

REV. C. C. JONES *to* LT. CHARLES C. JONES, JR.[8]
Walthourville, *Monday*, June 16th, 1862
My dear Son,

Your dear little one did not spend a good day yesterday, nor a good night last night: did not sleep well. She had two large evacuations yesterday—one in the morning, the other in the evening—which exhausted her a good deal; and the emaciation continues. Called in the doctor again. He lanced her gums for her eyeteeth, which she bore quietly, the operation seeming to be a relief. Mother says if it were not for removing her so far from the doctor and yourself she would take her down to the Island and spend two or three weeks there for the salt-bathing and for the benefit of the change. She intends using a salt bath here. We feel very much concerned for the issue of her complaint, following a severe attack of measles and connected with teething, and in the debilitating heat of summer. We must use every means, and ask a blessing upon them and hope for it.

Your mother left her yesterday morning with your sister and went to church. Your Uncle Henry had me to baptize his last fine infant, five months old. . . . In the evening at family worship we sung in remembrance of you "Come, My Redeemer, Come." And Mother said: "My dear child, I wonder what religious privileges he has enjoyed today."

3 P.M. Our dear baby continues about the same. Is *feeble* today; has little or no appetite. We will write you every day, and should you not hear from us, conclude she is as usual. But her sickness is of such a nature that she might not survive a severe attack of it but a few hours.

Little Daughter has got through the measles wonderfully well, and all the women servants of Daughter's household are up today, all having had the measles *strongly*. We all unite in much love to you. Take care of yourself in this trying northeaster.

Your ever affectionate father,
C. C. Jones.

Lt. Charles C. Jones, Jr., *to* Rev. C. C. Jones[8]
Savannah, *Tuesday*, June 17th, 1862
My dear Father,

It is with deep sorrow that I learn through your kind letter of yesterday, this morning received, that my precious little daughter is not as well as when you last wrote. The only consolation I have in my absence from her is that she is in the tender care of you and of dear Mother, and that in your love and kindest treatment she will have the benefit of all that man can do. The issue is with the Father of All Mercies, and I can only pray Him in goodness—if it be His will—to spare her precious life and restore her to many days of happiness and of usefulness. Is there anything in the way of medical advice which I can procure for her here? Or is there anything else I can do to serve you and her in any particular?

I am glad to hear that Sister's little ones and the servants have recovered so soon from the measles. The present attacks of sickness and the unusual prevalence of disease are directly to be referred to the existence of this terrible war.

I feel, this blustering day, for our troops without covering, and often with but scant food, upon the soaked earth; and especially for the section of our battery on James Island. As yet we have no definite intelligence from those

262

detachments, but shall probably know more by the Charleston papers which reach us this afternoon. I am inclined to believe that Captain Claghorn is with that section. No telegraphic reports of any character today. It is thought that the enemy will soon renew the attack on James Island. Hoping, my dear parents, that all will yet be well, I am, with warmest love to you both and to all, and with many kisses for Daughter,

Your ever affectionate son,
Charles C. Jones, Jr.

MRS. MARY JONES *to* LT. CHARLES C. JONES, JR.[8]

Walthourville, *Tuesday,* June 17th, 1862

My dear Son,

Our precious little babe rested more comfortably last night, and I hope the diarrhea has been arrested; but she continues exceedingly feeble, and suffers from a total loss of appetite. Although we try every imaginable kind of nourishment, she shakes her little head and puts it away with both hands. During the day she is most quiet and patient, often amused with the children. The doctor has commenced giving her tonics, and I would feel encouraged if I could only see the emaciation arrested and a little craving for food.

No one knows how much my heart is bound up in this precious child. It is nearly one year since I received her as a sacred legacy from her dying sainted mother. In that brief period of alternate hope and fear for the young life which I trust I have sought to cherish in every way, she has been to me a precious little comfort, rewarding every care with the affection of a loving little heart. I have often felt that my life was perhaps too much bound up in the life of this little one; and if my Heavenly Father should see fit to remove her from my arms to His own bosom, it would be a crushing blow. . . .

Little Mary Jones has recovered well from the measles. Charlie is just taking them, we think. And all your sister's servants who were taken down at the same time are all out at their accustomed duties. The weather continues very cool and damp. I am sighing for the warm sunshine, that I might take my dear little baby into the fresh air. If it were not for removing her from you so far, and from the care of Dr. Stevens, in whose skill we have confidence, I would take her immediately to the Island for change of atmosphere and salt-bathing, which I feel assured would do her good. Last night I put her into a bath of warm salt and water with beneficial effect.

The bell rings for dinner, and I must close. Be sure and send your clothes as soon as they are cut. Father, Sister, and Robert unite with me in best love to you. Kisses from the children, especially from your own little Mary Ruth. God bless and preserve you, my dear son!

Ever your affectionate mother,
Mary Jones.

263

REV. C. C. JONES *to* LT. CHARLES C. JONES, JR.[8]

Walthourville, *Wednesday,* June 18th, 1862

My dear Son,

Your dear baby was very feeble all day yesterday, as Mother wrote you. The doctor is doing his best, and Mother is calling all her experience into practice, and we hope on the whole the little sufferer is no worse today. You would scarcely know her pale and emaciated countenance and form—not above half her size in full health. Understands everything and appreciates all you do for her, but too languid to enjoy anything.

Mother watched with her until four this morning, when I relieved her that she might get some sleep. When Baby woke, she was surprised to see me lying in Mother's place, and did her best to look around me to find her grandmother. She has been very quiet all the morning. The doctor thinks she is no worse, and if we only could get her to eat something we should feel better. But she seems to relish nothing, and Mother has to give her what she thinks best for her regularly.

The only thing we need and which we cannot get out here is some *brandy*. We use it as an external stimulant; and if you could send us a quart bottle of it, care of Mr. Joseph Miller, No. 4, we would be glad to get it. The doctor recommended sponging the baby in whiskey; your mother told him she had been applying the burnt brandy and cloves, and he said it was just as good.

Everybody is interested in the dear child, and everything will be done for her that can be done. And if anything is needed, will let you know. I pray the Lord to spare us the great affliction of her loss, if it be His holy will. Our hearts are very full at times on her account and on yours.

Your two last interesting favors came this morning. The James Island battle was gallant. That is the way: give the wicked enemy no time nor place to entrench; push him everywhere, anyhow. Hope South Carolina will come out yet. A repulse at Charleston and Savannah would be a great blessing. Your not being with your section of your battery on James Island was wholly providential, and so you must consider it. What does General Mercer want with a thousand Negroes? Where is he going to fortify? On a heavy scale, it would seem. The enemy begins to taste a little of the practicability of subjugation by *invasion. We* cannot invade—beyond freeing the border states. The war is now beginning in reality with the Lincolnites. I hope they will find the coveted prize too large for their grasp. We can get along—if true to ourselves—without England or France to help us. My opinion is, McClellan will not fight at Richmond, but siege it out and environ the city with impregnable lines and force General Lee *to evacuate!* This is his design. Will our generals suffer themselves to be whipped in this way? And what a blow the loss of the city would be to us! McClellan is deceiving them with feints—nothing more. . . . All unite in much love to you. As ever,

Your affectionate father,

C. C. Jones.

Savannah, *Friday,* June 20th, 1862

My dear Father,

I am in receipt of your kind favor of yesterday, and cannot express the deepest anxiety which I feel on account of the continued illness of my precious little daughter. It pains me to the bottom of my heart to know that she still continues to be so feeble, and manifests as yet no signs of returning health and appetite; and it costs me many an hour of sincerest regret that I am unable to be with her in this her protracted and severe sickness. I can only pray—and that earnestly and repeatedly—to God that He would bless all the tenderest care and attentions of you, my dear father and mother, to her full and speedy recovery. Has her bowel affection been completely checked? Is there anything in the way of food in Savannah or elsewhere to be procured that you think will tempt her appetite? I send by express one gallon best brandy, which I trust will reach you in safety and without delay. It is directed to you, care of Mr. Miller.

Philo Neely has been here with her children for the past day. She came down to pay her husband a visit, who is connected with the Oglethorpe Siege Artillery stationed at the battery at the foot of the Bay. She desires her special remembrance to you both, my dear parents, and sends many kisses for Mary Ruth.

Our recent victory on James Island appears to increase rather than diminish in its results. I understand today that in their retreat not a few of the Lincolnites were drowned in crossing an intervening creek. Some were also shot in the water. The genuine Yankee was scarcely seen among the dead—mostly foreigners, the Scotch features predominating. Some of the oldest families in Charleston suffered in that battle. That is a misfortune which we have had to encounter during the entire course of this war: our best men are in the field, while we meet in the unequal contest hordes of mercenaries, not one in ten of whom belongs to the race entailing the present miseries, and upon which the avenging rod should descend. Our detachment still remains on James Island. The health of the men is pretty good. Captain Claghorn is expected in this city this afternoon. He has been suffering a great deal of late from dyspepsia, and I understand has had no little sickness in his family at Athens.

If we may credit the reports, a rupture between the U.S. and England appears to be imminent; but I have no question but that the ingenuity of Seward and the cringing policy of that degraded nation will readily afford some apology which, while it disgraces in the eyes of the world, will prevent anybody from "being hurt." For one I desire to see no foreign intervention, and fully concur with you in the conviction that if we are only true to ourselves we will be able, with the blessing of Heaven, to whip our own battles and secure our own freedom. That issue, obtained under such circumstances, will be far more valuable than if secured by the assistance of others. Our national existence will be all the more firm, and the satisfaction and honest pride of victory far greater.

I regret to learn that General Joseph E. Johnston is suffering much from his wound. He has been spitting blood, and a portion of his right lung is involved; but his recovery is anticipated. It is said that G. W. Smith, one of our good generals, is suffering from a stroke of paralysis, which—for the present, at least—incapacitates him from the discharge of active duties.

General Mercer desires the thousand hands, I believe, to strengthen our fortifications on the river and to dam around one or two of the batteries to keep the water out. Our troops on those river battalions are already experiencing the ill effects of their unwholesome locations. . . . With warmest love to you both, my dearest parents, and to all at home, and with tenderest kisses for my precious little daughter, and every hope and prayer for her restoration to health, I am ever

Your affectionate son,
Charles C. Jones, Jr.

MRS. MARY JONES *to* LT. CHARLES C. JONES, JR.[8]

Walthourville, Friday, June 20th, 1862

My dear Son,

Through God's mercy I am enabled to say that our precious little one is decidedly better today than she has been since her sickness. So ill has she been that I knew she could not be with us long if the disease was not arrested. Today she notices and will take her boiled milk without constraint. She is still upon the list of topers—a small portion of burnt brandy being necessary three or four times a day. Dr. Stevens has been very attentive in her case, and he is an excellent family physician.

Your father has not been able to leave her until today. He went down to Montevideo; and soon after breakfast we were gratified by the arrival of Sister Susan and Mr. Buttolph to spend the day with us. I have just left them a moment to send you this line. Jimmie and Willie have recovered finely from measles, and so has Little Daughter; but Charlie coughs dreadfully, and they are not fully developed with him. I am uneasy until they do appear. The servants all doing well up here.

Your sister and aunt, Robert and Mr. Buttolph unite with me in best love to you, with sweetest kisses from your own little daughter. We shall look with special interest for tidings of the section of your battery. Daily I implore the deliverance and blessing of Jehovah upon my beloved and suffering country. And I have faith to believe when His wise and just purposes are accomplished—although they may be through great and merited sufferings—that He will own and establish us a free and independent nation.

Ever your affectionate mother,
Mary Jones.

Savannah, *Saturday,* June 21st, 1862

My very dear Mother,

I cannot express my happiness upon the receipt of your kind letter of yesterday to find that my precious little daughter is so decidedly better. May God in mercy continue the good work of her restoration to perfect health!

During her protracted illness I have often feared, my dear mother, that your continued and unceasing watchings, and the confinement in the sick chamber, united with your tenderest anxieties on her account, must have affected your own health and strength. I trust, however, that you may in her improved health find comfort and rest, and that the nights of apprehension and the days of uneasiness and of hourly ministrations to the every want of the little sufferer may be soon succeeded by periods of quiet with all their refreshing influences. I never will be able to express one moiety of the thanks which I owe to you for all your great kindnesses.

Is there any whooping cough on the Sand Hills? I trust not, for if Mary Ruth in her enfeebled state should contract that disease I fear that she would not possess physical strength sufficient to withstand its exhausting effects. As I write, a poor little child not two years old in an adjoining room is laboring and almost suffocating under the influence of that trying affection.

Hope that the gallon of brandy reached you without delay. You will find it a very superior article, and I trust its use will realize every expectation.

We have no telegrams of interest today. There appears to be a general calm for the time being, which in all probability is indicative of a marshaling of forces and a general preparation for future enterprises of moment. General Stonewall Jackson has been heavily reinforced, and will soon with his characteristic energy assume the offensive again.

I regret to find that this question of foreign intervention, which has already proved a source of so much evil to us, is again revived, and that the eyes of not a few are turned to nations beyond the seas to bring deliverance from our present dangers. For one I am loath to indulge in any such expectations, and I am unwilling to believe that in the achievement of our ultimate national existence and political independence we will have to acknowledge our indebtedness to foreign aid. Our future, under such circumstances, will be less honorable, our triumph less perfect, our self-gratulations less pleasing; and it may be that this very intervention may materially involve complications which in after years will inure to our hurt. Rather would I see our redemption from the thralldom of our enemies purchased at the expense of blood and treasure; wrought out by our own strong hands and brave hearts; compassed by our own protracted self-denial and heroic endurance, with no reliance save upon the outstretched arm of Him who ruleth alike amid the armies of heaven and among the inhabitants of earth; assisted by no power save the merciful interposition of the Father of All Strength, who will recognize the right and cover the heads of those who fear Him in the day of danger. We are at all times prepared to hold honorable intercourse with sister nations of the earth. We are ready to enter upon legitimate commercial relations with them, and if they apply in the proper way, their applications will meet with a cheerful response.

Enclosed I send a copy of a lithograph representing in a humble way the first great meeting of the citizens of Savannah when they realized for the first time the necessities for a grand revolution. The occasion has never had a parallel in the history of our city; and as an humble memento of an eventful past this rude lithograph will in after years possess no ordinary interest. The individual "spreading himself" with every conceivable energy and earnestness from the balcony of the clubhouse may be Colonel Bartow or Judge Jackson; or it may be the subscriber, then mayor of the city. We all spoke, using that balcony as a rostrum, on that night to the assembled multitudes, who swayed to and fro on every hand like the sea lifted by the breath of the tornado. We added fuel to the flame; and that meeting, it is said, contributed more to secure the secession of Georgia and to confirm the revolution in adjoining Southern states than almost any other single circumstance of the times. It was followed by similar demonstrations throughout the length and breadth of the cotton-growing states. It evoked unmeasured surprise and condemnation from the Northern press. It stayed the hands of our sister city Charleston, and gave an impulse to the wave of secession which soon swept with a rapidity and a strength, indicating no returning ebb, all over the land. But few copies were struck off—say, a thousand—and they were widely circulated throughout the country.

I hope that little Charlie will soon be up and well again. With warmest love to you both, my dearest parents, kindest remembrances to all, and many kisses for my precious little daughter, I am, as ever,

Your affectionate son,
Charles C. Jones, Jr.

Lt. Charles C. Jones, Jr., *to* Mrs. Mary Jones[t]
Savannah, *Tuesday,* June 24th, 1862

My dear Mother,

I have just taken Mr. Ward by the hand, who returned this afternoon. The vessel in which he arrived from Nassau ran the blockade and got safely into Charleston harbor. I send the Charleston *Mercury,* which gives the particulars. He is looking remarkably well, and I am most happy to see him. He leaves his family in Rome. All well.

Tomorrow will be the birthday of my dear little daughter. May Heaven grant her many years of true piety and happiness upon earth! I sincerely trust that she is regaining her health every hour. . . . As ever,

Your affectionate son,
Charles C. Jones, Jr.

Walthourville, *Wednesday*, June 25th, 1862

My darling Papa,

Do you know that your little daughter is one year old today? I would like to put my little arms around your neck and lay my little head in your bosom and tell you how much I love you. Grandmama hopes that I will be spared to cheer your heart and to be a comfort to you. In the mornings she folds my little hands and teaches me to ask my dear Saviour to bless and keep you from all harm and to save your soul.

Today she has put a short dress upon me of white muslin trimmed with blue which she has made for my birthday. My sleeves are looped with pretty little bracelets that you used to wear at my age, and she has clasped my little blue sacque with your pin which holds the hair of my blessed mother and my angel sister, who have now been in heaven nearly one year.

Dear Papa, God has heard your prayers and made me almost well again. This morning I am very bright. Everybody is so good and kind to your little daughter. My little sister and Bubber Charlie are tender and loving to me, and will give me up their playthings. I cannot talk or walk yet, for I have been a sick baby; but I know a great many little things, play with my doll, and look at the books in Grandpapa's study. I love the birds and flowers and chickens and pussy and my dog Captain, and to walk with Susan in the bright sunshine or under the tall trees, and to ride in the buggy with Sultan.

Grandpapa has gone to see Aunt Susan and Uncle William and to Maybank. When are you coming home to see us? We all send love to you, with sweetest kisses and the true love of

Your own little daughter,

Mary Ruth Jones.

(pen in her hand)

Susan sends howdies for Master and George.

XI

Lt. Charles C. Jones, Jr., *to* Rev. *and* Mrs. C. C. Jones[8]
Savannah, *Saturday,* June 28th, 1862

My dear Father and Mother,

I have just returned from the telegraph office, and rejoice to say that all the reports from the momentous battle near Richmond are most favorable. We are successful at every point. The thorough rout of the Federal army is announced, and it is expected by many that McClellan will capitulate. I earnestly trust that we may not be disappointed in our anticipations. We have on several occasions—just at the heel of our heaviest engagements, and while the cup of absolute success seemed at our lips—had that cup dashed, and failed of the legitimate fruits of our victory, that I am fearful until the final announcements are received. I hope that the annihilation of that proud army may be complete—"horse, foot, and cannon."

Thirty-six hundred prisoners already arrived in Richmond, among them the Federal generals Reynolds, Sanders, and Rankin. Additional batteries captured. We have lost as yet no general officers, but I regret to see it announced that General Elzey is mortally wounded, and the gallant Major Wheat of the Louisiana Tigers killed. The former you will remember as Captain Elzey in command of the Augusta arsenal at the time that it surrendered to the state forces under Governor Brown, and the latter as the brave leader of the Louisiana Zouaves upon the plains of Manassas. The carnage on both sides has doubtless been terrible. Thus is the mournful cypress closely entwined with the laurel in the wreath of victory. So valuable an achievement must have been purchased at great cost.

But if we have in reality overcome, routed, and annihilated this grand army which for more than a year has been furnishing itself forth with every improvement in the munitions of modern warfare, perfecting itself in military art and discipline, proudly boasting of its invincibility and of its ability to crush the beleaguered capital of our young Confederacy under the leadership of "the young Napoleon"—an army which has absorbed the strength of our enemy's forces and stands as the representative of its military power, we may well indulge in congratulations of the most honorable and sincerest character, return our heartfelt thanks to the Lord of Hosts from whom the victory cometh, and with renewed vigor press forward toward the accomplishment of new enterprises until the independence of our Confederacy shall be firmly established. I presume there will be no lack now of a forward movement in following up the victory.

Additional news from Europe indicates the fact that France and England are more seriously than ever contemplating an armed intervention on the basis of a separation between the North and the South. Butler's infamous proclamation has produced no little effect, and given rise to open and emphatic expressions of indignation in Parliament. The cup of Yankee iniquity, already full to overflowing, must run over. A people setting at defiance all the principles of common justice, truth, honor, and ordinary humanity must be regarded finally—although self-interest and accidental circumstances may for a while delay the expression—as a perfect *outlaw* among the nations of the earth, and dealt with as such. Eventually, Seward's threats and the *Herald*'s lies, as the Arabian proverb has it, "like chickens will come home to roost."

General Lee's dispatch to the President announcing our successes is perfect.

I am indebted to you, my dearest parents, for a most delightful day. My sincere regret is that I cannot enjoy the privilege of being with you oftener; and I cannot tell you how much it rejoiced my heart to see the evident improvement in the health of my precious little daughter. With warmest love to you both, my dear father and mother, kindest remembrances to Sister, Robert, and the little ones, and many kisses for Daughter, I am, as ever,

Your affectionate son,
Charles C. Jones, Jr.

REV. C. C. JONES *to* LT. CHARLES C. JONES, JR.[8]

Walthourville, *Monday,* June 30th, 1862

My dear Son,

Your most interesting letter we have just read, and I agree with you that everyone who has an interest at a throne of grace should offer the sincerest thanksgivings to Almighty God our Saviour—and I add, with tears of gratitude—for His blessings which have so far attended our battle of Richmond. If we are made successful in defeating that long-cherished and petted and lauded army, it will be a most direct and signal manifestation of the Lord's approbation of our cause; and the effect in both hemispheres will be great. My faith in the final and favorable issue has never for an instant been shaken. May no delays nor mistakes of the powers that be in the cabinet and in the field deprive us of a victory which seems put within our grasp!

Your dear little one continues to improve. Yesterday at dinner, while a blessing was asking and her grandmother's eyes were closed, being seated in her lap, she stretched out her hand and helped herself to the whole loaf of rusk. I begged she might have a little piece, and it was given her under her grandmother's protest that it would not do her good. And so it fell out, for she passed an unquiet night and was not as well as usual. But she is up and about and interesting herself both in and out of doors. She has just had a nap on the bed in my study, with Elsie to brush off the flies.

Daughter received a letter from Mrs. Thomas Clay (Clarkesville) giving an interesting account of the death of Mrs. Benjamin Stiles, at the request of Miss Kitty, who, as we may well imagine, is in the deepest distress. Dr. Alexander used to say "we had only to live long enough to realize what the sorrows of life are, and what a world we live in." But there is a Balm in Gilead, and there is a Physician nigh.

I write principally to advise you, at Mother's request, of her purpose, God willing, *to take the cars for Savannah tomorrow—Tuesday, July 1st—and to be with you to tea,* and hopes you may be able to meet her at the depot, and that you will please *say to Dr. Parsons that she will see him on Wednesday morning.* All unite in much love to you. I remain, my dear son,

Your ever affectionate father,
C. C. Jones.

LT. CHARLES C. JONES, JR., *to* REV. *and* MRS. C. C. JONES[8]

Savannah, *Friday,* July 4th, 1862

My dear Father and Mother,

I had hoped that this, the anniversary of our former national independence, would have been rendered memorable in the history of our young Confederacy by the unconditional surrender of McClellan and his boasted army of invasion. It may be that such will be the case before this newly risen sun shall have performed his daily journey. For more than a week have our brave men withstood the shock of this tremendous battle, and by the help of the God of Justice the hostile legions of the aggressor have been driven back, one after another, in consternation and dread confusion. And even now the end is not. The Lincoln forces must have numbered nearly two hundred thousand men. To dissipate, annihilate, or put to flight such an overwhelming army—well appointed in every respect, thoroughly furnished with every appliance of modern warfare, supported by fortifications judiciously selected and erected under the personal supervision of accomplished engineers and bristling with numerous siege guns of recent patent, and capable of ready transportation and rapid concentration at any point of attack—cannot be the work of a day. Add to this the physical difficulties which are met at every step by our advancing columns in the matter of miry roads, deep swamps, thick woods, broken hills, and intervening rivers—and every pass, every obstacle stubbornly held by the slowly retreating enemy, whose rear guard, numerous and powerful, appears to be fighting with a valor worthy of a better cause; and the continued success of our brave men in the face of all these difficulties and dangers, and under such protracted fatigues, seems, as it in reality is, most wonderful. A short time must terminate this most sanguinary struggle, and we have every reason to expect most favorably to us.

If, however, we cannot today rejoice in the unconditional surrender of McClellan and the total annihilation of his army, we can with swelling hearts rejoice in the valor of our men and the success of our arms. We can in all humility and with unbounded thankfulness to Almighty God praise Him for the past, the present, and pray a merciful continuance of His great favor. We can hail with honor and with rejoicing the increasing glories of our young Confederacy, and with one acclaim shout in louder tones of living devotion, of renewed allegiance, and of sterner resolve: *Vivat nova republica!*

The effect of this defeat of their arms before Richmond must exert a most depressing influence upon the Federals. It must teach them the utter impracticability of any theory which looks toward a subjugation. It will strengthen the hands of the peace party in their midst. It will bring desolation to their hearts and sorrow to their eyes. It will completely upset all the boastful schemes, and give the direct lie to all the vain promises, of their corrupt administration. It will deal a blow from which the already shattered finances of that country cannot recover. Credit abroad will be depreciated. You already observe that gold in New York is now quoted at 108—and that when the first whisper of defeat was breathed in her streets and not heeded. Picture the scene when the hurricane of disappointment, rout, and almost annihilation shall lift its fearful voice.

The result in Europe must prove most favorable to us, and we will look with interest for reports from that quarter.

On our part this great victory—while it will cost many a pang to the state who has lost so many brave defenders, while many a sorrowing home will attest the magnitude of the sacrifice, and the voice of loud rejoicing and the paeans of success be hushed before the sounds of lamentation—will nevertheless give to us, one and all, assurance of the favor of God, of the greatness of our cause, of the value of the liberties for which we are contending, and of our absolute invincibility by the proudest force which our enemy may send against us. The tide has indeed turned. I trust that we have been sufficiently punished for our transgressions, and that the aveng-ing rod will be now lifted. You see our successes in Arkansas. James Island has been evacuated by the Lincolnites. Vicksburg still holds bravely out against the thunders of the mortar and gunboat fleet. General T. J. Jackson is by his activity replenishing our commissary stores, etc., etc., by valuable captures from the enemy. Thus the work goes bravely on, and I trust we shall soon hail the return of white-winged peace.

My dear mother, you will, I trust, pardon me for taking the liberty of opening the enclosed letter from Father, which arrived the morning you left. My anxiety to know how all were at home must be my excuse. I trust that you suffered no inconvenience from your ride on the cars, and that you are again feeling much better. The last act of mine in the city is to put this letter in the post. In a moment I will be on my way to camp. With warmest love to you both, my dearest parents, many kisses for my precious little daughter, and kindest remembrances to Sister, Robert, and the little ones, I am, as ever,

Your affectionate son,
Charles C. Jones, Jr.

Lt. Charles C. Jones, Jr., *to* Rev. *and* Mrs. C. C. Jones[8]

Savannah, *Monday,* July 7th, 1862

My very dear Father and Mother,

I am here for an hour or two on business of the company, and am just on my way back to camp. I write to assure all at home of my constant love.

We have a telegram that McClellan has been reinforced by Shields, and with an army of ninety to one hundred thousand men has posted himself very strongly some thirty-five miles from Richmond and offers battle. It is further announced that two of the greatest powers of Europe have officially notified the United States that the war must stop. Exchange in New York is quoted at 120, and gold at 109½. Buell is said to be advancing upon Rome, Georgia. Sickles' brigade (the brigade of the miserable Dan Sickles of New York notoriety, who you will remember shot District Attorney Key in the streets of Washington, D.C.) went into action in the recent battles before Richmond five thousand strong; and now not five hundred can be found— the rest killed, wounded, and captured! I have for some days felt no little anxiety about the ultimate result of our battles in Virginia. McClellan has doubtless suffered a terrific defeat, accompanied with tremendous losses; but his army has not been annihilated. We will look with the deepest concern for the issues of this the final struggle. We may hear more tonight.

We are all pretty well in camp. Tomorrow will be the anniversary of the death of my dearest Ruth. With warmest love to you both, my dear parents, many kisses for Daughter, and kindest remembrances to Sister, Robert, and the little ones, I am, as ever,

Your affectionate son,
Charles C. Jones, Jr.

The C.S.S. *Nashville* has run into the Ogeechee bringing a cargo of field guns, several fully appointed light batteries, Enfield rifles, etc., etc.—all the property of the Confederate States.

Lt. Charles C. Jones, Jr., *to* Rev. *and* Mrs. C. C. Jones[8]

Camp Stonewall Jackson, *Wednesday,* July 9th, 1862

My dear Father and Mother,

. . . The section of our battery which has been upon James Island for the past month or more returned yesterday—the men completely bronzed, but all well with the exception of two who were left sick in Savannah. The health of our entire command continues thus far to be pretty good. Every care is observed in keeping the encampment well policed, and in the removal as far as practicable of all local causes of disease. Surrounded as we are, however, by the low grounds, brackish marshes, and river swamps of this malarial region, we cannot but expect as the season progresses fevers and other indispositions of a serious character.

I understand that upon the dead Yankees found upon the battlefield on James Island were canteens well filled with water, whiskey, and quinine. Probably no army ever entered upon a campaign as fully equipped or as sedulously provided with every comfort, subsistence, and protection from disease as this Lincoln army of occupation. Everything—even the most trivial—indicates the enormous expenditure of money in its behalf by the Federal government.

The recent successes of our arms, by the blessing of God, have been even more remarkable and encouraging than were our former reverses depressing and unexpected. A degree of rather painful uncertainty still lingers about our final operations in the vicinity of our capital, and the reported reinforcements of McClellan may cost us yet many a brave life. Already is the loud shout of national exultation at thought of our immense victory almost hushed in the universal sorrows of private grief. At such great cost is liberty purchased; at such enormous sacrifices are the rights of personal freedom, national security, and private property secured.

The gallant defense of Vicksburg is rising into the true sublime, and the published order of General Van Dorn has the ring of the true metal about it. A thousand pities that this course had not been adopted in all our beleaguered cities and besieged fortresses long since. Many defeats would have been spared us, and the moral tone of our armies preserved from no little depression. The recapture of Baton Rouge is encouraging. The heavy cloud, dark and threatening although it still is, has lifted; and we already see, I think, through its rent folds the earliest dawn of national life and peace.

The warm days at our camp are succeeded by cool nights. I never have seen such heavy dews: tent as wet on the outside as though drenched with water. The mosquitoes and fleas are ever calling loudly for the exercise of true patience. Our horses have suffered terribly for the want of proper forage. This rice straw will not answer. We have already lost some six; and but for the approach of the time when we can obtain an abundant supply of fodder, I verily believe that they would almost all perish. We are now giving them some marsh grass. The unruly drivers, as a matter of punishment, are made to cut and bring it to the stables.

With warmest love to you both, my dearest parents, many kisses for my precious little daughter, and kindest remembrances to Sister, Robert, Mamie, and Charlie, I am, as ever,

Your affectionate son,
Charles C. Jones, Jr.

Walthourville, *Thursday,* July 10th, 1862

My dear Son,

Mother has so much to do that the lot of correspondence falls to me; and my only regret is that writing is not so easy and rapid as it once was. The gradual decay of the physical man is seen in the unsteady hand as well as in every other member of the body.

The series of brilliant victories which have been achieved by the Army of Eastern Virginia (as our President terms it in his admirable congratulatory address) has infused new life and energy into our citizens and soldiers; and there are few perhaps who would not desire to be able to say in after times at their own firesides: "We were in the battles before Richmond." But all cannot be the soldiers of our army. We must meet the enemy everywhere he presents himself; and though we never see his columns nor fire a gun, it will be the glory of every soldier that he stood in his lot with the noble patriots of the second and the greater revolution, prepared for battle whenever and however offered. The enemy that dares not set foot on shore for fear of the forces in readiness to receive him is as effectually repelled as if he had landed and been beaten back to his vessels; and the soldier who stands and waits does his duty as effectually as he who marches and fights. And indeed it is the severer part of the trial to the soldier to stand and wait. This has been your lot and that of thousands of brave men and patriots in various positions in the Confederacy. But you must sustain yourself with these reflections. . . .

We long to see the *finale* of McClellan's army. It will be difficult to force his position, and it will require great skill and resolution on the part of our commander in chief and his army. So far it has been a tremendous blow. May it please our Heavenly Father to continue his smiles upon us! The war is now fairly opened. Our malignant, unscrupulous, and determined enemy will call for succor and issue paper currency to defray expenses so long as the people under his despotic rule will respond to his calls and accept his compensation. Ours is the task to demonstrate, by divine aid, to that miserable people the impossibility of subjugation. I am sorry to see the subject of "foreign intervention" in the papers again. But enough for the present.

A public meeting of the citizens was called on the 8th at Hinesville to adopt some measures for suppressing if possible the escape of our Negroes to the enemy on the coast. *Fifty-one* have already gone from this county. Your Uncle John has lost five. *Three* are said to have left from your Aunt Susan's and Cousin Laura's; one was captured, two not; and one of these was *Joefinny!* Such is the report. The temptation of *cheap goods, freedom, and paid labor* cannot be withstood. None may be absolutely depended on. The only preservation is *to remove them beyond the temptation,* or *seal* by the most rigid police all ingress and egress; and this is most difficult. We have petitioned General Mercer to quarter Captain Thomson's company in our county. We need the corps, and trust he may be able to accede to our request. Our people *as yet* are all at home, and *hope* they may continue faithful.

Your dear little baby continues to improve, and is full of good nature; and we hope her ear will be effectually cured. Mother has put her into short clothes, and she is much cooler and more comfortable. Sabbath is Robert's Communion. I wish it were in your power to be here.

Mother has just come in. Your aunt's and cousin's Negroes were Joefinny, his brother Dick, and their nephew *Cato*. Cato is taken; the other two, with others, are said to be on the Island. Little Andrew, who married into the family, knew all about it and has told. I go to Dorchester this afternoon to see Brother Buttolph and family and to consult. My determination is to turn them over to the proper authorities and let them be tried and dealt with as the public welfare may require. Some example must be made of this matter. They are traitors who may pilot an enemy into your *bedchamber!* They know every road and swamp and creek and plantation in the county, and are the worst of spies. If the absconding is not stopped, the Negro property of the county will be of little value. Should you see General Mercer before our petition reaches him, tell him that we have petitioned for Captain Thomson's company. Do let me know your opinion on the proper disposition to be made of these absconding Negroes. What would you do with *white men?*

Glad to hear you are all still so well at camp. My kind regards to Captain Claghorn. All unite in much love. And kisses from your little daughter. Here is her love to you marked by her own hand: "Love to Papa." The Lord bless and keep you, my dear son!

Your affectionate father,
C. C. Jones.

LT. CHARLES C. JONES, JR., *to* REV. *and* MRS. C. C. JONES[g]

Calhoun, Monday, July 14th, 1862*

My very dear Father and Mother,

You will perhaps be somewhat surprised to see this letter located at such a remove from the spot where you suppose I am or should be. Not a case of desertion, however: I am here upon special duty to procure conscripts for our company.

And this is the famous camp of instruction where the unpatriotic are assembled from every part of the state, dragged from their shades of seclusion by the enrolling officers, the terrors and bugbears of the present day. You never saw such a collection of sick men in your life—if you will take the statements of the conscripts themselves. The lung of one "rose some ten years ago and busted," and he has not been a well man since, although even the most practiced eye fails to discover in his stalwart frame the most remote seeds of disease. Another reports himself as ruined by "numony," which "riz in his mouth and fastened his jaw so that he could not chaw good for five years." So soon as the back is turned you see this same fellow devouring most voraciously certainly not less than half a peck of green horse apples. And so they come—each with some woeful disorder which in his own estimation should most certainly exempt him from the operation of the Conscript Act, although these selfsame fellows find ample strength to loaf from year to year and attend to their own interests at home.

Calhoun is located on the state road in Randolph County some forty miles from the Tennessee line. Like all the little towns in Upper Georgia, it is not remarkable either for the cleanliness of its inhabitants or for anything else of an attractive character except the clear, cold water. The evil effects of the existing war are everywhere manifest. All the shops are closed. The sidetrack contains no less than thirteen engines and a number of cars formerly belonging to the Nashville & Louisville Railroad which have been left here for safekeeping and are now rusting in idleness beneath the summer suns and rains.

The trains are daily filled with conscripts and troops—the former reporting at the camp of instruction located three miles from this place, the latter going on to Chattanooga, many of them sick. You cannot imagine the terrible character of the atmosphere in these cars at night. It is enough to make a well man sick. Coming up here I spent the night upon the platform to take advantage of the outside air.

At present there are only a few hundred conscripts in this camp, and Major Dunwody tells me the probability is that the number will fall far short of the expectations of the government. I presume this may be accounted for upon the fact that finding the pressure of the Conscript Act upon them, many have availed themselves of the privilege contained in the act and have recently volunteered, thus accomplishing the objects of the act—to wit, filling up our decimated ranks—although not by men who would be technically known as conscripts. From the character of the men brought into service by the operations of this act, I should say that although our army had gained recruits, it had not been materially benefited by the accretions. However, although they are not the men upon whom a brave leader would rely for energetic, heroic action, they will answer as food for powder and understand how to use the spade.

The Oostanaula River runs in the vicinity of this village, and I am informed that its banks give frequent token of the presence of those ancient tribes who in former years possessed and loved these beautiful hills and valleys. I will not have an opportunity now for examining these monumental remains. Should I have leisure when this war is over, I hope to embrace an early occasion for doing so, and also for investigations in other portions of our state.

When passing through Savannah I met Bishop Elliott, who inquired very specially after your health, Father, and begged me to consent to accept the position of corresponding secretary of the Georgia Historical Society, an office recently vacated by the death of Mr. Tefft. He urged it upon me as the unanimous wish of the society.

In passing through Augusta I had the pleasure of a few hours with Brother and Sister Carrie. They with little Stanhope are all well, and the Doctor appears to be getting along prosperously. He has a very neat little carriage drawn by a fine horse: Titus as charioteer. His hospital engagements are exacting. I noticed in the cars and about the streets of Augusta quite a number of the wounded from Richmond; and singular to state, in almost every instance the wound was in the hand or left arm. . . .

I am, physically speaking, about as uncomfortable here as one can well be. Slept last night and the night before in a room with nine men—bed full of bedbugs, and the coverlet (here they do not indulge in the luxury of sheets) giving ample token that many days and perhaps weeks had elapsed since it had formed any companionship with the washtub. I will get away as soon as I can.

I hope, my dear parents, that all at home are well. With warmest love to you both, many kisses for my precious little daughter, and kindest remembrances to Sister, Robert, Mamie, and Charlie, I am ever

Your affectionate son,
Charles C. Jones, Jr.

Lt. Charles C. Jones, Jr., *to* Rev. *and* Mrs. C. C. Jones[g]

Calhoun, *Tuesday,* July 15th, 1862

My dear Father and Mother,

I expect to leave this place in the morning with twenty conscripts en route for Savannah. Have had a pretty laborious time of it, and my success under the circumstances has been somewhat remarkable. The only things pleasant which I will carry away with me are the memories of these beautiful hills, which have for the past few days gladdened the eye, and the recollection of this excellent water, which gushes in cool, generous, refreshing streams on every side. To think of ice would be to exhibit a degree of ingratitude unpardonable in the highest extent.

We are here almost dead to the outside world, and news of three or four days old would possess every imaginable novelty. Today Ex-Governor Foote, who passed in the train from Chattanooga, stated to a gentleman of this place then at the depot that Morgan would tonight burn the bridges across Green River, thus isolating the Federals, while General Bragg was rapidly advancing, and that we would soon hear of most important results.

I forgot to mention in my last a remarkable spring welling up from the solid rock located just at the foot of the hill upon which the conscript camp is pitched. It supplies the every want of four or five hundred men, and you can perceive no abatement whatever in its generous flow. It was famous even in the days of the Indians, and at a remove quite inconsiderable are still seen the traces of a large ball ground. Thus does every object in nature prove a speaking illustration of the truth of the Holy Scriptures: "The places that now know us will soon know us no more." Entire generations fade away as the flower of the field, while the trees which they loved still give back their answering welcome to the changeless air, and lend their refreshing shadows to another and a stranger race. The eagle eye that danced in joy at sight of this attractive spring is dull and glazed in death; and yet its limpid flow, unchecked by the lapse of time, is as pure and bright, as full of life and light, as though born of yesterday. Unclouded by the sad memories of former years, its sweet waters dance in the sheen of the same silver moon which more than a century ago invited the Indian lover and his dusky mate to this quiet retreat; and when shone upon by the beams of the selfsame sun, forgetful of the image of the heated brave with his nodding plumes and bent bow who so often here quenched his ardent thirst, reflect with equal certainty the gangling forms of Georgia conscripts, who loll in numbers upon the broad rocks which environ, voraciously devouring entire baskets of half-ripe horse apples.

Major Dunwody is most zealously discharging his duties here. They are arduous in the extreme, but he is remarkably affable amid a thousand and one questions reiterated by each newcomer, and does everything that he can to further the interests of the Confederacy. He is a brave little man, and most conscientious in the execution of his trust.

Ben Hardin Helm, I am told, is now a brigadier general, and is well esteemed as an officer.

Good night, my dear father and mother. With warmest love to you both, many kisses for my sweet little daughter, and kindest remembrances for Sister, Robert, Mamie, and Charlie, I am ever

Your affectionate son,
Charles C. Jones, Jr.

Lt. Charles C. Jones, Jr., *to* Rev. C. C. Jones[g]

Camp Stonewall Jackson, *Saturday,* July 19th, 1862

My very dear Father,

I am only today favored with your very kind letter of the 10th inst., the first intelligence I have had from those I love for many days. It gives me great pleasure to know that all are well, and that my sweet little daughter, by the blessing of a kind Providence, has entirely recovered from her recent and dangerous attack. May it please God in mercy to grant her many years of peace and piety, of usefulness and of true happiness upon this earth of changing joys and sorrows!

I reached camp on Friday morning at two o'clock A.M. with twenty-one conscripts, all able-bodied, active, honest men from Middle Georgia, a valuable acquisition to the strength of our battery. On Monday night next, D.V., I leave again for the camp of instruction at Calhoun to secure some twenty more, which will entirely fill the vacancies in our battery—vacancies to be caused by the discharge from our ranks, by virtue of the operation of the Conscript Act, of all men over thirty-five and under eighteen years of age some ninety days hence. I dread the repetition of the trip, but must perform it for the good of the company. You cannot conceive the change which has occurred in the comfort of travel caused by the present condition of the trains, crowded by troops well, sick, wounded, etc., etc. The atmosphere at night in one of those packed cars is enough to generate typhoid or any other kind of fever—the result of impurities in the atmosphere of the most appalling character.

You have observed our recent success in Tennessee. This, I am led to believe, is but an earnest of a forward movement on the part of our troops, who are heavily massed at and near Chattanooga, which will swell the triumph which now rests upon our arms. May we have the vigor, the courage, and the energy to press the advantages which have so recently and so signally been vouchsafed to us by a kind Providence!

It is a most mortifying reflection that intemperance exerted its baneful influences even in the very midst of our brilliant victories in the vicinity of Richmond; and that we were prevented from reaping the full reward of our achievements, and from compassing the full successes of our plans, by the drunkenness of some of our officers high in command. I do sincerely trust that the President will, instead of relieving them from command, see to it that charges are properly preferred and the delinquents dealt with as their enormous violations of everything true, honorable, patriotic, and right justly demand. The officer who is found indulging in liquor upon the eve of such a battle, or even during the progress of its exciting scenes, is a traitor to his country, a recreant to the high trusts reposed in him, and should be summarily punished—and that in the most public and emphatic manner. I had hoped that the recent orders upon the subject of intemperance in our army would have exerted their legitimate influence upon, and secured prompt obedience from, at least those who are entrusted with rank and authority. But recent events prove that certainly in some instances (let us hope they are but few) they have failed of working the proper results of reformation and of a just recognition of duty.

I deeply regret to learn that the Negroes still continue to desert to the enemy. Joefinny's conduct surprises me. You ask my opinion as to the proper disposition to be made of absconding Negroes, and also inquire what would be done with white men detected in the act of giving over to the enemy. If a white man be apprehended under such circumstances, he would doubtless be hung, and in many instances, if the proof be clear, by an indignant and patriotic community without the intervention of either judge or jury. In the case of a Negro, it is hard to mete out a similar punishment under similar circumstances. Ignorance, credulity, pliability, desire for change, the absence of the political ties of allegiance, the peculiar status of the race—all are to be considered, and must exert their influences in behalf of the slave. If, however, a Negro be found digesting a matured plan of escape and enticing others to do the same; or if, after having once effected his escape to the enemy, he returns with a view to induce others to accompany him, thus in fact becoming an emissary of the enemy; or if he be found under circumstances which indicate that he is a spy, it is my opinion that he should undoubtedly suffer death, both as a punishment for his grave offense and as an example to evildoers. In the case, however, of a Negro endeavoring to effect his escape to the enemy detected in the effort, my opinion is that he should not be put to death, but that he be taken to the county seat of the county in which the offense was committed and there *publicly* and *severely* *punished.*

I will embrace the earliest opportunity of seeing General Mercer. I think the petition just in all respects, and trust that it will be immediately granted.

I have written in much haste, but with warmest love to self, my dear father, my dear mother, my sweet little daughter, Sister, Robert, Mamie, and Charlie. As ever,

Your affectionate son,
Charles C. Jones, Jr.

Rev. C. C. Jones *to* Lt. Charles C. Jones, Jr.[8]

Walthourville, *Monday,* July 21st, 1862

My dear Son,

Your two favors from Calhoun we received last week, and congratulate you on the success of your mission. We could not tell where you were from the ceasing of letters until you turned up so far off. Many of the conscripts will do better in service than they promise for before entering. Good officers go far towards making good men. We need just now all the good men we can get, for our government seems moved to more vigorous action than ever.

Your dear baby is improving daily, getting back her flesh and her voice; and nothing interests her so much as the children. She will sit and play with Little Daughter and Charlie by the half hour, and is also much amused sitting on the matting in my study and scratching upon it with two pencils. Little Charlie is getting better also.

I mentioned in one of my late letters a public meeting held at Hinesville on the state of affairs in the county. Application has since been made to General Mercer to know what shall be done with Negro slaves absconding to the enemy when taken, and we understand he answers that he can do nothing as military commander. Something has to be done by somebody—and that efficiently—or things will grow into a bad condition. Can such Negroes be summarily dealt with under any acts of the state? Could they be taken up under the head of insurrection? Could their overt rebellion in the way of casting off the authority of their masters be made by construction insurrection? They declare themselves enemies and at war with owners by going over to the enemy who is seeking both our lives and property. They are traitors of the worst kind, and spies also, who may pilot the enemy into your bedchamber. It is those caught *going* that we wish to know what to do with;

those who are caught *coming back* may no doubt be treated summarily as spies. Please let me hear from you on this point so soon as you are at leisure.

We have lost another child at Montevideo—Little Lymus. Sick some time: inflammatory rheumatism, we think. And our faithful *Sue* is very sick. Mother has gone down today. She went down on Saturday and was very much fatigued by it, the weather has been so warm. I hope she may not be made sick. Robert has gone to his father's plantation today also. Daughter sends much love, and Little Daughter says: "Tell Uncle Charlie howdy for me." "My lo—" Tried to make the baby hold the pen to write her love to you, but she resists *in toto* after the first word, as you see. Hope a kind Providence has brought you safe home again.

Your ever affectionate father,
C. C. Jones.

LT. CHARLES C. JONES, JR., *to* REV. C. C. JONES[8]

Camp Stonewall Jackson, *Friday,* July 25th, 1862

My dear Father,

I found your favor of the 21st inst. had anticipated my return to camp, which was not accomplished until one o'clock this morning. I have just completed a flying and successful trip to Calhoun, Georgia—the second I have made—bringing with me an additional number of conscripts, sufficient to fill all vacancies in the ranks of the company which will be caused by the operation of the Conscript Act. I have slept and eat but little for the past seventy-two hours, and do not feel very bright this morning.

I had just returned from a similar detail when I was ordered by General Mercer again to repair to the camp of instruction and secure additional conscripts. As there was no examining surgeon at Calhoun, I took our battery surgeon, Dr. J. T. McFarland, with me. (Dr. McFarland was the surgeon at Fort Pulaski when that fortress was captured by the Lincolnites, and was for several months a prisoner in close confinement in the hands of the enemy, having recently been released and returned home under the general order, of late passed, directing that all surgeons shall be unconditionally released—an act of humanity and of simple justice.) Arriving at Calhoun, it was the work of but a few hours to accomplish my mission. I selected twenty-one good men (the complement required), had them duly enrolled, and started with them on Wednesday morning. . . .

Took tea with Mr. Rogers in Atlanta, and on my way up on a former occasion attended prayer meeting in his church. He and Mrs. Rogers are now keeping house. Her health is restored, and they live in much comfort. I enjoyed the hot rolls and good coffee, waffles and curd prodigiously after my semi-fastings at the rude wayside inns in Cherokee Georgia. He begged me to say to Mother and yourself that nothing would be more gratifying than to welcome you both beneath his own vine and fig tree and enjoy a

283

visit from you this summer. In common with others his church has suffered in consequence of the influences of this gigantic and unholy war.

Atlanta exhibits more signs of life and energy than any other city in Georgia. You would be surprised at the immense quantities of sugars, tobacco, etc., etc., there stored. Real estate has advanced to an enormous extent, and the probability is that when peace and happiness are again restored to our now distracted country, that the future of this city will be very bright. It contains even now a population of some seventeen thousand, and great improvements are constantly progressing. Fine stores with iron and granite fronts. Neat residences meet the eye on every hand. But a few years since, Atlanta was regarded as the home only of speculators, railroad hands, businessmen, demireps, and rowdies; but the tall spires of newly erected churches, frequent schoolhouses, and the increasing comforts of private residences, and the permanency of stores and public buildings give ample token that the rude infancy of this busy place has been superseded by an age of quiet, maturer civilization. It is even rumored that Atlanta may be selected as the future and permanent capital of our Confederacy; but of course this is simply a matter of speculation.

During my recent visit to Upper Georgia and almost to the confines of Tennessee I have seen and conversed with many persons recently from Kentucky and Tennessee. They with one consent represent those states as ripe for a general uprising in behalf of the Southern cause, as thoroughly disabused of those false impressions which the Lincoln government labored to infuse in the public mind, and entirely disgusted with Federal promises, Federal faith, and Federal rule. The mask has been torn from their faces, and the cloud lifted from their eyes. They now see clearly the unhappy results of their own indecision, and the almost fatal consequences of their self-deception, and are prepared with united effort to throw off the galling yoke of the oppressor. Forrest and Morgan have gone to the rescue, and numbers are flocking to their standards. The recent and rapid achievements of these dashing cavalry officers savor of a revival of the days of true chivalry.

Vicksburg still holds the combined fleet of the enemy at bay; and judging from the self-humiliating propositions which have recently been made to General Van Dorn by the commander of that fleet, we must suppose that its vaunted energy and power are fast ebbing away. I have even heard it suggested that the final capture of the entire fleet was by no means uncertain. Hemmed in between Vicksburg and Baton Rouge, which is now being heavily fortified, these hostile vessels, cut off from supplies, their crews dying under the influences of a purely malarial region and suffering every depression from repeated reverses, must, it would seem, unless something unforeseen occurs to prevent, eventually—and that at no distant day—surrender. The ram *Arkansas,* too, has been among them; and though they have seen her but once—and that in not a cloudless sky—they will probably never forget the introduction. Her conduct has added a bright page to our naval history, and her name will be associated with that of the *Virginia.*

Speaking of the *Virginia,* I am happy to see by the morning papers that the recent court-martial convened at Richmond for the trial of Commodore Tattnall have justified the abandonment and burning of that vessel under the circumstances, and have honorably acquitted the old commodore from the charges preferred. While I am glad to know that this has been done, I can never lay aside the regrets which one involuntarily entertains that this gallant vessel, in one day rendered famous for all time, should not have met with a fate more worthy her name and her daring heroism. Had a younger man been in command, her death struggles would in all probability have been encircled by a halo of the moral sublime and accompanied by such an illustration of fearless action that the world would have been amazed at the deed. But if the *Virginia* had lived in the waters which gave her birth, we would probably have had no "Onward to Richmond" on the part of McClellan; and the recent victories near Richmond would not have given to our arms assurance of their prowess, or to our country and the world an earnest, under God, of our ultimate success.

I learned from the agent of the state road that he had orders from the general government to furnish transportation for forty thousand men during the present and the coming week. The Army of the Mississippi is to be moved from Tupelo, Mississippi, to Chattanooga with a view to meeting and overwhelming Buell, who with thirty-five or forty thousand men is now said to be within thirty-five miles of the latter place. Buell whipped, an advance movement through Tennessee will occur, and thus both that state and Kentucky relieved from the hated presence of a detested foe. Twenty thousand of the Army of the Mississippi are said to be ordered on to Richmond. The President seems at last to have determined upon an aggressive policy. Lincolndom will soon feel for the first time the pressure of actual warfare. . . . Our fortunes have never been so prosperous as at this present moment, and if we are but true to ourselves and to the new policy which has been so auspiciously inaugurated, they will grow brighter and brighter unto the perfect end.

On the state road I had a long and interesting conversation with Governor Brown. Among other things he stated to me that that road would this year pay as clear profits into the state treasury the sum of six hundred thousand dollars. The government transportation over that road has been very heavy. The road itself is in capital order.

You ask me, my dear father, in your letter whether Negroes deserting to the enemy can be summarily dealt with by the citizens themselves under the acts of the state. I understand your question to be, whether in such cases the *citizens* can in public meeting condemn to death such offenders and have them summarily executed. A trial by jury is accorded to everyone, whether white or black, where life is at stake; and the trial by jury involves a trial by jury constituted in accordance with the laws of the state and before the judge competent to preside. Any other procedure, although possibly to a certain extent justified by the aggravated character of the offense and upon the grounds of public good, would in a strictly legal sense certainly be *coram non judice,* and would savor of mob law. Any punishment other than that involving a loss of life or limb could be legally inflicted without the intervention of judge or jury.

If General Mercer refuses to take military cognizance of such cases, and they occur during the intervals of the sessions of the courts, I cannot see what can be done except to take the law in one's own hand, and by severe punishment endeavor to prevent the recurrence of an evil whose influence cannot be overestimated. Terrible corporal punishment, accompanied with close and protracted confinement in the county jail, or public punishment followed by banishment from the county and sale in some distant part of the country, seem to me to be proper in cases where the offenders are apprehended under circumstances indicating a purpose on their part to desert to the enemy. If escape be attempted when ordered to halt, they should immediately be shot. No mercy should be shown where the party has once absconded and afterwards returns to induce others to accompany him in his act of desertion to the enemy. Under such circumstances the public good requires, in the absence of legal punishment, that the offender should be summarily dealt with—and that in a public and final manner; and for two simple reasons: first, to prevent effectually a repetition of the offense by the party himself and rid the community of his evil influence; and second, by the severity of the punishment and the publicity and promptness of its execution, to deter others from attempting the like. If insensible to every other consideration, terror must be made to operate upon their minds, and fear prevent what curiosity and desire for utopian pleasures induce them to attempt. If allowed to desert, our entire social system will be upset if the supremacy of the law of servitude and the ownership of such property be not vigorously asserted in cases where recaptures occur. The main object of the gunboats now lying along our coast doubtless is to encourage the escape of Negroes, and by stealing and reselling them aid in swelling personal wealth and in defraying the expenses of the present war.

I am afraid by this desultory letter that I have already trespassed too long upon your patience. I regret to learn that another death has occurred at Montevideo—another new-made grave added to the many which have so recently been dug in the plantation burial ground. Trust that dear Mother has recovered from her fatigue, and that Sue is better. Do, Father, accept my constant and warmest affection for self and Mother. Kiss my dear little daughter for me. Remember me affectionately to Sister, Robert, Mamie, and Charlie. And believe me ever

Your affectionate son,
Charles C. Jones, Jr.

Illustrations

The Rev. Dr. Charles Colcock Jones

Mrs. Mary (Jones) Jones

Charles Colcock Jones, Jr., at the time when he was a first lieutenant in the Chatham Artillery *(above),* and in the period after the War when he was active as a lawyer, historian, and biographer *(below).*

Mary Sharpe Jones and Joseph Jones in a daguerreotype taken sometime before the War *(above)*, and Joseph Jones in an oil portrait made from a photograph taken sometime in the 1880s *(below)*.

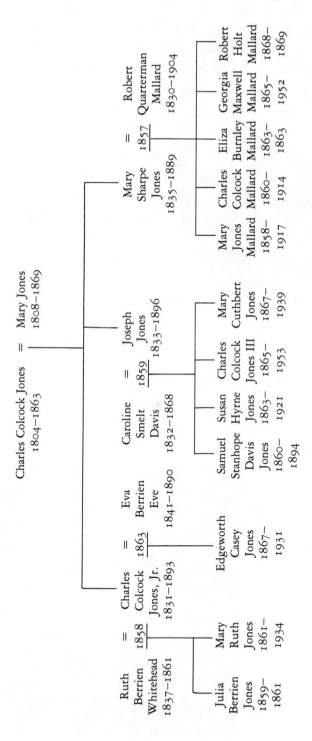

Charles Colcock Jones = Mary Jones
1804–1863   1808–1869

Ruth = Charles Eva = Joseph = Caroline Mary = Robert
Berrien 1858 Colcock Berrien 1863 Jones 1859 Smelt Sharpe 1857 Quarterman
Whitehead Jones, Jr. Eve 1833–1896 Davis Jones Mallard
1837–1861 1831–1893 1841–1890 1832–1868 1835–1889 1830–1904

Julia Mary Edgeworth Samuel Susan Charles Mary Mary Charles Eliza Georgia Robert
Berrien Ruth Casey Stanhope Hyrne Colcock Cuthbert Jones Colcock Burnley Maxwell Holt
Jones Jones Jones Davis Jones Jones III Jones Mallard Mallard Mallard Mallard Mallard
1859– 1861– 1867– Jones 1863– 1865– 1867– 1858– 1860– 1863– 1865– 1868–
1861 1934 1931 1860– 1921 1953 1939 1917 1914 1863 1952 1869
                    1894

The three generations of the Jones family in the 1860s. In 1870, two years after the death of his first wife, Joseph Jones married Susan Rayner Polk, with whom he had three children.

Mary Sharpe Jones, as she appeared shortly before her marriage in 1857 to Rev. Robert Quarterman Mallard.

Midway Church, Liberty County, Georgia, as it appears today.

The Joneses' Montevideo plantation house *(above)*, as it appeared some ten years after the War when it was no longer occupied by the family; the photograph, faded and indistinct, nevertheless gives a good idea of the architectural style of the house. The building housing the Midway Museum *(below)* was constructed in 1959 as a faithful replica of a slightly different style of plantation house typical of the neighborhood before the War.

CENTRAL RAIL ROAD

From Savannah to Macon, 191 Miles.

Passengers and Mail Train leaves *Daily*, both at Macon and Savannah, at 7 A. M., and runs through in 12 hours. Fare $7. Fare in Baggage Car $4 75. Way Trains, in Passenger Cars, from Station to Station 37½ Cents ; in Baggage Car, 25 cents. Children under twelve years of age, half price. Daily Line also between Savannah and Augusta ; Fare $6 50.

RATES OF FREIGHT.

On weight Goods, 1st Class 50 Cents per 100 lbs.
" " " 2d " 45 " " " "
" " " 3d " 40 " " " "
" " " 4th " 35 " " " "
" Measurement Goods 13 " " cubic foot.

For particulars in relation to freight the Company will always deliver (without charge) full printed rates. For Through Rates of Freight between Savannah, Griffin, Jonesboro' and Atlanta, the Company will also furnish full printed list, without charge.

L. O. REYNOLDS,
Chief Engineer
and Superintendent Transportation.

Trains, generally referred to in the letters as "the cars," played a vital role in family communications. This advertisement for the Central Railroad appeared in an 1848 *Census of the City of Savannah*. The Savannah, Albany & Gulf Railroad, to the south, figures more prominently in the letters, where stations are identified as, for example, "No. 3" (McIntosh) or "No. 4" (Walthourville). (See the endpaper map.)

"Birds-eye view of the coast from Savannah, Georgia, to Beaufort, South Carolina, showing the position of our fleet. . . ." The sketch, cropped here to show only the left half, appeared in the January 4th, 1862, issue of *Harper's Weekly*, with the numbered features being identified in a legend. There is some inaccuracy and distortion in the sketch, particularly in the area of Wassaw Sound (south, or in the sketch *left*, of Tybee Island) and Skidaway Island. The Isle of Hope, where the Chatham Artillery was encamped, lies northwest of Skidaway (no. 6 on the sketch), and both are on the right bank of the Wilmington River, rather than the left, as in the sketch. The spot identified simply as "Bluff" (no. 3) would be approximately where Charles Colcock Jones, Jr., saw "five Lincoln vessels" lying "in full view" in March 1862. Other features identified in the sketch and frequently mentioned in Charles's letters of the period were (1) Savannah, (8) Savannah River (with vessels sunk in the channel to impede passage of "the boasted Lincoln armada"), (9) Fort Pulaski, (14) Tybee Island, (16) Daufuskie Island.

Letter of February 2nd, 1863, from Rev. C. C. Jones to Col. Charles C. Jones, Jr. (See page 341.)

Arcadia March 16" 1863 -

My dear Son,
   Your Father has
passed a very bad nights and
I consider him critically ill. = I know
not if your Brother could possibly
come - but wish you to telegraph
him as early as you can. Your
Father has objected to sending
for the Physicians in the county -
& I am well aware if his true
situation was not understood
by them - rash practice would
be injurious, if not fatal. -
   Ever your affectionate Mother
     Mary Jones

Letter of March 16th, 1863, from Mrs. Mary Jones to Col. Charles C. Jones, Jr. (See page 356.)

Two views of the Andersonville prison camp. In September 1864 Dr. Joseph Jones was sent by the Surgeon-General of the Confederate States to inspect the camp. See his letter of September 22nd, 1864.

(Above) Labeled "Confederate ambulance wagon" in the book *Atlanta Illustrated* (3rd edition, 1881), this appears to be a sketch, made on the spot, of a burial detail. *(Below)* "Rebels moving south from Atlanta," sketched by D. R. Brown for the October 15th, 1864, issue of *Harper's Weekly*. See Mrs. Mary S. Mallard's letter of July 18th, 1864, describing her own family's flight from Atlanta.

View of Atlanta after its fall to the Union army, sketched by D. R. Brown for the November 26th, 1864, issue of *Harper's Weekly*.

XII

MRS. MARY JONES *to* LT. CHARLES C. JONES, JR.[8]
Walthourville, *Thursday,* September 4th, 1862

My dear Son,

Your last affectionate favor has been received. We have indeed cause for "profound gratitude" to our Almighty God and Redeemer for the recent discomfiture of our inhuman enemy. I can never rest when such tidings reach us until my knees are bowed in humble praise and thanksgiving to "Him who ruleth in the army of heaven and amongst the inhabitants of earth." Oh, when shall the day of our complete deliverance come? God grant that in that day we shall not only be purged from our former iniquities but be established in righteousness! When we look at the many professedly good men now arrayed against us, some might be led to doubt the truth of religion; but this is not so. Those men have departed from the precepts of the Divine Word, and are illustrating not the falsity of God's truth but their own inherent depravity. . . .

Your dear father went to the Island yesterday. Our affairs there are necessarily left to Andrew's fidelity. Providence has not yet opened up the way for the removal of our people, and as the time presses on when it may be absolutely necessary to do so, we become anxious, not knowing what distresses await all who live upon accessible points to the enemy the coming winter. I see that these arrangements weigh heavily upon your father, whose increasing feebleness is more and more evident. This summer he has lost both flesh and strength. I know that your brother and yourself will do all you can to relieve him of every care, and I trust the Lord will open up the way and provide a safe and suitable retreat for us and our servants. We have had great sorrows and great losses in their sickness and death this spring, and there are several now in feeble health from their severe illness.

When will you be able to visit us? If you would let us know, we could arrange so as to have our dear little daughter baptized at home, if it is impossible for you to spend a Sabbath with us. I ardently desire the performance of this precious duty and privilege on our part, and feel that it would be in accordance with the faith and wishes of her sainted mother in heaven.

The mail has just arrived, and with it, my dear son, your package, for which accept my sincere thanks. And enclosed you will find ten dollars. Please pay for the awls, etc., and your father's specs (the silver). And will you be so good as to purchase with the remainder for me as many pounds as it will of *washing soda for making soap,* and *bring* the same with you when you come. *You need not send it.* It is usually kept by any of the druggists or grocers.

Gilbert too has just come up with Tyrone, who is quite sick. And your father sends me a note saying that eight of Joe Anderson's Negroes left him on Sunday night, taking three others (making eleven). Their leader was his man James, who was cooking for the picket guard in Sunbury; and while they either slept or ceased to *watch* on Sunday night he took the picket boat and packed it with his own family and friends and left them minus breakfast on Monday morning! What shall be said if this is true of such coast guards! To mend the matter James's daughter went into the house and packed up all Bessie Anderson's best clothes and jewelry in her own trunk and took them away with her!

I observe various notices about Confederate money. Your father has over three hundred dollars in that currency, mostly twenty-, ten-, and five-dollar bills. The whole of the three hundred dollars you sent him from the sale of the cotton remains untouched—*all Confederate money.* And the two twenty-dollar bills you sent me from Lathrop are of the doubtful issue, but look genuine. What shall we do about them?

Your dear daughter is well and very bright. Little Charlie not so well today. I must close for the mail. Would you like me to send you some butter and okra? I have just completed the repairs of your shirts. Would you like buttons *sewed* on the bosoms? If so and you can send me six dozen pearl buttons, I will put them on. With much love from Robert and Charlie, and sweetest kisses from your little Ruth, and sincerest affection of

Your mother,
Mary Jones.

Excuse my trembling hand.

LT. CHARLES C. JONES, JR., *to* MRS. MARY JONES[8]

Savannah, Monday, September 8th, 1862

My dear Mother,

I am favored with your very kind letter of the 4th inst., and would have replied at an earlier date, but have been prevented from doing so in consequence of a severe cut, which almost severed the index finger of my right hand near the first joint. I was fearful at first that the first joint would have to be amputated, but I had the wound dressed soon after the accident, and it is now healing by the first intention. I was endeavoring to lift a large flat-bottomed inkstand, which had not been used for many months, from the table. It stuck hard and fast. I put my forefinger in its mouth to give me a greater purchase upon it, when it broke, and the upper edge of the fracture cut the finger very severely. Being very thick, I think no particles of the glass were given off, and therefore I trust the healing will be rapid and permanent.

The news from Virginia comes in slowly. We have gained a signal but not altogether a decisive victory. The conflict will, I presume, be renewed near Alexandria if our army presses in that direction. Removed as we are from the theater of active operations, and with but partial intimations of the character of the pursuit, we can but speculate as to results. My own impression is that the main body of the army will avoid Alexandria and Arlington heights and, crossing the Potomac higher up, invade Maryland, and, passing in the rear of Washington, subject that city to either a partial or total isolation. An excellent strategic point for occupation would be Harrisburg, Pennsylvania. This in our possession, Pennsylvania would furnish abundant supplies for our army, while Philadelphia, Baltimore, and Washington would be cut off to a very great extent from the rich tributes from the West which have ever furnished them with every necessary.

All we can do, however, in the absence of definite information is to pray for the continued mercies of the Giver of All Good, and repose continued and unshaken confidence in the great leaders and brave troops who have heretofore illustrated every virtue, every daring, and every endurance which belong to the noblest specimens of the truehearted, patriotic soldier contending for everything that is dear to him in principle and in country.

We have cheering news from Tennessee, and we look from that quarter for results even more decisive than in Virginia. Tennessee and Kentucky will soon be entirely relieved from the Lincoln yoke.

I have several letters from various portions of the state in reference to the sale of places, but none can be surrendered before 1st December next, and most of them 1st January—in consequence of the growing crop. I enclose the last received from Colonel Clark. Captain Spencer is now in Southwest Georgia near Thomasville, and has promised me to see if he cannot find a place there. Being perfectly acquainted with the localities, he thinks he may succeed. I am to hear from him in a very few days.

The Confederate money which you now have I do not think is spurious. The issue of which you speak will be at any time received at the customhouse and new bills given instead. So soon as I can come out I will receive the amount which Father and yourself now have and exchange the same for the new issue.

The shirts, I think, have holes in the bosoms for buttons. I do not think I would change them, as I have the studs to wear with them. The spectacles, awls, etc., if I remember, cost about $5.20. The balance of the ten dollars which you enclosed I will invest as you desire in washing soda, if to be procured in the city, and send the same to you by earliest opportunity.

I am sorry to learn that the Negroes of the county still continue to desert to the enemy. I am doing all that I can to ascertain some place of retreat for us. If I could only be relieved for a short time, I think I could succeed in effecting that object. I need some change too. I have had a constant and violent headache now for five days, and no cause for it that I know of. It exerts a very depressing influence, and at some moments almost takes my wits away from me.

I am very sorry to hear that Father is not as well as usual. Do give warmest love to him. Kiss my precious little daughter for me. And accept for yourself, my dearest mother, the constant love and gratitude of

Your affectionate son,
Charles C. Jones, Jr.

Kind remembrances to Robert and Charlie. Howdy for the servants.

REV. C. C. JONES *to* LT. CHARLES C. JONES, JR.[8]

Walthourville, *Tuesday*, September 9th, 1862

My dear Son,

Your sister and Robert have reached home in safety, D.G.; and your letter is at hand to Mother, enclosing one from Mr. Richard H. Clark, which is the most promising one we have yet had.

I am much concerned to hear of your *headaches*—in your letter and particularly from Robert. Now, there is a limit to exertion and confinement to business. The weather is hot and trying. You have had a laborious office for months at least, and no assistant allowed you. Headaches occurring with men under your circumstances are premonitions of severer affections and dangerous ones. You must therefore throw down your business for a time on *the score of health*, and relax until the tone of your system is restored to its healthy condition. Necessity knows no law. This is your duty and your right, and General Pemberton cannot deny you. Get a furlough and come out and see us, or take a trip off for your restoration somewhere. I am in earnest in this.

We regret to learn the cut on your finger. It must have been very severe, and hope it will heal "on the first intention." We are not our own keepers. Had you seen forty people put their fingers into that inkstand to disengage it from the table, you would have said: "Don't do that: if the glass breaks, you will ruin your hand."

Please hand the enclosed to Messrs. Claghorn & Cunningham, and present me kindly to Captain Claghorn when you see him.

Do stop and recruit. You do not know how glad we shall be to see you. Little Sister is full of life. Daughter thinks she has fattened very much. I hear her little voice downstairs playing; she has a language of her own. All send love.

Your ever affectionate father,
C. C. Jones.

LT. CHARLES C. JONES, JR., *to* REV. C. C. JONES[8]

Savannah, *Wednesday*, September 10th, 1862

My dear Father,

I am today favored with your kind letter of the 9th inst. with enclosure to Messrs. Claghorn & Cunningham, which I have duly handed to them.

Do thank Mother for her kind remembrance of me received by Robert. The groundnuts are remarkably large, and are very nice. It is a nut when fresh and well boiled of which I am very fond. Judging from the specimen sent, the yield of the ricefield must be very abundant. There are few grains of richer hue or more attractive view than the rice ready for the harvest. The peppers are very fine, but I am afraid of them. My rule is to eat nothing which may at any future hour remind me of the fact that I have eaten.

This morning I had a conversation with Mr. Gué, the clerk of Mr. Anderson, in reference to a sale of our cotton. He tells me that he thinks he can dispose of the same at forty cents per pound, and bagging can now be purchased at $1.25 per yard. He will have the refusal for some days of nineteen pieces. What do you think of the propriety of disposing of the cotton now in store on the places? Would it not be more prudent to sell than to take the chances of fire and perhaps of graver dangers during the coming winter? We will soon, too, have the addition of the incoming crop. I mention the subject for your consideration, and will abide by your views in the matter.

It is a most difficult matter to secure a place to which the Negroes can be removed. I have corresponded with gentlemen in various portions of the state, and have made every inquiry from the factors here, but without success. You will observe that in almost every instance the places offered in suitable localities are such as are considerably if not badly worn, and are only now exposed for sale with the hope of large profits on the part of the seller. As far as I have been able to judge, Randolph Whitehead's place as a retreat affords more advantages, despite the character of the lands, etc., than any I have yet heard of. It can remain for the present at least as a *dernier ressort*. His price is just what was asked for it before the war—a high figure, however, then. The greatest difficulties connected with the purchase are want of timber for plantation purposes and the exhausted condition of the soil. And yet Randolph tells me that ever since he has planted there he has never made less than five bales of cotton to the hand, and a sufficiency of provisions. A comfortable dwelling house is a great desideratum in the event of our being compelled to abandon the coast.

My own impression is that the principal danger to which we will be subjected will be the voluntary desertion of the Negroes. I very much doubt if the enemy will attempt to penetrate the interior except at strategic points. And the truth is, if God still favors our cause and inspires our armies and leaders as He has done in such a marked manner for some time past, the enemy will be forced to keep his troops for home defense.

The fall campaign opens on our part with a brilliancy and success absolutely wonderful. Contrasted with the position the Confederate States occupied three months since, our present is almost incredible. Already is the promise of our worthy chief magistrate redeemed, and the war is being carried "beyond the outer confines of our Confederacy"—Smith thundering at the gates of Cincinnati; Lee, Jackson, and Longstreet surrounding the beleaguered capital of Lincolndom and pressing to the rescue of Maryland. Ohio and Pennsylvania will both soon feel the presence of actual, present warfare; while a hasty retreat will be all that is left for the scattered armies of our invaders, who linger in uncertainty and fear in our borders, which they of late overran in such pride, strength, and exultation.

Every act in this drama but reveals more and more clearly the wisdom of our rulers, vindicates the energy and ability of the administration, and affords ever-increasing assurance of the favor of the Ever-Living God, to whom all thanksgivings are due, and are humbly and fervently paid by many a pious heart. Never in the annals of the world has a nation in such short period achieved such a history. Not two years old, and we have already performed such prodigies of valor, given such assurance of greatness, afforded such examples of moral heroism, individual action, and national prowess, and exhibited such proofs of high-toned patriotism, devotion to principle, and love of truth, that we search in vain among the pages of the past for a record to parallel it. Whatever else the nations of the earth may think or say or do, we have already wrested from them unbounded respect and admiration.

Have you noticed one very interesting fact in the history of this war—that the *pious leaders* have been specially blessed in all of their enterprises? If you will only reflect for a moment, the truth of this remark will become most evident. Stonewall Jackson, Lee, Stuart: pious men all—another illustration of the fact that the truly pious man is the best man for every walk and every emergency in life, and for the simple reason that he carries with him the favor of Him from whom alone all success and all strength can come.

As yet today we have no telegrams of interest.

Had the pleasure yesterday of taking by the hand Mr. Charles Jones Colcock, our kinsman, now colonel of a cavalry regiment in South Carolina, one of the most accomplished and agreeable gentlemen one might meet anywhere. He inquired very particularly after you and dear Mother.

Your watch, Father, is repaired and fully regulated, and only awaits a favorable opportunity to be sent home. Had I known of Robert's coming, I would have taken it from the jeweler's hands, but the shop was closed during his sojourn in the city.

Please say to Mother that just now there is no washing soda in the city, but I will secure it for her so soon as any can be had.

My head and finger are both better today. General Pemberton declines to relieve me from the court, and I am not sick enough to procure a physician's certificate. I trust, however, before long to have the great pleasure of seeing you, my dear parents, and my precious little daughter.

The Confederate money which you sent in is all *good*. It will be exchanged at the customhouse here so soon as the government remits new notes with which to call in and redeem the old issue. . . . My paper has all given out, and I must close. With warmest love to you both, my dear

292

parents, with many kisses for my precious little daughter, and kindest remembrances for Sister, Robert, Mary, and Charlie, as ever,

Your affectionate son,
Charles C. Jones, Jr.

Lt. Charles C. Jones, Jr., *to* Rev. C. C. Jones[g]

Savannah, Monday, September 22nd, 1862

My dear Father,

I this morning had an interview with Mr. Schley in reference to the purchase of his Buckhead place in Burke County. That plantation contains fourteen hundred and twelve acres, and he asks ten dollars per acre, one-third cash and the balance in one and two years. Will sell corn, peas, fodder, and mules, etc., on the place. Thinks it questionable whether he will be able to give possession much before the 1st January, although he may be able to do so before, in case he sees the opportunity clear for removing his Negroes to Texas. Mr. Schley tells me that one may reasonably calculate upon an average crop of about five bales of cotton per hand, and a yield of from eight to ten bushels of corn per acre. This year his corn crop will average twelve bushels. There are some hundred and fifty or two hundred acres of fine land yet to be cleared. The improvements upon the place are in fair condition. I am to embrace the earliest opportunity for going up and looking at the plantation with him. Health fair—on a par with other places in Burke; some chill and fever. Nine hundred acres cleared land, five hundred and twelve acres wooded land on the place. On the whole I like the prospects of this purchase more than those of any other place of which I have heard. Will be able to speak more definitely when I have seen and examined it, which I will endeavor to do at the earliest practicable moment.

Major Locke tells me that a little later in the season he will be prepared to purchase the cattle, and begs that intermediately they be allowed the benefit of the fields. The difficulty about a present purchase on the part of the government is simply this: there is a large supply now on hand—larger than the stock pastures in the vicinity of the city can conveniently sustain. So soon as that supply is somewhat diminished, the government will be prepared to enter upon new contracts of purchase. Intermediately the cattle fare better if kept upon the pastures and allowed the freedom of the fields upon the plantations. . . .

From what George tells me I almost fear to inquire how Tyrone is. His case is another illustration of the fearful indirect consequence of this unholy war.

We have most important dispatches from Virginia, but are in a state of painful anxiety in regard to the exact issues of that bloody battle at Sharpsburg, in which our loss is reported by the meager accounts already at hand to have been very heavy. Three brigadier generals killed and several wounded, among the latter our friend General Lawton. We can only hope and pray for the best, relying upon the tried valor of our troops, the known ability of our leaders, and the justice of our cause.

Nothing of local interest. We are still in the midst of this equinoctial, with its somber shadows and dripping skies. With warmest love to dear Mother, little Daughter, and all at home, I am, as ever, my dear parents,

Your affectionate son,
Charles C. Jones, Jr.

REV. C. C. JONES *to* LT. CHARLES C. JONES, JR.[8]
Walthourville, *Wednesday,* September 24th, 1862

My dear Son,

I agree with you that Mr. Schley's plantation is the most promising yet offered, and your personal inspection only can determine the purchase, in which of course you will be careful. It would give me great pleasure to accompany you, but think it would be too great an undertaking for me, as I have been retrograding considerably lately, and my symptoms are peculiar and more than ordinarily weakening.

It will be a question indeed *when* Mr. Schley gets his people off to Texas. The possession of the Mississippi by the enemy, and the regular passes into Texas estopped, will render removals very difficult and hazardous. *This matter,* in case of purchase, must be definitely and distinctly settled. Earlier than January 1st we should be on the ground—in *November early* if possible.

Clear the coast is the order of the day, for the enemy is making his arrangements to capture our remaining seaports and desolate to the utmost the country; and this will be the winter's work. Admitting we are favored in recovering the border states, in them he can do but little in the winter; and his campaign lies south and coast- and river-wise. We are having brilliant times North and West. If *the people* rise in Maryland, Tennessee, and Kentucky, the enemy must retire, and Missouri must follow; and we shall be, humanly speaking, stronger than ever. So may our Heavenly Father decree it for us!

Enclosed is a letter from your brother. I have marked some places. He is doing what he can in his circumstances to help us out. This removal presses heavily upon your dear mother, but I hope it may yet turn out that she need not leave her pleasant and long-cherished home. . . .

Am happy to say Tyrone is much better, though not out of danger. He was not expected to live at one time. Rest of the people at both places well. Busy harvesting.

Your baby is getting as hearty as ever. Begins to display temper, and sets everybody laughing when she essays to enter into conversation on subjects that interest her. Among other accomplishments is learning to kiss: opens her mouth and bites off the kiss from your mouth! . . . Mother, Sister, and Robert send much love, and kisses from your little daughter and niece and nephew.

Your ever affectionate father,
C. C. Jones.

LT. CHARLES C. JONES, JR., *to* REV. C. C. JONES[8]

Savannah, *Saturday,* September 27th, 1862

My dear Father,

I am in receipt of your kind favor of the 24th inst. with enclosed letter from Brother, and thank you for it. I am happy to know that Tyrone is better, and trust that his recovery may prove rapid and permanent.

I hope on next Saturday to be able to go up and examine Mr. Schley's place. The greatest difficulty connected with the purchase is that he will not be able to give possession much before the 1st of January next, in consequence of his having to gather the growing crop, etc. If we resolve upon the purchase of this plantation, we will have to arrange some intermediate disposition of the Negroes. . . . Early possession of any place selected is all-important. . . .

Yesterday we have the sad intelligence of the death of Spalding McIntosh (who married Sis Morris), an aide to General McLaws with the rank of major, and of the fact that both Randolph and Charlie Whitehead are wounded. This at the terrible battle of Sharpsburg. It is said by General Lee that the shock of this battle was more terrific than any which has as yet occurred in the present war. We held the honors of the field, but the long list of killed and wounded which has already reached us attests the severity of the struggle and the heavy price at which the victory was purchased. The present status of our army in Virginia and along the line of the Potomac seems involved in a degree of uncertainty which causes painful anxiety.

It occurs to me that our government ought, upon the termination of a general engagement of such magnitude and unquestioned importance, to furnish at the earliest practicable moment to the country at large at least an announcement of the general result. With the pressure of an active campaign of such proportions upon them our commanding generals of course have not the time to prepare elaborate reports; but a few lines will tell at the moment the fact of success or reverse and thus relieve the public mind. To know the worse, and to realize the true state of things, no matter how unfavorable, is always preferable to a state of disquietude and anxious uncertainty. Our nation has by past acts demonstrated the fact that with astonishing composure it can bear alike the joys of success and the disheartening influences of reverses. It seems scarcely proper, therefore, for our government to withhold authentic information in reference to past occurrences and accomplished facts, and thus to encourage a resort to the uncertain reports of letter-writers and the lying statements of Northern presses to satisfy the laudable desire of the people who are so nearly interested for a knowledge of the true status of affairs. Of course with the future operations of armies and with the anticipated plans of our generals we have no right to be made acquainted, for thus would those operations be often frustrated. I speak only of the duty of the government when the storm cloud has lifted from the battlefield to give the country at an early moment the result of the engagement.

No private dispatches, I believe, have as yet been received announcing the precise character of the wounds of Randolph and Charlie. I still indulge the hope that the report of McIntosh's death may not be correct. I obtained for him his appointment in the army. Until a very recent period he was connected with the 1st Georgia Regulars, and was recently promoted to the staff appointment which he now holds—or held at the time of his reported death. Maria Morris, his wife, was tenderly attached to him, and I feel deeply for her. . . .

I sent you on yesterday a copy of an Ohio paper which was handed to me by one of the returned Pulaski prisoners. They suffered much during their captivity, and were subjected to continuous and open insults. Finally all their trunks were broken open, and every article of value taken from them. They were thirteen days on the Mississippi River in returning. Captain Sims tells me that there were eleven hundred crowded on the boat in which he returned, and of that number near nine hundred had the diarrhea. You may imagine the condition of matters. The enemy, it appears, improved the opportunity afforded by the flag of truce used to convey the released Confederate prisoners to Vicksburg to provision several of their posts and garrisons on the line of the river—an act entirely characteristic of the race with which we are at war, devoid alike of everything pertaining to honor or good faith. Those returned officers (many of them) show plainly the effects of harsh usage.

You notice in the morning papers the announcement that Lincoln has issued his proclamation liberating the slaves of all rebels on the 1st January next—the crowning act of the series of black and diabolical transactions which have marked the entire course of his administration. I look upon it as a direct bid for insurrection, as a most infamous attempt to incite flight, murder, and rapine on the part of our slave population. With a fiendish purpose he has designedly postponed the operation of this for a future day in order that intermediately the mind of the slave population may if possible be prepared to realize and look forward to the consummation of the act proposed and thus prepare for the same. Practically, under present circumstances, I do not think the proclamation will have any effect. But this does not in the least detract from the character of the act, or lessen one iota the enormity of its crime.

You observe also that the eleven thousand prisoners lately taken at Harpers Ferry and released upon parole by Stonewall Jackson are to be sent out to the West to repel the threatened uprising of the Indians. The policy is openly avowed of rapine and desolation upon our coast and our borders whenever opportunity occurs.

The question occurs, what are we now to do with future prisoners captured from such an enemy? Are they within the pale of civilization? Are they entitled to consideration as prisoners of war? By the law of England an outlaw could be pursued and captured with hue and cry wherever found in the King's realm and killed at the first crossroad. Shall a less punishment be meted out to these robbers, murderers, plunderers, violators of virtue, and outlaws of humanity? By the statute law of the state anyone who attempts to incite insurrection among our slaves shall if convicted suffer death. Is it right, is it just to treat with milder considerations the lawless bands of armed marauders who will infest our borders to carry into practical operation the proclamation of the infamous Lincoln, subvert our entire social system, desolate our homes, and convert the quiet, ignorant, dependent black son of toil into a savage incendiary and brutal murderer?

Surely we are passing through harsh times, and are beset with perils which humanity in its worst phases has not encountered for centuries. The Age of Gold has yielded to the Age of Iron; and the North furnishes an example of refined barbarity, moral degeneracy, religious impiety, soulless honor, and absolute degradation almost beyond belief. *Omnia vestigia retrorsum.* It does indeed appear impossible to conjecture where all this will end. It does seem that only He who by a word calmed the tempest-tossed sea can bring light and order and peace out of the perfect moral, political, and social chaos which broods so darkly over the Northern states, give to our enemies a better mind, and assure us in the happy possession of our homes and loves and honor and property. Meanwhile we can only make a proper use of those means which He has placed in our power, and with a firm reliance on the justice of our cause, and with earnest supplication of His aid who saves not by many nor by few, offer every resistance to the inroads of this inhuman enemy, and illustrate every virtue which pertains to a brave, God-fearing people engaged in an awful struggle, against wonderful odds, for personal, civil, and religious freedom. . . .

Am happy to hear such favorable news of my dear little daughter. My daily prayer is that God will endow her plenteously with health and intellect and every attraction, but above all things that He will be pleased, even from early infancy, to convert her and acknowledge her as His child. With warmest love to self, my dear father, to dear Mother, Sister, Robert, and Mamie and Charlie, and with kisses for my precious little daughter, I am ever

Your affectionate son,
Charles C. Jones, Jr.

REV. C. C. JONES *to* LT. CHARLES C. JONES, JR.[8]

Walthourville, *Tuesday,* September 30th, 1862

My dear Son,

Your interesting letter of the 27th came yesterday. Would it not be well to make inquiries and see if possible Colonel Seaborn Jones's Tuckahoe plantation, which is offered *for rent,* before seeing or at least before deciding on Mr. Schley's place? Would not the rent of a fair place for a year on reasonable terms be better than a purchase at this time, and give us a further chance of looking out? I do not know how Colonel Jones's place is situated in respect to the railroad. I wish I could go with you, but cannot. You must do the best you can, and in deciding put all the advantages and disadvantages together and strike the balance. I consider the removal pretty much a permanent one, for by the time the war is ended the people will be so well fixed wherever they go that it will be a losing business to break them up again. . . .

Mr. Schley will find difficulty in taking his Negroes to Texas, unless we succeed in blockading portions of the Mississippi effectually. Our people must be off long before January, for from present appearances it will not be surprising if the enemy begins his campaign on our coasts early in the season. It will be a great relief when our people are *removed*.

It is not without full advisement that Lincoln has issued his Emancipation Proclamation. The conference of the governors sustains him in it, and in the renewal of the war with still greater vigor if possible. There is no other policy in all the old United States but the war policy. The old Northern Democratic party is nothing. Peace party there is none. Military dictatorship is a fancy; and the abolition and anti-South party waxes stronger and stronger. We have nothing but war before us. The enemy considers our subjugation but a question of time only. They can beat us and give us three or four in the game, for they say that they can call out three or four soldiers to our one, and their resources are as many times greater than ours, and consider us well-nigh exhausted now. Wonderful is it how they leave out in their calculations right and justice and God, who rules over the nations—even Him who can save by few as by many; and moreover, that the invader works at a disadvantage of three or four to one. Up to this hour we can say the Lord has been on our side; to Him let us constantly commit our cause.

Am happy to see that this execrable proclamation has been called up to notice in our Congress. I fully agree with you in your views of it. The war has become one for the perpetration of every brutal crime—for robbery, arson, and insurrection; and our government would be justifiable in putting every prisoner taken to instantaneous death, unless the war be wholly altered in its character and the proclamation be withdrawn. The Northern people will uphold the proclamation. England will uphold it, and so will France and every nation in Europe practically. There will be no remonstrances, no protests, unless great changes occur speedily. What Seward threatened them with if they interfered—the abolition of slavery and their loss of cotton, rice, and tobacco—is coming upon them without their interference. We must hope for the best from General Lee's army. A dreadful battle, that of Sharpsburg!

Mother and Sister go down this afternoon on a visit to Dorchester and the Island; also to see your Uncle William, who we hear has been and is still quite sick, but better. Tyrone still critically sick, though the doctor thinks some better. Am confined here on his account all the time.

Your dear baby is quite well. When I poured the water upon her head in her baptism, she meekly bowed it and never uttered a sound! Mr. Samuel Mallard took her in the twilight of the evening from her nurse, and she went and stayed with him and took him for yourself and was not inclined to leave him. She is getting a beautiful set of teeth, and her eyes are the very eyes of her mother. Some mornings she sits quietly through morning worship in the family. Mrs. Cay's tame deer came into the parlor last evening, and she was in an ecstasy.

Mother and Sister and Robert send much love. And kisses from your little one and Mary and Charlie. People generally well.

Your ever affectionate father,
C. C. Jones.

P.S. Did you speak to Mr. Gué to put by two pieces bagging for us—one for Arcadia and one for Montevideo? *Please do it.*

LT. CHARLES C. JONES, JR., *to* REV. C. C. JONES⁸

Savannah, *Wednesday,* October 1st, 1862

My very dear Father,

I am today in receipt of your kind letter of yesterday, and am happy to hear such good news from home.

I learn upon inquiry that the place of Mr. Jones is located *directly* on the Savannah River. It consists principally of river swamp, the highland being comparatively but little and sadly worn. Place very much out of repair, and the swampland (say, some four or five thousand acres) uncleared and subject to continual overflow. Mr. Jones wishes to *sell,* and asks some sixteen thousand dollars. The place is by no means a desirable one. It is, further, at quite a remove from the railroad.

Night before last, not having seen Brother and Sister Carrie for a long time, I went up to Augusta, breakfasted with them, and returned by the afternoon train, which reached the city last night. Found Sister Carrie and little Stanhope quite well. The Doctor had had a little fever, and was then suffering from headache. He was not looking as well as when I last saw him, but he stated to me that his present indisposition was temporary, and resulted from some night exposure to which he had been recently subjected. He is getting a very clever practice, and tells me he thinks he will be able to make both ends meet without difficulty. Dr. and Mrs. Leyburn were with them, and both desired especial and warmest remembrance to yourself, dear Mother, and Sister. Brother and Sister Carrie united in best love.

I was enabled to enjoy the pleasure of this hurried visit in consequence of the fact that the court-martial was dissolved in the afternoon of the 29th ult. But accompanying the order dissolving that court came another from General Beauregard assembling another, and reappointing me as the *judge advocate.* This court assembled today, and I have been all day trying causes before it. From all indications it appears that this is to be my occupation, at least for the present; and laborious as the duties are, I do not know but they are preferable to the duller engagements of camp life just at this time. It is especially true in military life that those who are bound must obey, and I endeavor to observe the rule that whatever is to be done should always be well done.

A little gunboat has been shelling below—down the river—this afternoon, evidently endeavoring to ascertain whether any new batteries had been erected by us, and whether any additional obstructions had been placed in the river. She has dropped down with the tide, and did not come up as far as the obstructions, or within range of any of our guns.

Randolph and Charlie Whitehead have both returned home. Randolph is badly wounded in the foot, and Charlie wounded in the arm. Poor McIntosh is said to have been horribly mangled, and was buried on the field. His wife is almost deranged. She had concentered all her affections upon him, and her heart, bereft of his loves, is desolate beyond description. . . .

I have seen Mr. Gué in reference to the bagging.

Do give warmest love to dear Mother, Sister, Robert, Charlie, and Mamie, and the tenderest affection and kisses to my precious little daughter. I am ever, my dear father,

Your affectionate son,
Charles C. Jones, Jr.

REV. C. C. JONES *to* LT. CHARLES C. JONES, JR.[8]

Walthourville, *Thursday,* October 2nd, 1862

My dear Son,

Yours of yesterday is at hand. A few more reappointments will give you a clear right to the judge advocateship. Am glad of it; it is better with its labors, as you say, than the monotony of camp life. You have time to be alone in your chamber morning and evening, and you have the great privilege of quiet Sabbaths and the services of the sanctuary. Those are special mercies in these times of war.

What a judgment is falling upon our country! When we view it in its extent, its ramifications, its intensity, its miseries, and its destruction and mourning and woe, it is enough to sober the most inconsiderate and soften the most obdurate and bring our whole people to humiliation before God, who is thus dealing with us. And while He has most signally and mercifully aided us thus far, yet His hand is still stretched out over us; for the war continues, and the enemy is laying his plans more resolutely and extensively to swallow us up. As we have survived his first great effort, trusting in the Lord may we not hope for a second deliverance? I have faith to believe we may.

The invasion of Maryland and the return of our army to Virginia I look upon *as a special providence in our behalf.* Success began to intoxicate, and incline many to cry out for invasion of the enemy's territory. General Lee was induced to make the experiment in the most favorable moment and upon the most favorable soil—at least one upon which the people were, to a good degree, at least, so friendly as not to rise upon us. He could advance but a little way. The people did not come to his standard. The enemy gathered with energy and promptness an army far outnumbering his and gave him the bloodiest battle (on their own ground, as they deemed it) ever fought on this continent; and nothing saved his army from defeat and ruin but the blessing of God upon his skillful disposition of his forces, and the indomitable courage of his men—men to be annihilated but never defeated! I hope this taste of invasion will be satisfactory—at least for the present. If the enemy with superior numbers and equipments cannot invade our thinly populated territories with large armies without being starved back if not driven back, how can we fare better invading a more densely populated country? The Maryland pear certainly is not ripe yet. When it will be, no one can tell. If we can free the other border states, it will be well. A desperate stand is to be made by the enemy to save both Tennessee and Kentucky. The fighting has not fairly begun there yet.

Will you be able to go up and see Mr. Schley's place on Saturday? Please let me know. I hope it may be in your power, for our time is running short, and we have much to do.

I understand Mr. Millen (brother of Mr. Berrien Millen) has a government contract for beef, and purchases cattle liberally. Do you know him? Am glad you secured the bagging. Will have the gins started in a few days.

Your visit to your brother must have been refreshing to both of you. Am happy to know he is doing so well.

Poor Tyrone still lingers. We had hope of him a few days ago, but he is no better now, and fear he never will rise from his bed! These repeated deaths are most afflicting to us. The doctor has been with him every day as often as he considered it necessary—always once, and most frequently twice, and sometimes three times a day.

Friday, October 3rd. Tyrone died this morning about four o'clock—another death from the sickness contracted on the batteries in Savannah last spring. Three out of the seven men sent have died. The general judgment has been heavy on our household, and of course on us. The last request Tyrone made to me on leaving him about nine or ten was to pray with him—our usual evening's parting. How it is with his immortal soul God only knows.

Robert sends love. Mother and Daughter not returned. Children well. Your dear child now playing in Mother's room.

Your ever affectionate father,
C. C. Jones.

LT. CHARLES C. JONES, JR., *to* REV. C. C. JONES[g]

Savannah, *Wednesday*, October 8th, 1862

My dear Father,

I am today in receipt of your kind favor of the 2nd inst., with postscript of the 3rd inst. announcing the sad intelligence of the death of Tyrone. I had hoped from last advices that although still sick he was nevertheless better, and that reasonable hopes of his recovery were entertained. The hand of affliction has indeed been heavily laid upon us. And where has it not fallen during the past eighteen months? We are in the hands of the Almighty, and it is our duty to acknowledge these His dispensations, and by repentance and in humility seek to make a proper use of them.

The advices from the West are not encouraging, and we appear to have met with a reverse at Shiloh. A battle is regarded as imminent between Bragg and Buell near Louisville, and we are told that Generals Lee and McClellan will soon meet again in deadly conflict. I see no cessation to present hostilities—unless some unlooked-for pressure is brought directly and forcibly to bear—except in absolute exhaustion. The mask is fairly lifted—and by their own hands—from the face of Northern duplicity and Yankee tyranny; and we can now expect from the Lincoln government nothing but renewed attempts and redoubled efforts to effect our annihilation. Their future operations will doubtless be characterized if possible by additional disregard of the commonest principles of justice, humanity, and religion. Devastation, ruin, insult, and barbarity will mark their footsteps. I have, under God, no fear for the final issue; but when our triumph will come, as matters now stand, can be known only to Him in whose hands are the issues of all things. The last victory at Manassas appears to have produced a profounder impression upon the European mind than any of the former which have been won by us.

The *Fingal* here is hastening towards a completion, and will vastly strengthen our river defenses. The guns are being mounted on General Mercer's line of fortifications around the city; and when the attack is made, as seems highly probable at no very distant day, I hope we will be able, by the help of God, to repel the invader with a loss and destruction which will not be soon forgotten. A naval expedition from Port Royal is advertised, but its destination is not given.

Mr. Schley will probably be here tonight, and I hope to be able to go up with him on Friday or Saturday. He has been very kindly assisting me by inquiries in Jefferson and Washington Counties, and tomorrow I will have the result, which you shall know so soon as ascertained.

The bagging is in store for us, and will be sent out any day you may wish. Cattle ought to be worth from fifteen to twenty dollars. Macpherson B. Millen is captain of commissary; his brother, of whom you speak, I do not know. Mr. Quarterman writes me that he can sell the cattle at Arcadia at fifteen dollars per head. Would it not be well to have at least a portion of the corn crop shelled and sold at once? I think I can make a contract for its sale here to the Quartermaster Department and obtain bags in which to sack it. One dollar per bushel.

By the train of tomorrow, Father, I send you a cask of pale Scotch ale—the only one in the city. I have tried to procure a cask of porter for you in Charleston, Columbus, and elsewhere, but without success. Be pleased to let me know what proportion of the bottles in the cask is good and what defective, as I am to pay only for the good. This can be done without much trouble as they are unpacked and used. If the article sent is not as good as you have had, you will excuse it when I say that it is the only ale which could be had, and was sold to me as a special favor. . . .

Do give warmest love to dear Mother, Sister, Robert, Mamie, and Charlie. Kiss my precious little daughter for me. And believe me ever, my dear father,

Your affectionate son,
Charles C. Jones, Jr.

LT. CHARLES C. JONES, JR., *to* REV. C. C. JONES[g]

Savannah, *Thursday,* October 9th, 1862

My dear Father,

I will try and get off from here so as to examine Mr. Schley's place on Saturday next. From a conversation had with him last night, if the plantation suits I think we will be able to purchase corn, fodder, etc., all on the place, and obtain possession at an early day. But you shall know all about it so soon as I can ascertain by actual examination. You may rely upon my doing the very best I can.

Nothing new here. With warmest love to all at home, I am ever

Your affectionate son,
Charles C. Jones, Jr.

LT. CHARLES C. JONES, JR., *to* REV. C. C. JONES[g]

Savannah, *Thursday,* October 16th, 1862

My dear Father,

I have just returned from Middle Georgia, and have purchased Mr. Henry J. Schley's Buckhead plantation containing fourteen hundred and twelve acres at ten dollars per acre, and also his present corn crop (say, four thousand bushels) at seventy-five cents per bushel.

The place is situated about one hundred miles, in round numbers, from this city, and is without exception the best place I have seen. It enjoys a fine reputation—none superior in that section. I rode over every foot of it before concluding the purchase. It contains about five hundred acres of as noble forest land as the eye can well discover in our state, is well watered, thoroughly ditched, and generally in fine order as to fences, etc., etc. We will need some four additional Negro houses. A steam sawmill is in the neighborhood where boards, etc., can be procured at a reasonable rate. A gristmill is located only about a mile and three quarters from the settlement, where, as is customary in that section of the country, all the grinding can be done for the place. There are a fine overseer's house, ginhouse with gin and running gear in capital order, screw, two corncribs, meat house, kitchen, dairy, four double and two or three single Negro houses—all frame buildings. Two churches in the vicinity—one Baptist, the other Methodist—where preaching is had at present every other Sabbath.

I took the whole of Mr. Schley's corn because I was getting it at a very reasonable figure, because he could not get it away, and because under existing circumstances I think the purchase a valuable one. It will doubtless be much higher as the season advances. It is not all harvested as yet.

The average yield on the place for the past twelve years, as shown by Mr. Schley's books, has been a little over five bales of cotton to the hand, and from ten to twelve bushels of corn to the acre. He has within the past two years taken in, at an expense of six hundred dollars, forty acres of the Buckhead swamp, which this year gives a yield of corn of thirty-five bushels to the acre. It is worth one's while to look at this field—a deep alluvial soil which seems to be almost inexhaustible. The rest of the place is above average, and I think the purchase a valuable one, and that by the blessing of God we may find it a safe, comfortable, and remunerative retreat for our people.

As to the question of possession, Mr. Schley tells me if at any time danger threatens, to send the Negroes up at once, and that they shall be quartered as best they can be with present accommodations. He will be through with gathering his crop by the 1st December, and will if possible complete the harvest and move away by the 15th December. He has promised me to accomplish this at the earliest practicable moment; and he is a gentleman of his word, and with that view will send hands from his lower place to assist.

I think at an early day we had better send the carpenters up and let them commence upon the new buildings which we will require for the accommodation of the people. And the people should be moved so soon as we can conveniently arrange for their removal—say sometime towards the first or middle of November. We cannot well send them at an earlier day, as we have to get out the growing and already matured crop. What Negroes you will send, Father, of course I will leave entirely to you. I expect to take mine from Arcadia, and such as Brother and Sister desire to send. But I will at the earliest practicable moment see you in regard to this matter and receive your wishes and instructions in the premises.

We can send the Negroes either by Central Railroad to No. 9½, where they will have to walk only about twelve miles to the place; or we can send them with wagons, etc., up the Louisville road, the distance of the plantation by that way being only one hundred miles from this city. Or perhaps what would be still better, we can send women and children, plantation utensils, bedding, etc., by rail, and let the men or a portion of them with a wagon, stock, etc., go up by way of the Louisville road. Your own judgment will indicate what had best be done. The removal will be a matter, I think, of not much trouble.

I propose, Father, to assume the entire responsibility of the purchase of the plantation: $14,120—one-third cash, balance in one and two years. I am unwilling that you should at your time of life, and in your present health, be troubled with any additional moneyed arrangements or new cares. If I live and have health, and these Yankees do not entirely overrun us, by the blessing of God I hope to be able to make the payments. If you can conveniently aid in the purchase of the corn, mules, and meat (which will prove quite an item of expense), I would be glad. And with the cotton which we have on hand, and the corn, etc., which we will be able to sell, I think we can do so without trouble. I am now making inquiries about mules, but will not contract for purchase before seeing you and ascertaining what portion of the stock we can conveniently carry up.

In reference to meat, which will be our greatest trouble, would it not be well at once to see what hogs we can purchase from the Negroes on the places and perhaps on those adjoining? We can then kill and cure below and send up by railroad.

I have this morning secured one keg shingling nails and half-keg flooring or rather weatherboarding nails—all I could find in the city.

In regard to the sale of corn, etc., from home, I can arrange with the quartermaster here to take all the corn we have to spare, if you think best, at one dollar per bushel, delivered at No. 3, Savannah, Albany & Gulf Railroad, the quartermaster furnishing bags in which to sack the corn.

We ought to take to Burke some thirty head of cattle. They can be easily driven up. I can purchase a wagon or two from Mr. Schley, and have also agreed to take his fodder, which is stacked in the field. We can sell our fodder here to the quartermaster, who desired it baled in bundles to weigh, say, three hundred pounds (from that to four hundred).

Mr. Schley's present overseer, a worthy man and a strict member of the Baptist Church, without children and with an excellent wife, represented to be an honest man and attentive to his duties, can be employed by us, I think, for a sum not much to exceed three hundred dollars for the ensuing year. Mr. Schley is pleased with him, and would have retained him had he remained on his plantation another year.

Referring to the conversation which we had at the depot, Father, when I last enjoyed the pleasure of seeing you, I presume Brother and Sister will require their proportion of corn, cattle, cotton, etc., sold from Arcadia, so that only a third of the amount therefrom realized can be appropriated toward the purchase of corn, etc., for the place in Burke.

The health of the place is fair—as good as is found in Middle Georgia—and I should say better than that of our plantations upon the swamps of Liberty. Mr. Schley this year has had to pay no medical bill except for services rendered by a surgeon in the case of one of his Negroes who was run over by a wagon.

I will endeavor, my dear father, to see you at the earliest practicable moment and learn all your wishes in the premises, which it will be equally my duty and pleasure to carry into effect as faithfully and as promptly as I can. I do wish that I could command my own time for about a week or more. I know that I could within that time accomplish much.

In the purchase of the place I have exercised my best judgment, and have done the best I could. If I may believe the opinions of others, I have secured a plantation far above the average. I would not exchange it for any I have seen in Middle Georgia, and I infinitely prefer it to Southwest Georgia. I have asked the blessing of God on the adventure, and trust with His blessing that we may find the investment safe and remunerative. For the present it must be viewed very much in the light of an insurance upon Negroes. . . .

I have written in great haste for lack of more time, and must beg you, Father, to excuse the rambling character of this letter. If there are any matters to which I have not alluded, if you will only indicate them I will give you all the information in my possession. Did the cask of ale ever come to hand? And do you find it good? How are all at home? Do give warmest love to dear Mother, Sister, Robert, and the little ones. Kiss my precious daughter for me. And believe me ever, my dear father,

Your affectionate son,
Charles C. Jones, Jr.

. . . Payments to be made when we take possession. Please let me know at what day you would prefer that the removal of the Negroes should take place, or about what time. I promised Mr. Schley to let him know in order that he might make his arrangements if possible to meet your wishes.

REV. C. C. JONES *to* LT. CHARLES C. JONES, JR.[8]

Walthourville, *Saturday,* October 18th, 1862

My dear Son,

Yours of the 16th Mother handed me last evening on my return from Montevideo, where I had been to see Phillis (Niger's wife), who is *quite sick,* Dr. Samuel Way in attendance. The affliction of sickness still continues upon us, and I pray that we may be made to understand and feel it and have it sanctified to us.

Your account of Mr. Schley's place is very satisfactory, and have no doubt that your purchase is a judicious one and as good as could well be made in any part of the cotton districts of our state. And the payment in three installments is more liberal than I had anticipated. And although you so generously offer to assume the whole payment for the place on your own account, yet I shall feel bound to render you every aid in my power to meet the payments as they come to maturity. I agree with you in preferring a location in Middle to one in Southwest Georgia. Am pleased to learn that there are five hundred acres of forest land (a specimen of what Middle Georgia was) and a steam saw- and a gristmill so contiguous. Most desirable advantages are these—and all not far from the Central Railroad. And *two churches* in the immediate vicinity, one of which I should like to have been *Presbyterian*—without intending any reflections whatever upon my brethren of the other denominations, with whom I have always cultivated the best understanding.

The purchase of the corn and fodder was exactly right, and indeed much of a necessity and a great convenience. The rate reasonable; and the surplus (if any) may be sold. Wagons are scarce, and if you can purchase one or two *good*, and on favorable terms, from Mr. Schley, you might do so. And feel the overseer's pulse and retain him, as he is a fixture and has the run of the place, and I presume an *exempt*.

Our corn can be sold at No. 3 depot to Mr. Millen, he furnishing sacks, at $1.25; and the fodder sold there also.

Monday, if the Lord will, I will shut up my beloved study and go to Arcadia and Montevideo and enter upon immediate arrangements to wind up matters, dispatch the carpenters, and prepare as many of the people for removal and at as early a day as we can, of which Mr. Schley shall have due advisement. I will then give you a statement of the whole—corn, cotton, peas, potatoes, rice, mules, cattle, sheep, and hogs.

Daughter has just come in to say the post office will close soon, and I must cease. We all congratulate you on your successful visit and return, and shall be truly glad to see you in person. All send love. . . .

Return of cask of ale: 4 dozen in good order, 1½ dozen three-quarters full; 1½ ditto half full; and one only broken. If the kindest and most unremitting attention of the best of wives and the best of children could have made me a well man, I should have been so long ago; and from my heart I appreciate it all, and thank you for it, and hope and pray God will reward you for it.

Mother begs you to send five dollars' worth of *hard* sailor or army biscuit for her. Borchert sometimes makes them if not to be had. She wants to see you very much. "*Insist* upon a furlough," Mother says. Please send out the money sent to be exchanged when you can. As ever,

Your affectionate father,
C. C. Jones.

Lt. Charles C. Jones, Jr., *to* Rev. C. C. Jones[8]

Savannah, *Tuesday,* October 21st, 1862

My dear Father,

I thank you for your kind letter of Saturday last, which has been duly received, and I am happy to know that all at home are so well—except Phillis, who I trust by this time is better. Am happy to think that my efforts to procure a suitable retreat for our people have been approved by you. Since the purchase my mind has been greatly relieved, and will be more so so soon as we can compass the removal of the people. Do let me know, Father, in what particular I can specifically serve you.

The notes have been exchanged, and Mother's "hard bread" purchased; but the express at present is not running on the Savannah, Albany & Gulf Railroad, so that I am at a loss how to forward them to you. I hope, however, that I may be able to see you on Saturday next, when I will, D.V., bring them out with me and have a full conversation with you in reference to matters and things.

We have nothing of local interest here. General Beauregärd is in the city, and the daily journals contain an account of his serenade and speech last evening. He makes a poor out at speaking—not an unusual occurrence among military men, although the records of the past furnish some brilliant exceptions. I learn that he will review all the troops of this district, or as many of them as can conveniently be collected here, on next Friday.

As at present advised, the tenure by which we hold Kentucky appears very uncertain: Bragg said to be in retreat, and before vastly superior forces.

I send you the Charleston *Courier*, containing a synopsis of the recent speech of Van Buren in New York City. Heavy Democratic gains at the North; but what do they signify?

With warmest love to my dear mother, Sister, Robert, and the little ones, and tenderest kisses for my precious little daughter, I am, as ever, my honored and beloved father,

Your attached son,
Charles C. Jones, Jr.

REV. C. C. JONES *to* LT. CHARLES C. JONES, JR.[8]

Walthourville, *Thursday*, October 23rd, 1862

My dear Son,

We are happy to hear that you will be with us, D.V., on Saturday. Try and stay till Monday afternoon.

Our corn and cattle ought to be sold as speedily as possible. Could you see the government officials before you come out? Corn is selling at $1.25 per bushel (sacks furnished) at the depots, weighing so many pounds (fifty-six, I think)—the fairest way to buy and sell all grains. If you furnish sacks and deliver in Savannah: $1.50. Cattle (good stock cattle): about twenty dollars round. The Maybank cattle (between forty and sixty head) were all fat for butchering when I last saw them some three weeks ago. Mr. Quarterman told me he had offered a part of the Arcadia cattle to Mr. George Millen at twenty dollars round. Had received no reply. We might pickle up some beeves for the people if we can get barrels for the purpose.

Could we charter a box car to take up our people (women and children and some men)—take them and all their baggage in at No. 3, *and have the same car go through to Central Railroad and right on* to No. 9½ or wherever they will get out? If this could be done, it would save time, trouble, and exposure. Would be glad to send off the first installment next week with the carpenters if they can be made ready. The car could be brought out the morning of the day, and be all *packed, provisioned,* and *passengered* ready for the afternoon train, which goes in now at 3 P.M.

The people we send up will require much room. Could they not take the place of as many of Mr. Schley's (who might vacate and go to his other place if it suited him) and help finish harvesting his crop?

All send love. Baby well. In some haste for the mail,

Your ever affectionate father,

C. C. Jones.

LT. CHARLES C. JONES, JR., *to* REV. *and* MRS. C. C. JONES[g]

Savannah, *Saturday*, October 25th, 1862

My dear Father and Mother,

I cannot tell you how great my disappointment at not being able to realize my cherished expectation of spending the day with you and all the dear ones at home. My arrangements were all made when a courier arrived announcing that the enemy were about to attack at Coffee Bluff. Our battery, the Guards battalion, and the 4th Louisiana Volunteers were ordered at once to take post there. Mounting Yorick, I reached the scene of anticipated danger, distant from this city some twelve miles, about sunset. Gunboats lying below, but no positive demonstrations made. Attack expected about 10 P.M. on the high tide. Tide falls, hour passes, and no attack. Expectations renewed of an attack at high water today. Another agreeable disappointment, and the declining rays of the sun this afternoon revealed the fact that the abolition boats were again quietly riding at anchor at their former positions in Ossabaw Sound and in Bear River. Slept last night without tent or blanket in an old field. Troop ordered back to their posts tonight, and I have just returned to the city, after a long and somewhat fatiguing ride, to enjoy the quiet and holy privileges of the coming Sabbath.

You have doubtless, my dear parents, noticed the happy accounts of the repulse of the abolition forces along the line of the Charleston & Savannah Railroad. I only wish that we could have surrounded, cut off, and butchered every one of the vile invaders.

I hope to see you some day next week. Do kiss my dear little daughter for me. Give love to Sister, Robert, and the little ones. And believe me ever, my dear parents, with tenderest and most constant affection,

Your son,

Charles C. Jones, Jr.

Mr. Schley consents that we send up the Negroes just when we please, provided they help gather the crop, etc. He will give *working hands* their board, and charge at rate of seventy-five cents per bushel for all corn consumed by nonworkers before the place is finally delivered. A fair proposition.

REV. C. C. JONES *to* LT. CHARLES C. JONES, JR.[g]

Walthourville, *Saturday*, October 25th, 1862

My dear Son,

We were greatly disappointed at not seeing you this morning, but we know you could not help it. Through divine favor we are all well today, and I write now to say that if the Lord will, I will be in Savannah by the cars *on Monday evening* and put up at the Pavilion if it is now open (if not, at the Pulaski) and hope you will still be in town, where I shall be glad to see you on our business matters. All send much love. As ever,

Your affectionate father,
C. C. Jones.

REV. C. C. JONES *to* LT. CHARLES C. JONES, JR.[8]
Walthourville, *Wednesday,* October 29th, 1862
My dear Son,

After my most pleasant visit to you I am again at home, D.G., finding all well, and Mother away on a business expedition at Maybank.

At No. 3 Mr. R. Q. Cassels, who is in charge of that depot, offered to purchase all our corn *for a government agent* at $1.25 delivered at that depot, *he furnishing sacks.* This is better than Major Hirsch's offer at $1.20, which we will be obliged to accept if you have positively engaged with him. I told Mr. Cassels that I would confer with you and let him know, and further that I would not sell one grain to speculators, and if he was in that line we couldn't sell to him. He replied that he was purchasing *for a government agent.* Now, who can he be—to offer five cents per bushel higher than Major Hirsch? Again, Mr. Cassels purchases by *weight*—a bushel rated at fifty-four pounds. Mr. Quarterman says he lost by this mode. You can let me know if you have positively engaged to Major Hirsch, and then I will see Mr. Quarterman before deciding.

Your sweet little baby is quite well, and all unite in much love.

Your affectionate father,
C. C. Jones.

MRS. MARY JONES *to* LT. CHARLES C. JONES, JR.[8]
Walthourville, *Wednesday,* November 5th, 1862
My dear Son,

. . . Last week I paid your uncle a short visit. He expressed the wish that yourself and brother would at once take possession of the servants intended for you by your aunt, allowing him a reasonable compensation. Said his will was made, etc., etc., and he was *very anxious* to see you. I asked if he wished me to confer with my sons upon the matter, and regarded what he was saying to me as a business arrangement. He replied yes, and desired me to write you about it. If his will has been legally executed, I should think it well for you to close in with his propositions for various reasons I have not time to name at this time.

By today's mail I received a letter from a *lady* proposing to furnish pork or bacon in payment for salt. Says she has plenty to kill, but no salt to cure. If we could make such an exchange it would aid us in supplying our people with meat. Whilst at Maybank for a day last week (whilst your father was in Savannah) I had a well dug in the salt marsh beyond the first bluff which promises a fine yield of brine, which turns out double the quantity of salt that the river water does. If we had more or larger boilers we could make a good speculation about the bacon. The lady wishes thirty or forty bushels!

Yesterday I turned out the *first blanket* from the loom, and eighty yards of cloth. I am trying with all the energy and means at command to have the people clothed.

Your brother is ready, and I must close. Our respects to Mr. Ward. Your father really enjoyed his visit to Savannah. Our united love. . . . In haste,

Your affectionate mother,
Mary Jones.

Lt. Charles C. Jones, Jr., *to* Mrs. Mary Jones[t]

Savannah, *Thursday,* November 6th, 1862

My very dear Mother,

I sincerely thank you for your kind note of yesterday, received at the hands of Brother, who left this morning for Charleston hoping to be able to return on Saturday next.

A few moments since, I had the pleasure of seeing Uncle John, who goes out to Walthourville tomorrow morning.

On Saturday next the 8th inst. I hope to be able to come out and see you and Father and my dear little daughter and all at home. Vallie Whitehead will probably accompany me; she is very anxious to see dear little Mary Ruth.

We have nothing of special interest here. This gloomy day keeps us within doors; but in a court-martial room we are but little affected by the dripping skies without. I hope the Yankee ironclads are experiencing the benefit of the dangers of the outside navigation, and that many if not all of them now venturing on their nefarious voyage hitherward may never live to tell the tale of their adventures.

Trusting so soon, my dear mother, to enjoy the privilege of seeing you and all the loved ones at home, I will then have the opportunity of congratulating you in person upon the success of your salt-making and cloth manufacture, so all-important under present circumstances. With much love to all, and many kisses for my dear little daughter, I am, as ever,

Your affectionate son,
Charles C. Jones, Jr.

Rev. C. C. Jones *to* Lt. Charles C. Jones, Jr.[8]

Walthourville, *Monday,* November 10th, 1862

My dear Son,

Our missing each other brought about a mutual and real disappointment on Saturday, but we were glad to learn that Miss Whitehead and yourself spent so pleasant a day, and that our sweet little baby interested you so much.

Mother is making every effort to have the people *clothed* who will form the first deportation, and has worked personally very hard, and has gone down today to Montevideo to finish off there and return this evening. Tomorrow, God willing, we purpose moving to *Arcadia* in order to be more immediately *in medias res,* where we hope to entertain Brother and yourself when you come out.

Mother and I appointed *tomorrow week, Tuesday the 18th,* this morning for the people to leave Liberty for their new home, and am glad it is the day that you have also appointed. *Let the 18th, therefore, be the day, if the Lord will.* And we will do all in our power to have everyone and everything ready. The car for us can be left on the track for us at No. 3, and we will have it all packed and ready when the train returns in the afternoon of the 18th. *You will see to the transportation from one depot to the other in Savannah, wagons, etc.,* and that a car be prepared on the Central Railroad so when you arrive on the evening of the 18th there will be no delay.

Mr. R. Q. Cassels declines taking the corn at $1.25. There is no sale for it out here. Major Hirsch is our only chance. *Can you not engage it to him at $1.20 and have the bags sent out at once to No. 3,* and we will begin to deliver forthwith. *The sooner the better.*

Our report from McIntosh County is that the abolition gunboats last week ran up Sapelo River, burnt Captain Brailsford's house, took off *every Negro* belonging to Mr. Reuben King at Mallow, and reduced the aged couple to nothing; and Mrs. Walker's tears alone prevented their carrying the old gentleman off. Captured one of the McDonalds at Fair Hope (the married one) *with a squad of armed Negroes,* and carried him off. His family and household and brother escaped. Burnt Colonel Charles Hopkins' house on the opposite side of the river, where they were fired upon and some of them killed by Captain Octavius Hopkins' company, and made off with themselves. We much need an intelligent, brave, and active commander of the cavalry corps stationed in the three counties to effect concert of action and celerity of movement.

Your Uncle John has just left for his plantation. Robert is at Presbytery in Bryan. We expected your brother today; has not come. Your dear sister sends you much love; and many kisses from the children. Their toys are delighting them now. Your little baby was the coldest infant I ever felt this morning at daylight. Had pushed down her covering, and Mother took her in bed an *icicle.* Half awake, she threw her arms around her neck laughing for the comfort of the change. Your Uncle John preached two admirable sermons for us yesterday. My respects to Mr. Ward; hope he is better. And our kind regards to Miss Val Whitehead.

Your ever affectionate father,
C. C. Jones.

LT. CHARLES C. JONES, JR., *to* REV. C. C. JONES[8]

Savannah, *Monday,* November 10th, 1862

My dear Father,

Through the kindness of the postmaster I have just received your letter of this morning, and am happy to know that the day named—to wit, the *18th* inst.—meets with your approval.

I leave tonight to arrange with Mr. Schley for the payment of the place, obtain titles, etc., so that in the event of my sudden death or any unexpected casualty there may be no question about title or possession. I propose to pay him ten thousand dollars on account the purchase moneys of the place, which will leave only $4120 due and payable two years hence. To secure this balance I will execute a mortgage upon the plantation to that amount. I will also go to Augusta and see what can be done in the matter of the purchase of mules. Will probably, D.V., not return before the last of the week. Will hope to be with you on Saturday next. If not, then on Monday morning, stopping at No. 3.

Brother will probably be with you sometime this week. He has doubtless gone to Augusta from Charleston.

You will of course think of all that is necessary for the Negroes to do in order to get them in readiness. I would suggest that all their clothing, pots, etc., etc., be thoroughly washed and put up in bundles of convenient sizes. If they have hogs we will purchase them; and we will have to make the best arrangements we can in reference to their little matters of property. I desire all my Negroes to go, as they are young, and their services will be required at once in putting the place in order. Do, if you can spare Porter and Pulaski, let them go up with William, as the services of the carpenters will be greatly and immediately required. Let them carry their tools. . . . Do not forget a bag or two of salt for the Negroes to take up with them.

I write in much haste. With warmest love to all, I am ever, my dear father,

Your affectionate son,
Charles C. Jones, Jr.

Have notified the railroad companies of the *day.*

I write Major Hirsch offering twelve hundred to eighteen hundred bushels corn at $1.20 delivered at No. 3, Savannah, Albany & Gulf Railroad, he furnishing sacks. If he accepts in my absence, he is to send the sacks out to that station marked "C. C. Jones, Jr., per Arcadia plantation."

313

XIII

Col. Charles C. Jones, Jr., *to* Rev. C. C. Jones^g
Savannah, *Wednesday,* November 26th, 1862

My dear Father,

Major Hirsch has not been in the city today, so that I have failed to see him in reference to the corn. He will, however, D.V., be here on the morrow, and I will then endeavor to effect a sale of, say, twelve hundred bushels or more, and also potatoes if I can.

I have not been assigned to any specific duty as yet, but probably will be on the morrow. Possibly as chief of light artillery on General Mercer's staff. But nothing definite as yet.

I trust, my dearest father, that you will gather strength. I cannot tell you how it pains me to the very bottom of my heart to see you so feeble; and I pray God night and morning that He would in great kindness stay the progress of your wasting disease, and spare your most precious life to us all and to future usefulness in the church and elsewhere.

I hope that my dear little daughter is better today. Regret that I missed Robert last evening. I had left the house, only a moment before he came, to get the syrup of ipecac for Baby. Nothing of interest here. With warmest love to self, dear Mother, Sister, and all, and tenderest kisses for my dear little daughter, I am ever, my honored father,

Your affectionate son,
Charles C. Jones, Jr.

Col. Charles C. Jones, Jr., *to* Rev. C. C. Jones^g
Savannah, *Friday,* November 28th, 1862

My dear Father,

Will you oblige me by sending by mail the copy of the London *News* which I carried out with me for your perusal, and which I left on the table in the parlor? It belongs to Mr. Ward, and he has promised the loan of it to some parties here.

The *Atlanta* is a perfect success. She dropped down the river last evening to a point near Fort Jackson, where she now lies. It is rumored that we will soon hear from her along the coast—possibly at Port Royal, or at the mouth of the Ogeechee—but with what certainty has not yet transpired. I presume the old commodore will be very anxious to make a demonstration if practicable.

I have been announced by General Mercer as chief of light artillery upon his staff, and have general charge of the light batteries upon the coast. It will require no little time and labor, I fear, to put some of them in good fighting trim.

We have nothing of special interest here. Am endeavoring to arrange for a sale of the corn—by no means a very easy matter. I think I can compass a sale of some potatoes at one dollar delivered at No. 3. Shall I do this? Cotton not yet worth fifty cents; it must go up higher.

I trust, my dear father, that all at home are well, and that my dear little daughter is quite relieved. Do kiss her for me. Give warmest love to Mother. And believe me ever

Your affectionate son,
Charles C. Jones, Jr.

COL. CHARLES C. JONES, JR., *to* REV. C. C. JONES[g]

Savannah, *Monday,* December 1st, 1862

My very dear Father,

I find that I can get for the corn one dollar per bushel delivered at No. 3, sacks furnished. This is offered by Major Locke. I think Major Hirsch will give $1.20. He is to let me know more definitely tomorrow, and I will then communicate the result.

I have fairly entered upon the discharge of my duties, and will be very anxious until I put all the light batteries in good order, some three of which are in not very perfect condition. . . .

We have nothing of interest here. Do give warmest love to dear Mother. Kiss my precious little daughter for me. And believe me ever

Your affectionate son,
Charles C. Jones, Jr.

MRS. MARY JONES *to* COL. CHARLES C. JONES, JR.[g]

Arcadia, *Monday,* December 1st, 1862

My dear Son,

I am happy to say that our dear baby is much better, and she has been out most of the morning in the sweet sunshine. I hope you received Mr. Ward's London *Times,* for which your father was greatly obliged.

Mr. Millen called today and engaged twenty head of cattle from this place at twenty-five dollars a head, and goes tomorrow to see the Island cattle, now at Montevideo. I hope we shall realize at least fifteen hundred dollars by their sale.

We commenced grinding the cane on Friday, and the mill works so well we will not be occupied with it longer than tomorrow or the day after, which

315

I fear will be too short a time to make it an object to our friends to come out for the purpose of syrup-boiling. I would insist upon their coming out this week if we were not obliged from the state of the cane to go immediately (as we are done here) over to Montevideo and grind the cane there, where we will be only marooning for a few days. I thought we should be longer at the business, and wish Mrs. Neely and Val and the little folks could have been with us; but you will understand how necessary it is to have the grinding done as soon as possible. And I want to enjoy their visit whenever it will suit them to make it without the hurry which might now attend it. Please remember your father and myself affectionately to them, with many kisses from their little niece. I hope we shall have at least three or four barrels of syrup for plantation use from the two places. Have not yet succeeded in making sugar.

Today at twelve o'clock a concert of prayer was proposed to be observed by the mothers, wives, and daughters of the Southern Confederacy for our beloved country, that we might be delivered from our enemies, and that the Lord would grant us *peace* in all our land. I can but believe that the prayer of faith has this day ascended as from one heart and one voice, although ten thousand knees have bowed in humble supplications at the throne of our Divine Redeemer, Jehovah of Hosts.

Your dear father unites with me in best love. And kisses from your own little darling. Our respects to Mr. Ward. Do when George comes out let him bring the basket and tin bucket. And will you write Mr. Sconyers to ask Stepney if he is willing to sell his poultry or pigs. Robin thinks they will suffer by being kept. I would buy them if he wishes to sell. In haste,

Your affectionate mother,
Mary Jones.

COL. CHARLES C. JONES, JR., *to* MRS. MARY JONES[8]
Savannah, *Tuesday,* December 2nd, 1862
My very dear Mother,

I am in receipt of your kind note of yesterday, and am truly happy to know that all at home are better, and that my precious little daughter is again restored to her accustomed degree of health.

Am also glad to hear that you have been able to effect such a capital sale of the cattle. Cotton, I understand, is worth sixty cents; it will probably be higher. I cannot at present get more than one dollar per bushel for corn. I think by next week it will be worth $1.20 from the government. I can get one dollar for potatoes delivered at the station in small quantities.

I will write to Mr. Sconyers in regard to Stepney's stock and poultry and let you know so soon as I hear from him. I expect to send George out before long, and will see that he carries out the basket and tin buckets.

There seems to be a perfect lull in this fearful contest—doubtless the hush which betokens the advent of a terrible storm. Our enemies are gathering their energies for some heavy demonstration somewhere along our lines. I trust in God that we may be able successfully to meet and repulse them.

My present position gives me a good deal of active exercise, as I visit the batteries on horseback.

It always rejoices my heart when I see and hear of these general assemblages of the people of this Confederacy for humiliation and prayer to Almighty God; and I trust that the fervent prayers of the wives and daughters of our land, offered with one consent on yesterday, may be graciously answered by the Lord of Hosts. War is a national judgment of the severest character; it comes from God, and is sent for wise purposes and to accomplish given ends. Among those objects perhaps the most important is the alienation of the hearts of the people from sin and worldliness, and a return of them to true contrition for past offenses, and the fear and love of God. It seems to me, as I look around me, that we have not even yet learnt the uses or accomplished the objects of this judgment. And this makes me tremble for the future. It does not do to trust in chariots or horses. There is a great Will behind all, over all, and directing all. For one I do try and humble myself before God, in all unworthiness and shamefacedness. And we can but hope and beg of Him that He will soon again lift up the light of His countenance upon us.

We have nothing new or interesting in the city. Do give warmest love to dear Father. Kiss my darling little daughter for me. And believe me ever, my dear mother,

Your affectionate son,
Charles C. Jones, Jr.

REV. C. C. JONES *to* COL. CHARLES C. JONES, JR.[8]

Arcadia, *Thursday,* December 4th, 1862

My dear Son,

Your two last letters have been received, from which we learn that you have entered upon your new military duties as lieutenant colonel of light artillery, and hope that you will be able to discharge them intelligently and honorably to yourself and usefully to your country, which I am well assured you will most conscientiously and faithfully endeavor to do.

Your solicitude for the declining state of my health, expressed not only in words but in acts, sensibly affects me. Few men have been more blessed than I with dutiful and affectionate children, and with a wife whose tender kindnesses know no remission; and could relief have come through all your devotion and constant efforts, I should long since have been restored to perfect health. But such has not been the will of God, and to that will it is my desire and prayer to submit cheerfully. My anxiety is that I may not be deceived in my hope of eternal life through Christ Jesus our Lord, but be prepared for eternity when the great change comes.

Your Uncle John left us this morning with the bulk of his people, all in excellent spirits and well stored in a box car. We rode with him to the depot and parted with him there. The exodus of Negroes from the seaboard is large. Abolition raids would scarcely pay expenses, and if the enemy knows this, those who remain on the coast will be the safer for the fact.

Mother informed you of the sale of twenty head of Arcadia cattle at $25 per head = $500: $250 paid, and the rest on delivery of the cattle tomorrow, I suppose. Sold also thirty-two at Montevideo—twenty at $25: $500; and twelve at $12 (small cattle): $144 = $644 delivered and paid for.

Corn is selling in the county at $1.20 to $1.25 to the troop, and *they haul it.* Selling for one dollar and then *hauling* to the depot is rather heavy work; and perhaps by delaying a few days we may secure more favorable terms. . . .

Little Sister is getting well again, and is the light of our dwelling. Mother is well. . . . Your Uncle William was here on Tuesday. Stays with Captain Winn at Dorchester. His people at Winn's also. Wish you would write him. Mother sends love. Kisses from your dear baby.

Your ever affectionate father,
C. C. Jones.

COL. CHARLES C. JONES, JR., *to* REV. C. C. JONES[8]

Savannah, Friday, December 5th, 1862

My dear Father,

Mr. Ward and myself are indebted to your kind remembrance for a delightful pair of mallard ducks, which arrived safely and in good order last night. Accept our hearty thanks.

Enclosed I send a letter just received from Mr. Sconyers, the overseer on the Buckhead place. You will be happy to see that all of the people are well. Please let me have the letter when you have completed its perusal.

You said to me that you wished a statement of expenditures already incurred on account Buckhead place. Enclosed you have the same. I have now entirely settled with Mr. Schley, with the exception of one note for $4120, given in payment of balance due upon purchase moneys of the place, which does not mature until 1st January 1865. Everything is now paid for upon the place. I owe in bank between six and seven thousand dollars, but this I hope to pay before very long with proceeds sale of stock and such assistance as you can conveniently give me (say, three thousand dollars) and from my share of articles and crop sold at Arcadia.

Cotton is now worth between fifty and sixty cents. Do not let Anderson sell your cotton unless he promises those figures, as they can be got by other commission merchants on the Bay. I can get one dollar any day for the corn if sold to government, and hope to get more.

Nothing of special interest. I hope, my dear father, that you are feeling better. Do give warmest love to dear Mother. Kiss my precious little daughter for me. And believe me ever, my honored father,

Your affectionate son,
Charles C. Jones, Jr.

COL. CHARLES C. JONES, JR., *to* REV. C. C. JONES[8]

Savannah, *Saturday,* December 6th, 1862

My dear Father,

I am this morning in receipt of your very kind favor of the 4th inst., and sincerely thank you for it, with every acknowledgment of the good wishes you express for a proper discharge of the new and more important military duties upon which I have just entered. I hope I may have disposition, strength, and ability to perform them aright.

The sale of the cattle is a fine one. I think with you that we had better delay a sale of the corn for a little while. So soon as the present government restrictions in reference to the conveyance of private freight are removed, my impression is that we will get $1.50 for the corn, and also be able to dispose of peas and potatoes if there are any to be sold.

Yesterday evening I sent you a statement of amounts already expended by me on account Burke plantation as requested by you. I cannot fully express to you, my dear father, what a great pleasure and privilege I have regarded it to have it thus in my power to compass the wishes of yourself and dear Mother in the matter of the removal of and the securing of a new home for our people without subjecting you to any additional trouble or pecuniary risks. I trust that the investment may prove a safe and profitable one.

Am happy to know that dear little Daughter is so well again. Do kiss her for me. Give warmest love to my dear mother. And believe me ever, my honored father,

Your affectionate son,
Charles C. Jones, Jr.

REV. C. C. JONES *to* COL. CHARLES C. JONES, JR.[8]

Arcadia, *Monday,* December 8th, 1862

My dear Son,

Am obliged to you for the memorandum of expenses for the purchase and stocking of your Buckhead plantation thus far. I will do my best to meet the three thousand dollars you wish, and as much more as we can raise to help you out.

I fear the cotton left over from last year from Montevideo may not turn out as much as we anticipated. We have five bales *upland* packed in *round* bales—fine quality; had no *rope* to put in square bales. Will take your advice about the sale of cotton. If you can negotiate a sale for sixty cents it had better go; and we can get Mr. Anderson to deliver it as usual if *he* cannot do as well.

Kate (*William's* wife) begs to go with her husband. She has three small children, and Mr. Buttolph starts on *Thursday,* D.V., with all their people from Lambert and White Oak save a few left to get out the crop. Your Aunt Susan says she is willing to hire her to you. Please let me know your mind before that day. There will be a year's work on your place for the carpenters

319

to put everything in order, and it would be a great comfort to William to have his wife with him. The only difficulty is house room and *field* room. The force will have to be reduced as soon as the way is opened. As it now is, we are acting under necessity. Would like to draw back some hands for Montevideo—not at all to cripple your operations but to make some ten or twelve to keep up the place and make it profitable. And will do so, God willing, if circumstances admit of it.

But there is no light shining in that direction. Every prospect at home and abroad is for a *protracted struggle.* Lincoln's message breathes the same heartless, cold-blooded, and murderous fanaticism that first began and has marked the war; and he repeats the same false and unjust reasons for it, and winds up by remitting the war until successful from one generation to another! And when successful all the world will approve and God forever bless! The magnitude and transparency of the folly and the wickedness of our enemy estops all comment. I can only repeat our daily prayer that God would take our cause into His own almighty hand, and humble us for our sins and judge between us and our enemy.

Our friends are generally well. The county on the moving order. Your Uncle John off—pleasantly. Your dear baby hearty and very interesting; jabbers and scolds and has a word to say, but in her own tongue. Mother thinks when she begins to talk she will talk all at once.

The notice of your brother in Saturday's *Republican* is highly complimentary, and very strong. We have to take in sail at times, even with a fair wind: it may be too much for our ship and rigging. Hope to write him today.

Syrup crop at Arcadia: two of the large barrels (marked fifty) each filled up, and about ten gallons over. Splendid syrup. Report from Mother, who says she has acted as first directress. We go to Montevideo today to renew the boiling there. When we get through there, will know what we shall have to send up the country. We have lost by the delay in grinding. Mother sends much love.

Your ever affectionate father,
C. C. Jones.

I find a man may write with a *cold hand* but a *warm and cheerful heart.*
Much pleased with Mr. Sconyers' letter.

COL. CHARLES C. JONES, JR., *to* REV. C. C. JONES[8]
Savannah, *Friday,* December 12th, 1862

My dear Father,

In consequence of my absence from the city your kind favor of the 8th inst. was not until this morning received. I was sent under orders by General Mercer to Augusta for the purpose of procuring a light battery from the arsenal in that city for one of the artillery companies under my command, at present supplied with guns of an indifferent character. In consequence of this I fear I am too late to reply in time to your inquiry in reference to William's wife and her hire. I can now only say that I heartily endorse any arrangement which you have already made, or which you may see fit and proper to make in the premises.

I have not had an opportunity today to make further inquiries in reference to the prices of corn and cotton, but hope to do so tomorrow, and will let you know the result.

Saw Brother, Sister Carrie, and Stanhope in Augusta. All well. The Doctor went to the Buckhead place at my request to *vaccinate* the Negroes. He is in daily expectation of the receipt of his commission, and thinks it more than probable that he will be ordered to Charleston. In that event he may remove his family to that city, although as yet nothing definite is ascertained.

Have just received a letter from the overseer, Mr. Sconyers. All the people well, and getting along well.

We have nothing of special interest here. Good news—as far as it goes—from Virginia. My throat has been giving me a good deal of trouble lately. I intend getting Dr. Sullivan to examine it for me and place me under treatment. It has always been my weak point. I am most happy to know that dear Mother and my precious little daughter are so well, and sincerely trust, my dear father, that you are feeling better. Today I reviewed and inspected the Chatham Artillery, my old company; found everything in excellent order. In haste, but with warmest love to self, Mother, and little Daughter, I am ever, Father,

Your affectionate son,
Charles C. Jones, Jr.

COL. CHARLES C. JONES, JR., *to* REV. C. C. JONES[g]

Savannah, *Monday,* December 15th, 1862

My dear Father,

The telegraphic intelligence from Virginia and elsewhere, although of a cheering character, does not as yet give assurance of any decided victory.

We are now, in all human probability, just on the verge of that tempest which has for some time been gathering. In view of the paucity of our troops when compared with the immense hosts opposed to us, fortified with all the most approved appliances of modern warfare; in view of the further fact that we are almost entirely unable to procure better arms and more soldiers, it does seem that we can alone in God look for deliverance. It is a time for universal prayer. The recent battle near Fredericksburg, although nobly won, has cost us the loss of valuable lives—Cobb, Gregg, and (more than all) *Hood,* one of the bravest of the brave. Priceless is that liberty purchased at such a cost. Twenty-five hundred of our troops from this military district left the city last night—destination probably North Carolina or wherever else the storm cloud may hang most darkly. We are anxiously expecting tonight more intelligence from Virginia. Our capital is grievously beset. But I have an abiding confidence in the valor and ability of our generals, the almost miraculous courage of our soldiers, and above all in the justice of our cause and the favoring protection of Heaven, and will expect a timely deliverance from all our troubles.

A letter from Mr. Sconyers tells me that all the people are well and getting along without any difficulty. The morning's mail will, I expect, bring me a letter from Brother, which will give his impressions of the place and of the condition of the people.

Will you have the kindness, Father, to have a barrel of rice beaten out at Arcadia and sent to me here in order that I may have it shipped to Mrs. Harlow at Waynesboro? I promised the old lady to send it to her. She is poor, and will esteem the gift. And more than all, she was the aunt of my dearest Ruth and tenderly attached to her.

Has Mother made any arrowroot this year?

I hope to see you and dear Mother and my sweet little daughter very soon. Is there anything in the world that little Mary Ruth needs that can be procured for her? I trust that you are, my dear father, feeling better. Is there any way in which I can serve you? With warmest love to self, dear Mother, and many kisses for my dear little daughter, I am ever

Your affectionate son,
Charles C. Jones, Jr.

Stepney says he wishes his hogs and poultry if practicable sent up.

MRS. MARY JONES *to* COL. CHARLES C. JONES, JR.[8]

Arcadia, *Friday,* December 19th, 1862

My dear Son,

We received your kind favor today and the extra, which fills our hearts with humble and adoring gratitude to God for this renewed token of His mercy and goodness to us and our beloved country. I have not words to express the emotions I feel for this signal success in the outset of this last fearful and terrific assault of our enemies, when probably he has arrayed a force five or six to one, armed with all the deadly appliances of modern warfare to overwhelm and destroy us. Surely our strength to resist and overcome is immediately from above and in answer to prayer; and I believe if we trust in our Almighty God and Saviour and strive to perform our duty to our suffering land in His fear and for His glory, that our enemies will never triumph over us. I trust if we are successful in the present repulse that the day of deliverance and the restoration of peace to our bleeding land will not be delayed.

What comfort and encouragement is afforded by the fact that we have so many Christian, true, God-fearing commanders; and that in many regiments of our army amidst the temptations and horrors of war the Blessed Spirit has been poured out for the conviction and conversion of officers and men; and that they who may be said to be treading the courts of death have had opened up to them the gates of everlasting life! Have you read the deeply interesting letters of our esteemed friend Dr. Stiles giving an account of his labors? I feel thankful that in this great struggle the head of our army is a noble son of Virginia, and worthy of the intimate relation in which he stands connected with our immortal Washington. What confidence his wisdom, integrity, and valor and undoubted piety inspire! And Virginia—noble Virginia—although she delayed her action in the offset, has bravely bared her bosom to the storm; and not only her men but her women too have sustained the patriotism and generosity of the state. Oh, that our God would give us true repentance for our many, great, and aggravated sins, which have brought this awful judgment of war upon us, and speedily establish us as a nation in righteousness and peace!

Your father and I took our dear little baby with us and spent the day with your aunt and Laura at Flemington. Found them comfortably located, although the house is small. Mr. Buttolph not yet returned from Baker County. *Kate* (William's wife) was not sent with their people; and your aunt says she is willing to hire her if you desire to have her. I told her we expected to have you with us shortly.

Can you not be with us at Christmas? It would be a great pleasure to us to have all our children with us—not for merrymaking but thanksgiving! I like the good old custom of gathering all under the rooftree at least once a year.

Thanks for your brother's letter.

We have now three barrels of superior syrup, and some gallons over, between the two places. Your sister wishes eight gallons for her family's use; you ought (and your brother) to retain the same; and that, with what we shall need on the places below, will leave, I think, two full barrels for Burke. I will this coming week pickle another beef and have a barrel of pork ready, so that you can order them up whenever you please to do so. Your father says there is a crosscut saw here that might go up. Our gins were doing very little, but *Audley very kindly* sent Prophet this week, and he has put them in fine order; so we hope the crop will soon be ready for market and the people to go up with the oxcarts. I am now making the arrowroot. Would you like to have some of it for any of your friends? . . .

Do write me if it is impossible for you to be with us next week. If you cannot come, I must send you some sausages, etc. Tell me what day. Write me on Monday, for if you cannot come out, we will send Gilbert in, as I want also to send a box or package to your brother on Tuesday to reach him by Christmas. It is late, and I must close, with best love from Father and Mother. Sweetest kisses from your little Mary Ruth.

Ever your affectionate mother,
Mary Jones.

Col. Charles C. Jones, Jr., *to* Rev. *and* Mrs. C. C. Jones[8]
Savannah, *Saturday,* December 27th, 1862
My very dear Father and Mother,

I have just returned to the city after my delightful Christmas visit to you and to my precious little daughter. I cannot fully express to you, my dear parents, how much I esteem these visits home, with all the quiet loves and pure influences which dwell beneath the paternal roof. I always feel that I am made a better man by reason of the privileges there enjoyed. Never will I be able to answer for one of a thousand of the great kindnesses and unwearied goodnesses, my dear parents, which all my life long you have ever so generously showered upon me, and for all the precious influences of your Christian precepts and examples. But one thing is certain, and that is that you will ever have the warmest thanks, the sincerest love, and the most dutiful obedience of your affectionate son, who will ever esteem it his highest privilege to render you every honor and service that may lie in his power.

Spent Friday night with Arnold, and on Saturday morning reviewed Martin's light battery, and also visited the fixed battery at Genesis Point.

A letter from Eva, just opened, tells me that her father has sunk very perceptibly in the last few days, and that the physicians offer no hope of his bodily or mental recovery. She and Cousin Philo are in great affliction.

I learn nothing new tonight. Mr. Ward desires his especial remembrance, and begs that I convey his hearty thanks to you for your kind remembrance of him and for all the good things sent. Do kiss my little daughter for me. And believe me ever, my dear father and mother, with warmest love,

Your ever affectionate son,
Charles C. Jones, Jr.

The basket for Brother was duly forwarded by George on Friday night.

COL. CHARLES C. JONES, JR., *to* REV. *and* MRS. C. C. JONES[g]

Savannah, *Thursday,* January 1st, 1863

"Happy New Year," my dearest father and mother and little daughter, trembles upon my lips as I address you; and I find the voices of congratulation upon this the dawn of another twelvemonth almost hushed into the more subdued tones of sympathy as I think of the many shadows which are lengthening all over our land, and of the peculiar sorrows gathering about so many. But although the merry laugh does not ring out as usual upon the calm air of this earliest-born, beautiful day of the new year; although the present is filled with disquietudes, and the clouds of doubt and of apprehension gather about the future; although the year which died last night has left us no rich legacy of peace, no guaranty of happiness; although the harsh sounds of war are abroad in the land, and vandal armies are besieging the very portals of our temple of national liberty; although prosperity has forgotten her accustomed paths, and the white wings of security are no longer hovering about our shores; although the hand of disease is heavily laid upon some whom God and nature and every cherished association of the past have made very near and dear to us; although coming days and future expectations from which we would fain expect only the sweet sunlight of joy and of hope are covered all over by the uncertain shadows of apprehension and of solicitude—we will not yield to fear; we will not forget past blessings; we will not cease to be grateful for present mercies; but will hope on, confiding all things in the hands of Him who doeth all things well, remembering the exhortation of the inspired Preacher: "Let us hear the conclusion of the whole matter: Fear God, and keep His commandments; for this is the whole duty of man."

Although it is New Year's Day, I am and have been very busy.

General Bragg, in command at Murfreesboro, today telegraphs General Beauregard that in the terrific battle which is still raging there between our brave troops and the abolition hosts under their most accomplished General Rosecrans, that we have driven back the right and center of the enemy, capturing four thousand prisoners (among them two brigadier generals), thirty-one pieces of artillery, two hundred wagons, etc., etc. The battle still raging on the left, and with great loss on both sides. I sincerely trust the victory may be complete, decisive. Here is one *bright ray*.

I send the almanac of 1863, and beg pardon for not having done so before. The truth is, my dear parents, I have been of late very busy each day. Nothing more of special interest here. With warmest love to you both, my dearest parents, and many kisses for my precious little daughter, I am ever

Your affectionate son,
Charles C. Jones, Jr.

REV. C. C. JONES *to* COL. CHARLES C. JONES, JR.[8]

Arcadia, *Tuesday,* January 6th, 1863

My dear Son,

As this is my first letter to you in the new year, I must wish you a Happy New Year—happy first in your experience of the forgiving mercy and love of God in Christ Jesus our Lord; next, in your open profession of your Saviour, who endured the Cross, despising the shame, on your account; in the joy you will experience in keeping His commandments and glorifying His name and living submissive to His will; in the accomplishment of all your lawful undertakings; in the realization of your pure and anticipated enjoyments; in the affection and confidence of all your relatives and friends; in a word, in a life of usefulness, illustrating all the virtues and graces which belong to the Christian and which adorn the man. You have the best wishes and prayers of your parents for all these things for you, and for a blessed immortality when life is past.

We had a little family gathering today of your aunt and Cousins Laura and Lyman, your Uncle William and sister, and the little ones (five in number), whose merry voices filled the house all day. We expected Robert, but he did not return by the cars this morning, having gone to James Island to pay a pastoral visit to his church members in Captain Thomson's troop. Our enjoyment would have been greatly increased by the addition also of yourself and your brother and his family.

Your Aunt Susan says she will sell you Kate and her three children to go with William her husband if Kate will consent; and no doubt she will. In determining the price I suggested her choice of a friend and your choice of another, and if they cannot agree, let them call in a third; and if the valuation satisfies you both, then abide by it. She said Mr. Fleming, who knows the family, would be a good person to fix their valuation. If you are still of the same mind to purchase, you can appoint someone to act for you. Your Uncle William would, I imagine, be a very suitable one. You can, however, judge best. He would act for you no doubt with great pleasure. He regrets much that he did not see you in your late visit.

You must let me know how many cattle you wish sent up to Buckhead as early as you can. The crop is ground out at Montevideo, and Pharaoh hopes to run the crop close at Arcadia this week, and the sooner then they are off the better. Am selling corn here and at Montevideo at $1.25 delivered at the cornhouse door. Will sell all shelled up at that price, and then see how much more may be sold now in the ear.

Mr. Buttolph says you wrote to inquire if he would sell his cotton at forty-five cents delivered at No. 3 depot. Do not know what he will do. He speaks of visiting Savannah with samples to see what can be done. Mr. Gué says Floridas fifty cents and over, but Liberty County common cottons forty-five cents. Forty-five cents is an excellent price. Could you include us in a like offer? A part if not the whole we might sell for that price. From Montevideo we have some thirteen or fifteen sea island and five upland in *round* bales. . . .

Mother has suffered very much from her cold and cough, and is still suffering, although a little better of it. Little Sister well and growing more and more interesting every day. All unite in much love to you. My respects to Mr. Ward.

From your ever affectionate father,
C. C. Jones.

If the cotton purchaser will say fifty cents at the depot, we can make him up an excellent lot. Your Uncle John would come in, I think.

COL. CHARLES C. JONES, JR., *to* REV. *and* MRS. C. C. JONES[g]

Savannah, *Wednesday,* January 7th, 1863

My very dear Father and Mother,

I sincerely trust, in the absence of any very recent intelligence from home, that all are well—that you, my dear mother, have been relieved of your troublesome cold; that you, Father, are feeling stronger; and that my sweet little daughter is enjoying all the blessings of health.

I cannot say to you how busy I have been of late, and it would be difficult for me to recall a leisure moment during the past two weeks. On Friday of this week I have ordered in five of my light batteries in order that I may give

General Mercer an inspection and review. The line will be formed in rear of the Savannah jail fronting north, the right resting on Whitaker Street. I trust the parade and review will be attractive, and assure the general commanding of the efficiency of the light batteries in this command, and of their preparedness at any moment for actual service.

It is a matter of deep regret that General Bragg has not been able to put to flight the army of our abolition enemy in Tennessee. Inspired by such cheerful accounts from the battlefield as first greeted our eager ears, it was a sad disappointment to have the cup of general rejoicing so unexpectedly dashed from the expectant lips. I fear General Bragg is not the man for the position he now holds. We cannot afford, under God, to have drawn battles, and a strange want of success appears to have attended from the inception all his military operations. An officer may be a brave man, and what is termed a "fighting" man, and yet be incapable of handling large bodies of men in the field. There may be—and events appear to be demonstrating the fact—a vast difference in the abilities of Captain Bragg commanding with distinction a single light battery and General Bragg with a large army under his control.

The loss of the *Monitor* has been confirmed—another cause for sincerest gratitude to the Giver of All Good, who has so often and so signally turned the counsels of our enemies to nought. . . .

What do you think, Father, of selling our cotton at fifty cents? I think I can effect a sale at that figure, saving all freight, commissions, etc., etc., upon delivery of it at No. 3. Please let me hear from you on this subject. With warmest love to you both, my dearest parents, and many kisses for my precious little daughter, I am ever

Your affectionate son,
Charles C. Jones, Jr.

Cousin Philo Eve, my dear mother, in a recent letter from Eva begs me to return you her sincere thanks for your delightful arrowroot. It is enjoyed by Mr. Eve in his feeble health more than anything else which has been offered him for many days.

COL. CHARLES C. JONES, JR., *to* REV. C. C. JONES[t]

Savannah, *Thursday,* January 8th, 1863

My very dear and honored Father,

It is with sincere gratitude that I acknowledge the receipt of your valued New Year letter of the 6th inst., which reached me only a few moments since. Already have I enjoyed the pleasure of assuring yourself, my dear mother, and my precious little daughter of my earnest and heartfelt wishes and hopes for your every happiness, temporal and spiritual, during the changing seasons of this year upon which we have so recently entered. I beg again, in all sincerity and affection, to renew those assurances, with the fervent aspiration that it may soon please the Supreme Ruler of the Universe to restore the light of His countenance, to grant unto us a speedy, successful, and honorable solution of the present difficulties which surround us, and again assure us in the permanent enjoyment of those blessings social, moral, intellectual, and religious which have in so many instances been almost wholly suspended by the existence of this gigantic and inhuman war.

I trust that dear Mother may soon be entirely relieved from the effects of her protracted and terrible cold. I had hoped that she was before this quite well.

In reference to the cotton, I am authorized to say that *I can get fifty cents for it delivered at No. 3* provided I can make up a good lot. This is above the market value, as I hear of a sale today at forty-five cents. I think it may be best for us to close at this in view of the uncertainties of the future; and you may say to Robert, to Uncle John, to Mr. Buttolph that the offer is open to them. . . . If there are any other parties who wish to be included, I will beg you to mention them to me, and I will endeavor to have the same liberty extended to them. Let come what will, fifty cents is a fine price, and I would rather sell at that than take the uncertain chances of the future.

I will purchase William's wife and children, and will be prepared, Father, to give whatever price you may deem proper, or which may be regarded as fair by anyone whom you may name. I should think, without ever having seen the woman or children, that fifteen hundred dollars would be a fair price if they are all young and healthy. But I leave the matter in your hands to act for me, and will abide any decision in the premises you may deem fair and reasonable.

You do well to sell the corn, I think, at the price named, saving transportation, etc., etc. I presume it would not be well to send more than twenty-five head of cattle to Buckhead plantation, and ten yoke of oxen and two mules if they could be spared. Am glad to hear that Andrew and his family are so profitably employed.

Please, Father, let me know how many bales of cotton can be delivered at No. 3 from all the plantations named, in order that I may at once communicate with the purchasers. By the arrangement proposed we save all the expenses of freight to Savannah, drayage, commission, etc., which form no small item in the aggregate. If the proposition meets with a favorable consideration, the cotton had best be sent to No. 3 at the earliest covenient day after we have ascertained the probable amount which can be then delivered. One thing I will say to you, Father, in confidence: I would send no more cotton to Gué. I give you this advice *not at random.*

Tomorrow I expect to have a grand review by General Mercer of five of my light batteries. With warmest love to self, my dear father, to my dear mother, and many kisses for my precious little daughter, I am ever

Your affectionate son,

Charles C. Jones, Jr.

REV. C. C. JONES *to* COL. CHARLES C. JONES, JR.[8]

Arcadia, *Friday,* January 9th, 1863

My dear Son,

Yours of the 7th and 8th we have received—the last this morning; and I hasten to say that I will immediately communicate with the parties you have named in relation to their cotton and let you know as soon as possible—by Monday or Tuesday, I hope.

Today is your grand review. Nothing prevented my being present but my weakness and Mother's indisposition. It would have afforded me unfeigned pleasure to have witnessed it. I never saw the like.

Mother, I think, is a little better. She went to Montevideo this morning on business. Your dear child is getting quite hearty again, and her little mind develops daily.

The battles in Tennessee turn out better than expected. Certainly General Bragg has given the invaders a serious check. But without reinforcements what can he do? Rivers rising and railroads open. Stirring times are upon us. We have only to stand the braver and trust in God more perfectly. . . . Mother is pleased that the arrowroot has proved so acceptable to Mr. Eve. Am sorry he is no better. I remain, my dear son,

Your affectionate father,
C. C. Jones.

COL. CHARLES C. JONES, JR., *to* REV. C. C. JONES[8]

Savannah, *Saturday,* January 10th, 1863

My dear Father,

I am favored with your letter of yesterday, and am happy to know that dear Mother is better of her cold, and that little Daughter is so well.

The review and parade of my light batteries were highly praised by everyone. You have probably noticed the comments by the editors. It was the first appearance of a battalion of light artillery in the history of this state. I had on parade about four hundred men, three hundred horses, and twenty-six field pieces (six-pounder guns and twelve-pounder howitzers) with limbers and caissons complete. I desire here to commemorate the fact that during the entire parade, inspection, and review not a piece of harness became deranged and not a horse declined for a second its duty. This was quite remarkable, and is one of the strongest proofs I can give you of the perfect condition of the batteries. When in line of battle for inspection the battalion presented a front of between four and five hundred yards. The display in column of sections was very imposing, and all the movements of the battalion were characterized by precision and rapidity. From General Mercer I received congratulations and compliments. I wish very much, my dear father, that you and Mother could have been present. I think you would have been much pleased with the military display.

The cotton had best be delivered at No. 3 as soon as it is all ready; and when all has been delivered, if you will be kind enough to notify me of the fact, the purchasers will send out an agent and weigh and pay for the same.

The news is encouraging from the West. And Vicksburg, true to her heroic memories, still successfully resists the combined attacks of the enemy. Do give warmest love to dear Mother and my precious little daughter. And believe me ever, my dear father,

Your affectionate son,
Charles C. Jones, Jr.

MRS. MARY JONES *to* COL. CHARLES C. JONES, JR.[8]

Arcadia, *Monday,* January 12th, 1863

My dear Son,

I sent on Saturday to No. 3 to know if there was now an express to Savannah, and found there was none; so I am peculiarly gratified in having an unexpected opportunity of sending Mr. Ward and yourself a few fresh sausages by today's train, and now write a hasty line to assure you of the great pleasure we have felt at the success of your review. It would have given your father and myself great happiness to have been present, but his inability to move about without great effort prevented. I think, however, he continues to improve, and has gone today to see after our salt-boilers. My cold is something better after a day in bed on Saturday.

When will you forward the barrels of pork and syrup and the rice for Mrs. Harlow? Give us a few days' notice, as they are all ready to be packed, and have to be brought over from Montevideo.

I send you two of our Confederate tracts. Please present the one written by Dr. Thornwell to Mr. Ward; I am sure he will recognize in it one of the master minds of the age. The one *for you* your father and I have read with deepest interest; we can never have too much light upon "The Way of Life."

The oranges grew in McIntosh County, and are for your throat; for I am sure you are suffering after the review.

Your precious little daughter is well and very bright, and busy in the sunshine with the poultry and her dog Captain. As you will see, I am writing in great haste, and hope you will be able to read what is written. With kisses from your little Mary Ruth,

Ever, my dear son, your affectionate mother,
Mary Jones.

COL. CHARLES C. JONES, JR., *to* MRS. MARY JONES[8]

Savannah, *Monday,* January 12th, 1863

Upon coming home this evening, my dearest mother, I found your kind letter of this morning with the enclosed tracts and the accompanying package of delightful sausages, etc., etc. For them all please accept my warmest thanks. Major Porter called to see me a few moments since, and as the oranges were so fine, and such a rarity, I gave them to him to take to Mrs. Porter and Mrs. Gilmer, telling him where they came from. The sausages, etc., etc., will be a great treat. Mr. Ward is temporarily absent from the city, but I will keep his tract for him; and he will unite with me, my dear mother, in sincere thanks for your kind remembrance of us. Both of the tracts I have already read tonight with great interest and I trust profit.

Any day that the articles from Arcadia are ready they might be shipped, and I will see that they are reshipped here and forwarded to their proper destination.

I had to give on Saturday seventy-five dollars for a keg of nails weighing a hundred pounds. What think you of that? And fifty dollars per pound for iron!

I am purposing on the morrow a request that General Mercer allow me a leave of absence on Friday and Saturday that I may go up and see how matters are progressing on the place. I trust it will be granted, as I deem it very important that I should see just at this time what they are about and give proper directions, etc., etc.

We have nothing of special interest here. I have been so busy night and day for several weeks past that my head feels this very moment as if it contained a small water mill. . . . I am ever, my dear mother,
Your affectionate son,
Charles C. Jones, Jr.

Did you receive some time since a ten-dollar bank bill—a New Year's present for my dear little daughter?

MRS. MARY JONES *to* COL. CHARLES C. JONES, JR.[8]
Arcadia, Tuesday, January 20th, 1863

My dear Son,

I thought often of you on Friday night, exposed as I feared you were to all the severity of cold, and prayed that you might be protected from suffering and sickness. As it was a night remembered by me, you may imagine that I felt especially grateful, when yesterday's paper gave an account of the distressing accident on the Central Road, that you were in the up and not the down train.

I trust your visit has been accomplished with satisfaction. I am always anxious to hear from your brother, which we have not done for several weeks. I hope you saw and left him and his family well. He pays so little regard to his own health or comfort that I often fear his constitution will not stand such unreasonable draughts. How did you leave all your friends? Does Mr. Eve improve? Should you wish to send more arrowroot, I have plenty of it.

I hope our servants are doing well. We want to answer their letters very soon. The carts and boys are all ready for going up as soon as someone can be found to go with them. Is there anyone familiar with the route from the up country that could be obtained?

We have just received a letter from my brother, your Uncle John. He will be with us in a few days, and wishes to know if he could purchase Stepney's buggy to take with him to Baker. Stepney on leaving told me he did not wish then to part with it. It is a very good one, and in good repair. Your father says it could go along with the carts, attached or with one of the mules; and as such things are every day more and more scarce, we would like to know what you think about it. Shall it be sold or sent up? Perhaps you know his present wish about it, or might find it useful on the plantation.

Have you succeeded in getting spinning wheels and cards? I see an advertisement for *sheepskins* and offering cotton cards in exchange at the *Milledgeville* factory. I have collected some fine skins, and when the *hides* go up might send them also to Mr. Sconyers to be exchanged. We have reserved all the short staple cotton (five bales and a packet of sixty or seventy pounds and one bale of yellow—long) presuming that the purchasers wanted only *sea island.·* As soon as yarn comes down to reasonable prices we must bag *a bale* for weaving. I am just putting in a piece of cloth, but not having my usual strength makes it slow business.

I came from church on Sabbath with a chill; had high fever last night. Your father sent for Dr. Farmer yesterday. He prescribed. I am under the influence of medicine today, and strange to say feel better for the attack of fever. It has at least this effect: confines me to the room. . . .

Your father and myself were much gratified at seeing Mr. Ward, and hope he is feeling better. I had not seen him for many years, and perceived that not even a visit to the "Celestial Empire" had availed to keep off the *snowflakes* of time.

Your father will meet "the purchaser" at No. 3 tomorrow, and says he will inquire after a Mr. Butler, said to be a suitable person to take the carts, etc., to Burke.

With sweetest kisses from your own little daughter, and thanks to dear Papa for the New Year's gift, safely deposited in the savings bank, and the warmest love of your parents,

Ever your own mother,
Mary Jones.

COL. CHARLES C. JONES, JR., *to* REV. *and* MRS. C. C. JONES[g]

Savannah, *Tuesday,* January 20th, 1863

My dear Father and Mother,

I found all well at the plantation in Burke, and getting along cleverly: the people content, and busily and cheerfully engaged in the discharge of their accustomed and daily duties. Agrippa had been quite sick with pneumonia, but was up again, and it is hoped will in due time resume his duties. Betty is sorely burdered with the primal sorrow of her sex; I have left specific instructions that she have every attention in the hour of her trial. The nails having arrived, the carpenters will at once complete three houses and proceed with the fourth. Repairs are needed on the old houses; attention will be given to this at the earliest practicable moment. The girls and women are succeeding very well in plowing; Miley is preeminently successful. All are fat and hearty and cheerful. Have prepared some ten or twelve acres for *rice;* and we will want the requisite seed from Arcadia, and also any rice hooks which may be there. Every inquiry was made after you, my dearest parents, and little Daughter, every member of the family, and all of the servants. Adam expects soon to be married. The physical appearance of the people indicates, I think, already decided benefit from the change. Their greatest want is shoes. Mr. Sconyers is busily engaged preparing for the crop of the coming year. The wheat is all up—about twelve acres—and looks very well.

Returned by way of Augusta. Saw Brother and Sister Carrie and Stanhope. All well except Carrie, who had the day I left some fever, but I trust nothing serious. My dear Eva was most happy to see me. Her father grows no better; it is a sad sight to trace in his robust frame the progress of disease. Cousin Philo asked me, my dear mother, to thank you sincerely for the delightful arrowroot, which has been greatly relished by Mr. Eve. Brother wished me to inspect his hospital. I thanked him for the kind invitation, but remarked to him in declining it that I made it a rule never to view humanity in its abnormal conditions except when duty required that I should do so. The next morning he told me he was glad I had pursued the course I did; for upon making his rounds he discovered that a case of confluent smallpox had developed itself in one of the wards during the night. He has sent a pump and some cod-liver oil, which I will ship by tomorrow's train. The pump is for injecting meat with salt water; and he says, Father, that he will be able to procure more oil for you when your present supply is expended. The Doctor is in his usual health. Stanhope a bright, fine little fellow full of health and activity. Brother's position is just the one he desired. His pay as surgeon is ample for his support, and he is able to pursue his studies and investigations.

I forgot to mention that I paid the people for all the corn which they left both at Montevideo and Arcadia. So soon as the meat and molasses and rice are ready for transportation and are sent in, I will see that they are reshipped here.

Your note, Father, matures on the 29th. I send one for renewal, if you desire to run the one in bank for a longer period. If convenient, would it not be wise to pay it? The bank leaves this entirely with you.

How is my dearest little daughter? Do kiss her for me. And believe me ever, my dear father and mother, with best love,

Your ever affectionate son,
Charles C. Jones, Jr.

Howdy for the servants. Will Aunt Susan sell William's wife and family? He is most anxious for me to purchase them so that they can be together.

REV. C. C. JONES *to* COL. CHARLES C. JONES, JR.[8]

Arcadia, *Friday,* January 23rd, 1863

My dear Son,

We were happy to receive yours of the 20th this morning, giving so pleasant an account of your late visit to Buckhead and to Augusta, and of the good health of the people and of your brother and family. . . .

The Montevideo and Arcadia cotton has been delivered under my own eye; and enclosed are two checks on the Farmers' & Mechanics' Bank of date by Mr. Rogers—Montevideo: $2780.50 (fifteen bales); Arcadia $3336.00 (twenty bales)—endorsed over to you. I think with you the note in bank had better be taken up. Please take it up for me; and as the bank has been so accommodating, it will give me pleasure to put it in its power to do me another kindness of the same character should I require it. Send me also a check on your bank in Savannah or on any of the banks in Augusta for $100, which I wish to enclose your brother for Stanhope—a little present for the child which makes him equal with his little cousins, and which I have too long delayed. The balance take and put with the $600 already handed you for moving and plantation expenses towards the $3000. What remains of the $3000 will try and make up shortly. . . .

Have you engaged anyone to go up (white man) with the carts and cattle? Let me know at once. I have spoken to a Mr. Butler, a reliable man in Flemington, who may go for us. You said you wanted *two yoke* of oxen (four). Did you mean *two yoke (four only)* or two *sets (four to a set*—eight in all)? Twenty head of cattle will be enough to send up, as small cattle cannot be sent, and the large will *calve* this spring.

Shall prepare everything as fast as possible to be sent by the railroad—Negroes' things and all—as *no load* can be sent in the carts. On second thought it seems advisable for the interests of Montevideo to retain *July,* and perhaps will not send him up. Do not forget to answer your mother about *Stepney's buggy.* Will send you a statement in relation to the Negroes' corn, etc., left, that you may compare notes with your payment to them for the same.

Your dear child is growing every day, and begins to say words, and is the light of the house. You must come and see her as soon as you can. Mother has been very unwell for weeks with a cold; hope she is improving now. . . .

Your ever affectionate father,

C. C. Jones.

COL. CHARLES C. JONES, JR., *to* MRS. MARY JONES[8]

Savannah, *Friday,* January 23rd, 1863

My very dear Mother,

I thank you for your very kind letter of the 20th inst., which reached me yesterday. Previous to its receipt I had given you an account of matters and things at the plantation and of Brother and family in Augusta.

I will endeavor to find someone here who can take charge of the people and wagons, etc., etc., to go from Arcadia. As yet I have been unable to secure a fit person. Men are scarce.

In regard to Stepney's buggy, he does not wish it sold, and it will be a matter of great convenience for me to have it on the place. One of the mules can be driven up in it. Vehicles of all kinds are at present very scarce, and I would suggest that it be reserved and sent up with the carts and cattle.

I am having five spinning wheels made. They will be ready in a very short time, if not already delivered. Cards I have not, but we can exchange skins for them in Milledgeville; and if you will have the kindness, Mother, to send some skins up by the wagons, I will see that the exchange is made.

In reference to shoes for the people, I can have at a tannery on an adjoining place leather tanned upon these terms: send two raw hides to the tannery, and they send you one tanned in exchange. I can then in the county have the leather thus obtained made up into shoes.

If Mr. Butler be deemed by Father a suitable person to take charge of the wagons and cattle and Negroes, and his services can be procured, the sooner the train is started the better. He will have to take the Louisville road, cross over into Burke County (say, at the ninety-five-mile station), and then he will be only twelve miles from the plantation. . . . If Father does not think Mr. Butler a suitable person, I will send for the overseer, Mr. Sconyers, and make him come down and take charge of the people—which, by the way, may be the best plan after all. But the matter is submitted for his and your decision.

I am pained to hear, my dear mother, that you have been suffering so much, and sincerely trust that you are now quite relieved from your severe and protracted cold. I am happy to know that my dear little daughter is so well. Does she walk or talk yet? I trust that Father is feeling stronger. With warmest love to you both, my dear parents, and many kisses for my precious little daughter, I am ever

Your affectionate son,
Charles C. Jones, Jr.

If Daughter has not been vaccinated, will you please have it done? I enclose some choice matter which I wish used for that purpose, as I know where it came from.

If there be any spare old saddles on the places, please have them sent up with the wagons, as they are much needed.

COL. CHARLES C. JONES, JR., *to* REV. C. C. JONES[8]

Savannah, *Monday,* January 26th, 1863

My very dear Father,

I am in receipt of your kind favor of the 23rd inst., with enclosures as stated: say, check in payment of Montevideo cotton ($2780.50), check in payment of Arcadia cotton ($3336.00), both of which have been paid. In compliance with your request I have today taken up your note in the Bank of the State of Georgia for $800, which is herewith enclosed, and also have purchased check on Augusta payable to your order for $100. Total: $900, which leaves $1880.50 to be applied as you desire to the part payment of corn, etc., etc., on Buckhead place, for which, Father, please accept my warmest thanks. With this sum and my proportion of the Arcadia crop, together with the contributions from Brother and Robert, I will be able so materially to reduce my indebtedness in bank as soon to liquidate the whole amount, if life be spared, D.V.

Please tell me if any portion of the Arcadia cotton sold was owned by Uncle William, as I desire to account with Brother and Robert for their proportions at the earliest practicable day. If any portion be Uncle William's, be pleased at your convenience to let me know the exact amount in order that I may account to him for it.

I think the five bales upland can be sold possibly at the station at from fifteen to eighteen cents. I will inquire and let you know at the earliest practicable moment.

Twenty head of cattle will be ample to send up, and four yoke of oxen—say, eight in all. If an additional yoke could be conveniently spared, I would be very glad if it could be sent up with the others, as I would like to present them to George Owens, who has always been very kind to me, and is now planting not far from the Buckhead place.

I have promised Stepney to let him come down very soon and attend to some matters. He will probably be here next week. I am about to have my fine stallion Red Rover brought to Savannah for me to use as a parade horse. I have now so much riding to do that I am compelled to have two horses, and the price asked for suitable animals is so enormous that I must economize.

We have telegraphic advices of a very heavy demonstration on the North Carolina coast by the Federals. No positive intelligence as yet of any advance from the coast.

We have nothing of special interest in the city. I hope, my dear father, that you are feeling better, and that my dear mother is relieved of her cold. I am rejoiced to hear that my precious little daughter is so well. I trust that I may be able to see you all very soon. With warmest love to all at home, I am ever

Your affectionate son,
Charles C. Jones, Jr.

Rev. C. C. Jones *to* Col. Charles C. Jones, Jr.[8]

Arcadia, *Tuesday*, January 27th, 1863

My dear Son,

Have just received yours of yesterday, enclosing the note for $800 paid in bank and the check for $100 on branch of state bank in Augusta, and memorandum of receipt of drafts for the cotton sold. None of the Arcadia cotton belongs to your Uncle William. He had his cotton hauled and ginned at Captain Winn's, and I believe sold at the same time with ours at fifty cents. The money paid for corn sold *here* I will hand you when you come out—at $1.25; but no more (after what is now sold is delivered) at that price. It is now selling to government out here at $1.50, and if the troops give that to others they may give it to us. Government is buying up the corn in Southwest Georgia at one dollar per bushel—I presume to forestall speculation in the spring and summer.

You said you had paid the people for their corn left at Arcadia and Montevideo. Arcadia I know nothing about. The corn left by them at Montevideo is as follows: Porter 7 bushels; Jackson 12; Betty 12½; Rose 2; Pulaski 7; Peggy 2½; Sam 1. Total: 44. Jackson left 9 bushels rough rice not well winnowed, and Tom some to be winnowed and measured. This I presume you did not pay for. They beg to have it sent up for them. Will have it properly winnowed and measured off.

I think Mr. Butler a reliable man, and would take up the carts and cattle and mules carefully; and will see him, D.V., this week again. The rice for Mrs. Harlow and for your brother has to be put in bags for want of barrels (just as good), and will with the bacon and syrup and other matters belonging to the people be properly marked. The oxcarts can carry *no load* except provisions by the way and some hides and the sail of the *Duck* for a covering on the way. Stepney's buggy may be taken to pieces and put in the carts, or driven up by Mr. Butler with one of the mules or Stepney's mare if she goes up.

Am glad to learn Stepney comes down next week with your horse Red Rover. He can then come out and see after his little matters, and take everything along with him by the cars when he returns. This strikes us as a good plan.

Your Aunt Susan has declined selling Kate and her family on second thought; says she "would much prefer to hire her at a *moderate* rate." . . .

Mother, I hope, is some better of her cold, but the cough still distresses her.

Your dear child grows more and more interesting day by day, and we hope will walk and talk in a little while. Knowing what her early infancy was, she is a wonder of health and progress to us who have had the care of her from the beginning.

I will look out a pair of oxen for your friend Mr. George Owens and send them up with the rest. Mother unites in much love, and Baby sends kisses.

Your affectionate father,

C. C. Jones.

P.S. The pump and cod-liver oil have not come. Did you send them?

Mother's tea is nearly out. Please get a pound from Claghorn & Cunningham on my account of some I see they recently advertise, and send it out by Stepney for me.

I look with great solicitude to the movements in North Carolina. We shall be signally blessed if it pleases God to give us the victory there. And a repulse of the enemy will contribute still to help on a right view of matters North and West.

COL. CHARLES C. JONES, JR., *to* REV. C. C. JONES[8]
Savannah, *Thursday,* January 29th, 1863
My dear Father,

I am today favored with your kind letter of the 27th inst., and am glad to hear that the enclosures of the 26th reached you safely.

I have sent to Brother and Robert checks of *one thousand dollars each* on account their interest in the amount cotton sold. As yet I have not had a leisure moment to make up the Arcadia accounts, or to give them the exact statement of amounts to which they are respectively entitled, or to exhibit the precise sums which they should respectively contribute towards the feeding, clothing, and removal of their Negroes. The margin of corn sold will in all probability cover these expenses, and also the additional item of war taxes, which may, under the contemplated legislation of Congress, prove a very important item for the current year.

I am happy to hear that you will get $1.50 for the corn. It is worth that amount; for all supplies, in consequence of the redundancy and consequent depreciation of the currency, are already—and will be even to a greater degree—appreciated in nominal value. The memorandum of corn furnished in your letter as left by the people at Montevideo corresponds with the amounts for which I have settled with them respectively, paying at the rate of one dollar per bushel.

Bags will answer every purpose for shipping the rice, etc., etc. Stepney's buggy had best be driven up, and his mare might be sent with it. He will himself be down, I hope, early next week—probably before the wagons leave the place. It is the prudent plan, Father, to send no load with the wagons other than the provisions necessary to feed the animals on the way. If you will let me know some days before the articles are shipped per railroad, I will see that arrangements are made here for transshipment from one depot to the other. Let me beg also, Father, that you will furnish me if convenient with a list of articles.

I rejoice to hear that dear Mother is better. Her cold has been one of unusual severity. I am very happy to know that my dear little daughter is so well. I long to see all at home, and will embrace the earliest opportunity for spending a day with you. Do ask Mother if there is anything here which little Mary Ruth needs. I have not sent the box containing the pump and the oil because I feared to commit it to the tender mercies of the freight agent. I trust, however, that I will secure an early opportunity for forwarding it, and will at the same time send the tea.

You have already noticed the fact of the recent effort of the enemy to silence Genesis Point battery. The demonstration was more formidable than any hitherto made, and certainly one ironclad vessel was present and participated in the bombardment. Is it not remarkable that after a bombardment of over five hours no injury was caused either to the fort or the garrison? The object of the enemy evidently is to capture the *Nashville*, now ready for sea, armed as a privateer under the name of the *Rattlesnake*, and lying a few miles above the fort watching her chances for going to sea. A large reward has been offered by the Lincoln government for the capture or destruction of that vessel. We are not credibly informed that the attacking vessels suffered any damage from the fire of the guns of the fort.

The general indications from various quarters point to an increasing and widespread dissension in many parts of the North and West. Let us hope that they will ripen into a political revolution which will produce most important changes in our favor. We are strong in North Carolina, and it is confidently believed that we will be able successfully to repel any advance of the enemy. General Longstreet is there with his army corps.

I regret very much Aunt Susan's determination in reference to *Kate and her family*. The last time I was at the plantation William begged me very earnestly to try and purchase his wife and children, for whom he appears to cherish a strong attachment; and I held out to him the hope that I would be able to do so. I am anxious to purchase them, and still hope—unless Aunt Susan has some special reason to the contrary—that she will agree to sell them to me, in order that they may be with their husband and father. Should you see Aunt Susan at some leisure moment, will you, Father, see if she is positively resolved not to sell?

We have nothing of special interest here. With warmest love to self, my dear father, and to my dear mother and precious little daughter, I am ever
Your affectionate son,
Charles C. Jones, Jr.

COL. CHARLES C. JONES, JR., *to* REV. *and* MRS. C. C. JONES[8]
Savannah, *Sunday,* February 1st, 1863
My dear Father and Mother,

The quiet of the peaceful Sabbath has been disturbed by the sound of the enemy's guns, and the stillness of the sanctuary invaded by the harsh discord of hostile cannon. For the fourth time the battery at Genesis Point has been attacked, and this time again by an ironclad armed with eleven- and fifteen-inch guns. But the fervent prayers which have this day ascended to the Father of Mercies have been heard and answered. The bombardment of the fort lasted five hours, and wonderful to say, resulted in little or no injury to the work. Major Gallie, commanding, was killed, and seven privates slightly wounded. One thirty-two-pounder gun was permanently disabled. Necessary repairs to the earthwork were completed two hours after the bombardment had ceased.

The conduct of the garrison is worthy of the highest commendation. The men and officers behaved most gallantly, fighting hour after hour with the utmost deliberation and with the cool resolve never to surrender the fort, but to stand to their posts until every gun was dismounted, and then, retiring within the bombproofs, to use their small arms in the event the enemy attempted to land. The battery will be held at all hazards. Supporting forces are in the vicinity, besides one light battery and two sections of the "Old Chatham" along the river bank, to contest the passage in case the enemy's vessels pass the fort. The *Rattlesnake* and the steam tug *Columbus*, if the worst comes to the worst, will be sunk in the river above the fort. The armament will also be at once increased by the addition of a ten-inch columbiad.

It is a matter worthy of note that this is the first time that a *fifteen-inch gun* has ever been used in the history of actual warfare. The shells thrown from that gun weigh three hundred and thirty-five pounds. Think of an open earthwork resisting a bombardment from such a monster for five hours, and that enormous gun located in an impenetrable iron turret from whose sides our heaviest solid shot glanced harmlessly away, or when striking them full were broken into fragments. This ironclad was assisted by four gunboats and one mortar boat behaving in the most cowardly manner; for while the ironclad, confident in her invulnerability, approached to within some six or eight hundred yards of the fort, the latter vessels remained at a distance of over two miles—from that point, however, discharging their long-range rifled guns and mortars, which threw their projectiles full into the fort. The flags from the ironclad were all shot away, and not a rascal from within the secure confines of the turret dared show himself to replace them. The upper and back part of Major Gallie's head was all blown off—probably struck by the fragment of a shell.

This afternoon another ironclad appeared within three miles of the Thunderbolt battery accompanied by a gunboat. The former fired a few shell into an island just opposite and retired. We may have an attack upon that battery tomorrow. I went down with General Mercer to that point this afternoon. General Hunter has returned, assuming command of the Federal forces in this vicinity, and promises an early attack upon Savannah. The bombardment of Genesis Point battery will probably soon be renewed by the enemy. I trust that it will please God to give us courage and ability successfully to meet and repulse the invaders.

I send by George for you, my dear parents, two pounds of very excellent tea, which please accept as a little present. I wish that I had something better for you and for my dear little daughter, but I am now *a beggar myself,* and have told George to ask you to send us *anything to eat* which you can spare from the place. Our market here is miserable, and everything at the most inflated prices. George will carry with him the box from Augusta.

With warmest love to you both, my dearest parents, and many kisses for my precious little daughter, I am ever

Your affectionate son,

Charles C. Jones, Jr.

Ten dollars enclosed for my sweet little daughter.

What gallant deeds in Charleston harbor!

The general would not consent to my going to Genesis Point today, and for the reason that he wanted me in readiness with my light batteries to meet any demonstration of the enemy from the direction of the Isle of Hope, which is not deemed at all improbable.

I hope you will soon hear from the *Atlanta* and Commodore Tattnall.

REV. C. C. JONES *to* COL. CHARLES C. JONES[8]

Arcadia, *Monday,* February 2nd, 1863

My dear Son,

Your letter of this morning greatly relieved our anxiety. We supposed you had been at Genesis Point. Thanks be to God for His mercy! May our brave men be always so sustained, and those famous ironclads become to fortifications weak as other vessels! We with our state mourn the loss of *Major Gallie!* All honor to his memory, and I hope peace to his soul! How remarkable: but one killed in the action! What news from Charleston! May our *old commodore* be favored with some exploit suitable to his fame and character!

Mother thanks you over and over for sending the delightful tea. She has been as busy as possible to send you what she has *at hand* (as you gave her no notice) as follows: one bag potatoes, one ditto peas and pumpkin, four pieces corned beef, one ham, one gammon, one bag rice, one bag grist, one turkey, three fowls, one bag grist for Abram. Sorry no tanias. And groundnuts very poor.

A great deal of love to you. And a great deal of haste, for George is loading up and putting the horse in the cart. Baby well. Write every chance.

Your affectionate father,

C. C. Jones.

COL. CHARLES C. JONES, JR., *to* REV. C. C. JONES[8]

Savannah, *Wednesday,* February 4th, 1863

My dear Father,

I was agreeably surprised last evening by the pleasure of Robert's company, and am happy to learn from him that all at home are well. Mr. Ward and myself are under every obligation to you and dear Mother for your kind remembrance of us. The articles, I understand, have arrived by the freight train, and George will have them brought from the depot today. They will be of great assistance to us.

Letters from Augusta and from the Burke place this morning received state that all are well. Agrippa is up, but not strong enough yet to go into the field. I have directed that he be kept from exposing himself until the danger of any relapse seems overpassed. Betty is now in one of the new houses, comfortably located, and she will receive every attention when the day of her confinement arrives. We have ten plows running, and more will be going in a few days. Stepney leaves the station (No. 9½) with Red Rover in the freight train of tomorrow; so soon as he arrives I will send him out.

Brother says all are well with him, and that he has just completed and forwarded to the surgeon general an article on tetanus, which I presume will be a valuable contribution to the profession, especially at this time.

The Lincoln ironclads now on our coast are far more formidable than the *Monitor,* which fought with the *Virginia.* Commodore Tattnall has full descriptions of them. It was expected that the attack upon Genesis Point battery would have been renewed today. It has been delayed, however—I presume in consequence of this high northeast wind. We all wish that it would increase to a gale, and send the boasted war vessels disabled wrecks upon our inhospitable sandbars.

Both Savannah and Charleston are liable to be attacked almost any day. If the enemy makes a bold attack upon Charleston with their combined land and naval forces, it will be one of the grandest sights in the history of modern warfare. That city is now as ready with her defenses as she ever will be. We can trust neither in fleets nor numerous armies, but our eyes and hearts will be turned to the God of Battles, who saves not by many nor by few, but by His own omnipotent arm.

With warmest love to dear Mother, Sister, and the little ones, and special kisses for my precious little daughter, I am ever, my dear father,

Your affectionate son,
Charles C. Jones, Jr.

REV. C. C. JONES *to* COL. CHARLES C. JONES, JR.[8]

Arcadia, *Tuesday,* February 10th, 1863

My dear Son,

We hoped for a letter from you this morning, our last intelligence being that you were suffering with cold and fever; but the daily expectation of an attack from the enemy no doubt keeps you employed, and you have few leisure moments to spare. In the event of an attack our united prayer is that God would shield your person and your life, and enable you to do your duty to your country in His fear like a patriot and a Christian man, and in any event that you may be prepared for His will. If ever a people were called upon to put their assured trust in God, and to fight manfully to the last extremity for liberty, for humanity, for civilization and religion, we are the people. And God will bless us. This is my confidence.

Your Aunt Susan accompanies your Uncle John to the city, and have thought it best for you to see her in relation to Kate and her family and know her decision. And I have kept William a day over to assist in getting our shipment ready. And you could let me hear by tomorrow's mail, or by return of your uncle, about Kate; and if she is to go, I will see *her off with William*—the best way for her to go. The baggage or freight train will not go in again until Thursday; and will send everything in on that day.

The oxcarts (two) with ten oxen (eight for Buckhead and two for your friend Mr. Owens, which you can select), together with two mules, Stepney's mare and buggy and harness, bridle and saddle, two lumber chains, two draw chains, five yokes, two reap hooks, one wedge, one ax (Pharaoh's), five and a half cowhides, and one roll sheepskins left on Friday the 6th under charge of Mr. Jesse Butler. Were to have left the day before, but rain and cold prevented. Long and short forage sent along for man and beast. Pharaoh and Dick only sent. Cattle could not be sent: too poor, too cold, country too bare of forage. I give Mr. Butler two dollars per day and pay his expenses. I will settle with him. Gave him fifty dollars at his starting, which hope will be more than enough for everything. Shall write Mr. Sconyers of his coming and give him a list of matters under his hand.

Your affectionate father,
C. C. Jones.

MRS. MARY JONES *to* COL. CHARLES C. JONES, JR.[8]

Arcadia, *Tuesday,* February 10th, 1863

Enclosed, my dear son, is an order for the railroad dividend. When collected please pay for the *sugar mill,* and send me the balance. Also twenty dollars if you can get me some brandy or any good spirit for your father's use. Joe prescribed it; and such is his health that I see it is absolutely necessary for him. I send a nice glass bottle for it. Also $173.75 from the sale of corn at Arcadia. And your Uncle John kindly offers to take a small package which you can send George for to the Pulaski House. . . . Please send the brandy if possible by him.

Many thanks, my very dear son, for your present of the tea. It is delicious, and the only article of luxury I ever crave. Your precious child is well, and growing intellectually and physically. If you will send out the bags by my brother, I could return them filled with grists, etc., when you wish them. These are solemn times. May we all be stayed upon the Everlasting God! And may He guide and arm and shield you, my own dear child!

Ever your affectionate mother,
Mary Jones.

COL. CHARLES C. JONES, JR., *to* REV. *and* MRS. C. C. JONES[8]

Savannah, *Tuesday,* February 10th, 1863

My very dear Father and Mother,

I had the pleasure of seeing Robert, Sister Carrie, and Stanhope on Saturday last. They were all well. Brother is much interested in the pursuit of his professional engagements, and seems much pleased with his present position as surgeon, which renders him perfectly easy in money matters, and also enables him to carry on uninterruptedly his favorite investigations.

Poor Mr. Eve is failing rapidly, I fear. His eyesight is now seriously impaired, and he lies most of the time in an insensible condition.

It is thought that the enemy contemplates an attack upon Savannah, and we are using every exertion to prepare the city for a successful resistance. Troops are returning from North Carolina. Three regiments have already arrived, and more are expected this evening.

I hope, my dear parents, to be able to see you and my precious little daughter on Thursday of this week. . . . We have nothing of special interest today from the coast. . . . With warmest love to you both, and tenderest kisses for my dear little daughter,

Your ever affectionate son,
Charles C. Jones, Jr.

COL. CHARLES C. JONES, JR., *to* REV. *and* MRS. C. C. JONES[8]

Savannah, *Saturday,* February 14th, 1863

My very dear Father and Mother,

After my short but most privileged visit to you and to my precious little daughter on Thursday, I returned to Bryan on Friday, inspected the light artillery I now have in that county, visited Fort McAllister, and reached the city Friday evening. Found the artillery in very excellent condition.

The scars caused by the shot and shell fired by the enemy on the 1st inst. are still numerous in and about the fort, and will continue for many days to come. The battery there is now much stronger than it was on the day of the engagement. All damage to the traverses, bombproofs, and parapet has been repaired. In fact, the parapet has been strengthened by the addition of at least three feet of sand, and a ten-inch gun has been added to the armament. An effort is being made to secure torpedoes in the stream below the fort so as to blow up the ironclad when next she takes her position to bombard. I trust the attempt may be successful. One achievement of this character will inspire the abolitionists with a most wholesome dread of our rivers. The memory of the Yazoo torpedo is still quite distinct in their cowardly recollections.

Today, in company with Generals Beauregard and Mercer and other officers, I went down the river on an inspection of our advanced batteries. When at the obstructions, we could with our glasses see several of the enemy's vessels lying above Fort Pulaski. General Beauregard is very pleasant in his intercourse with his officers. I had considerable conversation with him, and he possesses by his manners and deportment the agreeable art of attaching his soldiers to him. He is a man of great physical power, capable of uncommon endurance, plain in his habits, temperate, entirely free from everything savoring of profanity or levity, easy of approach, deferential in his manners, and characteristically polite. Has a rapid, quick eye to positions, and possesses all the qualifications of a first-class engineer. I enjoyed the morning thus spent. He will probably be here for several days.

I sincerely trust, my dear father, that you are feeling better. I cannot tell you how pained I was from the bottom of my heart to see you so weak, and suffering so much from that severe cold. I hope, my dear mother, that you will soon be restored to your accustomed degree of good health, and that my precious little daughter is still well. I forgot to get a lock of her hair before I left. Will you have the kindness, Mother, to sever one for me and send it to me by some convenient opportunity?

Enclosed are some pistol caps which I promised Uncle John. They are in a separate envelope.

William, Kate, and their children were safely shipped on board the cars, and I doubt not reached home in due season.

We have nothing of special interest today except some telegrams in reference to the condition of matters and things in the West, which if true are very important. But we have long since learned to receive with no little distrust the unsupported statements of even the most "reliable" gentlemen. With warmest love to you both, my dear father and mother, and many kisses for my precious little daughter, I am ever

Your affectionate son,
Charles C. Jones, Jr.

Sunday Afternoon, February 15th, 1863. This morning early Stepney made his appearance. He brings the cheering intelligence that all the people are well and contented; that the boys and wagons have safely arrived; and that William, Kate, and the children reached the station without accident. For this, as well as all other and great mercies, grateful thanks to the Giver of All Good. Stepney goes out in the morning. He will see what hogs he can purchase in the county.

Your affectionate son,
Charles C. Jones, Jr.

COL. CHARLES C. JONES, JR., *to* REV. *and* MRS. C. C. JONES[g]
Savannah, *Wednesday,* February 18th, 1863

My dear Father and Mother,

We have nothing of special interest here. A review of the troops will probably be had by General Beauregard on Friday and Saturday, if he is not at an earlier day called to Charleston. I have not felt very bright today, but hope, D.V., to be better on the morrow. I write to assure you, my dearest parents, and my precious little daughter of my constant and most affectionate remembrance. The hog and pigs arrived, and were duly forwarded. As ever,

Your affectionate son,
Charles C. Jones, Jr.

MRS. MARY JONES *to* COL. CHARLES C. JONES, JR.[g]
Arcadia, *Thursday,* February 19th, 1863

My very dear Son,

Your affectionate favor was received by the morning's mail, and I am up beyond our usual hour to send you assurances of our daily—I may say *now* hourly—remembrances. It is our precious privilege in this dark hour, when we know not where the storm will burst or upon whom the shaft of death will fall, to bear you in the arms of faith to the mercy seat, to the Cross of our Almighty Redeemer. He hath all power in heaven and on earth; and I entreat Him to protect and shield my beloved son, and to give him an assured hope of His love and forgiveness and acceptance, and in the trying and responsible station which you now hold to give you wisdom and prudence and courage, that you may be armed for the conflict and never waver or draw back from duty. I know that you have and will render to your country the fidelity and devotion of a brave man and a true patriot; and my hope and confidence for your safety and protection are in God alone. Above all things may He lift upon you the light of His countenance, and prepare you for life or for death as His sovereign will designs!

What can I do for you? By Stepney, who will not leave before Monday, I will try and send you some poultry, etc. Do let me know whenever I can do anything here for your comfort.

Your dear father has been very much weakened by his recent cold; and the increased anxieties weigh upon him. Today I have packed several trunks with necessary clothing, and shall try and prepare for emergencies; for emphatically we know not what a day may bring forth. . . .

Stepney has been busy every moment since his arrival. The meeting between himself and his father was touching; the old man laid his hands upon him and sobbed aloud.

Next Sabbath will be our Communion at Midway, and wish that you could be with us. Your father and I ardently desire before we "go hence to be no more" that you should join us around the Lord's table.

Your precious child is very bright and well excepting the little eruptions, which result, I hope, from teething. We talk of you daily, and night and morning she folds her little hands to ask God's blessing on her dear papa. It is late, and I must close, with best love from Father, kisses from Daughter, and the constant affection of

Your mother,
Mary Jones.

REV. C. C. JONES *to* COL. CHARLES C. JONES, JR.[8]
Arcadia, *Thursday*, February 19th, 1863
Will you put the enclosed piece in the papers if you think it worth publishing?

Dr. Howe writes Robert cotton osnaburgs may be had in Columbia at sixty-two and a half cents per yard for Negro summer clothing. Mother asks if it will be well to engage at that price there.

Did you see the person from the Bainbridge factory?
C.C.J.

COL. CHARLES C. JONES, JR., *to* MRS. MARY JONES[g]

Savannah, *Saturday,* February 21st, 1863

My very dear Mother,

I am this morning in receipt of your kind letter of yesterday, and most sincerely thank you for all your precious remembrance of me, for all your best wishes, and also for the sweet lock of hair from my dear little daughter.

I have been pretty sick this week: high fever, cold, and sore throat. The attack reminded me very much of the one from which I suffered when Ruth and our little Julia were both so ill near two years ago. I was taken sick on Tuesday last. Dr. Sullivan has been attending me, and through God's great mercy I am up again, and although somewhat weak, this morning resumed office duties. As a general rule my system very rapidly recovers from any attack, and I trust that I soon will be quite well again.

I have just sent Father's article to Mr. Sneed, editor *Republican,* with the request that he publish and also furnish copy to *News* for publication. I read the communication with much interest, and I fully concur in the views therein presented.

Yesterday General Beauregard had a review of the infantry and cavalry forces in this vicinity. The display is said to have been very creditable, and the general commanding expressed himself as much pleased with the drill and discipline of the troops. In consequence of my illness the light artillery did not appear upon parade. If General Beauregard remains until next week, probably a parade for inspection and review of that arm of the service will be had. Today the general has gone to Genesis Point.

We have nothing of interest from the coast. In fact, the pickets from the lower points report fewer vessels than usual in the vicinity of Port Royal. A remarkable tardiness and indecision appear to characterize all the movements of the enemy. General Beauregard seems confident of our ability, under God, both here and at Charleston to resist successfully any attack which the enemy may make. All we need here is an additional supply of heavy guns and men to make the defenses perfect, or very nearly so.

So soon as the articles are shipped from No. 3 I will have them forwarded from this point. I have just purchased and paid for 1559 pounds cured hogsheads, which have been boxed up and sent to the place. This will be a great assistance; and I have given directions not to have this meat issued until summer, but to have it opened, resalted, hung up, and smoked. Latest advices report all well.

I wish, my dear parents, that I could come out and see you and my dear little daughter; but just at this time it is a difficult matter to leave the city, as it is not known at what moment one's services may be needed. I sincerely trust that Father is better of his severe cold, and that you, Mother, are rapidly regaining your accustomed degree of good health. I am happy to know that my precious little daughter continues so well. With warmest love to you both, my dear father and mother, and many kisses for my sweet little daughter, I am ever

Your affectionate son,
Charles C. Jones, Jr.

347

I think it would be well to engage the Negro summer clothing at sixty-two and a half cents.

I spoke to Mr. Hamilton about the purchase of the five bales cotton at No. 3, and he promised to let me know whether he would buy, and at what price. Will endeavor to see him again at the earliest practicable moment and learn his determination.

Col. Charles C. Jones, Jr., *to* Rev. C. C. Jones[8]
Savannah, Saturday, February 21st, 1863

My dear Father,

Since writing today I have seen the Messrs. Hamilton, to whom I had spoken in reference to the purchase of your five bales short staple cotton. They tell me that their factory is too far from the railroad to haul the cotton there. I think you can find a market here for the cotton at a reasonable figure—say, eighteen or twenty cents; and I would advise that you send it in, with any stained cotton you may have, to Messrs. Richardson & Martin, who will, I think, effect the best possible sale of it. If unmarketable here, the round bales (short staple cotton) may be shipped to Augusta and sold to the factories there. To them the shape of the bags can be no objection.

Nothing new. I am feeling stronger this evening. . . . With warmest love to self, dear Mother, and my precious little daughter, I am ever

Your affectionate son,
Charles C. Jones, Jr.

I hope to send Mother's tea out by Monday's express.

Rev. C. C. Jones *to* Col. Charles C. Jones, Jr.[8]
Arcadia, Monday, February 23rd, 1863

My dearest Son,

Your two favors of 21st came to hand this morning, and we were sorry to learn how sick you have been. May it please God to give you rapid return to health! But do not presume and expose too soon. Better not be present or command at the review and inspection of your arm of service than run serious risks of bringing on a relapse. Your throat needs special care. This is a gentle stroke of God's hand upon you to draw you to Himself, and not put off your open profession of the ever blessed Saviour. Death is doing his ordinary work around us; and many who saw the commencement of the war, and were exposed to its shafts, have been removed quietly and unexpectedly from life to the retribution of the life to come! May that day not find us unprepared!

Yesterday was our Communion at Midway. Six whites admitted. Full congregation of white and black for the times. On our return home found your dear little one, whom we had left in perfect health, with fever and

348

looking wan. No reason for it save cutting teeth that we can divine. She revived her spirits in the evening, and after a pretty comfortable night is without fever and as well as usual this morning; and we hope it will pass off.

The articles for Buckhead after delay got off in Saturday's train: one bag rice, Dr. J. Jones; one ditto, Mrs. Harlow; two bags salt, C. C. J., Jr.; five ditto rough rice, two barrels syrup, one ditto pork, one grindstone, one barrel sundries, two bundles and one box ditto. Stepney has succeeded after some effort in securing some hogs, and will leave, D.V., by the freight train tomorrow (24th) with them and some sundries in charge. His visit in giving such pleasant accounts of the change of the people has been of the nature of a public benefit. My only regret is that they are not *all* removed; for whether we are disturbed or not, we plant in uncertainty, and it becomes a year of anxiety all round.

Mr. J. W. Anderson is my factor, and presume ought to send him the few bales left, unless he gives me no assurance of being able to sell the cotton. If it were in a safe place, would as leave keep as sell it. It is very fine upland.

Your brother in a letter received this morning promises to pay us a visit between Tuesday and Thursday of this week, if the medical director of this division, Dr. Miller, will grant him leave of absence for a few days.

I think I mentioned Mr. Butler's return. Got up all safe. You can select the pair of oxen for your friend Mr. Owens when you go up. Jackson *knows* them all.

Mother says Stepney will *bring in your ducks* tomorrow, and that we will try and supply you with salt so that you need not buy any. Your purchase of the bacon is good. What did you pay? Any more to be had?

Your aunt and Cousin Laura dine with us. All well, and all unite in much love. . . . We were much gratified with your account of General Beauregard, and glad that you had so pleasant an occasion of making his acquaintance. My respects to Mr. Ward.

From your ever affectionate father,

C. C. Jones.

Mother says gargle your throat with *warm salt and water,* and put the *mustard plaster to your throat every night.*

COL. CHARLES C. JONES, JR., *to* REV. C. C. JONES[8]

Savannah, *Friday,* February 27th, 1863

My very dear Father,

I returned today from Augusta, having successfully accomplished the matter of business for which I was detailed. I will soon have here a splendid six-gun battery of twelve-pounder Napoleon guns, the very best field gun which can be employed in our section of the state. I also have notice from Charleston that two very fine rifled guns will be at my disposal tomorrow. Thus I am endeavoring to retire all the light six-pounder guns and to supply their places with weapons of larger caliber, longer range, and of more

349

improved pattern. I will spare neither time nor labor in rendering this arm of the service as efficient as practicable.

Your kind favor arrived during my absence, and I thank you, Father, sincerely for all your kindness. I feel today a little used up by travel, for I am not entirely strong yet; but I expect to be quite refreshed in the morning. My cold is much better, and my throat now gives me no pain.

I deeply regret to hear that my dear little daughter has had fever, and trust that the attack was only temporary, and that she is already quite restored to health.

Saw Sister Carrie and Stanhope in Augusta. Both quite well, and desire sincerest remembrances. Cousin Philo and Eva both well, but Mr. Eve is gradually growing weaker and weaker.

The articles have all been forwarded to No.9½. I find today a letter from Mr. Sconyers which reports the safe arrival of Stepney, etc., and also the fact that all the people are well.

We have nothing of special interest from the coast today. Do give warmest love to dear Mother. Kiss my precious little daughter for me. And believe me ever, my dear father,

Your affectionate son,
Charles C. Jones, Jr.

I congratulate you upon the Doctor's visit, and I trust that God will bless his medical skill to your great relief and comfort. Do remember me to him.

I paid fifteen cents for the hogsheads. Would have procured more, but there were no more to be had.

COL. CHARLES C. JONES, JR., *to* REV. *and* MRS. C. C. JONES[g]

Savannah, *Monday,* March 2nd, 1863

My very dear Father and Mother,

The enemy are lying in force in Ossabaw Sound, and threaten the batteries at Beaulieu and Genesis Point. What their absolute designs are we can only conjecture. We are endeavoring to be thoroughly prepared for any emergency—at least as thoroughly prepared as we can be with the men, arms, and ammunition at command.

We are sadly in need of a greater number of heavy guns. This morning I received two splendid Blakely rifled guns, with harness, limbers, and two hundred rounds to the piece, which I have turned over to my old company. This is a very valuable addition to the efficiency of that battery. I am also in daily expectation of receiving from the Augusta arsenal some twelve-pounder Napoleon guns, and am using every effort to improve, as far as lies in my power, the condition of the light artillery in this military district.

You have seen an account of the destruction of the *Nashville* by the ironclad *Montauk* in the Great Ogeechee River—perhaps in many points of view not an unfortunate affair for us. That vessel, with a drinking captain and a rough crew, has been keeping that neighborhood in hot water for many days.

Dr. Palmer preached twice yesterday in the Independent Presbyterian Church. Both very fine sermons. A letter from Mr. Sconyers tells me that all are well at Buckhead, and matters progressing favorably. I write in much haste, but with warmest love to you both, my dearest father and mother, many kisses for my precious little daughter, and kindest remembrances for the Doctor. As ever,

Your affectionate son,
Charles C. Jones, Jr.

I send per express some of dear little Julia's jewelry for her little sister, and also a pair of shoes.

Howdy for the servants.

COL. CHARLES C. JONES, JR., *to* REV. *and* MRS. C. C. JONES[8]

Savannah, *Tuesday,* March 3rd, 1863

My very dear Father and Mother,

The abolitionists, with three ironclads, four gunboats, and several mortar boats, attacked Fort McAllister this morning. They opened fire about half-past eight, and the engagement continued without intermission until near half-past four o'clock P.M. The last dispatch, which left the fort after the firing had ceased, reports that only two of our men were wounded during the whole of this protracted bombardment, and they only slightly. The carriage of the eight-inch columbiad was disabled by a shot from the enemy. A new one has been sent out; and the gun itself, which was not injured, will be remounted during the night and be all ready for action in the morning. The injury to the parapet of the fort is slight, and will be repaired during the night. The garrison is in fine spirits, and are determined to hold the fort to the last extremity. It is truly wonderful how mercifully and abundantly the good and great God of Battles has encircled our brave men with the protection of His all-powerful arm, shielding them from harm amid dangers imminent and protracted. To Him our hearts ascend in humble, fervent gratitude for the past; from Him we earnestly implore like favor in the future. If the Lord is on our side, as we honestly trust and believe He is, we will not fear what our enemies, with all their boasted strength, can do unto us.

The enemy seems determined to reduce this fort if practicable, probably with a view to the destruction of the railroad bridge. That little fort has thus far so successfully and so bravely resisted every effort on their part for its reduction that they will doubtless use every endeavor, as a matter of pride, to compass its destruction. There is no question of the fact that it is a remarkably well-constructed earthwork—well traversed. The lessons of the past and of the present so demonstrate. It is almost a miniature edition of Vicksburg. In like manner must all our defenses be conducted.

The dispatch to which I alluded above states further that the ironclads, etc., retired, apparently with a view to obtaining an additional supply of ammunition. They dropped down the river only a little way, and a store ship soon joined them and appeared to be serving out ammunition. The attack will doubtless be renewed in the morning; in fact, while I write from my office in the barracks at this 9½ P.M., I hear guns in the direction of Genesis Point. The enemy will probably continue the bombardment at intervals during the night, with a view to wearying our men and preventing the necessary repairs to the fort; and when the morning light again cleverly dawns, the attack will be renewed with vigor. We are supplying the deficiencies in ammunition caused by the expenditures of the day. It is thought that one ironclad was seriously injured. This may be, however, only *conjecture;* we hope such is the *fact*.

The land force on our side, now in the vicinity of the fort and prepared to resist any effort of the enemy to land, consists of the 29th Georgia Regiment, the sharpshooter battalion, two companies in the fort, our light battery, and some seven or more cavalry companies. With the natural advantages of the country these men, if they do their duty, ought to accomplish a great deal.

We have been reinforced at this point by the arrival of the brave General Walker. General Clingman reached the city today with his brigade of three regiments, and General Taliaferro is expected with his brigade. General Beauregard announces himself prepared to come over at any moment that his services are needed. I trust and confidently believe that we will, with the blessing of Heaven, be able successfully to defend the city from the expected attack, and to teach the enemy a fearful lesson which will not be speedily forgotten.

I am getting my light artillery in capital condition, and hope, when the opportunity presents itself, to render efficient service.

The Doctor came in this afternoon and is staying with us. Mr. Ward also returned by the Charleston train. Many, many thanks, my very dear mother, for your kind and most acceptable remembrance of us.

I am very much pained, my dear father, to hear that you are still so weak. All I can do is to hope and pray that you may soon be better, and that it would please God in tender mercy to us all to prolong your days, so precious to us all. . . . Do, my dear parents, let me know if I can do anything for you at any time, or for my dear little daughter. I wish very much to see you all, but at present it is impossible for me to leave the post of duty, for it is emphatically the fact that we know not what an hour may bring forth. . . . With warmest love to you both, my dear father and mother, and many tender kisses for my dear little daughter, I am ever

Your affectionate son,
Charles C. Jones, Jr.

REV. C. C. JONES *to* COL. CHARLES C. JONES, JR.[8]

Arcadia, *Wednesday,* March 4th, 1863

My dear Son,

Your kind favor of last evening reached us this morning, and afforded us the very information which we were anxious to receive—circumstantial and reliable. No paper from Savannah came.

Surely we have reason to bless God and take courage and fight more manfully than ever. The bombardment of Genesis Point is one of *the events* of this most eventful war. The failure of the vaunted ironclads will have a great moral effect. The enemy will have less confidence, and we stronger assurance, of being able with properly constructed fortifications and good armament, and above all with *brave men,* to repulse them. I look upon it as a special providence—an answer to prayer. Eight hours' bombardment with three ironclads and some six or seven mortar and gunboats, and only two men slightly wounded, one gun carriage injured, and the damage to the breastworks repaired in the night! We learn that the enemy has renewed the attack this morning. May it please God to help us through to the end, that they may be finally repulsed!

The effect of this affair will be most salutary upon our troops in Savannah and Charleston. Right glad am I to learn that you are still receiving reinforcements for the defense of the city, and that an excellent spirit prevails, and that our outposts are to be defended to the last extremity and the enemy fought inch by inch. That is the plan. We heard yesterday that the enemy were to be permitted to land, and the outposts were to be given up, and our forces retired within the line of the city defenses! What an idea! What would be the consequence? A regular siege approach, an accumulation of men and matériel, and the city in all probability captured! Never retire and confine ourselves within our defenses until we are forced to do it.

Am happy to know also that you are so much better, and exerting yourself with energy and judgment and with so much success in putting your batteries in the best order for service. They will no doubt play an important part if the conflict comes, and may determine the fortunes of the day—in which event I trust, my dear son, and pray that God would shield your life and your person and enable you to discharge your duty as a Christian man and as a true soldier and patriot. General Walker is a great accession. Do you observe the *mercy* in the Genesis affair? *Not a man killed;* not one *dangerously* wounded!

The presence of your dear brother with you at this time gives great comfort to Mother and myself, and must be so to you both. The Doctor would not delay, but went down to be with you and on hand with the staff of surgeons if there should be a necessity. I looked at all his fine cases of instruments, and told him I wished they might always be kept in the same capital order, but he never be called to use them on the field of battle. His visit has greatly refreshed us.

Your dear baby is quite well all to the eruption. *She walked alone for the first time Sunday, March 1st, 1863.* Mother, Daughter, Robert, and Miss Kitty Stiles all unite in love and respects to you both. The Lord bless and keep you both!

Your ever affectionate father (with a tired hand),
C. C. Jones.

COL. CHARLES C. JONES, JR., *to* REV. C. C. JONES[g]
                                  Savannah, *Thursday*, March 5th, 1863
My very dear Father,

I am this morning favored with your valued and interesting letter of yesterday.

Have just returned from the vicinity of Coffee Bluff, which commands a view of Genesis Point and Ossabaw Sound. The vessels of the enemy have retired, and are not to be seen. No renewal of the attack since the 3rd, although they presented a menacing front on the 4th; and now on the 5th they appear, for the present at least, to have abandoned any intention of recommencing a bombardment which by the blessing of God proved so futile. The moral effect of the resistance at Fort McAllister must produce a most salutary effect upon the minds of our troops, and dissipates entirely the fearful and terrible ideas with which the abolitionists have sought to invest their proud ironclads. Just now there are no demonstrations apparent on our coast.

A moment since, I had a conversation with Commodore Tattnall. It is his impression that it is not the intention of the enemy seriously to attack either this city or Charleston, but that their purpose is simply to attract attention here by assaulting our outposts, with a view to preventing our reinforcing the armies of the West, where a great battle will probably soon be fought, possibly in the vicinity of Murfreesboro. The news from that section this morning is quite cheering. Van Dorn is redeeming his reputation, which suffered somewhat in the affair at Corinth.

There is no intention on the part of anyone here *to abandon our outposts and retreat within the city lines* except upon an extremity; and the statement made to you to that effect was entirely incorrect. On the contrary, it is the firm resolve to hold every post to the last extremity, and dispute every inch of ground with the enemy; and by the blessing of Heaven, when the hour of battle does come, the abolitionists will find that they have an uphill business in any endeavor to possess themselves of this city.

The Doctor is busily engaged in visiting the camps in this vicinity. He is not at home except at night. He is staying with us. . . . I am sorry to hear that my dear little daughter still suffers from that eruption. The Doctor promises me to prescribe for her. Do kiss her for me. Give warmest love to dear Mother, Sister, and Robert, and the little ones. My special respects to Miss Kitty Stiles. And believe me ever, my honored father,
                                        Your affectionate son,
                                        Charles C. Jones, Jr.

MRS. MARY JONES *to* COL. CHARLES C. JONES, JR.[g]
                                  Arcadia, *Saturday*, March 14th, 1863
My dear Son,

Your uncle had walked a mile up the road to meet you, your precious little daughter to the far gate, and Father and Mother in the sunny front piazza awaited your coming, when to our great disappointment Gilbert returned with an empty buggy. I have looked for your visit with peculiar interest, for your dear father has been unusually feeble—more so than he has ever been. This week he has had fever several days and nights, which I hope has been caused by a large boil which has given him great suffering. In his enfeebled condition any additional pain or cause of excitement to his system shows itself immediately. I hope you will be enabled to visit us very soon. I cannot express the anxieties that are weighing on my heart.

Your uncle had been two days and nights with us, and on leaving requested me to send for him at any moment. Night before last I received a note from Robert, but your father was too feeble to be left alone. I wrote Brother William, and he came early in the morning, and has remained today to meet you, thus affording an opportunity for my going up yesterday to see your sister and the newborn granddaughter—a plump little lady, and your sister doing remarkably well. They are very anxious to obtain a nurse, as it is impossible for me to leave your father.

We regret sincerely to learn that Mr. Eve still continues in that distressing and hopeless condition. Such has been your father's and my own sympathy with Mrs. Eve and Eva under this heavy affliction that we have desired to write and express our feelings to them; but his feebleness and many occupations have prevented. Let me ask when you write that you will say how truly we do feel with and for them. And your father has often remembered him in our social devotions. Your brother has often told me what a man of benevolence, industry, and integrity he was. I trust it may be well with him not only for time but also for eternity.

What an admirable account this week's *Republican* contained of the fight at Genesis Point! Who wrote it?

Please, my son, if possible get me some quinine and an ounce of gum camphor. Enclosed ten dollars. If not enough, you must let me know.

Your father and uncle join me in much love, with sweetest kisses from your little daughter and many thanks for the box by express. The rings are her admiration. I have been looking for weeks for that promised visit from Mrs. Howard and Mrs. Neely. My love to them.

> Ever your affectionate mother,
> Mary Jones.

COL. CHARLES C. JONES, JR., *to* MRS. MARY JONES[t]

Savannah, *Monday,* March 16th, 1863

My very dear Mother,

Your kind letter of the 14th inst. is before me, and it greatly distresses me to know that my dear father continues to be so feeble and so unwell. He is scarcely ever out of my thoughts, and my constant and fervent prayer is that God would graciously stay his declining health and prolong his life, so precious to us all. I hope to be with you on Tuesday the 17th, and regret that

I should have disappointed you on last Saturday, although I do not remember to have appointed that day for coming out. Did I do so? That is usually a busy day with me, for all the weekly returns from the batteries have then to be digested and forwarded.

Have written a letter of congratulation to Sister and Robert. I sincerely trust that Sister may soon be restored to her accustomed health, and that the tender life of this little daughter may be prolonged, in the good providence of God, through many years of joy and gladness to her parents and friends, and of usefulness and of piety in her day and generation. I have secured a nurse for Sister in the person of Mrs. Smith, who goes out today prepared to remain the required period of time. Mrs. Hall, on account of previous engagements, could not leave the city.

I will attend to your request, Mother, and bring the quinine and camphor with me when I come.

The description of the recent bombardment of Genesis Point was written, I believe, by Major Locke, formerly the editor of the *Republican,* at present a major in the Commissary Department. It was a very excellent article.

Many thanks for your and Father's kind remembrance of Cousin Philo and Eva in their affliction. I will in my next letter to Eva express your sympathy, for I know how sincerely they will esteem this your remembrance of them.

Aunt Susan left the city on Saturday morning; I accompanied her to the depot.

It is thought that Charleston may be attacked upon the next spring tides—say, on or about the 19th inst. We may, I presume, expect heavy engagements at more points than one during the next sixty days.

Do, my dear mother, give warmest love to my dear father. Kiss my precious little daughter for me. And accept for yourself every assurance of the truest affection of

Your son,
Charles C. Jones, Jr.

MRS. MARY JONES *to* COL. CHARLES C. JONES, JR.[8]

Arcadia, *Monday,* March 16th, 1863

My dear Son,

Your father has passed a very bad night, and I consider him critically ill. I know not if your brother could possibly come, but wish you to telegraph him as early as you can. Your father has objected to sending for the physicians in the county; and I am well aware if his true situation was not understood by them, rash practice would be injurious if not fatal.

Ever your affectionate mother,
Mary Jones.

I wrote this early this morning, intending to send Gilbert immediately. Your dear father insisted I should wait until the cars came, thinking you would be in them. I now send hoping Gilbert will be two hours at least in advance of them. Telegraph Joe immediately: he is evidently growing more and more feeble. May God strengthen and uphold us all!

Your mother, in deep sorrow,
M.J.

Your letter has just come. We still conclude to send Gilbert, that you might telegraph your brother. Your father is very anxious to see him *if* he can possibly come.

XIV

COL. CHARLES C. JONES, JR., *to* REV. GEORGE HOWE[g]
Arcadia, *Thursday,* March 19th, 1863
Reverend and dear Sir,

At the request of my sorrowing mother I write to announce to you the saddest intelligence—of the death of my beloved and honored father. He fell asleep in Jesus on the afternoon of the 16th inst. without the slightest struggle. For several days previous he had been suffering from a severe cold, and was unusually weak. His nights during that period were almost sleepless. Respiration difficult. Amid all his physical infirmities his characteristic composure and cheerfulness never flagged.

On Sabbath morning the 15th inst. he took his usual ride on horseback. On the morning of the 16th, the day upon which he died, he dressed himself, came downstairs, and breakfasted with the family. After breakfast he walked out upon the lawn in front of the house, but soon returned very much fatigued. Retiring to his study, he seated himself in his accustomed chair and read from his favorite Bible. He was then exceedingly feeble. My mother and my aunt (Mrs. Cumming) spent the morning with him in his study. He conversed with difficulty, and although greatly oppressed with restlessness, which induced him frequently to change his position, and also with extreme debility, appeared perfectly calm and happy.

At two o'clock dinner was served in his study. He enjoyed the food prepared, eating with relish. Soon after dinner, addressing my mother, he alluded to some recent published order of General Beauregard as being very encouraging in its character, and referring to the present gigantic efforts made by our enemies to effect our subjugation, added: "The God of Jacob is with us—God our Father, Jehovah, God the Holy Ghost, and God our Divine Redeemer; and we can never be overthrown." My mother repeated some of the promises of the Saviour that He would be present with those who trust in Him, even when called to pass through the dark valley of the shadow of death. To which he responded: "In health we repeat these promises, but now they are realities." My mother replied: "I feel assured the Saviour is present with you." His answer was: "Yes. I am nothing but a poor sinner. I renounce myself and all self-justification, trusting only in the free and unmerited righteousness of the Lord Jesus Christ." Mother then asked if he had any word for his sons. He replied: "Tell them both to lead the lives of godly men in Christ Jesus, in uprightness and integrity."

His feebleness increasing, my mother suggested that it might prove a pleasant change for him to go to his chamber and recline upon the bed, to which he assented. Rising from his rocking chair, he took the arm of Mother and of my aunt. As he was leaving the study he paused for a moment and, smiling, remarked to them: "How honored I am in being waited upon by two ladies!" This was about half-past two o'clock in the afternoon. Reaching the chamber, he reclined upon the bed, suggesting to my mother and aunt the manner in which the pillows should be disposed so as to contribute best to his comfort. My mother commenced rubbing his hands and feet, the circulation in his system being very feeble. He called for his body servant and bade him relieve my mother; and after Tom had rubbed his feet sufficiently, Father said to him: "That will do now; put on my slippers." Which was done. And then: "You can go." Closing his eyes, he rested quietly one foot over the other, as his wont was to lie, and in a few moments—without a groan, without a single shudder, without the movement of a single muscle —fell asleep in Jesus, as calmly as an infant in the arms of a loving mother. He passed away so gently that the devoted watchers at his side scarce perceived when his pure spirit left the frail tabernacle.

In the morning, with the assistance of his body servant, he had dressed himself, as his custom was, in a full suit of black with the utmost neatness. In this habit he died: not a spot upon his pure white cravat, not a blemish or wrinkle upon his vestment. From the bed in his chamber, without a single change in his apparel, a half hour after he breathed his last, his precious body was removed with the utmost tenderness and placed upon the favorite couch in his study. There he lay, surrounded by all the favorite authors whose companionship in life he so much cherished, attended by the precious tokens of his recent labors, in the holy calm of the room he loved so well, until Wednesday morning at eleven o'clock (the 18th inst.), when his honored dust was carried to Midway Church.

In the presence of a large concourse of citizens and of Negroes a funeral sermon was pronounced by the Rev. D. L. Buttolph from the text: "How is the strong staff broken, and the beautiful rod!" After the ceremonies were concluded, his honored remains were interred in the adjoining cemetery near his father and mother and the graves of other near and dear relatives, beneath the solemn oaks which cast their protecting shadows over that consecrated spot.

My father had very evidently been contemplating for months and even years the near approach of death. Not very long ago he said to me: "My son, I am living in momentary expectation of death, but the thought of its approach causes me no alarm. This frail tabernacle must soon be taken down; I only await God's will." The following is the last entry which appears in his journal; it was penned only a few days previous to his death: "March 12th, 1863. Have been very weak and declining since renewal of the cold on the 1st inst. in church. The emaciation continues. Taste scarcely anything; feeling of emptiness but appetite for nothing, and a few mouthfuls suffice.

Throat quiet. Difficulty of throwing off phlegm from the lungs, or rather the bronchial tubes; lungs seem to lack power of expansion so as to take in air enough to oxidate the blood sufficiently; respiration quicker than common. Owing to this cause, sleep badly, being forced every few moments to shift position. Digestion yet unimpaired. My disease appears to be drawing to its conclusion! May the Lord make me in that hour to say in saving faith and love: 'Into thine hand I commit my spirit: thou hast redeemed me, O Lord God of truth' (Psalm 31:5). So has our Blessed Saviour taught us by His own example to do; and blessed are they who die in the Lord."

Feeling, my dear sir, that you would be deeply interested in an account of the last moments of one who ever held you in such especial regard and friendship—of one so noble in character, elevated in principle, pure in honor, true in affection, generous in thought and act, refined in feeling, cultivated in mind and manners, and exalted in every Christian virtue—I have been thus minute in detail. Were I to attempt a recital of all the holy memories which cluster around his closing hours, were I to repeat all the precious words which fell from his almost inspired lips, time would fail me. His death was little less than a *translation*.

And what shall I say of the delightful, the holy savor of his life? How shall I speak of the loss which has been sustained by the church, by the country, by the community in which he resided, and by his sorrowing family? My honored father was still engaged, as his feeble and declining health would permit, upon his *History of the Church of God,* the great labor of his life. It remains, in the inscrutable providence of Heaven, unfinished, although complete as far as he had progressed with it. A few chapters more and he would have concluded the last page. As it is, it is his last offering to the church—his final labor in the cause of his great Redeemer. So soon as circumstances permit, it will be given to the world just as it came from his trembling hand.

Never through all the years of failing health and of great physical infirmity has Father's intellect been in the least degree impaired. In fact, it appeared to be sublimated in proportion as his feebleness increased, gathering heavenly strength as day after day in his debilitated frame was foreshadowed more and more the image of the grave. To the last moment he preserved to a wonderful degree his characteristic cheerfulness. Time he never wasted. His obligations to his family, to his servants, to the community in which he resided, to nature (whose admiring student he was), to the church, to the country, and to the great God he so faithfully adored, he seemed never for an instant to forget. He lived ever an exalted life, and everyone confessed the purity of his example, the ennobling influences of his walk and conversation.

But, my dear sir, I need not speak thus to you who knew him so well—to you who so truly estimated his virtues. In the warmth of my own feelings I have written much more than I at first intended. You will bear with me, I trust; for I have always loved and honored my father almost to veneration and positive worship.

It is the special request of my dear and bereaved mother that you would at some convenient moment prepare an obituary of Father. We trust that you will be able to do so, knowing as we do your appreciation of his character, assured as we are from your long intimacy, constant association, and close friendship that to you he would with peculiar confidence have entrusted everything touching his life and his labors in his Master's vineyard. With the principal events in Father's life, his responsibilities and engagements, as well as with his characteristic and noble traits, you are quite familiar. Should you desire any facts or dates, or any additional information, my mother or myself will be happy to furnish them at the earliest moment. All expenses connected with the publication of the obituary, in any form you may desire, will of course be gratefully borne by us.

With our sincerest remembrances to Mrs. Howe and each member of your family, I am, dear sir,

Very respectfully and truly yours,
Charles C. Jones, Jr.

REV. GEORGE HOWE *to* MRS. MARY JONES[t]

Columbia, *Saturday,* March 28th, 1863

My dear Madam,

How shall I express to you the deep sorrow which takes possession of all our hearts at the loss of our dear friend your lamented husband? And yet *your* loss as far exceeds that of all others as your relation to him was more close and tender, and your knowledge of all that was excellent and endearing in him was more intimate and perfect. That you will no more see his face in the flesh, no more hear his voice uttering words of counsel, wisdom, and affection, be no more stimulated by his daily example and cheered by his presence, no more have the remnant of life's weary journey lightened by his sharing it with you, and the now lonely hours filled no more with those duties you owed him, is a grief into which no heart can ever enter but yours. But you know, my sorrowing friend, where to go for relief. There is One whose heart sympathized when He was upon earth with every form of human suffering, to whom you can now go with all your griefs, and who cannot and will not withhold from you His most precious consolations. That our dear friend should so sicken, and his lovely and useful life be terminated thus, was a part of the eternal plan of Him who is wise in counsel and wonderful in working.

How much will we all miss him—miss his elevated and cheerful piety, his devoted spirit, his active, energetic mind, his friendly greeting, playful humor, and pleasant, instructive talk! How will the church mourn, which he has served so long and well; his brethren in the ministry also, who knew him only to admire and love him! He has been to me always a friend most dear. I have been drawn to him more and more the longer I have known him. Pleasant have been the hours we have spent together, and the memory of them is sweet.

But he is in more blessed society now. The messenger whom God sends to call His people home came noiselessly, and without pain to him terminated his earthly career and opened all at once, without the sorrow of parting with loves ones here, the gate of paradise, and bore him to the presence of that Saviour he loved. His joy how great! His crown how glorious! His eternal house not made with hands how pleasant! Shall we not join him there? And how soon may that happy meeting be? How glorious, too, the morning of the resurrection! "For if we believe that Jesus died and rose again, even so them also which sleep in Jesus will God bring with Him. The dead in Christ shall rise first. Then we which are alive and remain shall be caught up together with them in the clouds to meet the Lord in the air, and so shall we ever be with the Lord. Wherefore comfort one another with these words."

We all feel for you and your dear children, and other friends and relatives to whom your departed husband was so dear. May God multiply to you and them the consolations of His grace now and evermore!

Your friend in affliction and sorrow,
George Howe.

P.S. I am indebted to Mr. Buttolph and your son for their letters, received just as I was leaving home to fulfill an appointment. Will write to them very soon.

MRS. MARY JONES *to* COL. CHARLES C. JONES, JR.[8]

Walthourville, Monday, March 30th, 1863

My very dear Son,

I cannot command a pen tonight, and must employ this pencil to send you a line by tomorrow's mail. I am thankful to hear of our dear friends in Augusta, and from our servants. I have wanted to write and tell the latter all about the last days of their honored master. But oh, my son, what language can I find to convey what I would wish expressed? How did they receive the sorrowful tidings?

You know, my son, the desolation which reigns in my heart. I feel at times if it was not (as I humbly hope) for the sustaining grace of God and the presence of my gracious Saviour that I could not longer sustain the weary and heavy-laden burden which life now appears—separated from my head, my guide, my counselor, my beloved husband, to whom my heart has been united in tenderest love for thirty-two years. I ask myself: can there be anything even in the form of duty left to bind me here? God only knows; and also knows how much my foolish, sinful heart deserves His chastening rod in this dark hour. I want to know and do His holy will, and to be comforted only with His love shed abroad in my heart.

I long to return to the solitude of my own home, and to live amid the memorials of our beloved and honored head. If your dear sister is well enough and Robert returns, I want to go to Arcadia the last of this week. She has been graciously sustained under this severe affliction; but for two nights she says it has come over her with such power as to deprive her of sleep; and today she has had a return of the chill, accompanied with fever. I sent for Dr. Stevens; he has just left, saying she needed no medicine. She is very calm now, and I hope will have a good night's rest. The dear baby is perfectly well and quiet, which is a great blessing.

Your own precious child has had an affection of the bowels for two days, but is nearly relieved: the effect probably of teething. The treatment prescribed by your brother has already relieved the eruption, and I hope will do her lasting good.

As soon as I go home, will see that the necessary articles for the women are prepared to go by *Porter* when he returns, which, my dear son, you can direct whenever you think best. On my way down will stop at Montevideo, and if his work is done there will write you so that he may not unnecessarily delay his time here.

When you write, present my affectionate remembrance and tenderest sympathy to Eva and Mrs. Eve. I will write Mrs. Eve as soon as I can command my time. Now it is all taken up in your sister's sick chamber and care of the children. Good night, my dear son! May the example and precepts of your sainted father be ever before you! Follow him, even as he followed Christ, through whom he hath obtained an entrance into everlasting life.

Ever your affectionate mother,
Mary Jones.

My grateful acknowledgments to Mr. Ward for his kind sympathy.

31st. The articles for Aunt (some twelve or sixteen bags—I cannot now remember the number) were shipped last week. Would you let George inquire at the depot if they have gone to Marietta?

By today's express we send a box to Miss Kitty Stiles, who will be a few days longer at the Miss Mackays'. She has in every time of need been the kindest of friends to Daughter and myself, and now offers to do what we require and could not have done. If you have a moment, do call and see her.

COL. CHARLES C. JONES, JR., *to* MRS. MARY JONES[g]

Savannah, *Friday,* April 3rd, 1863

My very dear Mother,

I am in receipt of your very kind letter of the 30th ult. and sincerely thank you for it. You are ever present in my thoughts and in my love, and my constant prayer is that you may in this our heaviest affliction experience that consolation which comes only from above. I trust that my dear little daughter is better again, and that Sister has quite recovered.

I had the pleasure of seeing Robert as he passed through the city, and was happy to know that he was so much pleased with Atlanta and the prospects of the church. It strikes me the call is a very important one, and should be *carefully and if practicable favorably considered.* I know of no field in the state which offers equal inducements for extended usefulness.

I hope to be able to see Miss Kitty Stiles this evening. She is a woman for whom I have always entertained the highest esteem. Hers is a friendship which may well be cultivated.

The anticipated attack upon Charleston has not transpired as yet; it was expected on the 2nd inst.

Enclosed, my dear mother, I send you a letter this morning received from Dr. Howe. You will read it with interest. Will you be so kind at some early leisure moment to give me in detail the facts which he there desires, and I will answer his letter fully.

Do, my dearest mother, let me know what your plans are, and if I can serve you at any time. You well know that I will always esteem it not only my highest duty but also my greatest privilege to love and minister to your every comfort. I address this hurried note to Arcadia, as you mentioned in your letter that you expected to return home the latter part of this week. I hope to see you some day next week, and will let you know so soon as I am able to fix the day. With warmest love and tenderest sympathy, I am ever, my dear mother,

Your affectionate son,
Charles C. Jones, Jr.

Many kisses for my sweet little daughter. Howdy for the servants.

MRS. MARY JONES *to* COL. CHARLES C. JONES, JR.[8]

Arcadia, *Saturday*, April 4th, 1863

My dear Son,

Tom has just arrived with your affectionate favor and the enclosed letter of Dr. Howe. I will endeavor at an early day to answer his inquiries as fully as I possibly can.

I know at one time your beloved and honored father had drawn up "family records" which included incidents of his own life and of various members of our family, which if now in existence would be of priceless value to us. But through the inscrutable (to us) but no less wise providence of God they all perished with his other writings in the fire which consumed our dwelling at Columbia, April 18th, 1850. I recollect asking him not long since if he had any memoranda of his early life and labors, to which he replied (as well as I now remember) that he had not. The period of his public services can be easily traced from his various reports; before the church and the world he has been known and read of all men. Full of grace and truth, his life has been one undeviating course of uprightness and integrity. He loved his Master and his Master's work, and sought to advance the Redeemer's Kingdom with all the lofty talents that were so preeminently committed to his trust. "Good and faithful servant," I believe that he has entered into the joy of his Lord.

When I think of him with the Divine Redeemer, so precious to his soul on earth, with saints and angels, with his own dear mother, Sister Betsy, your dear Ruth, and an innumerable company now gathered into the mansions of heavenly peace and rest, I know that our loss is his eternal gain. But oh, when no returning footstep falls upon my listening ear, no voice or touch of love and kindness, no cheerful greeting, no words of counsel or encouragement—that silent study, that empty chair, that vacant sofa where first we plighted our early vows and where he daily rested his weary and enfeebled frame, *that desk* where he labored so perseveringly, his Bible left open upon it, his spectacles just as he laid them down, his hat, his stick just as he placed them on the table in the entry—can you wonder that I longed to be here with all these precious memorials around me?

I left Walthourville at one o'clock yesterday and came immediately down to Midway—my first visit to that consecrated spot. . . . Your dear sister was much better and sitting up when I left. Robert was suffering from a cold taken in Atlanta. So soon as she is strong enough to ride thus far, they will all be with me. . . . I have great reason to be grateful—and trust I am—for my affectionate and dutiful children and many kind friends. You may be assured, my son, I shall call unreservedly upon you at all times. I have received the kindest letters from my brother, from your Uncle Henry, Aunt and Cousin Mary, and Dr. Howe. . . . I will try and acknowledge them when I feel able to do so.

Your precious child is quite well, and almost entirely relieved of the eruption. She is my dear little comforter—my precious one. Seeing me weeping, she cried as if her little heart would break, and when we came here ran into the study and looked all around as if searching for her "papa." Our people are all well, and kind and attentive as they can be. Your dear daughter sends her sweetest kisses. May the Lord bless and save you, ever prays

Your affectionate mother,
Mary Jones.

I had intended to send you Dr. Howe's letter to me, but will reserve it until we meet.

COL. CHARLES C. JONES, JR., *to* MRS. MARY JONES[8]
Savannah, *Saturday,* April 4th, 1863
My very dear Mother,

I am in receipt of your kind letter of this morning, and sincerely thank you for it. So soon as you are able to answer the inquiries suggested in Dr. Howe's letter, if you desire me to do so, I will put them in form and forward them to him. In this I may be able to save you some labor. Do, Mother, add any reflections or incidents which you may deem proper. As soon as practicable, every memory should be made permanent. It is a sad loss to us all, that burning of the autobiographical sketch of my dear and honored father—one which we can never repair and must always most earnestly deplore.

I knew that the sympathy of kind friends would find expression in word as well as in feeling, and it will afford me a great pleasure to read them when we meet. Major Porter wept as I told him of the last hours of Father; and Mrs. Harriss said to me that Dr. Axson on Thursday following the day of his death, at the prayer meeting, gave a full account of his wonderful and happy demise. Heavy though this affliction be, my dearest mother, dark though the clouds are on that side which looks towards us, we can but rejoice at the happiness upon which he has entered, and with tearful eyes think without sorrow of that great change which has freed his godly and glorious spirit from the frail tabernacle of flesh and translated it to the immortal blessedness of heaven—to the companionship of the saints of all ages whose characters on earth he so much admired; and to an immediate association with that Triune God whom he so dearly loved, whose sacred Word he so much revered and studied, whose sublimated doctrines and laws he so closely observed.

I will be with you, my dear mother, at the earliest practicable day. General Beauregard, I understand, thinks that the attack upon our coast cannot be very long delayed. He expects the demonstration to be made against Charleston, and says that city is prepared for it. We have nothing of special interest here. Do, my dear mother, let me know whenever I can serve you in any particular, no matter how trivial. With many kisses for my sweet little daughter, and much love for you, I am ever

Your affectionate son,
Charles C. Jones, Jr.

MRS. MARY JONES *to* COL. CHARLES C. JONES, JR.[8]

Arcadia, *Wednesday*, April 8th, 1863

My very dear Son,

Tom has just come in with your letter; it is a solace to hear from you thus often.

I am in *the study* today, with aching head, and far more aching heart, trying to gather up the cherished recollections of your honored father, my tenderly beloved husband; my blinding tears every now and then forcing me to stop and ask: "Of whom am I writing? Can it be true that I shall nevermore behold his face on earth?" You have passed through this agony; you know how I feel. But oh, my son, yours was the sundering of young and tenderest ties; our hearts were cemented by thirty-two years of life's companionship. And I can truly say I knew not a moment of unalloyed happiness whenever in that period we were separated.

It is very difficult with no memoranda at hand to write what I desire, but will be faithful in what I do say, and ask of my Heavenly Father guidance and direction. I will try and forward my letter to Dr. Howe to you before it is sent to him. I have found one copy of the tenth report, which is a review of his missionary work among the Negroes, and answers much that the doctor desires to know. I will forward it with the request that it be returned, as I have no other copy excepting the complete set now deposited in the Augusta bank.

I had not until your letter been informed of the attack upon Charleston. I feel the greatest confidence that our just and holy God will hear and answer the prayers of his suffering people at this time, and that our enemies will not prevail against us! But we should humble ourselves and lie low before the Cross. I trust the day of fasting and prayer was observed "in spirit and in truth" throughout our whole Confederacy. Where did you worship on that day? I never doubt the final issue except when I hear of the sin and profanity that prevails, the Sabbath-breaking and immorality which is practiced by men in high places, setting aside the good of society, the welfare of their own souls, and all that is pure and sacred in character and reputation. For all these sins we must receive judgments from the Lord.

I observe by today's paper Mr. Lathrop has *yarn* for sale. What does he ask? I would like to get *if at all reasonable* six bunches, two of them very fine and four medium size. They say it is impossible to obtain it from the factories just now. I shall try and do all we can to clothe the people at home, for I see no other prospect of supplying their wants. . . .

Your precious child is well and very lively; has been much of the time with me in the study. It is time for the mail, and I must close. What can I do for you? Do you not want a supply of grist or rice? I am thankful *your duties* still keep you in Savannah. May the Lord bless and keep you, and prepare you by His grace renewing and sanctifying your heart for life and for death!

Ever your affectionate mother,
Mary Jones.

COL. CHARLES C. JONES, JR., *to* MRS. MARY JONES[8]
Savannah, *Friday,* April 10th, 1863
My very dear Mother,

I am this evening in receipt of your kind letter to Dr. Howe with the accompanying reports, both of which I will have posted tonight.

I have just been ordered to Charleston, and leave at six o'clock in the morning, D.V. I am sorry, my dearest mother, that I will not have the pleasure of seeing you before I go; but I trust in God, if the enemy does attempt to land, that we may be able to drive the detested invaders back with fearful loss, and that I may be soon restored to your loves and your presence. Heaven bless you and my precious little daughter, and shield you both from every harm!

With warmest love to you, my dearest mother, and many kisses for my little daughter, I am ever

Your affectionate son,
Charles C. Jones, Jr.

MRS. MARY JONES *to* COL. CHARLES C. JONES, JR.[8]
Arcadia, *Tuesday,* April 14th, 1863
My very dear Son,

Your letter at leaving, with its precious enclosure, although it sent a pang to my heart, was a great comfort to me; and I have been sustained under an abiding conviction that my gracious Redeemer will care for and preserve your life. Oh, my child, in these solemn times, this hour of darkest grief to us, seek to know honestly and truly how stands the great account between God and your own soul. Surely it is time for you to settle this great question and to be decided for your God and Saviour.

I am glad your dear brother is in Charleston. I know in case of an attack he would wish to render every service to his suffering countrymen and to be near to you.

Could I not send you a box of eatables by express? *Write me about it at once,* and *how to direct it,* and I will send it immediately; some hams (boiled if you wish), dried beef, rice, and grist, and whatever I think would reach you in good condition.

There is an interesting state of religion in the Liberty Independent Troop. Many have professed conversion. I am sorry they are going away to Savannah tomorrow. Colonel Millen's battalion is to take their place.

I have had Lymus brought here that I might attend to him, and finding that he did not improve have sent for Dr. Farmer to come and tell me what I had best do for him. I am anxious to omit no attention to the poor fellow. He always appeared attached to your dear and honored father, and is a little younger. The other servants are all well and doing well. Shall I send Porter to Burke as soon as he gets through, which ought to be very shortly?

Mr. Lyons sent a message through Gilbert saying he would give two dollars a bushel for twenty-five bushels of rice. Not knowing anything about the price, I sent a note of inquiry to Mr. Cassels at the depot; his answer this morning is: "There have been no sales here, but it is worth from four to five dollars per bushel if good," and told Gilbert it would bring more in Savannah.

I have received a great many kind and sympathizing letters from friends. One today from General Cocke. . . . Oh, that it was granted you both, my dear sons, to sit as I do in this consecrated study and to talk together of our beloved and honored head, gone from us on earth, but forever with his Lord in glory! Your dear aunt is with me this week, and your sister will be as soon as she is strong enough to ride.

I hope dear Carrie will not feel too anxious about your brother's absence.

Dear little Mary Ruth, my comfort, is well and bright and, Sister Susan says, a very good child. . . . Love from your aunt, many kisses from your precious child, and for you both, my beloved sons, the abiding love and prayers of

Your sorrowful mother,
Mary Jones.

COL. CHARLES C. JONES, JR., *to* MRS. MARY JONES[g]
Camp W. H. T. Walker, *Friday,* April 17th, 1863
I am this morning, my dearest mother, in receipt of your very kind letter

of the 14th inst., and am very happy to know that you and my precious little daughter are both well.

I long to see you both, and wish I could tell when I may expect the pleasure of being with you. Just now we do not know whether we will be returned to Savannah within a short time or not. The impression prevails with many that the real attack upon Charleston has not yet been made, and that the enemy will return to the assault within a few weeks. If such be the belief at headquarters, we will in all probability be retained in our present position for some time. So soon as we ascertain more definitely, I will write you and also answer your kind inquiry whether you shall send the box of good things. It would be very acceptable, and as soon as we know what our movements will be I will write you whether to send it or not.

When Porter completes his work at Montevideo, I would be very glad for you to let him return to Indianola for at least a while.

Rice was worth when I left Savannah from six to eight dollars per bushel; I would not sell it for less than five.

I trust that Lymus may soon be better.

I do wish, my dearest mother, that I could be near and with you to render you every assistance in my power; but you see and appreciate the condition in which I am—the claims which are now upon me. It would indeed prove a great privilege for me again to revisit that home hallowed by such precious loves, and consecrated by memories the purest, the noblest of earth. My beloved and honored father is ever in my most cherished affection and veneration.

May the Good God watch over and preserve you, my dear mother, and my sweet little daughter! Kiss her for me. My love to Aunt Susan. And believe me ever

Your affectionate son,
Charles C. Jones, Jr.

COL. CHARLES C. JONES, JR., *to* MRS. MARY JONES[g]

Savannah, *Sunday,* April 19th, 1863

My very dear Mother,

I write only a line for the post in the morning to inform you that I arrived here, through God's mercy, safe this afternoon. My command has (part of it) returned, and the balance will arrive tonight and tomorrow. I sincerely trust that you and my sweet little daughter are both well. Do kiss her for me. And believe me ever, my dear mother, with sincerest love,

Your ever affectionate son,
Charles C. Jones, Jr.

I hope to see you very soon.

MRS. MARY JONES *to* COL. CHARLES C. JONES, JR.^g

Arcadia, *Tuesday*, April 21st, 1863

My dear Son,

I am truly happy to know that your command has been returned to Savannah, and trust you may soon be enabled to visit home.

Yesterday the Liberty Independent Troop (Captain Walthour), the Liberty Guards (Captain Hughes), the Mounted Rifles (Captain Brailsford) rendezvoused at Midway. . . . Captain Walthour proposed that they should have a parting service. The door of the venerable old church was opened. They all entered with their arms in hand and took their seats, filling every pew below and the galleries above. There were prayers offered, two addresses, closing with the doxology, the whole assembly rising and most of them joining. Mr. Buttolph said during the service perfect stillness was observed, and that the close was sublime. There has been a very interesting state of religion in the troop, and several conversions. I trust the Holy Spirit will abide with them and perfect His blessed work in their hearts.

The removal of this company leaves the entire coast of the county in a defenseless condition. The enemy might now at any moment land troops at Sunbury or the Island or on the North Newport, and there would be nothing but a few pickets to notify the battalion *stationed* thirty miles away in McIntosh County! Meantime they might capture citizens, desolate estates, destroy property, and steal all our servants remaining. I do feel assured if the general commanding knew our exact position we should have a different arrangement. Mr. Quarterman has just called, and says he and Mr. Norman and Colonel Gaulden have been appointed a committee to wait on General Mercer and present our claims; if he fails to answer, the object is to proceed to Charleston and see General Beauregard. The committee will be down in tomorrow evening's train; and Mr. Quarterman would be very glad, he says, of any assistance from you.

I wrote Mrs. Howard last week; have not heard from her. . . . Your precious child is well and very good and bright; she sends her sweetest kisses for her dear papa. Sister Susan unites with me in best love to you.

Ever, my very dear son, your affectionate mother,

Mary Jones.

COL. CHARLES C. JONES, JR., *to* MRS. MARY JONES^g

Savannah, *Wednesday*, April 22nd, 1863

My very dear Mother,

I am this morning in receipt of your kind letter of yesterday, and am happy to know that you and my dear little daughter are well, and that Aunt Susan has been with you in your hours of deepest loneliness and sorrow. Most sincerely do I wish that I could remain with you, my beloved mother, to relieve you of every anxiety, minister to your requests, and render you every assistance in my power. But the rules of this exacting service are upon me,

370

and I can only respond in heart and not in person to those claims which it will always be my highest pleasure and privilege to recognize and allow. . . .

The parting with the troops at Midway Church must have been an impressive season. I regret to learn the unprotected condition in which our immediate coast is left, and trust that the representations made by the committee may prove effective.

I heard from Indianola yesterday. All well, and getting along well. Martha expects to be confined next week. If the clothes are ready, Mother, they had better be sent up at once.

I hope to be able to spend the day on Friday with you if nothing unforeseen occurs to prevent. Will you please let Gilbert meet me at the depot? I am so happy to know that Sister will be with you; and it will be a great joy for me to see her too.

We have nothing of interest here. With warmest love to you, my dearest mother, and with tenderest sympathy in this our greatest sorrow, with many kisses for my precious little daughter, whom I am very anxious to see, and with affectionate remembrances to Aunt Susan, Sister, and the little ones, I am ever

Your affectionate son,
Charles C. Jones, Jr.

MRS. MARY JONES *to* COL. CHARLES C. JONES, JR.[8]

Arcadia, *Tuesday,* May 19th, 1863

My dear Son,

Your affectionate favor was this day received, and I will first reply to the business part. Mr. Buttolph will probably be at home the latter part of this week, as it is our Communion Sabbath at Midway, and he ought to be here on Saturday. Next week, I understand, he will go to Baker County. I think, D.V., of riding to see your aunt and cousin tomorrow for the first time in many months, and will write you again particularly when to make the desired arrangements. I ardently wish that you could be with us on Sabbath. We are to have two additions of young soldiers from Captain Thomson's company.

I do not think it possible for me to leave Arcadia next week, as I am overlooking and packing the books, and want to make a catalogue of them. It is now so cool and pleasant from the recent rains that I do not apprehend any danger in staying. Should there appear to be any, I will send the baby up to your sister as she requests me to do. She is so hearty I would not wish to expose her to an unhealthy atmosphere. I have had company so constantly that what I desired to have done is still undone. She speaks of her dear papa every day, and never forgets you.

I believe I told you that Mr. Butler could not take up the cattle. Would it be possible for you to put them upon the cars at the twenty-one-mile station

371

on the Central Road and let Mr. Sconyers meet them at the ninety-five-mile station? They could be driven easily to the twenty-one-mile station in two days, and take the cars that night. The mule-wagon could go along with the forage for the journey from there, and Gilbert knows the route. Syphax will accompany Porter when he returns, and they could take care of them on the cars. If this plan is practicable, you can so arrange for it. The cows are in fine order, and will be a comfort to the people and useful on the place.

Last fall before leaving the Island your dear father had all the fencing put in complete repair and left in the enclosure four cows and four calves and one bull. I thought it proper to send Andrew down this week to see how matters stand, and Gilbert has just returned with the report. (Brother William gave Andrew his pass.) He found the fence to the causeway gate taken down for some distance and removed; the gate propped open; Mr. Dunham's sheep and hogs driven in up to the dwelling house; and the hogs even in the courtyard. Behind the cornhouse a pen was made, into which was put a large hog, which was there fed, probably from the provisions left in the barn, as the doors had been forced and the peas threshed out. Every cellar door to the house had been broken open; also the smokehouse and kitchen doors. Upon Half Moon next to the Cadden hammocks Mr. Delegal, Mr. Anderson, and Mr. King had located themselves, boiling salt and using the wood for that purpose. Audley has recently purchased Dr. Harris's land just over the causeway (known as Dr. McWhir's tract) and located his salt-boilers at the head of the causeway. Andrew saw him and told him of the state of our premises. He sent me word that all he wanted was a note from you or myself, and he would see that our interest was protected in every way, stating that he would be at Midway tomorrow, where I could send it to him. And I have just written the following to him:

Dear Sir:

You are hereby requested and empowered to represent our entire interest on the Colonel's Island, and to forbid all occupation or trespass by any person or persons upon either tract of land known as Maybank and Half Moon. The Half Moon tract joins on to your land recently purchased and is divided from it from Gridiron bridge by a ditch running down to the marsh, the cedar hammocks along the shore from that point being attached to it, and the dividing line between them and the Cadden hammocks being a creek which empties into the Woodville River. Mr. Dunham has a right of way to the Cadden hammocks, which is indicated by the road leading to the causeway to said hammocks.

Respectfully, etc.

I felt that this was just to ourselves, and hope I have acted properly in the matter. This cruel war imposes strange duties upon us all, and I am willing to stand in my lot.

I could but admire the ingenuity of my servants and the protection afforded by them today in the case of a suspicious-looking character who came up and asked for food. They told him their master lived in Savannah, and they could not entertain him. They asked that I would not come down. I told them I could not send him hungry away, and ordered Kate to get some dinner for him. They made him sit in the piazza, and when he attempted to come into the house (as he said, "to see how it looked") Flora and Tom barred the front door. I could see him from the balcony, and when his dinner was ready they sent him by Charles a large plate of rice and pork, a bowl of clabber, and would not even trust him with a knife or fork, but gave him only an iron spoon. The poor fellow eat voraciously—the first, he said, in three days. When he finished, Charles politely told him if he would now start he would put him on the right road. I hope I did not violate any law of charity or humanity, but I had not the courage to let him remain. Charles and Tom managed so well that I gave them each a little reward.

The death of our pious, brave, and noble General Stonewall Jackson is a great blow to our cause! May God raise up friends and helpers to our bleeding country! In what striking contrast stands that of Van Dorn! The one is surrounded by a halo of glory; the other is shrouded in a pall of infamy. There is no man who violates the purity and sanctity of society that will not reap his full reward in the due course of time. He may not always lose his life, and may even be permitted to walk abroad with shameless effrontery and receive the countenance and friendship of those who have not the moral courage, the strength of principle, the fear of God to rebuke his infamous and injurious practices. But he will surely eat of the fruit of his own way.

I will write you again day after tomorrow of Mr. Buttolph's movements. And now, my dear son, good night! Sweetest kisses from your little daughter. May the Lord bless and save you!

Ever your affectionate mother,
Mary Jones.

MRS. MARY JONES *to* COL. CHARLES C. JONES, JR.[8]

Arcadia, *Thursday,* May 28th, 1863

My dear Son,

I have been prevented by the rain for two days from going to Montevideo. As there is a prospect of clearing, I will go and spend the night there and have the cattle, sheep, and hogs counted up early in the morning. I wish to do this before leaving for the summer. I am much perplexed at the thought of leaving people and place without some white protection and control. Would it be well to try and get Mr. Calder? Audley is boiling salt at the Island and would not, I fear, undertake it.

Mr. Quarterman advises me that it is time for our *tax returns,* which are now due. How shall they be made out, and will a few days' delay involve anything serious?

Mr. Buttolph is now at home. Will go to Baker before long, but will, I presume, be here all of the coming week. Any arrangements you deem best can be made.

It is not right for me to keep our precious little baby here longer than this week, and if the season had not been so cool and dry, I would have deemed it imprudent to be here to this late period. If you can be out very early next week, I will keep her to see her dear papa. If not, she had best change the air, and I will send her to your sister even if I am compelled to stay. Her little mind expands almost as rapidly now as the unfolding leaves of the evening primrose. She has startled me several times with unexpected developments. She has the warm and loving heart of her own dear mother, and I trust will be as truthful in character. Her perfect remembrance of your beloved father is wonderful for one of her age. She is a great comfort in this period of sorrow and desolation.

I hope you found our friends in Augusta well. I long to see my dear son and Carrie and the little ones; but really these are such troublous times, if one has a quiet and comparatively secure abode I think they ought to be grateful and remain contented without changing.

Mr. Russell, to whom we sent nine sheepskins to be exchanged for cotton cards some four months since, writes that they are not to be had. Can they now be had in Savannah? And at what price? Porter has made me a nice loom, complete all to the blacksmith's part. I have had him repairing house, etc. He is all ready for your orders, and so is the salt. I think we have on hand a year's supply, and had best send it up. Andrew is still boiling. I want him next week to go to Maybank and make up the line fence. Did you get my letter about the cattle?

Hope George arrived safely, and General Beauregard enjoyed the mutton. We feel honored to contribute to his entertainment. Can you get his autograph for me?

These are dark days! How long our cry for deliverance and peace will remain unanswered is known only to our Sovereign Judge, who sees how much our sins deserve His chastening rod! I see no hope or comfort but from on high. With sweet kisses from your little daughter and the love of

Your affectionate mother,
Mary Jones.

COL. CHARLES C. JONES, JR., *to* MRS. MARY JONES[8]

Savannah, *Thursday*, May 28th, 1863

My very dear Mother,

I returned last evening from Indianola, where I spent three days. Found everything suffering very much for want of rain. Corn and cotton both small but healthy. On Tuesday and yesterday generous showers were descending upon the thirsty earth, and this morning the skies are still overcast; so that I trust we will be favored with an abundance of rain, and that the fields will soon rejoice in the life and the vigor of a new existence. All the people were well, and everything appears to be getting along quietly and favorably. The crop was very clean, and seems to be properly attended. I have about six hundred acres planted in corn, and one hundred and thirty in cotton. Am planting heavily in peas. Betty's children—also the infants of Lizzie and Kate—are all well. Peggy had been somewhat sick, but was better. I gave out the Negro cloth on Tuesday night—an abundant supply. The wheat is nearly ready for harvest; hope to make some sixty bushels. Am just about to erect a grain house, and would be very glad, my dear mother, if you would let Porter return to the place to assist in its construction if you have no further use for him. I have made all the tax returns, and have *included Porter*. I also gave out summer clothing for him, leaving the same in Stepney's charge.

I have seen the railroad agent here, and he tells me that he will have two stock cars at No. 2, Central Railroad, any day I may name, giving him two days' previous notice. So, my dear mother, if you will let me know when it will be convenient for you to have the cattle driven up (say, thirty to forty head), I will see that the cars are ready at that station any day you may name, and also communicate with Mr. Sconyers so that he may have hands in readiness at No. 9½ to drive them to the plantation. Gilbert might take charge of them to No. 2, and Porter go along also. Please see that they are well fed before they start; and if practicable it might be well to send some fodder along with them. Do, my dear mother, if there is an old saddle and bridle not in use on the place, let that accompany Porter. Do not forget to have a *bull* sent with the cattle. Will you please ask Porter whether we have more than one crosscut saw on the places? I cannot get one here, and am using a borrowed one at Indianola. The cattle will be of great advantage to the people, and it would be well to have them sent up at the earliest practicable day.

In regard to the salt, any time you may find it convenient to have it shipped from No. 3 to this city I will attend to its transshipment per Central Railroad.

I find a letter from Mr. Buttolph under date of the 23rd inst., telling me that he expected to go to Baker "on Tuesday next," which was day before yesterday. So soon as he returns we will, my dear mother, attend to the probate of my dear and honored father's will. I write today asking that he will let me know of his return in order that we may arrange this matter as soon as convenient.

Spent a day in Augusta. Eva quite unwell. She and Cousin Philo desired their special remembrance to you and my dear little daughter. Your kind letter of sympathy has been received, and was very sincerely appreciated by them. They begged me to express their deep acknowledgments for your kindness. Brother and Sister Carrie and the little ones were all very well, and united in warmest love. The Doctor had been suffering from a cold, but was better.

When, my dear mother, do you go to Walthourville? Sister writes me that your room is all ready, and that they are very anxious that you should come up as soon as you can. Do you think it prudent for you to remain much longer at Arcadia? I trust that you and my precious little daughter are both quite well, and that a kind Providence is ever near, encircling you with His protection and filling your pathways with many and great blessings, even amid these darkest days of desolation and severest bereavement. . . . Do, my dearest mother, accept every assurance of my constant and warmest love. . . . Mr. Ward begs me to present his respectful remembrances, and to offer his sincere thanks for your recent kindness. As ever,

Your affectionate son,
Charles C. Jones, Jr.

MRS. MARY JONES *to* COL. CHARLES C. JONES, JR.[8]

Arcadia, Friday, May 29th, 1863

My dear Son,

On my return this evening found your affectionate favor. I am thankful you found our people all so well and satisfied. After the distressing experience of the past year it always appears a special mercy when I hear "all are well."

Yesterday I took my little companion. We called to see the old people at the salt-boiling and my Old Mama; found them faithfully employed at their post of duty. Thence to Montevideo, where we passed the night, with all the precious memories of the past around me—your beloved and honored father associated with, and I may almost say present in, every spot. Indeed, he is so constantly in my thoughts and affections that I often look around to see if I cannot meet his eye or hear his voice. I often sit at twilight in his lonely study and wish it was given me to behold his precious face and form once more on earth. . . . I have been very much struck by a remark of *Sue's.* Speaking of all the spiritual, the religious instruction given by your father to the Negroes, especially his own, she said: "Our dear master has not left any of us poor; he has given us all our property to live off until our Blessed Saviour calls us home."

It was a new and strange business, but I felt that present circumstances made it a duty to see into the condition of things before leaving for Walthourville, particularly as I feared you might not be able to do so just now. This morning rose early. After family worship had breakfast. *Jerry* was brought to the door. I mounted, rode to the cow pen, counted and took down in memorandum book the number of cattle present, which Cato reported to be all. But there is quite a discrepancy between his account and that of your dear father. I told him they must be brought up and recounted and the pasture thoroughly searched. Thirty-two head were sold last winter; six oxen sent to Indianola. From Montevideo some have died; four of five killed. But still the number is less than it ought to be. Twenty head were sold from this place, and four oxen sent up, which of course diminishes the number. I have directed Prime to have all up here tomorrow. *All told* with Cato's account we have only sixty-four head. This includes Maybank and

Montevideo. We had at *Maybank* alone last summer sixty-three. Have left there nine head—which I fear our good neighbor will take care of! I then *reviewed* the hogs. One large one dead; the remainder doing very well. Passed through the cornfields. Highland very good: putting around seed and plowing; lowland broken. Rice *destroyed* in the largest square from drought and the salt water. A fine rain today, and Cato concluded to replant, as the season is early enough. The sugar cane pretty good; wants work. Close pease good. Cotton just coming up in many places. The month has been so dry it could not sprout; but a heavy crop of weeds.

Everything is wanting work so badly that I do not see how we could spare Gilbert and the mules any time *next* week to drive the cattle. He could do so perhaps the week after, and that would delay Porter another week. Syphax expects to go with him to Burke and visit his family, and could help with the cattle. Mr. Buttolph will be here next week if you could come out in the early part of it.

I took what my own dear father would have called the "grand rounds," and wound up with counting the sheep and a return to my own department in the poultry yard and flower garden. The people are all well, and appear to be faithfully employed; but the whole crop wants work, owing to the peculiarly late and dry season. The rice is so important a crop, although we had not reserved much rice I thought it best to use it for replanting.

I think our dear baby ought not to remain longer here, and will take her up at once and return and remain here next week, if God spares my life. Will ship the salt early next week. And now good night, my son. You may conclude that your mother is tired after such a day's work—*too* much so to sleep.

Ever your affectionate mother,
Mary Jones.

What must I do about the tax returns?

MRS. MARY JONES *to* COL. CHARLES C. JONES, JR.[8]

Arcadia, *Monday,* June 1st, 1863

My dear Son,

I am this moment from Walthourville, and hasten a reply to your leter. Left our little babe not so well from a cold, but thought it prudent she should not return.

I will send up to Mr. Buttolph and ask him to appoint *Thursday* of this week for going to Hinesville, which will give you time for writing the ordinary and also letting us know if you can come out on that day. I could meet you at the cars, and Mr. Buttolph and Laura could meet us at Hinesville.

Providence favored my seeing Mr. Butler this morning. Next Monday, D.V., he will come here and carry the cattle accompanied by Gilbert to his house, start on Tuesday, reach the station (No. 2) on Wednesday, where if you will so arrange, the cars can receive the cattle that night. Porter and Syphax will go down Monday or Tuesday and be ready at the station for the cattle. You will make arrangements with Mr. Sconyers for receiving them.

This afternoon the oxcart will take to McIntosh Station one barrel and three large bags of salt (containing nineteen bushels of salt) for Colonel C. C. Jones; and one sack of salt marked "Mrs. Eliza G. Robarts, Marietta, care of railroad agent." This salt is *more* than a supply for a year hence, bacon curing included; so do charge your manager to be careful of it.

Write particularly what time the cars will be at No. 2. The cattle will be there, Providence favoring, on Wednesday evening. I write in haste.

Ever your affectionate mother,
Mary Jones.

MRS. MARY JONES *to* COL. CHARLES C. JONES, JR.[8]

Arcadia, Tuesday, June 2nd, 1863

My dear Son,

The Lord permitting, I will meet you tomorrow as desired at No. 3 (McIntosh Station). I have just written Mr. Calder. . . . Robert leaves for Mount Vernon tomorrow, and kindly offers to take Tom with him, where he will work for four months at tanning and shoemaking, and by fall, I trust, will have gained sufficient knowledge to make the plantation shoes. In haste,

Your affectionate mother,
Mary Jones.

MRS. MARY JONES *to* COL. CHARLES C. JONES, JR.[8]

Arcadia, Friday, June 5th, 1863

My dear Son,

Mr. Quarterman has just called, and I have handed him twenty dollars to give Mr. Butler, which I presume will be more than sufficient for the expenses of himself and Gilbert and the cattle to the twenty-one-mile station on the Central Railroad. . . . *Thirty* head of cattle will be driven—twenty from this place and ten from Montevideo. Mr. Butler takes them Monday afternoon to Flemington, and Wednesday afternoon they will be at the station ready for the cars. Porter and Syphax will leave this place on Tuesday and meet them at the appointed place.

Enclosed I send Mr. Cassel's receipt for the salt. Please have the sack for our dear aunt, Mrs. Eliza G. Robarts, forwarded to her. It is directed care of railroad agent, and will go right.

Last night I felt the loneliness and isolation of my situation in an unusual degree. Not a white female of my acquaintance nearer than eight or ten miles, and not a white person nearer than the depot! My mind (blessed be God for the mercy) is kept free from all the ordinary fears that distress the unprotected. And surrounded as I am by the precious memorials of your beloved father, and near the spot where his sacred remains repose, I am loath to leave. *Daughter* urges me to do so on the score of health, and perhaps I will go to Walthourville on Saturday.

Should Robert decide for Atlanta, I will then be compelled to think of some resting place for my dear little baby and self during the summer. Your brother and Carrie invite me affectionately to spend it with them. When the time comes, I trust the Lord will provide and lead me in the way that I should go. For thirty-two years I have had a strong arm to lean upon—a wise head to guide, a heart all love and tenderness to bless and make me happy. It is my constant prayer that I may not be permitted to murmur or repine, and that what of life remains to me here may be spent in the discharge of duty, in the love and service of my God and Saviour, and in preparation for the solemn hour of death. Great will be *our condemnation*, my dear son, if after such an example and such precepts we fail through neglect or indifference or the love of sin or the influence of this wicked world to secure eternal life through Jesus Christ our Lord.

Ever your affectionate mother,
Mary Jones.

MRS. MARY JONES *to* COL. CHARLES C. JONES, JR.[8]

Walthourville, *Friday,* June 26th, 1863

My very dear Son,

We were so happy to see you yesterday; and the dear baby calls with increased affection for her papa. I often wish she could make you a daily visit. I trust our Heavenly Father has spared and will continue her precious life for great usefulness on earth. All else but the time we have spent in God's service and doing good will vanish as a dream when we take our last review of life's pilgrimage. . . .

Today I received the enclosed letter. *Please return it* and give me your views. Ought their use of the wood and occupation to be limited to such a length of time, or shall we allow them to stay as long as they desire? They speak of Mr. *Dunham's consent* to their digging wells. I sent Audley a plot of Half Moon, which includes the hammock where their wells are located; so they are wholly on our land. If you think it best *for me* to answer the letter, I will refer them to that plot in Audley's possession. I feel that what I desired is accomplished by the letter *in part*—a just and respectful recognition of our ownership. They made a request through Audley to be allowed to use the wood cut. I replied that they must communicate by writing, and we would then answer; and if they had been at great expense, I did not object to their doing so at one dollar per cord including what they had and would use.

Your sister and Robert unite with me in best love to you. Kisses from the little ones, especially your own.

Ever your affectionate mother,
Mary Jones.

Will you communicate with Mr. Ward while he is in England? If so, would it be improper to request him to make the inquiry what it would cost to secure the *copyright* and have published your father's *History of the Church of God* in London or any other place in England? It is my fervent desire to give the work as early as possible to the world. We could also take a copyright for the Confederacy to be published here as soon as the state of the country will permit. I should be under great obligations for any suggestions for the accomplishment of this desirable end.

COL. CHARLES C. JONES, JR., *to* MRS. MARY JONES[g]

Savannah, *Thursday*, July 2nd, 1863

My very dear Mother,

I am today in receipt of your very kind letter of the 26th inst., and am truly happy to know that all at home are well.

The letter of Messrs. King and Delegal is very respectful, and on the whole is all I think that we can ask of them. I would say to them that they can have the privilege of boiling salt on the premises, paying for all wood already consumed at once and hereafter monthly at one dollar per cord—the privilege to continue until 1st January next, and no oak wood to be cut by them. If you desire me to do so, I will write them for you. Audley would be a very good person, perhaps, on your part to estimate the amount of wood already consumed, if there is any question on that point. If you would prefer my communicating with them, please let me know, and I will do so at once.

Saw all friends at Augusta this week. Left Eva quite unwell, but I trust she soon will be better. Cousin Philo pretty well. The Doctor was looking badly. He purposes a visit to his friend Colonel Johnston at Sparta the ensuing week, and I trust the change will prove beneficial to him. Carrie and the children are well. They all desired sincerest remembrances to you.

Today is the second anniversary of the death of our sweet little Julia. How do all the sorrows of that saddest period come back over my soul with all the realities and freshness of but yesterday! And yet I never think of her otherwise than as a little angel only *lent* to earth, not *given*. How precious the thought that her safety for all time amid the eternal joys of heaven is secure!

General Lee appears to be pressing onward, and with marked success, into Pennsylvania. The enemy will now have a taste of actual warfare. We have a telegram today announcing the exchange of the crew of the *Atlanta*. With much love to all, and kisses for my dear little daughter, I am ever, my dear mother,

Your affectionate son,

Charles C. Jones, Jr.

MRS. MARY JONES *to* COL. CHARLES C. JONES, JR.[g]

Walthourville, *Friday*, July 3rd, 1863

My dear Son,

Your affectionate favor has just been received. This is indeed to us the period of sad memories; and yet what mercy mingles with the bitter cup! We are not mourning without hope. Our beloved ones, although absent from us, are present with the Lord. The Divine Redeemer who washed them in His own Blood, who clothed them in His own righteousness, who accomplished His sovereign will with them on earth, hath now received them into the mansions of everlasting glory and blessedness.

> With us their names shall live
> Through long succeeding years,
> Embalmed with all our hearts can give:
> Our praises and our tears.

It grieves me to hear that my dear Joe looks so badly. I know he is working himself down; I received a letter this week from him telling of his labors. I hope he will now take a little rest. And dear Eva, I am sorry to learn, is not well. A little change will do her good. You told me she spoke of visiting her friends.

Yesterday I had a long and fatiguing ride. Went both to Montevideo and Arcadia. Servants generally well. Little Andrew asks on account of his wife to remain a day or two over his week. I told him he might stay until Thursday of next week, when he will come in and go to Burke on Friday.

I will be much obliged to you to answer the letter of Messrs. King and Delegal. They speak of getting "Mr. Dunham's consent to dig wells." Please refer them to the *plot* of *Half Moon* which is copied from the original and now in the possession of Mr. Audley King, which will determine the lines.

Our peaceful little village assumed quite a military aspect the first of the week. On Sabbath Captains Hughes's and Walthour's commands arrived en route for the Altamaha. They departed Monday morning; and about one o'clock of the same day the trumpet announced the arrival of the Terrell Artillery, with *whom you are acquainted.* They encamped in the academy yard, around and about us on all sides; and more gentlemanly soldiers I think could not be found. They spoke of their *colonel* in the highest terms; said he was "mightily beliked," and "the boys would die by him"; all they wanted was to meet the enemy. In the afternoon they drilled, much to the admiration of all present. (I did not go out.) Both dinner and supper were provided for them, which they enjoyed, and departed Tuesday morning with their guns and standard decorated with fresh bouquets amid prolonged shouts, leaving behind their assurance that "the Yankees should never reach Walthourville." They excited not only admiration but confidence, and carried away our fervent prayers and best wishes for the divine protection and complete success if called to meet the enemy on the battlefield.

Your shirts, I hope, will *last longer than the war.* Do let me know whenever I can do anything for you. I am writing in great haste for the express. Love from your sister. Sweetest kisses from "Papa's daughter," as she calls herself.

> Ever, my dear son, your affectionate mother,
> Mary Jones.

MRS. MARY JONES *to* COL. CHARLES C. JONES, JR.[8]

Walthourville, *Tuesday,* July 7th, 1863

My dear Son,

Our mail carrier was unusually late this morning, leaving me but a brief period to say that I will with pleasure attend to the making of the articles, and only wish it was in my power to furnish all you need. From long service and no recent replenishing, the stock of house linen has run low at home; but you may be assured it will give me pleasure to assist you in every way that I can, and I hope you will let me know whenever I can do so. Send the articles, and I will see that they are made as early as practicable.

Our hearts are anxiously looking for tidings from our army, which seems in peril at so many points. "God is our refuge and our strength!" Robert has a prayer meeting every Tuesday night expressly for the country and our army in its present situation. Held at private houses; tonight it meets at Judge Fleming's. The appointments are made at the request of individuals. We can but hope that "He who will be inquired of by His people" will hear and answer their prayers. If ever there was an hour for urgent supplication, it is *now. . . .*

This day is the anniversary of our dear Ruth's death; I should say her peaceful departure to her heavenly rest. I would gladly know, my beloved child, if you have fulfilled her one great desire for you: *"Seek Christ, and seek Him now."* Oh, that He might indeed be formed in your heart—the hope, the foundation, the tried cornerstone of your affections and your happiness for time and for eternity!

I would gladly write more, but must close. You need not buy any more things for Baby unless I write for them. She is amply supplied, and if the shoes do not fit I will return them, for I am going to have some nice little ones made for her here. She sends sweetest kisses to dear Papa. Love from all.

Ever your affectionate mother,

Mary Jones.

I will hand you the bankbook when you come out. When will that be?

Eleven Negroes left this village Saturday night for the enemy; three have been caught.

MRS. MARY JONES *to* COL. CHARLES C. JONES, JR.[8]

Walthourville, *Tuesday,* July 14th, 1863

My dear Son,

I have this moment returned from Montevideo, and hasten to send you a basket per express. Hope the lamb will be good. The melon is from your sister, sent to her by Mrs. Fleming. The herbs you can give for the use of the sick soldiers; also the flaxseed. I thought they might be useful, and are just dried from my garden.

The bundle arrived by express, and I will make the articles as you desired. One pair of Baby's shoes she can wear; the other will not fit at all, so I return them at once. Please exchange for fully a size larger. Now that she is so constantly on them, her little feet are not so fairylike as they were.

My dear son, not a moment passes that my thoughts are not with you or my bleeding country in some form. How long will this awful conflict last? And to what depths of misery are we to be reduced ere the Sovereign Judge of all the earth will give us deliverance? It does appear that we are to be brought very low. May the Lord give us such true repentance and humility before Him as shall turn away His wrath and restore His favor, through the merits and intercession of our Divine Redeemer! I do bless God for the spirit of true patriotism and undaunted courage with which He is arming us for this struggle. Noble Vicksburg! From her heroic example we gather strength to hold on and hold out to the last moment. I can look extinction for me and mine in the face, but *submission* never! It would be degradation of the lowest order.

May Jehovah bless and preserve you, my dear child! Love from your sister and the children, with many kisses from your dear daughter and the true affection of

Your mother,
Mary Jones.

Little Mary has just said: "Grandma! Is that an elegant basket! I think Uncle Charlie will ask Beauregard to eat dinner with him."

Will you let George get me two dollars' worth of *black varnish* from the painters and keep it until you come.

COL. CHARLES C. JONES, JR., *to* MRS. MARY JONES⁸

Savannah, *Wednesday,* July 15th, 1863

My very dear Mother,

It was a sore trial for me to pass so near both this morning and this afternoon without seeing you, my precious little daughter, and the dear ones at home. But my orders were imperative, and I had in their discharge to forgo that pleasure. I said to Robert, whom I had the gratification of meeting at the depot, that I might not return before tomorrow; but I was able to compass the object which carried me out in time for the return train.

Many—very many—thanks, my dearest mother, for your kind remembrance of me. I must find some good friend tomorrow to help me enjoy all of these good things. They are indeed a treat. Do thank Sister too for the nice watermelon.

No news from Charleston today. The heavens above us are indeed dark; but although for the present the clouds give no reviving showers, let us look and pray earnestly for His favor who can bring order out of chaos, victory out of apparent defeat, and light out of shadow. All these reverses should teach us our absolute dependence upon a Higher Power, and lead to sincere personal and national repentance.

Daughter's shoes I will, D.V., exchange on the morrow, and will also procure the varnish, not forgetting to take good care of the basket. My head is

383

a little heavy from the hot suns of the Altamaha swamp; but I could not let your kind letter remain unanswered a single night, or sleep until I had returned you, my dear mother, my grateful acknowledgments for your kind and special remembrance of me. Kiss Daughter. Love to all. And believe me ever

Your affectionate son,
Charles C. Jones, Jr.

Tell Mamie I wish General B. was here to enjoy the nice mutton, but that he is so busy fighting the Yankees that he cannot come.

MRS. MARY JONES *to* COL. CHARLES C. JONES, JR.[8]

Walthourville, *Thursday,* July 16th, 1863

My dear Son,

We were greatly disappointed to find we should not see you this afternoon as we had anticipated—and I had promised your little daughter the pleasure of meeting her dear papa at the cars. But I am glad your business did not require you to remain all night at the Altamaha.

She becomes every day increasingly interesting: understands a great deal, and begins to show her own will in many ways. I do not think she will ever be a difficult child to govern. She discovers a decided taste for books, and will amuse herself with them at set times. For instance, as soon as prayers are over in the morning she calls out "Book!" and goes to the table where her favorite book of pictures stands and goes to reading in her own way. I would like a primer or spelling book with pictures for her, as she seems to prefer them to the common picture books. She often reminds me of her father in his infancy. Books were your playthings; at one time you always slept with one.

I fear your mutton was scarcely eatable today, it was so warm.

I am grieved to hear of Adam's illness. He was in feeble health a long time after his return from the fortifications on the Savannah River—was one of the number who were so ill last spring; and I think with God's blessing your brother was the instrument of saving his life at that time.

Will you be so good as to send, or bring me when next you come out, the last dividend from the railroad and the twenty-five dollars recently deposited? I might require them during the summer. Robert will be down before long, and could bring the money if you do not come out.

I would like you to request Audley King to act for us in the salt business, as he could judge of the amount of wood used and receive payment, being on the *spot.* Did the gentlemen say at what time they commenced boiling? They must use over a cord a day. It might be well to understand how they estimate the consumption of wood. Audley has quite a business young man associated with him—Mr. Collins, nephew of Mr. Mitchel of Darien.

Today's paper contained a very handsome acknowledgment from the Terrell Artillery of the hospitalities of Walthourville. . . . The last prayer meeting for the country Robert read the 74th Psalm; look at it. . . . I have felt very sad *today*: it is four months since your beloved father died. I realize every day more and more my desolation. With best love from all,

Ever your affectionate mother,

Mary Jones.

What think you of my idea of printing the *History* in England?

Col. Charles C. Jones, Jr., *to* Mrs. Mary Jones[g]

Savannah, *Saturday,* July 18th, 1863

My dear Mother,

I am this morning in receipt of your kind letter of yesterday, and can but reiterate my sincere regrets that I was unable to stop and see all at home upon my return from the Altamaha. My orders were, however, imperative.

It makes me very happy to hear such good accounts of my precious little daughter. May she be ever a perpetual joy to us all! And may it please God mercifully to surround her with every blessing—social, temporal, and spiritual! Never, my dear mother, will she or I be able to thank you sufficiently for all your great kindness. May the Lord reward and bless you for all your goodness to us!

The dividend from the Central Railroad Bank and the twenty-five dollars received for wood have both been deposited to your credit in the Bank of the State of Georgia, so that you will have to draw a check for what amount you desire. You can make that check payable either to my order or to that of Robert, and the amount will be sent out by the earliest opportunity.

Will you be kind enough, Mother, to send me at your early convenience *a recipe for making Ogeechee limes?* One of Eva's good friends has promised to put up some pickles for her, and also some Ogeechee lime preserves if she can obtain a proper recipe for the latter. And she has requested me at your convenience to obtain the same from you and forward it to her.

I will write Audley in reference to the wood, etc., as you desire. I will read the 74th Psalm. Tell Robert when he comes in that he must stop with me.

It might be well, Mother, under ordinary circumstances to have Father's church history published in England; but it would not now be practicable either to transmit the manuscript in safety or to pay the expenses of the publication. Exchange can only be purchased at a most ruinous rate—say, nine hundred percent. So soon as peace returns, our first duty must be to give this last labor of love of my beloved and honored father to the church, the country, and the world.

It is hard to realize that he has lain more than four months in that silent home prepared for all the living. And yet not *there;* for he is in a far higher, a far happier place, even in the bright heavens above, and in the companionship of the Lord Jehovah, of the Blessed Saviour whom he so much loved, of the Holy Ghost who was ever the Comforter to him, and of the dear departed who have gone before, and of the good and the great, the saints of all ages made perfect in glory. It is hard indeed to think that we will no more here be

385

blessed with his presence. May we be enabled through grace to meet him hereafter!

Nothing new from Charleston. Rain every day. With warmest love to all, and many kisses for my precious little daughter, I am ever, my dear mother,

Your affectionate son,
Charles C. Jones, Jr.

The mutton was a little touched, but we enjoyed and thanked you very much for it.

I will try and procure a primer for Daughter.

MRS. MARY JONES to COL. CHARLES C. JONES, JR.[8]
Walthourville, *Tuesday,* July 21st, 1863

My dear Son,

You have in the above recipe the manner in which I *used* to make Ogeechee limes. I have tried to be explicit, and hope it will be understood. If I only had the sugar I would send you something better than a dry recipe.

These are emphatically times when, "having food and raiment, let us be therewith content." I bless the Lord every day of my life that although I am a refugee from my own pleasant homes, still I am not a houseless wanderer as thousands of my noble countrywomen are, but am still surrounded with the comforts of life. And what is far above all these things, the lives of my beloved children are still spared.

Last evening just before sunset I heard the sound of the bugle, and just under my window two cavalry companies were dismounting—the commands of Captain Walthour and Captain Hughes. Most of them, having friends within reaching distance, dispersed in all directions. Robert and your sister being still away, I had to do the honors of the house. Seven of the friendless soldiers took supper; four stayed all night; and seven had breakfast at five o'clock this morning. A supply of melons, figs, curds, fresh butter, etc., having just come up from the plantation, I placed them at their disposal, and enjoyed the pleasure of seeing them appreciated.

This morning a poor fellow evidently in pain crawled through the paling and laid under the shade of the tree. He was a teamster, and had been injured yesterday in the back. I sent his breakfast and something to relieve the pain. His reply was: "He thanked the Lord there was one friend in the world to care for him." He still lies upon the grass under my window.

One of the melons is so fine I cannot resist sending it to you. With sweetest kisses, and thanks for the primer from your daughter,

Ever your affectionate mother,
Mary Jones.

XV

COL. CHARLES C. JONES, JR., *to* REV. *and* MRS. R. Q. MALLARD^t
Savannah, *Tuesday,* August 4th, 1863

My very dear and afflicted Sister and Brother,

Not until a late hour last night did I learn the sorrowful intelligence of the death of your precious little daughter. I did not even know that she had been sick, having returned to the city only last evening after an absence of more than a week. A warm brother's heart sympathizes most tenderly with you in this your hour of special bereavement. I know from sad experience the depths of those shadows which rest upon the parents' heart when the child we love—whose life is knit to that of the fond father and generous mother by the most enduring and intimate ties, cherished by the purest, truest affections —is summoned from our embraces in obedience to the call of an all-wise but inscrutable Providence. I do feel for you most deeply, and my eyes are filled with tears.

And yet is not the loss purely personal? Is not death, to that bright redeemed little spirit, great gain? In this the day of your special bereavement, what a mitigation of the great affliction to feel that all is well with her, that her salvation for eternity is certain, that no matter what rude alarms, what trying ills, may be in store for us in the future, she at least has by a good God been taken from the evil to come! The last entry, you remember, our beloved and honored father ever made in his diary was commemorative of her birth. He never saw her in life, but she is with him now. In that bright world above he has already welcomed her pure spirit; and there, in the living immediate presence of that great Redeemer who while on earth said: "Suffer the little children to come unto me, and forbid them not, for of such is the Kingdom of God," will they joy in the smile of the Lord. She is not lonely there. Ruth and little Julia and all the dear departed who have gone before are with and near her, and the endless companionships and unspeakable privileges of heaven are hers. There is every consolation in the thought that she is saved—an angel in heaven; and thus when we weep, it is only for ourselves, only for the light of the dwelling gone out at early dawn, only for the companionship so dear which can never on earth be renewed. You both are Christians, my dear sister and brother, and have free, full access to the source of all consolation—to the Father of All Mercies, who doth not willingly afflict, and who will bind up the bruised reed. May His sustaining grace be ever present with you to support and to comfort!

Earnestly did I desire to be with you today, but the indications of a possible attack upon this city at no distant day prevented my leaving Savannah. But although absent from you in person, my heart and tenderest sympathies have been and are with you. God bless you both, and the precious little ones who are still spared, and prepare us all to meet the dear ones in that better world where there shall be no more tears or partings or sorrows.

Ever your affectionate brother,
Charles C. Jones, Jr.

COL. CHARLES C. JONES, JR., *to* MRS. MARY JONES⁸

Savannah, *Tuesday,* August 4th, 1863

My very dear Mother,

I have just written Sister and Robert a letter of sympathy. I was greatly surprised and deeply pained to learn last night of the death of dear little Sarah Burnley. I knew not even of her illness, and great was my regret that I did not enjoy the privilege of being with you today. Do let me know of her sickness and her last moments. For yourself, my dear mother, accept my sincerest sympathies in this new affliction which has come upon us all. . . .

I returned only last night. Yesterday I visited Indianola. Martha's infant better, and all well except Adam, who improves slowly. Crops looking fair. Too much rain for some localities. By the express of yesterday I sent a sack of flour, ground from the wheat made at Indianola, for yourself and Sister. I think you will find it very nice, and hope that you will all enjoy it.

Saw Rev. Mr. Porter on the cars yesterday, who told me that he was going out to Liberty today or tomorrow to dissolve the connection existing between Robert and the Walthourville church in order to permit him to go to Atlanta. He expressed great regret at his leaving. You will doubtless see him while in Walthourville. Robert will, I fear, find it a difficult matter to secure a house, as the city is crowded to overflowing, and rents are at a high figure. His congregation will have to render him essential assistance.

In passing from Augusta to Atlanta I spent a night at General Toombs's with my dear Eva, who is now there on a visit to her friends Mrs. Toombs and Mrs. DuBose. She was pretty well, and very happy thus unexpectedly to see me after our protracted absence. Providence permitting, we will probably be married about the 5th of November. She desired her special remembrance and love to yourself and Sister, and her thanks for the recipe. I know you will love her very dearly, for she is absolutely attractive in every particular, and has a heart as pure and tender and full of affection as dwells in woman's breast. She is as perfectly devoted to me as I am to her, and I trust that Heaven will bless our mutual affections.

We are anxiously anticipating demonstrations on our coast, and are as active as we can be. Dark days are upon us, but we must look to God and gird up our loins. There is a wonderful lack of patriotism in many of our people. The greed of gain is the present curse of the country.

How is my precious little daughter? I am so anxious to see her, and hope to be able to do so before long. God bless her and keep her in His special care, and reward you, my dear mother, for all your kindness to her and to me! Kiss her for me. With best love to all, I am ever

Your affectionate son,
Charles C. Jones, Jr.

Enclosed I send a letter from Betty to you.

MRS. MARY JONES *to* MAJOR *and* MRS. JOSEPH JONES[t]

Walthourville, Thursday, August 6th, 1863

My dear Children,

It has pleased our Heavenly Father again to send the Angel of Death into our family circle; and the precious little one who received your beloved and honored father's last blessing on earth has been the first to join him in heaven.

About the middle of the past week our little Eliza Burnley appeared unwell with slight bowel affection. On Friday afternoon fever came on, but she was quiet and apparently free from pain. On Saturday morning the doctor was sent for. . . . He visited her three times a day, but the fever did not abate, although she was frequently drenched in copious perspirations. Sabbath afternoon I felt that her case was hopeless. . . . We sent for Dr. Stevens, and he kindly remained with us until her happy spirit took its departure from your sister's arms below to the bosom of the Divine Redeemer above on the morning of the 3rd at half-past five o'clock.

The little form was beautiful in death. Many kind friends from the village gathered around with tears of sympathy and words of comfort. The children were asleep when she died, and although in the room we did not think it proper to awake them. They were removed and dressed in another room, and when Daughter told them their little sister was dead, Charlie said: "Mama, has God sent for my sister already? And have the angels carried her up to Grandpapa?" He was surprised when he went into the room to find her little body in the crib, and afterwards asked to have it removed into another room, where hung some shades to the windows which he admired. He said they were "so beautiful the angels would like to come in at those windows to carry her away." Little Mary was devoted to the baby; would wait upon her, and was never happier than when permitted to draw her in her carriage. She asked to arrange the flowers about her, and did so. Frequently in life we have gone into the room where the baby was sleeping and found her wreathed around with cedar or flowers by her. Little Sister would insist upon standing at her side and fanning her, saying: "Birdie seeping." She was the center of love and attraction to the whole house.

Your sister bows in submission, but it is a heavy sorrow. Robert says: "I know, O Lord, that in faithfulness Thou hast afflicted me."

The funeral was held by Mr. Buttolph on the morning of the 4th, and we took the precious little form to Midway, where we laid her by the side of your father, in a line with your Uncle John Jones, Jr.'s, grave.

Yesterday by previous appointment Presbytery met here and dissolved Robert's connection with this church as a pastor, declaring it vacant. It was his intention before the baby's death to have preached in Atlanta the coming Sabbath; he will not now leave before next week. It is necessary for him to go up before removing his family and see what arrangements can be made for a house, etc., etc. I do not think they can move before September. When they do leave, if it suits your convenience, I desire very much to come up and see you.

It was one of the sweet anticipations which often crossed my thoughts to have my two darling little granddaughters, so near of an age, in my arms together. May the Lord in mercy spare your loved one to you! Although she was best prepared to go, we shall long miss her. She came in tears, when all were sorrowful around her, but she never added one pang. She was a precious little comforter while she tarried with us.

Your sister and Robert unite with me in best love to you, with many kisses for my dear grandchildren, and love and kisses from the little ones here. Your aunt and her family are well. Howdies for your servants; their families are all well. The Lord bless and keep you and yours, my dear son and daughter!

Ever your affectionate mother,
Mary Jones.

Your letter has this moment come. I hope dear Carrie will write me in your absence. I should think this the best season for going to Virginia.

MRS. CAROLINE S. JONES *to* MRS. MARY S. MALLARD[t]

Augusta, *Monday,* August 10th, 1863

My dearest Sister,

My heart aches as I begin this letter of sympathy to you, for it comes home to me sadly that sympathy nor tears can do anything to heal a heart sore with sorrow so recent as yours. I can only give you what I have: grief and tears for your loss. . . . My heart answers to yours, dear Mary, with a quivering sharp pang of realization as I look at my own precious baby and feel what anguish I too might suffer. And with that realization which only a mother can feel my heart bleeds for you. . . . They say no earthly love is taken away until it has accomplished its work. She has unsealed the fountain of tenderness in all around her, and now she has gone to be another link in the chain that draws you to heaven. . . . A tender and beautiful recollection to your little ones she will always be, and make heaven seem nearer and more real to them. I do not doubt it will make an impression upon Mary's heart that she will never lose, with her quick apprehension and strong feelings.

I hope, dear Mary, you will soon be with us. I have been looking forward to seeing yourself and our dear mother with all the little ones, and now more than ever desire it. You must stay here and recruit while Mr. Mallard makes the necessary arrangements in Atlanta. Your brother left special injunctions with me to add his urgency to mine that you would come at that time. He had left when Mother's letter was received; and how much he will feel with and for you, you know him well enough to understand. Dear Mary, receive my love and sympathy and tears. And believe me

Your ever tenderly attached sister,
Caroline S. J.

MRS. MARY JONES *to* COL. CHARLES C. JONES, JR.[8]

Walthourville, *Thursday,* August 20th, 1863

My dear Son,

No letter from you since we parted makes me extremely anxious. I hope you are not sick—alone and with no one to write me of the fact. Your sister suggests that you may have been ordered to Charleston; if that was so, I think you would have informed us. . . . Do, my child, let me know if you are still unwell, and if you desire it I will come down any day and nurse you. Make George sleep near your chamber while you are sick in case of needing his services.

I went to Montevideo day before yesterday. All well but Lymus; he continues very feeble. Cato stripping fodder. Our rice a failure from early drought; the river too salt to flow at the proper season. Audley called up and paid me fourteen dollars from Messrs. King and Delegal for July. He is doing well for himself, making, he told me, six hundred dollars per day. . . . I have no doubt the Island will become an attractive point, and whenever you are able to come out I would suggest what I think will benefit ourselves as well as our neighbors. With the exception of that owned by Audley, we own all the wooded land on the western (which is the safe) side of the Island.

Robert did not come today as we expected. Tomorrow will be the day of fasting and prayer appointed by our Christian President. May the Blessed Spirit prepare one and all to come with true repentance, humility, and faith to the throne of mercy, that we may find grace and obtain strength to help in this time of our sorest need! I see no mode of deliverance but by the almighty power of God through the merits and intercession of our Lord Jesus Christ, who is the Prince of Peace.

We received letters from your brother yesterday from Richmond, Virginia. Please, my son, tell George to take the bundle of *flaxseed* over to the Wayside Home, and to send the bowl, etc., when an opportunity occurs. Excuse my trembling hand. Sister unites with me in best love to you. Kisses from the little ones, especially your own.

Ever your affectionate mother,
Mary Jones.

MRS. MARY JONES *to* COL. CHARLES C. JONES, JR.[8]

Walthourville, *Saturday,* August 22nd, 1863

My dear Son,

I felt greatly relieved to hear that you had no return of fever, and through Robert that you were looking well again. I can never sufficiently thank and praise the Lord for His goodness and mercy in sparing my dear children to me whilst so many are mourning their loved ones slain upon the battlefield or laid in their graves by the hand of disease!

Robert was in time for his pulpit exercises. We had two services—more in the form of prayer meetings—which were peculiarly appropriate to the due observance of the day. We can but hope from our present circumstances of peril and deep distress that our nation was constrained to keep the fast as unto the Lord, worshiping in spirit and in truth, humbly confessing the sins which have drawn this heavy judgment upon us, and looking to God alone for deliverance. . . .

A letter from your Uncle John to your sister received today says he has been much engaged in preaching to the Texas Rangers stationed at Rome. Thirty have professed conversion, and the good work still continues. These revivals in our army are certainly the highest proofs we can possibly desire or receive of the divine favor. I can but regard as the darkest sign of the times this talk about reconstruction and submission, and the spirit of speculation, fattening upon the miseries and wants of a suffering land. We are anxious to know how affairs are in Charleston.

Our dear little Mary Ruth has been quite unwell all the week from cold. She is much better today. Should she not be quite relieved, I will not leave her tomorrow, which will be our Communion season at Midway. Our servant Niger hopes to unite with the church; your beloved father's death, he says, turned his thoughts to God. As our blacks could not bear the journey to and back in one day, I directed Gilbert to bring up the mules, who are good travelers. He will be up this afternoon; and hoping that you may be able to come out on Monday, I will keep him to take you down to the camps and the Island should you come. If prevented, I will hear from you.

I think it will be best for us *not to allow any more* use of the wood at the Island for one dollar per cord, but charge so *much a month*—say, fifty or a hundred dollars according to the use; for it does not appear possible to arrive at an estimate of the consumption. The profits of the consumer are so great they ought to be willing to pay a fair amount for the wood. This, I believe, is the plan adopted, and it appears just and right. If Mr. Collins wants to boil there, we will place a stipulated price per month.

With best love from us all, and kisses from your precious child,

Ever your affectionate mother,

Mary Jones.

You can get the butter at any time. I will send Patience word to have it ready for you.

COL. CHARLES C. JONES, JR., *to* MRS. MARY JONES[8]

Savannah, *Saturday,* August 22nd, 1863

My very dear Mother,

Your kind favor of this date has just been received. I am truly sorry to hear of the indisposition of my dear little daughter, but rejoice to hear you say that she is better. I trust it will please God soon to restore her to her accustomed degree of good health.

The day of fasting and prayer was very generally observed in our city. All places of business were closed, ordinary avocations suspended, and all the churches open. It was a Sabbath in our land. Dr. Axson gave us an excellent sermon, which I would be happy to see published and disseminated throughout the length and breadth of our beleaguered land. I understand the bishop's sermon was full of interest.

I had hoped, my dear mother, to have been out the early part of the coming week, but will be somewhat delayed in equipping and putting in order a light battery which has just reported to me from Florida. So I cannot say on what precise day I can be with you. Will, however, give you notice.

We have nothing of special interest from Charleston except the fact that two enormous Blakely guns recently arrived in Wilmington are on their way thither. These guns are vastly more powerful than any in the possession of the enemy, and when placed in position will most effectually disable any vessel in the attacking fleet. Each gun, independent of the carriage, weighs forty-nine thousand pounds, and throws a solid shot of nearly eight hundred pounds! Think of that! Such monsters are a novelty in the history of warfare. They cost, I understand, seventy-five thousand dollars each. In consequence of their extreme weight it is a very difficult matter to transport them; but every effort is being made to bring them forward at the earliest practicable moment and place them in battery at the most advantageous points. God grant that they may arrive in season to accomplish the safety of the city and the discomfiture of all her enemies!

The abolitionists shelled Charleston from Morris Island—a distance of over four miles—with their Parrott guns on night before last. Several shell fell in the city, and one of them set a house on fire. Can history furnish a parallel to such an act of inhumanity? Think of an enemy in the dead of night, without the slightest intimation, shelling a city filled with women and children and noncombatants! And yet this act is simply characteristic of the infamous race who have upon every occasion insulted our women, murdered our citizens, plundered our homes, robbed our plantations, desolated our fields, and filled the land with enormities such as are not remembered in the annals of savage warfare.

I hope to see Mr. Collins about the wood for his salt, and will act upon the terms suggested by you. Am happy to hear that Uncle John has been so much blessed in his ministrations of the Word to the soldiers. Similar reports come forward from various branches of our armies, and we are called upon to thank God for this evidence of His great favor. With much love to self, my dear

393

mother, and all at home, and many kisses for my sweet little daughter, I am ever

Your affectionate son,
Charles C. Jones, Jr.

MAJOR JOSEPH JONES *to* MRS. MARY S. MALLARD[t]

Richmond, Virginia, *Wednesday,* August 26th, 1863

My dear Sister,

Yesterday I received a letter from Carrie informing me of your recent affliction. This is the first intelligence which I have had of the death of the dear little one; and I deeply sympathize with you, my dear sister and brother, in this severe trial. Notwithstanding that the beautiful little flower has been broken from the parent stem, and the cheerful little light has gone out, and there is a vacant place in the little cradle and in the hearts of the fond parents and of the dear little sister and brother, still the Christian is able to find comfort. At any time—but especially in these times of uncertainty and bloody war—we can but say that these little angels have been removed by their all-wise and merciful Father to His own bosom from the evil to come. The blessing of her sainted grandfather was not long delayed, and now she is with him in perfect peace and happiness, secure forever from all the rude storms and temptations of earth. . . .

Amidst all our recent afflictions we have great and unnumbered blessings for which to be always thankful. What greater blessing could ever have been bestowed upon children than the kind care, noble example and instruction, and sacred memory of our dear father? And now that he has been removed from us, we can look back upon his life and see at every step the merciful dealings of God with him and his little family. I think that there never was a calmer, more useful and elevated, or more honored life devoted to the service of the Creator. He lived for eternity and not for time, although for others his labors embraced the relations of both; and he was always actuated by the desire to promote the best welfare of his fellow men, temporal and spiritual. What greater blessing than the inheritance of such sacred memories?

I hope, my dear sister, that your health has been entirely restored. You must come up and pay us a long visit. The change will do you good. I am very glad to know that Brother Robert will accept the call to Atlanta. I think that the climate in this elevated region will work a revolution in your health. Besides this, the place is an important and rapidly increasing one, and bids fair to become one of the largest manufacturing inland cities.

Carrie writes me that she will in the course of a few days be in our new rented house. I regret that I am not with her to assist, but in these times of war we cannot command our time as we would.

My present labors are severe and arduous, but they are invested with great interest. I have been greatly struck by the cheerful endurance of our poor sick soldiers. Amongst the thousands which I have visited—many of them, too, with hospital gangrene dissolving their poor limbs and exposing quivering muscles, arteries, and nerves—I have not heard one word of discontent or despondency. Words of submission and complaint are reserved for those who stay at home and enjoy the security afforded by these noble men who stand as a living wall around the homes of the Southern women and children. As long as such noble men compose our armies, we can never be conquered.

If Providence permits, I hope to turn my face homewards in ten days or two weeks. With warmest love to you and Brother Robert and the little ones, I remain

Your affectionate brother,
Joseph Jones.

COL. CHARLES C. JONES, JR., *to* MRS. MARY JONES[8]

Savannah, *Monday*, August 31st, 1863

My very dear Mother,

I have just been ordered by General Beauregard to Charleston to take command of the light artillery on James Island. I leave in the morning, D.V., not to return, I expect, if God spares my life, until the existing difficulties are settled.

My position is one of great responsibility, and I hope that I may have strength given me from above properly to discharge all the duties which will devolve upon me. All our help cometh from God, and every day do I realize more and more forcibly my every dependence upon Him. May He in mercy watch over and bless with His protecting care and love you, my dear mother, my precious little daughter, Sister, Brother, and all who are near and dear to me! I will hope to do my duty under every circumstance; and you will all remember, whatever may befall me, that I love you all with a true, warm, big heart, and from the bottom of that heart thank you all for your great and never-ceasing kindness and goodness to me all my life. Please let me know if my dear little daughter should at any time need anything.

A detailed statement of my affairs I leave in my tin box in the safe of the Farmers' & Mechanics' Bank in this city.

I regret very much that I did not enjoy the privilege of coming out as I expected to have done, but it was an impracticable matter, and now this order prevents me from accomplishing my contemplated visit this week. I will write you so soon as I can after getting over, and will tell you how to direct your letters to me. Do kiss my precious little daughter for me. Give much love to Sister, Robert, and the little ones. And believe me ever, my dearest mother,

Your affectionate son,
Charles C. Jones, Jr.

395

COL. CHARLES C. JONES, JR., *to* MRS. MARY JONES[8]

James Island, *Thursday,* September 3rd, 1863

My very dear Mother,

I came over to this island on yesterday under orders from General Beauregard to take command of the light artillery, of which there are here some six light batteries and two siege trains. I am located at the headquarters of General Taliaferro, and am as pleasantly situated as it is possible for me to be under the circumstances. Today I am going to ride around the lines with the general, and when I return I will take the earliest opportunity of giving you an account of the situation of matters. This morning I write simply to tell you that I am well, and to assure you and all at home of my constant love and truest remembrance. Do kiss my precious little daughter for me. Give love to all. And believe me ever, my dearest mother,

Your affectionate son,

Charles C. Jones, Jr.

Do write me as soon as you can, directing your letters to me at Charleston, care of General W. B. Taliaferro.

COL. CHARLES C. JONES, JR., *to* MRS. MARY JONES[8]

James Island, *Friday,* September 4th, 1863

My very dear Mother,

Nothing of an unusual character has occurred in the progress of this siege within the past two days with the exception that the enemy this afternoon paid some attention, with the *Pawnee* and a gunboat, to our southern lines, shelling and then retiring. Heavy firing still continues between the hostile forts on Morris Island; and our batteries at various points on this island are endeavoring to annoy the enemy. As you view Morris Island from the batteries in advance of our quarters and from Secessionville, you can almost imagine that you are looking upon *Staten Island;* there is such an aggregation of shipping of every sort and description, and such a collection of tents, etc., that the island presents the appearance of a continuous village. I have assumed command of the light artillery on this island. If any attack is made by way of James Island, I will have my hands full.

There is not a moment of the day or night but the boom of heavy ordnance, the smoke of our batteries, and the bursting of shells can be seen and heard. I regard the fall of Fort Wagner as a mere question of time, and think the policy of holding it longer a questionable one. . . .

Our present location is very filthy. You never saw such quantities of flies; and bad smells are everywhere. Should anything unusual occur, I will write you at once. Do kiss my precious little daughter for me. Give love to all. And believe me ever, my dear mother,

Your affectionate son,

Charles C. Jones, Jr.

There is no saying when this siege will end. We hope for the best.

COL. CHARLES C. JONES, JR., *to* MRS. MARY JONES[8]

James Island, *Sunday,* September 6th, 1863

It is Sabbath morning, my dear mother, but it is a very difficult matter to realize the fact. All day yesterday, all last night, and all day up to this hour, Battery Wagner has been subjected to a most terrific bombardment. Over one hundred were killed and wounded within its walls yesterday. No human being could have lived for one moment upon its walls or upon its parade. Against it were hurled the combined projectiles fired from the ironsides and the various mortar and Parrott batteries of the enemy located at different points on Morris Island. As their shells in numbers would explode in the parapet and within the fort, Wagner would seem converted into a volcano. Never was any battery called upon to resist such a bombardment, and I fear that it is now held more as a matter of military pride than anything else. It is very questionable whether this should be done.

In full view of everything on yesterday afternoon, from Battery Haskell, which was firing upon the enemy, I witnessed the progress of the siege. The gunnery of the Federals was wonderful. Wagner could not answer a single shot. The enemy last night assaulted Battery Gregg, which is located on the extreme north point of Morris Island, and were repulsed. God be praised for that; for had Gregg been carried, the entire garrison at Wagner would have been captured. I would not be surprised if the enemy assaulted Wagner tonight. That portion of the parapet looking towards the south of Morris Island has been knocked very much to pieces, and the sand crumbled into the ditch. In the very nature of things it cannot be held very much longer.

As a port of commercial ingress and egress Charleston is gone; but my impression at present is that the enemy will never be able to obtain possession of the city itself. It may be destroyed in whole or in part by the shells of the enemy, but it is questionable whether they can ever hold it as a site. The inner defenses are as yet intact, and the large Blakely gun is nearly mounted. Three ironclad gunboats are in the harbor, ready to attack the enemy in the event of their endeavoring to enter with their fleet.

We know not what a day may bring forth, but I trust that we may all be enabled, by God's blessing, to do our heroic duty under any and every circumstance. This life is a terrible one, but must be endured. Do, my dear mother, kiss my precious little daughter for me. Assure all at home of my sincerest love. And believe me ever

Your affectionate son,
Charles C. Jones, Jr.

COL. CHARLES C. JONES, JR., *to* MRS. MARY JONES[8]

James Island, *Wednesday,* September 9th, 1863

My very dear Mother,

I write simply to assure you and my dear little daughter and all at home of my constant remembrance and truest love.

The enemy yesterday attacked, with the ironsides and four monitors, Fort Moultrie, and were repulsed after a severe and prolonged bombardment. Last night an assault was made by them in barges upon Fort Sumter. The assault was signally repelled. We captured nineteen commissioned officers, one hundred and two noncommissioned officers and privates, and six barges. It is supposed that we killed and wounded and drowned between two and three hundred of the rascals. Our ironclads performed signal service. We captured also the flag which floated from Sumter when that fort was surrendered by Anderson, and which the enemy had brought in the expectation of again planting it upon the walls of that fort.

Day before yesterday I proceeded to the Stono with three light batteries to engage the sloop of war *Pawnee;* but she would not come within range, and after firing a few random shots retired.

Through God's great mercy I am still quite well. I think matters are assuming a rather more favorable aspect, and if the enemy will only delay a little longer any contemplated attack by the way of James Island, we will have completed a new and formidable line of defenses. The enemy will find it a very difficult matter to enter the harbor. What I most fear is the partial destruction of the city by the long-range Parrott batteries of the Federals located on Morris Island. The scoundrels are busy as bees placing them in position, and apparently are training them upon the city and our James Island batteries. Our batteries are always firing, night and day.

Do, my dear mother, kiss my precious little daughter for me. Give best love to all at home. And remember me ever as

Your affectionate son,
Charles C. Jones, Jr.

I have had no letter from home yet.

MRS. MARY JONES *to* COL. CHARLES C. JONES, JR.[8]

Walthourville, *Wednesday,* September 9th, 1863

My very dear Son,

Your affectionate consideration in writing is the greatest relief my anxious heart can have. Day and night my thoughts are with you, and my poor prayers ascending to my Covenant God, my Almighty Saviour, for His blessing and protection to my child. Even your little daughter, today at noon, being in the room with me, of her own accord knelt by a little trunk which was yours in infancy and said: "Pray God bless Papa!" Will not this cry enter into the ear of the Lord of Hosts? I believe that it will. And may He enable you savingly to trust in Him with all your heart! And may you be endued with wisdom and courage and strength equal to your day of responsibility and of peril!

I feel that nothing could be more solemn than the circumstances which now surround and the events that may await you. Let me tell you here, my son, that I am prepared to come to you at a moment's warning; and should you suffer in any way by wounds or disease, nothing shall keep me away from you. And I hope you will never deceive me about yourself. I write not thus to depress your spirits; my hope and confidence in God is firm. I know you will do your duty—and that bravely; and I believe He will guard and shield you. Ever look up unto Him, and pray for the unerring guidance of the Holy Spirit. In the basket which I am sending you today I have put a few Testaments and tracts. . . . Can I do anything for you in Savannah in attending to your house or any business which would assist you in any way? I will gladly serve you; only let me know it.

I am trying to do all I can to meet the wants of our people. Owing to the excessive rains our salt-boiling has been almost a failure the three past months. I have about ten or twelve bushels which I will send up before long. If the *boilers* could be had, I would remove *Andrew* back to the Island, where he could do much more at it. Do you know of any boilers that could be purchased?

As all hope of your coming out just now was abandoned, I went down to the Island on Monday, spent that night with your uncle (who has been quite sick with one of his old attacks but is better now), and returned to Walthourville yesterday.

Dr. Harris wrote me a very respectful letter last week proposing, if I would allow him to occupy Maybank house, that he would protect the place and keep things in repair as well as he conveniently could, wishing only planting land for a garden, and saying that he would even furnish firewood from his own land. I have allowed him to do so, and really feel it a kind providence, protecting the house that has been so dear to us from the certain ruin and decay which seemed awaiting it from the outrages of the lawless soldiers, who had commenced to break in glasses, doors, blinds, etc., and who kept it constantly open and exposed to the weather. Dr. Harris says he will vacate whenever I desire it. His family consists only of his wife and himself and a few servants. I reserve the Negro houses beyond the spring, as we may want them if we boil salt there or allow anyone to do so.

Audley has allowed a company of salt-boilers to settle on his land, and for that privilege and the use of the wood on ten acres they pay him six hundred dollars. They are probably making that amount each day. They now want to know if we will sell them wood. I wrote Audley yesterday that our oak wood in ordinary times would bring us, sold at the landing, three dollars a cord; and considering the enormous profits made by them I felt it but just and right that they give us three dollars a cord for oak wood which is just to their hand, and two dollars for the pine; and he might state these as the terms upon which they might have it. Messrs. King and Delegal make, I am told, about five or six bushels a day, ask twenty-five dollars a bushel, and pay us fourteen or fifteen dollars *a month* for the wood which they consume! I told Audley we had not been anxious to locate salt-boilers on the Island, but I felt that it had now been thrown open to them, and I think we may now avail ourselves of the many situations we have for that purpose. Audley was offered three thousand dollars by a gentleman a few days since for a situation on his land; he refused, as he had no room. I told him as we had, he should have referred him to us.

Today I send for you, through the distributing commissary of Savannah, a basket of provisions containing a boiled ham, biscuits, butter, potatoes, green sweet oranges, one dozen candles, and a bottle of blackberry prepared for medicinal use (excellent for all *bowel affections*—prepared with *brandy,* consequently a *strong article*), some horse-radish, etc., etc., which I trust will reach you safely and be acceptable. The potatoes are a present from the little ones. I must now close to get the basket ready. Your sister and Robert unite with me in best love, with the sweetest kisses from your own child. God bless and protect you, my dear son, and make you useful in our just and righteous cause!

Ever your affectionate mother,

Mary Jones.

COL. CHARLES C. JONES, JR., *to* MRS. MARY JONES[g]

James Island, *Sunday,* September 13th, 1863

Accept my sincere thanks, my dear mother, for your kind remembrance of me. The basket of good things has safely arrived, all in nice order. Manna in the wilderness was never more gratifying to the famishing children of Israel than are these most acceptable articles to our corn-fed mess. We have not enjoyed such a meal since we have been on the island as that which this morning graced our primitive table beneath the shadow of this large live oak. Contemporaneously with the arrival of your gift came another generous basket from Cousin Philo, so you see for the time being we are in clover. These kind and substantial remembrances from those we love are highly prized at all times; but especially during these monotonous periods of "sobby corn dodgers" and antiquated beef do they receive a most hearty and marked welcome. General Taliaferro and all of us are in the best possible condition this morning after our unusually bountiful breakfast.

The tracts and Testaments, too, are most welcome. Already are they in the hands of the mess, and as it is Sunday, several are this moment busy reading them. So soon as I conclude this short note I am going to devote myself to them. I am sorry to say we have no church here today. Persons at home can scarcely realize how grateful and valuable these contributions of Testaments and tracts are to our soldiers in the field. They are eagerly sought after and carefully read, and I doubt not but that many a good seed thus sown springs up and bears fruit an hundredfold.

The enemy has been very quiet for the past two days, but they are without doubt busily engaged in maturing their plans for future and further operations. We will probably hear from their new and altered batteries in a very short time.

We are anxiously expecting the result of that anticipated engagement between our forces and those of Rosecrans. That will be a most momentous struggle for our cause and country, and we cannot overestimate the disastrous results in the event of our defeat. *We must, under God, gain the victory there;* and it becomes us one and all fervently to implore the Lord of Hosts to crown our arms with a signal triumph.

There is no speculating upon the question when or how this siege of Charleston will end. We are being reinforced from General Lee's army. Gillmore is also receiving troops from Meade's army. The Yankees are bent upon the capture of Charleston—if such a thing can be accomplished by a limitless expenditure of men and munitions of war. We are weaker in all respects than they are save in the nature of our cause and the inspiration of our troops and—let us hope—in the favor of a just God.

How is my precious little daughter? Do kiss her for me. Give love to all at home. And remember me ever, my dear mother, as

Your affectionate son,
Charles C. Jones, Jr.

P.S. Under existing circumstances I presume Robert and Sister will hardly be able to go up to Atlanta unless the way is very clear for him to do so. I should think he ought to await the issue of the impending struggle—at least so far as a removal of Sister and family and household is concerned.

MRS. MARY JONES *to* COL. CHARLES C. JONES, JR.[8]

Walthourville, *Monday,* September 14th, 1863

My very dear Son,

Your favors of the 9th and 10th have just been received, and I bless the Lord for His mercies to you thus far! The repulse at Sumter was heroic. We should be gratified for the least expression of the divine favor. I am sad to think our men and means so defective; and today a rumor has reached us that the Blakely gun has burst. I trust it will prove false, and that in that gun we will have an effective engine for the destruction of our vile invaders.

Robert is just leaving for Atlanta. I trust "neither bonds nor imprisonment" may await him there; but affairs are assuming a most decided aspect in Upper Georgia. Your sister and the family will not probably leave before the first or middle of October. Should your brother return, I want to make him a visit before frost, *D.V.;* but I am unwilling to be moving about in the present aspect of affairs. Robert preached his farewell sermon yesterday. It was a solemn occasion: seven years of his early ministry closed! He gave a review of his ministerial work and its results in that period. He certainly has been permitted to accomplish much good, which we trust will endure through everlasting ages! It is with great reluctance this tie is severed between him and his people.

Your precious child is as hearty as she can be: all vivacity. Talks of her dear papa daily, enters into the plays with the children, acting her part sometimes as a housekeeper, then a cook, but most frequently as a baby, calling little Mary and Charlie "Mama" and "Papa," which gives them an air of great importance as they undertake her management.

I hope the basket has reached you safely. I write in haste only to assure you of our abiding love and remembrance. . . . God bless and save you!

Ever your affectionate mother,
Mary Jones.

MRS. MARY JONES *to* COL. CHARLES C. JONES, JR.[8]

Walthourville, *Friday,* September 18th, 1863

My dear Son,

For several days we have had weeping skies, and now the rain is falling fast. It *comforts* me to feel that the winds and the waves may be made instruments for our defense by Him who holds them in His almighty hand. Then again I think of my poor boy beneath the thin cloth tent, or exposed upon the open field to the tempest if not to the deadly fire of the inhuman foe.

Today I feel unusually depressed about our future prospects: the occupation of Chattanooga by Rosecrans and his fortifying and making it the base of operations; the various points from which he can draw men and means and supplies; and the devastation which may be inflicted upon our state, like those upon Mississippi, through raids; the giving up of one important point after another by General Bragg, falling back all the time with the delusive expectation of some advantage to be gained; and especially in the present instance, to my plain understanding, he appears to have totally mistaken the designs of the enemy and failed to anticipate his movements. It may all be right; I am of course incapable of judging. But thus it appears. And if we have not the power to prevent the enemy from occupying our strongholds, how are we ever to dislodge them and drive them out when once they have gained possession? And the history of our war has been that whenever they have been allowed a foothold they have maintained it. Their advances upon our territory are fearful!

Do not, my dear son, suppose that my spirit quails beneath the dark clouds which appear to curtain our political horizon on almost every side. No. I believe we are contending for a just and righteous cause; and I would infinitely prefer that *we all* perish in its defense before we submit to the infamy and disgrace and utter ruin and misery involved in any connection whatever with the vilest and most degraded nation on the face of the earth. We cannot pretend to fathom the designs of Infinite Wisdom touching our beloved and suffering Confederacy. It may be our sins will be scourged to the severest extremity—and we deserve it all. But I also believe when that wicked people have filled up the cup of their iniquity, God will take them in hand to deal with them for their wickedness and to reward them according to their transgressions.

I am happy to know that you received the basket in good condition, and that its contents have contributed to your comfort. Next week we will send you another supply. I wish the committee would bring us the basket back; it is so difficult to get anything of the kind. But that, I presume, would not be done. What would you like to have? Would you prefer a ham raw or boiled?

You have never told me who compose your mess. I want to know everything about yourself and situation. General Taliaferro is a Virginian, of course. Your dear father had a friend of that name whom he valued much for his deep piety and many amiable traits. They were classmates in the seminary at Princeton. In 1847, when we visited Virginia and your father was a member of our General Assembly at Richmond, one very charming day we took a trip down the James River, and on board the steamer made the acquaintance of a young U.S. officer of that name. I think he was then on a recruiting service for the Mexican War. We always cherished a very pleasant recollection and impression of him and the kind attentions which he showed us in pointing out the many magnificent estates that then graced the hillsides and beautiful valleys that bordered the river, all of which was perfectly familiar to him. To this day the green heights of Shirley and cultivated fields of Brandon, etc., etc., are before my mind's eye. Alas, for the change which has passed over them! I have a kind of fancy that your general may once have been that young officer.

It is particularly gratifying to me to know that the Testaments and tracts were so kindly received. My dear son, never forget your accountability to the heart-searching, the ever-present God, your Maker, Preserver, and Redeemer. And may God enable you to set an upright and Christian example before all with whom you are associated! What a blessing from above that our army is composed of so many who are truly godly men! The example of our noble Jackson (although some are found envious enough to detract from it) is worthy of imitation by our officers of every grade. He dared to honor the law of his God at all times and in all places and circumstances.

Your precious child is perfectly well. Today she came to my side with a little piece of palmetto which she was stripping with her tiny fingers and said: "I—plait—hat—for—my—papa." She is busy with the children from morning to night, when she is ready for an early supper and a good rest.

All friends are well. *Tom* made his appearance two weeks since, Mr. McRae sending him down with the men who were to work in Savannah—a month earlier than I expected him. He has quite the air of a *graduated tradesman*, and is tanning and making lasts preparatory to making shoes. I hope he will succeed. Could we get leather in Burke? Your sister unites with me in best love. Also Charlie and Mamie. Sweetest kisses from your little Mary Ruth. Howdies from all the servants. How is George?

Ever your affectionate mother,

Mary Jones.

Did you make any positive arrangement with Mr. Cassels about wood? He is on the Island and expects to get it at one dollar. But he ought to pay two dollars, and if you did not agree *positively,* I will charge that.

COL. CHARLES C. JONES, JR., *to* MRS. MARY JONES[8]
James Island, *Saturday,* September 19th, 1863

My very dear Mother,

Your very kind letter of the 14th inst. has been received, and I am very happy to know that all at home are well. The Blakely gun has burst, and is entirely valueless. Its mate will not be brought forward from Wilmington. They are both represented as being exceedingly defective in the theory of their construction.

I am glad to hear that Sister and the children will not go up to Atlanta immediately, and trust by God's help that before the 1st October the enemy will be entirely expelled from our state. Gallant reinforcements have gone forward from General Lee's army.

Eva writes me that Brother's youngest child has been very sick, but that it was better on the 15th and she hoped would recover. The Doctor had been telegraphed for from Richmond. She asks, my dear mother, when she and Cousin Philo are to have the pleasure of seeing you in Augusta, and begs me to remember her affectionately to you. I hope that I may be able to secure a leave of absence for the last of October. You know we are, D.V., to be married on the 28th of that month. I hope, my dear mother, that you may be able to be there at that time.

Everything is comparatively quiet here. The enemy appear to be making extensive preparations for the reduction of our batteries on Sullivan's Island, and for that purpose are mounting numerous and heavy guns upon Batteries Wagner and Gregg and at intermediate points. The attack, when made, will probably be a very severe one, and will be sustained by both land and naval batteries of the enemy. Yesterday with two long-range rifled guns I endeavored to annoy the shipping of the enemy in Lighthouse Inlet. I fired some twenty shot at them, but the distance was so great that it was impossible to tell whether any damage was done.

The air is quite chilly this morning, and the sky overcast. We will probably have more rain. I am so happy to hear such pleasant and interesting accounts from my precious little daughter. May a good God have her and you, my dear mother, and all at home in His especial favor! Do kiss her for me. Give love to all. And believe me ever

Your affectionate son,
Charles C. Jones, Jr.

MRS. MARY JONES *to* COL. CHARLES C. JONES, JR.[8]
Walthourville, *Thursday,* September 24th, 1863

My dear Son,

Yours of the 19th was received yesterday. What suspense hangs upon every hour my anxious heart only could tell. And what a relief when the mailbag reveals a letter in your own handwriting! God be merciful to you, my child, and enable you to do your whole duty to Him and to your country!

I fear I did not thank you as I intended for your deeply interesting account of the bombardment and evacuation of Battery Wagner. It must have been sublimely terrific. I have read it to a great many friends. Mr. Buttolph and Robert thought it ought to be published. You may be assured it shall be preserved. I am keeping all your letters—especially at this period—for your little daughter; if her life is spared I know she will have a head and heart to appreciate them. . . .

I am grieved to hear of the illness of Carrie and your brother's babe. Robert wrote us that Stanhope had been suddenly ill, but was relieved. I have been hoping to make them a visit, but times are so perilous it does not appear prudent to be moving about.

Our friends in Marietta are thrown into very uncomfortable circumstances. Their church at the end of the lot has been converted into a hospital, and the bare necessities of life scarcely to be obtained.

Do assure Eva of my true affection. I shall love her as a daughter, and hope I may be regarded as her second mother. My best regards to Mrs. Eve. I hope a kind Providence may permit the consummation of your marriage at the appointed time. If I can assist in any of your arrangements, I hope you will let me do so. Gilbert will be at your service. I think your house will need thorough cleansing, with whitewash *in the cellar,* before it is occupied.

I have been hunting for your winter undervests. You must have them in Savannah. Do dress warmly at this season. Are you wanting drawers? I could get some made of *unbleached sheeting* for you—of good quality and warm.

By today's train your sister and myself send a *box*—the largest we could find—with a few things for your comfort. We are puzzled for baskets, etc.; it is not now as formerly. The tracts for distribution we trust will prove little messengers for good to those who receive them. I have a bushel and a half of clean rice for you. Would you like it forwarded to James Island? . . .

I told you *Tom* had come home a month *earlier* than I expected him. We have just received a letter from Mr. McRae stating the reason. He says for several weeks Tom conducted himself so well and learned his trade so fast they were greatly pleased with him, but he commenced going off at nights across the river contrary to orders. Leather was missed from the shop. He was known to have made shoes at night and sold them. Finally several pair of finished shoes were missing from their shop; and suspicion falling on Tom, he thought it best to send him away at once before he got into more serious difficulty from his dishonesty. He says Tom with proper tools can make an excellent shoe. I always knew him to be an unfaithful boy, and one that gave your dear father much trouble. But I felt an interest in him from the fact that he had been his personal attendant, and wanted to make him a tradesman on that account. *Situated as I am,* I could not keep an unprincipled servant about me. Tom is now tanning hides, and some that were commenced in the spring are nearly ready for use. When ready I would like to place him under Mr. Sconyers' eye, where he can be controlled and make the plantation shoes. I have not and will not say a word to Tom about this matter *yet.* I had promised to let him go and visit his mother, and when he does so he can remain.

Peter (Martha's husband) proves to be a great rogue; he married in a few weeks after his return from Indianola. I gave him money to go. *Patrick* also is said to be married.

I am doing all I can in the weaving line. Your sister will provide for her people, so I trust we may make out for the whole. I fear we shall make but little at Montevideo: the rice is pretty much lost; not a pound of cotton picked in yet. I would be glad if you could find time to direct a line to Mr. Jackson. I believe he will try to serve us, but I fear he will rely too much upon *Cato, who I know* must feel himself under authority. I am sorry, my son, amidst the weighty affairs which claim your time and attention to bring any of my little concerns before your mind. I am and will try to accomplish all I can for the good of all concerned. *Clothing, shoes,* and *salt* are *my aims.*

Your sister unites with me in best love to you. Love from the children. Sweetest kisses from your daughter.

Ever your affectionate mother,
Mary Jones.

COL. CHARLES C. JONES, JR., *to* MRS. MARY JONES[g]

James Island, *Thursday,* September 24th, 1863

I am this afternoon, my very dear mother, in receipt of your kind and interesting favor of the 18th inst., and am truly thankful to know that all are well at home.

We are rejoicing and thanking the Father of All Mercies for His great favor in having granted us the victory in Upper Georgia. I trust that our triumph is complete. If such be the fact, we cannot overestimate its beneficial results. But as yet I must confess my mind is not clear as to the ultimate results of that immediate struggle. We have a powerful army, an accomplished general, and a rough country to contend against in securing the fruits of the victory. Let us trust, however, that He who has blessed us and inaugurated this good work will continue it even to the perfect end. This He is able to do, and to Him be all the praise and glory given. A decided success just at this time—and in that important direction—will most materially change the whole aspect of our national affairs. That army of Rosecrans is composed of finer material than any other the abolitionists have in the field. They are to a very great extent Western men, descendants of Virginians and Tennesseans and Kentuckians, men in whose veins flows blood at least to some degree kindred with our own. In vanquishing such an army we have to all human appearances overcome our worst enemy.

I read to General Taliaferro, my dear mother, your account of your meeting in 1847 on the James River the young U.S. officer on recruiting service, and of his civilities to you and my beloved father on that occasion. He immediately recalled the circumstance. *It was* our present general; and he begs me to present his respectful regards to you, with his acknowledgments for your kind remembrance of him. My associations with him are of the most pleasant character. Our mess consists of the general; his brother, Captain Taliaferro, A.A.G.; Captain Twiggs, inspecting officer; Lieutenant Cunningham, ordnance officer; Lieutenant Redmond, A.D.C.; my adjutant, Lieutenant Whitehead; and myself. We are all in tents except the general, who sleeps in a room of a partially dilapidated house near our encampment. We eat and sit in the open air beneath a wide-spreading oak tree; and of late, during these cold days and chilly evenings, we have gathered around a cheerful campfire. My associations here are as pleasant as they can be under like circumstances, and I am continually brought into contact with all our generals and prominent officers here on social terms of the most agreeable character. Our encampment is marked by good order and sobriety.

No, my dear mother, neither morning nor night do I ever suffer anything to interrupt my religious exercises—reading the Scriptures and earnest prayer. These I recognize as my first duties and highest privileges. At all times we are liable to death, and the tenure of life is each moment and in every place uncertain; but nowhere else is one brought to realize that fact so forcibly as when he is in the presence of the enemy, and liable at any moment to confront the immediate dangers of the battlefield. The consequence is that with the sober and the reflecting mind a situation of this character, so far from alienating the mind and thoughts from the contemplation of religious subjects, on the contrary induces the calmest thought and the most serious reflection, and leads us practically to realize the fact of our every dependence upon the goodness and the mercy of a superintending Providence.

While I was writing, a nice box of good things arrived from my dearest Eva. She is always so kind, so good to me. I will try, my dear mother, and return the basket to you. I know they are very hard to be procured. You can scarcely realize how sincerely your acceptable remembrance of us was appreciated. We are literally upon short commons, and these good things from home are indeed highly prized. We will look with eagerness for the coming of the other one which you have so kindly promised.

There has been no change in the military status of affairs here since I wrote you this morning. A letter from Augusta tells me that Stanhope is much better. The Doctor has returned, and he and Carrie are anxiously awaiting your coming. Do kiss my precious little baby for me, and thank her for her kind remembrance of her loving papa. I did say to Mr. Cassels that the wood would be one dollar per cord, as in the case of Mr. Delegal; but I have written him herewith a note which, my dear mother, you can enclose him if you think best. Salt is commanding such a high price that two dollars per cord would not be too much; and after the 1st January I would charge Messrs. Delegal and King that price. Do they pay regularly? With warmest love to all, I am ever, my dear mother.

Your affectionate son,
Charles C. Jones, Jr.

MRS. MARY JONES *to* COL. CHARLES C. JONES, JR.[8]
Walthourville, *Tuesday*, October 6th, 1863

My very dear Son,

Not a line from you for more than a week! My anxieties are so great I fear they run ahead of all reasonable expectations. I fear you may be sick, James Island is admitted to be so unhealthy. The papers give us no accounts of the advance of the enemy, but I know that perils encompass you on all sides. If I could not look up and beyond these dreadful apprehensions which often weigh me down, I should indeed be miserable; but I know that God reigns, and I can commit my dearest ones to Him as a faithful covenant-keeper who will never leave nor forsake them.

We have had colds prevailing, and our dear little daughter has had some fever from hers, but is very bright today. I sent for Dr. Stevens on Sabbath, rather to consult him about a dose of medicine than any uneasiness about her. She is daily expanding in her thoughts and feelings. I often wish she could cheer you with her merry laugh and cheerful prattle. She certainly has a wonderful love for her dear papa; scarcely ever hears the sound of the cars without saying you have come.

Porter and Niger from Indianola arrived on Saturday. Have not seen them yet. They sent me word that *Adam* died last week. I trust he was prepared for the great change; he had been a professor of religion for several years. Was one who contracted that severe disease of which so many died at the fortifications on the Savannah River, and I do not think he has been perfectly well since.

The ladies have just been sending off various supplies today for the sick and wounded in the late battles. I hope you got your box last Saturday week. We want to send you again this week. The mail closes, and I must stop to be in time. Robert returns next week. I want to go to Augusta the third week in this month, but have not decided the day. I am very averse to moving about. Your sister unites with me in best love. Kisses from the little ones.

Ever your affectionate mother,
Mary Jones.

MRS. MARY JONES *to* COL. CHARLES C. JONES, JR.[8]
Walthourville, *Wednesday*, October 7th, 1863

My dear Son,

Yours of September 29th was received today and relieves my anxiety, although I am sorry to know that you are not well. Do, my child, use every care to preserve your health. Be sure to *dress* and *sleep warmly*. I have always observed that these cool changes in early fall if not provided against would surely be followed by sickness in our climate.

Your drawers I will cut out and have made as soon as I possibly can get someone to do them. In the meantime I will mend up the old ones and send them to you *next week*, as from various causes I will not be able to send you anything this week as I promised to do. The baby's indisposition and my own will prevent my going below this week to collect the little matters designed for your comfort.

The ladies of Walthourville sent today to our sick and wounded in Atlanta one rice tierce, one barrel, and one box filled with good and useful articles and many delicacies, which I hope our noble and suffering soldiers will enjoy. There is nothing in this world too good for those who are shedding their precious blood and giving their own lives to defend and protect us from ruin and misery. Oh, when will it please our Father in Heaven to hear the cries which ascend from our suffering and afflicted land!

Robert mentions being at the funeral of your valued friend General Helm. The services were conducted by the Episcopal minister. His widow is now in Atlanta, where he was buried. He says he felt inclined to call and see her, but was afraid it would be intrusive. I hope he will do so, for he is "a son of consolation." If I knew where to find his honored mother, Mrs. Helm, I should feel like writing her. Truly does my heart grieve with both of them.

My son, nearly all of your classmates at Cambridge who were your personal friends are no more. One by one they have fallen in manhood's prime. God in love and mercy still prolongs your days. I trust it is that you may yet glorify Him on earth by a consistent and devoted Christian life. It is a great comfort to me to know that you observe your morning and evening devotions, reading the Scriptures and prayer. . . . Every night when I put your baby to sleep she says: *"Sing Jesus Christ."* Already has she learned to lisp that precious name. God grant that it may be engraven on her heart!

I was happy to know that you had made a visit to Augusta, and left dear Eva and all friends well. Gilbert will be at your service when you call for him. Would you desire me to go to Savannah and see about the removal and fixing of your furniture? If so, I will do it with pleasure, and postpone my visit to Augusta until November. I know it is so difficult to get anyone at this time to do such things; and I feel now that my life and time are only valuable as I can make them useful to my children, the church, and those who are dependent upon me. Write and let me know what I can do for you. I hope Mr. Lamar will make good the wear and tear upon your household goods. *Use,* I presume, does not mean *abuse.*

I have not yet seen the servants from Indianola. *Tom* has been doing very well thus far; has made eight pair of shoes for the children, besides mending, and over a dozen lasts of various sizes, all of which display quite a genius in design and execution. I will make him for the present complete the tanning and make up some shoes for the needy ones here. He is certainly a smart boy, and learned well in Mount Vernon.

Do when you write tell me what your command consists of, and what is General Taliaferro's on James Island. Present my respects to the general. I am happy to know that you are associated with a gentleman and officer of whom we formed so pleasant an impression; and the position he now occupies proves his country's estimate of his worth and ability. I do not wonder that he remembered your beloved father, for I think no one could forget his appearance and manners. They strikingly illustrated his noble character.

Time and paper fail. Nearly 12 M. All in bed but your mother. Love from your sister. Kisses from your own child. The servants send many howdies, and are always inquiring after you. God bless and save you, my dear son!

Ever your affectionate mother,
Mary Jones.

MRS. MARY JONES *to* COL. CHARLES C. JONES, JR.[8]

Walthourville, *Thursday,* October 8th, 1863

My dear Son,

Yours of the 5th is just at hand. I will do all in my power to help you. It is now rather late in the week to make arrangements for sending Gilbert, as Sabbath intervenes; but I will go to Montevideo tomorrow, D.V., and direct him to go down to Savannah on Monday accompanied by Tom. I will, if God wills, take Flora and be there on the 15th or 16th, as many hands are said to make light work. I hope all things will be in readiness. Grace and Adeline will, I presume, be there also to assist in washing and cleaning. You had best order a barrel of lime sent to the lot at once for the use of the boys in cleansing the kitchen and servants' rooms and yard. Do you wish the carpets put down? Perhaps Eva would prefer to arrange according to her own taste. I will just see to the purifications.

As I shall be much engaged, I do not care to have any friend know of my being in town, and would prefer to stay quietly at Mr. Ward's, or your own house as soon as it is habitable. Our little ones still have colds. I hope you will soon be well. I will direct Gilbert to go to Mr. Johnson for the keys, etc. With our united love,

Ever your affectionate mother,
Mary Jones.

COL. CHARLES C. JONES, JR., *to* MRS. MARY JONES[8]

James Island, *Monday,* October 12th, 1863

My very dear Mother,

I am today in receipt of your dear letters of the 7th and 8th inst., and am sincerely indebted to you for all your great kindness. Amanda has also promised me to do anything that she can to assist in putting the house in order. Johnson, my clerk at the barracks, will execute any directions which you may give. Your room at Mr. Ward's will be all ready. They will commence moving on the 15th; and I cannot tell you, my dear mother, how grateful I am to you for giving me at this time the invaluable benefit of your kind supervision.

The back parlor Eva wants me to have as a study, and desires all the books arranged there in their respective cases. My cabinet can also stand there. The third room on the first floor we will, D.V., use as a dining room. The front room upstairs I presume Eva will use as her room, and I would be glad if it could be put in order for us, as we expect to come down to Savannah just after our marriage. I would also be glad to have all the carpets put down at once. . . . I have asked Johnson to have all necessary whitewashing done, and I also enclosed him one hundred dollars to defray expenses connected with removal. I will send any more should it be needed. I am very anxious to save all the gas fixtures in my former house. Mrs. Harriss has a complete list of all articles turned over to Mr. Lamar, and Amanda will get it from her and show it to you. Grace and Adeline will be relieved from Mr. Lamar's service on the 15th inst. Do, my dear mother, give just such directions as you may deem best. I am but too happy to think that you will be there.

I hope to be able to spend at least a day in Savannah before going up to Augusta. On what day will you go to Augusta? I trust, my dear mother, that you will not deny us that great pleasure, and I hope that Sister and Aunt Susan will accompany you.

Will you please if convenient have my books and clothing and glass, etc., sent in, and also my boxes of Indian remains, and my cabinet, so soon as the house is ready to receive them. Will you also be good enough to bring in with you my seal and key, that I may place it upon my watch. I am deeply obliged to you for the services of Gilbert. I think that Johnson will prove very valuable to you in carrying out any directions which you may give.

I deeply regret to learn that you and my dear little daughter are still suffering from severe colds, and trust that you both will be soon entirely relieved and restored to perfect health.

My command here consists of six full light batteries of four guns each. I have under my command about six hundred men—a command which I would not exchange for that of any brigadier general on the island. General Taliaferro is the ranking brigadier general on the island. He desires me to present his acknowledgments for your kind remembrance of him.

I am happy to hear that Tom has been behaving himself so well, and trust that he will give no further trouble. . . . Do kiss my precious little daughter for me. Love to Sister and the little ones. And believe me ever, my dear mother,

Your ever affectionate and obliged son,
Charles C. Jones, Jr.

MRS. MARY JONES *to* COL. CHARLES C. JONES, JR.[8]
Walthourville, *Tuesday*, October 13th, 1863
My dear Son,

I am in receipt of your two last favors, and reenclose you Mr. Cassel's letter. As you suggest, perhaps it would be best to allow him to remain until

1864 upon the terms which he considered as agreed upon, cutting pine alone. I did not know that they had been positive; neither did I know that he had anyone associated with him. Did he mention that fact when he applied for a place on the Island? I feel that no individual has a right to secure a privilege for himself apparently when he has associated others in the business whose claims are afterwards urged. We must inform Audley of the permission until 1864. If we allow it, the Island will be denuded by the salt-boilers. I feel that the terms I suggest are just and right. Salt now commands thirty-five dollars per bushel! Audley told me there were others wanting wood, and that the companies on our land gave each of them fifty dollars a month for the *use* of *the water*.

As the gin had to be fixed (trunks, casts, etc.) I have kept Porter back until done. He said William and Niger could go on without him. When he returns I will forward the salt on hand—or earlier if you wish it. I will send what I have, and Mr. Sconyers must use it prudently, but plentifully in curing the bacon. I would be glad if he would collect for me a barrel of black walnuts. He could send them in one of the molasses barrels, and I will return it with syrup. I wrote hoping to secure a barrel of flour in Atlanta, but have failed. Will you be able to let me have a sack from Indianola for winter's use?

A letter yesterday from my dear Joe tells me he would soon be with you. I long to see him and his dear family.

Yesterday Gilbert and Tom left for Savannah with two large trunks and two boxes with all your articles here excepting the cabinet and books, etc., at Arcadia. I gave Gilbert not only a pass for the railroad but one to Mr. Johnson at the barracks and in the city for the removal of your furniture from Mr. Lamar's on the 15th under Mr. Johnson's direction. Tomorrow, D.V., I hope to go down myself with my maid Flora, and will be at the house to receive the articles on the 15th. I am glad you have furnished a list of your household effects. I will take up my abode at Mr. Ward's as you invite me to do, and hope we shall be favored in accomplishing the desired object.

I write in haste for the mail. You can write me in Savannah your wishes about anything you desire. All well today, through divine goodness! Robert expected tomorrow. With our united love, and kisses from your daughter,

Ever your affectionate mother,
Mary Jones.

Wish I could have seen your review.

MRS. MARY JONES *to* COL. CHARLES C. JONES, JR.[8]

Savannah, *Monday,* October 19th, 1863

My dear Son,

Your favor of the 16th is at hand this morning, and I presume you would like to know the progress of your business affairs. Gilbert and Tom were sent down on Monday the 12th. On Tuesday the 13th *Mr. Johnson* (and here ere I forget let me say no one could be more faithful and attentive to your interest or polite to your mother) commenced moving, so that when I arrived with my maid Flora on the 14th your furniture, etc., was all in your new hired house.

The cars were crowded; the train slow. I did not reach Savannah until after dark. Mr. Wells was in the cars, and obtained a carriage for me at the depot. Mr. Ward's faithful servants were at their posts, and received me hospitably. I went to my room, and having taken a basket of provisions, my tea and breakfast were at hand. That night it rained, thundered, and lightninged. I was sleepless, and after due efforts to forget myself struck a light and read. Rose at drumbeat. Went to the house in Mrs. Howard's carriage, kindly sent, for the streets were swimming. Soon found ample employment. Robert came during the day; and that evening, as all the blankets, quilts, etc., had passed into the washtub, I returned to Mr. Ward's. Your sister unexpectedly came in, and soon after Mrs. Winn, her daughter, and Mrs. McIver. My lunch basket was produced, and a very genteel entertainment drawn from it. They expected additional friends, so I have not returned there, but enjoyed the luxury of quiet and loneliness here. Your sister and Robert went out on Saturday, taking Tom with them. He was very unwell, and I feared might get ill. He has taken to tobacco, and I believe it makes him sick and stupid.

All the carpets are down. . . . Your bookcases, etc., look charmingly in the middle room. Four windows being to the front room and the shades not fitting, I have not put them up. . . . The gas fixtures are in place, but the gas not on yet. I am using candles, for which a patent for running away ought to be obtained.

Has it occurred to your mind that your whole household could not exist very comfortably on the ethereal substance called love? I have sent to Patience to get you some poultry, and ordered in your bag of rice. There is also not a knife or fork or spoon in the house but those of Adeline's.

This afternoon I will send for the oilcloth from Mr. Lamar's and have it put down in the upstairs entry, which is uncovered. Flora and Grace are cleaning and polishing the furniture today. Gilbert and Tom are washing glasses, etc. I hope all things will be ready to answer your expectations.

And above all, my son, may God add His blessing upon your marriage! If He has healed your breaches and again bestowed upon you a beloved companion, your first duty will be to *acknowledge Him in your family*. I do not wish dear Eva and yourself to dwell beneath a shelterless roof.

If, my dear son, circumstances should prevent my going to Augusta, I think you will understand them. I want to return home as soon as your house is in order. I long to see my darling baby. Your sister thinks they will go up very soon to Atlanta. I shall have to help her, and move myself to Arcadia. Many claims from all at home are upon me. It would be a great happiness to see you married, but I could add little to the occasion. Did you inform your Uncles William and John of the event? . . . In haste,

Ever your affectionate mother,
Mary Jones.

413

XVI

Mrs. Mary S. Mallard *to* Mrs. Mary Jones[t]
Atlanta, *Thursday,* November 12th, 1863

My dear Mother,

I snatch a few moments to tell you of our safe arrival and prosperous journey. We left Savannah on Tuesday morning at half-past five, and after a long day of slow traveling reached Macon at seven o'clock. We spent the night very comfortably at the Brown House. It was so late when we reached Macon that we thought it would be an intrusion to go to Cousin Mary's house; and then there was only one small hack that would take passengers to private houses, and this could not have accommodated ourselves and baggage. I saw Mr. Nisbet at the cars the next morning; he is larger than ever, and said Cousin Mary and Hattie were quite well. I regretted not being able to see them.

We arrived here last evening and went immediately to the Trout House; but Mr. Pease kindly sent his carriage and insisted upon our coming to his house, which we did, leaving all the servants except Tenah at the hotel. We expect to go to Marietta this afternoon. Mr. Pease has made an arrangement by which we will go immediately to Dr. Calhoun's house and thus avoid the necessity of the second move we anticipated. . . . Mr. and Mrs. Pease are very hospitable, and have invited us to remain until our furniture is moved; but I feel this would really be an imposition, for they have had a great deal of sickness among their servants; and now their niece is sick, and they fear it will prove a case of typhoid fever. I thought we had better go to Marietta and remain with Aunty until we could go to the house. I do not yet know what disposition will be made of the furniture until that time. Mr. Mallard has gone out hoping they will allow it to remain in the car.

The children have been quite pleased with the journey, though they begin to feel that they are a long way from Grandmama.

I was very glad Brother Charlie and Eva came from the up country in time for us to see them. I should have been delighted to have seen more of them, but it was impossible for us to remain longer. I think we will all love Eva very much.

Mr. Mallard has improved very much, though he is still very yellow. He is regaining his strength, and has a fine appetite.

Please excuse my writing the first part of this with pencil: I had no ink. The children send much love and kisses to dear Grandmama and Little

Sister. Love to Aunt Mary and Ellen if they are with you; also to Aunt Susan and Cousin Laura. Mr. Mallard unites with me in warmest love to you, dear Mother. Howdy for the servants.

Your affectionate daughter,
Mary S. Mallard.

MRS. MARY S. MALLARD *to* MRS. MARY JONES[t]

Marietta, *Monday,* November 16th, 1863

My dearest Mother,

The children and myself came here on last Friday afternoon. I found Aunty on the bed with a little fever; she looks rather thinner than when we last saw her, but is still cheerful and interested in all passing events. She has knit a pair of stockings for Mamie, and is now knitting a pair of socks for Charlie. . . . I was sorry to bring so large a family here, but we were at a loss to know what to do. I left Lucy with Mrs. Pease, as her servants had been sick and she was glad to have her assistance. Mr. Mallard was to have been installed yesterday, and expects to come here this afternoon. . . .

Yesterday we had a regular war sermon from a Dr. Elliott, a chaplain from Tennessee. His text was the curse of Ham, and his object to show that this was a religious war—the Bible arraigned against infidelity. He had a thorough knowledge of the Yankee character, and anyone that had ever lived among them could testify to the truth of his statements. Some of his ideas were novel. He thought it was a duty binding upon us all to bring the sons of Ham into subjection, and predicted that the day would come when instead of sending missionaries to Africa, overseers and taskmasters would be sent, and when the people were brought into subjection, then they would be Christianized. Another idea advanced was that families who freed their slaves never prospered, because it was a violation of the law of God. Excepting these odd ideas, it was a very good discourse, though not altogether suitable for the Sabbath.

All of the public buildings on the square here are converted into hospitals. It would do your heart good to see how beautifully they are kept. Everything about them is as neat and clean as possible, and very comfortable. I went through a number of the wards with Aunt Lou this morning. We took the children, and they carried little baskets of crackers and were greatly delighted to hand them to the sick soldiers. The cots are provided with very comfortable mattresses, and all have nice sheets and comforts made of homespun. Some wards have calico comforts, and there is a piece of rag carpet spread by the side of every cot. And the men were as clean as possible. The rooms are well ventilated, so that there is no odor of sickness, and the nurses are very attentive. Any want of attention is very severely punished. Last week a nurse was found sleeping, and the surgeon punished him by causing him to lie down with heavy logs of wood placed upon him. Another punishment is to gag them. Miss Lizzie Fraser has entered one of the wards as matron. She has gone in for the war, and receives forty dollars a month. Her business is to see that the food is properly prepared and dispensed. The nurses (men) and physicians attend to the diseases and wounds. She has nothing to do with them. Aunt Lou says I must tell you that if you were only here she could give you more than you could do; says she would give you Wards No. 8 and 10. Amongst the wounded is a Cherokee Indian; the children were very much interested in seeing him. The rooms are all comfortably warmed, and I think all who come to nurse their friends must be delighted to find them so well cared for.

Mamie and Charlie send their love to you, and say I must tell you they have been to the "hossipal" to see our wounded Confederate soldiers. They speak of you every day, and feel it is time for them to be going to see you again. They do not realize how widely we are separated. I do not like to think of this, dear Mother. It is just eight months today since dear Father was taken from us. It seems to me that years have rolled away since then. My thoughts are often with you in that consecrated spot at Midway.

I hope we will be able to return to Atlanta this week, and next week I hope we will be established in our new home. I am very anxious to be settled.

Aunty sends you many thanks for the cow. I presume it will arrive today. Mary Sophia can make feather flowers very prettily, and I think if she had the feathers she might be induced to make them. She is very anxious to get some, and I think if you could send some by Aunt Mary she would be delighted to have them. The small breast feathers and the feathers under the wings are used. Aunty, Aunt Lou, and Mary Sophia all send much love to you, and to Aunt Mary if she is still with you. . . . Do give much love to Aunt Susan and Cousin Laura. The children send many kisses for Grandmama and Little Sister. Tell Little Sister not to forget "Anna." Accept the warmest love of

Your attached daughter,
Mary S. Mallard.

MRS. MARY S. MALLARD *to* MRS. MARY JONES[t]

Marietta, *Monday,* November 23rd, 1863

My dear Mother,

I have not heard one word from you since we left, but presume letters must be awaiting me in Atlanta. Mr. Mallard left me on last Tuesday for Synod. He expected to have returned on Saturday to Atlanta in order to fill the pulpit yesterday. . . . I hope we will be able to go to Atlanta tomorrow.

Mr. Mallard made Charles drive the cow up here, for he found it would be delayed some days if he waited to send it by the cars, and it was only twenty-four miles and a plain road. Aunty begs me to return many thanks for it. They have had great difficulty in getting her to eat at all. She is now beginning to eat a little wet straw, but does not take to the washing at all. I hope they will be able to keep her, but unless she improves very much the milk will not pay for the feed. She has improved within a day or two, and now gives a teacup at a milking. The horse and cows all looked very badly after their journey, and I presume it will take them a week or two to recover.

We have all had severe colds; they seem to be prevailing. Charlie had quite a warm fever, and said to me: "Mama, I am afraid I will die." I asked him why he thought so; he said: "Because I am so sick." He had evidently been recalling his dear little sister's sickness and death. He is quite bright today, and I think will have no return of fever. Mamie begs me to tell you Aunt Eliza has promised her brother and herself two beautiful kittens for little pets. . . .

Aunt Mary wrote that a spy had been seen on Colonel's Island, and the salt-boilers had suspended operations for a time. Where did the spy come from—from the blockaders or Savannah? If there seems to be any danger of a raid, you must come right up to us.

Affairs appear rather brighter in the West at present. Some hope we may be able to capture Burnside; and if so, Rosecrans' army may be compelled to evacuate Chattanooga.

One of General Morgan's escaped men called here a few days ago. I did not see him, but Aunt Lou said he was a very handsome young soldier. He made his escape by crawling under the wall when the back of the guard was turned; and he said that any of the guards could be bought with ten dollars, and prisoners frequently escaped.

Do give much love to Aunt Susan and Cousin Laura; also to Aunt Julia's family. Aunt Eliza and Aunt Lou send much love to you. Kiss dear Little Sister for me. Charlie says tell Grandma some little dear pussies are playing with him. Mamie and himself send love and kisses to you. Accept the warmest love of

Your affectionate daughter,
Mary S. Mallard.

Excuse this paper: everything is packed up.

MRS. MARY S. MALLARD *to* MRS. MARY JONES*

Atlanta, *Wednesday,* December 2nd, 1863

My dearest Mother,

I intended to have written you some days ago, but have been so busy and so tired that I could not.

We left Marietta on last Friday morning. On reaching this place we found Mr. Pease at the depot superintending the removal of our furniture, so I came immediately to the house to receive the furniture while Mr. Mallard remained at the depot to load the drays. . . . I presume our furniture would have arrived in almost perfect order could we have removed it ourselves from the car; but unfortunately for us, the government needed the car just two days before we were ready, so they tumbled everything into the wareroom.

417

The result was a terrible scratching of everything and the breakage of one of the mahogany and one of the walnut chairs. I think, however, they can both be mended; and I hope to remove most of the scratches. The marble top of my drawers was broken in half. I will try and have it cemented.

What I grieve for most of all is the loss of my box of candles—that box which I made and put aside in July for Atlanta use. I trust it may come to light yet, though I fear it was stolen from the wareroom. This is a serious loss, for candles are six dollars a pound. Fortunately I had two or three dozen in another box.

I spent Friday here receiving the things. Mrs. Pease sent us a nice dinner and insisted upon our spending the night with her, which we did. Saturday was a most uncomfortable rainy day. However, we came over and have been here ever since. Mrs. Pease kindly sent us dinner again on Saturday, and on Sunday morning two loaves of bread and some butter. Mr. Pease sent some wood the day we arrived, and says he means to see that we are supplied. He has been as thoughtful and kind as possible; no one could have been more so.

Sabbath was a cold, windy, freezing day. We went to church morning and night, but it was so bitterly cold that only a few were out in the evening. The thermometer had fallen to 20°, and the wind blowing a perfect gale, so you can judge how we felt. After the evening service a gentleman remained and sought an introduction to Mr. Mallard, and requested him to call and see him the next day. He wished to see him "particularly for his own personal good." His name is Captain Alphonse Hurtel. Has charge of twelve hundred men, six hundred of whom are deserters, the rest Yankees. Mr. Mallard called at the prison and found that Captain Hurtel had been educated a Romanist, but in Mexico had seen the church in its power and corruption and had renounced the religion of his boyhood and become a skeptic. A few years ago he married a pious Presbyterian. Since then he has been converted, and he says one of Mr. Mallard's sermons has been blessed to him and determined him to make a profession of religion at once. His wife is in Mobile. Mr. Mallard thinks he will join our church at the next Communion. Is not this an interesting case?

Monday morning was even colder than Sabbath. When we woke, everything was frozen in our room. It was so cold I suppose our congregation must have been sorry for us, for five loads of wood were sent us during the day. Dr. Logan sent three, Colonel Grant one, and a Mr. Demarest one, directed to "Preacher Mallard." Mrs. Logan sent me a basket of nice Irish potatoes and two pieces of butter done up in Philadelphia style with a thistle stamped upon them. With the potatoes and butter was a pound cake sent by little Joe Logan to the children. Tuesday morning we had more butter sent by a Mr. Cole, and today Mrs. Pease sent me a loaf of bread and some fresh pork. So you see, the first week at the parsonage opens very pleasantly. Truly God has been very good to us, and I trust He will give us grateful hearts. If it were not for this terrible war, I would have more heart about this removal. Sometimes my strength almost fails me.

Mr. Mallard and Charles have been busy whitewashing, and I hope to get pretty well fixed by Saturday; but there is a world of work to be done both in and out of doors. I am on the whole quite pleased with the house. It has six rooms—four in the main building and two in the wing. I shall occupy the two in the wing, and intend to have a door cut between them, as they are very small, being only twelve by eleven feet. The other rooms are very little larger. The parlor is thirteen by fifteen four, and the drawing room a little smaller. They are neat and comfortable rooms, and I think we will find the house a warm one. It is quite near enough to walk to church. The lot is very large; indeed, I may say we have quite a field attached. The basement is very high; in it are two servants' rooms, a kitchen, and another room which I shall use as an open pantry and ironing room. I believe the Calhouns used it as a dining room. Besides these, there is a smokehouse and servants' room under one roof with a washing shed between. In this there is a large pot set in a furnace for washing. The fence around the lot is so dilapidated that the cows cannot be kept out. It will have to be thoroughly repaired before we can plant anything. I have been thus particular in my account of our arrangements, my dear mother, thinking you would like to know everything.

There is no special news from the front today. Fears are entertained for Longstreet's safety, his position being regarded as a very perilous one. Report says General Bragg has been relieved of his command at his own request. Our defeat was shameful and most humiliating. Mr. Bryson, who went to the front just after the battle, told Mr. Mallard it was the most disgraceful defeat of the war; that several regiments threw down their arms without firing a gun and ran when the Yankees advanced. It is said the South Carolinians were among the first to run. It was what we would have called "a regular skedaddle" if it had happened with the Yankees. Some say the army was demoralized before the battle because of insufficient food. I cannot vouch for the truth of this. I presume the men had no confidence in their general. I am glad he has been relieved of his command. It is very difficult to hear anything reliable. Our army is between Ringgold and Dalton, General Hardee commanding until Bragg's place is filled. The last accounts state the Yankees were retreating. I presume they are hastening to support Burnside. If we only had force enough to advance upon them, perhaps we might gain some of the advantages we have lost.

I left Aunt Eliza much better. She had taken several walks, and had missed her fever. Aunt Lou and herself were very kind to us; I do not know what we should have done if they had not kindly taken us in. The cow was improving. When I came here, I found that our own cow had fallen away very much, and does not give one-third as much as she did; but she is improving, and I hope will give as much as she did before.

I forgot to mention that the well is under one corner of the piazza. It seems a queer place to have put it, but it was dug there to be convenient to the kitchen. I would rather have it farther off. Red clay abounds here.

I have reserved the upstairs front room for you, dear Mother, and it is ready for you, and we are all waiting to welcome you. Poor little Charlie made up his mind last night to go to Arcadia this morning to see Grandma and Little Sister, and when I told him it was too far for him to go this morning, he had a cry about it. He said he wanted to go to Arcadia to see Grandma. Mamie says I must tell you she has a new front tooth and had one of the old ones pulled out, which she put under her head, and a heap of nice things came in its place. She says tell you she is learning to unbutton all her own clothes.

I have not seen Mr. Rogers yet. I have thought it charity in the people not to call, and hope none of them will call until next week.

You know how funny Mamie is about getting names wrong. Dr. Calhoun has taken everything away that he possibly could, and yesterday Mamie came to tell me Dr. *Cocoon* had sent for the lock on the chicken coop! Charlie and herself send love and many kisses to their dear grandmama and Little Sister. Mr. Mallard unites with me in warmest love. Howdy for the servants. Do give love to Uncle William, Aunt Susan, and Cousin Laura and Cousin Lyman.

Your affectionate daughter,
Mary S. Mallard.

MRS. MARY JONES *to* MRS. MARY S. MALLARD[t]

Arcadia, *Tuesday,* December 8th, 1863

My dearest Daughter,

Your long and most interesting letter was received yesterday, and told me your occupations just as I had imagined—putting to rights in all this bitter cold weather. I think of you constantly, and the fervent prayer of my heart ascends daily for God's blessing upon Robert in his new and at this time very peculiar field of labor and usefulness. . . . I have often wished you could have remained with me until January, as I was anxious for you to have done; and should the situation of Atlanta become more perilous, I hope Robert will consent *at once* to your coming immediately home.

Since the recent fright our coast has been quiet. I wrote you of the abandonment of the Island—although Audley tells me he hopes soon to resume his salt-boiling. I have no doubt the Yankees visit our shore whenever they are inclined. They went recently to Mr. O. Hart's in Bryan and took several of his Negroes away whilst he was at home.

I hope you have received all my letters. I have not written you for the past ten days, as I have during that time been in bed confined to the chamber with a severe cold, and am still keeping my room. The cold was contracted going to Montevideo *very early* an intensely cold morning last week to see a sick Negro (*Delia*). Everything was frozen, and we crushed through ice as the buggy passed on.

I feel so grateful to the good people of Atlanta for their remembrance of you in the *wood,* and especially to Mr. and Mrs. Pease. They have been true friends.

Joe wrote me he had to give thirty-five dollars a cord for most *inferior wood*. I know he must find it hard to supply his family. They have had a great deal of company, and Titus very sick with pneumonia and fearing measles. I shall expect them before long. Our friend Kitty is now with them, and they expected a visit from Edward's wife to see Kitty.

Cousin Mary and Ellen left me on Friday, both looking very well. They speak of a visit to Clifford and Maria before their return home.

Charles and Eva are quite well, and Mrs. Eve and Captain Edgeworth Eve are with them. Eva and her mother were to have come out on Monday, but I was too unwell to receive *Mrs. E.*

The servants, too, have severe colds and sore throats. I have had Phillis trying to cut out the Negro clothes, and she went to her bed yesterday.

On Monday *Rose* resumed her spinning. I thought your wheel, cards, work, etc., would perhaps get on best in the washroom, so she comes there every day and brings me the yarn at night, which I will send as soon as she has enough done. Mrs. Andrews sent by James thirty-one yards of cloth (striped) beautifully woven—the best we have had done. Said she would finish the rest as soon as the yarn came. I will send this up to your people in Burke (as the opportunity offers of doing so) with what I have, which is not half enough for their wants.

I really feel that I can hardly undertake what I have been doing, for my strength and—what is more, I often fear—my nervous system are failing. Oh, my daughter, the desolation of heart which I feel is beyond expression! The death of your beloved father every day presses more and more heavily upon me. To lose such a guide, such a companion, one so tender and sympathizing as a husband, with whom I had never a reserved thought, so wise in all counsel and arrangements—above all, my spiritual guide and instructor in things heavenly and divine! . . . I know that God is able to fill the void I feel within; but I fear the pressing burden of earthly care and occupation, the many and ceaseless calls upon time, all are bowing me down to this earth like a millstone about my neck. If I could only imitate your father's example whilst attending to all earthly duty! His conversation and heart were in heaven.

Tell my darling Mary and Charlie Grandmama loves them dearly and wants to see them every day and will write them a little letter soon. Little Sister talks of them constantly and sends sweetest kisses. She constantly asks where you all are, even to Abram. I must close, as I ought to be in bed. With best love to Robert and yourself, and kisses for the children, and howdies for the servants,

Ever your own affectionate mother,
Mary Jones.

I hope your candles will be recovered. . . . Tell Tenah Niger is quite well. When Robert has time, I would be glad to know if he could be hired to some good man and good work. The servants all send howdies to you and the children and to your servants.

MRS. MARY S. MALLARD *to* MRS. MARY JONES[t]

Atlanta, *Friday,* December 11th, 1863

My dearest Mother,

I have this evening received your letter written on the 8th. I am truly thankful to receive it, for I was beginning to fear you or Little Sister were sick. This is only the second time that I have heard from you since I left, and I think this is the sixth letter I have written you. I am very sorry you have been suffering from cold, and sincerely hope this attack will not prove as serious as that you had last winter; I remember how much you suffered, and how much flesh you lost. I don't think the climate of Arcadia is as healthy as Montevideo.

I wish, my dear mother, that you could be relieved of care, for I have long seen that your nervous system had more than it could bear. Ah, well do I know that your desolation of heart must increase; and as each month rolls by and brings its precious associations, our hearts are filled with deeper sorrow because our guide and counselor—our light—has been taken away. The 16th of this month will soon be here to remind us that we have passed nine such periods (and oh, how long they have been!) without our loving, sympathizing father. And then come the 20th and 21st—days peculiarly precious to you, filled with many hallowed memories. Pleasant memories and associations they are too; and although there is so much of sorrow when we feel they are gone never to return, still I feel we may have much real enjoyment and cheerful pleasure in recalling them all.

Last Sabbath evening Dr. Stiles took tea with us. I thought so much of my dear father. I wish you could be with us at this time. Dr. Stiles is about to commence a "protracted meeting," which will continue a week or ten days in the Baptist church (Dr. Brantly's). . . . Yesterday was an interesting day here, and I hope it was observed in Liberty, and presume it was; for if ever our people need to humble themselves, it is now. Mr. Mallard preached in our church in the morning. Dr. Stiles preached for Dr. Brantly. Our services closed in time for us to hear a very large fraction of the doctor's sermon. He labored to show that our nation must cry unto God or our cause was lost. In the afternoon there was a union prayer meeting held in our church. . . . I trust great good will grow out of this meeting to be held by Dr. Stiles. Perhaps our city may be saved by it, or in some degree prepared for any trials that may be in store for us.

Our last defeat was most disastrous to our cause. It is said our men did run in a most disgraceful manner. They were completely panic-stricken on the left wing. General Bragg is said to have done his duty bravely, and it is reported that he cut down one officer whom he could not rally. The officer will probably die. The report today is the Yankees have fallen back to Chattanooga and have burned and destroyed everything in the country. Our army is at Dalton. Atlanta is being fortified. Some think the next fall back will be to this place. Very dark days may be in store for us, but I trust God will in His merciful kindness keep the enemy from this place.

If it were not for this cruel war, I think we would find this a pleasant and interesting home. Mr. Mallard's field is extensive, and opens very encouragingly and pleasantly. Next Sabbath we will have Communion. Today two gentlemen called to see Mr. Mallard in his study; both desire to connect themselves with the church. . . . This afternoon an old gentleman called to beg Mr. Mallard to see his son, for whom he felt deeply concerned. The other night after prayer meeting a soldier spoke to Mr. Mallard and asked if he was the pastor of the church and said he wished to connect himself with it. I mention these things to show how encouraging and inviting a field it seems to be.

We have had a number of calls. I have made the acquaintance of some very pleasant people. Mrs. Hull called this afternoon. Mr. Rogers inquired very particularly after and sent his respects to you. I have been introduced to Mrs. Brantly, and she says I shall see her very soon. I think I shall have a very pleasant circle of acquaintances. Today a basket of sweet potatoes came from a Mrs. Gardner—a stranger to both of us, though a member of the church. She sent them a mile by her little son.

Our children have been quite well, and speak of you daily. Charlie cannot understand why I do not take him to Arcadia upon the days he appoints. As soon as your letter came this evening, Mamie ran to me and said: "Do let me kiss you for Grandmama." And Charlie came too, and after kissing me for you he said: "Now kiss me for Little Sister." Enclosed you will find what Mamie says is her letter and a lock of her hair which she promised you, and I think she says she has put in some babies for Little Sister and yourself.

We have had some very cold weather, and a few days of pleasant mild weather.

Charles begs me to say he gives his love to all the people, and tell Niger all are well, and Abram is getting very smart; and he wants Niger to intercede for his corn, which he left with Daddy Robin, and he wants him to sell it when the corn price rises. Charles also sends his best love to Mac. Tenah sends howdy for Niger, and says if she has any small hogs, he had better kill and cure them and bring the meat with him. Mr. Mallard will make inquiries about a place for Niger and write you. Did you ever receive the letter he wrote you about the cow? Kate has just come with her message, and begs to tell her sisters and father howdy for her, and begs her father if he has anything to spare please send it by Niger, and send the shoes she left with Augustus to be soled.

I am very glad to hear that Mrs. Andrews has sent home a part of the cloth. This will nearly clothe the people in the up country. I enclose twenty dollars. Will you be so kind, dear Mother, as to let Henry take it to Mrs. Andrews when she sends her bill? She promised to do these two pieces for money and the others for toll. I am glad it is nicely done. The other piece will be striped too. I think it would be well to send her another bunch of yarn before she completes what she has on hand, as it may secure her weaving it immediately. I wish we could spin by magic. It would assist us very much if we were near a carding factory. I am told there are a plenty around this place, but I do not know what they charge per pound. What do you think of yarn selling from thirty to thirty-five a bunch in Marietta? I priced it myself.

Everything is high. Wood has been sold at fifty dollars per cord here. We have bought some at the rate of forty dollars per cord. I have just engaged some tallow at three dollars per pound. This is much cheaper than candles at six dollars per pound. This is the common price for poor tallow candles. Everything else is in proportion.

The children send many kisses and love to Grandmama and Little Sister. Mr. Mallard unites with me in warmest love to you, dear Mother, and kisses for Little Sister. Howdy for the servants.

Your affectionate daughter,
Mary S. Mallard.

MRS. MARY S. MALLARD *to* MRS. MARY JONES[t]
Atlanta, *Monday,* December 21st, 1863

My dearest Mother,

I did not write you last week, as my time was greatly occupied in attending Dr. Stiles's preaching. He commenced on fast day, preached twice that day and on Friday night; and on Sabbath he began his "protracted meeting," and preached morning and evening every day last week and twice yesterday. He has labored very hard. . . . Whenever I hear Dr. Stiles I feel I am in the presence of a gigantic intellect. I wish everyone could hear him on the necessity of the humbling of the nation before God in order that peace may be secured. He says it is absolute folly for us to say: "We can't be conquered"; for God will overrun and conquer us unless we turn to Him and quit relying upon the valor of our men. . . . On fast day Dr. Stiles gave a full, clear account and justification of secession which is said to have been exceedingly interesting. I did not attend, as we had preaching in our own church.

I must believe the departure of a portion of the enemy from Chattanooga has been in answer to prayer; for if they had chosen to have pressed on, they might have been investing this city; for it is said our army is small and was too much demoralized to have made any desperate resistance.

Last night the government sustained a heavy loss here in the burning of half of the fairground hospital. There were forty buildings in all; about twenty were destroyed, but I believe no lives lost. A valuable bale of blankets was consumed. Dr. Logan told Mr. Mallard he presumed the loss to the government would amount to one hundred thousand dollars.

Mr. Pease's family have been greatly afflicted within a few days by the death of Miss Addie Peck, of whom you may have heard Mr. Mallard speak as having been the pet of the whole family. Her disease was typhoid fever—the fifth case that has occurred in the family. The others were servants; and Mr. Pease thinks he must have had something of the kind. Miss Peck took her bed the day we came up, and has never left it, though the family seemed to have no special concern about her case until within a week of her death. . . . Mr. Mallard conducted the funeral exercises in the church. Her body was taken to McIntosh County for interment. . . . Mrs. Pease thinks of going to the low country in a few days. I trust she will, for I believe if she does not, the fever will go through the whole family. And she is very much worn by her long nursing.

Mr. Mallard has just received your letter. We are truly sorry to hear that your cold has continued so long. I hoped to have heard you were quite well. I wish so much you could be with us; and if you continue so unwell, do, dear Mother, come up. The weather is very cold, but I think the atmosphere is dry and exhilarating. We have had frequent changes and rainy weather, but we have suffered very little from colds. Those who live here tell us the winter is unusually cold. I have found my thick leather shoes the greatest comfort I ever had, for the soil is red clay and retains the moisture a long time.

A few days ago my box of candles came to light most unexpectedly. James had packed it in the barrel of rice. You may be sure I was rejoiced to see it. The syrup is so little we think it had much better be kept for sickness.

We took tea by invitation with Mr. and Mrs. Rogers. Mr. Mallard spoke to him about Niger, and he said perhaps he would hire him. His work would be cutting wood and hauling it into town for sale. He said he would let us know in a few days, and said there would not be the slightest difficulty about hiring him here at remunerative prices if he came. I hope Mr. Rogers will take him. He seems quite sanguine about his ironworks, and says if the Yankees will only keep away three months he will be able to repay the stockholders. I believe Brother Charlie has some fifty shares in that concern. There is charcoal enough burned to run the furnace three months, and it will be fired this week. . . .

We are expecting Aunt Mary Robarts to spend tomorrow night with us on her way to Marietta. I received a letter from Aunt Lou a few days ago, and she says they are again much disturbed to know what to do about moving away. If they move they will sell their house and lot, for they say everything would go to ruin if left, and if the Yankees ever occupy the place, they will desolate everything. The difficulty is to know where to go. They have begged us to spend Christmas with them, and we think of running up for the day.

This place is being fortified, but unless some reinforcements are sent to our army, we will not be very safe. Our only hope is in God.

Do give much love to Aunt Susan and Cousin Laura; also to Uncle William and Aunt Julia's family. Mr. Mallard and the children unite with me in warmest love to you, dear Mother. I hope you will be quite well before this reaches you. If you should get sick, be sure and send for me, and I will come immediately down. Tenah sends howdy for Niger. Howdy for the servants.

Your affectionate daughter,
Mary S. Mallard.

MRS. MARY JONES *to* MRS. MARY S. MALLARD[t]

Montevideo, *Monday,* December 21st, 1863

My very dear Daughter,

I wrote Robert on the 18th, and on Saturday, feeling that a change was necessary to the recovery of health and strength, which have been failing since this attack of cold, I made the effort and came here—the first time for three weeks that I had been out of the house, I may say, having only walked into the yard once or twice in that time. The change, through divine favor, has been beneficial. Already I feel better, and have more enjoyment of food; and my cough and pain in the chest have greatly diminished. *This first* (after our marriage), this precious home had always peculiar charms for me. Your beloved father often asked if I was conscious of always singing as I came in sight of the house. That was purely an involuntary act; but there was an inward consciousness of emotions of peculiar gratitude and thankfulness to the Giver of every good gift for such an earthly home, and especially for him whose presence and kindness and affection made it all that my heart desired.

Yesterday was the anniversary of his fifty-ninth birthday, today the thirty-third of our marriage! And it was just such a cold, cloudless, brilliant December day as this. It was the first breath of winter upon the beautiful summer and autumn flowers that had lingered in the garden and were gathered to deck the bridal hall. That scene is now almost a vision of the imagination, and yet it is the reality in which I live. Life is now to me an empty shadow with the substance gone. Today I walked *alone* upon the beautiful lawn. I sat upon the blocks where he used to rest and mount his horse. I stood beneath the trees his own hands had trimmed. I listened to the song of the sweet birds he loved so well; saw his squirrels springing from bough to bough; recalled the unnumbered times when, side by side, we have walked together over every foot of ground, talking with unreserved confidence of all our plans for future improvement and usefulness. I could see him gazing up into the beautiful heavens above, or admiring the brilliant sunsets, or the stars as they shone forth in all their glory. He was never tired of contemplating the wonderful works of God. The whole creation was to his capacious mind, to his sanctified heart, the revelation of divine wisdom and goodness. None ever loved or appreciated or enjoyed the beautiful things of earth more than he did. Oh, my child, while grief for him and loneliness of heart must be the portion of my remaining days, I do bless my Lord and Saviour for the mercy and privilege of such a companionship, of such an association—that my lot was cast with such an eminent and godly minister. . . .

I received today a joint letter from Joe and Carrie. Stanhope, Titus, and Rose have all been sick with measles, and they feared the baby was about to take them. They were only waiting to see if she would take them to come and make me a visit, and will do so as soon as they possibly can, and I hope stay a long time. Kitty was still with them. . . . Charles and Eva wrote me they hoped to be out on Christmas—only perhaps for the day. She is truly a lovely and most affectionate person. How I wish you were all with me!

Little Sister has knelt down several times today in the midst of her play and prayed: "God bless Bubber Sissy." She was delighted with the paper babies, and misses the children a great deal. I am knitting a pair of socks for Charlie, and she comes very often to know if I have "done them for Bubber."

Niger was greatly pleased to hear from his family, and wants to see them. Sends "tousand howdies." The servants all inquire and desire to be remembered. We have had severe colds among them; Patience is now quite unwell. How do you get on with your new cook? The old one is quite in her element—coats tied up at the middle and flailstick in hand, mouth spread from ear to ear.

Our friends at Flemington and in the county are well. Dr. Palmer and family, I am told, are in the county; hope I shall hear him preach. Kiss my precious grandchildren, and tell them not to forget *Grandpapa* nor Grandmama. Little Sister loves them dearly. May the Lord bless and keep you all in peace and safety! With much love to Robert. Howdies for your servants.

Ever your affectionate mother,
Mary Jones.

MRS. MARY S. MALLARD *to* MRS. MARY JONES[t]
Atlanta, *Wednesday,* December 30th, 1863

My very dear Mother,

I received your welcome letter on Monday evening. Mr. Mallard wrote you on Tuesday, so I thought I would delay writing until this evening.

Aunt Mary Robarts came yesterday afternoon and spent last night and today with us. She intended to have gone to Marietta at two o'clock today, and did make the attempt, but the engine ran off the track just by the depot, so she was obliged to wait for this evening's train. We deposited her safely in the cars and bade her good-bye, thinking she would soon be on her journey; but to our surprise she returned soon after, bringing as an escort a refugee from Tennessee—a Methodist minister, most peculiar in his appearance. I suppose he must be an albino: *white—snow-white*—eyebrows and lashes and pinkish eyes. We invited him to tea, as he expected to remain until the next train; and then he had been very kind in assisting Aunt Mary. Mr. Mallard has just returned from the cars; they left in a pouring rain. On the platform Aunt Mary discovered Governor Brown and family, so she introduced herself and Mr. Mallard. The governor had a baby upon his knee trying to shake it into quietude, but failing in his efforts, Mrs. Brown gave it the natural source of comfort. As there was some doubt about the train, Aunt Mary followed in the governor's wake, so I hope she will arrive safely.

We spent Christmas with Aunt Eliza. A quiet, pleasant day: no one there except ourselves. We had agreed to dine together, so I carried up a ham and turkey. The children enjoyed hanging up their stockings, and Mamie said Christmas was a merry, happy day. Charlie carried a small bottle of cream to Aunt Eliza which he told her was to make "sillybubble."

When we returned next day, I found a fat turkey awaiting me—a present from Mrs. Coleman, one of our members. She is a very pleasant lady; I am sorry she is going away. But it is so difficult to get provisions that she is going to LaGrange, where her father resides. . . .

We feel quite anxious about Savannah, as reports have come that the Yankees have landed upon Skidaway. Do, dear Mother, if anything should happen to make you feel insecure, come immediately to us. It seems to be rather a general opinion that all the states must be overrun before the people are brought to a proper state of dependence upon God. Many think we must be humbled in this way before peace will dawn upon us.

The gentleman who took tea with us this evening was arrested in Tennessee, and with six bayonets at his breast was ordered to take the oath. He replied: "My life you can take, but my integrity you can't shake." He escaped while the Federals were plundering his father-in-law's house, stealing dresses and everything else; and such clothing as was useless to them they tore in shreds.

We have had very cold weather, but our people are very kind in sending us wood. This is a very great assistance. Mr. Pease says he means to see to it that we are supplied. He is very kind. His youngest child is now quite sick; they thought she would have died on Sabbath, but she is better now, though the fever still continues; and they are beginning to fear she has typhoid fever.

Dr. Stiles's meetings closed last week, and he went to Augusta to preach his sermon on "The State of the Country" in the Baptist church there. His preaching here was not attended with that awakening which we hoped for.

I am glad you are now at Montevideo, and hope the change may entirely restore you. It is certainly a more healthy winter climate; and then there is so much more to interest you there. I know you must feel as though Father were at times almost present with you. Every tree and plant upon that beautiful lawn is associated with him. It was a happy, happy home.

I am very sorry to hear Brother Joe and Carrie have had so much sickness; and yet it is a great relief to them to feel the children and servants have had measles. Kitty Stiles is in Macon now, and I presume she will soon pay us a visit.

The children are quite well; they and Mr. Mallard have enormous appetites and have all fattened. The children speak of you daily, and often appoint a time to go to see Little Sister and yourself. I do want to see her very much. Kiss her many times for us. The children send many kisses for dear Grandmama. . . . Howdy for the servants. The servants here send howdy.

Your affectionate daughter,
Mary S. Mallard.

MRS. MARY JONES *to* REV. R. Q. MALLARD[f]

Montevideo, Thursday, December 31st, 1863

My dear Son,

Your kind favor was received the day before I came here; also that of my precious child, which was so interesting I could not refrain from sending it in for her brother's and Eva's perusal.

I am glad upon the whole that Mr. Quarterman has rendered so favorable a report of the present crop. As regards myself, be assured I have not the slightest claim to prefer to any of the marketable part. The only assistance I would like is in provisioning Kate and Patience, who are fixtures on the place, and Little Ebenezer, employed with the oxcart and gin. For my house and other servants and horses (both long and short forage) I have had all brought from this place ever since I moved down to Arcadia this fall, and find it such a troublesome business that I shall endeavor to remain here as much as possible. Our crop here, with the exception of corn, is exceedingly small. We have made a plenty of provisions for use, but know not if there will be any to sell. The rice was a failure; I will be glad to exchange about ten bushels with you for seed rice. We had no manager here until very late in the season. With the exception of colds the people have been well at Arcadia, and Mr. Quarterman attentive to business. Porter put the gin in order, and it has been doing well until a day or two since; something about it broke, which he is now repairing. Henry appears very cheerful and attentive to all his duties. The fact of your present manager's being compelled to pass this place whenever he visits his own renders it very convenient. You had better be assured of benefiting yourself before you make any change. It is now a most difficult thing to get anyone to take charge of planting. In all this matter you are the best judge, and I know will try to do for the best. . . .

Say to my grandson Charles Colcock the little socks are for him; and he must send Grandmama word if they fit, so that she may knit him another pair. And if my little granddaughter would like a pair of stockings like them, only ribbed narrower, I will knit a pair for her, and she must let me know. Or would she prefer a pair of red and white mitts?

My paper is out. *A Happy New Year!* May *God's blessing,* which alone can make it so, ever abide with you, my dear children!

Ever your affectionate mother,
Mary Jones.

Kisses from Little Sister. The servants all send howdies. As soon as a place can be found for Niger, I will send him up. Have you tried the tannery?

429

MRS. MARY S. MALLARD *to* MRS. MARY JONES[t]

Atlanta, *Wednesday,* January 6th, 1864

My dear Mother,

Mr. Mallard received your letter containing the socks for Charlie last night. They are beautiful, and Charlie says I must say he is "must obliged" to you; that he means to wear the socks you knit to his papa's church, and those Aunt Eliza knit to Dr. Brantly's church! Mamie seems quite undecided which to choose—a pair of stockings or the mitts—so Grandmama will have to decide for her.

We have had intensely cold weather. On New Year's Day the thermometer was as low as six and seven degrees above zero—said to be the coldest weather known here since "the cold Saturday in 1834," when the mercury fell below zero. It was so cold that milk exposed for a short time to the wind froze at midday. I put out a little custard, and it was soon frozen into delightful ice cream. You may know how cold it was when the water remained frozen even in the room where we kept a constant fire. Today icicles are hanging from the houses, and the streets are glazed. I am quite reminded of our winters at the North, except that this climate is far more variable. Thus far we have all kept well.

Our horse and cow mind the cold very much—particularly the latter. Some mornings she will not drink her washing unless it is warmed. She gives us about two quarts a day; sometimes a little more. Everything is so enormously high that I am trying to make her assist in supporting herself and dispose of one quart.

Mr. Mallard is afraid he will have to send Jim back to Liberty, as we are now paying seven dollars per bushel for corn, and it is difficult to obtain it at all. We have not received our corn yet; it has been in Augusta for a month. I shall be very sorry if Mr. Mallard is obliged to give up Jim, for the congregation is so much scattered that it would be exceedingly difficult to visit them without a horse, and it would be impossible to visit those in the country.

Mr. Mallard went this afternoon to the tannery and engaged a place for Niger. Mr. Henderson, the proprietor, offers four hundred dollars a year and will clothe and feed. The tannery is in the city, a little more than a mile from our house. It is a steam tannery; hides can be tanned in sixty days. Niger will have nothing to do with the steam part; his employment will probably be chopping wood. It would be best to send him as soon as possible. Tenah is still well. I trust she will continue so until we have milder weather.

The recent abolition of the substitute system will soon make a great upstir in the land. I think some here are quaking. The streets here are crowded with men; I presume many of them are in government employ, but there must be some who ought to be in service.

Our gallant General Morgan's men are gathering at Decatur, six miles below this place. I presume they will fight with good will. We have felt quite anxious about the rumored attack upon Savannah, but I presume the report grew out of the fact that some state troops were ordered down there.

I am afraid we are going to lose Dr. Paul Eve from this place. He will probably get a position in Augusta, and will move his family either to the city or to some place in the country nearby. I am very sorry, for I like Mrs. Eve and think she would have been a very pleasant acquaintance. And Dr. Eve is a regular attendant of our church, not only on Sabbath but our weekly prayer meetings; and he makes a most earnest and feeling prayer. Mrs. Eve is a Baptist, though she is quite regular in attending our church. She is Dr. Eve's second wife.

I find my opposite neighbor, Mrs. Root, quite a pleasant lady. She is a member of Dr. Brantly's church, and I expect her husband is one of its most influential men. He is a large dry goods merchant.

You would be amazed to see how full all the stores are at present. They are flooded with calicoes and light spring worsted goods. The prices are of course high: black calicoes, six dollars; colored, eight dollars. The latter are a yard wide; the others ordinary width.

Charlie says if you will only send Little Sister here, he will play with her. Mamie begs me to tell you she is learning to sweep and put rooms to rights. I was very much amused with her yesterday. A Lieutenant McCoy called, and being extremely diffident, I suppose he must have winked his eyes a great deal. I did not observe him particularly, as other persons were present; but after he went, Mamie said to me with great gravity: "Mama, did you see those things Lieutenant McCoy covers his eyes with when he sleeps? Why, he never let them rest one minute! He kept doing them just so." And then she winked and rolled her eyes just like him. I did not know she was observing anyone specially in the room.

Mr. Pease's little daughter is improving, and the family expects to go to the low country next week if no more of them are taken sick. . . . The children send many kisses for Little Sister and yourself. They speak of you daily, and of dear Father also. Mr. Mallard unites with me in warmest love.

Your attached daughter,
Mary S. Mallard.

Mrs. Mary S. Mallard *to* Mrs. Mary Jones[c]

Atlanta, *Thursday,* January 14th, 1864

My dearest Mother,

We have not heard from you this week, but expect a letter tomorrow evening. Mr. Mallard received your letter approving the arrangement contemplated for Niger; you have before this received mine stating the precise terms agreed upon by Mr. Henderson, the proprietor of the tannery.

We have had a great deal of damp, uncomfortable weather for a week past. All our friends tell us this is an unusually severe winter. The icicles hung for days from the trees and houses, so you may imagine how cold it was. I do not know how the poor manage when fuel is so very high. We paid day before yesterday twenty-three dollars for a load of wood; this was at the rate of sixty or eighty dollars per cord. Thus far we have not been obliged to buy a great deal, thanks to the kindness of our people.

This afternoon we were served such a provoking trick by the express that I can hardly get over it. A box of oranges came for us last night, and not knowing it was coming we did not send for it this morning. So the expressman advertised it in the Memphis *Appeal* (an afternoon paper), and an hour or two after the paper was issued sold it as uncalled-for perishable freight. The *Appeal* is issued about two o'clock. We take the *Intelligencer*, but Mr. Mallard heard of the advertisement about five o'clock at Mr. Pease's store and went immediately to inquire for the box; and the man very coolly replied it was their rule to sell all perishable freight that was not immediately called for, and handed Mr. Mallard fourteen dollars. Said he sold the box for twenty. Upon inquiry, an express agent had been the purchaser and had gone to Augusta. The advertisement appeared at two, and I suppose before three the box was sold to the express agent to take immediately to Augusta to speculate upon, for oranges sell here at one dollar. I do feel highly provoked. We hoped if it had been sold to anyone in town we might have recovered it. It is said whenever these express agents want anything, they take it, and when called to account for the missing article, pay the valuation marked upon it. There may have been other things beside oranges in the box; I fear there was. I presume Mrs. Sam Mallard sent the box, and a letter from her, unless it had come directly through, would not have prevented this sale.

Mr. Pease says the express and telegraph are both humbugs and unreliable. Mr. Mallard has had a great deal of trouble trying to get some things through which Aunt Mary expressed from Liberty. The trunk containing wool and yarn has not gone yet, and the barrel of potatoes was sent and brought back and emptied in the streets all decayed. There was some wool in that, but I suppose they will affirm it shared the fate of the potatoes.

I received a note last week from Emily Green (formerly Howe) saying she was now living in Newnan and would come down and pay me a visit. She said she felt so strange among strangers that she longed to see some familiar face, and to see someone she loved. I have been expecting her all week, but presume the cold, wet weather has prevented. As soon as it clears, she will come. I shall be very glad to see her. Mr. Green is post chaplain in Newnan.

Mary Sophia will probably be here the last of this week, and will remain some days on her way to join her sisters in Screven County. Aunt Eliza is again agitating the question of a removal, and has written Uncle Henry to rent a house for her in Cuthbert. But in the meantime she has received a letter from him giving the high prices prevailing there and saying she would not have benefited herself by a removal there. I think there ought to be remarkable inducements that would make them leave their present situation. . . .

We have been trimming our vineyard today, and I hope we will have some nice grapes for you next summer, though the vines have been sadly neglected. I am afraid you could never be induced to cut your vines as unmercifully as they do here; almost everything is cut away except a few buds upon the new wood. Our lot is so dilapidated that unless we are able to put it in better order we will have no garden.

The children are quite well, and speak of you very often. Mamie begged me today "when she died to bury her by her Little Sister so she could be close to her and lie by dear Grandpapa too." Mr. Mallard unites with me in warmest love. Kisses from the children. What is Little Sister after these days?

Your affectionate daughter,
Mary S. Mallard.

MRS. MARY JONES *to* REV. R. Q. MALLARD^t

Arcadia, Monday, January 18th, 1864

My dear Son,

Niger has just left by this afternoon's train for Atlanta. At Savannah I have requested Charles to give him all needful directions, and you will take care of him after he reaches Atlanta, which I trust through a kind Providence he will do safely. Please get for me a written obligation from his employer for his food, clothing, shoeing, hire, and entire care of him in health and in sickness. I hope it may be so that he can be at your yard at night. He is a good man, and I hope will be preserved from evil.

Joe and Carrie and the children have been with me for ten days. He has left this afternoon with Eva and Little Sister on her first visit to her papa and "Mama Eva." I will write Daughter all about it at a leisure hour. With our best love to my dear child and yourself and the children. In haste,

Your affectionate mother,
Mary Jones.

REV. R. Q. MALLARD *to* MRS. MARY S. MALLARD^t

Arcadia, Thursday, January 21st, 1864

My dearest Wife,

Through a kind Providence I have reached this place safely, and find all well. The trip was quite a pleasant one, and unmarked by any incident worthy of record. I was glad that it was in my power to render Mrs. Pease any service; it was highly appreciated. The servants' baggage would have probably given her some trouble if I had not been along. . . . I went as I expected to your brother's, and received a very cordial welcome.

Eva was very pleasant. She acknowledged the receipt of your "sweet" letter (such, I think, she called it); urged her engagements, etc., as a reason why she had not replied sooner. She spoke of having read a beautiful letter from you to your mother which she had sent down for their perusal. We had some pleasant music in the evening. Among other songs she sang for me "Rock Me to Sleep, My Mother" and "Somebody Is Coming." The former was plaintive and very pretty; the latter I styled charming, and such it truly was as sung by her—in a peculiarly arch and merry style, with her eyes on the listener oftener than on the page. Last night her brother Berrien came down. He is very tall, and mind out of proportion. I was pleased with the serious way in which Eva rebuked him for speaking lightly of his former connection with the church. It seems he has given up all his religion. He had not forgotten the "lecture," as he called it, which Father gave him at Mr. Dowse's.

I had expected to have gone up to Walthourville this morning, but Mrs. Pease's friends sent for her to No. 3, so I concluded to get out at the same station. She offered me a seat a part of the way, but as there was a prospect of delay I walked to Arcadia. I found Aunt Susan, Cousin Laura, and the children as well as Carrie with your mother. We all wished for you to be here today. Mother was very glad to get the shoes, as Little Sister was nearly out. Mary Ruth is away on a short visit to Father and "Mama Eva." Mother minded the separation very much. She seems to look upon it (as she expressed it this morning when I told her how fond the child was of Eva) as "the entering wedge." I have handed your package to Aunt Susan.

You will be sorry to hear that two of our Negroes were implicated in the recent attempted stampede—Adam and Tony. Adam is now in military custody, and I suppose being punished by whipping. Tony has not, so far as I can learn, been captured yet. Mr. Delegal's boat was under his house, securely locked as he supposed, and the pillars too near to admit of its removal. But they dug down one of the pillars; but fortunately it was too wide to pass through the gate, and its creaking as it was drawn over the palings awoke Mr. Delegal. The most of Sister Sarah Quarterman's Negroes were concerned: her man Dickey the ringleader. He induced his wife (Brother John's Esther) to go. They will probably hang Dickey if he is caught.

I expect to go to Brother John's tonight and to Riceboro tomorrow. Your brother advises me to sell in Savannah by a broker, and will make all arrangements for me there. I met Niger in Savannah; he will wait for me until I return. I am anxious to be through and back as soon as possible.

If I can, I will write you again. My thoughts have been much with you. The Lord bless and preserve you and the "wee bairns"! Aunt Susan and Mother and all send much love. Aunt Susan thanks you for the pattern; it was the very thing which she needed, and is using it as I write. She bids me say that I (R.Q.M.) am but half welcome without you. Kiss the children for me.

Your loving husband,
R. Q. Mallard.

434

Arcadia, *Wednesday,* January 27th, 1864

My dearest Daughter,

You may be assured we were happy to see Robert. Would that you could have been with him! Only sorry for the cause of his visit, although I hope it will result in good. He will *explain all.*

I have had a great deal of company for some weeks, and been so busy as not to write you, as I design, every week. And you know how much I have to do, *all* centering in my poor self. The visit of my children has been very cheering. Your brother is now in Florida; I hope to keep them a long time. Your aunt and Laura and the children made me a visit of two days and nights last week. All well and doing well. Also your uncle; only he says you promised and *have not* written him. Miss Clay is now with us.

Eva came for Little Sister, and she has been in Savannah for ten days. You will know how much I must miss my baby and long to have her back. But it was right for her to visit her papa and "Eva Mama," who is as kind and tender to her as possible. She never forgets you and "Bubber Sissy."

Tell my dear little granddaughter I send her a dress. The *skirt* made one for *Mary* and *Ruth* and *Susan*. What three sweet names! . . . I have stolen a few moments to write, and now comes a call. With tenderest love for yourself, and kisses for my dear grandchildren, and much love from Carrie,

Ever your own affectionate mother,
Mary Jones.

Mrs. Mary Jones *to* Mrs. Mary S. Mallard[t]

Arcadia, *Friday,* February 5th, 1864

My dear Daughter,

I ought this moment to be in my bed, for I am nearly sick with a renewal of cold and general inflammation of the throat; but I fear if this leisure evening is not embraced I shall not have another just now. The only period when I have been alone was the three weeks when I was confined to my room and the house; and for the past month friends have been coming and going all the time. And during Robert's brief stay I felt that my time was so much taken up that I did not make half the inquiries I intended.

Yesterday Joe and Carrie left the children with me and dined with your uncle; today they have gone to Taylor's Creek for the day, and will spend the night with your aunt. They only took little Susan.

Dunwody, after a week in the county, returned this afternoon. I expected your Uncle John, but he did not come. This is the fourth time I have been disappointed, and hope nothing has occurred to detain him. Dunwody left quite in a gloomy state; unless he can get some appointment, he will have to return to the ranks as a private, which is not very pleasant to a young lieutenant! . . .

I am thankful to hear that Tenah is over her trouble, but am sorry you had so much company when you were so badly prepared for their entertainment. It is really at times a difficult matter to be "given to hospitality" with proper grace, especially when just removed to a new place. I trust your cow will make her appearance. Your brother's was missing several weeks; was finally found, but her milk was gone and has not been restored. I trust Robert's valuable cargo arrived safely, and fear the children's ginger cake in Niger's box was too stale to be eaten.

Carrie and Joe speak of returning to Augusta next week. He has been moving from one point to another; spent a week in South Carolina and another in Florida. I have enjoyed their visit and that of the dear children, and shall feel sad and lonely when they are gone. The baby is a darling *little* creature, and makes one think of our sweet little Eliza.

My baby is still in Savannah, and from all accounts is enjoying her visit. Her "Eva Mama" writes very lovingly of her, and Charles says she is "the light of the household." I hope this may not prove the entering wedge to taking her from me. I do desire that she shall know and love her own father and her mama, who is as kind as possible to her. It really is a great comfort to me to see her kindness and affection to the child.

I received your kind favor with the samples of gingham, and sent them to your aunt and cousin. They did not wish anything of the kind; and as I have been *compelled* to buy a bombazine which cost a price I am ashamed to mention, I could not well add to my wardrobe anything more at present.

I desire if possible to call and see Mrs. Pease, and feel grateful for all her kind attentions to you. Nothing but company or ill health or failure of cavalry, if Providence permits, will prevent.

Robert has given you all the news of the county. . . . Rose is diligent at her spinning, but Mrs. Andrews has not sent home yet the rest of the first pieces. Such a run of company has put a stop to my work in that line. Your brother has dyed me some white homespun a beautiful blue, and I will send Charlie some jackets from it when I send his homespun for pants, which I intended doing by Robert. But my poor head is so forgetful now.

Kiss my precious children many times, and tell them Grandmama longs to see them. With best love to Robert and yourself. Howdies from all the *servants here* and at *Montevideo*. Old Andrew and Sue were very much hurt at not seeing you before you left home. The old man says you know he was always a " 'sponsible man in the family." And now, dear child, good night. . . . May the Lord bless and keep you in His love and fear!

Your affectionate mother,
Mary Jones.

Mrs. Mary S. Mallard *to* Mrs. Mary Jones^t
Atlanta, *Monday,* February 8th, 1864

My dearest Mother,

I have not written you for a week. Constant company and many occupations have prevented. I have had company constantly for the past three weeks, and in that time have had frequent calls. Although I have returned a great many, I still have about twenty-four ahead.

I was greatly surprised by Cousin Lyman; did not know that he was near until he was in the parlor. We had a delightful visit from him; it was quite a treat to us.

We have all enjoyed the good things you sent us; they all came safely. The marmalade is very nice and the children have enjoyed their cake. The myrtle wax ornaments have been very much admired. I sent a part of the oranges to Mrs. Logan.

Niger seems quite satisfied and pleased with his work at the tanyard, which consists of hauling bark and cutting wood. He says his employer is "a pretty fine man." He wishes me to send word to his aunty that his baby is named Cinda. Tenah is doing very well; she has really been favored.

We have heard nothing further from our cow, so have concluded she is either closely shut up in somebody's yard or has been killed by the butchers. It is a great loss to us.

I have Kitty with me now, and am enjoying her visit. She looks better than I have ever seen her. Last summer she took the entire charge of the farm in Habersham, and was very active in the management of everything concerning it. She has a black linsey dress which she dyed herself, and it is a beautiful black. She seems to have succeeded remarkably well with her experiments.

Mr. Mallard received a note this evening from Mr. Buttolph in which he mentions Little Sister in connection with Brother Charlie and Eva, so I suppose she is still absent from you. How much you must miss her! I am glad you have had Carrie and her little ones with you during her absence. How I wish I could see them all!

I sent Mamie to Sabbath school for the first time yesterday, and she seems perfectly delighted. Miss Nannie Logan is her teacher, and Mamie says she is *too* pretty. The nice little books which she will have will always be a pleasant inducement to her to go. The Sabbath school is not in a very flourishing condition at present. The number of children who attend is very small, but I presume it will increase as the weather becomes milder. It has been so bitterly cold for several months that children could not be expected to come out. I am very glad to have Mamie go, and hope her interest will increase, for the association with other children will do her good.

Our town was in quite a stir on Saturday, though we knew nothing of it at the time. General Morgan arrived and made a very short speech at the Trout House. He is still here, but I presume will go where his men are collecting near Decatur. I should have liked to have seen him. Have you read the account of his escape written by 290? If not, I will send you a copy; it has been issued here in pamphlet form.

After Aunt Mary Robarts' return to Marietta, Aunt Eliza and all of them became very much exercised about leaving. There was quite a panic in the place, fearing that if the army should fall back, Marietta would be thrown within the Yankee lines. I believe now Aunty has *decided* to remain where she is; and I feel very glad she has, for I do not know where in these times she could be made more comfortable. And then she has so many kind friends there—though a number have moved from the place, amongst others Mr. William Russell. Aunty will miss him very much.

I wrote you week before the last about some ginghams here which are sold at five dollars per yard by the piece. If you would like to have a dress of this kind, I do not think you will be able to get anything cheaper, for many persons think dry goods will be higher. It is more difficult to bring in blockade goods. Mr. Buttolph carried a dress for Aunt Susan and Cousin Laura, and I have gotten three dresses for Miss Louisa. There were four dresses to the piece, but I let Kitty take one. I think I shall get a very black one for myself, and if you would like one of the same, do let me know soon.

Kitty desires much love to you. The children speak of you constantly, and often ask when I am going to take them to see Grandmama. They send love and kisses. Do give love to Brother Joe and Carrie if they are still with you, and kiss the children for us. Mr. Mallard unites with me in warmest love. I long for summer to come so that you may be with us.

Your affectionate daughter,
Mary S. Mallard.

Mrs. Mary S. Mallard *to* Mrs. Mary Jones[t]
Atlanta, *Monday,* February 22nd, 1864
My dearest Mother,

We have just returned from the country prayer meeting, where a few were assembled to pray for our cause. It is surprising how very few do attend, considering that it is a union meeting.

Mr. Mallard went up to Dalton on last Wednesday, or rather he spent that night in Marietta and went up the next day. It was bitter cold, and the engine became disabled, causing a long delay, which was anything but comfortable, as the windows of the cars were broken and there was no fire to be had. However, he reached Dalton in safety, and the next day walked four miles to the camp of the 25th Georgia. When he wrote, he said he was comfortably and pleasantly fixed and had preached twice that day and expected to continue the services the next day. Major Winn is now commanding that regiment, and Mr. Mallard said he had been very polite in having every arrangement made for preaching. . . . Dr. Stiles was with us a night last week, and he urged Mr. Mallard to go to the front, as he considered it most important that the army should have special religious privileges at this time. So he had come down to get some ministers to go up. It seemed such an imperative call Mr. Mallard felt it his duty to go. There is a great deal of interest on the subject of religion in the army, and unless this opportunity is improved, the time will have passed for doing them any good; for all believe the campaign will soon commence—perhaps in two or three weeks. Troops are daily passing down to reinforce General Polk. I trust he will be successful.

Yesterday afternoon we had a sight of General Morgan and his wife. We were in the Episcopal church, where Bishop Elliott preached and had confirmation; and General Morgan, being one of the congregation, attracted much attention. He was dressed in a handsome suit of black broadcloth, with nothing to indicate the soldier except his cavalry boots and black felt hat turned up on one side with a wreath-around-a-tree worked on it. He is very handsome, and his whole person and bearing is such as you would imagine should become General Morgan. His wife is very pretty, and I can assure you they are a dashing couple. Kitty and I were charmed with the general's dress, it was so unpretending and yet so elegant. I was glad I had Mamie with me. She is in perfect ecstasies at having seen General Morgan.

Dr. Quintard is now preaching in the theater, trying to gather a church; and I presume he will succeed, as he is an interesting preacher, and the people seem much pleased with him. Kitty and I went to hear him, and took Mamie with us. It was the first time she had ever seen the Episcopal service. Kitty asked her how she liked her church. She said: "I did not like it a bit. The people in your church behaved so badly: they looked in books all the time and kept talking, and the minister preached in a dressing gown." She wanted to know if the minister would dress himself in good clothes before he went into the street.

The regular pastor of the Episcopal church here is a very nervous man, and said to be an opium-eater and immoderate snuff-taker. On one occasion a little dog entered the church and so discomposed him that he sailed out of the pulpit and chased it up and down the aisles until he caught it, and then pitched it out and sent it squealing, much to the annoyance of his congregation.

We have had another taste of winter: cold, freezing weather. The apricot in the yard had commenced to bloom, and the flowers are completely killed. If the spell of warm weather had lasted a little longer, I presume we would have lost all our fruit. I hope we will have some nice grapes for you when you come next summer.

Kitty has been with me for the past three weeks, and will be with me for some time. I am very glad to have her with me during Mr. Mallard's absence. A letter from Brother Charlie mentioned that Little Sister had gone with Eva to Augusta, so I suppose she will not return to you until next week. She has made a long visit. Mamie insists upon putting in some babies which she has made for her. I don't think I told you what Mamie said about the dress you sent her: "Oh, I thank Grandma, and think this is my beautifullest dress!" She is going to Sunday school, and is quite delighted with her teacher, Miss Nannie Logan. Kitty sends love to you. The children unite with me in warmest love and kisses for you.

Your affectionate daughter,
Mary S. Mallard.

439

Atlanta, *Wednesday,* March 2nd, 1864

My darling Mother,

A long time has elapsed since I have heard from you. I have not had a letter for three weeks, and I can't help feeling anxious, thinking you may not be well.

I wrote you that Mr. Mallard had gone to the army—or "the front," as it is called here—to preach to the soldiers. His visit was much shorter than he anticipated, for while in camp the order came for three days' rations to be cooked and the troops to hold themselves in readiness for action. Mr. Mallard returned immediately to Dalton, and had the pleasure of seeing a great portion of General Johnston's army. And a grand sight it was. Mr. Mallard said the sight of the army filled him with hope; the men were all in good spirits and were comfortably clothed and shod. Mr. Mallard preached six times to most attentive audiences, chiefly to the 25th Georgia. He stayed in Willie Winn's hut. (He is now acting colonel of the 25th.) The soldiers had very comfortable winter quarters.

The result of the forward movement of the enemy you have seen from the papers. They undoubtedly supposed our army would fall back, and they would either gain an easy possession of Atlanta or, if unable to do that, entrench themselves at Dalton. They thought we had sent off so many to reinforce General Polk that we could not resist. Reinforcements had been sent to General Polk, but were speedily returned; and the Yankee prisoners were utterly astounded when they found their captors to be the very men they supposed with General Polk.

Mr. Mallard's visit to the army was very pleasant and refreshing to him. Dr. Stiles did not go up until the day the army commenced to move, so he did not preach at all. There were, however, a number of missionaries who preached.

Mr. Wood, who married Mary Jane Beck, was one of them. He spent a day with us, and told me that Charles Jones Beck had been wounded and taken prisoner at Gettysburg. When he was recovering, a companion and himself requested to be allowed to go upon the field to mark the grave of a friend. The request was granted, and they went out and did not stop until they reached Dixie, passing themselves as members of the 169th Pennsylvania Regiment. They had on hospital clothing, and were obliged to come out in them.

Charlie Pratt has joined Morgan's command. Dr. and Mrs. Pratt were here on last Saturday. They inquired particularly after you, and desired to be remembered to you. Mr. Pratt is looking old. Mrs. Pratt told me that the servant of Mrs. Pynchon who had returned to her owners from the Yankees had again gone to the Yankees, and this time taken all their other house servants. I presume it must have been a Yankee ruse, for the woman returned professing great penitence and loyalty. Said she had been convinced of her duty by reading the Bible and had returned to perform it, and during the months she remained was as humble and faithful as a servant could be. I presume the Pynchons will regret ever having received her.

Have you seen Dr. Stiles's sketch of Captain Thomas King? Kitty and I read it with great interest.

I have just had a delightful visit from Kitty. She has been with me four weeks, and returned this morning to Macon. She would have remained some weeks longer, but Edward had a furlough of thirty days, and she wanted to see him, and as it is will be with him only one or two days, as he went first to Savannah to see his wife and relatives there. Kitty may return to us after a week or two. . . .

I received a letter from Carrie this evening. She says her children are both well again. She seems to have enjoyed her visit very much.

Where is Brother Charlie now? He wrote me upon the eve of leaving for Florida, but did not say where he was ordered. I presume he was too late for the battle.

How much we have been blessed recently! The enemy seems to have been foiled in all his plans. Oh, that our people would recognize the hand of God in this and not be lifted up in their own strength!

The recent currency bill is making quite a stir in our town. I hope it will reduce the high prices, for I don't know what we are coming to. Think of giving three dollars per pound for ordinary beef, and choice pieces from four to five dollars per pound! It is ruinous.

Do give much love to Aunt Susan and Cousin Laura. I wrote Uncle William last week. Mr. Mallard and the children unite with me in warmest love and many kisses. Has Little Sister returned yet? The servants send howdy. Niger and Tenah have named their baby Cinda. Howdy for the servants.

Your affectionate child,
Mary S. Mallard.

Enclosed $33.35, being Niger's hire for one month.

Mrs. Mary Jones *to* Mrs. Mary S. Mallard[t]
Arcadia, *Saturday,* March 5th, 1864

My dearest Child,

I have not written you, I believe, for four weeks, during which time I have been constantly engaged nursing the sick, and with a continued run of company.

Immediately after Joe and Carrie left, *Fanny* was taken ill with pneumonia. I sent for Dr. Farmer; he thought she would not recover from the first. For twelve days and I may say nights I watched her case, doing all I could; but it was our Heavenly Father's good pleasure to call his servant home, and she departed in perfect peace and full assurance, through the Blood and righteousness of that precious Saviour she had loved and served for so many years. . . . Next, *Patience* has been in bed for two weeks: Dr. Way called in to her. Now improving but very feeble. Kate (cook) laid by for five weeks with a whitlow on her right hand. Still unable to use it. All this while company—sometimes seven or eight whites and three or four servants at a time. *Flora* my only effective servant to cook and wash. And the little "plagues of Egypt" in the house.

My responsibility and fatigue of these cases have issued in great prostration of body and spirit. On last Saturday a chill came on, followed by fever and pain (intense) in one side of my head, face, eyes, and teeth. Yesterday I was almost distracted; today I am up and feel better. Have taken blue pills and quinine, and hope I may not be laid in my bed again, if it be God's will. My eyes are so painful and inflamed I write with difficulty, and use a pencil.

My dear brother paid me a most delightful visit of a month, and returned on last Friday. It was a visit of true consolation and sympathy, and all the time we could command together was given to but one object—your beloved father. Oh, my child, no mortal may know the desolation of heart I feel!

Mrs. Eve and Eva came and brought my baby home. She talks of you all; saw your likeness the other day (the one taken North with Joe) for the first time, and said: "That is my Aunt Mary and my Uncle Joe." She was delighted with the paper babies, and said I must kiss Sissy for them.

Charles has written me but once since he was in Florida; he was in command of the light artillery about ten miles from Jacksonville and about four from the enemy. We cannot hear of any movement. All appears quiet. I am constantly anxious for my dear child; every movement is one of peril. God only can preserve him. I hope you and Robert remember him constantly.

Edward (Bess's husband) has been sick with a cold here for a week. The rest of the people are well. Henry brought the cloth home on Monday—the rest of the *first pieces*. I handed Robert the twenty dollars and kept ten to pay for it. Thanks for the $33.35; it comes in good time. I had no corn to sell, and have not sold the cotton. When the next month's wages come in, *you must keep them for yourself*.

Kiss my precious grandchildren for me. Best love to Robert and yourself. And howdies for the servants.

Ever, my dear daughter, your affectionate mother,
Mary Jones.

Mrs. Mary S. Mallard *to* Mrs. Mary Jones[t]

Atlanta, *Thursday,* March 10th, 1864

My dearest Mother,

I hoped yesterday's mail would have brought me a letter, but no tidings yet! I have had only one letter from you since Mr. Mallard was in Liberty. Perhaps I shall get one this evening.

I have been suffering very much this week from severe headache, and yesterday I was obliged to keep my bed, the pain was so severe. I am better today, though rather weak.

I think I wrote you that Kitty had returned to Macon to see her brother. A letter received from her this morning states that Cousin Mary and Mr. Nisbet are in great trouble on account of Hattie's having scarlet fever. One or two of their other children died of this disease, so no wonder they feel very fearful.

I am with you constantly now, dear Mother, as the anniversary of our greatest sorrow draws near. I have been dreaming frequently of my dear father. A few nights ago I thought we were all assembled in some familiar place of worship, whether at Midway or Walthourville I could not tell. A small congregation was assembled. Father was there—yourself, Brother Charlie, Mr. Mallard, and myself. We all seemed impressed with the idea that Father was soon to be taken from us. A hymn was given out to be sung, and we all joined in with trembling voices; but soon the notes died upon the lips of one and another and another until but one was singing, and soon that voice was choked. And there we all sat, weeping and sorrowing that he was so soon to be taken from us. . . . Today, according to the days of the week, is the anniversary of the birth of my dear little baby, though the 12th does not come until Saturday. These are days full of sadness; and yet I seem sometimes almost to hear a voice saying: "Why weep? They are with the redeemed, Blood-washed throng, singing the Song of Moses and the Lamb, and shall be forever with the Lord." I wish I could go to those two precious graves. They are not like ordinary graves; there is an individuality about them which I never thought a grave could possess.

Have you heard from Brother Charlie since he went to Florida? Where is he stationed? Where is Little Sister? Has she returned to you yet? Brother Charlie wrote me she would do so when Eva came from Augusta.

I have been very glad to see through the papers how signally the Yankees have been defeated in Florida. It is wonderful how their whole combined movement has proved a failure. It has turned out that their movement in the front was intended as an attack upon Atlanta—they thinking, of course, General Johnston's army was too much depleted to make any resistance at all.

What a diabolical attempt that was on the part of Colonel Dahlgren to liberate the prisoners, kill our President, and burn Richmond! A General Dahlgren, said to be brother of the commodore, has been attending our church regularly for some Sabbaths past with his family. They are very genteel, attractive persons in their appearance. Mr. Mallard and I intend calling upon them, as we hear they are going to remain here. It is said this brother gave our government the pattern of the Dahlgren guns invented by his Yankee brother.

Mr. Mallard received a letter from Mr. Quarterman day before yesterday telling us of Mom Fanny's death. I am truly sorry to hear of it; she is a great loss to the place, and will be very much missed. She was always so cheerful and so fond of her owners. Was she sick long?

Do tell Daddy Andrew that Charles has seen Abram, poor Dinah's former husband. He was working some miles from this place, and Charles met him once when he came in town. He had not heard of Dinah's death, and said he had never married until pretty recently, for he had always hoped something would turn up and he would be able to go back to Liberty. He sent a great many howdies to Mom Mary Ann and Daddy Andrew.

Our expenses were so heavy that Mr. Mallard has had to give up Jim. One of the army surgeons has him, and Mr. Mallard has the use of him on Mondays. We have never heard from our cow.

I have commenced gardening, and hope I shall succeed, for I see we shall be entirely dependent upon our own resources. One of my neighbors has given me some millet seed; I will enclose you some, for I think you have lost the seed. Mamie says I must tell you "Mrs. Root gave it to me, and she is a Baptist, and a member of Dr. Brantley's church." Mamie says you must be sure to come up, for you will get grapes, peaches, apricots, and cherries to eat.

Mr. Mallard unites with me in warmest love to you. The children send many kisses. Love to Aunt Susan and Cousin Laura.

Your affectionate daughter,
Mary S. Mallard.

MRS. MARY JONES *to* MRS. MARY S. MALLARD[t]

Arcadia, *Wednesday*, March 16th, 1864

My dearest Daughter,

Yesterday's mail brought me your affectionate letter. I knew that your thoughts would be with me at this time—from last Thursday night (which was in point of day if not of time the anniversary of the birth of your precious babe) to the present moment.

The events which marked that period of the past year have been enacted from hour to hour with a living reality. How sacred is every association with the precious life and death of your beloved and honored father! One year ago and that exalted life on earth was transferred from the duties and toils of earth to the rewards and enjoyments of heaven. Oh, to my desolate heart it appears as if ages had passed since we parted! His hat and stick are lying just as he laid them down on the morning of the 16th, 1863; and although I behold him not with mortal eyes, he is ever present in my tenderest love and recollections. For thirty-two years it pleased the Lord to honor me with his companionship—with his guidance, his support, his spiritual instruction, his wise counsels, his intellectual light and knowledge, his daily example, his prayers and his precepts, and all that tender and affectionate intercourse which as a wife I felt was the cherished boon of my life. Oh, that I had been found worthy of such a blessing!

I could not pass the day without a visit to our precious dead. All was sunlight: no shadows resting on their graves. The wreaths you placed there I have never removed, although I have put fresh flowers around them. But I felt that I could not take them away. I read this afternoon: "Eye hath not seen, nor ear heard, neither have entered into the heart of man the things which God hath prepared for them that love Him." Our beloved ones now see and hear and know. . . .

My dear brother's visit was very delightful, and I am glad we were much together in the early part of it, for when Fanny was taken sick I nursed or attended to her medicines day and night for eight days. And then Patience has been down for three weeks, and is still confined to her house, and much of the time to bed. I fear she will be an invalid for a long time. Yesterday I got a vial of iodine for rubbing her pains; it cost eight dollars. Kate is just out at her duties. Edward was quite sick for ten days; I *practiced* for him, and he has returned home. The result has been prostration, with fever and severe neuralgic pains in head, eyes, ear, and teeth; and I have been obliged to keep very close. I want to change to Montevideo as soon as Patience is better. Richard is now very sick with a mild form of pleurisy; Mr. Quarterman called in Dr. Farmer. I have just sent him a bowl of chicken soup and some stimulant, and he says he feels better. I have not been able to see him but twice.

Mr. Quarterman says he wrote you of Elvira's intended marriage; he appears to be very clever, and is very good-looking: a perfect row of ivory. . . .

We have had quite a military change in the county: Colonel Millen's battalion ordered first to Florida, then Virginia; and part of Colonel Colcock's and Major White's regiments have taken their places. Colonel Colcock's son is the acting adjutant to his men. He came last week and spent the evening with me, and I was very much pleased with him.

I hear but seldom from your brother. His last letter was from Camp Baldwin, four miles from the enemy and ten from Jacksonville. You may be assured I am in constant anxiety for him. May the Lord bless and save him, and make him useful in his country's cause!

I have now read with deepest interest Dr. Stiles's sketch of Captain King. *It must* do great good.

I cannot think why you have not received my letters. During the sickness I did not write for three weeks, but know I have written three or four times since Robert was here. I long to see you all. Tell my little grandchildren Little Sister talks constantly of them, and told me the other day: "I have a little baby in heaven." She has outgrown all her clothes, which I must alter. Eva is in Augusta. Kiss my children. Best love to Robert and yourself. Howdy for the servants. I have never been able to call on Mrs. Pease as I wished. . . . God bless you, my dear child, ever prays

Your affectionate mother,
Mary Jones.

MRS. MARY S. MALLARD *to* MRS. MARY JONES[t]

Atlanta, Friday, March 18th, 1864

My dearest Mother,

Your long-looked-for and welcome letter has been received; I cannot tell you what a relief it was to us when we saw your well-known handwriting. I am sorry to know you have been suffering so much from pain in your head and face; I expect it was the result of continued care and anxiety. You must have had a wearisome and trying time when the servants were sick. I am glad Little Sister has returned; she was absent so long I began to fear she was not coming back. Where is Eva? Has she returned to Savannah?

This has been a week of sadness and sorrow. I have thought of my dear father by day and by night. I have longed to be with you, and felt such a yearning towards that consecrated spot at Midway. I think when you come up you may be able to get such a marble tomb as you like. I have recently seen two very good ones in the marble yard, though rather plainer than you would like. I am glad Uncle John was with you so long; it must have been a great comfort. . . .

We have had another taste of winter: a great deal of ice and cold winds for several days past. Wood is so expensive that it always grieves us to find the weather getting cold. I am afraid the fruit will be injured. I had lettuce and radishes coming up, but think I have saved the plants by covering. The ground here so soon bakes and becomes hard that it is difficult for small seeds to penetrate the outer crust.

Two days ago we received a note from Mr. Rogers saying that he had shipped us six pieces of hollow ware from his Bellwood furnace. They have not arrived yet, so I do not know what they are. It is a handsome present in these days when iron is so scarce and valuable. I saw a spider and ironstand from his furnace; they were equal and I think better than any I ever saw. He has gone to Columbia now to fill some contract. His whole time and attention is given to these works. I think Brother Charlie has about fifty shares in the furnace. It will very soon pay a handsome percentage.

I look anxiously for the Florida news, and am glad to see the enemy have made no further demonstration, and feel thankful my dear brother has not been exposed in battle.

Mamie has just come in, and begs me to tell you she is going to Sunday school, and says you must write word what you think about it. She says she is making a quilt and growing so fat that you won't know her when you come. She is very much attached to her Sabbath school teacher, Miss Nannie Logan, and in compliment to her has named her doll (a boy) Dr. Logan. Mrs. Logan is a very pleasant lady. I only regret that we live so far apart. There is at least a mile between us, so that it would be impossible for us to be really sociable. I think I wrote you Mr. Mallard had to give up Jim, but still has the privilege of using him on Mondays.

If you have not sent the broken bunch of No. 10 yarn to Mrs. Andrews, please, dear Mother, keep it; for I shall have to knit some flannel shirts next summer for Mr. Mallard, and want Rose to spin me some more wool after the sheep are shorn. I think they are stronger with one thread of cotton, and it saves half the spinning. I have found my flannels great comforts to me this winter, and attribute my freedom from colds to them and the very thick shoes I have been wearing. I wear heavier shoes than I used to get for my

446

housemaids. The finer shoes are so exorbitantly high that many of the ladies wear these heavy shoes. I have found them very necessary in this muddy, rocky country.

I hope you receive all my letters. I write regularly every week. Kitty Stiles will probably return here in a week or two. My last letter from her stated that Hattie Nisbet had genuine scarlet fever, but was doing pretty well. They had a homeopathic physician attending her. Do give much love to Uncle William, Aunt Susan, and Cousin Laura. . . . Mr. Mallard and the children unite with me in warmest love to Little Sister and yourself.

Your affectionate daughter,
Mary S. Mallard.

MRS. MARY S. MALLARD *to* MRS. MARY JONES[t]

Atlanta, *Thursday,* March 24th, 1864

My dearest Mother,

The days that have elapsed since I last wrote you have been rather eventful, so I will give you a little account of them.

Sabbath evening we had quite a little gust of sleet and rain while the church bells were ringing, and many were detained at home. Mr. Mallard preached to a very small congregation and returned through the rain. The wind blew hard during the night, and the next morning dawned upon us cold, gloomy, and rainy. Mr. Mallard was prevented in his usual pastoral visits. About twelve o'clock Lucy announced that a poor lady with two children wished to speak to me at the door. I found a poor woman shivering with two little children crying with cold, a shabby broken-topped buggy and two poor horses before the door. The woman said she had been trying to find a place to warm and to have her horses fed, and she thought if she could only get to the Presbyterian minister's house, they would take care of her. I brought them in, and the children were soon at home, one in the chimney almost sitting upon the back log, and the other asking for bread, having had nothing to eat all day.

The poor soul began her story. She had come from Alabama (seven miles from Huntsville) with her husband and three children, driven away by the Yankees. They were making their way to the husband's relatives in Cobb County. We did not see Mr. Sullivan (that was the name), as he was engaged with the medical board endeavoring to get a discharge; and he had his eldest child, a girl of seven years, with him to take care of him. Mrs. Sullivan said he had been subject to epilepsy, and his mind was so seriously impaired that he was obliged always to take this child with him. I felt very sorry for her, for she was evidently in no situation to undergo extra fatigues. The Yankees had ripped up their beds, scattered the feathers and carried off the ticking, blankets, and coverings of every description, and had burned her own and her children's clothing. And the Union men had killed their cattle. All their provisions had been taken from them, so they were compelled to find another country. Whenever the Yankee officers were remonstrated with for burning and destroying property which was valuable only to the owners, their universal reply was: "I am sorry for you, but must obey orders."

Mrs. Sullivan said before the war they lived very comfortably in Huntsville, her husband being a lawyer (a pettifogger, I presume); but now, with the exception of a small box which they had sent ahead, they had everything they possessed in their buggy, and no change of clothing for herself or children. I gave her some little things, and when the little girl found there was a dress for her, she insisted upon putting it immediately on; and when I told her she could not put it on then, she raised her hand and would have dealt sundry blows if she had been allowed. Her mother told her she might put it on when she got home. She turned indignantly upon her: "We ain't got no home, and ain't goin' to no home. I want it on now!" (They were regular little crackers.)

After dinner Mrs. Sullivan went out to meet her husband, promising to return if they did not make up their minds to pursue their journey. We heard no more of them. She said that the Union men around Huntsville were faring just as badly as those who had remained true to the South, for the Yankees told them they had no use for men that would not stand by their country. This poor woman excited our compassion very much, and I presume it is one of thousands of instances. I hope they found some hospitable shelter, for it was a fearful night—very dark, and the wind blowing most furiously with gusts of rain and sleet.

The first news we had of our household next morning was from Lucy, who came in early with the announcement: "The robbers has been upon us last night! Forced open the hen house door and carried away all the poultry!" Charles came soon after, saying with rather a tone of triumph that they had left their "howl" (a prodigious pick used here upon the fortifications), and he had it and brought it as a trophy. (Charles must have manufactured the word *howl*.) The thieves had pulled the palings and come in, forced the door (or rather took it off its hinges after removing the board above), and had carried off two fine turkey gobblers, one guinea hen, all the roosters, and some ten or twelve hens, including the servants'. They did not disturb my ducks, I presume either because their hands were too full, or because only English ducks are raised up here. As soon as Charles found the poultry missing, he began looking about to discover where the rogues got in. Upon looking across the street, he found the neighbors examining their broken fence. *All* their poultry had been taken, and a pick similar to that found here was left there, showing that it was a regular thieving party. A neighbor a little farther down the street had everything stolen from their hen houses the same night. How many more suffered I don't know, for not being acquainted with the people, I have no means of ascertaining.

Things are coming to a fearful pass in this city. Mr. Pease says the exceptions are those who have not been robbed. In one instance they entered a smokehouse, opened barrels of wheat flour, emptied them into sacks, and carried off all the bacon. A very nice lady of our acquaintance had her smokehouse opened and all her lard stolen. These things are occurring every night. The night they came here was so fearfully windy and stormy that any amount of noise could not have been heard. It is supposed this kind of rascality is carried on by Negroes hiring their own time and those working upon the fortifications. They are aided, it is supposed, by low white men. Of course our police must be extremely inefficient. There are some soldiers who commit even worse depredations upon the neighboring farms and lots in the suburbs, putting guards around the Negro houses to prevent their giving the alarm and then robbing the hen roosts and taking off even the clothing of the Negroes. A few nights ago a man was knocked down and his boots taken; when he came to himself he was in his stocking feet. The gentlemen consider it unsafe to be much out at night.

I have a few hens left, but no rooster. When meat of all kinds is not to be had except at four and five dollars a pound, and scarce at that, it is a serious loss to have a large number of one's hens stolen, and two turkeys beside.

On Tuesday we had a very heavy snowstorm—as heavy at times as any I ever saw at the North. The whole earth was covered about four inches deep.

I must tell you before I forget of the children's remarks when they heard the robbers had been at the hen house. Mamie said we must get a parrot to stay at the door, and then when any strange person came to open the door, it would scream "Stealing! Stealing!" and then her papa would wake and shoot them with his pistol. Charlie proposed that we should build an iron house, and then "the naughty *India rubbers*" could not get in. They were both quite satisfied with their plans, and finally agreed that the chickens would be perfectly safe with a parrot at the door of Charlie's house built of iron.

March 25th. I commenced this last night, dear Mother, but did not finish. This morning the snow has disappeared from the ground. A number of tender buds and flowers have fallen from the fruit trees. I fear the fruit is seriously injured if not entirely destroyed, for the trees were encased with ice for two days. We indulged in the luxury of a little ice cream; I wished I could have sent you a saucer.

On Tuesday evening, when the ground was covered with snow, Mr. Mallard had to perform a marriage ceremony. He had received a note the day before from a lieutenant saying he was to be *"mared"* and wished him to perform the "serrimony." I received a generous supply of cake.

Last night Mr. Mallard attended a wedding in our church: Miss Mina Barnard to Major Morgan. Dr. Brantly performed the ceremony. The young lady said she must have an organ for the occasion, as the music would cover her embarrassment. The Baptist church has no organ, so they applied for the use of our church. An absurd and funny report was circulated through the town giving the order of exercises. Mr. Root, the Baptist deacon, was to have charge of the music; Dr. Quintard, the Episcopal minister, to perform the ceremony; Mr. Mallard give the bride away; and Dr. Brantly pronounce the benediction! This story was really believed by some.

449

I have seen very little of Mrs. Brantly, for she went to Augusta a week or two after she called, and will not return until the last of April.

I suppose Little Sister is delighted to be with "Danna" again. Kiss her for all of us. We all want to see you so much. I am sorry to hear Mom Patience is so feeble. Can't you bring her with you this summer? I think the change would do her a great deal of good. Kate has a room, and she could take part with her. Mr. Mallard and the children unite with me in warmest love to you, my dear mother, and many kisses for Little Sister.

Your affectionate daughter,
Mary S. Mallard.

MRS. MARY JONES *to* MRS. MARY S. MALLARD[c]

Arcadia, Wednesday, March 30th, 1864

My dearest Daughter,

Your last favor was received yesterday, and greatly interested us in the poor refugees you so kindly relieved. But I felt perfectly incensed at your repeated losses—cow and poultry all gone! If you think it could be done, I could send you up another cow and a few hens and turkeys. They are all very busy at this time laying eggs; not one setting yet. The poor geese, I believe for want of their accustomed feeding, have eaten up their own eggs, so we will have no goslings. I hope the turkeys will do well, as Kate tries her best with them. I despair of doing anything at Montevideo. Hawks and cholera are awful enemies!

Patience continues extremely feeble; I am anxious about her. Richard, after a serious attack of something like pneumonia, is again out this week.

Elvira was married Saturday week, *Henry officiating!* I gave her some substantials and a syrup cake and pone, and today in visiting Patience looked in upon the bridal decorations. Wreaths of China brier were festooned over the doors and around the room, and on the mantelpiece stood two bottles filled with large bunches of dogwood flowers. *Flora* was one of the bridesmaids, and Tom one of the groomsmen. I think she has married well.

I have just had a delightful visit from my dear Marion Glen and her niece Laleah Dunwody. Marion is a lovely Christian woman whose light is not under a bushel. She desired warmest love to yourself and Robert; wants to see you and your little ones.

Mrs. Andrews sent home another piece last week. . . . I will send her the last of the warp this week, and have your woolen yarn spun as soon as the sheep are sheared, which will be the last of April or first of May.

Your aunt and cousins came near being burnt out last Thursday. It was prayer meeting: Mr. Buttolph had walked; the ladies were at home. Whilst speaking, Mr. Cassels called to him: "Your house is on fire!" He closed without waiting for practical observations, benediction, or amen, and started to run home, but was taken up in a buggy. The house caught from a spark on the roof, and but for the mercy of God and the timely help of good neighbors must have been consumed.

Your brother wrote from Florida last week in fine spirits; says they are all fattening on good *pine smoke*. His direction is Lake City, care of Major General Patton Anderson. He is at Camp Milton, near Baldwin; the Liberty Troop with other cavalry are four miles in advance.

I have quite a mind to ask the refusal of the academy at Walthourville. In case the enemy compel you to leave Atlanta, it would be well to have a retreat. The servants all send a thousand howdies for you and your servants; Little Sister many kisses. Best love to Robert and yourself, and kisses for my dear children.

Ever, my darling child, your affectionate mother,
Mary Jones.

MRS. MARY JONES *to* MISS MARY JONES MALLARD[t]
Arcadia, *Wednesday,* March 30th, 1864

My dear Granddaughter,

Do you remember how your dear grandpapa's study looked—where the desk stood, and how the bright warm sunshine used to fall upon it from the windows that opened on the western side of the house in the wintertime; and when the spring came, the two old mulberry trees would spread out their green branches and shade them so beautifully? Do you remember how the books were arranged all around the room, and everything was in such perfect order and neatness? And where the rocking chair stood before the fire, where he used to sit and hold you on his knee when you came in to see him, or give you some pretty book with pictures to look at, or let you take a pencil and mark all over a piece of paper? . . . Grandmama is sitting alone in the study to write you this little letter and tell you how dearly she loves you and Brother Charlie, and longs to see you, and hopes, if God wills, to come and see you this summer.

Little Sister talks of you both; and sometimes in the morning she calls you when she first wakes up, and I think she has been dreaming about you.

I am very much pleased to hear that you go to Sunday school and love your teacher. You must obey all she tells you, and always say your lessons well. Can you read yet? Your Cousin Jimmie is very fond of his book, and comes regularly to his papa to be taught; and he is quite advanced in *The Young Reader.* The other day we went to Flemington, and Willie and Jimmie both repeated a beautiful hymn they had just learned, and did not miss a word of it—the hymn your mother and Uncle Charles and Uncle Joe used to say when they were small; so that Grandmama remembered it, and now writes it from memory for you and Brother to learn to say to me when I come up. Cousin Marion Glen, one of my dear friends, has been a week with me, and her niece Miss Laleah Dunwody, and she said a sweet little

451

grace for Little Sister to learn; and I write it down here for you to say when there is no one to ask a blessing:

> Lord, bless this food which now I take
> To do me good, for Jesus' sake.

And this is the hymn:

> My Heavenly Father, all I see
>   Around me and above
> Sends forth a hymn of praise to Thee
>   And speaks Thy boundless love.
>
> The clear blue sky is full of Thee,
>   The woods so dark and lone.
> The soft south wind, the sounding sea
>   Worship the Holy One.
>
> The humming of the insect throng,
>   The prattling, sparkling rill,
> The birds with their melodious song
>   Repeat Thy praises still.
>
> And Thou dost hear them every one;
>   Thou also hearest me.
> I know that I am not alone
>   When I but think of Thee.

I am sorry my paper is filled up. You must write me a letter very soon. Kiss dear Mama and Papa and Brother for Little Sister and Grandmama. And tell all the servants howdy for us.

Ever your loving grandmama,
Mary Jones.

Little Sister puts in the violets for Sissy.

XVII

Mrs. Mary S. Mallard *to* Mrs. Mary Jones[t]
Atlanta, *Thursday,* March 31st, 1864

My dearest Mother,

I am all alone tonight, and did I not know that it is a fact that this house is inhabited by tribes of rats, I should imagine myself besieged by robbers both great and small. We have the satisfaction of knowing that some fifty of the thieves and housebreakers who have committed nightly depredations are safely committed to jail.

Mr. Mallard left me on Tuesday for Cuthbert, where he has gone to attend the meeting of Presbytery. Uncle Henry invited him to stay with him, and he expected to do so. He will probably see Uncle John. He will not return until next week. Kitty Stiles will probably return with him from Macon. Hattie Nisbet has so far recovered from scarlet fever as to be able to sit in the parlor, and thus far has experienced no ill effects. I should have been glad to have had Kitty with me during Mr. Mallard's absence, for in these lawless days it is not pleasant to remain alone.

We have formed General Dahlgren's acquaintance. He commanded the first successful repulse at Vicksburg, and would have continued there; but General Lovell of New Orleans was placed over him, and he would not serve under him, so resigned. He has a son in Virginia who has passed through twenty-three pitched battles and has never received a wound. Is not this a wonderful providence? On several occasions comrades on either side have been killed, and still he was preserved unhurt.

There has been quite an interesting return of a young man in our congregation. His parents had heard nothing of him for nine months, and were almost beginning to mourn him as dead, when one evening, without any intimation, he walked into their sitting room. He had been a prisoner, and had written several times to his parents and bribed the sentinels to mail the letters, but they destroyed them. The young man says when he heard that he had been paroled and was to leave the prison the next day to be sent to the South, he felt as if he were going to heaven. I suppose we can scarcely imagine the relief and joy these poor fellows experience when they are released from those horrible demons.

Our weather continues cold and unpleasant, and some of the wise ones predict more snow in a few days. The cherry and apple trees are now in full bloom, and I hope we will have no more freezing weather, for most of our peaches have been destroyed, and it would be a calamity to have the cherries and apples killed too.

I received a letter from Aunt Lou two days ago; she mentioned that Aunt Eliza had been more unwell, and they had all suffered from colds. The girls had not returned; they are now on a visit to Cousin Clifford Powers and Cousin Maria Gilbert. They will probably stop with me on their way up.

What is the name of the Major Colcock in Liberty? Is he the same we saw in Charleston some years ago?

I have been very much relieved to see everything so quiet in Florida, and I hope my dear brother may not be exposed in battle.

The enemy are very quiet above us. The weather has been such that it would be out of the question to make any forward movement. Many believe that our army will soon fall back to Kingston, owing to the difficulty of transporting provisions. And the country around is entirely eaten out. Of course no one knows anything about it. General Johnston has proverbially been a man of his own counsel, and I presume no one knows what he will do with the army—advance, we hope, when the weather permits.

It is growing late, and I must go to bed, as I have been sewing pretty busily today. I send you a table which may be of some use to you in discounting old currency. It has been in our daily paper for some weeks past. Mamie and Charlie send their love and sweetest kisses to Grandmama and Little Sister. There is a cedar tree growing in the corner of the yard which Mamie says they call "Grandma"; and every day they run to it to get some cake and groundnuts and all sorts of nice things. Do give love to Uncle William. Did you hear him say he had received a letter from me? Good night, dear Mother. I feel that our Heavenly Father watches over us, and in His own good time we shall be united again.

Your loving daughter,
Mary S. Mallard.

MRS. MARY S. MALLARD *to* MRS. MARY JONES[t]

Atlanta, *Thursday,* April 7th, 1864

My very dear Mother,

You must excuse a short letter this time, as I am just out of bed, having been very unwell all week. I have suffered severely from headaches this winter; and the last two attacks I have been obliged to go to bed, and have felt quite weak in consequence. Yesterday I sent for Dr. Logan, and he has prescribed, and will put me on a course of tonics which he thinks will relieve me. My headaches are occasioned by nervous exhaustion, and I hope will not return.

Mr. Mallard has been away since last Tuesday week. I felt quite anxious about his not coming at the appointed time, but received a letter this evening saying he had felt it his duty to remain, as there was a precious work going on in Cuthbert. . . . He mentions that quite a number of lads and young men almost ready for the war are concerned. I trust and pray the Holy Spirit will be poured out in large measure, and that Mr. Mallard may receive a blessing which may extend to his church here. It has been in a very cold state. Oh, that it may be revived!

Mamie was delighted with her letter, and will answer it when I get well. Charlie and herself send many kisses for dear Grandmama and Little Sister. With warmest love,

Your affectionate daughter,
Mary S. Mallard.

MRS. MARY S. MALLARD *to* MRS. MARY JONES[t]

Atlanta, *Friday,* April 15th, 1864

My dearest Mother,

After an absence of two weeks Mr. Mallard returned yesterday afternoon. He had a delightful meeting in Cuthbert, and preached almost every day. . . . The interest was unabated at the close, so that all hope the good work will continue. . . . There is a revival in the Baptist and Methodist churches in Macon; also one in the Methodist church in Americus. And today news has come that a wonderful work is going on at the front near Dalton. What a blessing it would be if this good work could be carried on throughout our whole land! . . .

Kitty Stiles returned on last Tuesday, and will be with me for some time now.

Emily and Mr. Green spent a night with us this week on their way to visit Mr. Green's parents. They will return tomorrow and will take tea with us, as they are detained some four or five hours, the cars not connecting with the West Point train. Emily seems very well, and is pleasantly located in Newnan. . . .

Aunt Eliza has been very sick with a cold and something like rheumatism. Aunt Mary said if she had continued sick she would have sent down for Mr. Mallard and myself. Our spring is so cold and damp that I am not surprised at its affecting her health.

We have had a great deal of uncomfortable weather, and persons here tell me the season is at least one month later than usual. It is so cold that the seeds that have already come up grow very slowly. I have planted a large bed of Irish potatoes, which are coming up very nicely.

I wrote you such a short letter last week that I did not answer your last to me. You ask if you should send some chickens and turkeys. It is so late in the season that I do not think the turkeys would be very good, as the hens are laying, and I would rather not have my two gobblers sent up. In regard to the cow, unless we could get a *very fine* one from the low country, it would not pay to keep it. The rates on the railroad have risen very much, so that it would probably cost at least fifty dollars to bring a cow here; and then everything upon which we would feed a cow is enormously high. It is almost necessary for us to have a cow, though we do not yet see how we can get one. Butter is ten dollars a pound, and sweet milk from a dollar to a dollar and a half a quart. If we could get a cow that would give milk enough to make butter, it would be a great comfort to us.

You said in your last you thought of applying for the academy in Walthourville in case we should be driven from this point, so that there might be an anchor ahead. A letter which we received from Mr. Sam Mallard mentioned that Mrs. Ben Screven had rented it, and was keeping house there with Mr. Screven's two elder children; and she could only rent it conditionally, as the trustees held it open to a pastor as soon as one should come. I feel, dear Mother, that we are in the hands of Providence, and can only act up to present light. And should this field of labor be closed to Mr. Mallard, then we must trust Him for direction, and I believe He will take care of us. At present this place is in no particular danger, for the indications are towards a battle in Virginia, which all believe will be a most bloody struggle; though of course we none of us know how the tide of war will turn or what point will be most in danger.

I hope we will have a pleasant summer together. Mr. Mallard, the children, and myself are all longing for the time to come for you to be with us. When will you come? I have a sunny *little room* waiting for you. My only regret is that our rooms are so very small. . . . The cold has killed all our peaches, but we shall have cherries and a few apples and some quinces, and I hope our grapes will do well. . . . There are a plenty of Catawba vines here.

Kitty desires much love to you. She will probably return to Habersham this summer. Next Monday will be Mamie's birthday, so Kitty and I have been contriving a cloth head for the big doll as a surprise for her on that day. We locked the parlor doors while we were at work so that she should not find out what we were after, and she has been very curious to know what we could be doing.

Please, dear Mother, send me some pepper seed in your next letter. The paper of peppers I brought with me was entirely eaten up by the rats before I knew anything about it. Kiss Little Sister many times for us all, and accept our united love. Howdy for the servants. Tell Elvira I am glad to hear of her marriage, and wish her much happiness. How is Mom Patience now?

Your affectionate daughter,
Mary S. Mallard.

MRS. MARY S. MALLARD *to* MRS. MARY JONES[t]
Atlanta, Wednesday, April 27th, 1864
My dear Mother,

I wish you could have seen the delight of the children upon the receipt of the nice candy you sent them. It was a great treat to us all. Mamie seemed to enjoy her birthday very much. In commemoration of our own birthdays, which you used to celebrate so pleasantly for us, I made a plate of cake (boys and girls, rabbits, etc.), which gave Charlie and herself the greatest delight. Kitty manufactured a cloth head for my large doll, and this was another great source of pleasure, notwithstanding its ugly face. In addition to this, we were previously engaged to dine with Mr. and Mrs. Rogers, and there Mamie found Maria Whitehead, Mrs. Charles Whitehead's little daughter. The only drawback to her pleasure was a severe blow which she received the night before. She was running very quickly through the door, and struck her forehead just above the eye against the lock (or rather the iron place in which the catch fastens). She was going with a great deal of force—so much so that she was knocked down; and I think the cut went to the bone. It is about three-quarters of an inch long. I felt very much troubled, and we sent for Dr. Logan; but he was unable to come, but sent some sticking plaster, which Kitty and I put on; and I hope the scar will be small. Perhaps it will not show at all, for I put the lips of the wound very closely and carefully together. I cannot tell yet, as the plaster has not yet dropped off. She seemed to suffer no inconvenience whatever afterwards. . . .

You want to know what we think about the safety of this place. I think at present we are as safe here as you are in Liberty, and perhaps a little safer; though of course no one can predict what the changes of war will bring. Persons seem to have ceased fearing for this place, and many think General Johnston will soon make a forward movement into Tennessee. He has a very large army—some fifty thousand effective men—and is being daily reinforced. If we are ever driven from this place, I feel that Providence will direct us where to go; and it does not seem worthwhile for us to provide for that event. It would have been very pleasant for us to have spent a few weeks with you at home, but it was impossible for us to do so, for the season is too far spent. And it is so difficult to take children about at this time, for just now reinforcements are passing on to Virginia and elsewhere, so that the cars are used chiefly for their transportation. And then, dear Mother, you will so soon be with us that I would prefer deferring my visit until next winter, should I live until then.

I have heard from Marietta several times lately. Aunt Eliza has had several very severe attacks, and the last was of so serious a nature they thought she would have died. Hearing this this evening, I have determined to go up tomorrow morning and spend a day with her. She is aged now, and those who have passed their threescore years and ten sometimes pass away very quickly. I will leave the children in charge of Kitty and Mr. Mallard.

We have just succeeded in getting a cow, which we are trying now. I don't know how she will do. Her owners ask four hundred dollars for the cow and calf. This is cheap for this region, as cows command from six hundred to a thousand dollars.

We are all pretty well. Niger has been complaining of headache and cold, but is bright this evening. I gave him a dose of oil, and he has been quiet at home for two days. . . . He does not seem altogether satisfied with his place, because he can't make anything for himself. Says he has no fault to

457

find with Mr. Henderson, as he never meddles with anybody, and there is no kind of work there that would be too hard for him. He says you told him if anything did not please him he must complain to me, and that I might write you about it. His employment seems to have been chiefly job work—hauling tan bark, whitewashing, chopping wood, etc.

Mr. Mallard and the children unite with me in warmest love to Little Sister and yourself.

Your affectionate daughter,
Mary S. Mallard.

I would rather not have my woolen yarn mixed with cotton, as I find it is not so elastic as the all-wool and shrinks more. So please, dear Mother, whenever Rose is ready to spin it, let her put only wool. The rest of the broken bunch might be sent to Mrs. Andrews as we first intended. Yarn is forty to fifty per bunch.

Mrs. Mary Jones *to* Mrs. Mary S. Mallard[t]

Arcadia, *Saturday,* April 30th, 1864

My dearest Daughter,

I did not intend so long a time should pass before writing you, but I have been leading so irregular a life, with so many interruptions, that you must excuse me.

Your brother returned from Florida on last Wednesday week, the campaign having suddenly closed. I received a letter from Eva and himself on Saturday begging that I would come down and bring the baby, which I did on Tuesday, and returned today, having had a very pleasant visit to them. I was thankful to see the state of your brother's feelings, and hope that his thoughts have been specially directed, during the scenes through which he has recently passed, to the great and all-important subject. I know Robert and yourself ever bear him in remembrance at a throne of grace; and I feel more and more the power and efficacy of fervent, believing prayer. What a blessing to our army and our country! God in the outpouring of His Holy Spirit is giving us the highest token of His love and favor. What gratitude should fill our hearts as Christians for all these evidences of divine mercy! And we can but hope the day of our deliverance from our wicked foes is drawing near. I have never despaired of the final issue, but I have never before felt the dawn of hope so near. I trust it is not a presumptuous delusion! I have many interesting relics from the battlefield in Florida.

You will love Eva. She is a most lovable person, and a gifted mind. Her poetical talent is of a high order. She treats me with great affection, and loves Little Sister. It is very pleasant to see the attachment between them.

I received visits from many friends, but went only to the cemetery, where I took the baby. Dear little creature, she appeared to comprehend the object of the visit; gathered all the flowers and green sprigs in the enclosure and laid them on the vault. She looked up into my face and pointing to the door said:

"Is my dear papa in there too?" (She never forgets her "dear bessing papa," as she usually speaks of your beloved father.) Oh, my daughter, this afternoon *the truth* that he is not here—that I shall no more behold him in mortal flesh—came over me with awful power as I went to the vacant study! God grant that this may not be the sorrow which worketh death but that which bringeth forth the peaceable fruits of righteousness!

Your brother, although for the present returned to his old command, is in daily expectation of orders to some other point—he thinks either in Virginia or North Carolina. He is looking well, but suffers from rheumatism in the back and down his limbs, and has had neuralgic headaches. In Florida it was very wet, and he often slept in wet clothes on the ground.

I was truly sorry to know you had lost your cow, and that Robert had not the full use of Jim. I hope he has not sold him, but only *let* him out. We have had such a severe winter that the cattle down here could scarcely live. We lost a great many, and about twenty head of sheep and lambs, at Montevideo; here they have done better. But *often* this winter I have not had a drop of milk, and for months not a particle of butter saving an occasional saucer sent me by Sister Susan. As soon as the grass springs and they milk here, I will put up the butter for Joe and yourself, and think during the next month they may accumulate some for me to bring or send you.

Patience has been sick since the first of February, and is still feeble, although about. I want to let her visit her children at Indianola this summer, and will leave Kate in charge here. Rose, I presume, will be confined before long.

I will try and get your wool spun as soon as the sheep are sheared. Mrs. Andrews is now on the last piece. All have had clothing below. About ten yards, I think, was wanting for the children at Indianola. Would you like me to bring up the piece Mrs. Andrews now has—*the dyed warp?* She is an honest woman, and after her toll is taken out sends home more than I got from Mrs. Butler paying her for the whole. . . .

Time passes so rapidly I will soon have to be moving. Want to make all my dear children visits, if the Lord permits. Will spend a few weeks with Charles, the same with Joe, and then come up to you, if you are permitted to remain in Atlanta. Dear Aunty I want to see, and friends in Marietta.

Brother William has not been at church for three Sabbaths; he is suffering from his old pain in the back. Sister Susan and Laura are quite well. Mr. Buttolph went down to Savannah with me on his way to Charleston. He goes on invitation to preach to the Guards.

It is Saturday night, a heavy thunderstorm with hail prevailing. Good night, my dear child. May the Lord bless you all, and give you a peaceful and happy day of rest on His Holy Sabbath! With best love to Robert and yourself, and kisses for my grandchildren, and howdies for the servants,

Ever your affectionate mother,
Mary Jones.

459

Miss Mary Jones Mallard *to* Mrs. Mary Jones^r

Atlanta, *Thursday,* May 5th, 1864

My dear Grandmama,

I have been wanting to write you ever since your sweet letter came, but Mama has had so much headache that she could not write often, and could not lend me her hands until today. Mama has just read me your letter over again. I remember all about Grandpapa's study, and how, when I asked him for pretty books, he would let me go and take them out myself. And I remember how he used to kiss me in the morning.

I long to see you, and hope the Lord will take care of you, and that you will come up soon this spring to see us. I have some beautiful flowers on the mantelpiece, and the day you come to see us I will have more beautiful flowers for you to see. Tell Little Sister she loves flowers so much she must be sure and come up, because there are a great many more flowers in the woods up here. Apples and cherries are here, and if she will come she can get these. So make haste! Make haste!

I go to Sunday school every Sabbath, and love my teacher very much. She always gives me a pretty book to bring home, and Mama reads it to me. I can say the beautiful hymn you sent for Bubber and myself, and Mama is going to teach me to sing it. I am learning to read, and try to read "The House that Jack Built" and "Dame Trot" by myself; but some of the words are too long: Mama has to tell them to me. Bubber and I learned the grace you wrote for us—I mean the one Little Sister knows; and when Papa was in Cuthbert, Bubber used to put his head down and ask a blessing for Mama and me.

I will put in some beautiful honeysuckles in this letter for Little Sister, so that you may know what kind of flowers we have in our flowerpot. I love you, Grandmama, and send my love to Little Sister. This is all I wish to tell you. Mama, Papa, and Bubber all send love. Tell all the servants howdy for me.

Your loving little granddaughter,
Mary Jones Mallard.

Mrs. Mary S. Mallard *to* Mrs. Mary Jones^r

Atlanta, *Thursday,* May 5th, 1864

Dear Mother,

I have written almost entirely at Mamie's dictation; the language is her own. She was so full of flowers, and had so much to say of them, that I should have filled more than one sheet with this suggestive theme. I wish I could put my vase of wild azaleas before you—three varieties of pink and one deep orange. I have never seen any so beautiful.

I received your letter written upon your return from Savannah yesterday, and am glad to know you are well. Your visit to Savannah must have refreshed you very much. I cannot tell you how our hearts rejoiced at such tidings from my dear brother, and trust that He who began the work will carry it on and perfect it and make him a true child of God. This is a time when I think we have every encouragement to pray, for God seems very near and willing to bless our army, and has poured out His Spirit in a wonderful manner upon very many. I think the waking up of the churches at home one of the surest indications of peace we have ever had—or rather the strongest reason for hoping for peace.

We all fear the next terrible struggle, and I trust our people will not be so lifted up by our recent successes as to be led to vainglory and forgetfulness of our merciful Heavenly Father, the source of all these blessings. A battle is daily expected at the front, though some persons think this will be chiefly a diversion to prevent the troops being sent to General Lee. The Yankees are thought to have about eighty thousand men at Chattanooga, and General Johnston has about sixty thousand, all in fine spirits and expecting victory. I trust the battle will be decided very soon. No one seems to apprehend any danger for this place, for falling back is not General Johnston's policy. The committees here are getting ready and preparing themselves to go up to the relief of the wounded should a battle take place. . . .

I spent a day and two nights in Marietta last week. I found Aunty better than I expected to find her. She was up and engaged in knitting, and was cheerful, though I thought she stooped more than she did a few months ago and looked older and feebler. She had been very ill the week before with cramp and something like rheumatism. Aunt Mary seems to feel very anxious about her. Her friends are exceedingly kind to her; almost every day something is sent to her. The cow you sent them had a calf the day before I went up. They had not seen it, as it was at the house of one of their country friends, where they had put her to board until the calf should be born. They are all delighted, and hope she will give them a plenty of milk now.

I sent some homespun for Rose for diapers and baby shirts, and some spun cloth to make a frock for it. I also sent some homespun to Bess to make a frock for her baby. The bundles were put inside of some bags which Mr. Mallard sent Mr. Quarterman. Will you be so kind, dear Mother, as to ask them if Mr. Quarterman gave them the bundles? They were marked separately.

Mr. Mallard has not sold Jim. I do not think anything but the greatest necessity would compel us to do that. We could not afford to keep him, as corn is from eleven to fifteen dollars a bushel, and difficult to be gotten at that; so Mr. Mallard let one of the surgeons have him to use and keep, Mr. Mallard still having him on Mondays to use in pastoral visitation. Horses are selling from one to three thousand dollars, so any surgeon who wants a horse is glad to get one without having to purchase.

We all look forward to the time when you will be with us, and hope you will not tarry too long by the way. I think I have the best claim upon you. Kitty sends you a great deal of love, and says she is too sorry not to see you this year. She is still with us, and will not return to Habersham for a week or two yet. Thank you, dear Mother, for the pepper seed. My garden is very backward, though I believe not much more so than some of my neighbors'. Mr. Mallard and the children unite with me in warmest love to Little Sister and yourself.

Your affectionate daughter,
Mary S. Mallard.

I think I would like twelve yards of the woolen cloth Mrs. Andrews is weaving sent up here—that is, if all the others above and below have been served. Thank you, dear Mother, for giving it out to them.

MRS. MARY S. MALLARD *to* MRS. MARY JONES[t]

Atlanta, *Saturday,* May 14th, 1864

My dearest Mother,

You are no doubt sharing the universal anxiety felt in regard to the issue of the impending battles. We have had no telegrams from Virginia since the 10th, except one stating that everything has been filed and dispatches will be sent through as soon as practicable. I presume it is necessary to withhold news from the enemy. Kitty is still with me and in much suspense, for her brother is in Longstreet's corps and was most probably in the battle. I do not want her to leave until she hears of his safety. News can reach her so much more quickly here than in Habersham.

We are hourly expecting to hear the battle has commenced on our front, as the enemy are reported as being in full force not far from Resaca, which is sixteen miles this side of Dalton. They came by a circuitous route through Sugar Valley, and their present position has compelled General Johnston to change his whole line of battle. An immense number of wagons and provisions are being sent up, and many think General Johnston will advance if successful. The Yankees are said to have about eighty thousand, and our army is very large—probably seventy thousand. The men are in the best of spirits and very confident of success. We pray God that He will fight the battle for us, and that we may not be given over to vain confidence. The relief committees here are getting ready to go up and attend the wounded, and a portion of them went up yesterday to make arrangements. The hospitals are cleared of sick men, and all are getting ready for the wounded. Some men detailed for the purpose came here yesterday to beg for rags. All these things make us feel what a terrible thing war is. We will be in a dreadful predicament should General Johnston be unsuccessful or be compelled to fall back, but no one seems to contemplate this. All have the utmost confidence in his skill.

Dr Logan and Mr. Pease took tea with us last evening. Dr. Logan is a perfect gentleman, and very pleasant. I am sorry his family lives so far from me—too far for us to exchange visits often. Mrs. Hull is quite as far; I regret this too, for she has been very polite and kind to us. This place is so scattered that it is difficult to visit without a conveyance.

We have had some strawberries sent us this week, and have enjoyed them very much. Everything is acceptable in these scarce hard times. Think of our

462

paying ten dollars for two pounds of beefsteak! And this is the only thing to be had. I hear occasionally of chickens sold at eight to ten dollars apiece.

Mr. Mallard has had a call to go as chaplain to the 4th Georgia Cavalry, given by Colonel Avery. Of course he would not think of leaving his church. He has a large field among the soldiers who attend his church.

Mary Sophia, Lilla, and Ellen passed through day before yesterday on their way home. Mr. Mallard saw them from the Macon to the Marietta train. Lilla had her arm in a sling, having broken it while visiting Cousin Maria Gilbert. She was on horseback and fell in consequence of some horses' running and frightening her horse.

We are all pretty well except colds, induced by remarkably cold, cloudy weather. Kitty sends much love to you. Mr. Mallard and the children unite with me in much love to yourself and Little Sister. Howdy for the servants. Do, my dear mother, don't stay too late at Arcadia.

Your affectionate daughter,
Mary S. Mallard.

MRS. MARY S. MALLARD *to* MRS. MARY JONES[t]

Atlanta, Thursday, May 19th, 1864

My dearest Mother,

I wrote you late last week telling you we were in daily expectation that the general engagement would commence on our front. We are still in a state of expectation, though all believe it will take place in the next two days. Our army has been steadily falling back for a week past in order to gain good fighting ground and a position that cannot be flanked. The men are in the highest spirits, and express the utmost confidence in General Johnston. They are now at Kingston. Whether they will fall still further back no one knows, though it is conjectured the great battle will be fought at the Etowah River. Our army has had continued skirmishing—or rather it ought to be called a succession of small battles; and in every instance the Yankees have been handsomely repulsed with great slaughter. Our men have fought almost entirely behind breastworks, so that the most of their wounds are slight; that is, the surgeons call them slight, but they all seem terrible. Already about two thousand five hundred wounded have been brought down. Should a general engagement take place, our town will be more than crowded for a time. Those who are able to bear the journey are sent to other points. I trust our merciful Heavenly Father will fight the battle for us and crown our arms with success, for a reverse would be terrible: in all probability this place would go next. Should our army be victorious, it would be disastrous in the extreme to the Yankees, for they are so far from their base of supplies. They are pressing on in very heavy force. Our army numbers over seventy-five thousand effective men, and it is being constantly reinforced.

The relief committees from this place, Macon, Alabama, Florida, and elsewhere have all come up, and are very active in their attentions to the wounded. They seem to be provided with almost everything. I saw one of the gentlemen going around with a haversack full of tobacco distributing it to all who were out of it. Our ladies are very busy preparing and taking food to the depot to give the wounded before they are removed to the distributing hospital. Poor fellows, they seem so glad to get it. I was at the cars day before yesterday when the train came in, and it made my heart ache to see ten men stretched upon litters wounded in all portions of their body, but bearing all their sufferings without a groan. I observed one man particularly who had lost his leg conversing as cheerfully as though nothing had happened. There are comparatively few very severely wounded. Most of them are able to ride in the ambulances, and many of them to walk to the different hospitals. If you have any arrowroot to spare, please send me a little by express. I think by preparing it myself it will be very acceptable. Mr. Mallard went up to the front yesterday to assist in taking care of the wounded. I presume he will be down on Saturday, as the work is so constant and fatiguing they are relieved every day or two. Day before yesterday the lives of forty men were saved by the timely assistance of the committee. Humanly speaking, they would all have died. Mr. Mallard went off with a haversack of eatables, a tin cup, and canteen of whiskey.

A few nights ago, while Mr. Mallard was assisting with the wounded at the depot, a surgeon introduced himself as Dr. Webb, and asked if he had not married Mary Jones; that he had married Mary Castleman, and she had been in Atlanta; but it had not occurred to her that I might be here until after she returned to Forsyth, where Dr. Webb is stationed. At present she has gone North by flag of truce by way of City Point to get her baby, and Dr. Webb is beginning to wonder why she does not return. I cannot imagine what her baby could be doing at the North. I presume when Dr. Webb returns from the front he will call and see me. I should have liked to have seen Mary while she was here, and if she returns I presume I shall see her; but she is such a shrewd, managing person that if Dr. Webb does not mind, she will fix herself comfortably at the North and leave him to take care of himself until after the war.

Kitty has not heard from her brother yet, and of course feels very anxious about him. She will probably go to Habersham next week. I trust she will hear before she leaves.

The children send many kisses and love to dear Grandmama and Little Sister. The weather continues cool. Kitty desires much love. I received a letter from Cousin Laura last week. Give love to Aunt Susan and herself; also to Uncle William. With warmest love to yourself, dear Mother,

Your affectionate child,
Mary S. Mallard.

MRS. MARY S. MALLARD *to* MRS. SUSAN M. CUMMING[t]

Atlanta, *Friday,* May 20th, 1864

My dear Aunt and Cousin,

I am truly obliged to you for your letters just received. I cannot tell you how much concerned I am about my dear mother. I trust she is better; but if I should receive a letter from you tomorrow saying she is worse, I will take the next train and be with her on Monday. Do, my dear aunt, write me constantly, if only a line, and tell me *exactly what you think* of my dear mother. The communication is very direct now, and if allowed to pass by the military authorities, I could soon be with you. It is a great comfort to me to know that you are with Mother, and I know you will take every care of her. If she expresses any wish that I should go down, do let me know. Your letter came through very quickly—written on the 19th and received this evening (20th).

Mr. Mallard is still with the army attending the wounded. I do not know certainly when he will return, but presume tomorrow, as he expected to be back before Sabbath. It is the impression here that the battle must have commenced today; and if that is the case Mr. Mallard may feel compelled to remain longer. Our last news is that the army has fallen back in the neighborhood of the Etowah, and General Johnston has issued his battle order saying that he will now give battle and will fall back no further. And from all we can gather the army is in line of battle, so I suppose the contest will be decided by tomorow evening. I scarcely expect Mr. Mallard until after this battle is fought, unless the relief committee insist upon relieving those now engaged with the wounded. It is such heavy work that they send up six or eight new men every day. Of course it is an anxious time with us all, and a time for earnest prayer. If General Johnston is victorious, the Yankees must suffer terribly. All think he is able and will follow up any advantage he may gain.

I wish we had all the old rags from the households in Liberty. There is such a demand for them, and the citizens here have been so frequently called upon that they have very little to give. There is great demand for old sheets to spread over the wounded who are brought down on the cars. You can imagine the necessity for these: when limbs are amputated and the clothing cut off a foot or two above the place, something cooler and lighter than their blankets is necessary to throw over them.

Kitty expects to leave on next Tuesday for Clarkesville. She has heard nothing yet from Edward. His name has not been published in the list of wounded officers, so we conclude he must be safe; though of course nothing short of a letter from him would really be satisfactory.

Do give warmest love to my dear mother, and tell her if she wants me, I will come to her at once; and she must not hesitate to send for me. . . . Much love for yourselves and the children.

Your affectionate
Mary S. Mallard.

MRS. MARY S. MALLARD *to* MRS. MARY JONES[t]

Atlanta, *Friday,* May 27th, 1864

My dearest Mother,

I am truly rejoiced to hear through letters from Brother Charlie and

Brother Joe that you are decidedly better. I trust our kind Heavenly Father will soon restore you to your accustomed health. I cannot tell you how anxious I was about you; and nothing but my own sickness and the constant apprehension of the approach of the enemy kept me from going immediately to you. I felt very much relieved when I heard that Brother Joe had gone down.

I was quite sick in bed the first of this week, and am still quite weak. I have had a severe cold, which I suppose fell upon my bowels, causing me a great deal of pain and some fever.

We are passing through times of intense anxiety. We hope for a favorable issue, but none know how this campaign will end. The enemy are certainly very near us, McPherson's corps occupying Dallas. It has been a great disappointment to all that they should have proceeded thus far without a battle. General Johnston issued his battle order at Cartersville and undoubtedly intended to have fought there; but the false information brought by his scouts caused him to change his plan and lost him the opportunity. It is said they are laying waste as they come through. We have not heard much from Rome yet.

On Monday night, being restless and wakeful, I was startled by the ringing of our doorbell about two o'clock. I woke Mr. Mallard, and he went in his "disables" to find out who was there. To my astonishment I heard him say: "Yes, ma'am, I will open the door directly." I could not imagine what a lady could be doing there at that hour of the night, but soon found that Mary, Lilla, and Ellen had come down with a gentleman. I was very glad to see them, and we soon had them distributed. I sent Mary up to Kitty's room, spread a bed in the study for the gentleman, sent Mr. Mallard to the sofa in the drawing room and took Lilla with me, and made Mamie give her place to Ellen in the trundle bed. The girls came off without a particle of baggage, as the cars were too crowded for them to bring it. Mr. Bryson remained behind and brought it on Wednesday with the hospital stores. He insisted that the girls should be sent away, and has been as kind as a brother could have been, and went with them on Thursday morning to Fort Valley, and will take them to Perry. They will stay with Cousin Maria Gilbert. I think Mr. Bryson's going all the way with the girls is exceedingly kind, for they have a great deal of baggage, and Nanny with her baby.

I do feel deeply for my dear old aunty, brought to such trials in her old age; though Mr. Bryson, who left them last, says he believes Aunty is bearing it better than Aunt Mary and Aunt Lou. Aunt Mary especially feels it. The girls said Aunt Mary said she believed it would kill her for the Yankees to come to Marietta. "Indeed!" says Aunty. "*I* don't mean to die; it shan't kill *me!*" I was delighted to hear of this spirit, and hope she will be spared through it all. The enemy are moving a little southwest of Marietta, so maybe they will never occupy the place. I know they feel their isolation and desolation terribly now, for the mail has been stopped, and almost every family has left the place: not more than three or four left. They have been so long accustomed to having a number of daily visitors and to being shaken by a half-dozen trains a day that they will feel it terribly. We will watch our opportunities and send them letters whenever we can. The girls—Mary Sophia especially—did not wish to leave, but I think it was very wise to send them away. Their being there might have subjected the family to many more insults and much more trouble; and then they would have been so many more to provide for. They said the panic was very great in Marietta, and the difficulty of getting off very great. Some families waited three days at the depot before they could get off.

A number of persons have left here, though I do not think there has been anything like a panic. We have sent away all of our winter clothing, comforts, carpets, my sewing machine, and most of Mr. Mallard's books to Augusta to Brother Joe, so that if the army does not make a stand at this place, we will not lose everything. We all hope that General Johnston will be successful in driving them away from the city.

Mr. Mallard has been out all morning helping in finding shelters for the poor refugees who have come down here; and he says the last reliable information contradicts the report that McPherson's corps occupies Dallas. Our army is a little beyond that point, and day before yesterday had quite a little battle with the enemy, repulsing them handsomely. The cannonading was heard here. Mr. Mallard conversed with a gentleman who was present and under fire. He says our men behaved most gallantly and repulsed the Yankees in three charges. Our men were behind temporary breastworks. We lost about five hundred killed and wounded, the Yankees two or three thousand. Much of the heavy baggage of the army has been brought to this place, and the town is being quite filled up with army wagons and all the appendages belonging to the rear of an army.

I wish all the ladies in Liberty would send all their rags; they have no idea how much they are needed here, both for the present and the future. They could express the bundle to Mr. Mallard or to Mrs. Winship, president of the Atlanta Hospital Association. There are a great many wounded here now, and of course the number is daily increasing.

Do not feel too uneasy about us, dear Mother. If there is a prospect of the army's falling back to this place or of a battle occurring very near, I will go away with the children. It is a very difficult question to decide what to do. Brother Joe and Carrie have very kindly invited us to go there, but the place where we go must depend upon circumstances. If there is a prospect of a battle that will be decided in a week or two, perhaps I may go there until it is over. But if there should be a prospect of a siege, I think I would have to go to Liberty and take the servants with me. I pray that we may be directed aright and shown what will be best for us. I am living by the light of each day, and have everything so arranged that I could soon pack up my clothing. Of course if the Yankees ever reach this place, we must suffer heavy losses in furniture and everything else; but we are all in good heart and look for victory.

I presume Mr. Rogers' ironworks have been burned, as we know the Etowah works have been.

Kitty left me on Wednesday morning. The same morning Mr. Markham, a classmate of Mr. Mallard's, came here from the army sick, and is still here, though not confined to bed. I have had a full house all week.

I hope yet, dear Mother, that we will enjoy a portion of our summer in peace and quiet, and then we shall hope to have you with us. . . . I wish I could send you a draught of our cool delightful water; we need no ice.

Mr. Mallard and the children unite with me in warmest love. Brother Charlie writes me Little Sister is with them. Love to Aunt Susan, Cousin Laura, and Uncle William. Good-bye, dear Mother.

Your loving daughter,
Mary S. Mallard.

MRS. MARY S. MALLARD *to* MRS. MARY JONES[t]

Atlanta, *Friday,* June 3rd, 1864

My dearest Mother,

A letter received from Brother Charlie last night mentioned that you would go to Savannah today, so I will direct this letter there. I am truly thankful, my dear mother, to know that you are recovering your strength, and I sincerely hope a removal from care will soon restore you to your accustomed health. Brother Charlie has been very good in writing me, so that I have heard frequently from you.

We are passing through so much anxiety and perplexity that days sometimes seem weeks, and I scarcely realize how time is passing. We have been expecting a general engagement for the past two weeks, and it has not come yet, so that everyone has given up conjecture and now quietly awaits the issue. Our army is about thirty miles from this place, and the Yankees just in front of them. They have made several night attacks recently, and in every instance our men have driven them back with great slaughter. I presume you saw by the papers that seven hundred Yankee dead were left upon the field the night they attacked Cleburne's division. We too are losing many noble lives, though few in comparison with the enemy, for our men fight almost entirely behind breastworks.

Our town is rapidly filling up with the wounded. Some of the hospitals are entirely filled. Stores are being fitted up for hospitals, and I presume the city hall and other buildings will soon be impressed for the same purpose. I have been unable to go to the hospitals myself, as they are very far off, and I have not the strength to walk; but I prepare and send food to them. I have been sending for a week past to a ward filled with Texas men. They often send and beg me to send more arrowroot; sometimes requests come for onions, lettuce, and all manner of things. The bundle of rags and box of arrowroot came quite safely this evening, and will be very acceptable. I will keep the arrowroot and prepare it myself, for it is generally so badly prepared at the hospitals that the men will not eat it.

Mr. Mallard goes down tonight at two o'clock to the cars to assist in having the wounded carried to the various hospitals. There is a great deal of work to be done here now, not only with the wounded but with the refugees, who are here in great numbers. Mr. Mallard works constantly with the committee, and they are doing a great deal of good. They have quite a village of refugees dependent upon them for provisions, and many of them for clothing. The citizens of Savannah have been very generous in sending up rice and corn for them.

A most absurd piece has been published in one of our papers signed "Shadow," which describes a dreadful panic which the author says took place here some ten days ago. He describes the confusion and consternation of the citizens in a most exaggerated manner, and represents the whole population in a state of consternation and all moving off. The whole piece is a falsehood, for no such thing as a panic has ever existed here at all. Some few persons have moved away, and others have sent away articles of value and such things as could not be removed in haste; and this is the extent of the panic. Some of the Jews have removed their possessions, and a few Yankees have gone from our midst; but I believe these are the only men that have deserted the place. Mr. Mallard has been constantly called on the street by his engagements with the committee, and he says everyone seems to him to be earnestly at work trying in every way to alleviate the sufferings of those around.

I hear that the 5th Georgia Cavalry (Colonel Anderson) are to pass through here tomorrow, so I presume they will soon be in battle.

Thus far the enemy have never come to Marietta, and many hope and believe they never will. We heard from Aunty today. They are all well, though Aunt Mary and Aunt Lou say they are very much worn with anxiety. I feel deeply for them. Very few families remain there. The cars still run there, though the mail is stopped. As long as the cars run there and the wounded are brought down that way they will not feel utterly cut off. I have sent them two letters by private opportunity, and if you could write them we can get the letter to them.

I have had Mrs. General Cumming (Sarah Davis) with me since last Saturday. She came up hearing that General Cumming was seriously wounded. Colonel Cumming, his father, came with her, and has gone to the front to see his sons. When she came she expected to have returned in a day or two, but Colonel Cumming is still at the front, and she is awaiting his return. I believe she is almost half disappointed that she did not find the general slightly wounded, for she would then have taken him home with her. The hotels are such abominable places now that I am glad she is with us and not there.

Mr. Markham, the sick chaplain who has been with us recruiting, returned on Tuesday. He was very sick and feeble when he first came, but recovered very rapidly and returned quite well.

I must tell you of the preservation of our dear little children today. Mrs. Rogers called early this morning and begged me to let them spend the day with her; so she took them home, and while there a thunderstorm came up and the house was struck. No one was at all injured. The lightning, striking the bell wire, ran along and then down a portion of the plastering in the parlor. Mrs. Rogers and the children were in a room opposite (an entry between), and did not even feel the shock, though the report was very loud. It was a remarkable providence, and I regard it as such. Their preservation was wonderful. The house is a remarkably small one (only one story), and Mrs. Rogers says it has two rods, so that it is strange that it should have been struck.

I received a letter from Kitty this afternoon. She has reached home in safety. . . . It is growing late, so I must close. I am a great deal better this week; my strength is returning. The weather is delightful: the nights so cool that I always use a quilt. I wish you could have our cool water, it is so refreshing. Do give much love to Brother Charlie and Eva; I will write them in a day or two. Kiss Little Sister for us. Mr. Mallard and the children unite with me in warmest love. I long to have a letter from you once more.

Your affectionate daughter,
Mary S. Mallard.

MRS. MARY S. MALLARD *to* MRS. MARY JONES[t]

Atlanta, *Tuesday,* June 7th, 1864

My dearest Mother,

Mr. Henderson has just sent home $66.70, amount of Niger's hire for two months (from 1st of April to 1st of June). As Mr. Mallard is absent, I enclose you the amount. Niger was for several weeks at Stone Mountain gathering bark, but is again working at the tanyard.

I hope, dear Mother, that you are quite well again. I wish every day you could come immediately to us; I am sure the change would benefit you, and you would find drinking and bathing in our cool water a tonic in itself. I trust everything will be sufficiently quiet in a few weeks for you to come up.

Our dear old aunty has at last determined to move. Mr. Bryson tells me that the nearer the army comes to Marietta the more Aunt Mary's nerves give way; and he says such is their anxiety and excitement that he does not think it possible for them to remain. He has been a good friend to them, and is now doing all in his power to aid them. Mr. Mallard went up this morning to assist in getting them off, and I expect them tomorrow afternoon to spend some days with me before they pursue their journey. Mr. Bryson ascertained here that their household effects could all be conveyed as far as Macon for three hundred dollars. They have on hand five hundred dollars; and I told Mr. Bryson I knew their relatives would assist them. It is a dreadful trial for them to leave, and yet they begin to feel they could not brook the occupation of the place by the enemy. I do not know whether they have definitely determined where to go. I do feel very much for them. Aunt Lou dislikes leaving very much, for Joe just passed through today on his way to the front, and she feels she would not like to be far from him.

The whole of Colonel Anderson's regiment passed through today—or rather they marched today; they arrived two days ago. Fred King called to see us, and we saw several of the young men at church on Sabbath night. Mr. Porter took tea with us on Sabbath and preached for Mr. Mallard. He appears greatly improved in health, but not much so in figure, being dressed in cavalry uniform, even a round jacket, which exhibited his thin figure very funnily. The young men appear very much attached to him, and he labors very hard amongst them.

In view of the perils of the times our mayor has appointed next Friday a day of fasting and prayer. There are daily union prayer meetings held for the country. They are very interesting, but it is very discouraging to see a small house not half filled. One would suppose that no church in the city could contain those who would attend a union prayer meeting. The religious interest still keeps up in the army, notwithstanding all the fatigues of the retreat.

The children are quite well, and often ask if the summertime, when Grandmama said she would come, has not come yet. Charlie says he thinks it is winter, because if it were summer Grandma and Little Sister would be sure to be here. Good night, dear Mother. Be assured of the warmest love of your grandchildren and affectionate daughter,

Mary S. Mallard.

MRS. MARY JONES *to* MRS. MARY S. MALLARD[t]

Savannah, *Tuesday,* June 7th, 1864

My dearest Child,

Your aunt and myself came to town on last Thursday, and I have designed every day to write you, but my feeble condition and the constant calls from friends have prevented. Through God's mercy I have had no return of fever since it left me, and—what is even more remarkable after such a complicated attack of climate fever and pneumonia—my lungs are free from cough or pain. I presume the inflammation was thrown off. It was a great mercy that your brother was with me. . . .

We have a reported landing of the Yankees on Wilmington and Whitemarsh. No doubt they are enraged at the recent capture of the *Water Witch.* The troops are all withdrawn, and the defense of Savannah would devolve upon the light artillery. We are having most solemn and interesting prayer meetings every afternoon at five o'clock. Churches are crowded. Will not our Almighty Father, our Judge and Deliverer, hear and answer our cries for mercy?

Dear Eva has just come in and says: "Give a great deal of love to Sister." She is as kind and affectionate as possible to me. You will love her tenderly when you know her. Little Sister is quite well and bright.

Your last favor has been received. How thankful I am for the preservation of our dear little children from sudden death! I cannot tell you how anxious I am for you all in Atlanta, and for my dear aunt and cousins. What can I do for them? My heart is weighed down with their situation. Do let me know how I could help them. I pray constantly that you may all be guided by wisdom, and not suffered to remain exposed to that cruel enemy when you might get away. If there is any danger, do send Niger down to Liberty. . . . All unite in tenderest love to you and best love to Robert and the dear children. My heart yearns to see you, my dearest child.

Ever your own mother,
Mary Jones.

MRS. MARY S. MALLARD *to* MRS. MARY JONES[t]

Atlanta, *Saturday,* June 11th, 1864*

My dearest Mother,

I was truly glad and thankful to receive a letter from your own hand day before yesterday. I hope your strength will soon return. If things were only more quiet, I would insist upon your coming immediately to us, for I am sure the change at this time would do you more good than anything else. We are as quiet here so far as the situation of the house is concerned as if we lived in the country.

I wrote you that Mr. Mallard had gone up on Tuesday to assist in packing up Aunt Eliza's furniture. Mr. Bryson and Mr. Mallard packed up everything, and shipped it on Thursday. Mr. Mallard took Charles up to assist, and they were able to bring away everything belonging to themselves and servants. On Wednesday Aunt Mary and Aunt Eliza came here. Aunty bore the journey tolerably well, though she was very much exhausted, having been previously sick from an affection of her bowels. She was quite sick the day after she arrived, but is improving, though so feeble I do not think she will be able to move for a week. She is wonderfully supported under this trial. On Thursday Mr. Mallard came down with all of the furniture and all of the servants, and yesterday Aunt Lou came. The furniture was forwarded to Macon yesterday afternoon, Daddy Sam going with it to see that everything was properly cared for.

When Aunty left Marietta, they thought if no other arrangement could be made that they would go down to Flemington, as they said they had received a pressing invitation from Aunt Susan and Cousin Laura to go to them. They wrote to Mr. George Walker and requested him to receive their furniture and have it stored and if possible rent a house for them, that they might go to housekeeping. Yesterday afternoon they received a letter from Mr. Walker (not in reply to theirs, for he has not yet received that letter) inviting them to go to him should they deem it necessary to leave Marietta. This has determined them to go to Mr. Walker's and remain there at least for a while, until they can make some permanent arrangement. Aunt Mary asked my advice to help her determine, and said Mr. Walker had a very large comfortable house situated in Longstreet (Pulaski County) three miles from the Macon & Brunswick Railroad, that he was a man of large property, abundant means of living from his own plantation, plenty of poultry, butter, etc., and made a great deal of sugar and syrup, for she had seen fifteen barrels of sugar and more than that number of syrup on his place in the winter. Perhaps you had better not say anything about it, but I told her candidly I thought they would all be more comfortable there, and it would be far better to go there than to Flemington, although I knew Aunt Susan would give them as hearty a welcome and do as much for them as any relative they had. And they feel this. Aunt Eliza does not wish to go to Flemington if it can be avoided at this season, for she is so feeble that such a long journey would be exceedingly trying. And then she says it looks like taking her just so much nearer Midway graveyard.

Aunt Mary will leave on Monday for Macon, and from thence to Mr. Walker's to make all necessary arrangements; and when everything is ready and Aunty is strong enough, Aunt Lou and herself with the servants will go on. I do not think Aunty will be able to move for at least a week. I am very glad to think she has the prospect of going where there will be such an abundance of poultry and other things which seem very necessary to her now. It is a great trial to them to break up their pleasant home, for they feel it is a final move, and they do not expect ever to return. It is sad to see such a kind, hospitable family turned out of their own home. Aunt Mary begs me to say to you that the idea of being called by the hated name of *refugees* made them cling to their home until every male friend left the place—even Dr. Stewart, who had determined to remain. But when our army fell back, resting one wing on Kennesaw, they felt the enemy were at their doors; and they did not know to what straits they might be reduced, so got Mr. Bryson to come here and consult Mr. Mallard and Mr. Rogers and determined to move. Almost every family in Marietta has moved.

This move will necessarily be most expensive to Aunty. The expenses of getting the furniture to this place will be about seventy dollars. This Mr. Mallard and myself expect to defray. It will cost about one hundred and fifty dollars to move the furniture to Macon; how much more to the Walkers' I do not know. When there I presume they will be at no expense. They have taken all of their provisions and groceries with them, and will take Peggy, Will, Willis, and Bruce and Daddy Sam with them. Nanny and her child are with the girls at Cousin Maria Gilbert's.

I have been thus particular, my dear mother, for I knew you would want to know everything relative to the move and future plans. I fear Aunty will feel the quiet of the country very irksome, for she finds this place too quiet; thinks if she were in my place she would live more in the heart of the town to see all that was passing. Aunt Mary and Aunt Lou are pretty nearly worn out with fatigue and anxiety.

Our army is about three miles from Marietta, and was in line of battle yesterday; but whether it will result in an engagement it is idle to conjecture, for no one has the slightest idea of General Johnston's plans. I trust the battle will be fought soon, and that our arms will be crowned with success.

Yesterday, in accordance with a proclamation of our mayor, was observed as a day of fasting and prayer. The Baptists, Methodists, and Presbyterians united in the morning, and the services were deeply solemn and interesting. Addresses were made by a colonel from Texas (a minister) who commands in General Cleburne's division, and also by a chaplain from the Virginia army (Longstreet's command). Hearing him speak of Wofford's brigade, I begged Mr. Mallard to inquire if Eddie Stiles had been preserved through the battles. He said he knew him very well, and that he had behaved with distinguished gallantry, and the manner in which he handled his men had won the admiration of all. He had been preserved through all the battles and had been perfectly well. I trust the prayers offered yesterday will be answered, and our city spared.

There is a daily union prayer meeting here, but it is poorly attended. It is true that many of the ladies and gentlemen are occupied upon various committees ministering to the relief of the sick, wounded, and refugees. Still there is no excuse for a small attendance. I have not attended as many of them as I would like, for they are held a mile from my house, and I am not often able to walk so far.

It would be a great relief to us could we be assured General Johnston would not fall back to the Chattahoochee. Mr. Mallard says if he does, I shall have to go with the children and servants. I trust the necessity will not come. Brother Charlie and Brother Joe have both most kindly invited me to come to them, but I feel that I can form no plans for the future, for I do not know what a day may bring forth. If this place should be given up, of course we will have to seek another home. In that case it would not be right in these times of terrible scarcity and difficulty in living to take a household to anyone in a city; and the expense would be more than we could bear. If there is a prospect of holding this place at all hazards, then the children and myself would go away whilst the battle was undetermined; for we would not remain if there was any prospect of its taking place in or near the town. This is the way I feel about it, my dear mother; and I have tried to commit all these cares and anxieties to my Heavenly Father, and I trust He will make our way plain. The armies may keep their present position for half the summer. Everyone feels unbounded confidence in General Johnston, and the condition and spirit of the army is as good as could be desired.

I will cut up the pavilion you sent and take it to the hospital early next week. I know the men will be delighted to get pieces to spread over their faces and wounds. I think the flies of Egypt scarcely exceed the multitude abroad in this town.

Day before yesterday Niger came home discharged from the tannery. Mr. Henderson is breaking up his establishment here, and has no further use for his services. In your letter you say if there is any danger, send him home. We do not think there is any danger now, and write to know what you think best. Shall Mr. Mallard find some other employment for him? He begs to stay; says he would not like to go away as long as we are here. There is a great deal of gardening work to be done at this time, and until we hear from you, will let him employ himself in this way. There is a plenty of job work to be done, so he will not be idle until we hear from you.

Mr. Mallard wrote Mr. Quarterman last night to give out the osnaburgs to the people. I think there will be enough for *all* of the people at Arcadia. I am very glad we happened to have it on hand, for it would be difficult to get it at this time. Roswell factory is threatened, but I hope it will not be destroyed, for it would be a great loss. If the army falls much farther back it will be left exposed.

I have written you a long letter, dear Mother. . . . The children send a great deal of love to you and to Little Sister. . . . I hope you have received my letter enclosing Niger's hire. Aunt Eliza, Aunts Mary and Lou desire best love to you, and to Aunt Susan if she is still in Savannah. Mr. Mallard unites with me in warmest love to you, dear Mother.

Your affectionate daughter,
Mary S. Mallard.

MRS. MARY S. MALLARD *to* MRS. MARY JONES^t

Atlanta, *Thursday,* June 23rd, 1864*

My dearest Mother,

This morning Aunt Eliza and Aunt Lou left us for Macon on their way to Pulaski County. Aunty was so sick and feeble that at one time we feared she never would be able to leave us; but her spirit is very firm, and she was determined to reach her journey's end if possible. She has been with us two weeks, and as much as I would have liked to have had her remain longer, we felt it would be wrong to urge her to do so; for if anything like a panic should occur it would be almost impossible to get one so feeble away. I dread the effects of the journey for her, and most of all the seclusion of the country. I do not know how any of them will bear this, for they have so long been in the very center of news that they are very dependent upon it. They have a strong hope that they will be able to rent a very nice cottage of six rooms; there is also a nice vegetable garden all planted, and plenty of servants' accommodation on the lot. The whole town of Marietta has emptied itself: scarcely a family left. Our army is very near, and I believe some of the enemy's shells have already reached those houses next to Kennesaw. The shells now fall entirely over the mountain.

Your last sweet letter reached me on my birthday. Thank you, dear Mother, for it. These are indeed days of darkness and deep anxiety, and I am afraid I shall be among that class of women of whom it is said: "Woe unto them," etc. We have a very unsettled feeling about our future movements; they must depend in great measure upon the movements of the army.

A few days ago officers were impressing Negroes to work upon the fortifications at the Chattahoochee. Charles was of the number impressed. I was glad they did not take Niger, as we are daily expecting to hear from you about him. I wrote nearly two weeks ago to know what you thought best to be done with him, and hope to get an answer tomorrow.

I cut up the gauze you sent into convenient squares, and have given the most of them to the wounded men. You would have been amused to have seen two young crackers with their squares. One of them said he was "mightily proud of it," and the last I saw of him he was alternately covering his face and then folding the gauze to look at it. . . . You would be amazed at the number of wounded in this place. It is a constant source of regret to me that I am unable to walk to the hospitals, and I do not often have an opportunity of riding.

Thus far none of Captain Walthour's company have been wounded, though they have been in a number of skirmishes. Some of Captain Hughes's have been wounded, amongst the number a Mr. John Fennell, son of the person who used to keep a store at Riceboro.

I will direct this to Savannah. I trust, dear Mother, your strength is returning. I wish you would come to us next; I think the change would do you good. I know you would enjoy the cool nights and nice water. Mr. Mallard and the children unite with me in warmest love to you, and love to Brother Charlie and Eva.

Your affectionate daughter,
Mary S. Mallard.

We expect Brother Joe the last of this week.

MRS. MARY JONES *to* MRS. MARY S. MALLARD[t]

Savannah, Saturday, June 25th, 1864

My dear Daughter,

I have been hoping every day for a letter, but I know how much you have to engage your time. I have been scarcely able to write, and now do so in pain from rheumatism or neuralgia in my neck and head, which makes it very stiff, and with difficulty I turn or hold it either up or down. It has been so ever since my illness, and I fear it is becoming a settled affection.

On last Wednesday I made an effort and went home. Spent that night at Montevideo and the next at Flemington with our dear relatives there, who in all my sickness have shown me every kindness and attention. When I left home, Patience had to think of and pack everything; consequently there were some important matters forgotten. And then I wanted to see all the people once more before I left the low country. I found them all well; and all desire to be particularly remembered to Robert and yourself and the children. . . . I had told them on leaving I wanted all the butter at both places sent you as soon as they had enough to make it an object; from the state of the weather they have not made much, but I brought in a jarful done up in shucks which

I will express to you on Monday, and hope it may reach you safely. It was all that has been made at both Arcadia and Montevideo since I left. The next gathering I will send to Joe, thus alternating—if you find it worth the while to have it sent up. You must write me about it.

Rose spun your fine wool, which I brought up with me. Mrs. Butler had not sent home the last piece.

If Niger can find employment in Atlanta, I am willing for him to remain as long as you do, and wish you to make him useful to Robert and yourself at any time you may need his services. Please keep the wages that he may make for the present.

My strength returns slowly. If I had only been permitted, in God's providence, to be with you this summer, I know it would have been a great benefit, as well as the greatest happiness I could have had. As it is, the future is all uncertain. I have not appointed any time for going to Augusta. Carrie has had such a spell of nursing I fear to increase her cares. Eva expects to go to her mother, but she wants to delay as long as it is healthy here, for when she goes she cannot return until frost. I would prefer for the *benefit of my health* to go out into the country and board rather than remain in Augusta all summer. I expect certainly to make my dear Joe and Carrie a visit.

Your situation, my dear child, fills me with the greatest anxiety, and I do hope you will not tarry in Atlanta too long. All that I can do is pray for you.

The fearful condition of our armies on the front of our own state and Virginia fills every heart with trembling. Not a day now passes but we receive the sad tidings of some friend or acquaintance slain in battle. Our county is mourning many of her sons slain. Rev. Mr. Andrews and his wife were in deep sorrow for the death of a promising son killed in Virginia. Your Aunt Julia trembles for her boys now upon the battlefield. Colonel Joe McAllister is said to have died bravely. He was surrounded by the enemy, who demanded his surrender. He replied: "Only with life!" and continued to shoot down the enemy until overpowered. His last act was to hurl his pistol at their heads. . . . Major Thomson's remains are expected out in Liberty on Monday.

I have this moment received a letter from Cousin Mary. Aunt had arrived comfortably in Macon on the 23rd, where they would rest awhile and then go to Mr. Walker's. Cousin Mary hopes to rent a house belonging to Mr. Walker's son-in-law. Mr. Walker sent his wagons and had all their furniture moved and stored for them. I feel deeply for them, and rejoice that such friends and helpers are raised up unto them.

Charles and Eva unite with me in best love to Robert and yourself. Kiss my precious children for me. This is Little Sister's birthday. She says: "Tell Sissy and Bubber I send a letter to them."

Ever, my dear daughter, your affectionate mother,
Mary Jones.

Atlanta, *Friday,* July 1st, 1864

My dear Mother,

The express brought the jar and fans quite safely evening before the last. Nothing could be more opportune than the butter, for I had not a particle, and I am very much obliged to you for it. I have not sent the fans to the hospital yet, but know the men will be glad to have them, and shall get Mr. Dod to distribute them for me.

Brother Joe came up on last Saturday and remained until Wednesday, when Mr. Mallard and himself went to Marietta together. Mr. Mallard went as one of the aid committee to assist with the wounded. . . . Brother Joe was two weeks ahead of his secretary, so he came up to spend a few days with us and to offer his services for ten days in Marietta, where the chief field surgeon has his quarters. I should have been glad to have kept him quietly here, and would have liked to have persuaded him to do nothing for the next two weeks; but you know he must always be at work.

I have had Mr. Dod staying with me for a week past. He is the same who used to teach in Darien, and has recently come from Plaquemine in Louisiana, where he was settled and was living very comfortably, although under Yankee rule. He is quite an interesting man, and has left everything to come and labor in our army. At present chaplains can accomplish but little in the field, so he will probably establish himself in some hospital here; and he bids fair to be an earnest, laborious worker. I am truly glad he will locate here, for ministerial labor is sadly deficient in our hospitals here. Mrs. Dod is in Washington (Wilkes County), and is doing her own cooking. She has a son and daughter with her. I know of no one who has made greater sacrifices; and it has all been a voluntary offering on their part, for they might have remained. I see chaplains quite frequently, and have a weekly visitor in a Mr. Markham, formerly a pastor in New Orleans. Mr. Dod tells me he studied theology under my dear father's direction. He told me that he heard my dear father preach a sermon before the synod in Marietta on a Communion occasion which for beauty, simplicity, and effect upon his audience was unsurpassed; and the theme (as he expressed it) was "a simple narrative story of the Cross given by a feeling, loving spectator." Mr. Dod says the impressions made upon him by that discourse will never wear away. It is so pleasant to me to have anyone tell me their recollections of my beloved father. How I miss his counsels now!

Don't you think, dear Mother, you could come first to us and leave your visit to Augusta until later? We do not feel there is any immediate danger; and if there should be after you come, you could easily run down to Augusta. I want you to come while we are enjoying our vegetables; and I am sure a change at once to this climate would do you more good than later. I think even supposing the army falls back to the Chattahoochee, it will not do so for some weeks yet; so do think of it, dear Mother, and come immediately up. The last disaster to Sherman has been a very serious affair, and our cavalry is beginning to operate in the rear. We have had a few torpedoes at work upon the railroad track, so I hope we may yet be permitted to remain here.

I received a letter from Aunt Lou two days ago, and she says Aunty stood the journey remarkably well, and they are comfortably located with Mr. Walker, but have failed in renting the cottage they hoped to get. Already they begin to realize the utter quiet of the country, and long for a bit of news. I am afraid this will be a dreadful cross to all of them. Aunty misses her cool well of water. Aunt Lou says I must not be surprised to see her very soon, for she feels she must come nearer Joe. It is a time of great exposure to him, being in skirmishes every day. Aunty's house in Marietta has been taken by Bate's division for their hospital. Scarcely a family is left in Marietta.

The attendance upon our daily union prayer meeting is increasing. Some of the meetings are very interesting. . . . Do write soon, dear Mother, and say you are coming. The children send many messages of love. Mr. Mallard would unite with me in much love if he were here. I have written Eva by this mail thanking her for her handsome present.

Your affectionate daughter,
Mary S. Mallard.

XVIII

Mrs. Mary S. Mallard *to* Mrs. Laura E. Buttolph[t]
Augusta, *Monday,* July 18th, 1864

My dear Cousin,

You have doubtless heard through Cousin Lyman that we have left Atlanta—at least for the present—and are now numbered amongst the numerous throng of refugees. We had hoped to have remained longer in Atlanta, but when the order came to remove all hospitals in a few hours, and the enemy were reported as crossing the river within six miles of us, we thought we had better move our furniture while we could get transportation. And as it was, the granting of a car at that time was a personal favor to Mr. Mallard.

We made up our minds on Thursday morning, and by Friday afternoon everything was packed in the car and the house completely emptied, except one mattress and bedstead left for Mr. Mallard's accommodation. So you may know we worked hard. After everything was packed in the car, a telegram came from Brother Charlie saying expect Mother the next day. We did not know what to do, for everything had gone from the house, and we were compelled to go on ourselves; so Mr. Mallard telegraphed immediately to Mr. Nisbet to say we would leave that night for Augusta, and to stop Mother there. But unfortunately he did not receive it, and Mother had all the fatigue and anxiety of coming on and finding us gone. If we could have had the slightest intimation that she thought of coming, we would have made other arrangements. After a great deal of anxiety in Atlanta and fatigue and detention in coming here, Mother reached this place on Monday morning, we having gotten here the afternoon before.

We were detained in Atlanta by a serious accident which but for the mercy of God might have resulted fatally to some of us. We expected to have left at two o'clock Friday night, and intended to have walked to the depot; but Charles, without our knowledge, had borrowed a dray or four-wheeled wagon from one of the neighbors; and as we were excessively fatigued from the two days' packing, we thought we would ride down with our two trunks. Descending a steep little hill, I think something gave way about the cart, and it ran upon Jim, causing him to start off; and in a few moments we were all thrown out. The children were uninjured saving bruises upon their faces, and the skin was taken off of Mamie's knee. Mr. Mallard's foot caught, and he was dragged for some distance, but sprang back into the cart and disengaged his foot. I was seriously injured, being bruised in every part of my body from my head to my feet, with the exception of a portion of my back and stomach; and my collarbone was dislocated. I discovered something was wrong with it as soon as I was able to rise from the ground, and got Mr. Mallard to draw my shoulder back, which I knew would put the bones in position until a physician could be gotten. I suffered intensely, not only from the dislocation but from the other blows upon my chest, head, hip, knees, etc. But Dr. Logan soon bandaged me up, and advised our leaving at seven with our furniture. So Mr. Mallard opened the bedding and made a bed for me, and fixed a rocking chair so that I could sit down comfortably. It was well we were able to make this arrangement, for I could not have borne the journey in the passenger car. As it was, the bone was dislocated once after we started; and if I had been in a car, where I would have been compelled to have sat up, it would have nearly destroyed me.

Thus you see, my dear cousin, how narrowly our lives were preserved. I feel truly grateful that none of us were more seriously injured. We were two days in getting down here, and received a most affectionate welcome from Brother Joe and Carrie. Brother Joe is taking care of my arm, which will be bandaged up for six weeks, as the bone will not unite before that time. I am obliged to discard dresses, and look like a forlorn old lady sailing around in a sacque with one empty sleeve. I was quite a spectacle coming down on the cars, and often was asked: "Is you wounded?" I suppose they thought I was one of the unfortunate ones that had been caught between the lines when a battle was going on. I still suffer a good deal of pain, but this I must expect. I am truly thankful it was my left and not my right arm. Writing is about the only thing I can do, and that not very long at a time.

Brother Joe kindly let us store our furniture in his house. Mr. Mallard returned to Atlanta on Tuesday, and will abide the issue. If the town is evacuated, he will of course come away. I hope we may be able to return to Atlanta, but of course we will have to be governed by the movements of the army. Should Atlanta be evacuated, I think it probable we would go to Walthourville until some permanent arrangement can be made. I scarcely think yet of any future arrangements, as everything is so uncertain, and all turns upon the condition of affairs in Atlanta.

We found Carrie looking dreadfully, and the children both sick. Stanhope has been very sick, and is so weak that he totters around the house. Susie has been very sick also. Carrie went to The Hill on Saturday to spend a short time with her parents for the benefit of the change both for herself and children. I hope they will be benefited, for they are all very unwell.

I am truly thankful we have such a pleasant retreat. So many poor refugees are thrown out of their home without a shelter.

I think Mother intends enclosing a note in this to Aunt Susan. . . . Accept much love for Aunt Susan and yourself from

Your affectionate cousin,
Mary S. Mallard.

Augusta, *Friday,* July 22nd, 1864

My dear Sister,

We were happy this morning to receive dear Laura's letter to Daughter. It is almost the first tidings from Liberty since I left Savannah.

My passage through the state—up one railroad and down the other—was accomplished in such haste that I have been greatly exhausted by three days and nights spent in cars. The last thirty-six hours, between Atlanta and this place, we were detained by four crushed cars, heavily laden with government supplies and furniture of refugees, which could not be removed from the track a night and part of a day beyond the time of arrival. My stock of provisions had been completely exhausted before I left Atlanta. We stopped where not a drop of water could be had. I found a crust of bread in the lunch basket, which was shared with Flora. The most disagreeable part of the whole was walking quite a distance in the middle of the night—up embankments and down in ditches—to reach a relief car. I do not think my strength could have held out for the exertion had not a kind Providence brought to my assistance the strong arm of a young soldier, a lieutenant on furlough, who rendered me every necessary help. In all that journey there was not a human face I had ever seen before, and I felt desolate and lonely beyond expression.

Mr. Buttolph was so kind to me that I enjoyed his society and my trip up greatly. He has doubtless told of our adventures and given you the latest intelligence from the front. Every prospect darkens around us. This place, I fear, will feel next the presence of the enemy. There is so much to invite them in the government works and factories.

My dear daughter improves, but it will be a long time before she will use her wounded arm. Just now it is very painful: in the process of knitting. Her presence of mind and fortitude were wonderful, and it is a great mercy they were not all killed. Robert arrived yesterday, and Carrie and himself have gone today to visit Mr. and Mrs. Porter and Mr. Clarke's family at Beech Island. Carrie's children with Charlie have been quite sick; the boys are better, but little Susan Hyrne looks miserably. She has been threatened with cholera infantum, and is so feeble I would not be surprised if she is removed from this world of sorrow. Daughter and Carrie are both as thin as they well can be. These times of distress are preying alike upon young and old. The *situation* of my poor child makes her present trial peculiarly great.

I received a letter from Cousin Mary today. Aunt had been quite sick with fever, but was restored to her usual health. The girls were going to make a visit to Cuthbert. . . . Aunt and family I think will spend next winter between yourself and myself, and I want to do all in my power to make them comfortable. I expect Daughter and the children of course to be with me, for there is now no prospect of a return to Atlanta. Robert's church members have all removed. What the issue will be is known only to God. The outrages of the enemy at Decatur were awful!

482

I have not heard a word from Montevideo. Do inquire from Andrew if Mr. Jackson is still there or if he has been removed to the army. I am very anxious about my poor people, left in an unprotected condition, with none to think of or do for them. If my health had permitted and I could have remained in the county, I would not have left them. Those who have food and shelter and quiet homes in a protected region have reason for special gratitude.

Carrie and Joe, Daughter and Robert, with the children, unite with me in best love to yourself and Laura and Mr. Buttolph and the children. Remember us affectionately to Julia and Mary, Belle and Kitty; Audley and Kate when you see them. Love to Brother William from us all; I hope he is feeling better. Do let us hear from you soon.

Ever your affectionate sister,
Mary Jones.

MAJOR JOSEPH JONES *to* MRS. SUSAN M. CUMMING[t]

Augusta, *Saturday,* July 30th, 1864

My dear Aunt,

You will please accept the accompanying picture with the love of Carrie and myself. We regret that it is no better. Carrie's likeness does not, I think, do her justice. We send it to you chiefly on account of the little ones.

Sister and Brother Robert and Mother are now with us, and it gives us great pleasure to have this union of the families after the long separation. Sister's arm is slowly recovering, but still gives her much pain. Stanhope and Susan and Charlie, who have been quite ill, are all better and fast regaining their usual health and strength.

I returned a short time since from the Army of Tennessee, and if Providence permits I will leave for Richmond, Virginia, next Tuesday the 2nd of August. My report (third report to the surgeon general, C.S.A., on typhoid fever) is now completed; and as it contains much matter which would prove of value to our enemies, and as the communication with Richmond is uncertain, it becomes my duty to carry it on and deliver the volume in person to the surgeon general. This volume contains consolidated reports of the diseases, deaths, and mean strength of the Confederate armies from January 1862 to July 1863, and includes about six hundred closely written pages of royal quarto, and also contains a number of plates and maps. The labors have been numerous and continuous, and my health and strength has been greatly taxed. I have been greatly assisted in the manual labors by my secretary, Louis Manigault, of Charleston, South Carolina.

Carries unites with me in love to you and Cousins Laura and Lyman.

Your affectionate nephew,
Joseph Jones.

Please send the package to Uncle William at your earliest convenience.

Walthourville, *Monday,* August 22nd, 1864

My dearest Mother,

After bidding you good-bye we found the cars so much crowded that I could get no seat for some miles. I made a seat of my large shawls, pillow, and the overcoats, and rode very comfortably until we reached McBean's Station, where a lady got out. I took her place and gave mine to Brother Charlie, and Mr. Mallard sat upon one of the baskets. Lucy and the children located themselves very comfortably in the saloon, and I heard Mamie's little tongue all the way to Millen telling an old lady who shared the saloon with them all about the Yankees and about our living in Atlanta. . . . At Millen we waited an hour and a half. The children thought it fine fun to get up at midnight to play in the moonlight and eat watermelon. From Millen to Savannah we had a very comfortable journey, and I got down with less pain than I anticipated, though I was pretty thoroughly worn out by the time I reached this place. Brother Charlie kindly took us to his house and gave us a hot breakfast, which refreshed us very much.

The family here were all very glad to see us. . . . On Saturday a number of persons called to welcome us back. . . . The committee waited upon Mr. Mallard on Saturday evening, requesting him to preach for the church while he is absent from the Atlanta church. . . . Mrs. Screven thinks of going to her father's when Captain Screven leaves, which will be the 1st of September; so perhaps we may get back to the academy. Mrs. Screven has a little daughter about a month old.

I have heard nothing from Montevideo, as Niger did not come up on Saturday night. . . . I suppose you have seen through the papers that a whole company from Colonel Hood's command were captured in McIntosh. It is even so: thirty-five men and horses captured by marines. (The papers said by cavalry, but that was not so.) The Yankees were on foot, and it is said were exceedingly gentlemanly, allowing the prisoners to communicate with their families and to receive their clothing.

Mr. Mallard omitted one of Colonel Gaulden's acts in his flight from the Yankees in Riceboro, and that was this: being dressed in white clothes, someone suggested the Yankees would be sure to discover him going through the cornfield; so he stopped and smeared his clothing all over with black mud. This is said to be a fact.

I wish it had been so that we all could have remained together this summer, but I think Mr. Mallard did right in coming here. I hope poor little Susie is improving, and that Carrie has more rest. I think of them very often, and wish every day Susie had my piece of chicken. Lucy begs Flora to get her leather belt which she left in Sue's house and bring it for her. Please let Flora get our shoebrushes from Harry and keep them until you come. They were to have been brought, but were left out. Give much love to Carrie and Brother Joe from us all. I will write them very soon. Charlie will not believe he is in Walthourville because we have not gone to the academy. The children and Mr. Mallard unite with me in warmest love to you. Love to Eva and Little Sister.

Your affectionate daughter,
Mary S. Mallard.

I have not gotten over the fatigue of coming down, as I feel quite weak yet.

I forgot to have a pillow put in the small keg of crockery. Will you be kind enough, dear Mother, to take one out the bundle of bedding in the attic and have it put in? The keg is in the basement and contains my finest crockery.

MRS. MARY JONES *to* MRS. MARY S. MALLARD[t]

Augusta, *Monday,* August 22nd, 1864

My dear Daughter,

I have thought of you with great anxiety, and hope you did not wait long for a seat. Your brother wrote me saying you had all breakfasted with him in Savannah, and I trust through divine favor you are safely at your journey's end.

You know how unwell Carrie was for a long time before you left; I am sorry to inform you that she is now quite sick in bed with high fever. . . . Her extremely nervous condition for some time past has made me fear for her a serious attack of illness. . . . I have moved into your spacious apartment, and taken little Susie, crib, and Rose upstairs with me until her mother is restored. She was very good last night, requiring not more than three times to be up with a light. Stanhope is better. . . . Joe is much worn down, and a great deal to do; expected to go to Andersonville next week. Mrs. Cuthbert is sitting with Carrie, and I have left her to write you.

After you left I found a shirt, collar, and cravat of Robert's which I will have washed and bring or send as you desire. I had an affectionate letter from Marion yesterday, and hope soon to visit her in Washington. I must go and give Carrie her medicine. With much love to Robert and yourself, and kisses for the children, and respects to Mr. and Mrs. Mallard,

Ever your affectionate mother,
Mary Jones.

Do send this letter to Mr. Joseph Jackson.

MRS. MARY S. MALLARD *to* MRS. MARY JONES[t]

Walthourville, *Friday,* August 26th, 1864

My dearest Mother,

We are anxiously waiting to hear how Carrie is, and trust she is decidedly better ere this. I hope, dear Mother, that you will spare yourself as much as you can, and that your own strength will not give way under nursing. You know you are not as strong as you were previous to your illness. . . .

Yesterday we had Aunt Susan with us; she came over with Mr. Buttolph to Jacob Rokenbaugh's funeral. Cousin Laura and the children are quite well. Aunt Susan sends you many thanks for the Testament, and to Brother Joe for the picture; she was very much gratified by his sending it to her.

Aunt Susan has recently received a letter from Aunt Mary Robarts in which she mentioned that Aunt Eliza had not been so well, and she thought she was failing; and if she continued to grow more feeble, she thought of bringing her down in September, that she might end her last days with her friends, as they did not like to trespass too long upon Mr. Walker's hospitality. Aunt Lou had reached Longstreet with the girls. . . .

The company captured in McIntosh two weeks ago belonged to Colonel Colcock's regiment, and it is a great source of mortification. The reason assigned for their capture is that they were sent down without any knowledge of the country and were furnished with no competent guides; and as they relieved no pickets, they failed to put out pickets at some important point. A number of Negro men were taken off by the Yankees, but they refused women, children, and old men. They took off two men belonging to Mr. Shepard, and took Mr. Shepard prisoner, but afterwards released him on the ground of his being a noncombatant and over age.

I have not had an opportunity of sending your letter to Mr. Jackson yet, but will do so by Niger when he comes up on Saturday.

Mrs. Mallard is so much delighted with my Bible that she has begged me to enclose you five dollars and ask if you will be kind enough to get one for her. Mr. Mallard brought some of the soldier's Testaments with him, and will have an opportunity of sending some copies to Virginia by Captain Screven, who returns next week.

The children think it very strange we do not move over to the academy. Mamie told Mrs. Lowndes Walthour she was very glad to get back because all her property was here; and when we asked her where it was, she said with the greatest air of confidence: "At the academy lot." They send their love and many kisses to Grandmama, and love to Aunt Carrie, Bubber Joe, and Stanhope. I hope Susie and Stanhope are getting strong again; I wish they were here to run about in this sand. I think Mamie and Charlie have fattened since they came. My shoulder is still very painful at times. Dr. Stevens has recommended me to use a stream of cold water upon it, which I hope will strengthen it. Mr. Mallard unites with me in warmest love to yourself, Brother Joe, and Carrie. Love to Eva and Little Sister.

Your affectionate daughter,
Mary S. Mallard.

Mrs. Mary S. Mallard *to* Mrs. Mary Jones[t]

Walthourville, *Saturday,* September 3rd, 1864

My dearest Mother,

We have heard nothing from you since your letter of last Tuesday week telling us of Carrie's sickness. We hope from not hearing that she is getting quite well again.

I sent your letter to Mr. Jackson by Niger on Saturday. He says the people are all quite well. Daddy Tony continued to grow more feeble after you left until he was confined to bed. His leg swelled very much and gave him a great deal of trouble. Mom Sue attended to his wants and prepared his food for him regularly.

Mr. Mallard rode to Arcadia on Monday. The people are generally well except some fever with two of the children. Tom is now hired to Mr. Edward Delegal at two dollars a day, and found he wants him to make shoes.

We have nothing of special interest in our village. Mr. Mallard has entered upon his labors, and it is quite natural to minister to his old charge again, though he does so to great disadvantage in having no study.

I think we have all improved since coming down. The weather is very cool—quite like fall. I suppose you are enjoying the same change. How is little Susie? The children send love to Stanhope and herself and to Little Sister. Has Brother Joe gone to Andersonville yet? Mr. Mallard unites with me in best love to yourself, Brother Joe, and Carrie.

Your affectionate daughter,
Mary S. Mallard.

Mrs. Mary Jones *to* Mrs. Laura E. Buttolph[c]

Augusta, *Saturday,* September 3rd, 1864

My very dear Niece,

I ought long ago to have thanked you for your loving remembrance of me. My thoughts are daily with you all at Flemington, and I long to see you all. The memory of your kindness in my recent sickness especially dwells with me, and I am thankful to know you all continue so well. And I believe you are as *safely* located as anywhere in the Confederacy.

Augusta has presented a martial appearance today, and it is said fifteen hundred men have left to join the army in its present most critical position. These are from the factories, powderworks, etc., etc. There is a prevailing feeling of depression just at this time, but I trust the Lord will not forsake or deliver us into the hands of our enemies. One thing has greatly astonished me here—the *few* in number who attend the army prayer meeting, which is now held but twice during the week.

Joe has just returned from a visit to Carrie, who with the children has been staying for a week at Beech Island with Mr. Clarke's family. Carrie has been very sick and in most feeble health; I have felt very uneasy about her ever since I came up. And the children also have been very sick.

Mrs. Davis and Mrs. Cuthbert were in today. General Alfred Cumming has been seriously wounded in the hip, and they are daily expecting him home, as his father went on for him.

Colonel Edward Stiles was killed at Front Royal. Dear Kitty, what sorrow this will bring to her heart! And his poor wife!

Carrie and I have been much engaged preparing and taking refreshments to the hospitals. We went at first every day, but now alternate. In her sickness and absence I have gone alone. We are the almoners of Mrs. Smith and Miss Cumming. *Flora* is our cook. We take them among other things the purest and best of coffee; and you would be pleased to see how much good it does them, and to see the eagerness with which they receive and often solicit Testaments. I have distributed a number to them, and if I had them could give away a great many more. The Bible room is now filled with the Word of God for soldiers, and often on Sabbath there is preaching for them at the hospitals. I frequently meet with professors of religion among them, and generally in the morning find them reading their Testaments or see them laid on the pillows at the head of their little beds.

Eva is with her mother at present, and has not been well since she came up to Augusta. My little Mary Ruth is the picture of health and good spirits, and is with me at this time.

Last night Mr. Charles Dunwody spent with us, and returned to Washington this morning. I am hoping to visit dear Marion before long, and to go to Indianola, and just so soon as it may be safe, if the Lord wills, to turn my face homeward. I long to be once more near that consecrated spot, *Midway*. Oh, Laura, this world is all changed to me now! . . .

I will write my dear sister soon. Do give her our best love, and to Mr. Buttolph. . . . Kiss the precious children for me; and Little Sister sends them a kiss. Please give Brother William much love when you see him. Howdies for the servants, and remembrances to the kind friends around you. Do write soon to

Your ever attached aunt,
Mary Jones.

Mrs. Mary S. Mallard *to* Mrs. Mary Jones[t]
Walthourville, *Monday,* September 5th, 1864

My dearest Mother,

I was truly glad to receive your letter on Saturday and to know that you are pretty well, and Carrie improving. Mr. Mallard received a letter from Mr. Porter today written while Carrie was at Beech Island in which he says they are all improving and Susie sleeping all night "without a whimper," so I hope they will soon be well.

I am very much obliged to you, my dear mother, for the hat for Charlie, and am glad you were able to exchange the cap. Mrs. Mallard thinks she would rather not have the reference Bible if the print is smaller than mine, and wishes you to keep the money until Mr. Mallard goes this week.

Mrs. Morriss has written Mr. Mallard begging him to go to Augusta and preach her sister's funeral sermon on next Sabbath. As he was not in Atlanta when she died, and her parents were members of his church there, he has concluded to go, and will leave on Thursday or Friday. I am sorry he should have to make the journey again.

I scarcely think Colonel Edward Stiles could have been killed, as we have seen no notice of it in the Savannah papers, and I think the family there would have received some intimation of it through the public telegrams. I trust it is not so for poor Kitty's sake. It would be the greatest affliction that could befall her, leaving her almost entirely alone in the world. I know that Mr. Tom Cumming and Eddie were intimate and had promised to take care of each other, so I presume Mr. Cumming's servant must have known Eddie; and this is the only reason why I fear something may have happened.

I see by the papers General Cumming has been badly wounded. Is it a dangerous wound? I presume Mrs. Cumming will now have him at home.

Today we have had the dreadful tidings of the fall of Atlanta. What will go next? It grieves me to think of our beautiful church being desecrated if not destroyed by those horrible creatures. I presume they will endeavor to liberate the prisoners at Andersonville now, or move upon Macon. . . .

Niger came up on Saturday and says the people are all well except Mom Sue and Gilbert, who have had some slight fever. Niger has had a little fever also, but nothing serious. He says you have fine corn and fine rice, but the cotton is rather young to do a great deal before frost. He tells me a jar of honey was sent with the rice and butter. You never received it; neither did Mr. Cassels mention it in his note to you telling of the express charges. Possibly it may not have gone; I will get Mr. Mallard to inquire as he goes along on Thursday. Niger says July put "two *osnaburg* linens" in the bag of rice for his children, and wants to know if you ever saw them. Tell Flora Lucy inquired of Adeline about her clothes, and she says she did not send her new chemise that is now in Savannah. Lucy told her what Flora had received, and she said that was all she sent. So Flora may expect to get the rest of her wardrobe when she goes back to Savannah.

Thus far the Yankees have made no further demonstrations on our coast. Colonel Hood has placed another company in the same place that those were captured in McIntosh. There must have been gross negligence, according to the captain's own acknowledgment, though he was free of blame, being absent at the time.

I am truly sorry to hear Eva is so unwell, and hope she will soon be better. Do give much love to her. Tell Little Sister Sissy and Bubber send love to her and want to see her very much.

You would have been amused to have seen Mamie on Sabbath. As soon as church was out she spoke to Mrs. Judge Fleming, who kissed her and passed to someone else. But Mamie was not to be put off in that way. She pursued her and in a loud voice said: "Mrs. Fleming, Grandma sent her love to you and said I must give it to you." She then peered around but could see none of the other ladies to whom she intended to give your love, so she came out feeling she had not accomplished half as much as she intended.

489

I hope Mrs. Eve gave you some of her nice pears when she took you out visiting. I have had some very nice ones sent me by Mrs. Cay; she has had an abundance of them.

We are all pretty well here. . . . My arm improves very slowly. I have it out of the close bandages in a sling today for the first time. The bone is by no means firmly united.

How does Mr. Manigault like the idea of going among the smallpox Yankees? I hope Brother Joe will be careful and not make himself sick. It will be a laborious undertaking. Do give love to Carrie and himself, and kiss the children for us. Mr. Mallard unites with me in affectionate love to you.

Your attached daughter,
Mary S. Mallard.

DR. JOSEPH JONES *to* MRS. MARY JONES[t]

Camp Sumter, Andersonville, Georgia,
Thursday, September 22nd, 1864

My dear Mother,

At the close of each day my pen has been in my hand to write you, but I have been overpowered by fatigue. The labors here have been very arduous, but most interesting, and I trust important and profitable.

You can form some idea of the extent of the field when I mention the facts that there are at this time five thousand seriously sick Yankees, who are dying at the rate of more than one hundred per day; and almost all the well Federals—or those considered well by contrast—are suffering from diarrhea, dysentery, and scurvy. In the recent removals the sick have been almost necessarily left behind. Over thirty thousand men have been crowded into the confined space of twenty-seven acres, without a single shade tree and with scarcely a tent to keep off the rays of the Southern sun. From the crowding and filthy habits and condition of the men, their system in many cases has been so deteriorated that the smallest abrasion of the skin, as the rubbing of a shoe or the pricking of a small splinter or even mosquito bites, have taken on the most frightful gangrene; and in the hospital of the Confederate military prison over two hundred amputations have been performed for slight injuries followed by the most rapid and frightful gangrene. This day I visited two thousand sick within the stockade. Only one medical officer was in attendance upon these suffering and seriously ill patients. Scurvy, diarrhea, dysentery, and gangrene were the prevailing diseases. I hope that my labors may be the means of mitigating some of this suffering.

Whilst the Yankees have no claim upon our sympathies and upon our charities, still if prisoners are to be sacrificed, let the fact be distinctly stated beforehand, or else let the black flag be raised. When men surrender, the true policy—placing our action in no higher light—should be to treat them in such a manner that surrendering in battle will have no terrors. The fear of great suffering in imprisonment only renders our enemies more vindictive and more stubborn in battle.

Through a kind Providence my health and strength have continued excellent notwithstanding my most disagreeable and arduous labors. I hope in two days, D.V., to bring them to a close, and will then move to Macon. Mr. Manigault will be allowed to visit his family for a week, that he may attend to their removal. After his return to Macon I will spend a few days with you in Augusta. I desire to see you very much before you leave for the low country. I hope that your health, my dear mother, has been restored since your visit to Indianola. When I see you I will give a much fuller description of the Federals. With best love, I remain

Your affectionate son,
Joseph Jones.

Mrs. Mary Jones *to* Mrs. Mary S. Mallard[t]

Augusta, *Saturday,* September 24th, 1864

My dear Daughter,

I returned from Indianola a very short time after Robert and your brothers had left for the cars. It was a great disappointment to find I had missed them. And I had hastened back particularly on Monday hoping to meet Robert. His note, which I received, and for which please thank him kindly, explained the necessity for his early return. I rejoice that he has found a field of labor amongst his old and well-known former charge, and upon such agreeable terms. The Lord has dealt mercifully with him and his, although you have been called to personal sufferings and disappointment where you hoped for a permanent and pleasant home.

I had a most gratifying visit to the people, barring my own indisposition induced by the long hot ride and some other causes. I feared at one time I would be ill while there. Tell Little Daughter and Charlie while I was on my journey an old lady and gentleman—Mr. and Mrs. Partridge—were taking their large family of little ones across the broad road. I made Daddy Titus get down and catch me three of the pretty little creatures and put them into a tin bucket, where I gave them some crumbs of bread and sprinkled in some water, in which they dipped their little bills and drank. As evening came on, they missed their kind mother and began to cry. I made Daddy Titus get me some straw and tried to make a little nest, but with all my skill I could not weave it half as well as Mrs. Partridge would have done. But I wound it round and round, and then put them all into it and put my warm hand over them; and they put their little heads together and drew up close to one another and went fast asleep. They reminded me of the verse in your little hymn:

491

> Birds in their little nests agree;
> And 'tis a shameful sight
> When children of one family
> Fall out and chide and fight.

I did not have to put a "polster" between these little birds to keep them from "popping" into one another and getting angry when one touched the other, as some little children with sense and reason sometimes do. I sent them to Augusta the next day for Little Sister and Stanhope, but the journey was so long (and I was not there to take care of them) that one or two died, and I do not know what became of the other.

I am thankful, my dear child, to hear of your improved health. Carrie has returned greatly benefited from Beech Island; also the children. I am trying to persuade her to spend next week on The Hill. I expect, a kind Providence permitting, to visit Marion Glen at Washington week after next, going about the 3rd of October and returning about the 8th. And as soon after as practicable I will turn my face homeward. Eva is now on a visit to her friends in Sparta.

Last week our friend Kitty Stiles arrived very unexpectedly. She walked immediately to my room. She had just come from a visit to her sister in Carolina and was going down to see Sidney, who is very ill with typhoid fever—so ill that she has not been informed of Edward's death. Dear Kitty is looking well in bodily health, and bears her grief with great fortitude and Christian submission; but it is a heartrending blow to her. She feels most tenderly for Mrs. Edward Stiles, who she says is crushed. I presume she will write you of her plans.

I do so long to be once more at home. Dear Carrie is as kind and attentive as possible, but I feel it is best for me to have a home and to try to do my duty to those now dependent on me. Do write me all about yourself and the news of the county—I mean so far as the safety, etc., of the inhabitants is concerned. Carrie unites with me in much love to Robert and yourself, with kisses for the dear children, and from Mary Ruth, Stanhope, and Susie. Howdies for the servants.

Ever your affectionate mother,
Mary Jones.

MRS. MARY S. MALLARD *to* MRS. MARY JONES[t]

Walthourville, *Tuesday,* September 27th, 1864

My dearest Mother,

I was rejoiced to receive your welcome letter yesterday and to know that your fatiguing trip to Indianola had not made you sick. The children were greatly interested in Mr. and Mrs. Partridge and their family; Charlie seemed to think you had sent one of the little ones for him to pet. I am glad to hear that Carrie and the children were improved by their visit to

Beech Island, and hope the cool weather will brace them all and restore them to perfect health.

You will no doubt enjoy a visit to Washington very much. I have always heard it was a delightful place, and it will be so pleasant to see Cousin Marion. Do give love to her for us; and if you should see Mrs. Hull, give much love to her. She was very kind to us while we were in Atlanta. It must be a sore trial to her to think of her nice house being occupied by Yankees.

No one gained anything by remaining in Atlanta. I should like to know how much the exiles were allowed to bring with them; the newspaper accounts are so conflicting it is difficult to get at the truth. I hope our beautiful church will be spared, but I suppose it will share the fate of those in other places. Mr. Mallard received a letter from Mrs. Pease yesterday in which she mentions they are now living in the female college in Macon. . . . We have not gotten our horse yet, as Mr. Pease has been unable to get transportation for him. The cars have been so much taken up with government transportation that it is impossible for them to take private freight.

At this time everything is very quiet in the county. Last week one or two families moved away from Jonesville because the troops were temporarily withdrawn from McIntosh County and sent up to the Altamaha bridge; but they have been returned again, and all feel safe. The militia is disbanded at present so that the planters may have an opportunity of harvesting their crops.

Mr. Jackson was at Montevideo last week. All well there. Mr. Jackson's case will come before Judge Fleming on Saturday week, and everyone thinks he will be able to get out of service, as he has so many places in charge. There are really very few men to go into the militia, and several of them should be exempt for the sake of the many widows and orphans under their care. And then there would be so many Negroes left without a single white man to look after them if they are taken away; I mean such men as Mr. McCollough, Mr. Jackson, and Mr. John Mallard, all of whom have from six to ten places to look after.

Colonel Hood's regiment is still in these regions. Colonel Gaulden is still fussing about the militia, and is in command, and says when they meet again he intends offering them to General McLaws on *certain conditions*. Most persons think it will result in their being permanently disbanded; or at least they will retain their organization but not remain in camp, so that the planters will have an opportunity of attending to their business. . . .

I still have my arm in a sling, and it is only by comparing it with what it was a month ago that I can perceive the slightest improvement. My work is accumulating so much that I am obliged to use it some, although I never take it out of the sling. My other aches are very great at times. I have been hoping to be able to spend a little time with Aunt Susan and Cousin Laura, and I think I shall do so in a week or two.

Mr. Mallard's sisters, Mrs. Bacon and Miss Louisa, are now in Augusta, having been called there to see Mrs. Bacon's eldest son, who was taken ill on his way to Virginia. I do not know in what hospital he has been placed. He is quite young, and this is the first time he has left home for service. He was returning with Olivius Bacon to Captain Screven's company. I trust his life will be spared, for that family has been so much afflicted. Quarterman Bacon, who died this summer, was as affectionate as if he had been Mrs. Bacon's own child, and she leaned upon him very much. . . .

The children are looking forward with great eagerness to the time when we will all be with Grandmama at Arcadia. They send love and many kisses to you and to Little Sister; love to Aunt Carrie, Stanhope, and Susie. Mr. Mallard unites with me in love to Carrie. Love to Eva too. With warmest love and a kiss for yourself, dear Mother,

Your affectionate daughter,
Mary S. Mallard.

MRS. MARY JONES *to* MRS. SUSAN M. CUMMING[t]

Augusta, Thursday, September 29th, 1864

My dear Sister,

We were very happy to hear directly of you this week through Mr. Clay, who had recently made you a visit, the pleasure of which, so far as your family intercourse was concerned, seemed to have impressed him very pleasantly. I am thankful to know you have been so well, and that the children are so fat and hearty. I do long to see you all. And these cool nights give me hope of soon being at home, which after all is the best place for old people. My dear children here have been as kind as possible, showing me every attention in their power; but I often fear I have added a great deal to Carrie's cares, for she has been not only very sick at one time but extremely feeble, and the little girl so fretful and sick nearly all summer that she has had no opportunity of improvement. If they would allow it, I would take her home with me.

Joe has been at Andersonville several weeks investigating the most dreadful diseases amongst those infamous Yankees—smallpox, gangrene, etc. I do trust it will result in good to our own poor soldiers. He is now at Macon. Has his tent pitched near the female college, where he has access to the hospitals both in town and at Vineville. Has *Titus* as his cook and man-of-all-work, and Mr. Louis Manigault as secretary. I wish you could see the beautiful style in which Mr. Manigault prepares all the reports for the surgeon general at Richmond. I should say *transcribes,* as he only does the writing. Joe is most highly favored in this gentleman. He is also allowed two other assistants in his investigations, one a Mr. Ives and the other a son of Dr. Ford's. . . .

I had thought of making Marion Glen a visit next week, and wrote her to that effect. But on Monday she sent us by Major Minton her box of silver and valuables, saying they were apprehending a raid upon Washington. The bitter experience of going to Atlanta in the face of the enemy is too fresh in my recollection for me to attempt again either to embarrass my friends or expose myself, and particularly as I intended to take my little Ruth with me. So I have declined the pleasure of the visit for the present.

Carrie and I have been much interested in the sick and wounded in the hospitals here, and went to them near two months—as long as our supplies lasted. On last Sabbath Mrs. Bacon and Miss Louisa Mallard came up to see Mrs. Bacon's eldest son. We went with them to several hospitals before we found him and his brother Olivius, both sick. The ladies have just left with Mallard on sick leave for twenty days; Olivius is better and goes on to join his regiment in Virginia. Yesterday as I went in to see them in the morning I observed a poor soldier lying near them, evidently near his end. I gave him some blackberry wine, which he took from a spoon; and although he could not converse, I shall long remember the expression of his dying eyes as he would fix them intently on me. After dinner I went back. Only the narrow, naked pine bedstead remained. The poor soldier had been removed to the dead room to await interment, or perhaps to be sent home to his sorrowing friends.

Carrie unites with me in best love to you, dear Sister, to Laura and Mr. Buttolph, with kisses for the dear children. Stanhope and Little Sister send their love and kisses. . . . Howdies for your servants, and my own when you see them. Believe me

Ever your affectionate sister,
Mary Jones.

Mrs. Laura E. Buttolph *to* Mrs. Mary Jones^c

Flemington, *Wednesday,* October 5th, 1864

My dearest Aunt,

Mother has received your last letter, and says I must answer it immediately for her; and it is needless for me to assure you of the pleasure it gives me so to do.

We are to send for Cousin Mary Mallard to make us a visit next week; would have sent this week, but she desires to remain to their Communion on Sabbath and then come. . . . I have had my loom taken down, and Mother has furnished the room; so *we will still have a spare room,* and you must be sure and come to us just when you feel inclined. *A great plenty of room and a longing in our hearts to see your own precious self.* Do *not* tarry in Savannah: the yellow fever has been there for some time and seems to be on the increase. . . . If you could avoid Savannah entirely in coming home, *I* think it would be a good plan. Cannot your carriage meet you at some station? Sarah Jones reports its being *very sickly* in Savannah. I notice the number of deaths is double the number of last week. There are so many refugees there that a pestilence would be terrible.

Last week we were distinguished by a call from Colonel C. C. Jones and General McLaws. They were in the house before I knew they were at the gate, and found me in a simple white dress bearding palmetto. I was so glad to see the colonel that sometimes I forgot the presence of the distinguished general. And his quiet manner helped me to forget him more than once. Mother ordered a lunch for them, and while they were refreshing us we hope they were refreshed for their afternoon's inspection of militia, troops, etc. In the afternoon Colonel Jones delivered an impromptu address to the militia and the ladies on the part of the general—the most eloquent I have heard since I heard my dear sainted uncle near Riceboro address the soldiers. And Charlie looked so very like him: the fire of true eloquence gleaming from his eyes, every gesture grace, and all hearers spellbound—all wishing that nothing might break the silence. But the occasion was too grand for Colonel Gaulden not to deliver an address he had evidently prepared, and delivered in his own style and manner, wearing an old uniform that looked as if it had been in many a hard battle, and a red sash. He made the ladies and boys laugh and his men look *wilder* than ever, and as Cousin Mary Wells said, "drew a very *encouraging picture* for them of their gray hairs being laid beside their dead sons already in the grave." They were all drawn up in line fronting the church, the ladies sitting upon the church steps. You can imagine the scene. Strange that I was to hear my noble cousin speak for the first time under such circumstances! That one so gifted should be exposed to the bullets of the enemy! May Heaven shield his head in battle! And may God cover his head in all battles he may be called to pass through!

Dear Cousin Joe! While he is devoting his time to the sick and investigating diseases, I trust he will not wear self out. It will do Cousin Carrie good to come home with you, and we will all be so glad to see her and the children. Seeing one's friends is a pleasure the war must not deprive us of, it is such a great comfort. . . . I am sorry you have given up your trip to Washington; I wished to enjoy it through you. . . .

Little ones are well, and send love to little Mary Ruth, and say you must bring her with you to see them. And love to Stanhope and Susie. Mother and Mr. Buttolph unite in all that is affectionate.

Your ever attached niece,
Laura E. Buttolph.

MRS. MARY JONES *to* MRS. MARY S. MALLARD[c]

Augusta, *Wednesday,* October 5th, 1864

My dear Daughter,

Your last kind favor has been received, and I am thankful you all continue so well.

Yesterday *Mr. Ives* (a stranger to me, but now writing in Joe's office) called and inquired if I was in. Said he wished to know if *Dr. Mallard* had not married a member of my family. I told him the Rev. Mr. Mallard had—that he was not a "Dr." He said: "Oh, they call him so up here!" He had been sent by some of the Atlanta church members (a Mr. and Mrs. Whitner amongst others), as I understood him, to inquire if the report was true that *Mrs. Mallard* had died soon after she left Atlanta from the wounds she received when she was thrown out of a wagon. I told him we were very much obliged to the friends for their kindness in sending; and I was happy to inform them that although Mrs. Mallard had suffered and was still a sufferer from the injuries received, her life had been spared; and as she had recently been heard from, I hoped she was improving. I readily detected (as the gentleman's name would indicate) one of regular Puritan descent, so I thought I would end the conference by leaving him a little room for "guessing" what relation I bore to "Dr." and Mrs. Mallard.

Mrs. Bacon and Miss Louisa returned on last Thursday evening, taking Mallard home on sick leave for twenty days. The other brother, who was quite sick also but missed his fever, has, I presume, gone on to Virginia. Carrie, but for the state of her own health and the children and the illness of Sue's husband in the yard, would have insisted that the ladies should stay with her. But it really was impossible under the circumstances.

Carrie, I think, is completely worn down. She has been at The Hill since Saturday with her children. I am alone here with my dear little Mary Ruth, and in charge of Ralph, who continues very ill with typhoid fever. Flora and Harry have gone on a visit to Indianola; only Sue and Fanny and Susan constitute the household, and Sue has to be most of the time nursing her husband.

If a kind Providence favors my plans, I hope soon to return home. I had appointed this week to visit Washington, but Marion sent over her silver and valuables by Major Minton to Joe and Carrie's care, fearing there would be a raid upon Washington. The Atlanta *experience* was too fresh in my memory either to embarrass my friends or expose myself again, so I wrote declining the visit at present. I should have gone earlier, but I was feeling so feeble and sad I had no heart or strength for any extra effort, and now long to be at home. . . .

Mr. Manigault has been here removing his family to a house on this street; returns to Macon tomorrow. And Joe, I hope, will be with us on Saturday. I hope he will return before I leave. . . .

Things are going up every day. Calicoes (narrow) twelve dollars; wide, sixteen dollars a yard. Tea fifty and sixty cents a pound. And so it goes—up, up, up. It is wonderful how people live at all here. Wood eighty-five dollars a cord in the streets!

With much love for Robert and yourself, and kisses for my dear grandchildren, and from Little Sister. Remembrances to all inquiring friends.

Ever, my dear child, your affectionate mother,
Mary Jones.

Mrs. Mary S. Mallard *to* Mrs. Mary Jones[t]

Walthourville, *Friday,* October 7th, 1864

My dear Mother,

I had thought of you as spending this week with Cousin Marion Glen; but a note from Cousin Laura received yesterday mentioned that you had given up all idea of going. I am very sorry you have been unable to do so, for it would have refreshed you very much.

Uncle Henry called to see me two afternoons ago. He is now engaged in Savannah on some of Governor Brown's business, attending court-martial. He left Aunt Abby and the children quite well. Aunt Mary Robarts and the girls were with them at present, they having gone down to see if they could make any arrangement by which they could make a home in Cuthbert. Uncle Henry said they had partly perfected an arrangement by which they could get a portion of a large comfortable house. If they succeeded in making this arrangement, they would all come immediately down and go to housekeeping. If not, Aunty, Aunt Mary, and Aunt Lou expected to come to Flemington and remain some time in the county. The girls would go to Screven County to their aunt. . . .

I expected to go over early next week and spend ten days or two weeks with Aunt Susan, and will do so if Aunty does not come. I would have done so this week, but our Communion takes place on next Sabbath, and I did not like to be absent. And then I have been constantly nursing Tenah's baby, who has been ill for nearly two weeks past. I am still exceedingly anxious about the child, and do not know yet how it will terminate. She has had very high fevers and apparently some great difficulty in the chest, causing a most distressing and racking cough. Dr. Stevens blistered her chest two days ago. It has been a complicated case: I suppose partly climate fever. Charlie has been quite unwell this week from dysentery, but is quite bright again.

We are again debating whether we shall make an effort to get our furniture down. It is impossible to get transportation for Jim, so Mr. Mallard thinks of sending a servant to Macon and having him ridden across the country. The route would lay through Mount Vernon in Montgomery County. I thought I had brought down all of our clothing, but now that the time draws nigh for us to need them, I find a portion of our winter underclothing has been left. I think they are in the trunk of crockery in the attic. If we conclude not to bring the furniture, I shall be obliged to send for that trunk, though I fear it is scarcely strong enough to bear the journey in anything but a chartered car. I could not have the clothing taken out of the trunk, for there would then be nothing to pack the crockery with.

We are having frequent showers now, which interferes with the harvesting. I hear that Mr. Jackson has succeeded in getting exemption papers. He was at Montevideo last week. All well there.

Miss Louisa Mallard came up last evening. She seems to feel very grateful to you for your kindness to her sister and herself; says she does not know what they would have done if you had not assisted them. Mallard came home with her much better.

Do give a great deal of love to Carrie from all of us. Mr. Mallard and the children unite with me in warmest love to you, my dear mother. When do you think of coming down? Love to Eva and Little Sister.

Your affectionate daughter,
Mary S. Mallard.

MRS. MARY S. MALLARD *to* MRS. MARY JONES^t

Flemington, *Wednesday*, October 19th, 1864

My very dear Mother,

Mr. Mallard came over night before last bringing your note. I am truly glad to know that you are well and that Carrie has improved so much.

Our furniture has not yet arrived. The cost of a chartered car from Savannah to this place is *two hundred and eighty-eight* dollars, so Mr. Mallard concluded it would be best to have the furniture come by freight. He would have remained in Savannah until the car came down, but it was so uncertain when it would arrive that he did not consider it safe to remain, as there was so much yellow fever and sickness in Savannah. I will take good care of the things put in the bureau. We hope to be able to take the furniture directly to the academy.

Mr. Quarterman has gone to Virginia to look after his brother, Mr. Stewart Quarterman, who is severely wounded. As it was so uncertain when he would return, I took the liberty of opening your note to him, as there seemed to be a key in it, and I thought you might want something special done. Mr. Mallard went to Arcadia today to get the dress and shawl; so they will be sent by express tomorrow, and I hope they will reach you safely.

The weather is cool, and some persons saw frost ten days ago. There seems to be more sickness than usual in the county, though no serious illness that I know of. We are all anxious to see you, and longing to be with you, but feel it would be very imprudent for you to come down too soon. . . .

Everything seems very dark with us now, and we are anxiously awaiting the next telegraphic intelligence, for continued silence seldom indicates favorable news on our side. We have a rumor today from some "reliable gentleman" that General Hood's army has been surrounded, and our loss very great. We wait with sorrowful hearts to hear the truth. I hope it may prove only an idle rumor, for if we lose our army, our state is at Sherman's mercy. . . .

Your affectionate daughter,
Mary S. Mallard.

MRS. MARY JONES *to* MRS. SUSAN M. CUMMING[t]

Arcadia, *Friday,* December 9th, 1864

My dear Sister,

Will you be kind enough to send my candle molds if you are not using them, as I must try and prepare for nights of darkness. My lights have almost gone out.

My dear child left me on Tuesday. I did all that I could prudently to keep her, but she felt that she must be near Dr. Stevens. My anxieties for her are more than I can express. They will keep a horse on hand to send for me at a moment's warning.

God's dealings with me and mine at this time are very solemn. . . . You know Daughter's situation. Charles stands before a murderous foe, every moment exposed to death if called into battle; of this there can scarcely be a doubt, for their cannon are already firing at intervals. Joseph and his family are I know not where. Desolation has swept over Indianola; if any of our people are spared, they must be in great distress; not one word has been heard from them. And here I am alone with my dear little baby.

I am perplexed about this house. Ought the furniture to be removed? Books, etc.? *All* that I have is here. What arrangements do you think of making if the enemy advance upon the railroad and take possession of this section? . . . If the river did not run at our door, I would move back to Montevideo; for I will be constantly exposed here to stragglers. I try to be calm and hopeful, to trust in God and do the best I can; but sometimes my heart almost dies within me.

With best love to dearest Laura and yourself and Mr. Buttolph. Kiss the children for Little Sister and Aunt Mary. If convenient do let your cart call for the demijohns; I have no means of sending them.

Ever your affectionate sister,
Mary Jones.

MRS. SUSAN M. CUMMING *to* MRS. MARY JONES[t]

Flemington, *Saturday,* December 10th, 1864

My dearest Sister,

These are days of darkness, and if we could not call upon a merciful God we should be overwhelmed. God help and pity us! Your children, may they be under the shadow of the Almighty! Dear to me as my own, they are constantly on my heart. We must commit *all* to our God and pray Him to choose for us in all things. How I wish you were with us! I would come to you if I could help you.

We have been in great excitement here. Expect the enemy. We cannot go anywhere, but must stay and take whatever comes. Mr. Buttolph speaks of going into service. He is just going to see you. We heard you were at Montevideo.

Sorry you had to send for the molds. Many thanks for their use. The good Lord keep you and yours in perfect safety! . . .

Your ever affectionate sister,
S. M. Cumming.

MRS. LAURA E. BUTTOLPH *to* MRS. MARY JONES[t]
Flemington, *Saturday*, December 10th, 1864

My precious Aunt,

These are times when we can alone trust in God. And He is a *mighty Deliverer,* and will hear the cry of the widow and the orphan. . . . Captain Gignilliat told Aunt Julia it was an advantage to her being on the road; that the Yankee officers would station guards around the private residences while the army passed if requested. If it is God's will, I hope we may fall in with the best of them. . . .

The waste of provisions, starvation staring us in the face, is what I dread. Many have gone to Thomasville; but the crowd is so great there, and board a hundred dollars a day, we might as well die of want in one place as another.

Make Gilbert take care of and hide your horses. They kill all of those; and our men are now impressing horses, mules, and men. (Some of Wheeler's men were here yesterday.) They don't take oxen, so our oxen are to bring us provisions.

Mr. Buttolph says he will see you today. He must hide if they surprise us, and be on hand to take care of us. Cousin Robert must do the same for Mary. I hope they will get whipped at Savannah. May God shield my beloved cousin from death, and take care of us and all of our loved ones! . . . Kate went to South Hampton yesterday to be near Cousin Audley, and said if she only had someone with her, she would not feel afraid. . . . I hear most of the young girls have gone to Thomasville; Wallace Cumming has gone there with his family. . . . Mr. Buttolph says let house and all go, and come here and let us all be together. Willie said: "I will tell you what to do. Let us give the Yankees some of our little things, and they will love us and not kill us." May we be able to stand in our lot, with the blessing of God!
Your own niece,
Laura.

MRS. MARY JONES *to* MRS. SUSAN M. CUMMING[t]
Montevideo, *Monday*, December 12th, 1864

My dear Sister and Niece,

Your note has this moment been received. *I fear* your being cut off from your supplies. If you will come to us, and can get down to the station, I will send to meet you there whenever you appoint, or send our buggy all the way for you. We came here yesterday afternoon, and are trying to get some of our things over from Arcadia. One cart broke down. With our buggy and yours could you not come down at once?

Daughter is in bed today: overfatigue and anxiety. Robert is just leaving for No. 3; this goes by him. *God be merciful to us sinners!* For my poor child here, and my son in Savannah, my heart aches—and my bleeding country!
Ever yours, in warmest love,
Mary Jones.

XIX

Mrs. Mary S. Mallard *in her Journal*ᵗ

Montevideo, *Tuesday*, December 13th, 1864

Mother rode to Arcadia this morning to superintend the removal of household articles and the remainder of library, etc., believing that the Yankees were no nearer than Way's Station, and lingered about the place until late in the afternoon, when she started to return to Montevideo. It was almost sunset, and she was quietly knitting in the carriage, fearing no evil. Jack was driving, and as they came opposite the Girardeau place, now owned by Mr. W. E. W. Quarterman, a Yankee on horseback sprang from the woods and brought his carbine to bear upon Jack, ordering him to halt. Then, lowering the carbine, almost touching the carriage window and pointing into it, he demanded of Mother what she had in the carriage.

She replied: "Nothing but my family effects."

"What have you in that box behind your carriage?"

"My servants' clothing."

"Where are you going?"

"To my home."

"Where is your home?"

"Nearer the coast."

"How far is the coast?"

"About ten miles. I am a defenseless woman—a widow—with only one motherless child with me. Have you done with me, sir? Drive on, Jack!"

Bringing his carbine to bear on Jack, he called out: "No! Halt!" He then asked: "Where are the rebels?"

"We have had a post at No. 3."

Looking into the carriage, he said: "I would not like to disturb a lady; and if you will take my advice you will turn immediately back, for the men are just ahead. They will take your horses and search your carriage, and I cannot say what they will do."

Mother replied: "I thank you for that," and ordered Jack to turn. Jack saw a number of men ahead, and Mother would doubtless have been in their midst had she proceeded but a few hundred yards. (This must have been an officer; he was a hale, hearty man, well dressed, with a new blue overcoat, and well appointed in every respect.) Jack then drove through by Colonel Quarterman's, and not very far beyond met our picket guard.

It was now quite dark. When she came to the junction with the

502

Walthourville road, there she met a company of cavalry commanded by Captain Little. She informed them of the position of the Yankees, and entreated that he would give her an escort if but for a few miles. She told him the distressing circumstances of her family, and that she was compelled to reach her home and her daughter that night. He replied they were ordered to that point, and if she would stay with them or go with them they would protect her, but they could not send anyone with her. She again urged her distressing circumstances. He said: "The Boro bridge is burnt, and you may not go a mile before you meet the enemy. I cannot help you."

"Then I will trust in God and go forward!"

Meeting a servant of Captain Randal Jones's who had been with him in Virginia, he ran along with the carriage. He had been sent from the depot to inform his young mistress of the presence of the enemy. He rendered her very kind service, acting as a scout. He would dart forward, take an observation, and encourage her to proceed. Every moment she expected to meet the Yankees.

Passing from the public road, Mother turned up the crossroad by Tranquil Hill. At the avenue our picket was stationed, who informed her that the bridges on the causeway had been taken up, and her carriage could not cross over. Mother replied: "Then I must get out and walk, for I must reach home tonight if my life is spared!" She rode up to the dwelling house; Dr. and Mrs. Way came to the carriage and pressed her very kindly to remain all night. She had resolved to walk home when Mr. William Winn, one of the picket guard, rode up and informed Mother the bridges had been fixed so as to allow the carriage to pass over.

She hastened forward and met a picket near the crossroads by the Baptist church; saw no one again until reaching the hill above the Boro. Under the crack of the door she discovered a dim light, and taking the reins sent Jack in to inquire if the enemy was near. The reply was: "Yes, the Boro is full of Yankees." Turning up the Darien road, she made her way through an obscure and very rough road through the woods which had been used as a wood road, just back of our encampment. Jack was unacquainted with the way. The old horses completely tired out, so that with difficulty she passed into the old field back of the Boro into the road leading to our enclosure, reaching home after nine o'clock.

I was rejoiced to hear the sound of the carriage wheels, for I had been several hours in the greatest suspense, not knowing how Mother would hear of the presence of the enemy, and fearing she would unexpectedly find herself in their midst at the Boro.

Late in the evening Milton came running in to say a boy had met the oxcarts going to Arcadia and told them they could not pass, for the Yankees were in the Boro. It was a perfect thunderclap. In a few moments the boy was at the door confirming the intelligence; he was sent by Mr. Audley King and Mr. McCollough. Fearing a raiding party might come up, immediately I had some trunks of clothing and other things carried into the woods, and the carts and horses taken away and the oxen driven away, and prepared to pass the night alone with the little children, as I had no idea Mother could reach home.

After ten o'clock Mr. Mallard came in to see us, having come from No. 3, where a portion of Colonel Hood's command was stationed. Upon consultation the trunks were brought back. Mr. Mallard stayed with us until two o'clock A.M. and, fearing to remain longer, left to join the soldiers at No. 4½ (Johnston Station), where they were to rendezvous. He had exchanged his excellent horse Jim with Cyrus Mallard for a mule, as Cyrus was going on picket and he thought he would need a swifter animal. This distressed us very much, and I told him I feared he would be captured. It was hard parting under this apprehension, and he lingered as long as possible, reading a part of the 8th Chapter of Romans and engaging in prayer before leaving. It was moonlight, and Jack was sent forward to see if there was any advance of the enemy upon the place, as there was much open space to be passed over before he could reach the woods. Before parting he went up and kissed his children, charging me to tell them "Papa has kissed them when asleep." I had a fearful foreboding that he would be captured, and we stayed as long as prudence would permit in the front porch.

Wednesday, December 14th. Although it had been much past midnight when we retired, Mother and I rose early, truly thankful no enemy had come near us during the night. We passed the day in fearful anxiety. Late in the afternoon Charles came into the parlor, just from Walthourville, and burst into tears.

I asked what was the matter.

"Oh," he said, "very bad news! Master is captured by the Yankees, and says I must tell you keep a good heart."

This was a dreadful blow to us and to the poor little children. Mamie especially realized it, and cried all the evening; it was heartrending to see the agony of her little face when told her papa was taken prisoner. Mr. Mallard was standing in the porch of his own house at Walthourville when Kilpatrick's cavalry rode up and hailed him, demanding his horse. Supposing they were our own men (it being early and a very misty morning), he asked by what authority, when to his surprise he found himself a prisoner. The servants were all in the yard, and say he was dreadfully cursed by his captors, their language being both profane and vulgar. He was taken off upon the mule he had been riding. The servants then took the mules and wagon and in fear and trembling came down here. Mr. Mallard was captured before sunrise.

Mother sent Niger to South Hampton to ask Mrs. King to come to us immediately and to say the enemy was in the county. She was too unwell to come.

Thursday, December 15th. About ten o'clock Mother walked out upon the lawn, leaving me in the dining room. In a few moments Elsie came running in to say the Yankees were coming. I went to the front door and saw three dismounting at the stable, where they found Mother and rudely demanded of her: "Where are your horses and mules? Bring them out!"—at the same instant rushing by her as she stood in the door. I debated whether to go to her or remain in the house. The question was soon settled, for in a moment a stalwart Kentucky Irishman stood before me, having come through the pantry door. I scarcely knew what to do. His salutation was: "Have you any whiskey in the house?"

I replied: "None that I know of."

"You ought to know," he said in a very rough voice.

I replied: "This is not my house, so I do not know what is in it."

Said he: "I mean to search this house for arms, but I'll not hurt you." He then commenced shaking and pushing the folding door and calling for the key.

Said I: "If you will turn the handle and slide the door you will find it open."

The following interrogatories took place:

"What's in that box?"

"Books."

"What's in that room beyond?"

"Search for yourself."

"What's in that press?"

"I do not know."

"Why don't you know?"

"Because this is my mother's house, and I have recently come here."

"What's in that box?"

"Books and pictures."

"What's that, and where's the key?"

"My sewing machine. I'll get the key."

He then opened the side door and discovered the door leading into the old parlor. "I want to get into that room."

"If you will come around, I will get the key for you."

As we passed through the parlor into the entry he ran upstairs and commenced searching my bedroom. "Where have you hid your arms?"

"There are none in the house. You can search for yourself."

He ordered me to get the keys immediately to all my trunks and bureaus. I did so, and he put his hands into everything, even a little trunk containing needle books, boxes of hair, and other small things. All this was under cover of searching for arms and ammunition. He called loudly for *all* the keys; I told him my mother would soon be in the house and she would get her keys for him.

While he was searching my bureau he turned to me and asked: "Where is your watch?"

I told him my husband had worn my watch, and he had been captured the day before at Walthourville.

Shaking his fist at me, he said: "Don't you lie to me! You have got a watch!"

505

I felt he could have struck me to the floor; but looking steadily at him, I replied: "I have a watch and chain, and my husband has them with him."

"Well, were they taken from him when he was captured?"

"That I do not know, for I was not present."

Just at this moment I heard another Yankee coming up the stair steps and saw a young Tennessean going into Mother's room, where he commenced his search. Mother came in soon after and got her keys; and there we were, following these two men around the house, handing them keys (as they would order us to do in the most insolent manner), and seeing almost everything opened and searched and tumbled about.

The Tennessean found an old workbox, and hearing something rattling in it, he thought it was coin and would have broken it open. But Dick, the Kentuckian, prevented him until Mother got the key, and his longing eyes beheld a bunch of keys.

In looking through the bureaus, to Mother's surprise, Dick pulled out a sword that had belonged to her deceased brother and had been in her possession for thirty-one years. Finding it so rusty, they could scarcely draw it from the scabbard, and concluded it would not kill many men in this war and did not take it away.

The Tennessean found a large spyglass which had belonged to Mr. Mallard's father, and brought it out as quite a prize.

I said to him: "You won't take that!"

"No," said he, "I only want to look through it. It's of no use to me."

Dick went into the attic, but did not call for the keys to the two locked rooms. He took up the spyglass, and winking at me said: "I mean to take this to Colonel Jones." (Susan had told him Mary Ruth was Colonel Jones's child.)

Mother said to him: "Is your commanding officer named Jones?"

He laughed and said he meant to take the glass to Colonel Jones.

I said: "You won't take that, for I value it very much, as it belonged to my father."

Said he: "It's of no use to you."

"No, none whatever beyond the association, and you have much finer in your army."

He did not take it, though we thought he would have done so if we had not been present. He turned to Mother and said: "Old lady, haven't you got some whiskey?"

She replied: "I don't know that I have."

"Well," said he, "I don't know who ought to know if you don't!"

Mother asked him if he would like to see his mother and wife treated in this way—their house invaded and searched.

"Oh," said he, "none of us have wives!"

Whilst Mother walked from the stable with one of the Yankees from Kentucky he had a great deal to say about the South bringing on the war. On more than one occasion they were anxious to argue political questions with her. Knowing it was perfectly useless, she would reply: "This is neither the time nor place for these subjects. My countrymen have decided that it was just and right to withdraw from the Union. We wished to do it peaceably; you would not allow it. We have now appealed to arms; and I have nothing more to say with you upon the subject."

Mother asked him if he would like to see his mother and sisters treated as they were doing us.

"No," said he, "I would not. And I never do enter houses, and shall not enter yours."

And he remained without while the other two men searched. They took none of the horses or mules, as they were too old.

A little before dinner we were again alarmed by the presence of five Yankees dressed as marines. One came into the house—a very mild sort of a man. We told him the house had already been searched. He asked if the soldiers had torn up anything. One of the marines (as they called themselves) came into the pantry and asked if they could get anything to eat. Mother told them she had only what was prepared for our own dinner, and if they chose they could take it where it was—in the kitchen. They said they preferred to take it there, and going to the kitchen, they cursed the servants awfully, ordered milk, potatoes, and other things. They called for knives and forks, and having no others Mother sent out those we used; but they ordered Milton to take them immediately back and to tell his mistress to put them away in a safe place, as "a parcel of damned Yankees" would soon be along, and they would take every one from her.

We hoped they would not intrude upon the dwelling; but as soon as they finished eating, the four came in, and one commenced a thorough search, ordering us to get him all the keys. He found some difficulty in fitting the keys, and I told him I would show them to him if he would hand me the bunch.

He replied: "I will give them to you when I am ready to leave the house."

He went into the attic and instituted a thorough search into every hole and corner. He opened a large trunk containing the private papers of my dear father, and finding a tin canister, he tried to open it. Mother could not immediately find the key, and as he spoke insolently to her about getting the key, she told him he had better break it, but she could assure him it contained only the private papers of her husband, who was a minister of the gospel.

"Damn it," he said, "if you don't get the key I will break it. I don't care!"

In looking through the trunk he found a beautiful silver goblet which had been given to Mother by her dear little granddaughter Julia, and which she had valued as a keepsake. His eyes sparkled as he held it up and called out: "Here's something pretty, boys!"

Mother looked at him scornfully and said: "And would you take it?"

He said no, and put it quickly down, although we believe only our presence kept him from pocketing it.

One of the party came in with a secession rosette which Brother Charlie had worn at the great meeting in Savannah when he was mayor of the city. Mother had given it to Jack with a few letters to put away. As they were riding up he took it from Jack, and we were quite amused to see him come in with it pinned on the lapel of his jacket. This one was quite inclined to argue about the origin of the struggle.

One of them had an old cap—the helmet-shaped cap with horsehair plume belonging to the Liberty Independent Troop, and the jacket also, as we afterwards understood were those formerly used by the troop. Being blue with bell buttons, they could very well pass for sailors' jackets. They had rigged themselves from some house they had searched before coming here.

After spending a long time in the search, they prepared to leave with all the horses. Mother told them they were over seventeen years old and would do them no service. They took away one mule, but in a short time we saw it at the gate: they had turned it back.

After they left I found that my writing desk had been most thoroughly searched and everything scattered, and all my little articles of jewelry, pencils, etc., scattered. A gold pen was taken from my workbox.

Mother felt so anxious about Kate King that she sent Charles and Niger in the afternoon to urge her coming over to us, and told them if she was too unwell to walk or ride, they must take her up in their arms and let someone help to bring the little children. But they did not reach South Hampton, as they met a Yankee picket which turned Niger back and took Charles with them to assist in carrying horses to Midway, promising to let him return.

Friday, December 16th. Much to our relief, Prophet came over this morning with a note from Kate to know if we thought she could come to us. Mother wrote her to come immediately, which she did in great fear and trembling, not knowing but that she would meet the enemy on the road. We all felt truly grateful she had been preserved by the way.

About four in the afternoon we heard the clash of arms and noise of horsemen, and by the time Mother and I could get downstairs we saw forty or fifty men in the pantry, flying hither and thither, ripping open the safe with their swords and breaking open the crockery cupboards. Fearing we might not have a chance to cook, Mother had some chickens and ducks roasted and put in the safe for our family. These the men seized whole, tearing them to pieces with their teeth like ravenous beasts. They were clamorous for whiskey, and ordered us to get our keys. One came to Mother to know where her meal and flour were, insisted upon opening her locked pantry, and took every particle. They threw the sacks across their horses. Mother remonstrated and pointed to her helpless family; their only reply was: "We'll take it!"

They flew around the house, tearing open boxes and everything that was closed. They broke open Mother's little worktable with an andiron, hoping to find money or jewelry; it contained principally little mementos that were valuable only to herself. Failing to find treasure, they took the sweet little locks of golden hair that her mother had cut from the heads of her angel children near a half century ago, and scattering them upon the floor trampled them under their feet. A number of them rifled the sideboard, taking away knives, spoons, forks, tin cups, coffeepots, and everything they wished. They broke open Grandfather's old liquor case and carried off two of the large square gallon bottles, and drank up all the blackberry wine and vinegar which was in the case. It was vain to utter a word, for we were completely paralyzed by the fury of these ruffians.

A number of them went into the attic into a little storeroom and carried off twelve bushels of meal Mother had stored there for our necessities. She told them they were taking all she had to support herself and daughter, a friend, and five little children. Scarcely one regarded even the sound of her voice; those who did laughed and said they would leave one sack to keep us from starving. But they only left some rice which they did not want, and poured out a quart or so of meal upon the floor. At other times they said they meant to starve us to death. They searched trunks and bureaus and wardrobes, calling for shirts and men's clothes.

We asked for their officer, hoping to make some appeal to him; they said they were all officers and would do as they pleased. We finally found one man who seemed to make a little show of authority, which was indicated by a whip which he carried. Mother appealed to him, and he came up and ordered the men out. They instantly commenced cursing him, and we thought they would fight one another. They brought a wagon and took another from the place to carry off their plunder.

It is impossible to imagine the horrible uproar and stampede through the house, every room of which was occupied by them, all yelling, cursing, quarreling, and running from one room to another in wild confusion. Such was their blasphemous language, their horrible countenances and appearance, that we realized what must be the association of the lost in the world of eternal woe. Their throats were open sepulchres, their mouths filled with cursing and bitterness and lies. These men belonged to Kilpatrick's cavalry. We look back upon their conduct in the house as a horrible nightmare, too terrible to be true.

When leaving they ordered all the oxen to be gotten up early next morning.

MRS. MARY JONES *in her Journal*ᵗ

Montevideo, *Saturday*, December 17th, 1864

About four o'clock this morning we were roused by the sound of horses; and Sue, our faithful woman, came upstairs breathless with dismay and told us they had come upon the most dreadful intent, and had sent her in to tell me what it was, and had inquired if there were any young women in my family. Oh, the agony—the agony of that awful hour no language can describe! No heart can conceive it. We were alone, friendless, and knew not what might befall us. Feeling our utter weakness and peril, we all knelt down around the bed and went to prayer; and we continued in silent prayer a long time. Kate prayed, Daughter prayed, and I prayed; and the dear little children, too, hearing our voices, got up and knelt down beside us. And there we were, alone and unprotected, imploring protection from a fate worse than death, and that our Almighty God and Saviour would not permit our cruel and wicked enemies to come nigh our persons or our dwelling. We rose from our knees and sat in darkness, waiting for the light of the morning to reveal their purposes, but trusting in God for our deliverance.

New squads were arriving. In the gray twilight of morning we looked out of the window and saw one man pacing before the courtyard gate between the house and the kitchen; and we afterwards found he had voluntarily undertaken to guard the house. In this we felt that our prayers had been signally answered.

MRS. MARY S. MALLARD *in her Journal*[t]

Montevideo, *Saturday*, December 17th, 1864

As soon as it was light Kate discovered an officer near the house, which was a great relief to our feelings. Mother and I went down immediately, when she said to him: "Sir, I see that you are an officer; and I come to entreat your protection for my family, and that you will not allow your soldiers to enter my dwelling, as it has been already three times searched and every particle of food and whatever they wanted taken." He replied it was contrary to orders for the men to be found in houses, and the penalty was death; and so far as his authority extended with his own men, none of them should enter the house. He said he and his squad (there were many others present) had come on a foraging expedition, and intended to take only provisions.

Upon Mother's inviting him to see some of the work of the previous evening he came in and sat awhile in the parlor. Before leaving he discovered a portable desk on a table and walked up and opened it. She said: "That is my private property; it is here for my own use, and has only a little paper in it." He closed it immediately. (It had previously escaped observation and removal.)

The Yankees made the Negroes bring up the oxen and carts, and took off all the chickens and turkeys they could find. They carried off all the syrup from the smokehouse. We had one small pig, which was all the meat we had left; they took the whole of it. Mother saw everything like food stripped from her premises, without the power of uttering one word. Finally they rolled out the carriage and took that to carry off a load of chickens. They took everything they possibly could.

The soldier who acted as our volunteer guard was from Ohio, and older than anyone we had seen; for generally they were young men and so active that Mother called them "fiery flying serpents." As he was going Mother went out of the house and said to him: "I cannot allow you to leave without thanking you for your kindness to myself and family; and if I had anything to offer I would gladly make you some return."

He replied: "I could not receive anything, and only wish I was here to guard you always."

It was not enough that they should insult us by converting our carriage into a chicken-cart and take it away drawn by our own carriage horses; but they sent in to tell Mother if she wanted her carriage to send for it, and when they were done with it she might have it. We afterwards learned it was broken to pieces and left beyond Midway Church.

They took off today June, Martin, George, Ebenezer, Little Pulaski, our house servant Jack, and Carpenter Pulaski. Seeing the two last-named going away, Mother called to the soldier who had them in charge: "Why are you taking my young men away?"

He said: "They need not go if they do not want to."

She then asked: "Boys, do you wish to go or stay?"

They immediately replied: "We wish to stay."

She then said: "Do you hear that? Now, by what right do you force them away?"

They had Pulaski laden down with our turkeys, and wanted Jack to drive one of the carts. So they were all carried off—carriages, wagons, carts, horses and mules and servants, with food and provisions of every kind—and, so far as they were concerned, leaving us to starvation.

A little while after this party started, Mother walked to the smokehouse and found an officer taking sugar that had been put to drip. He was filling a bag with all that was dry. He seemed a little ashamed of being caught in the act, but did not return the sugar, but carried it off on his horse. He was mounted on Mr. Audley King's pet horse, a splendid animal which he had just stolen, and as he rode off said: "How the man who *owns* this horse will curse the Yankee who took him when he goes home and finds him gone!" He had Mr. King's servant mounted on another of his horses, and no doubt knew Mrs. King was with us and would hear the remark.

Immediately we went to work moving some salt and the little remaining sugar into the house; and while we were doing it a Missourian came up and advised us to get everything into the house as quickly as possible, and he would protect us while doing so. He offered to show Mother how to hide her things. She said: "We need instruction from Yankees, for we have never been accustomed to any such mean business." He said he had enlisted to fight for the *Constitution;* but since then the war had been turned into another thing, and he did not approve this abolitionism, for his wife's people all owned slaves. He told us what afterwards proved false—that ten thousand infantry would soon pass through Riceboro on their way to Thomasville.

Soon after this some twenty rode up and caught me having a barrel rolled toward the house. They were gentlemanly. A few only dismounted;

said they were from various of our Confederate States. They said the war would soon be over, for they would have Savannah in a few days.

I replied: "Savannah is not the Confederacy."

They spoke of the number of places they had taken.

I said: "Yes, and do you hold them?"

One of them replied: "Well, I do admire your spunk."

They inquired for all the large plantations.

Squads came all day until near dark. We had no time to eat a mouthful. The remaining ox-wagons were taken to the cornhouse and filled with corn.

Sabbath, December 18th. We passed this day with many fears, but no Yankees came to the lot; though many went to Carlawter and were engaged carrying off corn, the key of the cornhouse having been taken from Cato the day before and the door ordered to be left open. A day comparatively free from interruptions was very grateful to us, though the constant state of apprehension in which we were was distressing.

In the afternoon, while we were engaged in religious services, reading and seeking protection of our Heavenly Father, Captain Winn's Isaiah came bringing a note from Mr. Mallard to me and one from Mr. John Stevens to Mother, sending my watch. This was our first intelligence from Mr. Mallard, and oh, how welcome to us all; though the note brought no hope of his release, as the charge against him was taking up arms against the U.S. Captain Winn had been captured but released. We were all in such distress that Mother wrote begging Mr. Stevens to come to us. We felt so utterly alone that it would be a comfort to have him with us.

Monday, December 19th. Squads of Yankees came all day, so that the servants scarcely had a moment to do anything for us out of the house. The women, finding it entirely unsafe for them to be out of the house at all, would run in and conceal themselves in our dwelling. The few remaining chickens and some sheep were killed. These men were so outrageous at the Negro houses that the Negro men were obliged to stay at their houses for the protection of their wives; and in some instances they rescued them from the hands of these infamous creatures.

Tuesday, December 20th. A squad of Yankees came soon after breakfast. Hearing there was one yoke of oxen left, they rode into the pasture and drove them up, and went into the woods and brought out the horse-wagon, to which they attached the oxen. Needing a chain for the purpose, they went to the well and took it from the well bucket. Mother went out and entreated them not to take it from the well, as it was our means of getting water. They replied: "You have no right to have even wood or water," and immediately took it away.

Wednesday, December 21st. 10 A.M. Six of Kilpatrick's cavalry rode up, one of them mounted on Mr. Mallard's valuable gray named Jim. They looked into the dairy and empty smokehouse, every lock having been broken and doors wide open day and night. They searched the servants' houses; then they thundered at the door of the dwelling. Mother opened it, when one of them presented a pistol to her breast and demanded why she dared to keep her house closed, and that "he be damned if he would not come into it."

She replied: "I prefer to keep my house closed because we are a helpless and defenseless family of women and little children. And one of your officers informed me that the men were not to enter private dwellings. And it is also contrary to the published orders of your general."

He replied: "I'll be damned if I don't come in and take just what I want. Some of the men got wine here, and we must have some."

She told them her house had been four times searched in every part, and everything taken from it. And recognizing one who had been of the party that had robbed us, she said: "You know my meal and everything has been taken."

He said: "We left you a sack of meal and that rice."

Mother said: "You left us some rice; but out of twelve bushels of meal you poured out a quart or so upon the floor—as you said, to keep us from starving."

She then entreated them, on account of the health of her daughter, not to enter the house. With horrible oaths they rode off, shooting two ducks in the yard.

About half an hour after, three came. One knocked in the piazza and asked if Mother always kept her doors locked. She said she had recently done so by the advice of an officer; and Kate King said: "We have been compelled to do so since the house has been so repeatedly ransacked."

He said: "Well, I never do that and did not come for that." Asked if we knew Mrs. S—— of Dorchester, for he had turned some men out of her house who were ransacking it. He demeaned himself with respect, and did not insist upon coming in.

Upon one occasion one of the men as he sat on the bench in the piazza had his coat buttoned top and bottom, and inside we could plainly see a long row of stolen breast pins and jewelry—gallant trophies, won from defenseless women and children at the South to adorn the persons of their mothers, wives, sisters, and friends in Yankeeland!

One hour after, five came. Mother and Kate trembled from head to feet. It appeared as if this day's trials were more than they could bear. They knelt and asked strength from God; went down and found that three had already entered the pantry with false keys brought for the purpose. They immediately proceeded to cut open the wires of the safe and took all they wanted, amongst other things a tin kettle of eggs we had managed to get.

Mother said to them: "Why, you have entered my house with false keys!"

With demoniacal leer they said: "We want none of your keys," and tried to put in one of those they brought into the pantry door.

She told them: "Your soldiers have already broken the key in that lock, and it cannot be opened; but everything has already been taken." When they insultingly insisted the door should be opened, Mother told them: "Very well, break it open just as soon as you please."

She remonstrated against their coming over the house, and told them of the order of the officers. They replied none of their officers prohibited them from coming in, and they would be damned if they would mind any such orders, would be damned if they did not go where they pleased, and would be damned if they did not take what they pleased. Mother remonstrated, and in her earnest entreaty placed her hand upon the shoulder of one of them, saying: "You must not go over my house." Strange to say, they did not go beyond the pantry, and appeared restrained, as we afterwards believed, by the hand of God. They said they wanted pots and buckets, for they were in camp and had nothing to cook in. One asked for whiskey. To our amusement the man who stole the eggs stumbled and fell as he went down the steps and broke them all—but carried off the bucket. (Psalm 27:2—"When the wicked, even mine enemies and my foes, came upon me to eat up my flesh, they stumbled and fell.")

At dinner time twelve more came—six or seven to the door asking for flour and meal. Mother told them she was a defenseless widow with an only daughter on the eve of again becoming a mother, a young friend, and five little children dependent on her for food and protection. They laughed and said: "Oh, we have heard just such tales before!" They wanted to know why the house was kept locked; said it would only make it worse for us. (This had proven false, for when the doors were open it was impossible to keep them out.) Kate observed a large cravat upon the neck of one made of a black silk dress of hers which had been taken by one of them a few days before. Every species of men's clothing in our trunks and bureaus and portmanteaus was taken, but none of our personal apparel, for we generally stood by when they were searching our wardrobes. They took every piece of jewelry they could find. Twelve sheep were found shot and left in the pasture—an act of wanton wickedness.

Late in the afternoon more came and carried off the few remaining ducks. Going to the Negro houses, they called Cato, the driver, and told him they knew he was feeding "that damned old heifer in the house," and they would "blow out his damned brains" if he gave her another morsel to eat, for they meant to starve her to death. Pointing to the chapel, they asked what house that was. Cato answered: "A church which my master had built for the colored people on the place to hold prayers in the week and preach in on Sunday." They said: "Yes, there he told all his damned lies and called it preaching." And with dreadful oaths they cursed him. To Patience, when they were taking good and valuable books from his library (as they said, to send their old fathers at home), they said, when she spoke with honor of her master and his labors for the good of the colored people: "He was a damned infernal villain, and we only wish he was now alive; we would blow his brains out." To Sue they said, when she spoke of his goodness to the people: "We wish he was now here; we would cut his throat." They stole two blankets from July, and attempted to steal his hat. They took a piggin of boiled potatoes from Sue, and threw the piggin in the marsh when they had eaten them.

After all the day's trials, late at night came Kate's servant Prophet bringing her some clothing and chickens. We were rejoiced to see anyone. He reported South Hampton had been visited by a hundred and fifty men, who had taken all the corn given to the Negroes (three months' allowance), killed forty or fifty hogs and taken seven beef cattle, stolen all the syrup and sugar from the Negroes, and taken their clothing, crawling under their houses and beds searching for buried articles.

MRS. MARY JONES *in her Journal*[t]
Montevideo, *Thursday,* December 22nd, 1864

Several squads of Yankees came today, but none insisted upon coming into the house. Most of the remaining geese were killed by them. One attempted forcibly to drag Sue by the collar of her dress into her room. Another soldier coming up told him to "let that old woman alone"; and while they were speaking together she made her escape to the dwelling, dreadfully frightened and thoroughly enraged. The horrible creature then went to old Mom Rosetta; and she told him he had "no manners," and after a while got him away. Sue's running into the house sent a thrill of terror into Kate and myself, for we were momentarily expecting them to enter the house. My heart palpitates with such violence against my side that with pain I bear the pressure of my dress.

If it was not for the supporting hand of God we must give up and die. His precious Word and prayer sustains our fainting souls. Besides our morning and evening devotions Kate, Daughter, and I observe a special season every afternoon to implore protection for our beloved ones and ourselves and deliverance for our suffering country. I have often said to the enemy: "I pray not for revenge upon you, but I pray daily for deliverance from you"; and always felt amid my deepest distresses: "Oh, if my country was but free and independent, I could take joyfully the spoiling of my goods!"

MRS. MARY S. MALLARD *in her Journal*[t]
Montevideo, *Thursday,* December 22nd, 1864

About midday the two little boys Mac and Pulaski made their appearance, having escaped from the Yankees at Midway. One of the officers told Pulaski Mr. Mallard was at the Ogeechee bridge, and had been preaching for them and walking at large. They had put no handcuffs on him, and he was walking at large, and they gave him plenty to eat. We are all thankful to hear from him.

Pulaski says he asked for the well chain. They cursed him and said his mistress should do without it.

One squad who came to the house asked Mother when she had seen any rebels, and if there were any around here. She told them her son-in-law had been captured more than a week before, and he was the only gentleman belonging to our household.

Looking fiercely at her, he said: "If you lie to me I will—" The rest of the sentence Mother did not quite understand; it was either "I'll kill you" or "I'll blow your brains out."

She immediately stepped out upon the little porch, near which he was sitting on his horse as he spoke to her, and said to him: "In the beginning of this war one passage of Scripture was impressed upon my mind; and it now abides with me: 'Fear not them which kill the body and after that have no more that they can do. But fear Him who, after He hath killed, hath power to cast into hell.' I have spoken the truth, and do you remember that you will stand with me at the Judgment Bar of God!"

There were quite a number around. One man said: "Madam, if that is your faith, it is a good one."

She replied: "It is my faith, and I feel that it has power to sustain me."

One of these men threatened Cato with a pistol at his breast that if he did feed his mistress they would kill him; called her an old devil, and applied other dreadful epithets such as are used by the lowest and most profane.

Early in the afternoon the same officer called who had previously been in the house. He immediately inquired if the men had done any injury within since he was here last. Whilst he conversed with Kate and Mother his men were firing and killing the geese in the lot and loading their horses with them.

Before leaving he asked for a glass of water. Mother handed him a glass, saying: "I regret that I cannot offer a glass of fresh water, for you have taken even the chain from my well bucket."

He replied very quickly: "I did not do it. Neither did my men do it."

Having heard nothing from Mr. Stevens, Mother sent Charles to Captain Winn's (where he was staying) to ask him to come to us, as we were all in much distress. Charles returned saying Mr. Stevens would come, but was waiting for Uncle William, who had left Springfield the day before and walked to Dorchester; and they expected him the next day at Captain Winn's.

Friday, December 23rd. A day of perfect freedom from the enemy at our dwelling. Five or six rode through the pasture, but none came to the house or Negro houses.

Mrs. Mary Jones *in her Journal*[t]

Montevideo, *Saturday,* December 24th, 1864

As we were finishing our breakfast, which we always had to take in the most hurried manner with every window tightly closed upstairs in my chamber, five Yankees made their appearance from different approaches to the house. Kate and I went down, as usual, with beating hearts and knees that smote together, yet trusting in our God for protection.

One knocked at the door next the river. I requested him to go around to the front door, and—most amazing—he answered "Yes, ma'am" and went around. When the door was unlocked he said: "We have come to search for arms."

I told him the house had again and again under that plea been thoroughly searched; not the minutest drawer or trunk but had been searched.

He replied: "I would not like to do anything unpleasant to you."

A Dutchman said: "I have come to search your house, mistress, and I mean to do it. If you have two or three thousand dollars I would not touch it; but I am coming into your house to search it from top to bottom."

I told him the officers had said the soldiers must not enter private dwellings.

He replied: "There is no officer; we are independent scouts and do as we please." He looked up at the windows, and went around the front of the house, remarking in the most cruel manner: "This house will make a beautiful fire and a great smoke."

I said: "Surely you would not burn a house that was occupied!"

He replied: "Your soldiers would do it. I came here to fight, and I mean to do it." Then he insisted upon coming in.

I told him of my daughter's situation and entreated him not to come in, for she was daily expecting to be confined.

"Tell her to go to her room; we will not disturb her. We have not come to insult ladies."

I said: "If you are determined to search, begin your work at once." For they were pushing into the rooms, and with them an insolent little mulatto boy, who commenced running about the parlor. I called to the Dutchman and said: "Order that boy out of my house!"

He immediately stamped his foot and said: "Get out of this house and stay by the horses!"

They searched from the attic down. One of the party wanted to take a comforter, but the Dutchman said: "Let it alone." Another of them emptied out all my spools for weaving and took the bag.

They insisted two rebels had been here the night before, for a man had told them so. I assured them it was false. They then asked if I knew Mr. King, and insisted that he did come to the house, as his wife stayed here, and she knew where he was.

Kate told them she did not know.

The Dutchman said: "It's no use for a woman to tell me she does not know where her husband is."

Kate told him she was a member of the church and trusted a Christian, and would tell a lie to no man, even if he was an enemy. They then showed a pistol and blankets and wanted Kate to say they were her husband's, and gave her to understand he had been captured or killed.

Again they surveyed the house, asked if I knew North and South Hampton, said they had just burnt both places, that my house would be a beautiful flame, and that night they would return and burn it down. They then rode to the Negro quarters and spoke with Cato; told him to tell his mistress they would return and burn her house that night, and she had better move out.

My mind is made up not to leave my house until the torch is put to it.

About two o'clock Jack and Pulaski made their appearance, having been away just one week. They had been driving cattle for the Yankees. They met the same squad of men as they returned on the Boro bridge, and told the boys to come and tell Mrs. Jones they intended to return that night and burn her house down.

Our agony and distress are so great I sent Cato to Captain Winn and Mr. Stevens this afternoon to tell them our situation. We received a note signed "S," saying they did not think the threat would be executed, and that it was reported by the enemy that Savannah was evacuated two days ago, our forces going into Carolina and the Yankees capturing two hundred cars and thirty thousand bales of cotton and nine hundred prisoners.

We have all spent a miserable day, but have committed ourselves to Him who never slumbers nor sleeps. We are completely cut off from all creature helps, from all human sympathy. Helpless—oh, how utterly helpless! And yet blessed be God! We feel that we are in the hollow of His almighty hand. It is a precious, precious feeling that the omnipotent, omnipresent Jehovah is with us, and that Jesus, our Divine Redeemer and Advocate, will be touched with our sorrows.

The darkness of night is around our dwelling. We are all upstairs in one room with closed windows and a dim light. Our poor little children have eaten their supper. We have dressed them warmly, and they have been put to bed with their clothes on, that they may be ready to move at an instant's warning. My poor delicate, suffering, heart-weary child I have forced to lie down, and persuaded Kate to do so also.

Kept watch alone until two o'clock, and then called Kate, who took my place, and I threw myself on the bed for an hour.

May God keep us safe this night! To Him alone do we look for protection from our cruel enemies.

MRS. MARY S. MALLARD *in her Journal*^t

Montevideo, *Sunday,* December 25th, 1864

With great gratitude we hailed the light this morning, having passed the night. And no enemy has come nigh our persons or our dwelling; although there are appearances of horse tracks, which we have observed before, and believe they are often around at night to try and detect any gentlemen ("rebel," as they call them) coming here.

We were much alarmed towards morning by Sue's calling to have the house opened; Prophet had come bringing Kate some beef and meal.

At breakfast two Yankees rode around the lot, but seeing nothing to take away went away; and we were not further interrupted.

George and June came back, saying the ox-wagon had been cut to pieces and the oxen killed. They were carried to the Ogeechee, where George saw Mr. Mallard and says he preached to the Yankees.

Monday, December 26th. Saw no one all day. Towards evening we ventured out with the poor little children, and as we were returning saw one at a distance.

Tuesday, December 27th. No enemy today. Bless the Lord for this mercy!

Wednesday, December 28th. Another day without the appearance of the Yankees. Could we but know we should be spared one day we would breathe freely, but we are in constant apprehension and terror. Everyone that comes has some plea for insult or robbery. Was there ever any civilized land given up for such a length of time to lawless pillage and brutal inhumanities?

Thursday, December 29th. Free from intrusion until afternoon, when three Yankees and one Negro came up. Lucy ran into the house and locked the door after her, which seemed to provoke them. Three came to the door, and after knocking violently several times one broke open the door. Mother and Kate went down as soon as they could, and when he saw them he cursed awfully. They insisted upon coming in, and asked for that "damned wench" that had locked the door, threatening to "shoot her damned brains out," using the Saviour's name in awful blasphemy.

Nothing seemed to keep them from going over the house but Mother's telling them the officers had advised the locking of the doors, and the men had no right to enter the house, under General Sherman's orders. She told them the situation of her family and her daughter. One went into the parlor and pantry and into one or two other rooms; and one went into the room we are compelled to cook in, and crouched like a beast over the fire. He was black and filthy as a chimney sweep. Indeed, such is the horrible odor they leave in the house we can scarcely endure it.

The cook, seeing the party, locked herself into the cooking room; but they thundered at the door in such a manner I had to call to her to open it, which when she did I could scarce keep from smiling at the metamorphosis. From being a young girl she had assumed the attitude and appearance of a sick old woman, with a blanket thrown over her head and shoulders, and scarcely able to move. Their devices are various and amusing. Gilbert keeps a sling under his coat and slips his arm into it as soon as they appear; Charles walks with a stick and limps dreadfully; Niger a few days since kept them from stealing everything they wanted in his house by covering up in bed and saying he had *"yellow fever";* Mary Ann kept them from taking the wardrobe of her deceased daughter by calling out: "Them dead people clothes!"

Friday, Saturday, Sabbath, and Monday. No enemy came to the dwelling. They sometimes are at the cornhouse and do not come over. We view them from our upper windows taking the provisions and see them killing the sheep and hogs and cattle. We regard it as a great mercy when we are delivered from their presence within the house.

MRS. MARY JONES *in her Journal*[t]

Montevideo, *Tuesday*, January 3rd, 1865

Soon after breakfast three Yankees rode up and wanted to search for rebels and arms. They dismounted and sat upon the front porch. With much entreaty, and reminding them of the orders of their commander and the feeble condition of my daughter, they refrained from coming in.

One said to Kate and myself: "I guess you are too great rebels to go North, but if you will take good advice you will do so," and offered to get us a pass to Savannah if we would go.

I replied: "We prefer to remain in our own home and country."

Four others rode up and proceeded to search the outhouses. In the loft to the washroom they found some ear corn that we had concealed there to sustain our lives. They immediately commenced knocking off the shingles, and soon broke a large hole in the roof, those within hallooing and screaming and cursing to those without to come and see what they had found.

The one who had been speaking to us assured us they would do us personally no harm. I asked him to prevent their breaking down the house.

He called out: "Stop, boys!"

They replied: "We have found a lot of corn!"

"Well, you must let it alone." (I had told him we put it there to keep ourselves and the servants from starving.)

After this they ceased knocking off the shingles.

Seeing there was some trace of humanity in him, I related Mr. Mallard's capture, and that he was a minister of the gospel.

He asked: "What denomination?"

I replied: "Presbyterian," and asked if they had any professors of religion in their army.

He said: "Yes—many when they left their homes; but I do not know where you will find them now."

He was a Methodist, but had many friends who were Presbyterians; his parents Baptist. I asked him to stay and protect us while this lawless squad remained; but he said they must go, and rode off, while the others proceeded to gather all they wanted from the people's houses, making the Negroes fill the bags and take them out.

Sue in her kindness had hid away a few potatoes for the little children. She entreated for them, but they took every one, and tore a breadth from her new woolen dress which she was making and had sewing in her hands to make strings to tie up their bags of plunder. They have stolen even the drawers and petticoats of the women for that purpose; and sometimes they have taken their nether garments and put them on, leaving in their stead their filthy crawling shirts.

Having one ham, I had given it to Sue to keep for me. They found it; and being an old one they chopped it up and flung it to the dogs, Sue exclaiming: "Massa! You do poor Niggers so?" This was the only morsel of meat we had left.

They stayed a long while and finally rode off.

Wednesday, January 4th. At daylight my daughter informed me she was sick. She has been in daily expectation of her confinement for two weeks. I sent immediately for the servants and ordered my little riding pony, Lady Franklin, which the Yankees had taken and dragged several miles by the neck (because she would not lead) and finally let go, when she returned. And we have tried to keep her out of sight for this very purpose, saddled with my sidesaddle. Prepared a yellow flag for Charles (in case he met the Yankees) and wrote to Dr. Raymond Harris, three miles off and the only physician I know of in the county: "I entreat you to come to the help of my suffering child." Charles started before sunrise, going through the woods.

My heart was filled with intense anxiety and distress, especially as my child had an impression something was wrong with her unborn infant—the consequence of injuries received from a severe fall from a wagon, breaking her collarbone and bruising her severely, as they were making their retreat from Atlanta on the approach of General Sherman.

Dr. Harris, with a kindness and courage never to be forgotten, came without delay and in the face of danger; for the enemy was everywhere over the county. He looked very feeble, having been recently ill with pneumonia. Soon after being in her room he requested a private interview, informing me that my child was in a most critical condition, and I must be prepared for the worst. For if he did not succeed in relieving the difficulty, her infant at least must die.

I replied: "Doctor, the mother first."

"Certainly," was his answer.

He returned to her room and with great difficulty and skill succeeded in effecting what he desired. God, our compassionate Saviour, heard the voice of faith and prayer; and she was saved in childbearing, and at eleven o'clock gave birth to a well-formed infant—a daughter.

During these hours of agony the yard was filled with Yankees. It is supposed one hundred visited the place during the day. They were all around the house; my poor child, calm and collected amid her agony of body, could hear their conversation and wild halloos and cursing beneath her windows. Our dear friend Kate King had to meet them alone. She entreated that they would not come in or make a noise, for there was sickness in the house.

They replied: "We are not as bad as you think us. We will take off our spurs and come in." And one actually pushed by her and came in.

She stepped upon the porch and implored if there was one spark of humanity or honor about them that they would not come in, saying: "You compel me to speak plainly. There is a child being born this very instant in this house, and if there is an officer or a gentleman amongst you I entreat you to protect the house from intrusion."

After a while they left, screaming and yelling in a most fiendish way as they rode from the house.

Dr. Harris returned with Charles as a guide and reached his home safely, having met only one of the enemy.

In the afternoon a very large party rode up; said they wanted to know the meaning of the yellow flag which was placed over the front porch. Had we sick soldiers, or was this a hospital? I told them it indicated sickness in my family: my daughter was ill. One asked for matches; I had none to give. And taking Carpenter Pulaski, they rode to the neighboring plantations. They searched all the Negro houses, within and without and under, taking whatever they wanted. They have taken Gilbert's knife and watch and chain, July's pants and blankets, George and Porter's blankets and clothes, the women's pails, piggins, spoons, buckets, pots, kettles, etc., etc.

Thursday, January 5th. Three Yankees rode up in the forenoon and asked for me. I met them at the front porch. They wished to know if there were sick soldiers in the house.

"No, my daughter is sick."

They propounded the usual questions. I told them of the capture of my daughter's husband, and as they were Kilpatrick's men, asked if they would take a letter to him. They said they would; and I wrote telling him of the birth of the baby; and Daughter sent him her Greek Testament, Kate sent a letter North, and Mrs. King one to Clarence.

This man told me he was from Indiana; was a Virginian by birth. Said there was great dissatisfaction in the army on account of the present object of the war, which now was to free the Negroes.

Looking at me, he said: "Have you sons in the army?"

I replied: "Could you suppose I would have sons who would not defend their country and their mother?"

He said: "If your sons are now in that house I would not take them."

Understanding his trickery, I bowed and said: "I am happy to say you will not have the opportunity. If my sons are alive, they are far away and I hope at the post of duty."

We gave him the letters, which he put in one pocket, and the Greek Testament in the other, and rode off; but lingered a great while on the plantation, making the Negroes shell and grind corn for them, shooting down the sheep in the fields, some of which they skinned and carried away.

This man said his name was James Y. Clark, and was the only one of all we saw whose name we heard. A mere youth with him said he had a brother who had been a prisoner in Georgia, and when sick had been taken into a family and nursed; and whenever he met a Georgian he would treat him as well as his own men. They spoke more kindly than any we have conversed with.

Before going to bed—about twelve o'clock—Driver John came to say a letter sent to my brother in Southwest Georgia and letters sent by Kate to Mrs. King and a letter to my sister Mrs. Cumming had all been found on the person of Lewis, a most faithful man, who had come late the previous night to receive them. Flora had ripped up his sleeve and sewed them in. On account of his fidelity some of his own color informed the Yankees that he carried letters for rebels. They put him in custody, and while in their hands he managed to send the old man John to us to say they had taken our letters, and he wanted us to know it and be prepared for them if they came to trouble us. My letter contained only a truthful account of our present condition. These very men that spoke so fair to us this morning had our letters then in their possession and read them aloud at the Negro houses. Where will all this perfidy, insult, and injury to the helpless, the fatherless, and the widow end?

As night closes in upon us I place my darling little Ruthie in bed. Kate sees her little ones at rest; and Daughter with the baby is sleeping, and so are little Mary and Charlie. I often walk alone up and down the front piazza, to mark the light against the sky of the low lingering flame of the last burnt dwelling or outhouse. I can locate them all around on the neighboring plantations. I look with fear and trembling in the direction of our venerable old church at Midway. We hear the Baptist church in Sunbury has been consumed—burnt as a signal fire to indicate by the troops on this side the safe arrival of this portion of the army to that on the opposite shore in Bryan County.

Bless the Lord for the great mercy of nights free from the presence of the enemy! We would certainly go deranged or die if they were here day and night.

Friday, January 6th. No enemy appeared here today, but we have heard firing around on different places.

The people are all idle on the plantations, most of them seeking their own pleasure. Many servants have proven faithful, others false and rebellious against all authority or restraint. Susan, a Virginia Negro and nurse to my little Mary Ruth, went off with Mac, her husband, to Arcadia the night after the first day the Yankees appeared, with whom she took every opportunity of conversing, informing them that the baby's father was Colonel Jones. She has acted a faithless part as soon as she could. Porter left three weeks since, and has never returned to give any report of Patience or himself or anyone at Arcadia. Little Andrew went to Flemington and returned. I sent him back to wait on our dear sister and family and to be with his own. I hope he will prove faithful. Gilbert, Flora, Lucy, Tenah, Sue, Rosetta, Fanny, Little Gilbert, Charles, Milton and Elsie and Kate have been faithful to us. Milton has been a model of fidelity. He will not even converse with the Yankees, and in their face drives up and milks the cow, without the milk of which little Julia would fare badly, for she is just weaned. His brother, Little Pulaski, refused even to bring a pail of water, and took himself off a week since.

Saturday, January 7th. Forenoon. No enemy thus far. God be praised for His goodness and mercy! Our nights have been free from intrusion.

A keen northwester is sweeping over the lawn and whistling among the trees, from the branches of which the long gray moss is waving. The pall of death is suddenly thrown over our once cheerful and happy home. Not a living creature stirs in garden or yard, on the plain or in the grove. Nature wears a funereal aspect, and the blast, as it sweeps through the branches, is sighing a requiem to departed days.

As I stand and look at the desolating changes wrought by the hand of an inhuman foe in a few days, I can enter into the feelings of Job when he exclaimed: "Naked came I out of my mother's womb, and naked shall I return thither; the Lord gave, and the Lord hath taken away: blessed be the name of the Lord." All our pleasant things are laid low. Lover and friend is put far from us, and our acquaintance into darkness. We are prisoners in our own home; we dare not open windows or doors. Sometimes our little children are allowed under a strict watch and guard to run a little in the sunshine, but it is always under constant apprehension. The poor little creatures at a moment's warning—just let them hear "Yankee coming!"—rush in and remain almost breathless, huddled together in one of the upper rooms like a bevy of frightened partridges. To obtain a mouthful of food we have been obliged to cook in what was formerly our drawing room; and I have to rise every morning by candlelight, before the dawn of day, that we may have it before the enemy arrives to take it from us. And then sometimes we and the dear little ones have not a chance to eat again before dark. The poor servants are harassed to death, going rapidly for wood or water and hurrying in to lock the doors, fearing insults and abuse at every turn. Do the annals of civilized—and I may add savage—warfare afford any record of brutality equaled in extent and duration to that which we have suffered, and which has been inflicted on us by the Yankees? For one month our homes and all we possess on earth have been given up to lawless pillage. Officers and men have alike engaged in this work of degradation. I scarcely know how we have stood up under it. God alone has enabled us to "speak with the enemy in the gates," and calmly, without a tear, to see my house broken open, entered with false keys, threatened to be burned to ashes, refused food and ordered to be starved to death, told that I had no right even to wood or water, that I should be "humbled in the very dust I walked upon," a pistol and carbine presented to my breast, cursed and reviled as a rebel, a hypocrite, a devil. Every servant, on pain of having their brains blown out, is forbidden to wait upon us or furnish us food. Every trunk, bureau, box, room, closet has been opened or broken open and searched, and whatever was wanted of provisions, clothing, jewelry, knives, forks, spoons, cups, kettles, cooking utensils, towels, bags, etc., etc., from this house taken, and the whole house turned topsy-turvy.

Their conduct at Arcadia and our losses there I will tell at some other time.

Monday, January 9th. Yesterday the 8th was the Holy Sabbath Day. No enemy came nigh our dwelling. As has been my custom, the servants assembled—not in the chapel as formerly, that being rather far from the dwelling, but in the kitchen, which is large and comfortable. Seats were arranged around. My audience was composed mostly of women and children; a few men and boys and some strangers had called in. I read the Scriptures and one of my honored husband's sermons. We engaged in singing and prayer. To me it was a season of solemn worship. Also catechized the children. I have tried during this season of distress to remember God in the family and household.

About noon Dr. Harris sent his driver, Caesar, over with a kind note of inquiry after my daughter, saying they had been again treated most shamefully by the Yankees. They had robbed them of bedclothes, provisions, etc. I asked the doctor's acceptance of an Oxford edition of the New Testament and Psalms which I had preserved, "with grateful recollections of his kindness, courage, and skill in an hour of great peril and deep distress."

We understand that Colonel Hood has come in from beyond the Altamaha under flag of truce, and that a number of ladies and children with a few of their personal servants have left the county and gone south towards Thomasville. Although we see no way of relief to ourselves, we rejoice that others are delivered from this dreadful captivity.

No enemy today.

Tuesday, January 10th. We have been free from the presence of the enemy thus far today, although in great apprehension for several hours, as Sue came in at dinner time and advised us to hasten the meal, as she heard firing in the woods between this and White Oak, which is not much over a mile distant. It was reported they would return today with a large forage train of several hundred wagons going on to the Altamaha.

One thing is evident: they are now enlisting the Negroes here in their service. As one of the officers said to me, "We do not want your women, but we mean to take the able-bodied men to dredge out the river and harbor at Savannah, to hew timber, make roads, build bridges, and throw up batteries." They offer twelve dollars per month. Many are going off with them. Some few sensible ones calculate the value of twelve dollars per month in furnishing food, clothing, fuel, lodging, etc., etc. Up to this time none from this place has joined them. I have told some of those indisposed to help in any way and to wander off at pleasure that as they were perfectly useless here it would be best for me and for the good of their fellow servants if they would leave and go at once with the Yankees. They had seen what their conduct was to the black people—stealing from them, searching their houses, cursing and abusing and insulting their wives and daughters; and if they chose such for their masters to obey and follow, then the sooner they went with them the better; and I had quite a mind to send in a request that they be carried off.

Wednesday, January 11th. Our little babe is one week old today. Bless the Lord for His abounding mercy to mother and child—and to me, their only nurse (excepting the attendance of Lucy, who is very faithful by day and night). The precious little one gives no trouble, and the very care she brings calls my thoughts away from surrounding scenes of distress.

We have had another day of freedom from the enemy.

Our servants keep up communication with their neighbors around; and today it is reported (with what truth we have no means of ascertaining, for we never behold a human being) that the enemy nine thousand strong have gone down the Albany & Gulf Road to Thomasville; from thence will send out a raid on Southwest Georgia. This would prove a most disastrous move to our cause, as that is our great grain-growing and meat-raising region, the Commissary Department of our army in Georgia depending upon that section for supplies.

In our captivity we are in utter ignorance of all without. We know not the state of our cause or the condition of affairs in the Confederacy. Clouds and darkness are round about us; the hand of the Almighty is laid in sore judgment upon us; we are a desolated and smitten people. What the divine decrees concerning us are remain with Infinite Wisdom. We see not; we know not. But we cling to the hope that when our Heavenly Father hath sufficiently chastened and humbled us as individuals and as a nation in wrath, He will remember mercy, and that we shall be purged and purified in this furnace of affliction and brought out a wiser and a better people, to His honor and His glory. At present the foundations of society are broken up; what hereafter is to be our social and civil status we cannot see.

The workings of Providence in reference to the African race are truly wonderful. The scourge falls with peculiar weight upon them: with their emancipation must come their extermination. All history, from their first existence, proves them incapable of self-government; they perish when brought in conflict with the intellectual superiority of the Caucasian race. Northern philanthropy and cant may rave as much as they please; but *facts* prove that in a state of slavery such as exists in the Southern states have the Negro race increased and thriven most. We would point to the history of the British West India Islands, and to New England, with her starved and perished blacks. Not that we have done our duty to them here; far from it. I feel if ever we gain our independence there will be radical reforms in the system of slavery as it now exists. When once delivered from the interference of Northern abolitionism, we shall be free to make and enforce such rules and reformations as are just and right. In all my life I never heard such expressions of hatred and contempt as the Yankees heap upon our poor servants. One of them told me he did not know what God Almighty made Negroes for; all he wished was the power to blow their brains out.

Thursday and Friday, January 12th and 13th. We have had days of quiet, no enemy appearing.

The weather is charming, and has been so for four weeks. The atmosphere is brilliant and bracing: nights cold, mornings frosty, the noonday delightfully warm and balmy. I never saw more resplendent nights; the light of the moon is as the light of the sun.

Our dear little children have ventured out and are luxuriating in the sunshine. Sue, like a presiding genius, has them all around her and variously occupied. Some are making traps to catch the little sparrows, others plaiting rush baskets, arranging mimic gardens and houses. Their sports are all of a rustic order, and their little spirits soon react. I never saw them more cheerful and happy than they now are. But only let the watch cry be heard—"Yankee!"—and how soon they would turn pale and flee into the house for protection!

We see no living sign of animal or poultry saving one poor pigeon that taps at our window for food, one little frightened chicken that dodges at every sound under the shrubs in the flower garden, and one old goose who, faithful to her trust, keeps up her nightly watch and with shrill call rings out the hourly changes.

Mr. D—— called to see us, and confirmed the reported advance upon Thomasville and Baker County.

Kate received a letter, and Daughter one from Robert. He has been paroled for ten days, and is now staying with our kind friends Rev. and Mrs. Axson. Efforts are being made for his release. My poor child has had a sorrowful time, but she has borne her troubles with great fortitude and submission.

Zadok brought me a letter: everything confirms the raid south. The enemy are in full possession of Savannah; Negroes in large numbers are flocking to them. We fear our poor army is in a bad way. General Hood is reported almost annihilated, and supplies for General Lee's army greatly diminished. But our God is in the heavens, and we look unto Him. We wait for Thy salvation, Lord!

I know not where my own beloved sons are. May God protect and bless them!

At sunset I was sitting with the baby in Daughter's room. One of the servants came up and said an officer had called, and he looked like one of our men. Kate and myself went below immediately, and to our inexpressible joy found Colonel Hood. He had come under flag of truce to carry any of the inhabitants beyond the Altamaha, or to take them within the Yankee lines if they so preferred. He kindly expressed much sympathy with our situation, and offered to come and take us out as soon as my daughter could move, or to take Mrs. King into Savannah; also to take charge of letters to or from our friends. It was very touching to see the feeling of our little children to him; they evidently regarded him as a deliverer, and crowded into his lap and around his knees. It so happened we had ventured to make a little raised ginger cake, and had a little piece of corned beef in the house; so we insisted he should share it with us, and we put up the remainder for his journey. He told us the reported advance of the enemy upon Thomasville and Southwest Georgia was false, but gave us a gloomy view of our prospects in other parts of the Confederacy. He offered to forward letters to my son Colonel C. C. J. through General Cobb at Macon.

Sabbath, January 15th. We have had a day of rest. All the women and young people assembled in the kitchen, and we had a pleasant religious service, singing, reading the Scriptures, and prayer and a selected piece on true faith. They were all respectful and attentive. I strive to keep up the worship of God in the family, and believe that true and undefiled religion

527

alone is the great controller and regulator of men's actions. And especially at this time do I see the absolute necessity for all the restraints and influences which can be brought to bear upon the ignorance and perversity of this poor deluded people.

Monday, January 16th. Twenty-two months today since my beloved and honored husband entered into his everlasting rest. I bless my Heavenly Father that he is spared our present distresses. And yet oh, how desolate we are without him! My counselor, my earthly support, my spiritual guide removed when most needed! If this deepest, greatest of all sorrows was necessary to be laid on me, all that I can pray is: "Lord, perfect that which concerneth me, and let not my will but Thine be done."

Before Kate and myself had risen from dinner table Mr. Buttolph came. With joyful hearts we welcomed him, and rejoiced to hear from my dear sister and Laura and the children and friends at Taylor's Creek. He had walked from Flemington, and was greatly fatigued. He gave us many particulars of the infamous conduct of the enemy.

Soon after retiring there was a gentle knock at the front door. Throwing up the sash, we recognized J. A. M. K. He gave us cheering news of our army. General Lee has repulsed General Grant in several of his recent attacks, and General Sherman's advance upon Charleston has been met and driven back. We hear that the inhabitants of Savannah are straitened for food and support, and many of the most respectable ladies are compelled to make cakes and corn bread and sell to the Yankees to enable them to live. He told us negotiations for Robert's release had been successful, and he would soon return home via South Carolina. God grant that it may be so!

Audley remained but a short time and left, as it was unsafe for him to be here, although we believe the enemy have generally left the county.

Tuesday, January 17th. As Mr. Buttolph could escort and protect Kate, she concluded to leave us for Taylor's Creek. The oxcart came over from South Hampton and took her baggage, and she and Mr. Buttolph, with her children and nurse, rode in a little jersey wagon drawn by a mule. We are grieved to part with her; our mutual trials and afflictions, our mingled prayers and tears at a throne of grace, have all drawn us very near to each other.

It has been our custom to have a season of reading the Scriptures and prayer morning, noon, and night. Sometimes, when our hearts have fainted and our strength failed as we were surrounded by our foes, we have knelt and prayed together, and God has given us strength to meet and "speak with the enemy in the gates." I never knew before the power or calming influence of prayer. From the presence of our Heavenly Father we feared not to meet the face of man. We must have died but for prayer. However agitated or distressed when we approached the mercy seat, we always had strength given us for our day.

In all my intercourse with the enemy I have avoided conversation or any aggravating remarks, even when I felt a sword pierced through my soul. For instance, when they reviled the memory of my beloved and honored husband, or taunted me with the want of courage on the part of my countrymen (charges which I knew to be as base and false as the lips that uttered them), they always addressed me as an uncompromising rebel, and I never failed to let them know that before High Heaven I believed our cause was just and right. The isolated and utterly defenseless condition of my poor family compelled me often to use entreaties; but after the day was over I frequently inquired of Kate and Daughter: "Tell me, girls, did I act like a coward?"

Every development of the enemy but confirms my desire for a separate and distinct nationality.

Saturday Night, January 21st. On Thursday Mr. L. J. Mallard visited us. He is now with his family. Gave us various accounts of the enemy. They encamped near his house; at one time on his premises over a thousand. They entered his dwelling day and night. They were forced to obtain a guard from the commander of the post, who was stationed at Midway, to protect his family. The house was repeatedly fired into under pretense of shooting rebels, although they knew that none but defenseless women and children were within. And Mrs. Mallard, who is almost blind, was then in her confinement. They rifled the house of every article of food or clothing which they wished. Mr. Mallard had nothing left but the suit of clothes he wore.

On Friday Mr. Richard Axson sent a short note from Robert. His exchange had not been effected, but he was hopeful of success. Mr. Axson had walked to Savannah and obtained a horse from the Yankees.

Kate, Daughter's servant who has been cooking for us, took herself off today—influenced, as we believe, by her father. Sent for Cook Kate to Arcadia; she refuses to come.

Their condition is one of perfect anarchy and rebellion. They have placed themselves in perfect antagonism to their owners and to all government and control. We dare not predict the end of all this, if the Lord in mercy does not restrain the hearts and wills of this deluded people. They are certainly prepared for any measures. What we are to do becomes daily more and more perplexing. It is evident if my dwelling is left unoccupied, everything within it will be sacrificed. Wherever owners have gone away, the Negroes have taken away all the furniture, bedding, and household articles.

Monday, January 23rd. Sabbath was so inclement, had no services for the people. The house servants were all in attendance at family worship.

Today sent again for Kate, and she has come, apparently with her free consent.

Tuesday, January 24th. At sunset walked to the Negro houses and met our good minister, Rev. D. L. Buttolph. He had walked from Flemington, a distance of fourteen and a half miles. As water to a thirsty soul, so is the presence of a friend to us now in our captivity. The family were well, but he gives a deplorable account of their social condition. Nearly all the house servants have left their homes; and from most of the plantations they have gone in a body, either directly to the enemy or to congregate upon the large plantations in Bryan County, which have been vacated and upon which a plenty of rice remains.

Thursday, January 26th. Porter brought his wife, Patience, and their three boys over. She appears glad to return, although the outer pressure is so great it is difficult for anyone to stand up for duty and their owners.

Friday, January 27th. A clear, cold day. The wind was sweeping around the house and drifting the dried and fallen leaves into heaps. I looked out and saw two bending forms passing around to the front door. They looked like time-worn pilgrims. Who can they be? We discovered our friends in adversity, Captain Winn and Mr. John Stevens. They had walked four miles to spend the day with us.

We asked them up into Daughter's chamber, where we recounted our sufferings and trials. Mr. Stevens said he had read the Scriptures and Jay's *Exercises* daily to the captain, and they had been a great comfort. His mother when dying had given him her gold spectacles and her Testament and Psalms; and now in the night of sorrow they had been the means of light and consolation to them. May God sanctify their losses and distresses and convert them unto Himself!

We had a little coffee for sickness that we had hidden. I had a good cup drawn for them, and they left before sunset.

XX

MRS. MARY S. MALLARD *to* MRS. SUSAN M. CUMMING[t]
Montevideo, *Friday,* February 10th, 1865

My dear Aunt and Cousin,

Our hearts have been greatly cheered this afternoon by letters from Brother Joe and Eva, the first that we have received. Eva wrote for Brother Charlie, as his arm was very much inflamed with symptoms of erysipelas. He had been sent by General Hardee to reorganize General Wheeler's cavalry, and had been detained by his arm in Augusta. Brother Joe says Sherman's main army is at Springfield in Effingham County and in Robertville in Carolina, thus controlling the railroads to Augusta and Branchville. It is thought he will make a simultaneous attack upon both places. Large bodies of troops are being collected to resist the attack, and they hope Augusta may yet be saved. Eva and her cousin, Miss Bird, left Savannah the Sabbath before the evacuation upon a few hours' notice, taking only their trunks with them and all the servants. Library and everything else were left behind, and Eva has heard that the house is occupied by Yankee officers. Brother Charlie had heard of Mr. Mallard's capture, and General Hardee promised to do all he could to facilitate his exchange. But I despair, for both flags of truce have failed, and the Yankees have specified a particular person—a Mr. Dickson, brother of Major Dickson, U.S.A.

Uncle William came here on Wednesday in a little wagon like that Kate rode to the Creek in. We were truly rejoiced to see him, and are most happy to have him stay with us.

February 11th. I had my note partially written last evening when I was interrupted by the arrival of company: Eva and Bessie Anderson, with Tommy Gignilliat. The girls walked almost all the way from Dorchester, and will spend some days with us.

I am very much obliged to you, my dear aunt, for your kind offer of household goods, and *if* I ever have a home and house to keep, they will be most acceptable. Everything now turns upon the release of my poor captive. I have heard ever since the first of January that he was soon to be released, and you know the effect of hope deferred.

My little baby has been remarkably healthy, and gives as little trouble as could be expected for so young a baby. I have never desired to call her Louisa, but have always wanted her called Susan for you, my dear aunt, unless you preferred naming her Georgia Maxwell. We call her by the latter name, as

531

that seems to be your choice. She is a pretty little thing, and Mother says reminds her of your little Georgia. Her brows are quite dark and rather heavy for an infant. I do not know that Mr. Mallard has heard of her birth, for he has never alluded to her in any of his letters. The opportunities are becoming very rare now, and I dread all communication being cut off. Should you hear of anyone going down to Savannah at any time, please write Mr. Mallard a few lines and send it to Dr. Axson, for he would always know where he could be found. I presume he is again in prison, as his parole was out.

How I wish we could all be together, if only for a little while! There is so much to be talked over. What is our future to be? Brother Joe says they are hoping something from our peace commissioners (Stephens, Hunter, and Campbell) now in Washington.

Several families are starting today for the Altamaha: Mrs. Cyrus Mallard's and Mrs. Delegal's. Mr. Delegal's Negroes, Captain Winn's, and Mr. Cay's are being removed. I hope the enemy will not return upon us, and that Sherman's proclamation will not be carried into effect.

Our children have been remarkably well, and blessed with wonderful appetites. Mother and all the little ones unite with me in warmest love to you both and Cousin Lyman. Kisses for the children. Georgia sends many thanks for the shoes, sacque, and flannel.

Affectionately yours,
Mary S. Mallard.

MRS. MARY JONES *to* MRS. SUSAN M. CUMMING^t

Montevideo, Saturday, February 11th, 1865

My dear Sister,

Many thanks for your kind remembrance of us. The pork was delicious. I sliced it daily for Daughter, and the weather was so cool it lasted a great while. The children and myself would eat the sauce as butter for our bread.

Our dear old brother is badly off for pants and vests and shirts; we have tried to supply these articles. He appears to feel the sadness of the times very much, but has the consolations of religion as his support.

Daughter has written you all the news. We have heard nothing until yesterday. I am deeply concerned for Charles. . . . Oh, that he were truly and professedly a child of God! My dear child grows more and more anxious about her husband.

William, your driver, wishes to have your oxcart. Shall I send it there? We have been unable to find our oxen until yesterday. They are perfectly wild. We have now a cart, and are most grateful for your having loaned us yours, although we have been able to use it very little for want of oxen.

Andrew tells me if you were in trouble he would wish to be with you; but as you now have Augustus he wishes to stay below, as he can do more for his family. Please let me know your wishes. If you can do without him,

532

he is very necessary to us if we plant, being the plowman if we get a horse or mule.

With our united and best love,

Ever your affectionate sister,
Mary Jones.

Ask dear Laura to send my *manuscript book* by Andrew.
Brother William is minus tobacco.

MRS. CAROLINE S. JONES *to* MRS. MARY JONES[t]

Augusta, *Tuesday,* February 14th, 1865

My dearest Mother,

We have today received your third letter, and are grateful for the intelligence of your welfare, though deeply distressed at the thought of yours and our dear Mary's sufferings. I can never express to you how we have suffered in the thought of your situation. Joe has been ill with anxiety about you and the impossibility which has up to this existed of reaching and helping you. I trust this will not much longer exist. He and his brother, who is here for a few days, have been consulting and trying to devise plans for visiting you and making the arrangements you desire.

I hope you have before this received letters from both of them. Ever since the receipt of your first they have been writing, hoping that the same kind Providence which guided your letter to us would permit you to receive theirs. Joe doubtless told you of the many and vain efforts he had made to obtain a horse after his poor Lewis died at Indianola upon the occasion of his visit there immediately after Kilpatrick's raid upon Burke. He has tried in every direction, but what with the thefts of the Yankees and the necessities of Wheeler's men, there are no horses to be had. And as each effort has ended in failure, poor Joe has sunk deeper into his distress and depression about you.

My dear, dear mother, how can I tell you of our sympathy with you and our grief for your sufferings? Words and time would fail me to tell you, and it is so aggravated by the thought of how helpless we are to aid you. We have been constantly threatened with the approach of the enemy. Only last night it was rumored that two corps were marching upon the city. This morning it is reported they have struck their tents and are marching in the direction of Columbia, so that we do not know from day to day—hardly from hour to hour—what may be the result. The terrors of your position, though, it seems to me perfectly unequaled: alone in a remote place, surrounded by insurgents. It seems to me too dreadful, and it convinces me more and more of what I have always known: that my dear mother is a wonderful woman to have borne it as she has. And poor Mary—to have been called to suffer what is always such a trial to her under such terrible circumstances! I am rejoiced to hear that she and the baby are doing well.

Lest you should not have received Charlie's letters, I will tell you of Eva and himself. Eva came up from Savannah three days before the evacuation, and has been here ever since. She is tolerably well, though not in strong health. Charlie was on a tour of inspection and reorganizing Wheeler's men, and stopped here on his way, intending to leave the following day. But he has been detained by a troublesome boil on his bridle arm, which prevents his riding. So he has been in town, but occupying his time in writing reports on his previous inspections, principally in the Doctor's office. So I have had the pleasure of seeing him frequently. He has probably conveyed to you some idea of his indignation at the conduct of a former member of his household, and threatens condign punishment when a fitting time arrives, as it surely will, *he* thinks; and so do I.

Sherman's movements in Carolina are veiled in the same mystery as when he passed through Georgia. For many days past Kilpatrick has been threatening this place from the neighborhood of Aiken, and a large force of cavalry has been within sixteen miles of the town. We have not known at any moment whether the next intelligence would not be that the enemy were in sight. I have determined to stay and abide the issue. It seems to be the general impression that a populous town is safer than anywhere else; and then at this inclement season, if I went out, I should not know under what roof I and the children would find a shelter. Today for the first time in weeks there seems to be the impression that for the present at least they will not attack Augusta. But if they get the other places, I suppose they have only to come and take it when they are ready. Oh, for a victory! But that seems to be a forgotten word with us.

Joe is buoying himself up greatly on the thought of getting to you; and as he is a determined man and finds a *way* when he has a will (though he may have great *difficulty* in finding it), I should not be surprised if he rode in some fine morning through the gates of his beloved home and brought rescue to his mother and sister. And then my dear mother and sister must come to us and make their home with us (if the Yankees spare us) until the end of the war, and as much longer as they will.

I am too grieved about Mr. Mallard's capture. Oh, that he were free and with you! From time to time we have heard of him through persons coming from Savannah, and that he is well and bears his great trial with an effort at cheerfulness. A few days ago we heard a rumor that he was released. I hope it may be true—or a *presage* of coming release.

We would give a great deal to hear of Aunt's welfare and Cousin Laura's, and something about Uncle William Maxwell. How has he, at his age and with his infirmities, fared through this terrible time?

We both rejoice greatly in hearing of Gilbert's noble conduct. Joe has always said he knew he would prove faithful, and I used to say last year that I thought there was something really touching in his manner to you ever since the death of his master. He seemed to feel that he was specially responsible for looking after your interests, and there was almost a tenderness in his respect to you. I am sure Joe will never forget his faithfulness.

534

Little Stanhope listens with eyes full of wonder and dismay at the story of the Yankee outrages at Arcadia (which he remembers with the deepest interest), and how they stole everything from his "dear grandmother and Charlie Mallard." If he had the body, he has the soul to fight them to the death for these atrocities. He is very well, and told me only today I must let him go back to Arcadia and play with Ruthie and Captain. Susie, too, is very well, except that she is suffering from dreadful chilblains contracted on this damp ground. Her feet are very sore; but she is otherwise perfectly well and full of spirits.

Mary's baby ought to turn out a wonderful woman, having had the temerity to come in such adverse times. I want to hear all about it and what its name is. How is little Ruthie? Charlie and Eva are very anxious to hear about her. Little Mary, I can readily believe since all the experiences of the past months, is progressing rapidly in womanliness. Do, dear Mother, give my dearest love to Mary, kiss all the children, and take for yourself all the affection and devotion of

Your attached daughter,
Caroline S. Jones.

Joe sends a great deal of love. He is pretty well, only overworked. He has been working double-tilt for some time past, expecting to be broken up by the Yankees. He hopes he will soon be with you. Good-bye, dearest Mother.

C.

MRS. MARY S. MALLARD *to* MRS. MARY JONES[c]

Doctortown, Wednesday, March 8th, 1865

My dearest Mother,

After leaving you on Thursday morning we rode slowly along until we reached the foot of the Sand Hills. Soon after we got fairly into the sand our horses refused to go; however, with much urging and great difficulty we reached Mr. David Miller's. Mr. and Mrs. Miller were very glad to see us, and entertained us very kindly. They both desired me to beg that Uncle and yourself would stop with them on your way to Baker. In the afternoon we met some young men who had just come across the Altamaha, and they brought a most unfavorable report both of the river and the ford over Jones Creek near Mrs. Johnston's. Mr. Miller told us we could avoid this ford by going near Captain Hughes's and crossing what is called the Parker Ford, so we determined to try that route.

On Friday morning Captain Walthour called at Mr. Miller's and said he understood there was a flat at Captain Hughes's landing, and we could cross there and thus avoid the Doctortown route altogether; that he meant to make further inquiries and go that way, as he had a great deal of furniture to move. As we intended to go near Captain Hughes's in order to cross the ford at Jones Creek, this seemed a most pleasing arrangement.

Soon after starting on Friday morning our horse took stands again just by Mr. Cay's. At this moment Tommy Gignilliat rode up, and Uncle John asked him if he could give us any assistance, as there was no prospect of making our broken-down horse carry us to our journey's end. He very promptly said his brother had a mule at Mrs. Hart's and he would get him for us. In this he failed, but got one of Brother Sam's for us. It so happened our horse soon began to draw very well, but after a while Mr. Dunham's mule began to limp and fail so much we had to use the extra mule in the wagon. Our team was altogether so poor that we did not reach Captain Hughes's until dark—a distance of fifteen miles.

We were most hospitably received and entertained. They inquired most particularly concerning Uncle and yourself, and sent a most cordial invitation to you to stop with them should you take that route. We crossed Jones Creek on a bridge about a mile and a half from Captain Hughes's. Greatly to our disappointment we learned there was no flat at Captain Hughes's and no way of crossing there, so he advised us to go about twenty miles higher up and cross at Tillman's Ferry, where he felt sure there was a good flat and there would be no difficulty.

Accordingly we started on Saturday morning, hoping to reach Mr. Edwards', a good place to pass the night. But owing to our poor teams we did not get farther than Messrs. Hall's, two bachelor brothers about twelve miles off. They entertained us in true bachelor style, welcome to all their house afforded. They had a huge number of Negroes, but everything showed the absence of a lady's hand. Here again we were completely foiled in our plans, as Mr. Hall said he thought it doubtful if we could get a flat at Tillman's, and we might have to wait for it several days, as the ferryman lived across the river. But he said Mr. Edwards knew more about it than he did, so Uncle John wrote a note of inquiry, and he kindly sent it over for us. Mr. Edwards replied we might cross if we could get the wagons into the flat, but he was of the opinion we had better go to Nail's Ferry for safety, thirty-eight miles farther on. Our teams were so poor, and Mr. Hall said there was no prospect of buying forage on either side of the river, so Uncle John concluded to return to Captain Hughes's, as we seemed shut up to the Doctortown route. Mr. Hall fed our mules and oxen abundantly, and would not accept any pay.

We returned to Captain Hughes's on Sabbath evening, feeling it was really an imposition upon their hospitality; but they received us very kindly and seemed as if they could not do enough for us. Captain Hughes gave me a bottle of nice scuppernong wine of his own make, and Mrs. Hughes a bottle of wild honey for our journey. The captain had put up a large quantity of it.

On Monday we commenced our journey again, and were directed by a Mr. Chapman to a ford not far from his house where we could cross Jones Creek on a batteau, and the water there was not so deep as at either of the other fords. When we reached the ford, Uncle John sent Jack ahead on horseback to ascertain the depth. He found it would come into the front of the buggy, but the bottom was hard and free from holes. Uncle John, Ruthie, the baby, and myself went over in the buggy; Charles, Lucy, with my two children, went ahead on the batteau. We had to unload a part of the ox-wagon and take the things in the boat, which occasioned a delay of several hours. The oxen were so worn that they refused to go after traveling a few miles, so we had the prospect of being delayed within four miles of the river.

When within a half mile of the railroad (the point where we expected to dismiss the wagons and take a boat), we were most suddenly brought to a dead halt. Uncle John found to his utter amazement that a branch which was dry when he came was overflowed. A freshet had come down and the water was rising. This was indeed a new development, and bid fair to end our journey just here. Uncle John sent Jack ahead to ascertain the depth, and found it was so deep as to run over the back seat of the buggy, so that it would be impossible to get over dry. The oxen had given out a mile back, so the mules had to be sent back to assist them. There was no alternative: we could not cross, so we made up our minds to camp out.

My kind uncle went to work and soon had a nice little tent constructed and covered with the wagon sheet. The mattress was spread upon some green pine boughs, and the bundle of comforters and blankets opened. The four children and myself slept under the tent, and Uncle John in the buggy. Saving the rolling of the children upon the ground several times during the night, we passed a tolerably comfortable night in front of a regular campfire. My little baby took no cold. She has stood the journey very well.

On Tuesday morning Uncle John thought the water had risen three feet and was still rising, so he took Gilbert and rode to the railroad, hoping to flank this branch. But to his dismay he found it extended to the railroad; and as there was a trestle ahead, there was no way of reaching our destination from that side; so you may imagine our perplexed, puzzled state. At length Uncle John remembered the batteau at Chapman's Ford five miles back, and sent the mules for that.

In the meantime Brother Sam rode up, and soon after Captain Walthour, and in a little while his wagon loaded with furniture. It was a large wagon, and the captain offered to take the children and myself across; so we mounted upon the furniture and fodder and passed over safely, though most of the things in the body of the wagon got thoroughly wet. Brother Sam then brought us over to this place. We came in a small boat across Back Swamp, then walked from there to this place. The walking is heavy a part of the way, but I was agreeably disappointed in the trestles; they are floored, and the walking very good and not dangerous. The water is rising very rapidly—about eight feet in three days. My dear uncle remained on the other side with the servants and baggage in order to move today. It has been raining so hard this morning I fear he will be able to do but very little. (I suppose we had to walk about two miles. The baggage will not be carried so far, as wagons will meet it at the bridge.)

The children have all behaved very well and given as little trouble as could be expected of children of their ages. Your baby has been very good and happy, and walked the greater part of the distance over the railroad yesterday. Charlie and Mamie walked all of it. Ruthie and Charlie were so tired that they have slept all morning. I have borne the journey very well, though I am pretty tired today. I am thankful we have all kept well.

I will not say anything about our movements until Uncle John comes over. There are no letters here for you, and it is impossible to get a newspaper. Colonel Hood's men have been ordered to the next station, and unless they receive further orders will go on to Florida, as the Yankees twenty-two hundred strong are reported to have been moving upon Tallahassee; and it is also reported that they have been repulsed. If the last is true, Colonel Hood's men will not go off. It is reported that we have gained a victory in North Carolina, killing three thousand Yankees and General Kilpatrick. This needs confirmation, though it is said General Early of Virginia attacked in front and Beauregard in the rear. Colonel Hood told me this morning he did not credit Kilpatrick's death. He said the last paper, dated the 4th, states that Kilpatrick's cavalry had met a much larger force than they had anticipated, and had given Charlotte the go-by and were moving towards Wilmington. (Captain Walthour told me Kilpatrick was just such a man in appearance as Uncle Charles Berrien, and had just such a pompous manner.)

My thoughts are with you all the time, my dear mother. I hope we will soon be united again. Do make haste and come out. I feel more anxious than ever about Uncle William and yourself. . . . Nothing of Uncle John yet. The river is rising; I fear he will find it almost impossible to get over. If I hear nothing from him this evening, I will give this to Captain Screven, who is going to Liberty tomorrow; and if your buggy has not already returned, he will go in that. . . . If possible I will get Captain Screven to call and tell you what he knows of the route. The freshet here is a tremendous one, and there is no knowing when the river will be down. It is steadily rising, and I fear Uncle John will be waterbound on the other side of the river. Everything will probably get wet from the heavy rain.

Thursday. Last night was most inclement: tremendous rain accompanied with thunder and lightning. I fear my dear uncle must have suffered very much, for I know it must have been impossible for him to keep dry.

Should you come this way it will be necessary for you to bring some bedding, as nothing but an empty room can be had here. I applied yesterday for rations and am faring pretty well.

Captain Screven thinks of leaving this morning, and I will send this by him, and request Uncle John to add a line indicating the road he thinks best for you to take.

Clarence and Bayard King arrived last night. They were taken to Point Lookout in Maryland, and have been paroled. I saw Clarence.

I hope, my dear mother, you will be supported in your loneliness and that you will soon come out to us. I know how desolate you must feel, but I know the same kind Heavenly Father who has led us all along this dark path will abide with you and with my dear uncle. Ruthie says: "Tell Mama I send a love to her."

I fear you will hear nothing from Mr. Mallard through Zadok, for I hear the black pickets will not allow any Negroes to return. . . . None of the Negroes sent down recently have returned. They are becoming very strict in Savannah.

Mamie and Charlie and Ruthie unite with me in warmest love to Uncle and yourself. Baby Georgia sends sweet kisses to her dear grandmama. One of the soldiers sent her a little milk this morning. Love to all in Flemington and at the Creek. Captain Screven thinks he will not be able to call and see you, as he is now on his way to join his command. Howdy for all the servants. I have Lucy and Elsie with me; the rest are over the river.

Your affectionate daughter,
Mary S. Mallard.

Saturday Morning. The contents of my large yellow trunk are now being brought up thoroughly wet, and I fear many things entirely ruined—a beggarly account of my bonnet, and the children's hats all went under the water. I do not know the condition of the other trunks, as they have not been brought up yet. They did not fall in the water, so I hope things are not all ruined. Am I not unfortunate!

Uncle John tells me he has written you of all that happened at the river. He thinks this route altogether impracticable for you, and thinks it will be best for you either to come by Nail's Ferry or by Barrington. If you come through the country, then go by Taylor's Creek and from there to Mr. Henry Edwards' and from there to Nail's Ferry. Mr. Fennell has a map of Georgia, and you can trace the route upon that. If you wish to strike this railroad, then send Gilbert to Barrington and ascertain whether the waters are low. There is a good flat there and ferryman, and it is not very far to No. 7; and we understand the cars will be running to that station for some time to come. It is a great undertaking by whatever route you may choose. The embankment here is washing away so rapidly that it is almost impossible to come this way.

I have lost my box of candles, the children's tin tub, and some smaller articles.

Gilbert has come for the letter, so I must close. The children all speak of you daily, and send their best love and kisses. The servants are all well. Good-bye, dear Mother.

Your loving daughter,
Mary S. Mallard.

MRS. MARY S. MALLARD *to* MRS. MARY JONES[t]

No. 7, Albany & Gulf Railroad, *Wednesday,* March 15th, 1865
My dearest Mother,

We left Doctortown yesterday morning in the government wagons (two for the baggage and one for the family), and reached this station in the evening, having traveled about eighteen or twenty miles. We were very fortunate in getting these wagons, for if we had hired them, they would have cost us about two hundred dollars. Colonel Hood was not at Doctortown when we came away, but he had left directions that Uncle John should be furnished with transportation whenever he needed it, so we are indebted to him for it. To our great joy we saw the cars coming down this afternoon, and they are here tonight and expect to return in the morning; so we hope to be off by seven o'clock, and trust we will meet with no further detention.

We have been delayed a long time in our journey, but the causes have all been providential, and I trust we have not been impatient. We have all been blessed with health. The servants have stood the journey remarkably well. Mom Patience has walked all the way, and I have been surprised to see her bear the fatigue so well.

We are staying with a Mrs. Pettigrew, who has furnished us house room, and we do our own cooking. We managed in the same way at Doctortown. Should you come here, you might make the same arrangement, as it is a great saving of expense. This house is very open: large cracks in the floor and no sashes to the windows; but the fireplace is most ample, and lightwood abounds. It is so mild I do not think the children will suffer at all. My little baby continues bright and well, developing every day.

I heard through Tommy Gignilliat that Zadok had returned. Please let me know if possible whether he took my letter to Mr. Mallard; and send a copy of any letter he may have written. A servant of Uncle Banky's will take this to you; and if he returns before you come out, he might bring letters and mail them in Thomasville.

I wrote you from Doctortown telling you of my dreadful loss of silver. Perhaps you may not receive that letter, so I will repeat that portion of it. The silver trunk was one that went under the water, and when I opened it to have it dried, I missed all of my teaspoons (twenty-two in number), my gilt-lined gravy ladle, pickle knife and spoon, mustard spoon, and napkin ring. Did you have any teaspoons in your box? If so, they are all gone; not a teaspoon in the trunk. All of your dessert spoons are safe. The tacks in the hasp of the trunk looked as if they had been drawn, as they were so loose that Uncle John took some of them out with his fingers. He thinks the things were taken by one of the ferrymen (a soldier); for the trunk was alone with them an hour or two, and one of the men deserted the night after. Five deserted, and it is thought some of them made their way to the Yankees. It is bad enough to lose the silver, but worse to think of its being carried into Yankeeland! My bonnets went under and are pretty much ruined, and I have lost the box of candles in the same way. So you see, my losses have been very heavy. I cannot think that any of these articles were left out in packing the silver, though I would be glad if you would look into the teapot I left. And possibly these things may have been abstracted before we left, though I do not think this at all probable. Uncle John submitted the whole affair to Major Camp, and he promised to use every effort for their recovery.

I forgot to bring my woolen yarn. If you can find a place for it, please bring it.

Notwithstanding our many detentions, we have met with a great deal of kindness during our journey, and have been much blessed. If all are able to go through to Thomasville tomorrow, we will leave next morning. Uncle John will be just in time to fill his appointment in Mitchell County. I shall probably be obliged to go directly on, owing to the difficulty of procuring forage, and will reach Baker on Sabbath evening.

Tomorrow will dawn upon us filled with sad memories. How I wish, dear Mother, we could go together and spend the day by that sacred spot where sleeps our precious dead! Perhaps you may have this privilege, but I can be with you only in spirit. Two years have passed away, and oh, how long they have been! . . . Ruthie is quite well, and begged me to write you a letter this morning and say she wanted to kiss you. The children all unite with me in warmest love to Uncle and yourself. Howdy for all the servants.

Your affectionate daughter,
Mary S. Mallard.

I will write you by every opportunity, and will write my brothers as soon as I reach Baker. Good night. Do come soon. We are so anxious about you. You will need some cooking utensils by the way.

MRS. MARY JONES *to* MRS. MARY S. MALLARD[t]

Montevideo, *Wednesday,* March 22nd, 1865*
My beloved Daughter,

God be praised that my dear brother and yourself and the little ones and servants were preserved amid your many perils and exposures! I hope my brother will not suffer from the wettings and sleeping in the night air. I have suffered intense anxiety for you all, and could not hear one reliable word until Bayard came to see me.

To my inexpressible joy your dear brother arrived late Saturday night in his buggy, and Harry on horseback. He would have gone immediately on the next day to your succor, but was so tired from his own exposures he waited until Monday morning. And I had made every preparation for your relief in food, etc., and he left after breakfast, but to his great relief met Charles and Gilbert and George returning with the horse and mules. One ox died, and they were starving, and had to leave the buggy and wagons in the swamp. They were in great peril. Your brother is just starting this morning back with them, hoping to construct a raft and bring them over; for we must leave this country as soon as possible. Every day perils life and animals. God alone knows the end of all this trouble; every day it becomes worse with us. We have abandoned all hope of going as you did, and will try and make our way through the country. If we are foiled, will write whenever we can.

I gave you every piece of silver I have in the world to pack in the trunk, so if my spoons are missing also, they have been stolen. God's sovereignty appears in the minutest events of life. Truly, my child, you have had sorrow upon sorrow.

Zadok came the week after you left and said he had delivered your letter; that dear Robert was well and would be out the following week. Said also he saw *Clarence and Bayard* in Savannah. I was rejoiced to see him, and believed him and gave him a reward for his fidelity. It all turns out a falsehood, and I do not believe he ever went to Savannah. He has since left the place—it is supposed by water—taking two young women with him and a young man, two plows, and a grindstone. I presume he will settle in Bryan.

Your aunt and cousin will start as soon as they can get transportation. Hope we may all go together the last of this week or first of next. I want Joe out of this country. The Lord bless and reward my dear brother for all his kindness to me and mine! Best love to them all, and kisses for my precious little ones. Tell Ruthie "Danna" hopes to see all soon, and she must not forget to pray for her as she promised.

Ever your own mother,
Mary Jones.

In haste. God willing, I will bring an excellent horse and the old mule and my buggy.

MRS. MARY JONES *to* MRS. SUSAN M. CUMMING^t

Montevideo, *Saturday*, March 25th, 1865

My dear Sister,

Joseph went on Wednesday to the Altamaha with Charles, Gilbert, and Andrew. He constructed a raft on Thursday; brought over the buggy and wagons on Friday. Was unable to bring over the oxen on the raft; one had died. Consequently the wagons were left, and he returned with the buggy this afternoon.

His life and time are so precious, and horses so valuable, we have concluded to leave this place on Wednesday of the coming week, stay Wednesday night with Julia on Taylor's Creek, *D.V.* We hope most fervently you will all be able to move at the same time, and that we may be permitted to go together. We will have only our buggies, *and a one-horse cart* to help us with our baggage, provisions, etc., and *six* servants, one of them an infant. This is a very short notice and very limited conveyance, but we can do no better. I cannot even take Mr. Jones's papers that I value above all things. My heart is very sad. But God reigns!

Do let me know your plans. I would rejoice if you could go along now, and we would do all in our power to assist you on the journey. Have heard incidentally that my dear child and brother and the little ones have all arrived safely. With our united and very best love to yourself, Laura, and Mr. Buttolph and the children, believe me

Ever your affectionate sister,
Mary Jones.

MRS. SUSAN M. CUMMING *to* MRS. MARY JONES[t]
Flemington, *Saturday,* April 15th, 1865

My dear Sister,

You can scarce imagine the pleasure your letter gave us. John King met Charles on his return from South Hampton and brought it to us—that is, Mr. Buttolph and myself; for Laura and Susan Mary have been at Julia's since Monday. I feel most thankful that amid the perils and dangers of the way you had progressed so far, and trust you are safely lodged in Cousin John's hospitable mansion ere this, and recovered from the fatigues of the journey, and enjoying the society of the loved ones there.

You will be surprised to hear that our contemplated trip has been postponed, D.V., for six months. Mr. Buttolph's congregation have had a meeting and have proposed to furnish him subsistence, and are so earnest and urgent about it that it seemed to be a plain duty to remain—at least for that length of time—and then see what Providence may determine. In the event of Mr. Buttolph's being compelled to remove, transportation is to be furnished him. We had engaged transportation, and packing commenced, with the intention of leaving on Monday the 17th, and with the understanding that provisions must be carried for sixteen persons and eight horses, leaving very little space for anything else. We expected to go to housekeeping soon after our arrival; consequently were not a little perplexed what we should carry. But I feel that Providence has decided for us, and trust that we may abide safe under the shadow of His wing. And oh, that peace and His blessing may be vouchsafed us ere the time expires! . . .

Andrew came on Wednesday preparatory to our removal. All well, and at work as usual. I hope it will meet with your approval for us to keep Andrew up here; he can go down whenever needed. Augustus is to go on Monday with Mr. Fraser to No. 7 on his way to Southwest Georgia. I overheard him say he was going if it cost him five thousand dollars. Judge Fleming owns his wife, and he has behaved so well that we are under promise that he shall go. Sarey thinks if we stay she will drop a few seeds, and she and Andrew have been busy today planting a little of everything. They are willing to go or willing to stay; their minds are made up at present to stay with us. They have been such comforts and helps to us I hope no temptation will lead them astray.

Now that we are here, remember there is *room* in our *house* and room in our *hearts* for *you* and *yours.* Julia will take every care of the trunks. I saw them in her bedchamber. I have Mary's teapot and sugar bowl. Your bedstead at Arcadia I shall have brought here, and Mr. John Norman has moved up your

543

piano. Mr. Fennell is to look after our affairs; and if I hear or know of anything that I think will make it necessary, and send Mr. Fennell word to that effect, he is to move valuable things here or elsewhere as circumstances may show.

A Mr. Smith has just come here from Savannah, and says Richmond has fallen on the 5th after heavy loss on both sides. Mr. Rahn's son William was killed in North Carolina on the 8th of March. Mr. Grest's Swiss nephew and Mrs. Spencer's son Captain Spencer are dead. Oh, that these days of suffering affliction may be shortened for the elect's sake! . . .

There must have been a most joyful reunion between Mr. Mallard and his dear family. . . . Tell Mary I hoped to be able to bring the little dress for my name-child, but will try and get it to her by a safe hand—perhaps by her father. I feel so sad to think you are all so far from us; but I always felt that I could not go and leave you here, and am glad that Dr. Joseph came and arranged for you. . . . Our children talk very often of their cousins and meeting them in Baker. . . . Brother William seems quite satisfied at Julia's; says he suspects he has come to die with her. . . . Give my warmest love to dear Mary, Mr. Mallard, Cousins Jane and John, Mrs. Dunwody and Mary. Kiss all the little ones for Aunt Susan. Accept of a large share for yourself. And believe me, dear Sister,

Your affectionate sister,
S. M. Cumming.

MRS. MARY JONES *to* COL. WILLIAM MAXWELL*

Refuge, *Saturday,* April 22nd, 1865

My dear Brother,

We left Liberty on the 31st of March and reached the home of my dear brother on the 13th of April, where we received the warmest welcome. But as Robert and myself got out of the buggy everyone exclaimed in disappointment: "Where is Uncle? Where is Cousin William?" When I told them you had changed your mind at the last moment, they were all grieved to hear it. Brother John and Sister Jane had already placed a couch for you in a cool place in the entry. Even the little children felt it. Johnnie and Josie asked why Uncle Maxwell had not come; and the next morning the first question Ruthie asked on waking was: "Is Uncle drowned?" (I suppose she remembered the flood of waters through which they came.)

Much as I regretted your not coming with us at this time, I often rejoiced that you were spared the fatigue and exposure of the journey. We had to camp out several nights, and traveled often from daylight to dark, not making over sixteen or twenty miles. . . . After crossing the river at Nail's Ferry, we struck the railroad at Blackshear. Here my dear son Joseph, with Charles and the wagon, retraced their journey together as far as the Altamaha, when Joe took the road via Mount Vernon to Augusta, and Charles the river road to Liberty. You may be assured Daughter and the children were *rejoiced* to see Robert. She had been informed of his release through a letter from Charles. . . .

On Wednesday of this week we were all thrown into great distress. The Yankees were reported within ten miles of us and advancing with cannon. I thought of your remark: "Mary, I fear you are going into trouble." We have every reason to apprehend their raid through this country now that Columbus is in their hands. And God alone knows what will become of this land if they should desolate it as they did ours. Want and misery of every form must prevail. Corn is now selling here at fifteen and twenty dollars per bushel. The lateness of the season will prevent the hiring of any people, so that I am compelled to keep them here; and while my kind brother will do all in his power for us, his own provision crop last year was very short.

My dear brother, I am deeply concerned for my poor servants, and for the fate of my home, containing everything of value that I have in the world. Do if possible send an occasional message to my people. And say to Mr. Fennell if *there is the least necessity* I wish him to move *my carpets and trunks,* and the *large box* in the closet upstairs, and the box of pictures, and the books, and my bedding, to any point Audley and yourself might think safe. . . . If God spares my life and it is possible, I hope to return early in the fall to Liberty. Do ask Audley to do me the favor of writing me the condition of things at home and on the coast. Have you any soldiers scouting Bryan and Liberty? If you do not find it too great a tax, please send me a line to say how you are. We are expecting daily to hear of Mr. Buttolph's arrival and our dear sister and Laura and the children. *This is a far-off land;* I think a whole continent lies between Liberty and Baker.

Daughter and all the family here unite in warmest love to you and to Julia and every member of her family. Believe me

Ever your affectionate sister,
Mary Jones.

MRS. MARY JONES *to* COL. CHARLES C. JONES, JR.[8]

Refuge, *Tuesday,* April 25th, 1865

My dear Son,

Mrs. Randolph Whitehead called to see us this morning and mentioned that her husband would make an effort to reach Augusta. Through him I trust you will receive this communication. I hope, through the good providence of God, your brother has arrived safely.

We reached my brother's home on Thursday the 13th, where we received the warmest welcome. It was my intention so soon as I was rested from the fatigues of the journey to take your dear child with Susan your servant and proceed immediately on to Augusta, hoping that I would find uninterrupted communication by railroad from Albany to Augusta. The recent developments of the enemy have disappointed these plans, and I will have now patiently to await the turn of coming events. I would be very glad to know your will and wishes about our dear child. I have made every effort for her comfort and safety. *The report* of an armistice for ninety days has reached us; but in this *far-off land* it seems very difficult to obtain any reliable information of the state of the country. We have been in great fear of an inroad upon this section. God in mercy grant us protection and deliverance from such suffering!

I have brought with me twelve servants and Susan. The lateness of the season makes it very difficult if not *impossible* to hire them. *Jack* is the only one I have been able to hire as yet—for twenty-five dollars per month. Corn is now selling for twelve and twenty dollars per bushel, and I will have to purchase provisions for them at that price. Your uncle's provision crop last year was so short that he will not be able to furnish what I will need. In addition will be your sister's servants. But we will try and make some suitable arrangement for them all. We have failed to hire Susan as a weaver. Your uncle has kindly offered the use of a place distant about five miles (if the war continues) that our people might plant; but as we are without mules, plows, or hoes, that would not be practicable. I must depend on hiring.

Your aunt and Mr. Buttolph are expected this week with Laura and the children to make their home in Baker, probably for the war. I am thankful they have a home of their own to come to.

Your dear child said two mornings since: "I dreamed my dear papa had come for me." She speaks constantly of you and of her mama, and sends her sweetest kisses to you both. She is well and happy, and makes the eighth child in this family. They have a merry time. Daughter unites with me in best love to Eva and yourself and to Mrs. Eve. Your Aunt Jane is in *extremely feeble health*. Your uncle desires much love to you both.

Your affectionate mother,
Mary Jones.

Mrs. Caroline S. Jones *to* Mrs. Mary Jones[t]

Augusta, *Sunday,* April 30th, 1865

My dearest Mother,

Finding that Tom Clay is going down to Albany, I think it the most feasible plan for getting a letter to you that has yet offered itself to me, so I hasten to avail myself of it; for I fear the Yankees came between us just in time to intercept our last letter, and you may still be in ignorance of Joe's safe return home. He arrived here just a fortnight ago today, showing great benefit from his visit to you and his various journeyings, forming so desirable a relief from his usual labors and sedentary life. His spirits were lighter, I know, from the moment of being able to make arrangements for reaching you and doing all in his power to aid you in leaving the county. He wrote you the day of his return, and I wrote you twice, I think.

How my heart sank within me when I heard of the successive capture of Selma, Montgomery, and Columbus, fearing it was but a prelude to the devastation of the rich and coveted acres of Southwest Georgia, and that my dear mother and sister might again be called to pass through the trying scenes they have just passed! It was one great consolation among so many painful aspects of the subject that at least fighting and conquest were over for a time.

We are almost paralyzed here by the rapid succession of strange and melancholy incidents that have marked the last few weeks—the sudden collapse of our tried and trusted General Lee and his army, about which, sad as it is, I can feel no mortification, for I know he did all that mortal man could do; then the rumors of peace, so different from the rapturous delight of a *conquered peace* we all looked forward to; then the righteous retribution upon Lincoln. One sweet drop among so much that is painful is that he at least cannot raise his howl of diabolical triumph over us. The rumors of peace-terms negotiations are constantly being repeated, with now and then rumors of armed intervention from abroad, which somebody says is like medical attendance to a man whose throat is cut. It seems to be a very general impression that there is a strong outside pressure and threatened foreign complications which may account first for the armistice and then for these terms of peace of which we hear so often without knowing anything definite. Have we not fallen upon sad, sad times? At least, though, I will take comfort in the thought that you are safe from invasion where you are.

I trust you were well during your long and tedious journey, and that you had a happy reunion with Mary and the children. Tom Clay tells me he met you at some point on the road after the Doctor parted from you. We were rejoiced to receive intelligence of you of that date. How did Uncle William bear the journey? Do give much love to him from both of us. . . .

We are suffering here extreme embarrassment from the derangement of the currency consequent upon the war—or rather peace—news. Days ago Confederate money, according to the *government* gold standard, was 100 to 1. Today gold is 300. We got rid of all of ours speedily, the Doctor investing six months' pay in bacon and flour. You will be grieved to hear that our storeroom was broken into and one-third of our flour and every vestige of bacon we owned in the world stolen from us a few nights ago. It is our first misfortune of the kind, and but that now it is irreparable we should not feel it so much, so many others having suffered much more severely. I have taken the hint and moved what little I had left upstairs into the garret.

If you received my letter written just after Joe's return, you received my thanks for your many kind remembrances by him. For the sugar I was very grateful, having given that up some time since. The children were delighted with the groundnut cake, and Stanhope values his tin plate as if it were silver, and eats from it at every meal. . . . Dear Mother, you are in our thoughts and speech every day and many times a day. I hope the time is not distant when you will come to *this* home of yours. We shall be so glad to see you. I am writing late at night, having just heard of Tom's design of leaving in the morning; so being very limited in time, I am obliged to be very

547

hurried. Give a great deal of love to Mary, Mr. Mallard, and the children. What a shock of pleasure Mr. Mallard's return must have been to Mary! Give much love to Uncle John, Aunt Jane, and Uncle William. With a great deal of love from both of us,

> Most affectionately your daughter,
> Caroline Jones.

XXI

Mrs. Eva B. Jones *to* Mrs. Mary Jones[t]

Augusta, *Tuesday,* June 13th, 1865

Dear Mother,

It is with sad and heavy hearts we mark the dark, crowding events of this most disastrous year. We have seen hope after hope fall blighted and withering about us, until our country is no more—merely a heap of ruins and ashes. A joyless future of probable ignominy, poverty, and want is all that spreads before us, and God alone knowing where any of us will end a life robbed of every blessing and already becoming intolerable. You see, it is with no resigned spirit that *I* yield to the iron yoke our conqueror forges for his fallen and powerless foe. The degradation of a whole country and a proud people is indeed a mighty, an all-enveloping sorrow.

I have uninterruptedly sought forgetfulness, or rather *temporary* relief, from these present griefs in a most earnest application to study. Some fourteen volumes of history have claimed my recent attention. And yet the study of human nature from the earliest epochs affords one little comfort. How vice and wickedness, injustice and every human passion runs riot, flourishes, oftentimes going unpunished to the tomb! And how the little feeble sickly attempts of virtue struggle, and after a brief while fade away, unappreciated and unextolled! The depravity of the human heart is truly wonderful, and the moiety of virtue contained on the historic page truly deplorable. How often have these same sorrows and unmerited punishments that we are now undergoing been visited upon the brave, the deserving, the heroic, and the patient of all ages and in all climes! . . . Virtue, like the violet, modest and unnoted, blossoms in silence and fades softly away; the fragrance it threw on the morning breeze was very sweet and very rare; but the breeze died away, and the memory of the virtuous dies too. I fear you will think I am growing very allegorical, but really "the common course of events" is so out-of-date that it needs a few extra flourishes on everything we do at present to mark this most unnatural era. Had it not been for my dear books, the one comfort as yet unmolested (I do not refer to those we left in Savannah), I am inclined to believe I should have been constrained to apply for a suite of apartments in some lunatic asylum—if they too have not vanished with other national comforts!

Charles, thank Heaven, is very well and just the same immaculate darling he always was, but just now so deeply and exclusively busy at the plantation, earning his daily bread "by the sweat of his brow," that I only am occasionally enchanted with a flying visit. He received a week or two ago a letter from you which we were both rejoiced to receive, and which, by the way, he immediately answered, I enclosing a note. But after having written, some farther developments of Yankee policy being foreshadowed, he waited to see the results, and as he was suddenly called away, left me with directions "not to send the letter." I do not feel at liberty to do so until I hear more from him.

I suppose you have learned even in the more secluded portions of the country that slavery is entirely abolished—a most unprecedented robbery, and most unwise policy. So it must appear even to the ignorant. I know it is only intended for a greater humiliation and loss to *us,* but I should think that even the powerful and unconscientious conqueror would reap the ill effects of so unguarded a movement. However, it *is* done; and we, the *chained witnesses,* can only look on and draw inferences and note occurrences —"only this and nothing more." There has been a great rush of the freedmen from all families in the city and from neighboring plantations. Adeline, Grace, and Polly have all departed in search of freedom, without bidding any of us an affectionate adieu. All of Dr. Joe's servants have left save Titus and Agrippa and children, I think he told me. . . . We have lost many of our servants, but a sufficient number have remained to serve us, and as yet these appear faithful and anxious to please. On our plantation everything is "at sixes and sevens." One day they work, and the next they come to town. Of course no management of them is allowed. Our Yankee masters think that *their* term of slavery having expired, that the shackles they have abandoned, more firmly riveted, will do for us their former owners. And we meekly bow the head, receive chains and insults, and observe a mute and most submissive demeanor. Veritably like lambs we are led to the slaughter, and like sheep before the shearers we are dumb. And they *shear* ahead—in a manner most wonderful to behold.

Very shortly I will, D.V., leave "these scenes so charming" to forget in a summer sojourning among my best-loved friends some of these present miseries. After the annual delight of a Sparta trip I hope to visit some friends in Athens; and from thence I spend the remainder of the summer in the mountain breezes of Clarkesville with my dear aunt. I trust I'll find both health and flesh in the delightful summer retreat of my aunt, for I need both sorely—although I am a little stronger for the past few days, or rather *two days*.

I fear I am quite wearying you with my unusual volubility. My dearest mother unites with me in warm love to yourself and Ruthie. I suppose the little lady is grown entirely beyond one's recollection. Kiss her for me. I know her papa would send a very affectionate one for her were he here. Dismayed at the divers accumulations of great poverty, hopeless and in the depths of an abyss of despair, faintly I reiterate:

Affectionately yours,

Eva.

MRS. MARY JONES *to* MR. CHARLES C. JONES, JR.[8]

Atlanta, *Monday,* June 26th, 1865

My dear Son,

I wrote you on the eve of our departure from Baker, and forwarded the letter by express from Macon. I hope you have received it. As it was necessary for your sister and Robert to precede me, I remained—first with my friend Mrs. Mitchel and then with Mr. and Mrs. Nisbet—until Friday morning, when I came up with our dear little Mary Ruth. *Susan* was with me, and so far as I observed appeared as usual; but the night before I left, when I called for her at bedtime to attend upon the baby, she was missing, and I saw nor heard anything more of her. It was useless to delay my plans or make any inquiries after her, so I came up with Mary Ruth as I had designed doing. I wrote requesting you to meet her here, as I was unable to take her to Augusta myself and then to return immediately. Neither funds nor health would permit.

Your sister and Robert are living in Mrs. Coleman's house fronting McDonough Street. . . . We live in a *very, very* small cottage on the slope of the hill, with a vegetable garden in front. It has two rooms below and two small ones in the roofing. One answers to parlor and dining room; the other they have given to me; and your sister and Robert have the upper rooms. Our furniture is as primitive as possible: not even a bedstead as yet, and a little borrowed bedding.

Robert has just called for my letter, and I must close. Yesterday our precious child entered her fifth year. No doubt you remembered it. Soon after she entered the church she whispered gently: "Danna, are you going to baptize me again today?" God grant to her young heart the true baptism of the Holy Spirit!

I wish we had some sweet comfortable place to invite dear Eva to share this healthful climate with us. (The word *home* has died upon my lips.) I hope it will suit your convenience to come up shortly. Your sister and Robert unite with me in warmest love to Eva and yourself, with sweetest kisses from your child. Our love to your brother and Carrie, and affectionate regards to Mrs. Eve. Mary and Charlie send love to Uncle Charlie and Aunt Eva.

Your affectionate mother,
Mary Jones.

MRS. EVA B. JONES *to* MRS. MARY JONES[t]

Augusta, *Tuesday,* June 27th, 1865

Your last letter to Charlie, dear Mother, reached here some few days after I had written you quite an epistle, and while he was still at Indianola. He had been hard *at work* while there, his hands hard and burnt like a common laborer's. Yet he scarcely had a breathing space before, mounting cotton bales in a wagon, he started down to Savannah to try and make a little money, which article he is totally without and greatly in need of. He begged I would write you immediately and let you know the urgency of the case and say he would try if *possible* to get out to Montevideo. The reason of this great haste was, he had invested some of his Confederate money in two bales of domestics; and hearing he could get ten cents advance on the price here in Savannah—or rather, the market being overstocked here with that sort of goods and there being a dearth of them in Savannah—he, fearing a tumble in the price in that market so soon as these flatboats now building commence to carry freight, wisely seized this probably *best* opportunity, and is now on his way to Savannah in a most primitive style.

Of course you know there is no way for him, or anybody else scarcely, to make money now. He will not be allowed to practice his profession until he is permitted to take the oath. His wheat crop has utterly failed, and we are all as poor as church mice. The Negroes at Indianola wanted to give a little trouble during his last visit, but he soon straightened them up, and now they are behaving very well. We here have been most unfortunate, for being so near to the city, our Negroes are under all the baleful influences of the vile abolitionists (of which the worst specimens are in our midst); and they (the Negroes) work or not just as it best suits their convenience and pleasure. We have only a third-crop planted (that not worked); and our most promising fields are now under water.

Besides this, the Negroes and Yankees have broken into our smokehouse and swept it of *every piece* of meat. Not content with this great and to us terrible robbery, they have even entered with false keys our storeroom here, and have not left us a single ham. So we are now dependent on the market, and have to purchase every bit of meat we eat. Constant depredations are being made on the place, and we can obtain no *redress,* and are entirely at the mercy of the merciless.

I grow so wearied with all these troubles that I long so for the quiet of the up country, where I trust before long to be. I will now wait until my cousin, Miss Casey, is strong enough to accompany me. She has been dangerously ill with typhoid fever, which is spreading all over the city. I have heard that the Yankee surgeon mentioned a few days since a case of black vomit, which sounds something like yellow fever. Indeed, I should be surprised at nothing, for the city is kept fearfully filthy, and the cellars (many of them) continue filling with water from the springs in them caused by last month's great freshet.

Charlie will go to Atlanta so soon as he returns from Savannah. Another great reason for his going so immediately was that a friend had written us if he would go down *directly* he might be able to save *some* of his furniture, which was a great consideration to people who have now to earn their daily bread. It is pitiable the state in which we all find ourselves.

I saw the Doctor yesterday; he said Carrie and the children were quite well. All of their servants but Titus left them.

Do give my warm love to Mr. and Mrs. Mallard and the children. I trust they are all quite well. I know the pleasant climate of Atlanta will invigorate you all. Mother sends kind remembrances. We both send a warm kiss to Ruthie. I saw her aunt, Philo Neely, the other day. She came up for some *new things,* having just received from her father-in-law forty thousand greenbacks. But tell Ruthie she did not remember her, I fear.

Affectionately yours,
Eva.

I directed my last letter to Atlanta. I think it, however, reached that city before you did.

Have you taken the oath yet?

MRS. MARY JONES *to* MR. CHARLES C. JONES, JR.[8]

Atlanta, Sunday, July 9th, 1865

My dear Son,

A gentleman going directly to Augusta informs me that he will take this letter to you and see that it is safely delivered. I have written you three times since I left Baker and twice since my arrival here two weeks since, informing you and asking you to meet your precious child here, as it was not in my power to bring her to Augusta. I have not received an answer to either, and feel convinced they never reached you. One was by express and directed to Mrs. William J. Eve; the other two by mail.

Knowing through your last letter your great desire to have Ruthie with you, and fearing also to expose her longer to the climate of Baker, I left my dear brother's for the purpose of bringing her thus far to you. She will be a precious little comforter to Eva and yourself in these dark days of sorrow. I would bring her to you, but I have not the means to go to Augusta and return here, where I expect to remain until fall if I am then able to go to Liberty. *Of my present situation or future plans I will not now speak, hoping to see you as soon as is convenient for you to come to Atlanta.* I wish your sister was so situated that she could invite dear Eva to accompany you; but we are with the most limited accommodations, and in the smallest house you could well imagine. Robert's church was untouched, and the congregation fast filling up.

I have not received a line from your brother since we parted on the railroad. I know he has written. Have received one letter from Carrie and yours with a note from Eva.

Robert and your sister unite with me in much love to Eva and yourself, and to your brother and Carrie. Your precious child says: "Tell Papa and Mama I send my love, and kisses too." She grows daily more lovely and interesting. God bless you, my son, with the comforts of a true and living faith!

Ever your affectionate mother,
Mary Jones.

Augusta, *Friday,* July 14th, 1865

How very much have I been surprised, my dear mother, to learn that so few of our letters to you have been received! I have within the last three weeks written you two long letters.

In the last I told you of Charlie's going to Savannah in order to make a little money before leaving for Atlanta; for of funds we *too* were utterly *destitute.* He went down in a most primitive style, mounted upon some bales of cotton, of which our estate owned *six*—a mere pittance. But we were glad to have even that forlorn quantity. Charlie returned from Savannah on yesterday, and left this morning for his plantation to attend some urgent business. He will return very soon in order to go to Atlanta. I suppose he will leave the first of next week. I assure you he would have gone to see you and get Ruthie two weeks since but that we have *not* a *greenback.* And strange to say, the Yankees won't take our Confederate money!

Well, we are all down here as poor as poverty can make us. Besides the freeing of our Negroes (which deprives us of the greater part of our property, of course), the Yankees and Negroes together have stolen every piece of meat we had (about one hundred and seventy pieces), and we have not a *ham* even left. Then a variety of mules, sheep, and hogs; so altogether we are in a forlorn condition. I expect before long to become a very efficient chambermaid and seamstress, though the latter comes very hard to my poor unused fingers. Our ménage has been frightfully reduced; and of our numerous throng there remains a seamstress (who has had to lay aside her old calling to become cook, washer, and chambermaid) and one who attends to everything else about this unfortunate establishment. Adeline, Grace, and Polly were the first to assume freedom. To crown my misfortunes, which persistently attack me from all sides, Charlie and I had been laying aside carefully every few cents of specie that we could gather; and most tenderly did I keep it locked and laid away. To no one would I breathe of my few gold and silver dollars, when what was my surprise and despair the other day to find that my wardrobe had been *entered with a false key* and my forty-three dollars in specie gone—vanished, abstracted!

> 'Twas ever thus from childhood's hour:
> I've seen my fondest hopes decay.

One of our freedwomen expects shortly to enter the holy estate of matrimony, and has therefore indulged in some extravagancies and petty fineries. The question arises: Whence came the "filthy lucre" to purchase these indulgences? And my empty wardrobe echoes emphatically: *"Where?"*

Charlie will soon be with you and tell you all the news of Augusta and Savannah; also Indianola. I have been expecting to go up the country this whole summer, and my friends have been writing constantly for me; but I fear my recent loss will preclude my traveling to any extent. . . . I have some pretty little dresses for Ruthie, but will send nothing I have for her, as you say Charlie will bring her back with him, and it will be merely giving you additional trouble and take up more room in her trunk. I will try to get a servant to attend her, but I suppose as she is growing so fast I will *almost* be able to attend her myself.

Your letters coming this way have been more fortunate in reaching their destination than ours. Both of my last had Yankee stamps and were put in the post office. I saw Dr. Joe this morning; he told me he would try to find some reliable person who would see that you received this.

Charlie never looked better than he does now, and is if anything more adorable than ever. I fear I have spoiled him a little bit, though for *my life* I can't see that I have! We are both going to hard work and try to gain a livelihood some way.

My poor brother Edgeworth feels his glory departed, and lays aside the captaincy with a sigh as he opens an up-country store. He goes bravely to work, and says he'll gain an honest livelihood; and many of his best friends here are delighted with his independence and energy. But these times try men's souls—and women's too! . . .

Augusta is very unhealthy just now; there is a great deal of typhoid fever here. . . . Sallie Casey came quite near leaving this terrestrial a few weeks since; she had merely come down on a visit. . . . There were twelve Negroes interred yesterday; the city is crowded with them.

Do give my warm love to Mr. and Mrs. Mallard and the children. My mother sends her kind regards to all of you. With love for yourself and Ruthie,

Affectionately yours,
Eva.

MR. CHARLES C. JONES, JR., *to* MRS. MARY JONES[t]
Augusta, Friday, July 28th, 1865

My very dear Mother,

Daughter and myself safely reached Augusta yesterday afternoon at six o'clock. Eva met us at the depot. We had a long and hot ride, but Mary Ruth is as bright as a new little button this morning after a long and refreshing night's sleep.

This morning at one o'clock Sister Carrie again became a mother: a fine little boy whom they call Charles Colcock Jones after our beloved and honored father. The Doctor is in the best of humors, and both mother and child are doing, I learn, very well. Your kind remembrance came just in time, and for it all are very grateful. The Doctor thinks that the birth of this little stranger was hastened by Carrie's fall from the buggy, of which I told you. The little ones are both well.

Mrs. Eve has been sued by three of her house servants for wages—a most unwarrantable procedure. The truth is that unless something is done here, great annoyance will occur. We will all have to recognize the fact at once that our former slaves have been set free, that we have no further legal claim upon their services, and that if they continue with us we must pay for services rendered. The amount of the compensation will of course depend upon each particular case. I am just writing Mr. Fennell a full letter on the subject.

Eva returns her sincere thanks for your beautiful present, and unites with me in warmest love. Little Daughter sends her sweetest kisses for her dear "danna," to whom, under God, she owes everything, and to whom we can never be sufficiently grateful all our lives. Mrs. Eve desires kindest remembrances. She still suffers much from her cough. I trust, my dear mother, that you may be preserved from many annoyances during this distressing period, and that God will richly endow you of His great grace. Give our best love to Sister, Robert, and the little ones. Do, my dear mother, let me know whenever and in what way I can serve you. As ever,

Your affectionate son,

Charles C. Jones, Jr.

I send a few postage stamps.

MRS. MARY JONES *to* MR. CHARLES C. JONES, JR.[8]

Atlanta, *Thursday,* August 10th, 1865

My dear Son,

Yours of the 28th July did not reach me until the 3rd inst., and confirmed the happy announcement which had been previously made by Mrs. Smith and Miss Cumming of the birth of another son to your brother and sister Carrie. I feel truly grateful to God for this renewed mercy to my children, and have a peculiar love and drawing to my little grandson who is to bear the sacred and honored name of his grandfather. . . . Nothing but the state of my own health prevented my being with them.

For some time I have been conscious of a general failure, and since you were here have had two attacks of fever which confined me to bed. Robert, without my knowledge, brought Dr. Logan to see me, and I am now under his treatment. I am better, but feeble; hope there will be no return of fever. There has been recently a terrible *night atmosphere* around us, owing in part to proximity to camps and an enclosure with hundreds of condemned horses. And there is that universal pressure upon head and heart which all must feel.

I rejoiced to know that you arrived safely with my precious little Ruth. Tell her "Danna" misses her by day and by night, and is constantly listening for her sweet voice and her little step; and when she was sick she wanted her baby to rub her head and bring her a cup of cold water as she used to do. I trust she is well, and I doubt not very happy. No one can ever know what that child has been to me; but I wish her also to know and love her own dear father and her affectionate mama. I repeat what I have already said: she will be welcome to share the last morsel her "danna" has. Do, if Eva is not able to carry out her plans of going into the country, and you find she is likely to suffer from the change to Augusta—do let her return immediately to me here.

If able, I will try to visit Augusta before I return to Liberty. I want to see all my dear ones there, and if practicable would like to go to Indianola and see the people. I want to know their feelings. We have had a conversation with those of our household; *they are all expecting to return to their old home.* Tell Tom Daughter and I were very much pleased with the slippers, and I hope to see him before long. If an arrangement can be made for getting the leather, I will be glad if you will direct Tom to make for me eighteen or twenty pairs of plantation shoes. The people below are in great want. I sent nearly all I had made last year up to Indianola. If the piece of *calfskin* is suitable, he can make me a pair of walking gaiters. Do you think, my son, there is any prospect of recovering those hides put into the steam tannery at Savannah? The bull's hide was superior; I am entirely without a harness, and if it can be recovered, will use it for that purpose. Please tell all the people howdy for me, and that I want to see them all, and that we will try and do all in our power for them. Do let me know whenever you hear from below. When will Stepney return? . . .

Your sister's babe is better. She and Robert join me in much love to Eva and yourself. The children send kisses, and say Little Sister must come back soon. Many, many kisses for my darling child. And she must write and tell me what she is doing, and if she wants to see her "danna." I had a package prepared to send her by Mr. Cumming, but he did not call as he promised. My kind regards to Mrs. Eve. The Lord bless and save you, my son!

Your affectionate mother,
Mary Jones.

MRS. MARY JONES *to* MR. CHARLES C. JONES, JR.[8]

Atlanta, *Friday,* August 18th, 1865

My dear Son,

Your last letter was not received until yesterday. It had evidently been *torn* open either in this or the office in Augusta. This, I am told, is now frequently done to ascertain the sentiments of the people, so we will have to use great prudence. Alas, for our humiliated and degraded condition!

Robert has taken the oath; and as I have several interests to represent, would it not be well for me to do so at once before I go to the low country, where I may not have the opportunity of doing so, and yet might be put to some trouble about our landed property there if there should be any attempt at confiscation? Do write me about this if you can get a reliable *private* opportunity of doing so. I am suspicious of all communications *by mail.*

I have made a written contract with Flora to remain with me until the end of the year, and your sister and Robert have made contracts with their servants. They *all* design returning to Liberty, but will wait until the railroad to Savannah is finished. I am distressed at the thought of Lucy's leaving, for I fear your sister and her little children will miss her sadly. I would do anything in my power to retain her, but your sister thinks if she stays against her will she would be worse than useless. Tenah and her increasing family would be a burden in town. I mean to inform them plainly if they come below it must be to labor and be subject to control, either at Montevideo or Arcadia. I think they have an idea of possession. With regard to cultivating Montevideo, I will be compelled to increase the force there to do so successfully; and if I can do so from those who have lived there and are now at Indianola, I would prefer it to strangers. But of this we can arrange when you come down. Do write me what report Stepney brings when he returns.

I am anxious to visit the people at Indianola, but the time is drawing near for my return, *D.V.*, to Baker, which I hope to do the last of September or first of October. I cannot obtain any information of either the Central or Albany & Gulf Roads. Are they rebuilding? And when will they be in operation?

I wrote Eva and yourself letters last week, which I hope have reached you. I now send two worked flannels for my little darling. Do get them to her as soon as you can, for she will need them in early fall. I have been unable to get any flannel here; would like to have sent her four instead of two. My heart aches to see my precious child. . . . Kiss her again and again for "Danna," and tell her I will write her a letter for herself; and Bubber and Sissy and little Baby send kisses to her. Daughter and Robert unite with me in best love to Eva and yourself. Our kind regards to Mrs. Eve. . . . I have had no fever this week, and feel better under Dr. Logan's treatment.

Ever your affectionate mother,
Mary Jones.

MR. CHARLES C. JONES, JR., *to* MRS. MARY JONES[t]
Augusta, *Saturday,* September 2nd, 1865
My very dear Mother,

I am just in receipt of your kind letter of the 18th ult. and of the package for little Ruthie, for both of which please accept warmest thanks. I am rejoiced to know that you are feeling so much better, and I pray God that you may be speedily restored to perfect health.

I have been for a week past under the weather, but I am, thank God, better now. Returned only today from Indianola, where I have been for more than two weeks past trying to harvest the crop of provisions. Very little is done there when I am away, and even while I am there. No one hurts himself by hard work. People all well. Harriet and Miley both lost their infants. All the people are, I think, very anxious to return to Liberty in the fall. As yet I have not conversed generally with them on the subject. Now that they are all free, there are several of them not worth the hiring. Please name, Mother, which of them you wish at Montevideo, and I will try and get them for you. I would have gone to Montevideo before, but I have not been strong enough to undertake the journey.

You had better take the oath at once. You do not come under any of the excepted classes, and it is well as a matter of precaution that you pursue this course.

Stepney says all are well at Montevideo and at Arcadia, and that the crop looks very well. Mr. Fennell writes me that the Negroes are doing very little work.

The Central Railroad is completed to the forty-five-mile station, and I understand that they hope to have the Albany & Gulf Railroad in running order by the 1st October. In consequence of the fact, however, that no dependence can be reposed in the consecutive labor of the hands employed in the reconstruction, no definite time can be assigned for the completion.

Daughter and Eva are still in Sparta. Both quite well. I do not expect them back for two weeks. Eva writes me under date of the 27th enclosing warmest love from herself and Ruthie for you. Brother better. His family quite well. Mrs. Eve desires her special remembrance. I have failed thus far in securing a house in Savannah. Every place crowded. Do, my dear mother, let me know in what I can assist you. With warmest love for yourself, Sister, Robert, and little ones, I am, as ever,

Your affectionate son,
C.

Mrs. Mary Jones *to* Mr. Charles C. Jones, Jr.[8]
Atlanta, *Wednesday*, September 6th, 1865
My dear Son,

Evening before the last I asked Robert to walk with me to the graveyard; I wanted to find the grave of your friend General Helm, which was pointed out to us by the old sexton, who bears the significant name of *Pilgrim*. He is buried on the slope of the hill, and his grave marked by a marble head- and footpiece with this inscription:

Ben Hardin Helm
of Kentucky
Fell at Chickamauga
September 20th, 1863
aged 32 years.
He giveth His beloved sleep.

The hand of affection had evidently planted some flowers around the cherished spot, and a long-withered bunch of buds and evergreens lay decaying upon the grave, now overrun with wild vines. I had carried a beautiful bunch of flowers with me, and in his mother's name I laid it on his grave, and brought away a little sprig which I would like to send her if I had the heart to write her. How much I thought of poor George and the pleasant visit he made us on the Island, and the desolating changes that have passed over hearts and homes since then! Whilst my tears were falling upon the grave of the hero, I could not but remember the goodness and mercy of the Lord in sparing the lives of my two sons. Not far off in innumerable graves lay the remains of our noble and unrecorded dead, grown over by rank forest weeds: no name, no date, no place in history, no memorial but the undying love and remembrance of bereaved hearts.

My dear son, your sister has been quite sick for two weeks with severe neuralgic pains in head and back; has now two blisters, which have afforded relief, and just submitted to the extraction of four jaw teeth, and is much better today. I have been of course occupied with the little ones, and but little time for replying earlier to your last favor.

I hope dear Eva and my own little Ruth will enjoy the visit to Sparta. No tongue can tell how much I want to see my child. The children talk every day of her, and love her as a sister.

I expect, *D.V.*, to leave Atlanta on Monday the 2nd of October via Macon for Cuthbert, where I hope your Uncle John will send the buggy to meet me. After remaining a few days in Baker, or until suitable arrangements can be made, I will return to Liberty with those of our people who wish to go back. I hope the road will be in a condition for me to go from Thomasville to No. 3, but I can hear nothing of it. I could not undertake to go overland in a buggy for any consideration, but wish to carry the horse and buggy back on the railroad, and hope to get transportation for the Negroes. How I am to accomplish *all this alone I cannot now see;* but such is my plan. Flora and Milton will return with me from this place. I hope you will be able to meet me at Montevideo as you proposed doing, and organize some plan for the future. I have no home but that, and no means of support but what must come from planting; but my heart sinks at the thought of such an undertaking by myself and under such distressing circumstances.

Through Mr. Barnard I learn that large numbers of Negroes have returned to the county—six hundred, it is said, already; and that, *instigated* by *Cato,* the people at Montevideo had behaved in such a way that Mr. Fennell had been forced to call in the Yankees. They were doing better, and the corn crop was promising. Cato has been to me a most insolent, indolent, and dishonest man; I have not a shadow of confidence in him, and will not wish to retain him on the place. If I am to live there, I would like to have Stepney with me, if he wishes to do so, and a few others of my former servants: Sam and his wife and Hannah; if Patience remains, and Porter, I suppose they will want their children; and I would like to have Peggy with me, and William, and Tom if he will be obedient and industrious. But I feel that I cannot make any arrangements until we meet at Montevideo and see what is best to be done for the interest of all concerned. I must employ those who will be useful, but would prefer those I have known, provided they will be faithful.

I wrote General Wilson, and through General *Wild* he replied that as soon as the *bureau* was opened in Atlanta he thought I would have no difficulty in getting transportation. It has not yet been opened. About mules and horses he referred me to the quartermaster at Atlanta. How would it do for me to apply in Savannah? This place is too far off; I have made no application, as it would be useless.

Should you determine to return to Savannah, I hope it will be in my power to aid you in some articles for housekeeping. . . . Do write me very soon and tell me all you know of the Albany & Gulf Road. Your sister and Robert unite with me in best love to Eva and yourself and my dear baby. Howdy for the servants, and respects to Mr. and Mrs. Sconyers.

Your affectionate mother,
Mary Jones.

MRS. MARY JONES *to* HON. DANIEL PITTMAN[t]
Atlanta, Friday, September 8th, 1865

I do solemnly swear or affirm, in the presence of Almighty God, that I will henceforth faithfully support, protect, and defend the Constitution of the United States and the union of the states thereunder, and that I will in like manner abide by and faithfully support all laws and proclamations which have been made during the existing rebellion with reference to the emancipation of slaves. So help me God.

Mary Jones.

Sworn to and subscribed before me at Atlanta this 8th day of September 1865.

Daniel Pittman, Ordinary,
Fulton County, Georgia.

MRS. MARY JONES *to* MRS. CAROLINE S. JONES[8]
Atlanta, Tuesday, October 3rd, 1865

My dear Daughter,

I am in distress and perplexity, and write to ask your help. The authorities here promised me transportation for the freedmen who wish to go from this to Savannah. Now, on the eve of leaving, they inform us that it can only be obtained through the bureau in Augusta. Will you be kind enough to obtain from General Tilson the necessary papers for me? These people are really in distressing circumstances. They are without means, and wish to return home where they can obtain an honest livelihood.

Robert leaves for Americus in the morning, and Daughter is anxious for me to stay until he returns on next Tuesday. And as I have not heard a word from Charles, and not yet obtained transportation for the freedmen, I have concluded, my dear daughter, not to be with you until Wednesday of next week, the 11th inst. . . . Do drop me a line, and do your best to get the transportation and forward it to me immediately. Daughter unites with me in best love. Do let Charles know that I will not be in Augusta until Wednesday the 11th.

Ever your affectionate mother,
Mary Jones.

In haste. As I am myself a needy refugee, could you not get transportation for *myself* as well as the freedmen?

MRS. MARY JONES *to* MRS. MARY S. MALLARD[t]

Savannah, *Monday,* October 16th, 1865

My beloved Child,

Through the goodness of God your brother Charles and myself arrived safely here on last Saturday night, and I am with our dear friends Mr. and Mrs. Axson. Mr. Axson expects to attend Synod, and it gives me an opportunity of writing you. Carrie promised she would write for me from Augusta.

In consequence of cars off the track I did not arrive at Augusta until between ten and eleven o'clock at night. Charles had waited at the depot until nine; was taken with a chill and had to leave. But Titus was there to meet me, and I found Carrie with a bright fire and hot cup of tea and a most warm welcome. She and the dear children are looking better than I ever saw them, and Charles Colcock Jones, Jr., is a precious boy—fat and amiable: the best baby, she says, they ever had. She has heard but once from Joe since he reached Washington, and nothing of the trial yet.

Charles and I and the freedmen left Augusta Friday night at seven o'clock. Soon as we reached the Waynesboro depot, the rain came down in torrents and continued until we got to Waynesboro, where we took hacks twelve o'clock at night and rode until one o'clock the next day—a distance, I think, of fifty-five miles—when we took the car again. This was a car with a wooden seat running on two sides: no cushions and very rough. To transport our *baggage alone* cost thirty-seven dollars from Augusta to Savannah, and fifteen dollars apiece for passage money. Charles had to dispose of some of his Southwestern Railroad stock to enable me to get down. Flora and Milton had transportation for themselves but not their baggage. If the river had been up we would have taken the boats. We will go out to Liberty as soon as we can get a conveyance. . . .

Do thank Mrs. Hull for the delightful rolls; I ate nothing else coming down. And tell my dear cousin Joe's little children were delighted with her wafers. And your bountiful supply was shared with General Hardee and his daughter, who were our traveling companions from Augusta to Savannah. The railroad will not be finished probably before January. . . .

Tuesday. Last night, to my surprise, Dunwody came in and reported all well when he left. I was rejoiced to hear from my dear brother and family. Patience and Porter still in Baker. Dunwody brought on the buggy and horse.

We are hoping to get transportation in a U.S. wagon to Liberty. If so, will try on its return to send in your bale of bedding and Robert's box of books as far as Savannah. Dr. Howard offers to give them house room; and at any time that you order them up, he will forward them to you. He says the river will not rise before January, and by that time the Central Railroad via Augusta will be finished. As it will cost you nothing to get these things to Savannah, it bethought me a good plan for helping to get them thus far on the way to Atlanta. Dr. and Mrs. Howard live in Jones Street between Whitaker and Barnard. He intends moving to Atlanta another year, and says as Robert is to be his pastor, he must take care of your things.

Reports from Liberty are very dreadful. I can only go and see for myself; and if I am endangered by staying, I must seek a home elsewhere. . . . Oh, how I shall miss you all! Sometimes that dreadful loneliness seems more than I can bear. . . . Your letters to me had best come directed to Rev. I. S. K. Axson, D.D., *for Mrs. C. C. Jones,* until we get a mail to Liberty. . . . Kiss my precious children over and over for me. And the best of love for yourself and Robert, with grateful recollections of all your love and kindness. . . . Do write me all about yourself and the children, and take care of your health.

Ever, my dear daughter, your affectionate mother,
Mary Jones.

Mrs. Mary Jones *to* Rev. R. Q. Mallard[t]
Savannah, *Tuesday,* October 17th, 1865

My dear Son Robert,

Dr. Axson and Charles and all with whom I have conversed think the *History* ought not, and probably cannot, be printed under four dollars per volume: eight dollars for the two volumes. *So please fix the price at that rate. If printed otherwise, you could take your pen and alter the circulars before they are distributed, making four dollars per volume, eight dollars for the two.* I must trouble you to distribute the circulars, if ready, both at Synod and the assembly if you are there. If you fail to go, perhaps some friend would interest themselves to do so. I would be glad to receive some of them, but shall be so isolated it will not be possible for me to do much. Do keep an account of any expense you may be at, and I will see that you are refunded.

If you see or hear from Joseph, do let him know that Mr. Rogers has kindly offered to furnish the paper for the first edition, and wishes to know how large it will be and when required, that he may order the paper. I have written Joseph on the subject, but fear he may not have received it. . . .

Ever your affectionate mother,
Mary Jones.

Mrs. Mary Jones *to* Mrs. Mary S. Mallard[t]
Montevideo, *Wednesday*, October 25th, 1865

My dearest Daughter,

After many days' delay in waiting for transportation your brother succeeded in getting a carriage and wagon, and we reached home on the evening of the 20th. The road was exceedingly rough. We expected the buggy to meet us at the courthouse, but Gilbert did not get the message in time, so we had to take the carriage all the way.

We stopped at Midway and stayed as long as we possibly could. I felt grateful that I was permitted once more to kneel by that precious grave. Everything within was untouched, only much overgrown with weeds and bushes. But it was distressing to see the condition of the church: doors and windows open, shutters off; and the sheep had evidently taken shelter in the aisles. Every house around the church was destroyed.

We reached home about dusk, and found the servants apparently glad to see us. But Mr. Fennell soon informed us that freedom had done its work here as elsewhere. We found George, July, and young Gilbert had left for the Albany & Gulf Railroad; and Jack, who had just arrived a day or two before, had left for Savannah in company with Dick and Anthony from Indianola. Mr. Fennell reports not one-fourth work done in months, and a system of stealing here and at Arcadia regularly carried on. At Arcadia the whole of the cotton had been stolen, and all from here, although we had scarcely any.

I wrote you that I would send in the bedding and books; but as we failed to get a U.S. wagon, I was unable to do so, but sent by return of the small wagon which brought our baggage two mattresses and one feather bed. I did not send pillows and bolster, as the bundle was large, and I knew you could do without them.

Charles begs me to say to Lucy he sends best love to her, and wants to see her, and will come up as soon as the way is open and he has the means. At the present rates and mode of conveyance it is very difficult and very expensive to get along. It cost me over one hundred dollars to get out here, and had also transportation for the servants. You have no idea how expensive traveling is. Your brother has advanced me the means, or I could not get along.

I find everything in good preservation here, but a great deal to put to rights. Do not know when Patience and Porter will come. Sue, Flora, and Milton compose my household. We have not yet made any arrangements for another year. I hope you insist on Niger's paying for his room. I am not at all anxious to have him or his family, but if they come and will attend to their work, I will do the best I can by them. If not, they will find no home either here or at Arcadia.

Charles will see about renting Arcadia when he returns from Savannah. He goes in tomorrow, D.V., to meet Mr. Ward and determine his future arrangements. . . .

As usual, I write in haste. It is after twelve o'clock at night, and I must close. Will write our beloved relatives as soon as I have seen a few friends and heard the news. Give my warmest love to them. Best love for yourself and Robert, and many kisses for my dear grandchildren.

Your affectionate mother,
Mary Jones.

MRS. MARY JONES *to* MRS. MARY S. MALLARD^c

Montevideo, *Tuesday,* November 7th, 1865

My dear Daughter,

Hearing that Mrs. Winn would go to Savannah day after tomorrow, I embrace the opportunity of sending you a line. We have still no mails, and I have not had a line from you since I left Atlanta. Have written you several times. Robert's kind favor from Augusta has just reached me, but not the circulars, or the letter with information of my brother. I have been exceedingly anxious to hear from him and to know if I may expect Porter and Patience.

The past has been quite a week of trial. *Sam* (Sue's husband) came from Savannah and announced his intention of taking her to a *farm* near Savannah. I spoke with Sue and reminded her of Sam's want of fidelity to her, and the unjust and unkind manner in which he had often treated her. She, however, decided to go; and I told her if so, I preferred she should go at once; whereupon she withdrew Elizabeth in the midst of our last rice-cutting, and they have been for a week beating rice and grinding and washing and walking about at large. I told Sue if she was ever in want or ill-treated, she must return to me. She replied: "No, ma'am, I'll never come back, for you told me to go," thus in a saucy way perverting my remark. As Sam's farm was not exactly ready for their reception, today a cart drove up, and they left to remain at Mr. Lyons' at Riceboro for the present. Although Sue has been disrespectful to me and shown a very perverse spirit, I do remember all her former fidelity; and I am truly sorry for her, for I believe she will feel the loss of her comfortable home. Flora announced if her aunty went she would not stay by herself, so I presume when it suits her convenience she too will go. Even Gilbert (through his wife Fanny) has the matter of change under consideration. What is Charles's ultimate design I cannot tell. I spoke with him soon after I came home and advised him as strongly as I could to go to Atlanta, and he told me he would do so. I hope he will on Lucy's account. But I am thoroughly disgusted with the whole race. I could fill my sheet with details of dishonesty at Montevideo and Arcadia, but my heart sickens at the recital, and a prospect of dwelling with them. For the present it appears duty to do so.

It is a great comfort and support to have your brother with me. He will go to Augusta very soon, and meet Mr. Ward in Savannah. I am told they are proposing to run him for Congress. When last in Savannah he was approached on the subject by some of his friends, *but declined*. I should regret very much to see him enter political life at this juncture of *his life* and the disturbed condition of the country, to say nothing of pecuniary considerations. We are all bankrupt, and only industry and economy will enable us, with God's blessing upon us, to earn a support.

My precious child, I think of you constantly, and wish you had one-half of this large and comfortable home and furniture. When you will ever be able to get anything from here is uncertain, as they are so slow in completing the Central Railroad. The Albany & Gulf Road is done to No. 4 from Doctortown, and I believe they are working also from the Savannah side. I have not had time to examine your crockery, but from the view taken hope the most of it is saved. I have no doubt many things could be sold if people could pay for them.

Your brother sent all his furniture to auction and sold it. Only a very small part remained, and that very much abused. With the proceeds he has bought me a pair of mules and wagon. His library and Indian remains are saved.

We have been trimming up, and the garden and lawn are looking beautifully. Tomorrow we begin to grind cane, and I wish the children were here to enjoy it. I will have some nice stalks saved to send them if possible.

Last Sabbath we took the mule and buggy and attended church at Flemington. It was Communion, and a full attendance. Mr. Buttolph preaches but once, as many persons walk, and they cannot begin before twelve o'clock. They have organized a Presbyterian church, and only await the meeting of Presbytery to have it regularly constituted. . . . Julia and her family and your uncle were out. . . . They are all coming down very soon to South Hampton, and then your uncle will be with us. I hope I may only have someone left to cook and wash! . . .

Do give warmest love to our dear relatives at the Stone House; I will try and write them a long letter very soon. We are now going to dine and ride to see Mrs. Winn and get her to take our letters into Savannah. Kiss my precious children for Grandmother. Oh, how I have missed you all! . . . *Milton* has been a comfort to me since I returned; hope I may keep him. . . . Mr. Alexander and our dear Marion Glen are to be married! . . . Remember me to Mrs. Hull and all inquiring friends. With best love for Robert and yourself, my darling child, and remembrances for Ellen and the servants,

Ever your affectionate mother,
Mary Jones.

MRS. MARY JONES *to* MRS. MARY S. MALLARD[t]
Montevideo, *Monday*, November 13th, 1865

My dearest Daughter,

Although I have been on my feet all day, and it is now near twelve o'clock at night, I must send you a line by your brother, who expects to leave in the morning in company with Mr. Owens, who arrived night before the last. And Audley has been with us all day and is spending the night. And tomorrow I expect your uncle.

Your letter was handed to me on Sabbath, and I was rejoiced to hear from you, but sorry to know that you are still suffering from your teeth. I wish they were all removed and you had a painless set.

The conduct of Patience and Porter is strange, but I am not surprised. I am glad you wrote your dear uncle not to send any of the people from Baker. I do not wish them, and will probably be able to hire very few, and expect by January I may not have one of my old servants about, unless Gilbert remains. This is very sad *and* perplexing, but I trust the Lord will provide for me. Your brother will write your uncle for me about Patience and Porter. I think Robert will find a very sorry account of Mr. Quarterman's management at Arcadia and the conduct of the people.

I hope to write my dear aunt and cousins very soon; I have been so busy, have not had time. Tell my dear little granddaughter I will be very proud of her letter, and she must certainly send it. Tell Lucy Charles and her mother and all the people send howdies for her and Tenah. I think you ought to make "Mr. Niger" pay like a "gentleman" for his many privileges. Do look if I left my knitting. And would be glad if when Robert comes down he would bring my quilt patches and scraps from the trunk. I wrote asking that he would not receive any more money, but only get subscriptions. I am very much obliged for his interest and efforts. Good night, my darling child. With much love to Robert, and kisses for my dear children, and howdies for the servants,

Ever your affectionate mother,
Mary Jones.

MR. CHARLES C. JONES, JR., *to* MRS. MARY JONES[t]
Savannah, *Wednesday*, November 15th, 1865

My very dear Mother,

We safely arrived in Savannah after a wet and rough ride between five and six o'clock P.M. Found Mr. Ward here. Gilbert did not return today; I thought it best to let Rescue rest for the day, as the trip had been fatiguing. He will, D.V., go out in the morning, and will carry the salt, which, being Liverpool, I hope you will find excellent. I have given Gilbert $5.00 and a pair of shoes ($2.50), and send a pair of shoes for Charles ($2.00); also for Mr. Fennell two handkerchiefs ($1.00). I mention these amounts so that you may, if you please, make a memorandum of them, so as to see exactly how we stand with them in case of any settlement. . . .

Letters from Eva. Ruthie is the picture of health and happiness, but Eva has been suffering very much, and I fear is no better. The attending physician advises a colder climate and an early change if practicable.

Mr. Ward will not resume practice in Savannah. He has made every arrangement for opening an office in New York, and has offered me a full copartnership with him. The prospects for success, under God, appear flattering. It seems a providential opening for me in more respects than one. I believe that if I go, I will be able better to provide for your comfort, my dear mother, than I otherwise could. I would also be able to meet the desired change for the benefit of Eva's health. I believe that your health would be greatly benefited by a change of air next summer, if not sooner. I will see Eva on the subject, and will prayerfully ask advice from above. It is a great change—a grave undertaking. I want to do what is best for you, my dear mother, and my dear wife and our sweet little daughter. The more I see of Savannah, the more am I convinced that there is—for the present, at least—but little prospect for aught else than a living. If practicable, I must try and do more. If I do conclude to go to New York, it will, D.V., not be before the middle or last of December.

A letter from Mr. Sconyers tells me that matters are progressing at Indianola only tolerably well. I will go there and see what can be done in reference to the Negroes. I am also making inquiries in reference to the sale of our plantations.

I told Gilbert to look around and see for himself the condition of things. He tells me he has been doing so, and that from all he can see and learn, he feels that home is the best place for him and his family. He will tell you all, and has promised me to do all that he can for you.

Dined with George Owens today, and took tea with Major and Mrs. Porter. All friends well, and unite in much love. I expect to leave for Augusta on Friday morning. Do, my dear mother, let me know if you need anything. God knows that my highest human wishes, hopes, and desires are to conduce to the comfort and happiness of yourself and my precious wife and child. To this I will sacrifice everything; and for the attainment of this end I am prepared now and always as He gives me strength to attempt all, to endure all, and to labor without ceasing. I hope to see you again, D.V., within three weeks. Remember me to all friends. Do not forget to prepare that biography of dear Father. With warmest love, I am ever, my dearest mother,

Your affectionate son,
Charles C. Jones, Jr.
May the good God have you ever in His special favor and protection!

Mr. Charles C. Jones, Jr., *to* Mrs. Mary Jones[t]
Savannah, *Thursday,* November 16th, 1865
My very dear Mother,
I have offered Montevideo plantation for sale (exclusive of furniture, crop,

animals, and farming utensils) at thirty thousand dollars in specie, Arcadia tract at fifteen dollars in specie per acre, Maybank tract for eight thousand dollars in specie. In case any of the parties desiring to purchase come out, you will thus know the terms proposed. The places should not be sacrificed. If they can be sold for what we conceive their full value, it may be well to let them go. The descriptions, etc., are in the hands of Messrs. W. H. Burroughs & Company of this city. They will communicate with me before anything is definitely determined upon.

I leave, D.V., in the morning for Augusta. With warmest love, I am ever

Your affectionate son,

C.

Gilbert tells me that he will do his whole duty, and stand by you to the last. He says Anthony and Dick have gone back to Indianola.

MRS. MARY JONES *to* MRS. MARY S. MALLARD[t]

Montevideo, *Friday,* November 17th, 1865*

My darling Child,

I wrote you this week by your brother, but hearing that Fred was going to Atlanta, I could not miss the opportunity of sending you a letter. I have been busy the most of the week grinding cane, but we have been much interrupted by rain, which has fallen in torrents. The day your brother went into Savannah it poured all day. Gilbert has just returned, having slept on the road last night, the situation of the roads and bridges preventing his reaching home.

Your brother will doubtless write you of his future plans and prospects. I trust the Lord will guide him aright. If he were only a truly converted man—a Christian—my heart would be at rest for him. I hope you do not forget to pray for him; God's Spirit can and I hope will regenerate his heart. He has in his life been called to deep sorrows, and is now enduring an entire prostration of pecuniary means after having acquired an independent support. It is very painful to me to know that I have it not in my power to aid either of my dear children, and that they have all to struggle hard to maintain their families. It is with peculiar sorrow that I think, my dear child, of your uncomfortable situation—not even a carpet on your floor or a pair of andirons in your chimney, and the severe winter soon to set in.

The Albany & Gulf Road, I am told, will not be in running order before February, and the roads to Savannah are almost laid aside. But I see by today's paper brought by Gilbert (for we have no mails) that Captain Charlie will soon be running to Riceboro, and also that freights up to Augusta via the boats have been reduced. Have you received your bedding sent to Savannah by return of the wagon in which we came? I sent two mattresses and one feather bed. The bundle was so large I had to remove the bolsters and pillows I had put in for you, but I knew you were supplied in pillows. Do write and let me know if you wish anything shipped at any time by the vessel.

The military authorities have been sending out a squad of soldiers to detect stolen articles from the crackers and recover them. I wish your things could be recovered. And I would be glad to get all my chairs and kitchen things back.

As I wrote you, Sue had left. She is still at the Boro, and I am told has hired Elizabeth to work at Dr. Samuel Jones's. Flora is in a most unhappy and uncomfortable condition, doing very little, and that poorly. . . . I think Flora will certainly leave when she is ready. I overheard an amusing conversation between Cook Kate and herself; they are looking forward to gold watches and chains, bracelets, and *blue veils* and silk dresses! Jack has entered a boardinghouse in Savannah, where I presume he will practice attitudes and act the Congo gentleman to perfection. Porter and Patience will provide for themselves. I shall cease my anxieties for the race. My life long (I mean since I had a home) I have been laboring and caring for them, and since the war have labored with all my might to supply their wants, and expended everything I had upon their support, directly or indirectly; and this is their return.

You can have no conception of the condition of things. I understand Dr. Harris and Mr. Varnedoe will rent their lands to the Negroes! The conduct of some of the citizens has been very injurious to the best interest of the community. At times my heart is so heavy I feel as if it would give way, and that I cannot remain. But I have no other home, and if I desert it, everything will go to ruin. Mr. Fennell has done all he could to protect my interest; but he is feeble physically, and I do not know that he has any special gift at management. I believe him to be an honest and excellent man. We planted only a half-crop of provisions here, and they did not work one-fourth of their time. Judge the results: not a pod of cotton planted, and all I had stolen, and the whole of that at Arcadia gone. You know I wished Little Andrew to return to Montevideo after Mr. Buttolph decided not to go to Baker, as he was our best plowman. He did not do so. Wanting help at this time in grinding cane, I wished him to come down. He did so, stayed part of a day, and walked off. I have not heard of him since. This is a specimen of their conduct. It is thought there will be a great many returning to the county; I do not believe so. . . .

I hope Robert received your brother's letter in reference to the circulars. All we want at present is to obtain subscribers. The work probably cannot be published under a year. I have requested Joseph to confer with Mr. Rogers about the paper he so generously and kindly offered to give for printing the first edition. Do let him know where Mr. Rogers is.

I have just called Charles and asked if he had any messages. "He sends love to Lucy and Tenah, and begs to be remembered to you, and says he will make an opportunity to come and see them before long." This is the sum and substance of his message. It is impossible to get at any of their intentions, and it is useless to ask them. I see only a dark future for the whole race. . . . Do write me all about yourself and the dear children and Robert and the church. . . . Kiss my precious grandchildren. If they were here they should eat sugar cane all day and boil candy at night. . . .

Ever your affectionate mother,
Mary Jones.

MR. CHARLES C. JONES, JR., *to* MRS. MARY JONES[t]

Augusta, *Sunday,* November 26th, 1865

My dear Mother,

Before leaving Savannah I wrote you a letter telling you of the proposition which had been made me by Mr. Ward to join him in New York in the practice of the law. I have had the matter under very careful consideration, and have concluded to accept. I find Eva's health very delicate; and her physicians advise as necessary a change at the earliest practicable moment to a colder climate. We hope to sail from Savannah by the 20th prox. if possible, and expect to be with you within the next two weeks. I trust thus, my dear mother, if God spares my life, to be able to secure a home and a support for you. And you know, wherever I go and whatever I do, that I am always your devoted son, ready and most anxious at all times to do all in my power for your comfort and happiness; and further, that my house is always your home.

I called up all the Negroes at Indianola, and the only ones who expressed a willingness to go to Montevideo were: Clarissa and her children (May, Chloe, John, and Jane), Sam and his wife, Big Miley and her girls (Phillis and Lucy), and Silvia and her husband (Billy). All the rest say that they are going they do not know where exactly, but all nearly decide upon a return to Liberty. The women are the controlling spirits. Stepney and Pharaoh are very desirous of going to Arcadia, there to work upon any terms imposed. They were all greatly staggered when I told them I expected to sell Arcadia. Little Tom has ever since my absence been working on his own account upon the adjoining plantations. He says he is going with his father to Liberty, and his father expects to return to White Oak with Martha and the rest of his children. William, Kate, and family expect to go to Liberty, but not to Montevideo or to Arcadia. Abram purposes the same thing. Robert and family, Niger and family, Pharaoh and family, and Hannah expect to do the same thing. Maria is going to hunt for Dick. Rose says she is going with Cato. Little Miley goes with her husband. Mary goes with her husband. Elsie and family go to Syphax. Hannah goes with Pharaoh. Peggy wishes to go with Sue. Dick and Anthony have already left the plantation. You thus have all their expectations. The very best of them are those who wish to go to you at Montevideo. I will make all necessary arrangements. Tom says he will go down to Montevideo in two weeks, and will then make the shoes for the people—that he cannot do so without measures. This, I think, is merely an excuse. I have for you about a hundred yards of cloth, and all the Negroes who come down to you have received shoes and clothing. Will be able, I think, to supply you with corn from Indianola.

571

Will write you again very soon. Ruthie is very well, and sends sweetest kisses to her dear "danna." Eva unites in warmest love. Brother and family all well. Have attended to all your commissions, and will explain everything when I come. I am ever, my dear mother,

Your affectionate son,
Charles C. Jones, Jr.

MR. CHARLES C. JONES, JR., *to* MRS. MARY S. MALLARD^c

Augusta, *Thursday*, November 30th, 1865

My very dear Sister,

Upon my return from Liberty I posted for you a letter from Mother which you have doubtless received before this. I remained about three weeks with her at Montevideo, and did all that I could to make her comfortable and repair the damages which had been caused by the enemy. Everything was progressing pretty well when I left, and the servants were orderly, respectful, and at their work. The use of this free labor is an absolute experiment; and while I hope that by March next we may be able to control it to at least a limited extent, I very much fear that for some time to come there will result but little profit from its employment. Poverty and severe legislation can alone render it available. At Arcadia I found everything at loose ends. I think it best for all concerned that this place be sold at the earliest practicable moment, if such sale can be negotiated upon advantageous terms. I am offering it at fifteen dollars in gold per acre, but very much doubt if such a sum can be realized. The Negroes on the place have done nothing for the past year, and Mr. Quarterman has been of little service. All the cotton has been stolen.

Eva's health for four or five months past has been very delicate, and the physicians advise a radical change of scene and air at the earliest practicable moment. Mr. Ward and myself expect to open a law office in New York City on the 1st of January next, and I expect to sail for New York with Eva and Ruthie from Savannah by the 20th December. The condition of Eva's health urges me mainly to the move. I find also in the depressed condition of affairs in Savannah that there is a chance there only for a bare subsistence. I utterly failed also in securing a house. It is a grave change; and it is with a heavy heart, my dear sister, that I contemplate an absence from all who are nearest and dearest to me, and from my native state. I go to New York also as a pauper upon borrowed money. But I hope that the motives which impel me there are correct. I have endeavored to seek guidance from above in determining the grave matter; with God's blessing I trust that we will succeed. Every energy will be devoted to the prosecution of the duties which will devolve upon me, and I hope that I may be able to secure there a home for Mother, where you will always find your room ready, and warm hearts waiting to welcome you.

I am sorry that we will not probably see you before we leave. Did you receive the bundle of bedding? I shipped it from Savannah. We leave here by the 10th to spend a week with Mother. Enclosed please find a photograph of our beloved and honored father; it is one of a number which I had taken in Savannah. I trust, my dear sister, that you are better, and that God will deal graciously with you and yours. Eva and Ruthie unite with me in warmest love to self, Robert, and the little ones. . . .

Your own brother,
Charles C. Jones, Jr.

MRS. MARY JONES *to* MRS. MARY S. MALLARD[t]

Montevideo, *Saturday,* December 9th, 1865*

My dearest Daughter,

I feel even at a late hour that I cannot close the record of the past week without sending you a line before retiring; and think I will adopt the plan of writing you daily if I can, so as always to have a letter on hand for the opportunity that may offer through friends of sending it to you.

The past has been a troublous week, and yet one of mercies too. In the midst of perplexities I have had friends to counsel and to cheer me. Your aunt and Jimmie have been with me for two weeks, and your uncle came on last Tuesday. Mr. Buttolph has been here frequently, and Emily and Mr. Green spent a day with me last week. Yesterday Sister Susan left, and Mr. Buttolph today.

On Monday of this week Anne and Dr. Adams came and brought your last letter. Your aunt and I were just going over to the Retreat at the time. They did not tarry long. We started as soon as they left, and had just reached the turn of the road by the chapel when, discovering Sam (Sue's husband), we stopped and hailed him. He came up and presented a *yellow* letter marked "Official Business," addressed to your brother. I opened it and found an order from the bureau stating that as we had refused to pay Sue and her niece wages, we were now ordered to do so or show reason at that bureau for refusing—at fifteen dollars per month for the two from August 1st! We returned to the house, and I replied in full to Colonel Sickles, and made Sam take the reply immediately back with him to Savannah. What the result will be I cannot imagine.

We then proceeded to the Retreat and spent the day until sunset cleaning out the graveyard, which was a perfect wilderness. We cut away the trees which were injuring the tombs, and put the yard in complete order. I hired two axmen that did good service, as there was much to do.

I believe I have written you that we spent a day the week before at Midway, and put our precious enclosure there in perfect order. I have been thankful to show this mark of respect and affection to our beloved ones who are in their peaceful graves. Oh, how peaceful when compared to our days of sorrow and perplexity! When I had finished I went alone into our old church and knelt before the pulpit and there pled with the God of our Fathers that He would not forsake His ancient heritage, but remember the desolations of His own Zion; and although parted and scattered He would once more be favorable unto us, send us help from the sanctuary, and strengthen us out of Zion. . . .

And I am happy to tell you when Mr. Buttolph came this week he put a paper into my hands. It was an invitation to renew his work at Midway and preach two Sabbaths in the month, for which they give four hundred dollars; and I presume will give quite as much at Flemington. They now furnish a most liberal supply of every kind of provisions—meats, corn, flour, syrup, potatoes, butter, etc., etc.

I will here close until Monday, D.V.

Monday Night, December 11th. I resume, my dear child, this letter. We spent a quiet Sabbath at home reading to your uncle, and had five boys in the Sunday school in the afternoon.

To return to the record of the past week. On Thursday morning Flora informed me she wished to leave immediately for Savannah. I asked the object of her visit. After some hesitation she said it was to meet Joe, but she would return. I gave her some money, and she left as soon as she had eaten her breakfast. Today I hear she did not go to Savannah, but is still in the county. About midday Patience appeared at the Negro house, and came over and attended to the rooms until Saturday morning, when she went off by sunrise, since which time only Kate and Milton are about me, and Gilbert at the stable. I am doing all the chamber work with Kate's assistance. Patience evidently designs setting up for herself, and has settled herself at Arcadia. She complains that during all the summer old Daddy Robin never received any allowance; and when the crop was shared, although strangers were brought in, he did not get a particle of corn and rice. The management on the place *has truly been astonishing!* Mr. Quarterman told me he believed *Henry* was the person who stole the cotton. The sooner that nest is broken up the better. My heart is pained and sickened with their vileness and falsehood in every way. I long to be delivered from the race. And yet if it be God's will that I remain here, I pray that He would give me a spirit of submission. You can have no idea of their deplorable state. They are perfectly deluded—will not contract or enter into any engagement for another year, and will not work now except as it pleases them. I know not from day to day if I will have one left about me or on the place. Several of them refuse positively to do any work.

December 25th. I would be glad to write the usual "Merry Christmas" to my dear children in Atlanta. I can truly say: "With God's blessing may you ever have many and happy ones!" I have just a moment to send off this sheet.

Yesterday we had preaching at our venerable old church, and are to have it every other Sabbath. All of Robert's family were there and well excepting Mrs. John and Mrs. Cyrus Mallard. The latter has been quite sick.

Steamers are now running three times a week to Sunbury, connecting by a line of hacks to Walthourville via Riceboro. If you wish, I can send your carpets or anything you wish in that way; but there must be someone in Savannah to receive and forward them. . . . We have now a company of Yankees at Riceboro, and I hope they will keep order.

Your brother has not yet arrived. I have been so anxious about him I have not slept for ten days more than a few hours at night. . . . Your uncle is very feeble; sends you his best love. My warmest love for Robert and yourself, and many kisses for my dear grandchildren. Write often. Best love to all at the Stone House. In haste,

Your ever affectionate mother,
Mary Jones.

MRS. EVA B. JONES *to* MRS. MARY JONES[t]

Augusta, December 1865

As Charlie tells us it will be, he thinks, almost impossible to take Ruthie out, in the present condition of the roads and derangement of all traveling facilities, to see her dear grandmama, I must write to tell her of the health, sayings, doings, progress, and arrangements made for the comfort of the little one that I know is so dear to her grandmama. She is and has been the picture of health ever since you sent her to me in August last, and I think as merry and happy a little child as I ever saw. She is at present full of going to "New *Yark,*" as she calls it, and cannot be bought out of the fancy for going there.

We both sincerely regret that you cannot see Ruthie before she leaves. I think you would be very proud of the way in which she says her little verses. She repeats eight pieces of poetry, among them all the kings and queens of England down to the reigning monarch, Queen Vic, whose name she pronounces with great gusto—quite beautifully for such a *young personage.* Then I always tell her historical stories, and only a very few at a time, lest her little mind would be confused in hearing too many different ones. I endeavor to inculcate the greatest veneration for truth, to the exclusion of the quantities of foolish fiction prepared for the *injury* (*I* think) of infant minds of the present day. She knows the stories of "The Little Princes," "Richard the Hunchback," "Columbus and His Discovery of America," of "Alfred the Great," "Romulus and Remus," and the mythological tales of "Pyramus and Thisbe" and "Narcissus" (which she will always tell you are "not true"), and tells many of them *very well.* I wish her to know how to use good language, and so always make her tell me the last *old* story before I tell her a new. She says her catechism very well, and also her psalm and hymn. She knows quite a number of Bible stories. She has already made quite a reputation for herself, and talks quite learnedly of kings and queens. At the same time you must not fear, as I hear Mrs. Battey does, that her mind is being overburdened; for I assure you no one would take more care of that than I—the difference between her and other children being merely that she has been taught in the form of stories a *little history,* and they generally hear only of "Jack the Giant-Killer" and other equally silly tales of the nursery.

I am trying in every way possible to do my duty in *every respect* towards this little one that *you sent* to me and her father *brought;* and I trust I am succeeding. She has a clear, bright mind, a most lovely disposition; and although I am a "cruel stepmother," she is remarkably fond of me, and thinks I am quite an *institution,* although *I* say it who should not.

I have her little wardrobe all fixed up splendidly, and did it all myself; and everybody says it is beautiful. I have braided and made for her a dress and cassock of magenta delaine, all lined, the covering wadded. Then she has a reps alpaca gray paletot, lined and wadded, that I also made; three beautiful little braided sacques (my work again) lined warmly for New York; her buff suit; and an embroidered merino, a present from my dear cousin, Mrs. Bird. I have made her a pretty little balmoral, over which she wears a looped-up dress; balmoral boots coming high over the ankles; worsted stockings and leggings. She will be warmly provided for on the steamer. Everything has been made with an eye to the New York winter. Her two hats, which I trimmed myself, are *beauties,* and so pronounced by everybody. One is a beautiful leghorn I *had,* fixed over in the latest shape and trimmed with the new blue real lace and a *gold* buckle, also the inevitable *plumes.* Her other, a traveling hat, is like a little boy's cap trimmed *à la napoléonne,* and is very becoming. I have also a warm little worsted bonnet for her to wear on deck. I have dwelt on her wardrobe at some length, knowing that whatever other people might think, this would be interesting to you, as it is to me. I think if Ruthie could read what I have written, she would beg me to mention the fact of her having two standing collars and some cuffs to which she is greatly devoted.

She is beginning to use a great many big words and old-fashioned phrases, and *patronizes* people to some extent. The other day she was standing in my light, and I said, in the regular "cruel stepmother" style: "My dear, I *know* your head is empty, but it is not in the *least* transparent." She slowly moved away, pulled up a rocking chair, and said, looking at me quite steadily: "No, Mama, my head is *not* empty; it is *full* of *sense*—and of all that *poetry* you taught me *too!*" Triumphantly she concluded this phrase, and all a poor "cut-up" individual could do was to succumb and kiss her gracefully.

I trust that when you join us in New York in the spring you will find her *greatly* improved in every respect. There are the faintest indications only of her yearly eruption, and I think the Northern winter and a summer sea-bathing must certainly cure that entirely.

I wish it were possible for you to meet us in Savannah so you could see the child; she is so sweet and smart, I regret that you cannot see how much she is improved. Notwithstanding all my ill health, I keep her constantly with me. We are rarely separated. She has, however, made little or no progress in her letters, or rather, spelling. I teach her only orally, but she can count to fifty in French and to one hundred in English. I intend to teach her some French verses soon, so as to accustom her to the pronunciation and accent. So much can be done towards removing from study the hardship and lack of interest that most children discover. I want to make learning a pleasure and a pastime to Ruthie if my health permits. I never will allow her to repeat her verses if she shows the least want of interest in them.

I believe you may well rest content on the subject of her being prepared for the cold winter. She has plenty of warm blood, fine health; and if clothes can keep people warm, she *has them* of every sort and description.

I regretted so much that Charlie was unable to see Mrs. Mallard. She only came down for one day, and had left her baby to say good-bye to him. She is entirely lovely and lovable, I think. And with such a daughter and *such a son* as Charlie is, you must be a very happy mother. I have no doubt that Carrie would here announce to you and the public *generally* that the Doctor was of all the brightest and the best. But I allow no such thing. Nobody—not even his brother—shall come near him when I speak of his perfections. He is quite an angel—though I believe I am the only one that has found *that out!*

With warmest kisses from your sweet little grandchild, kind remembrances from Mother, I am

Affectionately yours,
Eva.

MR. CHARLES C. JONES, JR., *to* MRS. MARY JONES[t]

New York, *Friday*, December 29th, 1865

My dearest Mother,

I embrace the earliest opportunity of announcing the fact of our arrival in this city, through God's mercy, in safety. As I wrote you, we sailed in the *San Salvador*, leaving Savannah on the 23rd inst. In consequence of unusually rough weather and continued fogs, our passage was protracted, and during a considerable portion of the time quite uncomfortable. To escape the violence of the storm we ran into Port Royal harbor and remained at anchor there one night. We reached the city last evening. Found our rooms at 132 East 16th Street all ready for us, through Mr. Ward's kindness. And now, in our office for the first time this morning, I write my first letter to you.

Eva and Ruthie stood the voyage pretty well. Eva is so feeble that she suffered not a little; but Ruthie, with the exception of a few hours during the violence of the first storm, was as well and lively as she could be. She made friends with everyone, and laid everybody and everything under contribution for her amusement and pleasure. She won the hearts of all, and made the captain of the steamer her special playmate.

We are comfortably located, at least as much so as our present means will allow. Our office is on Broadway near Trinity Church. We hope to do a good business, and will, God helping us, bring to the discharge of all duties devolving upon us our every energy and attention. I hope, my dear mother, soon to be able to provide a home and a support for you. Come to me whenever you can, and let me know if I can serve you in any way.

Eva, who will write you very shortly, and Ruthie unite in tenderest love and kisses. And I am ever

Your affectionate son,
Charles C. Jones, Jr.

Direct your letters to me care of Ward & Jones, 119 Broadway, New York.

XXII

MRS. MARY JONES *to* MRS. MARY S. MALLARD[t]

Montevideo, *Wednesday,* January 17th, 1866

My dearest Daughter,

I write a line hastily, having just completed the "week's wash" with the use of the machine, and Kate and Milton to help, and Pulaski to bring water. The boys worked cheerfully to the tune of "I'll Away, Away." Try it: it goes finely to the up-and-down motion of a washing machine.

Since Flora left I have had Elsie waiting on me, but I think her mother influenced her to leave on last Sabbath. Porter wanted her to stay with me. Patience has acted very badly; and no one has done more to keep the servants away than Sue, as I believe.

Charles informs me he wishes to go as soon as possible to Atlanta, and Lucy must be looking for him. As he goes via Augusta and could take charge of your things, write me immediately what you would like sent up. Captain Charlie is expected daily, and he might go to Savannah on board his vessel and take charge of books or any articles sent, and at Savannah they could come up on the steamer to Augusta. The only trouble is the means. *If I had them,* you should not be without your furniture. But I am penniless.

Charles writes me from New York he hopes to sell Arcadia. I presume he has corresponded with your brother and Robert and yourself on the subject. I think as you are all away from the county, it would be best to do so, for the place has been running down very fast and is becoming very dilapidated. As landed property there is none more valuable in Liberty County. The Negroes have ruled there entirely this year.

Do *write immediately* if I shall send any things by Charles. . . . Give much love to our dear relatives at the Stone House. Your uncle is quite feeble, and I have to watch over him daily. . . . Audley has written Robert about Dr. Wells: he was a surgeon in the Federal army! I feel that we want our own men to fill posts of honor and profit, not those who have brought us to grief and ruin. . . . Kiss my precious children. And best love to Robert and yourself from

Your ever affectionate mother,
Mary Jones.

Thank you, my dear child, for the stamps and the breakfast shawl—a perfect comfort to me, and I live in it.

Savannah, *Wednesday,* January 17th, 1866

My beloved Mother,

I am here on a matter of business which I hope to be able to conclude in time to be with you on Monday next. If not on Monday, then on Wednesday. I will come, D.V., by way of Sunbury.

I left Eva, I trust, improving, and Ruthie in perfect health. She has sent you her likeness, which I forward in advance.

I will probably bring out with me a German, who goes out to look at the plantations. I hope that I will be able to lease or sell Arcadia to him. He will also look at Montevideo and the Island if you desire it.

With tenderest love, and overjoyed at the prospect, God willing, of being so soon with you, I am ever, my dear mother,

Your affectionate son,
Charles C. Jones, Jr.

Mr. Charles C. Jones, Jr., *to* Mrs. Mary Jones[t]

New York, *Sunday,* February 11th, 1866

My very dear Mother,

Enclosed is a photograph of your dear little Ruthie, which she sends with warmest love to her dear "danna." I think you will agree with us that the likeness is excellent; and I am persuaded that Eva deserves great credit for the artistic design of the picture.

I reached New York only yesterday after a most tedious journey by land. On my return I stopped for two days at Indianola and found matters progressing there much more favorably than I had expected. I have about twenty hands under contract, and they appeared to be working well and in good spirits. Silvia and Billy, Pharaoh and Lizzie have concluded to remain in Burke for the present year and have entered into the contract. They are the only ones of our former Negroes who remain with me, all the rest being strangers. I trust by this time that you have received the corn. I directed Mr. Sconyers immediately upon the receipt of the cotton seed to have the bags filled and shipped. Should you need more, my dear mother, just send the sacks back again, and they shall be replenished. I have lost heavily in hogs by the colera—or *cholera,* as the word is generally spelled.

Brother I found in Augusta looking badly. Sister Carrie and the children were all well. Spent a day in Atlanta with Sister, and was very glad to see that she was looking much better than when we parted. The little ones were all in perfect health. All anxious for Robert's return.

I returned by the way of Knoxville and Lynchburg—a long, tedious route with many interruptions and much discomfort. I find Eva looking better. I trust that this change of scene and air will very materially conduce, by the blessing of Heaven, to the early and complete restoration of her health.

I hope, my dear mother, that everything is progressing as favorably as could be expected, and that God is dealing mercifully with you. Do let me know whenever I can serve you in any way. . . . Eva and Ruthie unite in warmest love to yourself and Uncle William.

Your ever affectionate son,
Charles C. Jones, Jr.

MR. CHARLES C. JONES, JR., *to* MRS. MARY JONES[t]

New York, *Saturday,* February 24th, 1866

My very dear Mother,

I have had not a line from you since bidding you good-bye at Montevideo. You may imagine, therefore, how very anxious we are to hear of and from you, and to know that you are well, and that God is graciously favoring you. Please write us as soon as you can and tell us of everything at home, and particularly of your precious self.

Through God's favor I have thus far been able to sustain my family here in comparative comfort, for which we desire to be very grateful. Eva, I hope, is gradually becoming stronger, although she is not as well as I could wish. Little Ruthie is the picture of life, health, and happiness. She improves in her lessons, and is beginning to spell very well. She repeats a great many little pieces of poetry, psalms, etc., and does not forget her catechism. She often speaks of her dear "danna," and sends sweetest kisses. . . . We are confidently expecting that you will come on and spend the summer with us; and if Providence favors us, I hope to make such arrangements as will secure your comfort and happiness. Do, my dear mother, let me know if there is anything you need. . . .

How are matters progressing at Montevideo? Mr. Sconyers writes me that the fifty-seven bushels of corn were duly shipped from Indianola. I trust that they reached you safely. Whenever you need more, send and get it. Were Messrs. John W. Anderson & Sons able to sell the rice at a good price? I saw them on the subject while in Savannah. How is it with Rescue? I hope he recovered, although I feared from your note, received while at the Pulaski House, that it was all over with him. I trust that you received in due time the package left by me with Messrs. John W. Anderson & Sons in Savannah, to be forwarded to you by earliest opportunity. It contained two pounds of the best tea I could find in the city for you, my dear mother, a pipe and tobacco for Uncle, a suit of clothes and a watch for Gilbert, and a vest for Niger. I trust that Gilbert still remains faithful. I wrote requesting you on his account to let Old Andrew and Mary Ann have allowances of corn, and that I would respond for the amount thus expended. Did Mr. Broughton make his appearance in good season, and are you pleased with him? Pharaoh and Lizzie, Old Billy and Silvia concluded to remain at Indianola for the present year. Have you been able to procure as much cotton seed as you require? Do, my dear mother, let me know if I can advise or serve you in any way. I ardently wish that I was nearer, where I could enjoy the privilege of seeing you often and of relieving you of every burden.

What we have to do is, as far as practicable, to make the Negroes content and happy, and induce them in the present change in their status to realize the obligations devolved upon them. The President's veto message has been fully endorsed here by large and enthusiastic meetings. I send you a copy of the *Times* giving a full account of everything. I do not think that Congress will be able to pass the bill over his veto. This veto is a great matter for the South, and we ought to honor the President for the manner in which he has discharged his duty. . . .

We have nothing of special interest here. The weather is delightful, and reminds us of the pleasant airs and bright suns of our loved Georgia. . . . Eva and Ruthie unite in tenderest love and kisses. Remember us affectionately to Uncle William and to any inquiring friends. And believe me ever, my dear mother,

Your affectionate son,
Charles C. Jones, Jr.

Mr. Charles C. Jones, Jr., *to* Mrs. Mary Jones[t]
New York, *Monday*, February 26th, 1866

My very dear Mother,

Some two days since, I wrote you a long letter, and now add a line simply to enclose you a not very good likeness of a certainly not very handsome fellow. Well, if the picture is not as handsome as it might be (and for this the original is far more to blame than the artist, although the latter has painted the right eye of a Tipperary bully after an Irish wake instead of the mild, reflective optic of an anxious attorney), this counterfeit presentment will at least remind you of one who loves you very dearly, and earnestly prays for your every success and happiness.

I have thus far tried in vain to persuade Eva to have hers taken; but she, indulging in a little display of mock vanity, says: "Wait, Charlie, until I grow a little prettier." As this consummation so devoutly to be wished is, however, very near at hand, I think you may expect her likeness very shortly.

She and Ruthie unite in warmest love and tenderest kisses, with our love for Uncle. I am ever, my dear mother,

Your affectionate son,
Charles C. Jones, Jr.

I hope you received the likeness of Ruthie sent some two weeks since.

Mrs. Mary Jones *to* Mrs. Mary S. Mallard[t]
Montevideo, *Monday*, February 26th, 1866

My dear Daughter,

The whole plantation was astir at the dawn this morning—men and women moving lighter articles on their heads, and the carts carrying the heavier. Captain Charlie lies in the stream, and will move ashore this afternoon and take all aboard; and I hope they will all reach you in safety. I had a jug of syrup all prepared to send the children, but it commenced fermenting, so I concluded as the people had worked so cheerfully to share the greater part to them. And there was little prospect of its reaching you in such a disturbed condition. And if I live, D.V., will fill and send the jug full of syrup in the fall.

I had to boil all the marmalade hastily over; and Kate being sick, it was done by Lucy and badly burnt, but hope you and the children will enjoy it. Your aunt has sent you a wool mattress, and I have also sent you one, and a pair of pillows and bolster. The children's little mattress was too black and worn to send. I would have sent a trundle bedstead, but Robert thought it not worth the expense of carrying. The only articles left which could not be packed are some jars, a few kitchen things, and some chairs badly broken. You will see what I have sent you. I would have sent the entire dozen of chairs, but you know I lost two dozen of my chairs at Arcadia, and some of my bedding, and during the war used up four wool mattresses for the Negroes. The bedding which was sent you I directed Flora to put up last spring, and had not time to see what was in the bundle. We arrived late at night, and it went off by daylight the next morning, and I believe you did not get it for months. I thought Flora had put up a hair mattress, but find she did not. I have sent you a piece of new carpeting for your entry. My own carpets begin to be worn, having been fourteen years in use—all but the one bought in Augusta. And two were cut up for the *ingrates*.

Robert will tell you of my domestic affairs. I sometimes feel that nothing but stern necessity keeps me here, to which is added the abiding desire and aim to be enabled to publish your father's work. . . .

Lucy was very much troubled to hear Georgia had missed her so much. She has had quite a time nursing Charles, who has not done a full day's work since he *contracted* this year. She has a bad cold, she says *contracted* by being up so much with Charles. Could you not write to Augusta and get Sue to cook and wash for you? She is a good servant, and I think as Niger is in Atlanta would like to be with you, and be permanent. If you favor the idea, *write at once,* for her scamp-brother Pulaski wants to bring her down on Mr. Lyons' plantation. I believe after all it is best to keep the old ones if they will serve, and think you would like Sue. . . .

Ever your affectionate mother,
Mary Jones.

MRS. MARY JONES *to* MR. CHARLES C. JONES, JR.[8]

Montevideo, *Monday,* February 26th, 1866

My dear Son,

I have been most anxiously hoping to hear of your safe arrival in New York, but as yet we have no mails, and it is only occasionally I hear of an opportunity

582

to Savannah. One is this moment presented to send you a hasty line of love and remembrance.

Do not let my child forget her "danna." Every day I am missing her more and more, and only the fact that she is contributing to your happiness reconciles me to my loss. I hope you returned Eva my warmest thanks for the likeness, which stands upon my table, where daily I look upon it. She is so much grown, and has assumed such an air of girlhood, that I can scarcely recognize my baby. I hope it may never be necessary to cut her beautiful hair.

By Captain Charlie we last week received your most valuable gifts. Accept my sincere thanks for the delicious tea, and your uncle's for the beautiful pipe and tobacco. You never saw anyone in your life more delighted than he is with the pipe. No stranger even can be any time in the house but he goes and brings it out and shows it with the greatest admiration. He says I must tell you he never smoked anything to equal it, and never saw as beautiful a one. And Gilbert is the proudest fellow in the world of his watch and suit of clothes. Says he means to *"hang to you to the last."* He desires me to give you a "tousand tanks." You may be assured I shall not suffer his parents to want, and have told him to call for any assistance they need.

Niger was very much pleased, and thanks you for his vest. *Today* he returned from Arcadia with a load of pistol shot in his left hand. Coming home he was in company with a man who had a pistol, which Niger attempted to fire at a wildcat, and put the load in his own hand. I sent him immediately over to Dr. William Wells, now at South Hampton; and he has just returned with a note saying the injury might cause him much trouble, and he would not be able to work for some time. He extracted the load and some shot; Niger would not consent to the use of the knife, so other shot remain. So much for their use of firearms!

Charles also has been laid up for some time, but upon the whole we are, I am thankful to say, moving quietly on. Mr. Broughton has arrived, and so far pleases me well. He appears to know his business, and attends to it, which is saying much for any man. He has just called for my letter, so I must close. . . . Warmest love to dear Eva and yourself, and my best wishes and prayers for her entire restoration to health. . . . Tenderest love and kisses for my child, and much love from your uncle, and remembrances from the servants.

Ever, my dear son, your affectionate mother,
Mary Jones.

MR. CHARLES C. JONES, JR., *to* MRS. MARY JONES[t]
New York, Thursday, March 8th, 1866

My very dear Mother,

I cannot express to you our happiness upon the receipt of your kind letter of the 26th ult.—the first we have had since I bade you good-bye. We are rejoiced to hear of your good health, and that everything at Montevideo is progressing so quietly and pleasantly. May God in mercy watch over and protect you and favor you in all things! I am glad that the bundle from Savannah reached you safely, and that the articles contained gave pleasure to those for whom they were intended. . . .

I write in great haste, and will write you more fully very soon. When will the Albany & Gulf Railroad be opened? Is there anything, my dear mother, that I can do for you? Eva is not so well today; her general health, however, I think is better. Daughter is very well. They both unite in tenderest kisses and love. Remember us affectionately to Uncle. And believe me ever, my dear mother,

Your affectionate son,
Charles C. Jones, Jr.

MRS. MARY JONES *to* MRS. EVA B. JONES[g]

Montevideo, *Friday*, March 16th, 1866

My dear Daughter,

This is the return of our sorrowful anniversary, and with the indulgence of my own grief come very special remembrances of yourself and your dear mother. I think it a remarkable coincidence that both your father and my dear Charles's father were removed on the same day. How sadly it presses upon my heart that my dear children have now no one on earth to pray for them and influence them by example and by precept as their devoted and godly father did! I have often heard the petition from his lips: "Let us not forget the dead." God grant that it may be answered in the case of his own children, that they may "not forget the dead." I see in my dear son the noble, generous, and affectionate traits of his beloved father, but my heart yearns to see the decided evidences of Christian character and principle. Would that as a family we were all united to Christ, and had the love and service of God as the great end and aim of our lives! Then could we indulge the blessed anticipation of a joyful reunion in a brighter, better world. *Do when you write tell me where you worship on the Sabbath.*

I had spent the day mostly in my room, reviewing not only my afflictions but God's many undeserved mercies to me, when at its sorrowful close three letters were brought me, all from my very dear son—one containing his own most excellent likeness, and another the precious little picture of my darling child. It is perfectly lovely. Your conception and arrangement is admirable, and you must have practiced even the expression of her little face to have succeeded so admirably. I do thank you for it, my dear daughter, more than I can express, and for all your tender love and care of that sweet child. And I ever pray that you may be rewarded for it. It may be the fruit of my love and partiality, but I have always felt she was an unusually lovely child. Charles does not mention your ever having received either of my letters, or my letter to Ruthie. I hope she will soon write to her "danna" a long sweet letter and tell me all she does. I have a great deal to tell her, and will write very soon. Tell her Mom Lucy and Daddy Gilbert were delighted to see her picture. Mom Kate exclaimed: "Missis, is that your baby that you raised? Do give me one to keep in my *bus-som!*"

Did Charles carry the calico dress I sent her? And did it fit? I had my fears that he did not think it worth carrying. If it reached you, you saw it was unfinished. Although I sat upon the doorsteps in the broad light, I could not see to put on the braid or make the buttonholes. My eyes failed me entirely. Do let me know what work I could do for her. If you would send me her length, I would make her some chemises and pantalets. I have nothing of the kind as a guide. I doubt not you can in every respect do far more and better than I could for her; but if there is anything I could do to promote her comfort, it would give me happiness to do it. God bless her! How I should like once more to fold my child in my arms, and to know that she still loves me!

We have as yet no mails or post office in our county. This week the Gulf Road was opened, but we have no one loyal enough to be entrusted with the *U.S.* mail. I think the Scripture is literally fulfilled in our case: "Because of swearing the land mourneth." Without an oath we cannot have a mail or a post office, a railroad conductor, express agent, or any civil officer. How long will this continue? The Northern clergy who are so active in political affairs had best take that text, using for their illustrations Federal oaths, and for their practical inferences Southern wrongs and oppressions. It is only as some kind friend brings me a letter do I hear from my children. Not one word until this day had I heard from my son Charles since he reached New York. And not a line from Atlanta and Augusta for a month! I have learned to live without newspapers, but I cannot without hearing from my children.

It rejoices my heart to hear that your general health improves, and I pray it may be restored and established. Charles does not mention his own health; I hope he has quite recovered. I was very uneasy about him when he left me. Please do not let him use much tobacco; I cannot resist the impression that it will undermine his health if he uses it to excess.

Sister Susan is quite well, and always desires love. So does my friend Mrs. King. . . . With best love from Uncle and myself to you and Charles, and many, many kisses for my darling child, ever believe me

Your affectionate mother,
Mary Jones.

I shall *confidently* look for *your picture. Do not disappoint me.* Why did you not send it?

MRS. MARY JONES *to* MR. CHARLES C. JONES, JR.[8]

Montevideo, *Monday,* March 19th, 1866

My dear Son,

You may judge of our isolation when I tell you I had not heard a word from you since you reached New York until this past week. But your affectionate letters have all come at once, and now I feel like a starving person made happy and comfortable by a warm, hearty meal. This abominable *oath-taking* still embarrasses all our political and social arrangements; in dear Eva's letter I send a text for Dr. Spring or Dr. Tyng or any other Federal D.D. I have also not heard excepting through your letter a word from your brother or sister, and I feel assured they have written. I wrote you acknowledging the valuable presents to your uncle and myself and to Gilbert and Niger, with which all are delighted, and grateful to you for. The tea is delicious, and often refreshes my weary spirit.

And now I must thank you especially for the likenesses. Yours is excellent, although I still fancy as I look at it that you are not entirely well. Do, my child, watch the influence of tobacco upon your constitution. Literary and sedentary men confined to studies and offices cannot indulge the habit as those who lead active lives in the open air. You see *mother-like* I cannot feel that *a word* is sufficient for the wise; where the heart rules it has to speak many and often. . . . The picture of my little darling delights my eye, and I think I can hear her saying, as her little hand lies extended: "See my mother's little crooked finger." The expression of her face is exactly what it should be, listening to the voice of the seashell in her hand. And why did not Eva send me hers too? I shall not feel that the compliment is complete until she does so; and I shall be anticipating its coming in every letter. I will accept her as she is, without waiting for additional charms.

I am thankful, my dear son, to know that your business has been such as to enable you to support your family, and that the desire of your heart is granted in the improved health of your dear wife. I trust and pray that it may be God's will to restore her to perfect health. You made some allusion to housekeeping. Would not such a step be premature, involving increased care to Eva and heavy expense in furnishing, etc.? I know it is far more comfortable to have your own home, and often houses ready furnished may be obtained at moderate rates.

You most kindly speak of my visiting you this summer. It would be a great pleasure, but I do not indulge the anticipation for a moment, and you must not for the present year think of it. If God spares my life and you ever have a home there at some future day, I know it would give me great happiness to see you in it. I have at present no plans for the summer. Shall stay here as long as possible—perhaps the whole of it. Everyone should now conform to their circumstances. My great desire is, if my life is spared, to see your father's work given to the church and to the world, that it may accomplish its mission of good, and to have the means of erecting a suitable monument at Midway.

Your aged uncle, too, requires not simply attentions but *watchful care.* I was so long accustomed to the fluctuations of your beloved father's health, and got so accustomed to observing the least change, that it is perfectly natural for me to watch over the old gentleman—to see just when he ought

586

to rest or retire, or needs a cup of tea or a glass of *milk toddy;* or when I should sit by him and stir up the old fires of memory, talking of Sister Betsy and past days of happiness, or throwing forward some comforting anticipation of brighter and never-changing, never-ending ones to come. Now that my precious baby is no longer with me, it is of God's mercy that one object is left to claim my daily care and attention, so that what others might regard differently I do as a blessing, as it makes me feel that I am not living entirely for self.

We are getting along pretty well on the plantation. *So far* we have never had a manager that in all respects suited me so much as Mr. Broughton. He would have planted corn ten days since, but waiting for coal tar, he has commenced today. . . . The people have worked well, but Niger was two weeks out of the field from the pistol wound in the left hand, and Charles has not done a full day's work this year, his ear and head still affected. . . . Thus our little number has been materially reduced. Sam does well as foreman, and Gilbert is as faithful as ever. I have told him your wish about his father and mother, and he will have the corn whenever he wishes. Andrew is preparing a fine crop for himself, and you may be assured they shall not want. Under a new system I am trying to inaugurate such measures as will regulate the future, and in my performances try to exceed my promises. I would be glad if I could give them meat, but have it not. They get syrup weekly as a gift, and have had beef once, and things cooked occasionally for them.

My faithful friend *Rescue* died the third day after he was taken. We are now unable to leave home excepting on Sabbath.

It will grieve you to know that Peggy, the faithful and devoted nurse of our little Mary Ruth, died recently of smallpox in Savannah, and I am told in circumstances of great want and neglect on the part of her husband Henry. She was in Sue's house; but she too, I am told, was afraid to go near her. She told me herself she came from Burke to be with me here, but her aunt and sister were the means of keeping her away. You know she came to see you, and you told her when you got a house in New York you would send for her. The servants tell me she repeated to them what you had said, and told them as soon as you sent she was going to New York to be with her "little missy." I think she was as devotedly attached to the baby as any nurse I have ever seen. Do tell her all about poor Peggy's death, and how much she loved her and wanted to come and take care of her. Poor thing, she told me when you sent for Silvia if she had been able, she would not have let her go to wait on "Little Missy," but would have gone to Augusta herself. I do not know where her little child Eva Lee is, but presume Flora or Sue has her.

Yesterday after an illness of two weeks *Rosetta* died from pneumonia. Her children were devoted to her; her old husband Sam has been with her since Robert came; and all her children but Abram were around her dying bed. She has long been a member of the Baptist Church, and expressed to me a good hope that through her Saviour her peace was made with God. I tried to do all I could for her, and her life has probably been prolonged by nourishment and stimulants. . . .

My brother Henry spent Saturday night with us; is doing well in Baker. Your Uncle John has accepted the call to Griffin. I must close. Do ask Eva to write me all about Ruthie. Our respects to Mr. Ward. . . . Your uncle unites with me in best love to Eva and yourself and Ruthie, for whom tenderest love and kisses from "Danna." Gilbert and the servants desire to be remembered. God bless and save you, ever prays

Your affectionate mother,
Mary Jones.

MR. CHARLES C. JONES, JR., *to* MRS. MARY JONES[t]

New York, *Friday,* March 30th, 1866

My very dear Mother,

Your kind and welcome letter of the 19th inst. has just been received, and you can scarcely imagine the delight which it gives us to know that you are well and unharmed amid the changes of this transition period. . . .

I am peculiarly touched by the sad fate of Peggy. She well knew that I was prepared to do all I could for her comfort, and that I offered her a home for life. I never can remember except with the deepest gratitude her kindest attentions to little Ruthie, and her absolute devotion to her in the darkest hours. My effort was to persuade her either to remain at Indianola or come down to you at Montevideo. She would have done the one or the other, but was influenced to a contrary course by her friends. Poor thing, freedom brought sad fates to her door. What will become of her child!

I am glad to hear that everything is getting along so well at Montevideo, and hope that as the period of transition wanes, matters will become better suited. Have you a mail yet to Riceboro? I have heretofore sent my letters to the care either of Dr. Axson or of Messrs. John W. Anderson & Sons. . . .

Enclosed, my dear mother, I send you a check for one hundred dollars. It is my individual check on the National Bank of the Republic payable to your own order. I think you will have no difficulty in using it. All you will do is to endorse it by writing your name on the back, and either of the storekeepers in Riceboro will cash it for you. . . .

Give our love to Uncle, and accept for yourself, my dear mother, our united love and tenderest remembrances. Remember me to all the servants. And believe me ever

Your affectionate son,
Charles C. Jones, Jr.

MR. CHARLES C. JONES, JR., *to* MRS. MARY JONES[t]

New York, *Monday,* April 9th, 1866

My very dear Mother,

On the 30th ult. I had the pleasure of enclosing to you, under care to Rev.

Dr. I. S. K. Axson, my check for one hundred dollars, which I trust reached you in due course of mail and will prove serviceable. In the absence of any information on the question whether or not the post offices at Riceboro and at No. 3, Albany & Gulf Railroad, have been resumed, I send this as usual to the care of our reverend and dear friend.

I deeply regret to learn, through a letter just received from Sister, that her little ones have of late been suffering so severely from whooping cough. Little Georgia especially has been critically ill, and I judge from Sister's account of her present condition that she is still in no little danger. I sincerely trust that they may all soon be restored to perfect health.

Brother writes me that he will soon be with you. I hope that you will make him stay a long time, for I am quite satisfied that he is sadly in need of rest and recreation. I frequently indulge the hope of being able myself to see you, perhaps the last of the present month or during the next. We have some matters of business which may require my presence in Savannah about that time, and I am awaiting developments; so that I may kill two birds with one stone. Every arrangement as yet, however, is uncertain.

Eva and Ruthie are both quite well. Daughter is becoming quite interested in her little books, and begins to spell quite well in words of one and two syllables. She speaks often and tenderly of her dear "danna," and prays for her night and morning. Eva's health, I think, is decidedly improving, and little Ruthie is as well as she can be. I think, under God, this change of climate and scene has been of great benefit to them both. Yesterday we had snow all day, and the weather today, although bright, is quite cool.

We are somewhat at a loss in regard to our plans for the summer. Our landlady goes out of town on the 1st May up the Hudson, increasing her rates, and making it a condition precedent that her rooms there be engaged from May 1st to November 1st. This we are not inclined to comply with. There is a great tendency of the New York population to the country through fear of the cholera, which, it is believed, will prevail here during the summer months. The consequence is, all the country houses within accessible distances for business purposes within the city are commanding very high rents.

We have nothing of special interest. We are getting along pretty well in our business, and we have great cause for gratitude to the Giver of All Good. I trust, my dear mother, that you are well, and that everything at Montevideo continues to move on smoothly. Do let me know if at any time I can serve you in any way. Eva and Ruthie unite in warmest love to self and Uncle. And I am ever, my dear mother,

Your affectionate son,
Charles C. Jones, Jr.

MR. CHARLES C. JONES, JR., *to* MRS. MARY JONES*
New York, *Monday*, April 23rd, 1866

My very dear Mother,

I often wonder whether my letters reach you regularly. They are written certainly every week, and are usually directed to the care of Dr. Axson. Enclosed is a letter from Eva which will tell you of herself and our precious little Ruthie. It is with the deepest gratitude that I report them both well. Ruthie is as bright and as rosy as possible; her health has never been better. Eva, too, has grown much stronger, and is better than she has been for years. The change, through God's blessing, has been most beneficial to them both.

I have just rented a house on 84th Street opposite the Central Park. It is quite in the country and yet in the city. The Eighth Avenue cars pass every five minutes within one square of the dwelling, and the time from the house to my office is just one hour. The house is a pleasant one, and I hope the locality will prove healthy. It will certainly be much cooler than in the city. In Central Park, too, Ruthie will have ample room for play and for fresh air. Eva is very busily engaged securing furniture, and we hope to get into the house by the 7th of May.

And now, my dear mother, I must insist upon your coming on and spending the summer with us. This is the *very least* you can do, for you know your room will be always ready, and we will be only too happy to welcome you. Brother will be coming on, I expect, in June, and he will be your escort. Now, you will not deny us this pleasure. I am quite sure, under God, that the change will be very beneficial to you. . . .

Our business matters are progressing favorably. I have been very hard at work ever since I saw you. I hope to see you during the next month if business arrangements will permit. All unite in tenderest love to self and kind remembrances to Uncle. And I am, my dearest mother, as ever,

Your affectionate son,
Charles C. Jones, Jr.

MRS. MARY JONES *to* MR. CHARLES C. JONES, JR.[8]

Montevideo, *Friday,* May 18th, 1866

My very dear Son,

For over three weeks my longing eyes and heart have waited to welcome your coming. As weeks wear away I fear you may not be able to leave New York, and particularly as you have just gone to housekeeping. . . . For three successive weeks I have had a noble wild turkey hung up in the dairy for you. The last was so fine I kept it four days hoping you would be here to enjoy it. During your brother's visit and since we have had five as fine as you ever saw. I have requested that no more be killed this season *unless* you come. Mr. Broughton says he has two gobblers waiting for you. I have preserved the feathers to some of the finest, and intend having a large fan made for the firm at 119 Broadway to fan *"Southern claims."*

Hoping still to see you, I will not even begin the endless details of plantation life. We have had it very dry, and the season is unusually late. Cotton just fairly up, and rice not all planted. I have had some severe trials with the people here, but trust through divine strength and guidance matters will go right in future. . . .

Did you get my letter asking you to bring me three padlocks? . . . And we are entirely without scales or steelyards for weighing. I saw Fairbanks (or some such name) very highly recommended; it was said they were not expensive, and yet would weigh a bag of cotton.

I do not propose, *D.V.*, leaving here before the middle or last of June, when I will go to Augusta. Your sister writes to say my room is all ready in Atlanta. And I am truly grateful, my dear son, to Eva and yourself for your kind invitation to pass the summer with you. Holding so large a part of my heart as you do, you place a great temptation before me in such an invitation. Your brother goes on in July.

I am so desirous to have your father's *History* published at once, fearing some accident might occur to the manuscripts, that I wish to dispose of so much of Central Railroad stock as will meet the expense of publication. This can be done either in Savannah or Augusta when I go up. Your brother says he will have time to attend to the publication while he is at the North, and we will try and get Dr. Howe to correct the proof sheets.

Your uncle requests you to try and effect a sale of his plantation near the Island (Springfield). There are three hundred and twenty-five acres, a most healthy and desirable place of residence, fish, oysters, etc., etc. Says you know all about it. He will take ten dollars per acre. It would be a great matter for the old gentleman if you could sell it.

He unites with me in best love to Eva and yourself. Kiss my precious child for me. The Lord bless and keep you, ever prays

Your affectionate mother,
Mary Jones.

MRS. MARY JONES *to* MISS MARY RUTH JONES[8]

Montevideo, *Friday*, May 18th, 1866

My darling Child,

"Danna" has just come in from the garden, where she found this sweet spring rose, almost the last of the season. It looked so beautiful and was so fragrant it made me think of the precious flower I have blooming far away in New York. So I thought I would sit down and write you a little letter, and put the sweet rose in it, and send it to remind you of your Southern home.

You have not forgotten *Monte-willio-way*, have you? There are no wicked Yankees here now to torment us as they did last winter, when for one month we were all prisoners in our own home. The doors and windows stand wide open now; and the bright sunshine peeps in, and the cool breezes filled with perfume from the tea-scented olive and the sweet roses and flowers of the garden come freely through the entry and halls. The avenue of oaks, the grove, the lawn are all beautiful; the laurels in full bloom. The little squirrels are once more cheerful and happy, and all day long are chasing each other round and round and up and down the trees. Day and night the sweet little birds are singing their songs of praise and thanking God for His kind care of them. You know we had but one old goose left from our flock of seventy. She was very lonely until about two months since we got another; and now they have two little "doozé," as you used to call them. The father and mother take them out walking and picking grass upon the lawn, and are so proud of them. They will not let dog or cat or duck or chicken come near them. The only pigeon left by the Yankees that used to tap at the window for corn and pease flew away and brought home another, and now they have a fat little squab just fledged.

Your dog Captain faithfully guards the house at night. He sleeps sometimes in front on a bed of dried leaves; and when "Danna" hears a noise she throws up the glass and calls, "Captain! Captain!" and he answers with a loud, hoarse bark. His fierce voice makes people afraid of him, but he never bites, for he belongs to an amiable family. Little *Hero,* the colt, grows finely, although he has had to take care of himself since his mother, Lady Franklin, was stolen this winter from the pasture. But he is a brave little fellow, and can whip the largest mule in the stable whenever he fancies the corn and fodder. We have a merry set of calves and little lambs, and Daddy Gilbert is now taking off the warm winter jackets of the old sheep.

Your dear papa has no doubt told you that your nurse Peggy was dead. She took care of and nursed you for the first year of your life, and loved you very dearly. She wanted to go to New York to wait on you, but it is the will of our Heavenly Father that she should not live even to take care of her own child. I hope poor Peggy was a Christian and has gone to heaven.

My darling, "Danna" misses you every day of her life. She keeps your little chair by the side of hers in the parlor, and often wishes you were here to fill it. But I daresay you are better off where you are, your kind mama takes such good care of you, and teaches you so many pretty and smart things, and you live in such a great city, and see so many beautiful things. And then I know you are a great comfort to your dear papa, who is working hard to support Mama and his little daughter, and "Danna" too. You must never forget when he comes home weary and tired to run and meet him with a happy face and a warm, loving kiss, and to do all you can to obey and make him and Mama happy. You must put your little arms around them and kiss them both for me.

You will think this a dull letter, but I hope it will remind you of your home. Never forget, darling, to love the Blessed Saviour and to pray that He would love you and make you His own dear child. May God ever bless you! You must write soon to

Your own loving "danna,"
Mary Jones.
Mom Kate and Daddy Gilbert send you howdies.

My very dear Mother,

I am this morning in receipt of your precious favor of the 18th inst. with its sweet enclosure to little Ruthie, which I have also read with deepest pleasure and interest, and which she will not hear read until I get home tonight. She will at that time, however, be up; and her loving little heart will be very thankful to her dear "danna" for her kind and special remembrance, for all the bright and calm views of that blessed home consecrated by so many memories of happiness and comforts and privileges, and for the sweet rose, redolent of those delightful perfumes which always linger with peculiar richness and delicacy about the garden at Montevideo. She will write you very soon and thank you sincerely for this pleasure. Only last evening she came to me and said: "Papa, hold my hand and let me write a little letter to Danna."

She is the only one (except Eva's wild Irish girl) in the entire household who has not been sick within the past few weeks. Eva and Mrs. Eve are both now quite unwell, and Polly has been very sick. Yesterday I was badly used up with my old enemy. But I hope we are all on the mend. The spring has been a very unpropitious season, abounding in chill winds and cold rains. As I write I am reminded by the whistling winds and cloudy skies more of the dark days of September than the mild hours of May. I presume, however, that summer will soon be upon us in good earnest, for the changes here are, when they occur, very decided.

I have been very hard at work since I have been in New York. We breakfast a little after seven. I reach my office about nine o'clock or a little before, and never leave it until half-past six, which brings me home to dinner about half-past seven.

We are pretty well fixed in our new home; and again, my dear mother, let me urge your coming on and spending the summer with us. Your room is all ready. It is designated as your room, and all you have to do is to come on with the Doctor and occupy it. You well know what a hearty welcome awaits you, and I am quite confident that a change of scene and climate will be most beneficial to you. Remember, we are confidently expecting your coming.

I still hope to be able to come to Georgia during the month of June. My movements have been delayed in consequence of the nonpassage of a law of Congress which will facilitate the transaction of some business of importance committed to our care. If the bill passes, I will go at once to Savannah, and will then enjoy the great pleasure, which my heart craves so sincerely, of being with you.

I regret deeply to hear that you have been subjected to "severe trials" at Montevideo, and heartily unite with you in the hope that they are now overpassed. The transition in the status of the Negro has been such a marked and violent one that we cannot wonder that he does not at once adapt himself rationally and intelligently to the change. He has always been a child in intellect—improvident, incapable of appreciating the obligations of a contract, ignorant of the operation of any law other than the will of his master, careless of the future, and without the most distant conception of the duties of life and labor now devolved upon him. Time alone can impart the necessary intelligence; and the fear of the law, as well as kindness and instruction, must unite in compelling an appreciation and discharge of the novel duties and responsibilities resting upon him.

My advices from Indianola are of an unfavorable character. The season has been cold and wet. Cotton seed has been scarce and of an unreliable quality. The consequence is that everything is backward, and the stand of cotton very irregular and bad. So far as I can learn, the Negroes have behaved pretty well, although on this point Mr. Sconyers has not written me particularly for several weeks. I wish very much that I could visit the place. Have had to furnish bacon, which has been and will continue to be a heavy expense.

In reference to the sale of the Central Railroad stock, my dear mother, for the purpose of publishing Father's manuscript, if you will allow me to suggest, I would advise against its present sale, and for two reasons. First, I am in possession of facts which lead me to believe that a dividend will be declared before very long which, while it will benefit you very much, will also materially enhance the value of the stock. We have just compromised a very heavy claim in favor of the road, which I think will enable the company to declare a dividend. Second, now is not as favorable a season to sell as we may reasonably expect a little later; nor is it a favorable season to have printing done here. Labor and materials are both high. I think next winter we shall see the rates of labor and materials more reasonable. I would be loath also, Mother, to part with that stock, the annual income from which you will need, and which is the very best security in Georgia. By next fall, also, I hope I may be able to *assist* in the expenses of the publication, if not wholly defray them. No one can be more anxious than I am to see the valued labors of my beloved and honored father given to the world, and I would not for one moment suggest any hindrance in the consummation of that most desirable object. But my impression is, unless there be some special reason in the case unknown to me, that it would be more advantageous to delay the publication until next fall. At all events, do not sell the stock now, as it can be done at any time by power of attorney, which I can prepare for you at any moment. The longer the sale is delayed the better.

I hope, my dear mother, that you have found leisure and strength this past winter and spring to prepare Father's biography, or at least to collect and arrange the materials and note your own specific recollections, which will of course be far more valuable than those of anyone else. This I deem a very important matter, and I hope that you will have strength and leisure to accomplish it.

I have promised the Georgia Historical Society to prepare an account of the fortifications erected around, and of the military operations connected with, the city of Savannah during the last war. Have you any journal or newspaper or written accounts or memoranda with the loan of which you could favor me? I have thought that perhaps my letters to yourself and Father from 1860, or say 1859, to the close of the war would prove of some value to me, and enable me to fix certain dates which otherwise I might find trouble in doing. May I ask the favor of you at some early leisure moment to gather up those letters and memoranda of every sort and kind in your possession and send them on to me by express at your early convenience? I will be greatly obliged to you if you would do so. The express freight on the package I will pay here.

Please say to Uncle that I will do the best I can for him in the matter of the sale of his plantation, but that the season is so far advanced that I doubt whether a sale can be effected before fall. Assure him, however, that I will do all that I can.

The scales and padlocks I will look after. Do, my dear mother, let me know if you want anything, and if I can do anything for you. You know my highest pleasure and privilege are to serve you in every way in my power. All unite in tenderest love. Hoping, my dear mother, that every blessing will ever attend you, I am ever

Your affectionate son,
Charles C. Jones, Jr.

MRS. MARY JONES *to* MR. CHARLES C. JONES, JR.[8]
Montevideo, *Monday,* May 28th, 1866

My very dear Son,

Your valued favors by General Lawton reached me last week. They were sent by Captain Charlie Thomson, who delivered them faithfully; and I am most grateful to you, my dear child, for the enclosure of fifty dollars. You have done everything that it was possible for a son to do for a mother, and you really must not continue to make such drafts upon your hard-earned resources. I know you must now have calls for all you make, and it distresses me to feel I may be increasing your cares. I have always tried to make my personal wants as few as possible; and if the Lord is mercifully pleased to prosper us with anything of a crop, I trust I shall be able with economy to make a support from the plantation another year.

Sometimes I am *encouraged; never* very hopeful, from the unreliable character of the laborers. To give you an illustration: Several weeks since, when I thought all things prosperous, Gilbert came and informed me that July and Jesse were going that morning to Savannah with a copy of the *contract,* which they had requested and I had furnished them. Soon after, *Sam* came up on the mule, saying the people one and all had declared they would not strike another lick with the hoe; they were dissatisfied with the contract, and thought I meant to deceive them. I told him to go into the field and order them every one—men and women—to come to me. They did so. I met them on the front steps and inquired kindly but decidedly into the cause of

595

such conduct. They had one and all evidently been poisoned by someone, and July and Jesse were ringleaders in the affair. I was extremely weak at the time, as it was soon after my sickness; but I felt it important to act promptly in the presence of the people. So I told July and Jesse immediately to take up the line of march for Walthourville, where the agent of the bureau lives; and directing Gilbert to get the buggy, I asked Brother William if he would accompany me, as he had been a witness to the contract. The old gentleman was so incensed at their conduct he said he would go a hundred miles with me.

I arrived, of course, before the men, and laid the case and the contract before Mr. Yulee, the agent. He made some shifting remarks about "public opinion" and its being customary to give "half of the crop," etc. I told him the provisions of my contract had been suggested by a Federal officer then acting as a bureau official, and endorsed and approved by him as such. I then asked if he would furnish me a legal standard for contracts. He said they had none.

"Is my contract, then, a legal one?"

"Yes, madam."

"Are the people, then, not bound to comply with its terms?"

"Certainly."

"I now, then, sir, appeal to you as the agent of the bureau to restore order upon my plantation!"

He then rose and wrote a summons for July and Jesse to appear before him, and told me if the people did not return to their duty he would put the instigators into irons; and if that did not answer, he would send them to Savannah and have them put to work with a ball-and-chain upon the streets. I told him I desired nothing of the kind—only the return to order and duty on the place. Soon after we left, July and Jesse arrived, and I received by their return a note saying they professed perfect satisfaction with the contract and promised to return to their duty.

Since this outbreak things have moved on very well. I have told the people that in doubting my word they offered me the greatest insult I ever received in my life; that I had considered them friends and treated them as such, giving them gallons of clabber every day and syrup once a week, with rice and extra dinners; but that now they were only laborers under contract, and only the law would rule between us, and I would require every one of them to come up to the mark in their duty on the plantation. The effect has been decided, and I am not sorry for the position we hold mutually. They have relieved me of the constant desire and effort to do something to promote their comfort.

I am not only satisfied but much pleased with Mr. Broughton. He understands his business and attends to it, and is an excellent planter and manager, especially for these times, commanding respect and obedience in a quiet but decided way. Gilbert has maintained his fidelity on all occasions, and Kate and Lucy are great comforts to me. . . . We are now suffering from a most protracted and distressing drought, and if we do not have rain within a few days, the provision crop must be greatly injured. We have been able to plant but one square of rice, and that is very slim. We are now planting the inland swamp as you cross in going to the Darien road. The Negroes in this county have suffered for want of food, and many are now working simply for provisions. If it had not been for the corn you have sent me, I would too have been in great distress. Mr. Sconyers writes me he has sent me thirty bushels of corn and two of pease, which I am glad to get for planting. . . . Our stock of cattle is carefully watched by Mr. Broughton. Your uncle took a look at them this evening and says they are very fine. I wish I could send you a plate of fresh butter every morning. Do write me if there is anything I can send you from home; and if I can help Eva in any household articles (bedding, etc.) it will be my greatest pleasure to do so. I wrote you of the crop at Arcadia; it is doing well. Last week I made our tax returns.

On Saturday night I received your most affectionate letter, my dear son. It would indeed rejoice my heart to see you and dear Eva and my precious child. I am thankful you are once more in your own hired house. May God's blessing rest upon you in it, and make it to you the abode of peace and happiness! Tell dear Eva she does me too much honor in selecting for me her best chamber; that must not be. I do long to see you, but I do not know how to write about coming on until I reach Augusta. Does Mrs. Eve expect to spend the summer in New York with Eva and yourself?

Mrs. John Barnard told me on Saturday that Adeline was very much inclined to go to New York to cook for you. Do you wish to have her? I think she would be a comfort to you. I cannot get over the feeling of confidence in those born and raised with us. If I can do anything in that line for you, let me know it. I have no doubt you could secure black servants here if you wish them.

Tom is now in the county. I have seen him but for a short time. He came down with a fine double-barreled gun, and is helping his father at Lyons'. *Anthony* has left for *New York*. Tom tells me both *George and Jack* are dead, which makes three gone of our personal servants. Tom is now a carpenter. Did you allow him to keep all the shoemaker's tools you bought for him? Or are they still yours, although his possession?

As I have written you, my dear son, I wish to sell so much of my Central Railroad stock as will enable us to print your father's *History* at once. The way seems providentially opened for your brother to attend to the printing this summer. I am so much more familiar with his handwriting than anyone else, I have thought if I am permitted to visit you this summer and the work is printed in New York, if there was any obscurity I might make it plain.

We are still without any regular mails to Riceboro.

Your uncle has been very feeble recently, and expects to leave this week for Dorchester. *D.V.,* I expect to leave either the 14th or 19th of June for Augusta. He desires you to sell his place if possible, as I wrote you, saying if a purchaser can be found, he will name titles, etc. He feels leaving

Montevideo; says there is no other place where he will be so comfortable or so much spoiled. I am sure there is nothing on earth I would not do for him.

Please do not forget the padlocks, etc.; and I will be glad to have seven pounds rutabaga turnip seed and some drumhead cabbage. You must be tired of this scrawl. Best love to dear Eva and yourself. Kisses for my baby. God bless you, my dear child, ever prays

Your affectionate mother,
Mary Jones.

The servants send many howdies.

MR. CHARLES C. JONES, JR., *to* MRS. MARY JONES[8]

New York, Monday, June 4th, 1866

My very dear Mother,

Your last kind favor has just reached me, and we are truly happy to hear from you and to know that you are well. I am distressed to learn that you were some time since so much troubled and annoyed by the misconduct of the people at Montevideo, but rejoice with you that you have of late found them more obedient and attentive to their duties.

The accounts which I receive from Indianola are very unsatisfactory—only a half-crop of cotton planted, and that in very inferior condition. Late spring, cold rains, and bad seed have united in causing a very indifferent stand, even in the small quantity planted. Some of the Negroes work pretty well, some very well, and some again very indifferently. And so the story runs generally.

I will send on the padlocks and garden seeds by express, D.V., in a day or two. The package will be directed to you, No. 3, Albany & Gulf Railroad, as I presume the express has resumed its carriage on that route.

I am truly sorry to hear of the death of George and of Jack. They were both good servants, and I would have been glad to have assisted them all their lives by every means in my power. I had hoped to have gotten George here. We are anxious that Adeline should come on and cook for us; and some two days since I wrote Amanda Howard requesting her to see Adeline and induce her if she could to come on at the earliest practicable moment. I hope that she will succeed in doing so. We expect to hear from her on the subject very shortly. She will, I think, be a great comfort to us; and I believe with her and Polly, who has proven herself a very treasure, that we will get along very well, D.V.

I have already written you in relation to the sale of the Central Railroad stock. If you conclude to sell a portion of it, I would postpone the sale as long as possible, and would not sell at any rate until definite arrangements had been made with the publishers as to price, time of payment, etc. The payments would in all probability not have to be made until after you had received one dividend. I beg to refer on this subject to my letter of the 28th ult.

598

I think I let Tom have some tools. He had a great many of his own. I do not think he has any to which he is not entitled.

Enclosed, my dear mother, please find a check in your favor on the Bank of the Republic in this city for fifty dollars. I wish that it was for an hundred times that amount. You will have no difficulty in negotiating it. It is, as you will perceive, payable to your order.

And now, my dear mother, you must let us again renew our earnest entreaty that you come on and spend the summer with us. Your room is all ready, and we are depending upon your acceptance. We can take no refusal, and shall after your arrival in Augusta expect you to let us know exactly when it will suit you to come on.

On the 28th ult. I begged you to send me all my letters addressed to dear Father and yourself since 1859 that you can conveniently find. My object in desiring them is this: I am preparing for the Georgia Historical Society a brief history of Savannah for the past five years, and also for the Chatham Artillery an account of the part borne by that battery in the struggle for Confederate independence. Those letters, as they probably from time to time referred to passing events, will in all probability furnish me with a thread for the respective narratives. If you have also, my dear mother, any printed or written notices or documents touching the local history of the company or of Savannah during the period alluded to, I would be very glad to receive them. Please forward to me, 119 Broadway, New York, care of Ward & Jones, at your early convenience.

Through God's mercy we are all up again. Nothing of special interest. Pray, my dear mother, let me know if you wish anything, or if there is any way in which I can serve you. Tell Uncle that I will do all that I can to compass the sale of his place. All unite in tenderest love and warmest kisses. And I am ever, my dear mother,

Your affectionate son,
Charles C. Jones, Jr.

Kindest remembrances to Uncle and all relatives and friends. Howdy for Gilbert and all the servants.

MRS. MARY JONES *to* MRS. MARY S. MALLARD[t]

Augusta, *Wednesday,* June 20th, 1866

My very dear Daughter,

I left Montevideo on Thursday morning in the wagon (the buggy being fairly worn out and laid by for repairs) to No. 3, where I dined with Mr. Augustus Fleming; and under the kind escort of Mr. Buttolph we reached Savannah about six o'clock. Accepting the invitation of our valued friends Dr. and Mrs. Axson, I stopped with them, receiving most hospitable entertainment. In yours and Robert's name I gave them a pressing invitation to visit you this summer, knowing what sincere pleasure it would afford you to entertain friends so valued, and to whom you are under so many obligations for kindness to Robert. Laura had been in Savannah about a month with her numerous friends, and was greatly improved.

I saw Major and Mrs. Porter and all their connection, and was to have gone up in company with Marion Alexander and Dr. and Mrs. Robson on Friday night to this place; but a disappointment in the hack caused me to remain until Saturday morning, when I came up *alone,* your brother meeting me with a hearty welcome at the cars. And Carrie and the children did so at the house. I felt grateful to find them all so bright and well—excepting your brother: he is very thin and *worked down;* looks very badly. Carrie very busy and full of work. We have *hired* a sewing machine, and I am going to try and help her, but do not know how I shall manage without you to arrange it for me.

Carrie and Joe are much disappointed that Kitty passed through Augusta without their seeing her. It would be a great pleasure to me to see her. You know I have always considered her one of my loved and valued friends.

I have thought, my dear child, constantly of the call to New Orleans, and made it a subject of daily prayer that *God* would direct Robert at this time by the special influences of the Holy Spirit, that no false motives may influence his feelings or blind his judgment, but the glory of Christ's cause and Kingdom may be the grand and ultimate aim of his life in this and all other decisions. I can but have a preference for the climate of Atlanta when I think of you and the dear children; and then too I shall feel if you go to New Orleans that I shall hardly ever see you, if I am spared to live longer in Liberty. But this is all personal. There can be no doubt of the importance of his present location and the growing influence of Atlanta. New Orleans must be a trying climate to the constitution, although Randolph Axson tells me the summer is delightful, winter damp and sometimes very cold. Says the church to which Robert is called is beautifully located in the American part of the city. Says living is about as expensive as Savannah, and he prefers New Orleans to any other place. But I presume Robert has ere this written you fully of all things.

Your brother Charles has given me a most pressing invitation to visit him when Joe goes on, and seems to feel hurt at the thought of my not accepting it. Joe thinks of going on now not before August or September. My mind is perplexed about it. I do long to see my dear baby so much.

Carrie and your brother unite with me in best love to you and to Kitty and the dear children, and to Aunt and Cousins Mary and Lou and Sophia and Lilla and Ellen. All friends send much love to you and them. I left your uncle at Dorchester for the present. Excuse my miserable writing.

Ever, my dear daughter, your affectionate mother,
Mary Jones.

XXIII

MRS. LAURA E. BUTTOLPH *to* MRS. MARY S. MALLARD[t]
Flemington, *Tuesday*, July 17th, 1866

My dearest Cousin Mary,

A long time has transpired since a line passed between us, and I think it is now time to make up for lost time. Of course your engagements have been so varied and numerous that I am the only one to blame, and my seeming neglect has been neither willful nor voluntary.

I long to hear directly from you and your loved ones, who have ever been cherished in my warmest affections. I trust dear little Georgia has entirely recovered, and that you feel like yourself again. I hope Cousin Robert may remain in Atlanta, as the place is so healthy, and destined to be the greatest city in the state. New Orleans seems so far off that although the advantages may seem greater, still the climate in summer must be depressing. I have felt the heat of the few past days very much here.

Mr. Buttolph has gone to the North to see his aged father. He sailed in the *Tonawanda* on Saturday for Philadelphia, and expects to be absent two months. And I trust that he will enjoy himself extensively and derive all the advantage he can from the trip. The Yanks have clipped my wings, so I could not accompany him. Mr. W. J. Way took daguerreotypes of the children for their grandfather to see. . . . What do you think of our going to Williamstown, Massachusetts, to live? It seems to me I would stagnate there; but the children will have to be educated, and *if* Mr. Buttolph is called there, I don't know what the result *might* be.

We had a few showers last week, which may save the corn crop in a measure; but it is very dry. The swamps are all dry, and the vegetables all dried up. Gilbert came for Mr. Buttolph's horse and took him on Saturday to Montevideo. He said all the people there were well, but the starving people who had no work were "very plenty."

Mr. Buttolph saw Uncle William in Dorchester the last Sabbath but one. Quite well. . . . Uncle is to make Dr. Robson and Cousin Audley a visit on the Island and then come to us. His room here is nicely fitted up with Mother's cottage furniture and waiting for him with a warm welcome.

If you go to New Orleans, Aunt Mary's children will be scattered, and it will require time to journey from one to the other. I presume by this time she is with you; do give her our warmest love. . . .

I enclose you a photograph colored by Mrs. Cheves of Savannah. They were so poorly taken and the paper so miserable that the paint blotted, and you may not recognize the lady with red hair and red eyelashes! It is the best I have to send. Annie said: "You can't make me believe that is Miss Laura—*the eyes is dreadful!*" And Mother thought it was one of the Pratts.

Mother, James, Willie, and Susie unite with me in much love to Aunt Mary, yourself, and Cousin Robert, Mary, Charlie, and Georgia. Love to Kitty Stiles.

Your ever affectionate coz,
Laura E. Buttolph.

MRS. MARY S. MALLARD *to* MRS. LAURA E. BUTTOLPH[t]

Atlanta, Saturday, July 28th, 1866

My dear Cousin,

Your letter containing yourself was received with great joy, and I must return you many thanks for it.

I have done very little letter-writing for some months past. My poor little Georgia has required such undivided attention that I have done little else than mind her. She has been improving for a week past. She had a severe attack of cholera infantum about six weeks ago which reduced her very much and brought her very near death. Dr. Logan has despaired of her life three or four different times, but through the mercy of our kind Heavenly Father she is improving, and we hope will get well. She is very interesting, though the most timid child I ever saw in my life. She will allow no one to touch her except Mr. Mallard and myself and the children. I have only been waiting for her to lose the invalid look to have her photograph taken for Aunt Susan and yourself. She says any single word and begins to connect them. Yesterday she put her little foot in my bed and said: "Mama, scratch it." She is too weak to walk much alone.

I have placed your photograph in my album, though I do not think it does you justice. I think the blotting of the colors and the peculiar color of the hair must change the expression, though I think it like you and am very glad to have it. Mamie knew it immediately. I want one of Cousin Lyman now. . . .

I wish you could have gone North with Cousin Lyman. The change would have done you good. I can't say I would like to think of you living in such a far-off Yankee place as Williamstown!

Our New Orleans arrangements are in uncertainty. Mr. Mallard accepted the call, and requested this church to unite with him in requesting the presbytery to dissolve the pastoral relation existing between them. They refused to do this, dissenting from him in the correctness of their conclusion. He immediately wrote the Prytania Street Church informing them of the action of this church, and received an answer saying they would prosecute the call with all energy. As Presbytery does not meet until the 27th of September, the matter cannot be decided until then; though Mr. Mallard still thinks it his duty to go to New Orleans, as no new facts have been developed to change his decision. New Orleans has always seemed to me a long way off, though it is, in fact, only forty-eight hours from this place. And if the Gulf Railroad is ever completed, we will be just as near Liberty from that point as from this. The greatest drawback is the yellow fever; and I feel that is to be greatly feared. Dr. Palmer sent me word yellow fever was a humbug, but I cannot be induced to believe any such idea as that.

My dear mother is here now, and looks remarkably well. She expects to go North with Brother Joe the middle of August. This arrangement will cut short her visit to us very much. I am so sorry she is going, though I know she is most anxious to see Brother Charlie and Ruthie. . . . Mother and Mr. Mallard unite with me in warmest love to Aunt Susan, Uncle William, and yourself, and many kisses for the children. We really must write each other often.

Your affectionate cousin,
Mary S. Mallard.

MRS. MARY JONES *to* MRS. MARY S. MALLARD^t

New York, *Friday,* August 17th, 1866

My dearest Daughter,

I would have written you before this, but the fatigue consequent upon our long journey has almost laid me aside. Think of it: at least thirteen or fourteen hundred miles accomplished in four days and a half—day and night in the cars!

We reached Chattanooga at six o'clock and left at 9 P.M. for Nashville, where we arrived a little after sunrise and enjoyed a nice breakfast at the St. Cloud Hotel, which is served entirely by white servants; and everything was clean and nice and arranged in the eating line after the present approved style of separate tables and ordering whatever you wish, which comes up hot and in a variety of small dishes. Your brother after breakfast went out to see Dr. Eve; I laid down after a bath and took a refreshing nap. After Joe came in we walked to the capitol, a magnificent structure, not much injured by the Yankees, although the grounds around were entrenched and fortified; but almost every tree has been cut down by them, which makes it excessively hot and glaring. Dr. Eve called after dinner (Mrs. Eve prevented by an injured finger); expressed himself much pleased at the prospect of having your brother in the medical college. And by the by, they had already announced him upon their catalogue, which was taking time by the *forelock. Despairing* of the *vacancy* they had *anticipated,* to secure his services they had created a new professorship, which he will fill. I do not at this time remember what it is. We were much pleased with the appearance of Nashville, and I trust it will prove a wise and judicious move for my dear son and his family.

We left Nashville at six o'clock, traveled all night, and reached Cincinnati at one o'clock on Friday, expecting to make a close connection and go

603

immediately on to arrive on Saturday in New York, but found to our great disappointment we would be detained ten hours. And what was most distressing, the whole place was pervaded by the cholera panic, which disease had that day taken off forty-nine. The first object I saw from the window of the great saloon of the depot (which is also a kind of hotel) was an open wagon with eight coffins. And the dining room where we went to take our dinner was filled with the odor of chloride of lime; and the presence of disinfectants was evident all over the building, where several fatal cases had occurred. Not far off, in the same street, an entire family had died; and a friend who went to nurse them had been so frightened that he almost had the cholera and was speechless: probably something like paralysis had been induced. The horror which sat upon the countenances of wives parting from their husbands, parents from children, friend from friend, now that the king of terrors was in their midst, I thought might bring home to them some conception of the distress and misery they had brought upon us, fleeing from our beloved homes and friends, and writhing beneath their desolations of all we hold dear. The whole city appeared awe-stricken: not a smile, not a word, as they passed up and down in solemn silence. The whole atmosphere appeared tainted; and one of the waiters told me beef killed overnight was unfit for market the next morning.

We left Cincinnati a few minutes before eleven at night, taking the Great Erie & Western Road. The cars are of magnificent proportions, and sleeping cars all curtained and arranged with every comfort. But we did not go into them; your brother thought in case of cholera it would more likely be there than the open cars. We traveled uninterruptedly day and night, changing, I think, but once—a distance of eight hundred miles through a country cultivated, rich, and beautiful. The scenery at times was very fine.

As I mentioned, the ten hours' detention in Cincinnati threw us into the Sabbath, and we did not reach your brother's door until about one o'clock. He gave us a most hearty welcome, as did Eva; and my little Ruth was delighted to see me. She could not express her joy for excitement. She has been around me all the time. Asks constantly about Bubber and Sissy. Said: "Danna, what made you cut Bubber's hair off? It was so beautiful!" She evidently thought they would come with me. Tell Charlie she reads beautifully in easy reading, and is a remarkable speller. She sits down and studies her lessons entirely alone, then comes up and recites them. I find her much grown and much improved: a little lady in her manners. She undertakes the entire care of me when we walk out, showing and explaining everything and warning me of all danger.

I found Mrs. Eve and Eva all prepared for a trip to Newport for the benefit of sea-bathing, especially to Eva. Tomorrow will be one week since they left. Your brother saw them safely down and returned the next day. They are enjoying themselves; Eva, I trust, has the prospect of permanent benefit to her health. . . . I am now in charge of the house until her return.

Your brother has a delightful house. It is as quiet as the country: beautiful views from every window, and Central Park (that wonder of this country) near enough to walk every day in it—if I only had the strength. But I feel completely used up by the journey, and never in my life more inactive. I cannot walk a square without the most distressing sensations. I hope it will be better with me soon.

We are a great way off from the stores, which I have been but once to; and finding some warm winter skirts (balmoral), I bought *one for you* and *one for myself*. Goods, so far as I see, are as cheap in Atlanta as here.

Your brother Joseph found it impossible to stay this far, as he had to meet the doctors at night, and has put up at the St. James Hotel. He will probably visit Philadelphia and confer with the publishers there about the *History*.

On Sabbath we attended Dr. Scott's church, and your brother has taken a pew and will worship there. I am greatly delighted at this. Dr. Scott is a most earnest and engaged and godly minister. I was greatly moved and interested in all the pulpit exercises. I wish that Robert could hear him and see the manner—so solemn and earnest. He preaches long sermons, and makes great use of the Scriptures, requesting the congregation to read along with him, explaining the chapter at the same time. Yesterday he *called* to see me, and I greatly enjoyed his visit. He spoke with so much respect and affection of your beloved father. I told him of Robert's call to New Orleans; he says it is a noble field, and excellent people in that church. Says you need not have the first fear of the climate. The more I hear and see, the deeper is the impression that Robert has made a wise decision. I do hope the presbytery will not embarrass his move.

Your brother unites with me in best love to Robert and yourself and the dear children. Ruthie sends love and kisses. Your dear letter and the enclosures have been received. Am truly sorry Tenah's baby is dead. . . . Much love to dear Aunty and Cousin Mary and Lou, Ellen and Lilla.

Ever your affectionate mother,
Mary Jones.

MRS. MARY S. MALLARD *to* MRS. MARY JONES[c]

Atlanta, *Tuesday,* August 21st, 1866

My dear Mother,

Tomorrow will be two weeks since you left us, and still we have no tidings of your arrival. I hope the fatiguing journey has not made you sick. I presume Brother Joe has accepted the call to Nashville, as his name has been announced in the papers as professor of pathology. His name is placed first in the list of professors. . . .

I can write only a few lines, as I am myself very feeble. On last Wednesday I had my teeth extracted—nine in all. Six were taken out while I was under the influence of nitrous oxide gas; and had I stopped there, I do not think I would have suffered a great deal. But the three roots had to be extracted without the gas, as it was too tedious and difficult an operation. It was a tremendous shock to my nervous system; but Dr. Logan was with me, and with the aid of brandy and chloroform (taken internally) I got through, but soon after became insensible, and continued so for fifteen or twenty minutes. Mr. Mallard was very much alarmed, though the doctor told him he did not think there was any danger. It proceeded from nervous exhaustion and loss of blood. After an hour or two Mr. Mallard put me in a carriage and brought me home. The poor little children were frightened to see me lifted out and brought into the house in their father's arms. I thought I had more strength for the operation than I really had. I feel a kind Providence has been very merciful to me in watching over and preserving me thus far. I am glad you were not here: I know you would have suffered so much anxiety. I am taking muriate of iron, and hope gradually to recover my strength. I have been up most of every day since, and all of yesterday and today.

All of Aunt Eliza's family well; they have an increase of boarders. . . . How is Eva's health? I hope improving. Much love to Brother Charlie and herself and Ruthie. . . . Mr. Mallard and the children unite with me in warmest love to you, dear Mother. Mamie says to bring Little Sister back with you. Love to Brother Joe. Tell him he must not work too hard.

Your affectionate daughter,
Mary S. Mallard.

MRS. MARY JONES *to* MRS. MARY S. MALLARD[t]
New York, *Thursday,* August 30th, 1866
My dearest Daughter,

Your last affectionate favor has reached me, filling my heart with gratitude for God's mercy in *sparing your life* under such suffering and (as I believe) direct exposure to death. You must have been in a most critical situation. I hope your health will be improved in the end.

By the time this reaches you, your brother will have returned through Atlanta and given you accounts of himself and of us, and above all of the prospect we now have of your beloved father's work going immediately to press. I have written Dr. Howe asking the great favor of his revision and correction as a Biblical scholar and divine. Your brother here will receive and correct the proofs, and then forward them to Dr. Howe. I trust he will be able to accede to our request. I feel very happy in the prospect of its publication, and trust I shall be able to meet the liabilities involved. It will probably cost twenty-five hundred dollars to stereotype the work.

Day before yesterday I received a letter from your Cousin Laura informing me of the death of our beloved and aged relative, your Uncle William. . . . I presume they have certainly written you all the particulars. There is no one left to mourn for him as I will—no one else whose desolation and loneliness was cheered and protected by his presence and companionship. I had hoped—selfishly, I acknowledge—that God would spare his life on earth many years to come; although he told me before I left home: "Mary, you will never see me again; when you return, it will be to shed a silent tear on my grave." Oh, how I shall miss him—from his place on the sofa and around the hearth, from the family altar and the head of the table—miss his counsel and protection in that sad and lonely home where the very care and attention he claimed at my hands was a blessing! God alone knows what my future will be. I commit my way to Him, and pray and believe that all things will be ordered for me.

I have been very unwell since being here—at times greatly depressed in mind and body. Joe returned in so short a time I did not have the strength to accompany him back. *Do, if Mr. Pease or any of your personal friends come on to New York, let me know it.* I shall be anxious for an opportunity of returning in a few weeks hence, and know of no one here going South. Mrs. Eve speaks of returning, but I do not know any of their arrangements. She and Eva are expected by the boat from Newport in the morning. I hope Eva will return improved in health and strength.

My dear little Ruthie has been my roommate since her mama went away. She has improved in every respect, and spells wonderfully well and reads very correctly. Tell Charlie she is ahead of both Stanhope and himself; studies her lessons by herself and stands up and reads and spells right off. She speaks with great affection of the children, and always says I ought not to have cut her bubber's hair off, it was so pretty. When I showed her the likenesses, she pointed at the right one and said: "That is Uncle Robert."

Have you heard anything more from New Orleans? My dear child, I feel that I must return by way of Atlanta; for when we part this time, I know not when or where the next meeting will be.

I have thought a great deal of my dear old aunt. How much she will feel Brother William's death! Do give her and my dear cousins much love. . . . Your brother unites with me in warmest love to Robert and yourself and the dear children. Kiss them all for Grandmother and Little Sister, who loves them dearly and talks of them. Do write soon. God bless you, my child!

> Your affectionate mother,
> Mary Jones.

Mrs. Mary S. Mallard *to* Mrs. Susan M. Cumming[t]

Atlanta, *Friday,* August 31st, 1866

My dear Aunt,

A few days ago Aunt Eliza sent us Cousin Laura's letter containing the sad intelligence of Uncle William's death. How remarkable that he should have been permitted to spend his last days where Aunty died ten years ago! I doubt not this was very pleasant to him. It makes us very sad to feel we shall never see him again. He was at Montevideo the last weeks I spent there, and I shall never forget the submissive, quiet spirit that characterized those days. It was really touching to see his gentleness. I think he has longed to depart for some years past. I pray that we may all be ready when the summons comes. . . .

Brother Joe has accepted the call to the medical college in Nashville, and will commence his lectures there the 1st of October. I presume he will return very soon from the North, as he will have to move his family. I hope it is a wise move. He will have the prospect of a more certain and ample support in Nashville, and the climate is better than that of Augusta. In these days of pecuniary prostration the question of support for a young and increasing family becomes a very serious one.

Our New Orleans movements are still undecided, and will not be determined until the meeting of Presbytery, which takes place the 26th of this month in Griffin. I am most anxious for the matter to be decided, for the uncertainty is very painful to me. The church here will use every effort to have the presbytery retain Mr. Mallard. . . .

Aunt Eliza has been more unwell of late, but still keeps up her interest in life and things around. Think of it—she is now knitting socks for her great-grandchildren! . . .

My little Georgia has been improving quite rapidly for the past three weeks. I am now able to get sweet potatoes for her, and they seem to have done her digestion good. She runs all about, and says anything she pleases. If Mamie attempts to control her in anything, she says in the most positive manner: "Now, Mamie, hush!" It has been a struggle for life with her since February, but I begin to hope now that her little life will be spared to us.

If you should see Gilbert or anyone from Montevideo, please tell them to say to Lucy that Tenah and Niger have lost their baby, little Lucy. She was sick about a week. They felt it very much, for she was a remarkably fine child. . . . Please write soon. Mr. Mallard and the children unite with me in much love to Cousin Laura and yourself and kisses for all the children. How I wish I could come down and see you!

Your affectionate niece,
Mary S. Mallard.

MR. CHARLES C. JONES, JR., *to* MRS. MARY JONES[t]

New York, *Monday,* October 22nd, 1866

My dear Mother,

I have been anxiously observing the heavens, and am very glad to think that you enjoyed a pleasant and smooth passage. Please let me know how you stood the voyage, and whether you have entirely recovered from the fatigue, and whether there is anything which I can do for you. I am very desirous of knowing also how you found matters at Montevideo. Do let us hear from you as soon as you can.

I returned from Washington this morning after a fatiguing sojourn of three days in that unpleasant city. Found Eva better and little Ruthie quite well, but with her face somewhat swollen from toothache. Eva is to take her to the dentist to have it filled. They both unite with me in warmest love.

We have nothing of special interest. The skies are becoming overcast, and I am glad to think that you are safely on terra firma again. Do, my dear mother, let me know whenever I can serve you. As ever,

Your affectionate son,
Charles C. Jones, Jr.

MR. CHARLES C. JONES, JR., *to* MRS. MARY JONES[t]

New York, *Monday*, November 5th, 1866

My very dear Mother,

I am in receipt of your esteemed favor of the 26th ult., and sincerely rejoice to know of your safe arrival at home, and of your good health. We sincerely trust that you have quite recovered from the fatigues of the sea voyage, and that in the end you will derive benefit from its effects.

Am sorry to hear of the influences of the severe drought; but a dry season as a general rule is, I believe, favorable for the cotton in the marsh, and I hope that what has been lost on the high ground may be made up there. Those best advised are of opinion that cotton will during the coming season command a high price, so that it is all-important that every pound should be saved.

Before I forget it, let me say that from all I can learn of the present status of the commission merchants in Savannah, I think you will find *John L. Villalonga* perhaps the best person to whom you can commit the sale of the cotton. If you conclude to send to him, you can enclose the accompanying letter. I know that he will be glad to serve you, and I believe that he will faithfully and efficiently attend to any business entrusted to his care.

All that can be done for the mules with the distemper is to have them well cared for and have their noses smoked with the fumes of tar and burnt feathers. It is a severe affection, and will reduce them greatly; but as a general rule they will recover. They should have a plenty of forage.

In reference to the sale of the cattle, I think that you would do well to reduce the stock, retaining what you may deem necessary for the supply of the table, etc., etc. They should now command a fine price—or rather a little later in the autumn.

Please let me know Mr. Broughton's determination for another year so soon as he lets you know it.

Have you, my dear mother, heard from Miss Kitty Stiles yet? I do hope that she will come and spend the winter with you. . . . Eva, I hope, is gradually growing better. Little Ruthie is the picture of good health. They both unite with me in warmest love. . . . As ever, my dear mother,

Your affectionate son,
Charles C. Jones, Jr.

Howdy for the servants.

609

MR. CHARLES C. JONES, JR., *to* MRS. MARY JONES^c

Washington, D.C., *Saturday,* November 10th, 1866

My very dear Mother,

Here I am again, a petitioner in favor of the plundered Confederate. The hindrances and procrastinations attendant upon all efforts to bring the matters in question to an early and favorable adjudication are even more frequent and annoying than the famous "law's delays." I am hoping, however, for at least partial success.

I write now simply to assure you of my constant love and remembrance, and indulging the hope that God is mercifully preserving you from every harm. I hope to hear fully from you at your early leisure. I expect to be in Georgia soon after the 20th of December.

Just before I left New York on Thursday last, Mr. Scribner exhibited to me a sample page of Father's *History.* I think you will be greatly pleased with it. So soon as I return, I will commence, D.V., correcting the proof sheets, and will do all in my power to see that this is faithfully and accurately done. I will send you the first specimen page I can. . . . I hope to get back to New York the coming week.

Do, my dear mother, let me know if there is anything you wish, or anything that I can do for you. With warmest love, I am ever

Your affectionate son,

Charles C. Jones, Jr.

MR. CHARLES C. JONES, JR., *to* MRS. MARY JONES^c

New York, *Tuesday,* November 20th, 1866

My dearest Mother,

I am this morning in receipt of your kind favor of the 13th inst., and am very glad to know that you are well.

I assure you that I feel most deeply for you in your present loneliness, and I would esteem it the greatest privilege if you would come and make your home with us. You know your room is always ready; and all you have to do is to come on and occupy it. I think in justice to yourself and to your children that you ought to divest yourself of all these cares and spend your time with us, where you have every right, and where you ought to know everything will always be done for you that can be done.

I regret to hear of the death of the mule, and must try and supply its place for you at an early day.

In reference to Mr. Broughton, I think that his services for another year should be secured at whatever reasonable price he can be induced to take. Under the circumstances five hundred or even six hundred dollars would not be above the value of his services, and I would engage him at once. So long as we retain the place we must have a competent man there; and you need a prompt, responsible, and reliable man. His presence is an absolute necessity, and I would not hesitate for a moment. He would probably be able also to command labor, and that will be a very important matter. . . . Have you spoken with him in reference to giving him an interest in the crop, he furnishing the labor and managing the place? . . . I hope to be with you in December, and will then put in proper shape all business matters. Meanwhile whatever arrangements, my dear mother, you may deem advisable can be carried into effect.

I will do the best I can here to find a purchaser for Montevideo and Arcadia, but I fear that there will be little chance at present for effecting an advantageous sale. The Island also I will try and sell.

I leave for Washington again tomorrow morning. My business there requires great attention, but is most unsatisfactory. Any dealings with the departments are subject to numerous annoyances and vexatious delays.

In reference to a factor, I believe that Mr. Villalonga or Messrs. Tison & Gordon or the Andersons will do you justice. Tison & Gordon are excellent factors and very responsible men. Villalonga is a Floridian and an energetic factor. I would sell such of the cattle as you do not need whenever a good price could be obtained; and you will be sure to get this in the present scarcity.

The Central Railroad and Banking Company of Georgia will, we are informed, declare a dividend by the 15th prox. Do not part with that stock: it is the best investment we have.

Father's *History* is in the hands of the stereotyper, and I am correcting the proof sheets. I do not think that he could ever have read over the manuscript after Mr. —— copied it. Mr. ——'s copy is very defective: sometimes words and even portions of sentences left out, and at other times the sentences so confused that I am at a loss to know the meaning. But I will do the best I can, and give all my nights to the task of correcting the proofs and making the work as perfect as I can under the circumstances. The manuscript should have had a thorough revision before it was placed in the hands of the publisher. I hope, however, to get along with the publication without serious difficulty. You may rely upon the fact that I will do all in my power, and in doing this will feel that I am discharging a sacred privilege and duty.

Eva has again been quite unwell. Ruthie is the picture of good health. Both unite in tenderest love. And I am ever, my dear mother,
Your affectionate son,
Charles C. Jones, Jr.

Mr. Ward desires his special remembrance.

Mr. Charles C. Jones, Jr., *to* Mrs. Mary Jones[t]
Washington, *Friday,* November 30th, 1866

My very dear Mother,

I have been here for the past ten days attending to some important business, in the transaction of which I have been subjected to the most constant and perplexing delays. Aside from every other consideration, it is a matter of great annoyance to me to be here at this time, and yet I cannot help myself. I hope to get away by the middle of next week, and I hope to get away from New York for my trip home by the 20th of December.

I sincerely trust, my dear mother, that you are well. I long to be with you. Do let me know if there is anything in which I can serve you. . . . My absence from New York delays the correction of the proof sheets of Father's *History*. This I very much regret, but I cannot help it, and upon my return will do all I can to make up for lost time.

There is nothing of special interest here. Members of Congress are flocking in. This is the last place one can visit for anything like pleasure. With warmest love, my dear mother, and hoping soon to see you, I am ever

Your affectionate son,
Charles C. Jones, Jr.

MR. CHARLES C. JONES, JR., *to* MRS. MARY JONES[t]

Washington, *Monday,* December 3rd, 1866

My very dear Mother,

. . . In consequence of my engagements here for the past two weeks, I have been unable to correct any more of the proof sheets of Father's church history. I think upon examination it is quite evident that Father never read over—at least carefully—the copy made by Mr. ——; and that copy is in many respects very carelessly done. I never saw the manuscript. It was placed by Brother in the publisher's hands, and contracts made for publication. It is probably too late now to withdraw the work. I can probably make all the requisite corrections, although the amount of care, attention, time, and responsibility involved will be very great. But this I will endeavor to assume, and will do the very best I can. You may rest assured that I will not allow any imperfections other than such as absolutely inhere in the work (if any there be) to appear. I will correct the proof sheets with reference books at hand. Brother was so urgent in the matter, and had had the manuscript so long in his possession, and seemed so absolutely confident that it was in all respects ready for the press, and was withal so imperative in the matter, that I said nothing after expressing to him my sober, sound convictions of what was proper in the premises. The sequel has thus far fully justified the propriety of the views then expressed—at least to my mind. But, Mother, you must not let the matter trouble you, either pecuniarily or otherwise. I have assumed the responsibility of everything, and if I live and have health and strength, I will endeavor to present the manuscripts in a truthful and proper manner to the public. There are many alterations in style which I think should be made, but as these affect to a certain extent the genuineness of the publication, I will leave the manuscript as I find it, confining my corrections to manifest clerical errors. I will see the printer so soon as I return to New York, and will then write you fully. I think that I will be able to manage matters.

By all means *deny consent* to the establishment of a schoolhouse upon Arcadia land. It would, in the present condition of things, be but an opening to complications, losses, etc., etc. If Stepney will assume the planting of Arcadia upon proper terms, I think with you that there will be no use for the intervention of Mr. Mann. It would only detract from any profits which might be realized to give him any interest in the matter. I do not believe that his overlooking them would do any good to the laborers on the place. Stepney is familiar with Arcadia and knows how to cultivate the place; and if he will act with his former fidelity, I do not see that we could do better for the present than to employ him for this purpose. If he will furnish the labor, seed, etc., he should respond to us for one-third of the crop, he and the laborers assuming all expenses. In other words, the land should earn at least one-third of the crop produced. He will probably see you on the subject, and when I come out in December I can put everything into shape. At present I would make no agreement with Mr. Mann.

Uncle William's estate will, in the absence of a will, go to his next of kin; and someone will have to take out letters of administration. Captain Winn would be a good person to do this. I do not know who his next of kin are. He could find them out, I presume, without difficulty by advertising after he had been qualified as administrator.

Last Thursday I went to Mount Vernon and paid my respects to the home and tomb of General Washington for the second time in my life. The first time, you will remember, was when we all visited the sacred spot in 1839. I could recall the very spot where Father stood and made those lifelike sketches, the loss of which we can never cease to deplore. Everything remains unchanged, and the object of the association is to keep the house, outbuildings, and premises generally in precisely the same form and condition as that in which they were left by the general. Miss Cunningham was there. She had suffered vastly in the travel, but had had quite a satisfactory meeting of a number of the vice-regents. Efforts are to be made to make collections in behalf of the association, which is sadly in need of funds. She inquired most affectionately and particularly after you, and desired her kindest remembrances. I spent an hour in her chamber. She was in bed, and evidently very weak. Enclosed I send you a sprig from the flower garden at Mount Vernon. The box from which it was plucked is said to have been planted by the general himself.

I am tired to death of this place, and I hope to get away by the middle of the week, or by the last at furthest. Do, my dearest mother, let me know if there is anything in which I can serve you. By last advices Eva and Ruthie were pretty well. With warmest love, I am ever

Your affectionate son,
Charles C. Jones, Jr.

. . . If you have not already decided upon your factor, I think you will find that Messrs. *Tison & Gordon* would do you ample justice. They are excellent factors and responsible men.

Montevideo, *Wednesday,* January 2nd, 1867

A Happy New Year to you, my darling child, and to Robert and the dear children! May our Divine Lord ever abide with and bless you all! The skies with us are very dark: no ray of sunshine since *last year.* It is all in sympathy with our national and domestic gloom. Everything is dark within and without.

Your brother reached Montevideo on Friday last, giving me a most agreeable surprise. It has been raining ever since his arrival, yet he has been hard at work doing all he could with this wicked and perverse generation. This evening, we trust, they have consented to some terms of agreement.

Your brother went to Arcadia yesterday and was most pleasantly received. Stepney is coming back to take charge of the place, and they all engage to do their best the coming year. The place is well filled up with many valuable laborers, and it is hoped they will do better this year than the last. Mr. Mann makes a return of about a *bag and a half* coming to the place, with about twenty-five bushels of corn and a little rice, which I will try to sell. Also the cotton as soon as it can be ginned. I have paid all the taxes on the place, and the corn will meet them.

The most of the people on this place will remain, and Niger and Tenah go in with them. Gilbert will stay as last year, but puts his son to a trade; and Fanny retires as an invalid. Mr. Broughton with great reluctance consents to stay, but begs even now to be released.

My dear child, the anxiety and distress experienced about these people and my situation here cannot be told. Sometimes I feel in utter despair and desperation, and I would rejoice to sell the place tomorrow if I could. Only *one sacred tie* to Liberty would then be left. I feel that my way is gradually hedged up, and I daily ask my Heavenly Father to lead me in "the right way." I forgot to say that Kate announced today that she must go with her husband next year. I hope to persuade her to the contrary. Lucy is very faithful, but they often groan being burdened with freedom. The changes which surround me are marvelous.

Last week I made a visit to your aunt, and found her on the eve of a domestic "January Revolution": Anne gone, and Matilda going, to Savannah. They hoped to secure a good cook and washer. Mr. Buttolph's relative Lyman has presented him with a marvelous washing machine and a wringer. The clothes (from a blanket to a cambric handkerchief) will pass through and come out nearly dry. The cylinders are covered with gutta-percha, and you can sit at the machine and wash and read. Laura has improved in health, but is not strong. Your aunt is quite well, and always busy.

I do so wish you could get a call for Mr. Buttolph in New Orleans. How happy we should all be if only permitted to live near each other! Think of it—I have not been once on Sabbath to dear old Midway since I came back. No way of getting out! Two of the mules dead, and the third too poor to use!

I must close, as I am completely exhausted with the day's excitement. Our best love for Robert and yourself. Many kisses for my dear little grandchildren. Affectionate regards to Dr. and Mrs. Palmer and their family. I heard from Dr. Howe last week. All well.

Ever, my dearest child, your affectionate mother,
Mary Jones.

MR. CHARLES C. JONES, JR., *to* MRS. MARY S. MALLARD[t]
Montevideo, Wednesday, January 2nd, 1867

My very dear Sister,

You see I am here with Mother in our dear old home—now, alas, so changed. The disastrous influences of this recent war have wrought sad vicissitudes, and where peace and order and content once reigned there are little else than disquietude, turmoil, and desolation.

After a very perplexing day the freedmen here have at length come to terms, which, if not absolutely desirable, are at least the best which could be secured, and, everything considered, may be regarded as tolerably fair, if fully carried into effect. I have endeavored to persuade Mother not to bother herself with the ingrates, but to shut up shop and make her home with her children. But she is loath to do this, and concludes to try free labor another year. Stepney is to return to Arcadia and plant the place with some thirty hands, we to receive one-third of what is made, and to supply nothing. This is the best I could do; and I hope, with the blessing of Providence, that we may find the arrangement at least tolerably remunerative. I regard the whole matter as an experiment in behalf of the free Negro. Labor in this county is in a very demoralized condition, due in a great degree to the inefficiency of the white men, who are led by the Negroes instead of endeavoring to direct and control their services.

Have not seen Eva and Ruthie for more than two weeks. Hope that the next week will find me on my way back, for I long to see them.

Enclosed I send two letters of introduction for Robert, one to General Beauregard and one to General Wheeler. Upon my return to New York, D.V., I will send some circulars of our new firm, which I will feel greatly indebted to Robert if he will distribute as he may think proper among the influential businessmen of his acquaintance and congregation in New Orleans. I hope, my dear sister, that you are already comfortably and pleasantly located in your new home, that you have been kindly welcomed, and that every blessing will attend you, and that Robert's ministry will be sanctified to great good.

Father's *History* is in the hands of the printer, and I hope the first volume will be out in the spring. The correction of the proof sheets occupies all of my time. The manuscript was never corrected by Father, and is in many respects very defective; but I will do the best I can.

All friends here are well, I believe, although the weather has been so inclement during my visit that I have been nowhere except to Arcadia. Mother still has Lucy and Kate and Gilbert with her. Niger and Tenah are here. Mother unites with me in warmest love to self, Robert, and the little ones. And I am ever, my dear sister,

Your affectionate brother,
Charles C. Jones, Jr.

My address is: P.O. Box 6049, New York City.

Our new firm will probably be *Ward, Jones & Whitehead,* the latter member a New York lawyer of probity, character, and considerable distinction. Now, if you have any good cases you wish thoroughly "ventilated," just send them on.

I have just made up and entered for Mother in the family Bible the entire family record; and I deem it but an act of simple justice to apprise you of the fact at this the earliest moment that the space allotted for *births* is *entirely filled, and there is no room for a single further entry.*

MRS. MARY JONES *to* MRS. MARY S. MALLARD[t]

Montevideo, *Tuesday,* January 8th, 1867

My dearest Daughter,

Your last affectionate favor has been received. You know not how your letters cheer and comfort my heart in this utter loneliness. Your brother's visit of a week was very precious, and our parting very sad. It rained incessantly whilst he was here. Yesterday we had a glimpse of the sun, but today the heavens are darkened with clouds: every now and then a scud of cold rain, and every evidence of continued bad weather. All is gloom without, and not much light within.

I sometimes feel I must sink under the various perplexities of this situation, and know that if God should withdraw the hope and confidence which I trust He permits me to entertain in His infinite wisdom and special guidance, that I should be truly desolate and miserable. I have struggled hard to bear up under the severe losses, the sad reverses, and I may almost say pecuniary ruin of our temporal prospects. I have tried to live here that I might protect and not sacrifice this our home from any feeling of loneliness or isolation, or from motives of ease and deliverance from care. I have labored to preserve it as my only home, and what might in God's providence be a home to my dear children. And even now I am not willing, if I can prevent it, to have it sacrificed. But I feel that God is hedging up my way here; and I have come to the determination that if a purchaser can be found, we must part with our beloved, our long-cherished home. I do not see how I can keep it up, dependent as I am upon a manager for the oversight and upon the false and faithless freedmen as laborers. If there was hope of improvement in the future, I could endure any temporary trials; but I am convinced the condition of things will grow worse and worse. There is nothing to make it better—at least with the present generation; and by what means the Negro is to be elevated to an intelligent and reliable laborer I cannot see. The whole constitution of the race is adverse to responsibility, to truth, to industry. He can neglect duty and violate contracts without the least compunction of conscience or loss of honor; and he can sink to the lowest depths of want and misery without any sense of shame or feeling of privation which would afflict a sensitive Caucasian.

As I wrote you, I have not even had the means of going once to church to Midway this winter, and I do not feel that I ought to incur the expense of a horse, for I am trying to do all in my power to defray the expense of publishing your beloved father's work. Although your brother has found business in New York, his expenses are very heavy, *and he is in debt;* so that I feel he is unable to bear the pecuniary expense and also to give his entire evenings to the corrections, which he says are so very great that he is employed every night from the time he reaches home until twelve and one o'clock in correcting the proofs. He has to look out the references and often supply sentences, as he finds the manuscripts of *that* Mr. —— exceedingly defective. Your brother Joe has sent him the original copy, and he thus hopes to have it finally in order, but is convinced your father never read the copy over as it came from Mr. ——'s hand. Of this I cannot say, as the year following we had to leave our home, and your father deposited the manuscripts in the bank in Augusta for safekeeping, and there has been no opportunity since of reviewing them. Both Charles and myself desired Dr. Howe to see them before they went into the publisher's hands, but Joe opposed delay, and we yielded. I wrote Dr. Howe from New York, but received no reply until a few weeks since. It would evidently be a great demand upon his time; and although he did not refuse, I could see it would be a great consumption of his time and attention. I will write him soon. Your brother Charles hopes he will be able to make out and get the first volume in print by the spring. If Dr. Palmer fills his appointment from the General Assembly to Europe, I would like to ask the favor of him to take a copy of the work with him.

From the excessive drought our crop here, although better than our neighbors', *will not meet the expenses of this place the past year,* all things taken into consideration. Mr. Broughton has consented to remain another year, but I have to increase his salary to four hundred dollars, and as yet no increase of laborers, and a decreased system of labor. But there was no alternative: the place must be protected until disposed of.

I wish it were so that the furniture and books could be divided and sent to you and your brothers as you each needed and desired. Do write me what you would like to have, and also what would be the probable cost of transportation in a vessel from Savannah to New Orleans. There are certain things I would like to retain if possible; and I would not like to see the library sold. Many persons in this county need furniture, but they are too poor to pay for it.

617

I have not yet made a formal contract with the people. Gilbert will stay on his old terms, but withdraws Fanny and puts Harry and Little Abram in her place and puts his son Gilbert out to a trade. Cook Kate wants to be relieved of the heavy burden of cooking for two and wait on her husband. Lucy sighs and groans. But I presume these old damsels will remain with me for the present. I have no young ones about even to pick chips; and having walked out, I have just returned with the end of my sack filled with cedar and live-oak chips, which are giving out their fragrance and warmth.

Do write me your views and feelings on all these points. I have really so little to write of beyond my own troubles that I seldom think it profitable to be thus disturbing even my own children. During all my life it has given me pain to make drafts upon the sympathy of anyone.

I hope your black and white help will dwell in peace and not leave you. I would value Kate for her attachment to you and try to keep her. . . . Can you not get a little girl from some orphan asylum bound to you for a certain period that would nurse Georgia? It will injure your arm seriously to carry her so constantly.

Kiss the dear children for Grandmother. Best love to Robert and yourself. Lucy, Kate, Tenah, and Gilbert all desire remembrances, and Gilbert sends many thanks for Robert's gifts to him. . . . Do write soon and often to

Your ever affectionate mother,
Mary Jones.

MR. CHARLES C. JONES, JR., *to* MRS. MARY JONES[t]

New York, *Tuesday,* February 5th, 1867

My very dear Mother,

Today we see the earth for the first time since my return. It is very like the first blush of Spring, although I very much fear that we will still have many fierce struggles before Winter fairly resigns his scepter. . . . We have nothing of special interest here. Everything is dull, and the future appears uncertain. Business matters are not as flourishing as they might be.

Father's work is being as rapidly printed as the nature of the case will permit. You have no idea how defective the manuscript is. The manuscript was in no respect ready for the printer, and I am quite certain that Father never read it over. I am doing the best I can, but the style and construction of sentences are often so involved and faulty that it is hard to preserve the original. Frequently, too, wrong citations occur (owing to the negligence of the amanuensis) which have to be corrected, and omissions of important words which have to be supplied. Father appears rather to have *noted* what his thoughts were than to have embodied them in finished sentences. How deeply we deplore the fact that his life and health were not spared to perfect what he began! The first volume will, I hope, if the printer does not delay, be out sometime in the spring or summer.

With warmest love, I am, my dear mother,

Your ever affectionate son,
Charles C. Jones, Jr.

MR. CHARLES C. JONES, JR., *to* MRS. MARY JONES[t]
New York, Friday, February 22nd, 1867

My very dear Mother,

I am very anxious to know that you are well, and that God is dealing kindly with you. How are matters progressing at Montevideo? And is there anything that I can do for you?

Everything here is covered with snow to the depth of more than a foot. Eva and Ruthie are completely housed. They are both pretty well, and unite in tenderest love and remembrance. Ruthie is reading in her Bible, and gets along very well.

Over two hundred pages of the first volume of Father's church history is in type, and I hope that the whole will be stereotyped within the next month. The labor of correcting the manuscript and the proof sheets consumes three to four entire evenings each week. My impression is, in view of the cost of publication and the condition of the manuscript, the second volume of which I fear will be in worse condition than the first, that we had better wait awhile after the publication of the first volume until we see whether there will be any demand for it, and until the manuscript of the second volume has been properly read and corrected. I hope there will be ready sale for the work, although I fear from the impoverished condition of the South, and the nature of the work, that the sale will be more limited and tardy than we could wish. I trust, however, that in this apprehension I may be mistaken. Mr. Scribner will do all that he can, I believe. . . .

After I left Indianola the Negroes grew tired of picking cotton, and consequently instead of gathering the fine crop of over one hundred bales which was produced, not much more cotton was picked than sufficed to pay expenses. And I have meat and corn to buy for the present year. I am planting this year with about sixteen hands, and will sell so soon as I can get anything like a fair offer.

With our united love, my dearest mother, and hoping that you will let me know if there is anything I can do for you, I am ever
Your affectionate son,
Charles C. Jones, Jr.

MR. CHARLES C. JONES, JR., *to* MRS. MARY JONES[t]
New York, Sunday, March 3rd, 1867

My very dear Mother,

I am this moment in receipt of your favor of the 25th ult., and am thankful to God for His merciful preservation of you in health and from every harm.

I regret to hear that the freedmen are not working as you could wish. There is no redress in the matter except to discharge them, and this leaves one in a worse condition than before. Under the present legislation of Congress I look forward to no stability in this labor, at least for the present. I hope that Mr. McDonald will not disappoint you in the care and attention which we have a right to expect of him. Your purpose to plant an additional amount of corn with Gilbert and Andrew is very good.

All reports we have from the South are gloomy. I have endeavored in vain to effect a sale of our real estate. Parties here do not wish to invest at the South when so many better lands, and at cheaper rates, are offered in the West. The passage of this Reconstruction Bill over the President's veto also complicates matters very materially. . . .

The first volume of the church history will be stereotyped during the present month. The cost of stereotyping will be about twelve hundred and fifty dollars. Could you spare five hundred of this amount from the sale of the crop at Montevideo without inconvenience to yourself? If you can, I will make up the remaining seven hundred and fifty. The stereotypers will probably expect pay within two or three weeks. If the sum named will inconvenience you, Mother, let me know, and I will make an effort to borrow the whole amount here. . . . I would not mention the subject to you, but I have not now more money than I know what to do with; and it is about all that I can do to meet my expenses. The failure of the Negroes in Burke to gather in my crop has disappointed my calculations; and we find great difficulty in collecting the debts due us for services rendered to the South.

All my evenings are employed in passing Father's *History* through the press, and I have spared no pains to make the edition as accurate as possible.

Eva and Ruthie are both quite well, and unite in tenderest love and remembrance. Eva will not go South this spring. In her delicate state of health she could not stand the travel. We are expecting her mother on during the present or the coming month. We are snowbound again: everything completely covered.

Do, my dearest mother, let me know if there is anything I can do for you, or if there is anything you need. I will write you again fully very soon. Many thanks for the sweet tea olive. Its delicate perfume brings back so vividly all the dear memories of "Home, Sweet Home." Love to Aunt Susan and Cousins Laura and Buttolph and the little ones. I am so glad that they have been with you.

Ever your affectionate son,
Charles C. Jones, Jr.

MRS. MARY JONES *to* MRS. MARY S. MALLARD[t]

Montevideo, *Monday*, March 4th, 1867

My dearest Daughter,

To think over three weeks have passed since I wrote you a line! Your precious letters are a great comfort to me. They cheer my spirits and divert my thoughts from the daily pressure of care and perplexity, which I do assure you do not diminish.

I have felt at times that I must give way. The contract made is of the simplest kind and at the lowest rate—one acre to the women and two to the men, and the ground plowed, only corn and cotton planted; and yet they dispute even the carrying out and spreading the manure, and wanted a plowman extra furnished. And the fences are not yet made up, or the land prepared for planting. Mr. Broughton, too, appears very unwilling to give himself any trouble to enforce their contract. I sometimes feel that things cannot continue at their present rate, and this morning had a decided talk with him. He has accumulated business and not added one to the force here, but asked for higher wages. I have to give four hundred dollars, with no increase of force and diminished quantity of labor. I could do no better. The contract was at his suggestion, and I presume he thought it would save him trouble, of which he is evidently afraid. Gilbert is very faithful, and so is Charles. They are the exceptions. . . . But we will turn to a more pleasing subject.

Your dear aunt and Jimmie have made me a visit of over three weeks, which I greatly enjoyed. It was a time of great perplexity, and her presence and company greatly cheered me. Your aunt is very well and cheerful, and speaks soon of going to Savannah and probably to Macon. . . .

Last week I went to Maybank, and called upon Mr. and Mrs. Lewis, and spent the night at Woodville. Kate and Audley are trying to make themselves comfortable. They occupy three houses, and hope soon to have their dwelling put up; but labor is very high and very scarce. He has two white men laboring on the farm; no Negroes yet excepting day laborers. . . . Our dear old home would almost break your heart. As I rode up, Mr. Dunham's sheep were eating down the beautiful flowers as they were putting out; and the whole place, wooded and cleared, has been burnt. Indeed, if our *enemy* is not removed, the forest on the Island will be entirely destroyed by his repeated burnings. And he is making free use of our lumber—cedar, oak, and pine.

Did I write you Stepney has charge of the planting at Arcadia? But all under contract.

My dear child, I have been deeply pained to hear of Robert's continued suffering from his head. I am the more uneasy knowing that he is so uncomplaining. Do try repeated use of tincture of iodine, and then cold bathing after the surface is well from the iodine. Perhaps coffee disagrees with him; it always affects my head and nerves. I believe green tea much better for a student.

And my precious little Georgia—to think she remembers me! Tell her "Danma" has braided her a beautiful gold-colored cambric with black, and will send it by express as soon as she goes to Savannah. I am so thankful she has recovered from pneumonia. I wish you had Tenah in New Orleans.

I am going to write Mary, and will close, with warmest love to Robert and yourself and the dear children. I *think* Mr. Buttolph *would* accept a call to New Orleans.

Ever, my darling child, your affectionate mother,
Mary Jones.

621

Montevideo, *Monday,* March 4th, 1867

My very dear Granddaughter,

I received your letter a few weeks since while Cousin Jimmie was with me, and it gave me great pleasure to see how well you could write. And Cousin Jimmie read it, and his grandmother told him he must learn at once to write. . . .

I am happy to hear that Brother and yourself go to school and have so excellent a teacher. You must love and respect her and try to improve by all she teaches you. I want you to tell her Mama has written me about her, and I desire my best respects to her and feel very grateful to her for the kind interest she takes in my little grandchildren.

I wish, my darling, you and Brother were here now. The hand of our kind Heavenly Father seems stretched out in so many beautiful objects around. The trees have put on their new robes of green, and the bright and beautiful flowers are smiling in the sunshine and generously throwing out their sweet odors to every passing breeze. The two pigeons are here still, and come at my call to eat their breakfast and dinner from a little shelf at the pantry door. There is a remarkable chanticleer in the yard who is very proud of his gay feathers. One half of his plumage is bright red and black, and the other half mottled and striped, and he looks as though two different birds had been cut in two and stuck together.

Poor Captain died from eating part of a diseased mule that had died in the pasture.

Your good old nurse, Mama Lucy, asks constantly after you and Charlie, and says you must love your books and study hard. And Tenah wants to see you all, and Abram told me today he wanted to see "Marse Charlie" and "Miss Mamie." You must never forget these servants that were so kind to you all. Tell Kate her mother has been very sick, but she is better now, and all the rest of her family are well; and all they with the people here send many howdies for her. And Daddy Gilbert thanks Papa for what he sent him, and sends many howdies for you all. And so does old Daddy Andrew.

I hope you will write me again soon. . . . Kiss your precious mother and father and brother and Georgia for Grandmother; and know that she loves you all tenderly and longs to see you.

Your affectionate grandmother,
Mary Jones.

Mrs. Mary Jones *to* Mrs. Mary S. Mallard[t]

Montevideo, *Friday,* March 15th, 1867

My darling Child,

I have just returned from a very hurried business visit to Savannah, weary and feeling very sad. All things conspire to make me so, especially the return of this most sorrowful period of my life. Oh, how long, how long it has been since your dear father was taken from us! I feel at times as if I must die from the weight of grief which presses on my heart. The unshared burden! Here I am utterly alone. The goodness of God alone comforts and sustains my poor soul with a conviction that for the present I am in the path of duty, and hoping to accomplish the cherished wish of my heart.

Your brother writes me the first volume of the *History* will be through the press this spring, but Mr. Scribner is uncertain whether to give it now to the public or withhold it until fall. The cost of stereotyping that volume will be twelve hundred and fifty dollars. I have just sent all I had from the sale of the cotton over and above what I am at present owing.

The Arcadia cotton (one bale) was sold in the seed to Mr. Mann and realized one hundred and sixty-eight dollars. You request your part sent to your brother to aid in the publication, which I will do. We made here ten light bales of white cotton for *all* concerned and two of stained. Could it have been gotten early to market it would have commanded a good price, but it is now very dull. But I was obliged to sell, fearing also that it would be no better. You know I lost all my mules, even to the little colt (Dove's last representative). I will not by a great deal meet my last year's expenses, and our provision crop was so short I fear many on this place will soon be in want. The freedmen—nearly all of them—went to Savannah for their money; and although they need *bread*, almost all of them, Gilbert tells me, bought either a musket, double-barreled gun, or revolver! They all bear arms of some sort in this county. Such is the limited nature of my contract on this place for the present year—with no increase of laborers, but great increase of the manager's salary, and evident *decrease* of effort on his part—that I have really very little hope of realizing anything from the place the present year. The only advantage is the protection of the place in view of sale; but such is the state of the country even *that* may not be advisable, although if a good offer presented, I do not think I would hesitate.

While in Savannah I saw Kitty. She is looking remarkably well and cheerful, and will make me a visit before long if possible. I stayed with *our dear* and *tried* friends Dr. and Mrs. Axson. All sent warmest love to Robert and yourself. . . .

March 16th. An opportunity presents itself of sending this immediately to the office at No. 3, and I close hastily this morning. In Savannah I sent by express a little dress for my dear little Georgia. "Danma" braided it for her. I am grieved to hear of her ill health. Do use constant rubbings of sweet oil, camphor, and hartshorn over her little chest and lungs and spine. I am greatly troubled about Robert's state of health. *Do make him rest all you can.* I hope the blisters will help him. Let him use the liniment also down the spine and give up drinking coffee and use tea. . . . Your letters are a great comfort to me, and cheer my heart in this far-off wilderness. God bless you, my beloved child, and your dear husband and precious children! . . . Servants all send howdies.

Ever your own loving mother,
Mary Jones.

623

MRS. MARY JONES *to* MRS. MARY S. MALLARD[t]

Montevideo, *Monday,* April 22nd, 1867

My darling Daughter,

This is the tenth anniversary of your marriage, and I am too weary to do more than assure Robert and yourself of my warmest wishes for many happy returns. I have thought a great deal of you today, and sought in a special manner at the throne of grace for the divine blessing upon you both and upon your dear children. May the Lord make you conscientious and faithful and wise in training them up! It is a great and responsible work to educate a family. Habits and manners formed in childhood generally abide through life; and certainly the principles of faith taught in youth will shape the conduct and character for time and for eternity.

I am greatly delighted with the likenesses. Robert's is excellent. Everyone says you look *broken*. Dear little Georgia's is a sweet picture, and "Danma" loves to look at her dear little baby sitting up like a little lady. *Tenah* was delighted to see it. I do long to see you all, but *when* is known only to Him who ordereth all our ways.

23rd. Yesterday was a great mass meeting (political) of the freedmen at Newport Church. I am told there never was such a turnout in this county. They were addressed by Rev. Campbell, the former governor of St. Catherines, now owner of Belleville plantation (McIntosh County), where he has a colony of his own color (black). . . . They erected a stage under the trees near Mr. Law's monument, and had three flags (U.S.) displayed over their heads. Campbell urged them to hold fast to the Radicals and give the Democrats a wide berth. This is the onward progress to (I fear) a war of races.

And yet I am more hopeful than I have been for a long time. I think the bill of our governor, and that of the governor of Mississippi, will test if we have any semblance of a constitution or any law in the land. I believe the whole government to be nothing more nor less than a great stranded whale, whose flounderings are just beginning to appear. I must believe that He who ruleth in the army of heaven and among the inhabitants of earth is about to defeat the counsels of the wicked and bring to confusion the iniquity of this nation. I do feel at times a *strange hopefulness.* . . .

Your brother has sent me the printed title page to your dear father's *History,* and the first volume will soon be stereotyped. I sent him all the money (one hundred and sixty-eight dollars) that came from Arcadia—yours and Joe's and Charles's part—to aid in the publication. I will try and defray the whole expense. Your brother says he has given his entire winter to the work, generally being engaged until one o'clock in the morning.

Your Uncle John writes very sadly of Sister Jane's health. Your aunt has just returned from her visit to Savannah, Macon, Marietta, and Griffin. I must close. Tomorrow, *D.V.,* we meet to clean out the graveyard. Miss Clay spent last week with me, and sends love. Remember me to Dr. and Mrs. Palmer. Tell little Mary I am looking for a letter from her. Do encourage her to write. Kiss the dear children for Grandmother, and best love to Robert and yourself. If *possible* do influence Kate to marry and keep her; she certainly is attached to you. Lucy, Kate, and Gilbert all send howdies.

Ever, my dear child, your affectionate mother,

Mary Jones.

Sam (Lucy's father) died in March.

MRS. MARY JONES *to* MRS. MARY S. MALLARD[t]

Montevideo, *Wednesday,* May 15th, 1867

My dearest Daughter,

Your last kind favor, with the letter of my dear granddaughter, has been received. You cannot know how precious and acceptable your letters are to me. I hear nothing, see nothing, but as my children write or send me papers. Recently I have, however, been favored with visits from many friends.

Did I write you that Miss Clay spent a week with me? She was so cheerful, so delightful in every respect, that I was greatly refreshed by her society. If God spares our lives next winter, I think if I am here she will be much with me. She says she wants to write a book, and I tell her this is the place to do it in. She really has not even the comfort of a chamber to herself at Richmond, where they have built a rough house which has been more than filled. I do not think at her time of life that she is called upon to make sacrifices that involve entire personal ease and quiet. All but one—and he a man—of their former servants have left. . . . When she came, she brought me half a dozen bottles pure London ale and some nice black tea (about half a pound). Feeling the need of some tonic, I have taken a little of the ale, and thought it did me good. But I cannot bear—and do not like—anything stronger than *tea.* I may not leave here just now, and if I stay will take some kind of tonic to give me a little strength.

Sabbath week was our Communion at Midway, and Rev. Mr. Comfort from Valdosta preached for us all day. . . . He is a Virginian, and a regular F. F. V.—that is, he belongs to the best aristocracy in the world, one of those noble and pious old Presbyterian families of Virginia. . . . Mr. Buttolph brought him and spent the night with me. I was greatly interested in his visit. Being acquainted with many friends whom he knew, and having traveled over the mountains and valley and visited the springs of Virginia, we had many subjects of conversation. He was in Princeton Seminary when the war broke out. Was closely watched; had to leave secretly; made his way through much difficulty; arrived in Alexandria at the very time *Jackson* killed Ellsworth; reached our forces and entered as a private, in which capacity he served until he was licensed and became a chaplain. His health is very feeble; has rheumatism—owing, I presume, to exposure in the army. . . .

On Sabbath morning I went to Flemington and worshiped; it was also their Communion. . . . I stayed all night with your aunt and cousin. . . . Your aunt was absent about six weeks with James and Willie; visited our relatives in Marietta and Griffin. Sister Jane continues in very ill health; my brother writes very gloomily of her condition. She has been sick for two years, and is now most of the time in bed. Mary Sophia had just been confined at Aunt's and had a little daughter. They have several boarders, and hope for as many as they can accommodate in summer.

Sister Susan and Laura and Mr. Buttolph have very kindly invited me to spend the summer with them, and so have Joe and Carrie. I am really at a loss what to do. It would be a great happiness to see my dear children, and I know they would do all in their power for me; but I really feel as if the expense of traveling is more than I ought to incur—and cannot unless I am able to raise the means.

I have tried to live as economically this winter as possible, that every means might be furnished to the publication of the *History*. The first volume will cost thirteen hundred dollars; I have been only able, with the hundred and sixty-eight dollars contributed by your brothers and yourself, to send on seven hundred and fifty dollars. I have been making every effort to sell my cattle and sheep to raise the money, but without success.

Last week your brother sent me the first clear stereotype pages of the work, and my eyes rested upon them with feelings of devout gratitude to God. My first impulse was to fall upon my knees and render thanks that I had been permitted to see the desire of my beloved husband accomplished, and to know that the valuable labor of the last ten years of his life would be given to the church and the world.

Your brother Charles has labored very hard to prepare the work for the press. His entire evenings have been given until one o'clock in the morning before he could retire. Says he has not been able this winter to open a law book at night. My constant prayer has been that God would bless these efforts to the good of his own soul. In his last letter he says it has been a hard struggle to support his family. The most of their business is from the South; consequently a great difficulty in collecting.

A friend tells me *Eva* is to be *confined* in July, and said she supposed I knew all about it. But not a *hint* even has been given to me. I understand she wishes only her particular friends informed. If they mean to surprise me, I ought not to anticipate the information; and if designedly withheld, it certainly would not be very pleasant to make inquiries. So the matter must rest with themselves. There are wounds in life very painful.

I am glad you have taken off black. Your dear father did not approve of wearing it for a long season of years.

You do not write me what your plans are for the summer. Do let me know if Dr. Palmer thinks of going to England. I would like so much to place your father's work in his hands if he does go. I hope it may have a European as well as American circulation.

Last night there was a large meeting and registering of names at Riceboro. A Yankee Negro the speaker. Assurances given that the coming year forty acres of land would be given to each, and our lands confiscated and given to them, to whom they justly belonged. All here were present. A fearful state of things! Where will it end?

Tell Kate her family are all well and send howdies. Her father and mother say they want her to come home to them. I am really grieved she has acted so. Tell her I hope if possible she will marry the man and try and lead a better life; that I wish her well, and she can never prosper in sin. . . . Kiss the dear children. Best love to Robert and yourself.

Ever, my dearest child, your affectionate mother,
Mary Jones.

MRS. MARY JONES *to* MRS. MARY S. MALLARD[t]

Montevideo, Wednesday, June 5th, 1867

My darling Child,

I was thinking of your birthday and dated *the 12th,* which, when it arrives, if your mother is alive you may be assured she will be thinking of you and praying for you and wishing you every good and happiness for time and for eternity.

I have been suffering intensely over a week with pain in the arm and shoulder that was injured *ten years* ago. It has caused me to think of your sufferings, which have been so extreme, and which I doubt not you will always feel in your broken bone. On Sabbath I was in bed all day, and am now suffering so much I can scarcely write. It has been owing to sewing very steadily and brushing out the dining room with too much energy. I really fear I have injured some of those old ligatures that were ruptured. I am not at ease in any posture night or day.

For weeks we have had most trying weather: excessive rains and hot sultry atmosphere. The planters are complaining of grass and injury to the crops. One night last week we had a terrible thunderstorm that struck two trees, almost touching the cattle and sheep pens, just back of Sue's and near to Caesar's house. But God mercifully shielded man and beast and shivered only a cedar and a pride-of-India.

My dear child, my heart will be very anxious for Robert and yourself and the dear children this summer. I fear especially as those floods have deluged the land around New Orleans. If yellow fever should appear, you and the children would not certainly remain; and yet how could I counsel you to leave your husband? May God protect, guide, and preserve you all!

It rejoices my heart to hear of Robert's encouragement in the church. He has a wide field of influence. May the Great Shepherd enable him to fill it to divine acceptance!

You have never told me if Dr. Palmer goes to Europe this summer. Please let me know in your next, and remember me to them.

Tell my dear granddaughter I am waiting for her next letter, and look for one from *Charlie also.* I send enclosed one written to me from my little Ruthie with her own hand, and the first she ever wrote. I want Charlie to see it, and *then please send it carefully back, for I value it very much.* You can keep it until I reach Nashville, *D.V.,* where I feel I will be much nearer to you.

I have two pair of linen sheets that I want to send you, and thought it might be best to take them on to Nashville. Write me at once what would be the best way of getting them to you. If you *write immediately*, I will get your letter before I leave. I am anxious to go up the last of this week to Flemington and visit your aunt, and make arrangements for leaving the middle or last of June, if my arm gets better. Laura is in Macon with Susie on a visit to Mrs. Nisbet.

Tell Kate her family are all well. I have never told them a word of her situation. She ought to write them.

In any allusion to Eva's situation, *I must request you not to say a word of my having written you,* as I am not informed by her or Charles. I presume it is her wish to keep it thus. I sent her on a bed and mattress, and your brother has recently sent me a barrel of various nice and useful things in housekeeping. Business is dull with them, and he finds it hard, as everybody else does, to meet expenses. Mrs. Eve is with them, and I have heard would make her home in New York.

I have written in scraps, resting my arm. The servants all send many howdies for yourself, Robert, and the children. Tenah longs to see them, and seems ready to cry whenever she speaks of you or them. *She is huge!* With warmest love to Robert and yourself, and kisses for the dear children, and howdy for Kate. God bless you, my child!

Your own mother,
Mary Jones.

I wrote you your dear father's *History* would be out in the fall. Charles has sent me specimens of the stereotyping. The size of the printing is excellent. Does it not rejoice your heart?

MRS. MARY JONES *to* MRS. MARY S. MALLARD^c

Montevideo, *Monday,* June 24th, 1867

My darling Child,

Kind Providence favoring my plans, I will leave home in the morning and go down in the freight train to avoid night riding through the swamps, as the passenger train leaves at four o'clock in the morning.

By the express tomorrow I will send you two pair of linen sheets *for your own use,* which will add to your comfort in that hot climate; one of your old books for Charlie and one for Mary; a lace *crazy Jane* for Georgia; and Bloomfield's Greek Testament (which was your dear father's) for Robert. I trust it will prove useful to him in his study of the Scriptures.

Your kind favor with the valuable enclosure from Robert and yourself has been received, and I am truly grateful to you both for your kind and generous remembrance of me. My great grief is that I can do nothing for my children now, and am only a trouble and expense, although I desire to be as little burdensome as possible.

Much as my heart yearns to see you, my dear child, my judgment is against your coming to Nashville and returning to New Orleans in July. I fear it would be dangerous to do so, and might induce severe illness. If our lives are spared, the General Assembly meets in Nashville in November, and then perhaps you could come up. You know not, my dear child, how I long to see you; but I dread your exposure this first year in that climate.

Did you know that Carrie had *expectations* during the summer or fall? So she writes me. And your brother in his last letter for the first time tells me Eva expected to be sick the middle of July or first of August.

I forgot to say the chemise is for you. I bought it in New York. Hope it will fit you. You will see the sheets are marked, and you can alter to your own name. When your uncle was leaving last summer, I handed him fifteen dollars and told him I had sold his linen sheets (which he did not want) for that amount. He was much pleased, but did not know who bought them. I am told Mr. William Stevens, your old teacher, has administered on his estate.

By the by, it just occurs to me to ask if Robert has any remembrance of having paid whilst Arcadia was in his charge a medical bill to Dr. Farmer for attendance upon *Fanny,* who died. It was in February 1864. He has recently sent me the account, and as he was always very prompt in collecting his bills, I thought this might have been paid. Please let me know when you write about this matter if Robert has any recollection of it.

Tenah has been very sick, and looks badly. She is in a family way. Lucy also is not well. She has just come in, and says she wants to see you and the children "worse than bad." I think Niger has his fill of planting. She and Tenah send many thanks for the presents. They have not come yet.

For six weeks we have had floods of rain. Crops almost lost. Until yesterday the sun had not shone for ten days. . . .

I must close, with much love to Robert and yourself, and kisses for my dear grandchildren. I will look for Charlie's letter. And send me Ruthie's.

Ever your affectionate mother,
Mary Jones.

XXIV

MRS. MARY JONES *to* MRS. MARY S. MALLARD[t]

Nashville, *Saturday,* July 20th, 1867

My dearest Child,

I have been one week in this place. Found your brother and Carrie and the children all well and looking well; the children much grown. I had a pleasant journey on, with kind friends meeting me at every point.

Spent a week with your uncle and family. Sister Jane much improved, with prospect of permanent recovery; looked, I thought, as well as usual. Your uncle very thin, and looking much older; perplexed with the uncertain prospect of support from his church. Whilst in Griffin the examinations in the college where Johnnie and Josie attend occurred, and I was highly delighted with their standing and proficiency. In Josie's department he was the only scholar who stood *perfect* in everything (studies, deportment, etc.). They were the best speakers, and the vice-president said they were model boys. I felt truly proud of my nephews, and trust they will be great comforts to their parents. . . .

In Atlanta I was met by Dr. Wilson. . . . Your uncle had sent a sketch of your dear father's missionary labors to Dr. Wilson at my request; and since being here I have been diligently occupied making such extracts from his reports to the Association for the Religious Instruction of the Negroes as would illustrate his life and labors as a missionary. I am especially anxious that this period of his life should appear in its true light and importance. . . .

I spent three days with our relatives in Marietta. Our dear old aunt enjoyed my visit. Had no fever, and was up all day excepting her usual nap, and sat until some time after dark in the porch. . . .

I thought a great deal of you in Atlanta. The place much improved: all life and bustle, and population larger than before the war. . . .

My dear child, I am filled with pressing anxieties for you and Robert and the dear children. Oh, that the Lord would shield you all from that dreadful disease! Do write me constantly, if but a line. I am thankful to feel if you should be taken sick I could come to you. . . .

Your brother and Carrie unite with me in best love to Robert and yourself and to the dear children. I am looking for Charlie's letter, and he must send me Ruthie's. The Lord bless and preserve you all!

Ever your affectionate mother,
Mary Jones.

New Orleans, *Saturday,* August 3rd, 1867

My dear Aunt and Cousin,

A letter received from Kate King yesterday mentioned incidentally that Cousin Lyman had been ill. She "supposes I know dear Mr. Buttolph has been ill for weeks." I had not heard anything about it, and am grieved to hear of it, and hope he has quite recovered. . . .

Thus far we have had a healthy summer, though many have constantly predicted an epidemic; and I have heard the remark many times: "This is yellow fever weather." There are a few cases every week and also some cholera, but really nothing to speak of. I think the highest number of deaths that have occurred in one week from yellow fever have been five. This, you see, is proportionately very small. I have known of only one case within my acquaintance, and that was a young man living near us. He had it very lightly, and is quite well again. Still we are very watchful; and if anyone should be unwell about the house, I should put them to bed and send for the doctor, as everyone has impressed it upon us that everything depends upon taking the fever in time.

The last ten days of July were very warm. Now we are again enjoying pleasant breezes and agreeable nights.

Two weeks ago Mr. Mallard preached at Pass Christian, one of the retreats on the Gulf shore. One of our deacons owns a place over there, and invited Mr. Mallard to come over and take a week of rest and preach to the Presbyterians spending the summer there. The houses at Pass Christian are strung along the beach for five or six miles, one house deep. Everyone has a bathhouse in front of their lot, and the water is so shallow that they have to be put a quarter of a mile and more into the water in order to have it deep enough. Mr. Mallard says you can wade a hundred yards and then be not more than waist deep in the water. . . .

The gentleman with whom Mr. Mallard stayed is one of the wealthiest in our church. He is chief partner in the leading jewelry establishment here, and his family enjoy all the comforts of wealth. I must tell you of a conversation that Mamie and his little daughter had at a party. Mamie had carried a shabby little brown fan to the party. (I did not know she had taken it with her.) Katie Griswold said to her: "What made you bring such a fan? Suppose you were going to a wedding; would you carry that fan?"

"Yes," says Mamie, "for I have no other."

"Well! You ought to be ashamed of yourself. I would get a nice white satin fan and carry that. Why don't you buy one?"

Says Mamie: "I haven't the means."

"Why don't you get your father to buy you one?"

"Because my father has no money to spend on fans."

"Well! Why don't you get somebody to get you one? Ask some of your relations to buy you one!"

Says Mamie: "My relations and friends are all poor, and they could not give it to me."

Katie, not knowing what to say, said: "You ought to be ashamed of yourself to carry such a fan; and you ought to get another."

"Well," says Mamie, "if you are so anxious for me to have a fine fan, why don't you get one yourself and give it to me?"

Thus ended the conversation. Imagine Mamie's telling the child of the wealthiest people in the church her father had no money to spend on fans, and all her relations were poor! It was very funny.

While I write, Georgia has twice put her hands on the soot of the chimney, so that she might have an excuse for playing in the water under pretense of washing them. She requires a great deal of management, and has been sick so much of her life that we feel she is almost a baby yet. . . . I have a little strap which I find very useful as a regulator, and took it to the breakfast table the other morning. Mr. Mallard asked her what it was brought there for. She replied instantly: "To whip Papa."

I suppose all of your children have grown so much. I long to see all of you, but when we shall all meet I cannot tell.

Recently some of the gentlemen of the church have had six large-sized photographs taken of Mr. Mallard, and they were kind enough to send us one. It is very handsomely finished in India ink, and is a most pleasant and satisfactory likeness. I would give anything if I had one as good of my dear father.

I do not know whereunto the expenses of this place will grow. Think of small pods of okra being sold at fifteen cents per dozen, four tomatoes for ten cents, peaches a dollar and a half per dozen, watermelons (not large) for seventy-five cents and upward without limit, five or six small sweet potatoes for ten cents. Don't you wish you could dispose of a hundred bushels at that rate?

We are quite on the progressive order here. The last improvement made by our military master, Phil Sheridan, took effect yesterday. The city council was removed, and several colored aldermen appointed. It is beyond endurance. I never felt as I do now how desirable it would be to be beyond the rule of these wretches. I tell Mr. Mallard I hope if he gets a call from this place it will be to Canada or somewhere out of Yankee bounds. For the present it is our duty to await the issue, and I only hope they will hasten on their schemes and by this means bring an end of some sort.

Do write me soon. While Mother was in the county I did not write you as often as I ought, for I knew you heard of us through her; but now I will write more frequently. Love to Aunt Julia's family, and sympathy, too, in their troubles. Mr. Mallard and the children unite with me in best love to you both and to Cousin Lyman and the children.

Your affectionate niece and cousin,
Mary S. Mallard.

We have no news from Eva yet.

Mrs. Laura E. Buttolph *to* Mrs. Mary S. Mallard[t]

Flemington, *Saturday,* August 10th, 1867

My dearest Cousin Mary,

We were so glad to hear of you and your loved ones and to know that the fever was not raging in New Orleans as the papers reported.

I am sorry to see that you are progressing the wrong way in New Orleans as we are here. No redress in cases of difficulty with the freedmen here; and stealing seems to be the order of their day, until people find it next to impossible to live. Stock of all kinds killed. No meat, no butter, very little meal. Negroes starving with laziness. Military paralyzing all efforts to make them work. Country ruined: South has no future! Things worse and worse. No help as far as I can see. People generally dissatisfied with their homes; too poor to go away. Seasons unfavorable; too poor to live at home! . . . We have no potatoes, corn, or anything else. We rented out our places, and the crops having all failed, we will realize nothing. The people have no money to pay Mr. Buttolph's salary, and as it is impossible to live on air, of course, I do not know what we shall do. Hope Mr. Buttolph will get a call where those who preach the gospel can live of the gospel. . . . Cousin Audley has recently had a difficulty trying to get some of Ben's sons to work, and been heavily fined. The Nigs get the best, and are in the majority in this county. . . . Mr. William Norman intends removing his large family to Florida; says it is impossible to live here, the Negroes steal so and kill his stock. . . . And things must get worse and *worse here.* Sorry to send you so black a picture of the reality of things! . . .

I suppose you have heard that Charlie's Eva has a son, and Charlie is greatly delighted. He does not say what his name is to be. He was born on the 27th of July. . . . Mother, Mr. Buttolph, and the children unite with me in *best* love to you and Cousin Robert, Mary, Charlie, and Georgia. . . . Mother says she is so much obliged to you for little Georgia's likeness; also for yours and Cousin Robert's. How much pleasure these shadows give us! Write soon to

Your own cousin,
Laura E. Buttolph.

Mrs. Mary Jones *to* Mrs. Mary S. Mallard[t]

Nashville, August 1867

My dearest Daughter,

Last night I had a dream that caused me great anguish in sleep, and I woke up shivering as though I had a chill. I thought your dear father had died, and they were taking him away without permitting me to look upon his face!

Soon after breakfast your letter came, telling me of dear little Georgia's illness from yellow fever. My heart has been so sad, so heavy, all day I could scarcely occupy myself. I told your brother I wanted to go immediately to you. He said what my own reason approved—that I might only increase your trouble; for in all probability, going at this season into New Orleans, I would more readily contract the disease and be only an additional trouble. . . . I can but hope that the disease may not extend in the family, and if it does, as it is not prevailing in an epidemic form, that this may prove a favorable period for that terrible acclimation which I believe all must undergo who live in New Orleans. Darling little Georgia, she had a sorrowful birth and has had a suffering life. I hope you are enabled to supply Kate's place, as this is about the time for leaving.

Carrie is far from well, and is often cast down at her coming day of trial. And my dear Joe looks and is truly very feeble; I am seriously concerned for his health. I have been constantly busy since I reached Nashville. The weather has been excessively hot, but the city is thus far free from cholera, which prevailed so fatally here at this time last year—which is due, as their best citizens acknowledge, *under God,* to your brother's unwearied efforts for the health of the city.

Many thanks for Laura's letter. She gives a dark picture of our once happy home. I really think Mr. Buttolph would do well to remove North, where his father still lives, and he has a large circle of excellent relatives. But it would ruin our church in Liberty. He has sold out their interest in Baker to Mr. Thomas Fleming. . . . Good night, my dear child! I will write Mary and Charlie soon, and am very proud of their letters. Your brother and Carrie unite with me in warmest love and sympathy to Robert and yourself and the children. Kiss them all for me. God bless and protect you all!

Ever your affectionate mother,
Mary Jones.

Mrs. Mary S. Mallard *to* Mrs. Susan M. Cumming[t]

New Orleans, *Thursday,* September 12th, 1867

My dear Aunt,

I take it for granted you are anxious to hear from us at this time. I know you see reports of the epidemic here and know that we are exposed.

We have had no new cases of fever since Georgia's attack, though we are surrounded by it on every side. The yellow fever increases, but not rapidly, and thus far the deaths have been chiefly confined to foreigners. . . . Our most experienced physicians pronounce this a very mild epidemic. The cases, though very decided, yield easily to treatment. The weather has been so pleasant and the skies so beautiful that it has been almost impossible to believe there could be poison in the air.

I received a letter from Aunt Mary Robarts this week in which she mentions Cousin Lyman had been invited to preach for their church with a view to a call. I do hope the way will be open for you to move. Aunt Mary says Marietta has revived very much. Liberty County is hopelessly ruined, and I cannot see anything to make a continuance there desirable. And then there is another phase of the up country: it can be made a white man's country, which the coast will not be—at least for many years. If you get established there, perhaps you may have to entertain some New Orleans friends occasionally!

Brother Charlie has written begging us to go to New York until winter, but at this time it would be far more dangerous to leave than to remain; for the fever would almost certainly be developed, and it might be where we could not procure either competent medical attendance or good nurses. Most of the nurses here are colored, and some of them very efficient. We have a man engaged should Mr. Mallard take the fever. Our friends here are very kind in offering their services. There is a great deal of kindness and hospitality among these people, and a certain degree of freedom in calling upon each other in time of need that is very pleasant. I trust we will be preserved.

I will write you when I can. We are all very cheerful and hopeful. You must pray that we may be kept in faith and our minds stayed upon God. Mr. Mallard and the children unite with me in much love to yourself, Cousin Lyman, and Cousin Laura and the children. . . .

Your affectionate niece,
Mary S. Mallard.

MRS. MARY JONES *to* MRS. MARY S. MALLARD^t

Nashville, Wednesday, September 18th, 1867

My darling Child,

I cannot sleep—have been lying awake thinking of you, and now rise and light the gas, that I may send you a line by the morning's mail. Oh, the goodness and mercy of the Lord to you and to me, that He should be keeping you in perfect peace amid "the pestilence that walketh in darkness and that wasteth at noonday"! Only dear little Georgia has been smitten, and her disease has been healed, so far as I now know. And yet fearfulness and trembling often seizes me as I think: "Perhaps this moment my children are laid upon a bed of sickness." Fearful and distressing! . . .

Carrie still keeps up, and is working bravely. She has a woman in the house who works the sewing machine, and this week we hope to do wonders. She had not made the first preparation when I came, and *nothing* over from Charlie, and has had all her own underclothes to make up; so you may imagine there was plenty of work to be done. Yesterday I took Stanhope to a tailor and had a winter suit cut for him, and today, D.V., I am to cut another by it for him, that he may be prepared for cold weather. The children all look well and have improved much. Susie is very pretty and interesting, and is much more manageable. Stanhope reads very well, and is anxious to go to school. . . .

You last favor has been received. It is my only relief to receive your letters. Nashville continues healthy, but oh, so hot! Plenty of mosquitoes at night, with certain other little *night robbers,* who as I lit my gas scampered away in every direction. *God be with you all, my dear child!* Carrie and Joe always unite in best love to Robert and yourself, and the children speak of you all constantly. Kiss my dear grandchildren.

Ever, my dearest child, your affectionate mother,
Mary Jones.

I am glad to know Kate is with you. *Tell* her *howdy.* I was sorry she acted so wickedly, but I never told any of her family, or anyone at home.

MRS. MARY JONES *to* MRS. LAURA E. BUTTOLPH[c]

Nashville, *Monday,* September 23rd, 1867

I did not intend, my dearest niece, that one day should pass without replying to your last dear favor, and yet over a week has done so.

You can scarcely imagine how busy I have been all the time. I found Carrie with all her preparations to make, and we have been trying to get all the little ones prepared for winter. I have been making various new and refitting old garments. The past week Carrie was taken so unwell I thought it would all be over in a short time, but she is up again, and it may be deferred for two weeks.

Above all this is my constant anxiety for my beloved children in New Orleans, from whom I hear three or four times a week. Heard on the 16th and 18th. Dear little Georgia quite recovered, but Robert and Charlie were both sick with the fever. My precious child yet preserved, and little Mary. She writes that Robert and Charlie were both doing well. . . . They were surrounded by kind and efficient friends and nurses, who did not allow her to sit up at all; and day and night a gentleman was in the house to procure medicines and attend to the wants of the family. . . . Robert was taken on last Saturday week, and when it was announced to the congregation by one of the elders on Sabbath, they immediately called a prayer meeting on his behalf; and the elder told the congregation that none of them were to call at the minister's house unless they went as nurses, that they must not go to ring the doorbell and disturb the family, that not even Dr. Palmer would be permitted to see Mr. Mallard unless he went to nurse, and there would be people enough to inform them of his situation. She says if she desired it, one of the ladies would come and relieve her of housekeeping. I never heard of greater kindness than they have received. They have an excellent physician, and the epidemic is pronounced of a mild type. But oh, to think I am not permitted to be with my precious child in this season of sorrow and suffering! Nothing but the assurance on her part and that of Joe that I would only be increasing their distress keeps me away. I dread to hear that Daughter has taken the fever. I am sure in her situation it must go very hard. . . . It is prevailing generally with great fatality throughout Texas.

Thus far Nashville continues healthy, and in providence it is ascribed to the efforts of the health officer in removing all causes of disease. It has been very hot recently, and very dry; and just now mosquitoes abound. I greatly miss the cold delightful water of Upper Georgia.

Daughter enclosed your last letter, and the news about Marietta filled my heart with *sorrow* and with joy. Should our good pastor leave Liberty, the church would be utterly broken; and yet I know the people do not by any means support him. Mr. Buttolph has set us all a noble example of suffering patience under trials and reverses; and I have felt in God's own time and way a door of relief would be opened to a wider field of influence and a surer prospect of support. For myself, if you move away, *my precious dead* will be the only tie remaining to bind me there with a desolated home. I fear there will not be enough made this year at *Montevideo* to pay the manager! . . .

Joe and Carrie unite with me in best love to my dear sister and niece and Mr. Buttolph, to Jimmie and Willie and Susie. And their little cousins here send love and kisses. I long to hear from you all. Your letters are a great comfort to me, and my heart is with you in warmest love. . . .

Your ever attached aunt,
Mary Jones.

Politically things are in a dreadful condition here.

Mrs. Laura E. Buttolph *to* Mrs. Mary Jones[t]
Flemington, *Wednesday,* October 2nd, 1867

My dearest Aunt,

Your valued letter came day before yesterday, and was like cold water to our thirsty souls! Even the children danced around me when I said: "A letter from my precious Aunt Mary!" And containing so much good news!

May our Heavenly Father bless and spare all of our loved ones in New Orleans and bring them safely through that terrible disease the yellow fever! So glad Cousin Robert and Charlie were better, and the good people so efficient and kind. I do like that elder who gave such sensible directions. Truly they are *warmhearted Christian* people, and no mistake. . . . It would only be feeding the fever if you were to go, and might at this season prove fatal to you, besides increasing their *anxiety and care.* I have heard that one in Mary's case usually has it light. I only trust it may prove so with her, and that little Mary's case may be as light as Charlie's.

Mother gives her very best love to Cousin Joe, and says she congratulates him on removing everything that was *usual* or *unusual,* and hopes that he will receive ample remuneration for finding out all those noxious vapors and preserving life in Nashville; that she considers honor an empty puff these days; that Solomon is wise in saying: "Money answereth all things"; but don't think she is getting to be a "flighty, worldly-minded woman."

Mr. Buttolph returned mentally and physically refreshed by his trip to Marietta. He was officially informed that so soon as the pastoral relation was dissolved between Mr. Palmer and the church, he would receive a call to it. The presbytery will meet on the 10th of this month, and so soon as the door

637

of this cage is opened, D.V., these birds will, I think, fly out. Aunt Eliza says she will live two years longer if we go there. She completed her eighty-second year on Sunday. . . .

Mother, Mr. Buttolph, and the children, who talk of you every day, unite with me in love to you, dear Carrie and Joe and Stanhope and Susie and Charlie. Mother says this is her letter to you.

Your affectionate niece and sister,
Laura E. Buttolph
S. M. Cumming.

REV. R. Q. MALLARD *to* MRS. MARY JONES^t

New Orleans, *Thursday,* October 17th, 1867

My dear Mother,

About this hour (3½ o'clock P.M.) Mary was taken sick on Monday last. She has therefore just completed the *third day* of twenty-four hours, considered one of the crises of the disease, perhaps the principal one. Her attack has not been of a severe character, and her symptoms have been favorable with one exception. No nausea, no obstruction of natural functions; she has, however, been suffering very great pain in her back, hips, and limbs (principally the latter two). It is pronounced neuralgic in character, and I fear it will not be entirely subdued until she is able to change her posture and sit up. I have today heard of a case similar to hers in this particular of a lady now convalescent. Her pains prevented sleep last night and this morning, with the exception of a few naps. As soon as the doctor could be had, he administered a remedy which has given her ease. It will have to be repeated probably in the course of the afternoon and night if the pains return with severity. Thus far there have not been, so far as we know, any tendencies to a danger peculiar to her situation. I hope that she may have a quiet night. Of course I feel, and must continue to feel, deeply anxious about one who has grown every year if possible more precious to me. Mary is in good spirits and is hopeful of recovery, through God's blessing.

Charlie has had a slight attack of fever—the result of some unknown imprudence. Mamie and Georgia well. . . . Mamie is quite thin and pale but in fine spirits.

My dear Mary unites with me in warmest expressions of love to yourself and the other members of the household. Continue to pray for us that a merciful God may continue to deal tenderly with us, His undeserving servants.

Affectionately your son,
R. Q. Mallard.

Friday Morning. I did not get an opportunity for mailing this yesterday, and I therefore add a postcript one day later. Mary suffered some pain again last night, but has been quiet since midnight and has had considerable *refreshing* sleep. The doctor was here in the evening and was much gratified at the effect every way of the opiate administered, and directed its repetition if the pain returned. Its effects have now died away, and as she is quiet and almost free of pain, I hope that she will escape further suffering. Charlie bright and waiting for breakfast.

REV. R. Q. MALLARD *to* MRS. SUSAN M. CUMMING[t]
New Orleans, *Saturday,* October 19th, 1867

Dear Aunt Susan,

I rejoice that I have the glad news to communicate of my dear Mary's convalescence. She was taken sick with the yellow fever on Monday last, and the doctor pronounces her today "through the attack" and (to use his language) "well." Every soul on the premises—Addie, Lucy, Kate, Catherine, the children, Mary, and I (nine cases in all)—have been carried safely through. Have we not infinite cause for gratitude to God for His great mercy? Oh, magnify the Lord with me, and let us exalt His name together!

Yours affectionately,
R. Q. Mallard.

MR. CHARLES C. JONES, JR., *to* MRS. MARY JONES[t]
New York, *Wednesday,* October 30th, 1867

My very dear Mother,

Your last kind favor has been duly received, and I thank you sincerely for it. We have indeed cause for the greatest gratitude to our good Father in Heaven for His special kindness to our dear ones in New Orleans. Well do I know how heavily anxieties on their account must have pressed upon you. Now, however, that the sunshine of returning health appears once more settling upon the household, I hope that you will feel quite well again.

I cannot bear, my dear mother, the thought of your returning to Montevideo to remain any time there. The county is in entirely too unsettled a condition; your position will be altogether too lonely and isolated; and, in a word, I would not subject myself to the discomforts and uncertainties of even a temporary residence there. You may also rest assured that no profit will, under existing circumstances, be realized from planting operations in Liberty County. The decline in cotton and the uncertain nature of the labor cut off all hope—at least for the present—of remunerative adventures in this behalf. At the best estate, profits will not pay you for the disagreeabilities of a residence there.

I have endeavored in vain to interest a single purchaser. Parties will not buy, and for very good reason. Who does wish to buy in a county in such an unhappy condition as that in which our beloved South now is, and in a climate far from healthy during the warm months of the summer? I must confess my heart is very heavy when I think of the present and the future of the South. I have no doubt but that Reason, at present dethroned, will

639

eventually resume her sway; but intermediately what commotions may come before the white race regains its suspended supremacy? Who can tell? No one will wish to be there who can reside elsewhere. My impression is, my dear mother, that it would be best to sell out all the stock and perishable property at Montevideo and rent the place if a responsible party presents himself. Negroes and Negro labor are so entirely unreliable that a sum certain is far better than a speculative interest in the results of labor. I hope to be with you the last of December or early in January, and will do all I can to assist you. Meanwhile, if you have any offers, please consider them.

I am at a loss to know what to do with my Burke place. It is under mortgage for five thousand dollars, and if sold it would not probably pay the mortgage. The only resources I have are from my profession, and our receipts have been very limited of late. I must confess the prospect seems very dark. . . .

Do, my dear mother, give up all intention to remain at Montevideo during the coming winter, and come and divide your time with your children, who will be only too happy to welcome you, and will esteem it the highest privilege to have you with them. Let me know if I can do anything for you. The Central Railroad will declare a dividend of five percent in December. This will help you.

Eva is badly pulled down with her little boy, and is not very strong and well. She does not get rest enough. Ruthie and Casey are both pictures of good health. . . . All unite in tenderest love. And I am ever, my dear mother,

Your affectionate son,
Charles C. Jones, Jr.

MRS. MARY S. MALLARD *to* MRS. MARY JONES[t]

New Orleans, *Thursday,* October 31st, 1867

My dearest Mother,

I am thankful to be able to write you once more. Great have been our mercies: nine cases of that terrible fever in our household, and all recovered, while so many mourn the loss of one or more members of their families. . . . Persons living here say there never has been so sad an epidemic as this. In previous years the mortality has been comparatively small among the natives and higher classes; but this season it has fallen heavily upon the most respectable, and numbers of natives have died, and a remarkable number of children have fallen. We have lost ten by the fever out of our congregation, and now a young lady of seventeen is dangerously ill.

I was taken sick so late that Mr. Mallard has been kept from taking any trip abroad. If possible he will spend a few days across the lake next week. . . .

We will probably have to move from this house next week or the week after, as this with the furniture will be sold on the 15th of November. We will have to furnish for ourselves, and will be able to do so on a very small scale and by degrees, getting only what is absolutely necessary. I am sorry to give up this house, as it is very convenient, though rather far from the church. The other house is pleasantly located in the midst of our people, and I think we shall like it very much.

We are all anxiously looking for the time to come when you will come to us; and we hope, dear Mother, nothing will prevent your coming as soon as possible. I wish it could have been arranged so that Mr. Mallard could have met you in Atlanta. He is writing you in regard to the *History;* I long to see a copy of it.

I would write more, but have not strength. Until day before yesterday I had not been out of my room. I am rejoiced to hear Carrie is doing so well. Give a kiss of love and welcome to the little stranger for us all. The children all unite with me in much love to Brother Joe, Carrie, and the children, and warmest love for yourself. . . . Tomorrow will be All Saints' Day, one of *the days* of interest in New Orleans. The cemeteries will be visited and tombs decorated. I regret I shall be unable to see any of them. The whole city will be given up to the duties of the day.

Your loving daughter,
Mary S. Mallard.

MRS. MARY S. MALLARD *to* MRS. MARY JONES^t

New Orleans, *Thursday,* November 7th, 1867

My dear Mother,

I write you once more to Nashville, not knowing the time you expect to leave.

We have had delightful cool weather for a week past, and some say a little frost. The return of cool weather is doing much for the restoration of our invalids. I am improving slowly, and hope to be able to go to church next Sabbath, which will be our Communion. . . . The yellow fever has almost disappeared from the city, and persons are returning. In a few weeks the city will be full of the summer birds, and I feel we shall have a population totally out of sympathy with the suffering and afflicted ones who have been here during the epidemic.

Mr. Mallard went to Pass Christian on Monday to spend a few days with Mr. Griswold, and will return tomorrow. Even a few days out of the city will be beneficial. Pass Christian is about six hours' run by steamer on the lake shore.

We expect to move on next Tuesday, and then I shall make a change in my household. Kate said to me a few days ago: "I wish to tell you if you will give me twelve dollars per month I will stay with you; but if not, I have had good offers and I will find another place. I had twenty-five dollars offered me to wet-nurse, but I won't nurse for anybody."

"Very well," I said, "if you have had these fine offers, you had better take them. I cannot afford to give you twelve dollars for what you do and support Catherine too."

"Well," said she with a very impertinent air, "I will find another place."

Ever since we came here we have paid her nine dollars a month, and she had not been here two weeks before she incapacitated herself for her work, which was cooking and washing; and the greater part of the time I have had to hire a woman two days every week at a dollar a day to wash and iron; so that I have really paid all the time from thirteen to seventeen dollars per month on her account, besides having the annoyance of her situation and dirt and the screaming of her child. After her confinement I allowed her to return before she was able to work. Then I nursed her child and herself through yellow fever; so that altogether she has been a very expensive servant to me. I have had the comfort of having her here without change, and she did very well while we were sick; though I am now convinced that her *situation* had a great deal to do with her remaining, and I am pretty certain she is entering upon the same life again, which of course would forbid my retaining her. It is too bad. I have warned her and dealt faithfully with her, but she will follow her own evil ways. I have seen for some weeks that she was becoming disaffected and surly, so that it did not surprise me when she gave notice she would leave. Since then she has not found the fine offers she spoke of, and I think she is quite miserable; but I shall make no effort to retain her, although I feel very sorry for her, and shall continue to do what I can for her.

As far as I can judge, Adeline, my white woman I took care of while she had yellow fever, seems truly grateful; and she has offered to do my cooking and washing with the assistance of a woman one day whom she offers to pay out of her own wages. This will be a great relief to me, for she seems to be a quiet, honest woman and says "she don't want me to distress myself." I hope she will prove what I think she is. It will be easier for me to get someone about the house. Adeline is now doing my washing and most of the housework. Kate does the rest and cooks. I am very glad Adeline has offered to cook, for I feel always comfortable when that department is filled. I don't feel able to go into the kitchen, and that is something that has to be attended to. Housework can be postponed. I tell the family the day I have no cook they will all eat lightly! I will make a cup of tea or coffee on the gas, and they can have that with bread and cheese and milk and crackers. I shan't consider hot soups, etc., healthy.

We received a letter from Mr. Mallard's brother John a few days ago giving a deplorable account of the poverty of the people in Liberty. He says many of the sick have continued weak from the want of nourishment, and no prospect of matters improving. They are all very sad about Mr. Buttolph's leaving, but he (Mr. Mallard) says he feels he is in the path of duty, as they cannot support him. Do, my dear mother, remain as short a time as possible in the county. It is even more desolate than last year. Make your arrangements as soon as possible to come to us. Can't you come by the middle of December? We all long to see you.

The children are getting strong again. I let them run in the square and yard as much as possible to try and get their health as quickly as they can, as I want them to begin school again as soon as we move. They send love and kisses to dear Grandmama. Good-bye, dear Mother.

Your loving daughter,
Mary S. Mallard.

MRS. MARY JONES *to* MRS. MARY S. MALLARD[t]
Montevideo, *Tuesday,* November 19th, 1867

My darling Child,

Here I am, through God's mercy, once more at our dear old home.

I arrived on Friday week and went up to Flemington. The following Monday your aunt, Willie, and Susie and myself, driven by Gilbert, went to the Island. Audley is filling up the Island with white laborers, and is encouraged. Kate has the wife of one of the workmen as her cook; but she has been often doing her own cooking, and has no nurse for her infant, an uncommonly fine babe (*Robert Lewis*).

Last Sabbath was a deeply solemn and sorrowful day at Midway. Our beloved and faithful pastor, connected with us for thirteen years and four months, broke to us the emblems of our Redeemer's love for the last time. Now perhaps for the first time in the history of our venerated sanctuary the living teacher is withdrawn. So far as we are concerned, silence will reign within those consecrated walls, or even a more deplorable end may await them. And our precious, our beloved, our sainted dead must sleep in the solitude and neglect of a wilderness. My heart felt as if it would burst at this last great affliction which it has seemed best for the Great Head of the Church to send upon us.

Mr. Buttolph and his aged father, now eighty-eight, came home and spent the night with me. They will leave the county on Tuesday the 26th. Through Major Wallace they have cars direct to Atlanta and free tickets for all the family; and I know it will cheer your heart to hear that kind Mrs. Smith, now in Canada, has given your good aunt this year one thousand dollars in greenbacks. Mr. Fleming bought their place and has sold profitably all their stock, etc., etc.

It is true, my child, this county is in ruins. The people are becoming poorer and poorer; I know not what is to become of them. My situation here is just this: one bale of cotton and about twenty bushels of corn made by the freedmen employed. Gilbert, whom I hired, has made me some more corn, but one-third is rotten. No rice at all, nor potatoes to speak of. And a salary of four hundred dollars to pay the manager! I had a talk with him last night and offered to turn everything into his hands, but he will not hear to it; and although I have furnished everything besides for his support and comfort in health and sickness, and he has really done nothing so far as labor is concerned on the place, he has not the honor or conscience to say he is willing to share in any degree the total loss of the year. I am totally at a loss what to do with the place, and am trying to sell cattle and sheep to meet expenses.

And now you must write me the best way of going to New Orleans, and what it will cost to take me there. If I only had the means, would send you just what you need to furnish your house. I must send you the Brussels carpet and a bedroom carpet and some bedding if no more. Would you be willing to pay the express on the carpets? Write me candidly and at once and tell me, my precious child, *when* you expect to be sick. I must bring on your father's papers; I could not leave them. All else—books, pictures, bedding, etc., etc.—must remain. Charles will be here 1st of January, and I could not leave before he comes. I am so much perplexed and distressed at my situation, and leaving the place unprotected (for Mr. Broughton will not manage for us again); and if I can get Mr. Alexander, I will do so. *Do write immediately; I have not a moment to spare.*

Bless the Lord for His mercy in your spared lives! Saw all of Robert's sisters and his brother on Sabbath. All looking well. Warmest love for Robert and yourself, and many kisses for my grandchildren.

Ever your loving mother,
Mary Jones.

MRS. MARY S. MALLARD *to* MRS. MARY JONES[t]

New Orleans, *Tuesday,* November 26th, 1867

My dear Mother,

Your letter written from Montevideo is at hand, and I hasten to reply without waiting for Mr. Mallard to go to the railroad office to inquire the best route here, etc. He will do so this afternoon, and then I will write all particulars. You must not trouble about your expenses here, for we had intended expressing you the amount, and will do so soon. We are truly grateful to you for the carpets and bedding, and will gladly pay the express. All that will be necessary will be to direct to Mr. Mallard, Third Street between Coliseum and Chestnut Streets, and take a receipt. We will pay at this end. The carpets will be the greatest help to us, and the bedding; for such things are above the purse of common people.

I am truly sorry to hear of the deplorable condition of affairs at Montevideo. Would Mr. Alexander be willing to rent the place? Even a small rent would be better than planting yourself and finding things at the end of the harvest worse than nothing. Such is the demoralized condition of the Negroes in Liberty that until half of them die of starvation they will not realize the necessity of earning their bread in the sweat of their brows. Would Audley like to extend his white colony to Maybank? If some of the outbuildings had been spared, something might be done there with white labor; for the climate is so healthy, and the advantages of the salt water so great.

The condition of Midway is distressing. I often think of our dear ones sleeping in the graveyard there, and thought how desolate it would be when there was none to minister in the sanctuary. I feel thankful the sainted ones whose bodies rest there were spared all knowledge of the future. And now they enjoy perfect rest and joy; and "their ashes our Father's care will keep."

I feel anxious, my dear mother, you should leave the county as soon as possible. Now that Aunt Susan and all the family have left, it is too desolate for you to remain; and yet I know it is a tremendous trial to leave so comfortable a home. Still there is nothing but the house. Everything else is changed—and *permanently* changed while our political condition remains what it is. You must make our house your home, and we will try and do all that we can to make you happy. I think you will like this place; the only objection to it is the want of a more invigorating climate.

How did the Negroes appear when you returned this time? Do they still seem to retain any of their former attachment? At this time the "Black-and-Tan" Convention is holding its sessions in this city. One of the papers calls them the "Bones-and-Banjo" Convention. A black Negro occupies the chair, and white and black are sprinkled alternately through the house. These are the men to frame a new constitution for the state! I think the sooner the Radicals run their race the better.

What time in January will Brother Charlie probably come South? I hope early, so that you can make your arrangements before the winter is too far advanced.

I am rejoiced to hear of so much assistance being given Mr. Buttolph in transporting his family. Major Wallace is a Presbyterian and a noble man. Mrs. Smith's gift to Aunt Susan is most generous. I have always thought she was a noble woman, and wholly unappreciated by the Davis family. I do not believe there is another member of the family that would ever think of recognizing Aunt Susan's connection with them. This gift will be a great help to the family. When will Cousin Laura be confined?

I think I shall be sick about the 11th of February—certainly not later than the 15th. I feel sometimes as though it might be nearer, for I have never recovered my activity since the yellow fever, and suffer a good deal at times from those horrible cramps. You know what they are.

My white servants seem quite cheerful and contented in my service, and if they will only remain so, I shall be satisfied. My young German house girl requires constant supervision, but she is so pleasant-tempered and respectful that I hope to make something out of her. She is too new a broom for me to know yet; it is common for all of them to run well for a month.

Mamie and Charlie commenced school today. In a short time the school will be moved within two squares of us, for which I am very glad, as the children are not entirely strong and very susceptible to colds, and we have a great deal of wet weather after January.

I wish you could come on before Christmas. The stores of New Orleans are worth seeing on Christmas Eve, and the crowd that throngs Canal Street is as interesting as the articles on exhibition. . . . Love to Aunt Julia's family. Mr. Mallard and the children unite with me in tenderest love for yourself. Howdy for the servants.

Your affectionate daughter,
Mary S. Mallard.

MRS. MARY JONES *to* MRS. MARY S. MALLARD[t]

Montevideo, *Thursday*, November 28th, 1867

My darling Child,

Not one word from you since your letter directed to Nashville! I wrote you fully before I left that place, sending two blue merino sacques for Mary and Georgia. Have they ever arrived? My heart aches to hear from you.

If I only had the means of transportation, here is a house full of furniture that could be so useful to you, but it is utterly out of my power. One bag of cotton and forty-two bushels of corn made on this place. And no work done by the manager—not even the spring work. And yet, although he has been cared for and supported, he claims his salary as though he had done his duty and made a crop. I never saw less *true* feeling on the part of a man. At Arcadia they will make about half a bag and some corn and fodder for sale. How much I cannot tell; perhaps enough for taxes. I will tell you as soon as sold. It has been the most disastrous year I ever knew.

I have made no positive arrangements yet for this place; will probably get Mr. Alexander to take charge, and let Gilbert be the foreman. Charles and Lucy promise to move over to the lot and take charge of the house and lot.

Do write me fully the route to New Orleans and the expense of getting there. And write me the time you are expecting to be sick. Do write at once—and *particularly.*

Next week I will try and express the Brussels and one other carpet to you, which will, I hope, be a help to you. Write me what bedding or anything else you want that could come by express without being too expensive. I am trying to pack and arrange the books, furniture, etc., so that if I never am permitted to return, they can be sent to those who will wish them. There is no sale for anything of the kind here. It is the poorest community, and becoming worse and worse. The rod of affliction is still heavy in temporal affairs, and that heavy stroke of losing our beloved pastor is now added.

Day before yesterday (Tuesday) I went up and dined in company with your dear aunt, Mr. Buttolph and his father, and the two boys and Susie. At one o'clock the cars came; and it was an affecting sight to see them leaving, and a long line of weeping and sorrowing ladies, gentlemen, young men, and children left at the side of the vacant track, now sheep without a shepherd. For the first time in its history I believe our venerated church has none to break the Bread of Life. I feel that I am more utterly alone than any being in the county; I am linked only to my beloved and kindred dust. Being unable to do more, I am going to put up the brickwork of a tomb at Midway. It will not prevent a monument as soon as I am able.

646

I have risen at three o'clock to write, as I do not usually sleep beyond that hour now. *Do write me at once the route and cost of journey to New Orleans,* and time of getting there. And above all write me of yourself. . . . With warmest love for Robert and yourself and the dear children. I am provoked at Kate's ungrateful conduct; she deserves to be sent away. Hope if she stays she will do better. If she could see the ragged and starving ones here, she would value her place.

Ever your own affectionate mother,
Mary Jones.

MRS. MARY JONES *to* MRS. MARY S. MALLARD[t]

Montevideo, *Sunday,* December 1st, 1867

My darling Child,

I wrote you fully before leaving Nashville; have written you twice since I reached home. Was rejoiced to receive your last on Saturday night; had not heard so long from you.

Before leaving Nashville I wrote to little Mary and sent through the mail two blue French merino sacques that I had cut and embroidered on the machine—one a walking sacque for her, and a house sacque for Georgia. You do not mention getting them. Robert had best inquire particularly at the office. They were put in the very last of October or first of November. If they do not come to light, I will write on to Nashville about them.

Do write me at once the *best route* to New Orleans, and *the expense of getting there,* and *when you expect to be sick.* I long to be with you, and am doing my best to arrange business here so as to leave early in January. I will send you the Brussels and a bedroom carpet, and if the expense of transportation was not too great, would send you furniture *complete* for your drawing room, etc., etc. Would you be willing to pay the express on the Philadelphia sofa and the six chairs to match those you have? It is impossible to sell here: people are too poor to buy. I will send on a bed and mattress with the carpets if the express is not too high.

I write in haste this morning, hoping for a chance to the mail. Do answer these inquiries one and all *immediately,* for my arrangements depend on your reply. With best love to Robert and yourself, and kisses for the dear children,

Ever your affectionate mother,
Mary Jones.

MRS. MARY S. MALLARD *to* MRS. MARY JONES[t]

New Orleans, *Saturday,* December 7th, 1867

My darling Mother,

Your last letter, dated December 1st, has just arrived, and I hasten to reply. Mr. Mallard opened your letter at the office, and finding you had sent the parcel by mail, he inquired particularly, but the postmaster said nothing had ever come. I am truly sorry, for I fear the pretty sacques are lost. Neither they nor your last letter from Nashville have ever been received. It is too bad.

Mr. Mallard inquired about the routes here. There are two, and the expense from Savannah here is about the same by either. One is by way of Macon, Columbus, Montgomery, and Mobile; thus far by railroad. At Mobile you take a steamer to this place, or rather to the Pontchartrain Railroad, which is only half an hour's run from the city. Sometimes the passage from Mobile is very rough, and persons are made very seasick. When it is calm it is very pleasant to those who enjoy water carriage. The boats are very fine. The other route is entirely by railroad, via Chattanooga, where you will take the Memphis & Charleston Railroad to Grand Junction; from there to Canton, and on to New Orleans. The time occupied is three days and six hours. This is considered by the general ticket agent here the best route, as there are fewer changes; and when they do occur, you only step from one car to another; and there are sleeping cars all the way. The fare by either route is forty dollars from Savannah. There you could obtain a through ticket. We expect to express on the first or second day of January forty-five dollars, which we will direct to you, No. 3 (McIntosh Station). I am sorry we cannot do it at once. Whenever you fix the time for leaving, write us some days previous so that Mr. Mallard can meet you at the depot. Or else telegraph from Savannah.

We are truly obliged to you for the carpets and bedding, and will gladly pay the express on them. Thus far we have not been able to form any idea of the cost of bringing furniture, as the clerk here says there are so many ways of estimating express freight—sometimes by weight and sometimes by bulk. I do not think we could pay the express on the furniture in the next six weeks; but if you could leave the chairs and sofa so that they could be sent afterwards, we would be very glad to have them. The very association would make them valuable. Should anything occur, in the meanwhile, and we can find out definitely about the cost, I will write immediately; or if you should see the express agent at the other end and he could give any idea, we would like to know. Having to furnish from the beginning, anything is acceptable. I tell Mr. Mallard I wish he could be called upon to perform some wedding ceremonies; but I despair, as he has had only one since coming to the city.

Mr. Mallard is under the impression you can check your baggage by the Grand Junction route all the way through. This would be a great relief, as it is the greatest source of trouble to a lady.

I think I shall be sick about the 11th or 15th of February—not later. I do long for the time to come when you will be with us. It is so long since I have seen you, I think I have grown old in the meantime.

I wish I could get the pictures. Could you fix them so that they might be sent for? We can get them after a while, I know. I only wish we had the means to bring everything that would make you comfortable and remind you of home.

It is Saturday night and growing late. All are in bed except myself, so good night, my dear mother. Tenderest love from us all. I have written you three times since knowing you had left for Liberty; hope you will receive the letters. I hope your last from Nashville will yet come to light. Howdy for the servants. I have not seen or heard a word of Kate for nearly three weeks, so don't know whether she succeeded in getting a place or not.

The citizens here hope much from our new commanding general—Hancock. He is said to be a gentleman, and opposed to the Radicals. He has just assumed command, and has already removed the Negroes from the jury. Many of our best men have called upon him, feeling he was, as it were, on a common platform in favor of justice to the South and opposed to Radicalism.

Your loving daughter,
Mary S. Mallard.

MRS. MARY S. MALLARD *to* MRS. MARY JONES[t]
New Orleans, Friday, December 20th, 1867

My dearest Mother,

This is my dear father's birthday, and tomorrow will be the anniversary of your wedding day. Days full of tender and pleasant memories! I wish you were here to spend them with us.

Little Georgia speaks of your coming constantly, and is making her arrangements. She says "she is going to buy a pretty bed for her dear grandmother, and she will sleep with her downstairs and love her all times." She is still a peculiarly shrinking child, and I think her early fright of Yankees has left a distrust of her fellow men. She imagines she will have the entire charge of your room, and says you "will come tomorrow day right in the cars."

Thus far our winter has been exceedingly mild, and the weather perfectly charming.

The entire loss of crops throughout the state has depressed and (the businessmen say) almost paralyzed all trade in the city. They say there never has been such a financial distress since the city was built. Very little cotton to be bought, and no price to be gotten for what is produced. I think the Radicals will be convinced of their folly. I see by the papers there are fifty thousand workmen out of employment in New York. Only such home arguments can appeal or affect the Northern politicians. . . .

Last evening Mr. Mallard was called upon to perform a wedding ceremony for two of the colored citizens. In this state the legal forms are very peculiar, and accompanied with a good deal of trouble. The marriage certificates have to be signed by the bride and groom and at least three witnesses. Mr. Mallard said it was very amusing to see these Negroes. Of course he had to explain to them the nature of the document. Two of the attendants could write, so they were greatly puffed up by their attainments, and with quite a condescending air brought the bride and her husband to make their marks.

The colored ladies and gentlemen are entitled to all the privileges of full citizenship, though it did not occur to them the minister ought to receive a fee!

We have a commander here now—General Hancock—who is disposed to refer all cases to the proper civil authorities, and thus far promises to do justice. He has received much attention from the citizens, and is disposed to take counsel of prudent, sensible, prominent citizens of the place.

I hope, dear Mother, you have received my letter telling you the opinion of the railroad agent here that the best route to New Orleans from Savannah is by Chattanooga, where you take the Memphis & Charleston Railroad to Grand Junction, and then on to Canton and down to New Orleans—railroad all the way. The expense is the same by either route: forty dollars. The changes are less frequent by the Grand Junction route and more easily made by a lady, as there is merely a change of cars. The other route (by Columbus and Mobile) is a very pleasant one, but you are a part of a day and night on steamboat. The boats between Mobile and this place are very fine, and considered safe boats. The difference in time is only a few hours. You must write or telegraph from Savannah which way you will come and at what time you will leave, so that we can know when to meet you. Mr. Mallard will send you by express on the 1st of January forty-five dollars directed to No. 3.

The children are well except colds. I think you will find them grown. Think of it, dear Mother—eighteen months have nearly elapsed since we have seen you. . . . Mr. Mallard and the children unite with me in warmest love. Love to Aunt Julia's family when you see them. Howdy for the servants.

Your loving daughter,
Mary S. Mallard.

MRS. MARY S. MALLARD *to* MRS. MARY JONES[t]
New Orleans, *Thursday,* December 26th, 1867
My dearest Mother,

Your letter and the bales by express arrived on Christmas Eve. The bales were apparently in good order, but when we opened the bedding we found the whatnot completely crushed, much of it broken into inch pieces; and the table legs are also completely broken. Not one shelf even of the whatnot remains; nothing but the top boards of the tables are safe. Yesterday being a holiday, nothing could be done; but this morning Mr. Mallard will go to the express and see if anything can be done—though we fear not, as the receipt was given for a bale of bedding and one of carpets, and to all appearances they were delivered in good order. The express freight upon the two bales was nearly forty-five dollars. I am so sorry the whatnot and tables were broken, for aside from their being such pretty pieces of furniture, the association made them so valuable. We are truly obliged to you, dear

Mother, for the carpets and bedding. I have not opened the carpets yet, as I could not put them down for some days. Mr. Mallard will inquire at the express and then add a postscript to this at the office. There are so many changes in the route here that I scarcely think it would be worthwhile to risk any more furniture or perishable articles. I presume the bale of bedding was put at the bottom, and the weight of freight upon it crushed the whatnot.

I had intended writing a long letter this morning; but just here I have been stopped by company, so I cannot write more and have this in time for the mail.

If the box of pictures could wait until February, we could then be better able to pay the freight upon it. We are obliged to do things by degrees in these days of cash transactions.

Yesterday was as mild as summer, and if it were not for the general financial gloom resting upon the city, I suppose it would be a "merry" Christmas. . . . There seems to be a general apprehension that there will be serious trouble with the Negroes in the country, many of whom are roaming around like Indians. Having made nothing, they are living upon the cattle, and it is thought they will soon make inroads upon the scantily filled barns of the planters. I fear there will be a like condition of things in Liberty, and I am so anxious for you to come away as soon as possible.

The children are well except Charlie, who has an attack of jaundice, which makes him uncomfortable and gives him very yellow eyes. All unite with me in tenderest love for yourself.

Your affectionate daughter,
Mary S. Mallard.

REV. R. Q. MALLARD *to* MRS. MARY JONES*

New Orleans, *Thursday,* December 26th, 1867

My dear Mother,

I have seen the agent of the express, and learn from him that the company are not responsible for the damage done to the whatnot. As the receipt called for a bale of bedding, they are only accountable for the safe delivery of it as such. He says it would have come safely even unpacked, and for no higher freight. I am very sorry that it should have been broken, as it was a memento of happier days.

I send you by express today to No. 3, Albany & Gulf Railroad, forty-five dollars, which I hope will reach you safely. Wish that it was a hundred. . . .

Your affectionate son,
R. Q. Mallard.

Coming via Chattanooga, Grand Junction, and Jackson, you can check your baggage all the way through.

REV. R. Q. MALLARD *to* MRS. MARY JONES[t]

New Orleans, *Friday*, December 27th, 1867

My dear Mother,

I had carried to the express office and left to be forwarded to you a package of forty-five dollars when the dreadful tidings came of the calamity which has befallen your son in Nashville. I know that you will appreciate my motive in diverting this amount, which I had intended for your expenses hither, to the more pressing necessities of my afflicted brother. I am sorry that the expense of moving and furnishing has so straitened me as to forbid my doing what I should like for both.

Lest by any accident the letters from Nashville have not reached you, I would say Carrie writes that they were burned out on last Friday, barely escaping with their lives.

Yours affectionately,
R. Q. Mallard.

MRS. MARY S. MALLARD *to* MRS. MARY JONES[t]

New Orleans, *Thursday*, January 2nd, 1868

My darling Mother,

A Happy New Year to you from your children and grandchildren! Yesterday was bright and beautiful, and I hope it may be an omen of the coming year. It is customary for the gentlemen to pay their respects to the ladies on New Year's Day. Not deeming it very becoming in me to be sitting up (for shapes), I excused myself yesterday. I really was not well enough to be dressed all day.

I received a letter from Aunt Mary Robarts yesterday announcing the birth of another son on Christmas morning—Cousin Laura's fourth boy. . . .

The box containing one hundred copies of my dear father's *History* arrived day before yesterday; and next week our indefatigable little sexton will commence his labors. He will undertake the sale of them, as we think nothing can be done except by special agency. The book would be entirely buried and lost sight of if it were placed in the bookstores. Mr. Mallard has sent a circular to almost every member of his church, and I hope some copies will be sold. If it were not for the extreme poverty of the people, I have no doubt that a number could be disposed of; but for many here, formerly wealthy, the struggle is for daily bread.

I hope, dear Mother, your next letter will tell us you have appointed the day for leaving Liberty. We long to have you with us. The children are daily expecting and talking of your coming. Georgia thinks she is to have the sole management of everything concerning her "danmother". . . . All unite with me in warmest love.

Your affectionate child,
Mary S. Mallard.

Mrs. Mary Jones *to* Mrs. Mary S. Mallard^t

Montevideo, *Monday,* January 6th, 1868

My darling Child,

Robert's and your last two favors have been received. I was truly gratified at his disposition of the forty-five dollars, and I know how much good it will do in aiding your poor brother and his family. I am sorry to think you were at so much expense for the articles sent by express, and that what I intended as good proved to be such a loss in the whatnot and tables. But keep the pieces: I am a great hand to *repair;* and perhaps they can be glued, as it is only for ornament.

What shall I say of your dear brother's and Carrie's losses? I am almost cast down beyond measure on their account. Unless Carrie's family can help them, I do not see what they are to do! I have sent them all the money in my power, and as soon as I can hear their plans, will send them some bedding and household matters (sheets, towels, etc., etc.). And there are the good books here which I have desired to share with you all, as I have repeatedly written and said. Furniture is out of the question; it is too expensive to send. I have been making a catalogue of the books and packing them in boxes, which has been a fatiguing business, as it all passes through my own hands. . . .

Your brother came on Christmas Day and stayed with me until the following Tuesday. Eva and her mother and the children were in Augusta, and would spend the winter South. He returns immediately to New York.

He writes me from Savannah saying the route via Mobile was considered the best. I was also told so yesterday by the gentleman whom I saw at Walthourville as I went to worship there. Grand Junction, he said, would be quite out of the way. Oh, how I *dread* the undertaking! It seems so strange! And yet will not God provide for me as He has done in days that are past? In almost every other journey I seemed to have friends or places that I knew ahead of me. Now I am going to entirely strange places until I reach New Orleans. If I only knew someone to call upon in *Mobile* in case of trouble, and to see me on the steamer! Traveling *alone* becomes more and more unpleasant to me, and no one knows how I feel my lonely and desolate situation.

If possible I wish to leave this county on the 14th, and Savannah as soon as I can arrange my business there. The cars run every other day from No. 3, so that if I do not go, *D.V.,* on the 14th, I may not do so until that day week. But I will write on the eve of leaving.

Miss Louisa called and dined with me on last Thursday. . . . She brought a bag of pecan nuts for the children, which I will *try* to get in the trunks. . . . The pictures are all ready for transportation; I will take and leave them at No. 3 if they cannot go before I leave. . . . Do, my precious child, take care of yourself. I long to be with you, and am anxious every moment on your account. The Lord be with you and bless you and yours! . . .

Ever your affectionate mother,
Mary Jones.

653

DR. JOSEPH JONES *to* REV. *and* MRS. R. Q. MALLARD[t]

Nashville, *Wednesday,* January 8th, 1868

My dear Brother and Sister,

You will please accept my thanks for your affectionate and valued favor and generous gifts. The package containing forty-five dollars and the valuable bundle of clothes reached me safely by express. The presents of dear little Mary as well as Charlie's kind prayers and good wishes are gratefully remembered. I fear, my dear sister and brother, that you have robbed yourselves; for I know that your expenses, especially after the past season of protracted and dangerous illness, must be very heavy.

Through a kind Providence the future looks bright. As soon as my dear wife and children could be comfortably clad and prepared for the journey, I carried them to Augusta, where they will remain for the present during the cold weather. If Providence permits, I will perfect the necessary arrangements for their return in the spring. Carrie suffered from cold and high fever during the journey down, but when I left Augusta on the 2nd she was much better. She has borne the distressing calamity with Christian resignation and wonderful cheerfulness. Her calm, uncomplaining conduct has elicited universal admiration from her numerous friends.

After parting with Carrie in Augusta, I rested last Thursday in Marietta with my dear relatives. Aunt Susan was suffering severely from the effects of her labors in moving: a rheumatic affection of the muscles of the neck and back. I prescribed for her, and in accordance with my advice she went to bed. Cousin Laura was doing well, and her last baby is a fine healthy boy. Cousin Lyman's father is still with him—an aged gentleman of near ninety years. I am told that the Presbyterian congregation is delighted with our good cousin, and the people have exerted themselves to make the family happy and comfortable. The parsonage is being renovated, and as soon as the repairs are completed, they will move from Aunt Eliza's, where they are now staying. My dear old aunt is feeble but cheerful. She is confined to her bed most of the time. Cousins Mary and Lou still continue cheerful, charitable, and kind, and the best of daughters and housekeepers. Our dear friends and relatives in Marietta gave me a most hearty welcome, and sincerely sympathized with us in our recent calamity. It gave me great comfort and pleasure to meet with them.

I have rented an office in Church Street near the corner of High Street. Through the noble exertions of my kind friend Dr. Eve, many of my most valuable works were preserved. The library was on the lower floor, immediately in the rear of the store which was burnt. We lost all the furniture, wearing apparel, and all my surgical instruments. Nothing was saved except from my library and a small room back. I am truly thankful that the manuscript of my honored father was not with me at the time of the fire, as it would certainly have been destroyed. The box in which it had been placed was consumed, together with many of his letters and memorials. I would rather have lost everything in the world than this manuscript. I am thankful beyond measure for this great mercy.

The fire appears to have been the work of an incendiary—of one of the tenants of the store immediately beneath our sleeping apartment. As the individual was unknown to us even by sight, and as the goods had been insured for at least four times their value only four days before the fire, it is thought that the sole object was money! Whilst our losses have been heavy, and whilst it was a terrible experience to my precious wife and little ones to flee in their nightdresses from the burning house at the dead hour of night in the rain and wade in the cold mud of the streets in their bare feet, at the same time we have abundant cause for rejoicing in the salvation of our lives. We should all have perished but for the fact that I was aroused immediately upon the first alarm of fire. I had been up until a late hour arranging my library and office, and had just fallen into a gentle sleep when the alarm was sounded. It would be impossible to express the anxiety of my dear wife when we found that our dear little Susie was missing. I left Carrie standing in the street and rushed into the house and rescued her from the suffocating smoke. My feelings have always been peculiarly tender towards Susie since her extreme illness.

Our friends in Nashville have been most kind and sympathizing. Dr. and Mrs. Eve have done everything in their power for our comfort. We feel more attached to Nashville than ever. My hearty consent was given to the present visit, although it breaks up my cheerful home and leaves me very lonely, because I hoped that it would give Carrie a season of comparative freedom from care, in which she might prepare her dresses and the clothing of the children.

I trust that this affliction may be blessed to our spiritual good. "The judgments of the Lord are true and righteous altogether." "Except the Lord build the house, they labor in vain that build it. Except the Lord keep the city, the watchman waketh but in vain. It is vain for you to rise up early, to sit up late, to eat the bread of sorrows, for so He giveth His beloved sleep." We feel that we have every cause for the most devout gratitude. With warmest love, I remain

Your affectionate brother,
Joseph Jones.

MRS. MARY JONES *to* MRS. MARY S. MALLARD[t]

Savannah, *Saturday,* January 18th, 1868

Thus far, my darling child, am I spared on my way to you. The closing up of my life at home has been very painful. I am here with our ever kind and dear friends Dr. and Mrs. Axson, and expect to leave in the evening train of Monday the 20th via Macon, Columbus, Mobile. I trust God for a safe and prosperous journey. You will know when I ought to arrive, and I know Robert will meet me at the depot. Your friends here all send warmest love. Kiss my dear little children for Grandmother. And with best love to Robert and yourself,

Ever your own affectionate mother,
Mary Jones.

655

I thought it best to attend to the box of pictures, and have shipped that and two trunks of my own from No. 3. Mr. Fleming thought I had best pay for them at the other end of the road, and said he had no doubt if Robert would say they were private papers of a minister and ask it, they would grant a reduction. They weigh heavily, and I will pay for them when I come.

I have engaged a slab, and leave an inscription to be placed upon it. Wish I could have consulted you all, but I could not leave your father's grave uncared for, and have done the best I could.

Ever your mother,
Mary Jones.

Epilogue

So ENDED the Georgia world of Mrs. Mary Jones—"a skeleton world," she had called it three years before, where "the bright prisms of hope which once encircled every object and gilded every scene have faded tint by tint, until dark shadows are resting where sunbeams played. Of early possessions and enjoyments I have seen an end; riches have taken to themselves wings and flown away; I am a captive in the home I love, and soon must wander from it—an exile in my native land." In those bitter days of March 1865, isolated at Montevideo and still recovering from the ordeal of Kilpatrick's raid, Mrs. Jones had sought consolation in calling up a happier past:

Memory's buried stores lie all exhumed before my eye. My husband brought me to this his home a young and happy wife—happy, oh, no mortal tongue can tell how happy in his love and confidence, how blessed beneath his influence and with his guidance and companionship. The thrilling joys of those bright days do even now affect this withered heart: his precious words of love, his smile of approbation or encouragement as toils and cares came thronging up the way of life, his godly example, his pious teachings, his tenderest sympathy, his unwearied efforts to alleviate every sorrow, to supply every want, to anticipate and gratify every wish. The most refined, confidential, and affectionate intercourse of thirty-two years made my existence blessed beyond the common lot.

Beloved children were the gift of God to us, and in the sanctuary of home they were nurtured and trained. We were enabled to secure the best of teachers for their intellectual and moral education, and received our reward in their improvement and appreciation of those advantages; whilst their obedience and affection crowned our earthly happiness. The chapel where they passed their schooldays is still standing in the bright sunshine; the twigs they planted have grown to lofty trees; the garden where they reaped their little golden harvests, although grass-grown, is still upon the gentle slope; the museum where so diligently were gathered their scientific spoils, their stuffed birds of varied species (all the songsters of our native forest), their Indian remains, and nameless curiosities, is overgrown with rose vines. Fragments of their well-worn books are scattered upon the shelves, and in the drawers are treasured specimens of drawing and early composition. Their little chairs are with me still, to image up their infancy and childhood. The plain, the grove, the woods are here, but they no longer echo to their cheerful voices; their prayers, their songs, their youthful sports all are hushed. . . .

When first we came to this now beautiful home, it was a rough and uncultivated field. A few large live oaks and small trees dotted here and there the rude enclosure.

The spacious dwelling has been built and every improvement has been made under our own eye; every tree and flower planted by our own hand. And now that I see them stretching in shady avenues, or grouped in thickly wooded groves waving their lofty branches above our heads, or blooming in rare beauty or with exquisite perfumes, they are all to my heart more than the common forest trees or garden plants. I have loved and cherished them; they speak to me as with living voices of the ever-present past. That cedar of beautiful proportions in front of the dwelling was planted by my husband with his own hands. I see him bending to the task, and daily look upon it as the chronicler of thirty years. Those magnolias in the rear were named Charles and Joseph. Traces of Daughter's mimic garden still remain in sweet mistle and rose bushes, in bulbs that annually spring from their hiding places. That magnificent live oak, from which a twig was never cut, was set out by our faithful house servant Jack before his own cottage door. Old Daddy Jupiter planted that leaning oak at the turn of the avenue "to be remembered by."

These living memorials remain, but the hands that placed them there are moldering where "no work nor device is found." The halls of this mansion no longer echo to the master's step. The chair is vacant at the board and around the hearthstone. The precious study consecrated to spiritual and intellectual toil is closed, the desk unused and the books all packed. The chapel bell no longer rings out its welcome invitation to saint and sinner. The voice of the priest in his own household no more is heard in prayer and praise or unfolding the mysteries of divine revelation. The servants that used so faithfully and pleasantly to wait around us are (many of them) dead or scattered or sadly and willfully changed. All things are altered. "Abroad the sword bereaveth; at home there is as death." "The adversary hath spread out his hand upon all our pleasant things." The enemy has destroyed every living thing; even the plainest food is made scanty. His robberies and oppressions force me from my beloved home, where it is no longer safe or prudent to remain. And I must leave it in my advancing years, knowing not where the gray hairs which sorrow and time have thickly gathered will find a shelter, or the fainting heart and weary body a resting place, or any spot that I may ever again on earth call home.

These gloomy words Mrs. Jones had written in her journal in March 1865, on the eve of her departure from Montevideo for her brother's place in Baker County, the "far-off land" from which she feared she might never return. As we have seen, she did return the following October, but only to struggle for two disastrous years against well-nigh impossible odds, until in November 1867 it became obvious that she must abandon the home she had cherished so long—"smiling Montevideo," to which she had come as a young wife more than three decades before.

I have risen at midnight and thrown wide the closed shutters of my chamber window, that I might look upon my beautiful earthly home. The clear bright moon is approaching its full-orbed proportions; it has passed its meridian in the heavens, and its declination is towards its diurnal repose in the west. From the diadem of night is reflected the magnificent light of countless brilliant stars, some of greater, some of lesser magnitude. Jupiter sits unrivaled upon his imperial throne. Orion displays his martial belt of peerless gems. Sweet Pleiades have paled beneath the moonbeams, whilst the polar star gives out its cold unchanging rays of white. Beautiful Venus still veils her matchless charms behind the orient sky, waiting to harbinger the coming moon.

Nature below is in perfect repose. Not the faintest zephyr stirs the sleeping forest leaves. Not a waving shadow breaks the entire outline of houses and groves. The giant oaks and lofty pines are perfectly daguerreotyped upon the lawn, whose even surface, still thickly strewed with autumnal leaves, reflects a golden tint; whilst the pure white walks of the garden stand out like silvery highways. Not a sound is heard to break the profound stillness of midnight, saving an occasional tinkle of the bell as Pretty Maid shakes her head or changes her place in the cow pen, or our faithful gander, who keeps his sentry watch in the poultry yard, calls out the passing hour.

I alone seem awake in the vast universe around and above. And yet I know that I am not alone: I feel encompassed by countless evidences of an omnipotent, omniscient, omnipresent Deity. Oh, the sweet and precious consolations that have often flowed into my soul—far from living friends and kindred and all the joys and supports and sweet sympathy of my beloved children! Yes, here in this utter solitude my Heavenly Father hath given me songs of rejoicing even amid the utter loneliness and desolation of a widow's heart and a widow's home.

So Mrs. Jones had mused in her journal on December 9th, 1867, only a few weeks before her departure for New Orleans. Small wonder that she found the "closing up" of her "life at home" so "very painful." Despite "the sweet and precious consolations" of "an omnipotent, omniscient, omnipresent Deity" she grew increasingly despondent as the fateful day approached; and her final Sabbath in Liberty County was inexpressibly sad. "I have felt that it might be the very last I should ever spend at my once happy and privileged home, which now appears more like the grave of my buried hopes and affections than as the dwelling place of living and attractive associations. The scenes of the past have been coming up in rapid review. They are so painful in contrast with the great changes that are now upon my heart and life!"

It was not, to be sure, a homeless fate to which Mrs. Jones was destined in January 1868; but it was a fate to which, understandably, she was never to become fully reconciled. Removed in her sixtieth year from the world she had known from childhood, set down in a world that must have seemed to her exotic indeed, she survived but fifteen months, secure though she was in the warmth and affection of her daughter's New Orleans home. Once, in December 1868, she returned briefly to Liberty County, where she saw completed the work on her husband's tomb at Midway—"the most beautiful marble slab I ever saw: very thick, without spot or blemish. . . . As the clear sunlight of heaven fell upon it without stain or shadow, I thought how emblematic of the glorified spirit washed white in the Blood of the Lamb and clothed in the spotless robe of a Saviour's righteousness." But her plantation affairs she found in wretched condition: "Everybody and everything," she wrote Mrs. Mallard on January 8th, 1869, "is at the lowest ebb in Liberty

—due, I think, to want of decision and energy on the part of the men. No concert of action, no public sentiment. . . . The place is beautiful—but oh, how sad! And every day some new perplexity. My child, be thankful your lot has been cast elsewhere." Late in January 1869 she returned to New Orleans; her health steadily declined, and on Friday morning, April 23rd, 1869, after an illness of less than forty-eight hours, she died peacefully at her daughter's home. Scarcely two weeks had passed since the death of Robert Holt Mallard, born on March 3rd, 1868; and Mrs. Jones was buried beside her infant grandson in the family vault in Lafayette Cemetery.

On her deathbed Mrs. Jones had been questioned by her daughter: "Mother, have you any wish in regard to resting at Midway? If you have, it could easily be done." Mrs. Jones had replied: "I have always said, 'Where I die, there let me be buried'; for 'at the last day we shall all be raised in a moment, in the twinkling of an eye.'" And so it came to pass that Mrs. Jones's body remained in New Orleans. For several months her children debated the wisdom of sending her back to be buried beside her husband at Midway; but the removal was evidently judged to be impracticable. In a letter written to his sister from New York on January 19th, 1870, Charles Colcock Jones, Jr., speaking of "our dear and sainted mother," virtually settled the question for all time:

With reference to the removal of her remains, I think this ought not to be done at present. She lies now in your own tomb, with her own precious grandchild, whom she loved so tenderly, by her side. Under all circumstances it seems to me that this is a most fitting resting place. You will agree the more readily with me, I think, in this particular when you reflect upon the almost deserted condition of Midway burial ground. My own wish would be, one of these days, to remove Father from that graveyard and inter him in the Savannah cemetery. Private burial grounds and country churchyards are not the best places wherein to deposit the dust of those we love most. They are, in the country, so liable to change and neglect that in nine cases out of ten, under the eyes even of the second generation, they fall into decay and desolation. The absence of the law of primogeniture, the want of local attachment in the American mind, the facility with which alienations of real property are accomplished, the shifting nature of our population, seeking new homes as inclination, ambition, or interests may suggest, all unite in rendering these private burial grounds and cemeteries of small country churches unstable. . . . I think, my dear sister, that Mother had better remain where she is, in your own tomb, for the present at least. At some future day the removal may be made; but I question the expediency of carrying her back to Midway churchyard.

When one recalls the months and years of unremitting toil which Dr. Jones devoted to *A History of the Church of God,* and the veritable obsession with which his widow pursued the arduous task of seeing her husband's manuscript through the press, it is peculiarly affecting to note that the first volume, published by Charles Scribner late in 1867, enjoyed little favor with the book-buying public and hence was never followed by a second. From the beginning the work seemed strangely ill-starred: as we have seen, the box containing one hundred copies which reached New Orleans on the last day of 1867 was entrusted to the "special agency" of the "indefatigable little sexton" of Prytania Street Presbyterian Church, since, as Mrs. Mallard observed, "the book would be entirely buried and lost sight of if it were placed in the bookstores." During the spring of 1868 few copies were sold; by July 14th Mrs. Jones herself reluctantly conceded that "the sale has been so limited I do not know when we will be able to put out the second volume; times are very hard, and it is difficult to interest friends in good books." Eighteen months later, on January 19th, 1870, Charles Colcock Jones, Jr., wrote his sister opposing further publication:

More than a year has elapsed since the first volume was issued. An edition of five hundred copies was printed, and the larger portion of it remains unsold, with little or no inquiry for the work. Due advertisement has been made, and efforts used to give circulation to the work; but even *at home* and where Father was best known there is literally no inquiry for the work, and the copies on hand remain upon the shelves of the booksellers unsought. Even the immediate members of the family, and clergymen who were in personal communication with Father, have not purchased copies. . . . My own judgment has always been averse to the publication; but as a matter of respect to Mother, and in deference to her wishes, I did what I could in passing the first volume through the press.

Now and then a copy of the *History* was sold during the succeeding decade; then, on August 19th, 1881, nearly fourteen years after its publication, Mrs. Mallard wrote her daughter Mamie from New Orleans:

I received a letter from your Uncle Charles three days ago saying he had received $132 from Scribner (proceeds of the sale of your grandfather's book); and he sent me a check for the whole amount, as he desired to relinquish his portion in my favor, and wrote your uncle here desiring him to do so also, which he did this evening. . . . This was a wonderful surprise, for I had no idea there ever would be anything realized upon the book; and your uncle thinks this will be all, as there are a number of copies on hand and no call for them. I feel that the book accomplished one good end in giving occupation and interest to your dear grandfather's invalid life.

The death of Mrs. Jones was a fundamental shock to her children. A link with the past had been broken: no near relative remained in Liberty County to preserve the family places from decay and ruin; and distance made it difficult if not impossible for the children to return. It is a poignant fact that Mrs. Mallard never again saw her native county after her flight from Montevideo on March 2nd, 1865. Bound to New Orleans by the responsibilities of a growing family, she enjoyed the respect and love of her husband's congregation and set an example of Christian benevolence for the whole community. In 1875 she suffered an attack of pleurisy from which she never fully recovered; some six years later a serious relapse left her a semi-invalid. In November 1888 she was prostrated by an attack of pneumonia, after which she was almost continuously confined to her bed; the following May, at her physician's advice, she was carried to Marietta, Georgia, where at the home of Miss Louisa Robarts she died on August 31st, 1889, aged fifty-four, surrounded by numerous relatives and lifelong friends. Her body was returned to New Orleans and placed in the family vault in Lafayette Cemetery. Meanwhile her husband had continued his New Orleans ministry; from 1866 to 1877 he had served as pastor of the Prytania Street Presbyterian Church; from 1879 till his death twenty-five years later he served as pastor of the Napoleon Avenue Presbyterian Church. On January 19th, 1893, he married Amarintha Mary Witherspoon, daughter of a Presbyterian clergyman. Three years later he was elected moderator of the General Assembly of the Southern Presbyterian Church meeting at Memphis in 1896. From 1891 to 1904 he was editor of *The Southwestern Presbyterian*. His two books, *Plantation Life Before Emancipation* (1892) and *Montevideo-Maybank: Some Memories of a Southern Christian Household in the Olden Times* (1898), describe scenes and incidents of life in coastal Georgia immediately prior to the Civil War. He died in New Orleans on March 3rd, 1904, aged seventy-three, and was buried beside his first wife.

Both of the Mallard daughters continued to reside in New Orleans; the son, Charles Colcock Mallard, a civil engineer associated with the Southern Pacific Railroad, held prominent administrative posts at various points in the West throughout a distinguished career of thirty-five years. He died unmarried in New Orleans on November 24th, 1914, aged fifty-four. His elder sister, Mary Jones Mallard, for some years conducted a school for small children in New Orleans. She never married, and after her father's death she lived in the household of her younger sister, Georgia, who had become the wife of William Kimsey Seago on November 17th, 1896. Mary Jones Mallard died in New Orleans on May 7th, 1917, aged fifty-nine; Mrs. Seago, born during a Yankee raid at the height of Sherman's march through Georgia, lived to be nearly eighty-eight. After a long and active career in church and charitable work, during which she served as editor of the Woman's Auxiliary Department of *The Christian Observer*, official organ of the Southern Presbyterian Church, from 1924 to 1939, she died in New Orleans on December 7th, 1952, survived by four children.

Neighbors of the Mallards almost from the beginning of their New Orleans residence were the family of Mrs. Mallard's brother, Dr. Joseph Jones, who in the summer of 1868 was elected professor of chemistry and clinical medicine in the Medical Department of the University of Louisiana (later the Tulane University School of Medicine), a post he held till his retirement in 1894. Through his researches and publications, particularly in tropical medicine and general hygiene, Dr. Jones gained an international reputation; in addition to scores of articles in technical and professional journals he published, in four enormous volumes, his monumental *Medical and Surgical Memoirs* (1876–1890), embracing the chief investigations of a long career. He was a member of numerous societies, both scientific and historical; and he held many distinguished and responsible posts: he was visiting physician to the New Orleans Charity Hospital (1870–1894), president of the Louisiana Board of Health (1880–1884), and president of the Louisiana Medical Society (1885–1886); in 1889 he was appointed surgeon general of the United Confederate Veterans. A few weeks after his removal from Nashville to New Orleans his wife Carrie died suddenly, on December 4th, 1868, leaving four small children: eighteen months later, on June 21st, 1870, he married Susan Rayner Polk, daughter of the Rt. Rev. Leonidas Polk, bishop of Louisiana and lieutenant general in the Confederate army. Three children were born of his second marriage: Hamilton Polk Jones, Frances Devereux Jones, and Laura Maxwell Jones. In 1892 the University of Georgia conferred on him the honorary degree of doctor of laws. At the time of his death on February 17th, 1896, in his sixty-third year, he was regarded as one of the leading professors of medicine in the United States and one of the profoundest scientific men of his generation. He was buried in the family vault in Lafayette Cemetery, New Orleans.

His eldest son, Stanhope Jones, was also a physician, receiving his degree from the Medical Department of the University of Louisiana in 1883. After a brief period of medical practice in association with his father he died prematurely on July 24th, 1894, in his thirty-fourth year, leaving three motherless children. His younger brother, Charles Colcock Jones III, a mining and metallurgical engineer, graduated in mechanics from Louisiana State University in 1884 and in mining and metallurgy from Lehigh University in 1887. In 1902 he removed to California, where he became prominent in the development of the iron and steel industry; he died in Los Angeles on April 28th, 1953, in his eighty-eighth year. His sister, Caroline Susan Jones (formerly Susan Hyrne Jones), left New Orleans soon after the death of her father in 1896, joining her stepmother and two half-sisters in Chestnut Hill, Pennsylvania, where she taught at Springside School until her death on June 14th, 1921, aged fifty-eight. The younger sister, Mary Cuthbert Jones, married Dr. Julien Trist Bringier on January 21st, 1896, resided at Tezcuco, her husband's plantation on the Mississippi River near Donaldsonville, Louisiana, and died aged seventy-one on May 27th, 1939.

Meanwhile in distant New York Charles Colcock Jones, Jr., had risen to considerable distinction in the profession of law. In the spring of 1877 he returned with his family to Georgia and fixed his residence at Montrose, a fine antebellum mansion in the village of Summerville (now part of Augusta). Here he continued his legal practice and pursued his literary career; as biographer, historian, and archaeologist he gained nationwide recognition, and a substantial series of publications established his fame as one of Georgia's most prolific and successful writers. His longer works illuminate the history of his native state: *The Monumental Remains of Georgia* (1861), *Historical Sketch of the Chatham Artillery* (1867), *Antiquities of the Southern Indians* (1873), *The Siege of Savannah in December 1864* (1874), *The Dead Towns of Georgia* (1878), *The History of Georgia* (1883), published in two large volumes, and *Negro Myths from the Georgia Coast* (1888), beautifully dedicated to the family servants he had known as a youth. In addition he published essays and discourses on a variety of subjects, including some dozen annual addresses delivered before the Confederate Survivors' Association, an organization which he founded in 1879 and of which he was till the time of his death the only president. His archaeological and historical collections were accounted among the most complete of his day. He was twice complimented with the degree of doctor of laws: by New York University in 1880 and by Oxford University (Georgia) in 1882. His wife Eva died suddenly on October 25th, 1890, two weeks before her forty-ninth birthday; three years later, on July 19th, 1893, he followed at the age of sixty-one. He died universally respected and greatly lamented, and was buried with signal honors beside his second wife in Summerville Cemetery.

Both of his children survived. Ruth Berrien Jones (formerly Mary Ruth Jones) had become the wife of the Rev. Samuel Barstow Carpenter, an Episcopal clergyman, on February 13th, 1890. For some years he served as rector of the Church of the Atonement and the Church of the Good Shepherd in Augusta; and after his death in 1912 his widow continued to occupy the family residence, Montrose, until her death on July 17th, 1934, aged seventy-three. Her half-brother, Charles Edgeworth Jones (formerly Edgeworth Casey Jones), inherited his father's taste for literature; he graduated from the University of Georgia in 1885 and later studied Greek and Latin at Johns Hopkins University without receiving a degree. He was the author of several tracts, including *Education in Georgia* (1889) and *Georgia in the War* (1909); he also published a memorial essay on his father in 1893. After a quiet and studious life he died unmarried in Augusta on October 30th, 1931, aged sixty-four.

"Our affairs here are in sad condition," wrote Mrs. Jones from Montevideo during her final visit in January 1869. "It is well we came, and it will be necessary—painful and expensive as these visits are—for the protection and preservation of the house, etc., to be here at least once a year." Mrs. Jones never again saw her "dear but desolate home"; she died in New Orleans in April 1869, leaving the care and responsibility of the plantations in Liberty County to her eldest son, Charles Colcock, who administered affairs as best he could till his death twenty-four years later. In December 1869 he made the first of many annual visits to Montevideo; he described his experience in a letter from New York on January 5th, 1870:

I returned from Georgia yesterday. My visit to Montevideo was very pleasant but very sad. My beloved mother was not there, and my dear father—he too was gone! Lucy and Charles and Niger have all been very faithful, and have done their best. Everything was in much better order than I expected to find it. The people were delighted to see me, and I left them all in good heart and promising to do their best. Lucy is still in charge of the house, Charles of the lot and oxen, and Niger of the plantation. Stepney is in charge of Arcadia, and I have requested Audley King to do the best he can with Maybank.

Mrs. Mallard, we have seen, never returned to Montevideo after leaving it in March 1865, though for a time, at least, she evidently entertained some expectation of a reunion there with her brothers. "I hope if you visited Georgia that you spent some time at Montevideo," wrote Charles Colcock from New York on April 15th, 1871: "do not forget our plan to spend a month or two there next winter." Unfortunately the happy plan did not work out; and with the passage of the years the likelihood of a reunion at Montevideo steadily decreased. On January 2nd, 1882, Charles Colcock wrote his wife of his annual visit:

Here we are at the old homestead, sadly marred by the disintegrating influences of time, disfigured by the devastations wrought by the recent hurricane, and yet beautiful under the beams of this calm moon and filled with memories pure and consecrated. Overshadowing all is a cloud of sadness each year growing deeper and darker as the influences of inexorable decay become more and more apparent. The garden long since has become a wild. The dwelling, once so bright and cheerful, has already grown discolored, and is in parts sadly out of repair. Even the trees are growing old, and some of the largest, which the tempest has spared, are dying. The entire region is strangely changed. It is peopled only with the phantoms of things that were, and present images are a mockery of the blessed idols once here enshrined. The lesson is repeated everywhere: "The places which now know us will soon know us no more forever." Earthly visions—the truest and loveliest—endure but for a season, and then evanish into the realm of shadows. Everything grows insubstantial with the flight of years, and in the end lapses into something near akin to nothingness. The true, the beautiful, the good alone survive in divine revelations; these we cherish, and they alone amid the general wreck savor of immortality.

In June 1880 the Mallards' former manservant James died leaving a family of nine; early in 1885 Tenah, beloved nurse of the Mallard children, died leaving four girls and one boy. Charles Colcock wrote his sister from Augusta on January 11th, 1886:

Upon my recent visit to Liberty I was sorely distressed at the desolation which had been caused by the floods and the continued rains of last fall. The entire rice crop had been swept away, and the cotton and much of the corn rotted in the fields. The consequence of all this was that I did not collect enough to pay taxes and defray the cost of the extensive repairs which I have found it necessary to put upon the old homestead. At Arcadia the same cause brought about like results, and I was disappointed in realizing the small balance due on account of the sale of lots. . . . Lucy is growing older, but seemed pretty well. Niger has consoled himself with another wife—a widow with some five children. These, added to what Tenah left, are sufficient to people a small plantation. He wisely keeps the two families apart.

And so time continued to take its toll. On his annual visit early in 1888

Charles Colcock found "everything in a situation more depressed and impoverished than usual. . . . Lucy has been crippled up with rheumatism, and although now somewhat better, is scarcely able to move about. The visit was a sad one to me."

For a few more years, until his death in 1893, Charles Colcock continued to maintain the house; thereafter it quickly fell prey to the depredations of the neighboring poor, white and black, who tore out mantels, seized cornices and moldings, carried off stair rails and floorboards, and eventually so despoiled the house that little was left for the winds and the rains to destroy. Montevideo was said to be the last antebellum plantation house in Liberty County to survive the ravages of war and time. Shortly after the turn of the century the place was sold out of the family, and the elements soon completed what the vandals had begun. Today there is no house at all: nothing remains of the splendid mansion that once knew human laughter and human tears; and little in the surrounding wilderness suggests that this was once the seat of wealth, refinement, and learning. To the visitor who knows the past it is a heartbreaking spot. In the tangle of forest growth he traces the rough lines of a brick foundation; in mimosa and magnolia and holly, now monstrously overgrown, he sees vestiges of a garden once laid out with affection and taste. A mile distant the plantation gates still stand, mute evidence of a day that is dead; and streamlined trains, chrome-plated in the sunlight, streak past bound for New York. The rest is silence. The North Newport River still glides on, thoughtless that a way of life has vanished from the earth.

The fate of Midway Church promised for a time to be no less disastrous. Near the end of the war Kilpatrick's cavalry, encamped at the church for six weeks, penned their horses and cattle in the cemetery, appropriated the church as a slaughterhouse, used the melodeon as a meat block, and rifled the cornerstone of its contents. During the succeeding years the church shared the ruin and desolation of the surrounding area; in October 1865 Mrs. Jones found it "distressing to see the condition of the church: doors and windows open, shutters off; and the sheep had evidently taken shelter in the aisles." After the removal of the Rev. Mr. Buttolph in November 1867 and the virtual dissolution of the church, the white membership reluctantly withdrew to worship at the various retreats. Churches were established at Walthourville in 1855, at Flemington in 1866, and at Dorchester in 1871; after the war the fourth retreat, Jonesville, disappeared altogether from the scene. Midway Church was leased to its Negro members, who agreed in return to keep the building in repair and the cemetery in order; some six hundred Negroes organized a separate congregation under the pastorate of the Rev. Joe Williams, a clergyman of their own race, and continued to worship at Midway for twenty years. Mr. Lazarus John Mallard, selectman of Midway Church from 1854 to 1867 and also clerk of the session, described the condition of the church in a letter to his former pastor on October 9th, 1868:

We have not worshiped at Midway since you left, but still consider ourselves members of the old church, and are loath to give up the idea that we will yet some day return to that sacred spot hallowed by so many associations. . . . The old church is still used by the Negroes. The graveyard is now in unusually good order—kept so by the colored people as some compensation to us for the use they have of the church.

Last week I was permitted to visit the much-loved spot. It so happened that Simon the old bell-ringer was passing along the causeway, on which I had just finished some public work. I invited him to a seat in my wagon, with the request that he would go up with me to the old church and ring the bell for me, that I might hear it as in former days. You could hardly imagine—and I could hardly describe—my feelings to you. I stood upon the steps and listened. Where are all those who obeyed that bell and once came at its call into the House of the Lord? I walked up and down the aisles, marking the pews where once a solemn and worshiping assembly sat. Where are they now? All gone—some one way and some another, and many to their long last home. Shall the like of what we have seen never again be witnessed within these walls? Shall that *sacred* desk, made so by the faithful who have there stood, never again be occupied by another who shall break unto us the Bread of Life? Here in this house hundreds received their first serious impressions, and hundreds were built up in their most holy faith; saints have been strengthened, and sinners converted to God. Many and such like thoughts flashed across my mind, and I could have wept over the desolations which have been visited upon our ancient Jerusalem. How unsearchable are the judgments of God, and His ways past finding out!

Although Midway Church was never formally dissolved, the removal of Mr. Buttolph marked its practical extinction as a place of public worship for whites; the last annual meeting of the Midway Church and Society was called in December 1865, and the last entry recorded in the session book was dated October 1867. Ten years later an attempt to sell the building failed: the white membership had hoped to invest the proceeds and apply the income to maintenance of the cemetery, then rapidly falling into decay. Finally, on March 9th, 1887, after a lapse of more than twenty years, the Midway Church and Society resumed its annual meetings; and it has continued to meet annually ever since.

At the meeting in March 1888 it was resolved that the cornerstone of the church, laid at the centennial celebration of 1852 and later rifled of its contents by the Federals, should be relaid with appropriate ceremonies at the next annual meeting. Accordingly Colonel Charles Colcock Jones, Jr., then living in Augusta, was invited to deliver an address at the old church on March 13th, 1889. The day appointed proved to be so rainy that hardly a score of persons appeared; but the address was delivered, and the Savannah *Morning News* next day pronounced it "one of the noblest efforts of the orator-historian." After vividly sketching the centennial celebration of 1852 Colonel Jones paid tribute to "the sterling patriotism, heroic devotion to principle, and great sufferings" of the Midway colonists during the Revolutionary War; he then detailed "the overwhelming ruin and sad changes" which prostrated "this once noble and happy community" during the late struggle for Confederate independence.

Although the tide of active, intelligent life appears in large measure to have receded from this long-accustomed shore; although shadows still gather about us, and the gloom of disaster hangs heavily above plantation and highway; although the voice of the pastor is seldom heard within the porches of this almost deserted temple, and the dust of silent Sabbaths settles noiselessly upon the altar and pew; we will nevertheless here set up a column in remembrance of all that has been, in praise of those who sleep within the ivy-mantled walls of this churchyard, in commemoration of the deeds and virtues of our ancestors, and in confident expectation of the rehabilitation of this now wasted community. . . . In relaying this cornerstone let us express and cherish the hope that no untoward events or undue procrastination will delay the consummation of our laudable design, but that the purpose which we this day inaugurate may be speedily accomplished. Thus by a physical embodiment of the exalted memories and valuable traditions of this people, and by symbolizing the general gratitude, will we stimulate a fuller, a prouder recognition of the virtues and the valor of the days that are gone, and encourage nobler efforts for the rehabilitation of a region formerly so favored, and for so many years the abode of refinement, of industry, of morality, of patriotism, and of civilization. [Address Delivered at Midway Meetinghouse in Liberty County, Georgia, on the Second Wednesday in March 1889 (Augusta, 1889), pp. 18–20]

In view of the pitiless rain on the ceremonial occasion and the consequent thinness of the audience present, it was thought advisable to postpone the actual relaying of the cornerstone until a more propitious day; thus on May 8th, 1889, the people reassembled and the cornerstone was laid by William Augustus Fleming, captain of the Liberty Independent Troop, after a sermon by the Rev. James Stacy, then pastor of the Presbyterian church at Newnan, Georgia:

And though the former order of things may never be restored, and this building, hoary with age and rich in historic renown, as well as sacred memories, may tumble in ruins, and even these tombs and monuments, which mark the last resting places of many loves ones, whose moldering bodies lie slumbering in this camping ground of the dead, be completely obliterated, yet if the descendants of this people, conscious of the mighty responsibility resting upon them, and inspired with fresh vigor and zeal from the monuments of the past, instead of spending the time glorying over bygone achievements, or indulging gloomy forebodings about the future, would diligently and laboriously apply themselves to the task before them, they may yet continue the work so gloriously begun by their forefathers and even make the record of the old church still more illustrious. And it is possible, in some way unknown to us, that God may in the future raise up even here, out of these moldering ruins, another church and clothe it with the vigor and freshness of former years. But if this be not His will, if the time of her active life be past and she is to live only in history and story, then let the influence of her embalmed life continue ever to linger like holy fragrance around this sacred spot, a silent witness of the past and a source of inspiration for the future; in either case a benediction to the world, and to all who shall come after. [*History of the Midway Congregational Church* (Newnan, Georgia, 1899), p. 260]

In his now classic *History of the Midway Congregational Church* Stacy gave a graphic account of the early fortunes of the Midway settlement, reproduced numerous records of the church, and summarized her astonishing contribution, past and present, to the intellectual and spiritual life of America. On the threshold of its second century the original structure was, he wrote, in a state of remarkable preservation, partly because it had been, according to contract, "built of the best wood," and partly because it had been solicitously maintained and repaired throughout the years.

But time has commenced doing its work. It fills the heart with intense sadness to visit the old spot and see the decay that is going on. For twenty years the old church building was given the colored people, the only compensation required being that they should care for the cemetery. During that time the yard became very much neglected. Many of the monuments were allowed to fall; others were upturned by trees growing up beside them. In the burning of limbs and rubbish and grass many of the monuments were smoked and greatly marred, insomuch that at the end of that time the contract was rescinded and the church used only by the whites at the annual reunions in March. The cemetery now presents much of a neglected appearance, many of the inscriptions being wholly illegible on account of a covering of moss which has been accumulating upon them. No one, however, can visit the place and look upon the old church, standing solitary and alone at the junction of two roads, without a single home in view, her worshipers all gone, her doors closed, her careening steeple still pointing heavenward, with the tops of her faded monuments silently lifting up their heads from underneath an arch of pendant moss and peering over the massive brick wall which encircles the resting place of her dead, without feeling that he is standing upon sacred ground. [pp. 219–220]

This distressing picture of the old church was not long in prompting its friends to action. In 1905 a subscription committee was appointed and a letter of solicitation was addressed to every known descendant of the Midway community; among the contributions received was a personal check from President Theodore Roosevelt, great-grandson of General Daniel Stewart. Soon a sum was raised sufficient to restore the cemetery to order, straighten the "careening steeple," and secure the walls of the church from total collapse. For fifty years these restorations checked further decay; then in 1956, when it became necessary to widen the highway separating the church from the cemetery, the church was moved forty-two feet to the east and at the same time meticulously restored inside and out. The Georgia Department of Highways bore the cost of moving the church and part of the cost of restoration; the balance of the cost was met by voluntary contributions of friends.

Meanwhile in 1946 the Midway Museum Society had been organized under the sponsorship of the St. John's Parish Chapter of the Daughters of the

American Colonists, with the participation of the Liberty County Chapter of the United Daughters of the Confederacy; its objective was "to perpetuate for posterity the memory of the Midway colonists through the medium of a museum." A nationwide campaign realized sufficient funds to purchase a museum site directly behind the church; this site was donated to the State of Georgia, and on it a commodious fireproof structure in the style of a typical antebellum plantation house was erected by the Georgia Historical Commission to preserve records and relics associated with Midway history. The museum was dedicated on November 29th, 1959; it is operated and maintained by the State of Georgia under the supervision of the Georgia Historical Commission; it is regularly open to visitors, and a small admission fee contributes to its maintenance.

And so the spirit of Midway Church lives on today, not only in the beautifully restored house of worship built by stalwart Calvinists in 1792, not only in the handsome museum established to perpetuate a glorious history for the instruction and delight of generations to come, but also in the countless sons and daughters of the early communicants, now scattered far and wide across the nation and the world, who cherish the memory of a worthy past and everywhere occupy positions of honor and trust. The church is no longer open for regular services; but each year the Midway Church and Society meets on the second Wednesday in March; and each year on the last Sunday in April hundreds of loyal descendants of the Midway community gather at the church for what is known as the Midway Celebration. In the morning a distinguished clergyman, not necessarily a son of Midway, preaches a sermon and administers Communion from the original service; later a basket lunch is spread in the neighboring grove, where friendships are renewed and ancestral deeds are recalled; in the afternoon a memorial service is held in the cemetery across the way, and flowers are placed on the graves of the honored dead.

Long after his pilgrimage to the old church, long after his scrutiny of treasured heirlooms in the adjacent museum, today's visitor is disposed to linger in the peaceful moss-draped cemetery across the highway to the west. Here, surrounded by a solid brick wall six feet high and eighteen inches thick, the forefathers sleep in the shadow of majestic live oaks more venerable than the church itself. Perhaps no other spot of equal size encompasses the dust of as many men and women who have shaped the destiny of the state and the nation. In less than two acres of ground lie the remains of at least twelve hundred persons, among them Nathan Brownson, delegate to the Continental Congress, member of the Federal Constitutional Convention, and governor of Georgia; John Elliott, United States senator; John Elliott Ward, first United States minister to China; and Louis LeConte, eminent botanist, father of Professors John and Joseph LeConte of the University of California. A tall shaft in the center of the yard, erected by the Congress of the United States and unveiled in 1915, honors the memory of two Revolutionary heroes, General Daniel Stewart and General James

Screven. And here and there, in tombs of varying design and elegance, lie the ancestors of the Mallards, the Quartermans, the Bakers, the Ways, and the Winns—heroic men and women who braved the perils of the wilderness and risked the tomahawk of the savage to enjoy the blessings of civil and religious liberty. Their touching inscriptions tell the story of frail humanity for more than two hundred years. One such inscription, cut in a marble slab surmounting a bricked-up tomb, evokes a peculiar interest:

Sacred
to the memory of
Revd Charles Colcock Jones D.D.
Born in Liberty County, Georgia
December 20th 1804,
Departed this Life at Arcadia Plantation
March 16th 1863

———

Twice a Professor of Ecclesiastical History
and Church Polity in the Theological
Seminary at Columbia, South Carolina.
Three years the corresponding Secretary of
the Board of Domestic Missions
of the Gen. Assembly of the Presbyterian Church.
His life was employed in Self-denying and
devoted Labors for the evangelization of the
Colored population of his native
County and State;
and in awakening in behalf of this great work
the sympathies and efforts of the South.

———

The devoted Husband and Father, the firm friend &
Kind Master, the public Benefactor, the zealous
Evangelist, the profound Theologian, the learned
Author, the pure Patriot, and the exalted Christian.
In his Character
were combined all those virtues and traits
which dignify, ennoble, and benefit mankind.

———

He walked with God and was not, for God took him.
How is the strong staff broken, and the beautiful rod!